D1567539

MESOAMERICAN WRITING SYSTEMS

Joyce Marcus

MESOAMERICAN WRITING SYSTEMS

Propaganda, Myth, and History in Four Ancient Civilizations

Princeton University Press
Princeton, New Jersey

Library of Congress Cataloging-in-Publication Data

Marcus, Joyce.
    Mesoamerican writing systems : propaganda,
myth, and history in four ancient civilizations /
Joyce Marcus.
        p.   cm.
    Includes bibliographical references and index.
    ISBN 0-691-09474-8
    1. Indians of Mexico—Writing.   2. Maya—
Writing.   3. Indians of Mexico—
Names.   4. Maya—Names.   5. Indians of
Mexico—Politics and government.   6. Maya—
Politics and government.   7. Ethnohistory—
Mexico.   8. Ethnohistory—Central
America.   I. Title.
F1219.3.W94M37   1992
970.01'072—dc20   92-9091
                                         CIP

This book has been composed in Linotron Aldus

Princeton University Press books are printed on
acid-free paper and meet the guidelines for
permanence and durability of the Committee on
Production Guidelines for Book Longevity of the
Council on Library Resources

Printed in the United States of America

10   9   8   7   6   5   4   3   2   1

Dedicated to the departed giants
who were so generous with me

Henry Berlin
Alfonso Caso
Tania Proskouriakoff
Alberto Ruz
Eric Thompson

Such a group will not be seen again

CONTENTS

ILLUSTRATIONS

TABLES

PREFACE

The late V. Gordon Childe, in attempting to establish the criteria by which an archaic civilization could be defined, listed writing among his top ten (Childe 1946, 1950, 1951). Today we know that not all early states had writing. At least three major civilizations of Peru—the powerful Moche, the urban Chimu, and the imperialist Inca—did not have writing. The civilization of Classic Teotihuacán in the Basin of Mexico, flanked on the south by states that had used writing for centuries, achieved its greatness with only the slimmest evidence for hieroglyphic writing.

This book is about the four principal high cultures of Mesoamerica that *did* use writing. From north to south, these were the Aztec, Mixtec, Zapotec, and Maya (Kirchhoff 1943). Even these cultures were not, as some have claimed, "literate" civilizations, for we have no reason to believe that the commoners who made up the bulk of the population could read and write. Rather, as we will see in this book, writing was a *tool of the state*. An elite minority, consisting of hereditary rulers with their priests and scribes, monopolized the ability to read and write, just as they had monopolized a number of other skills and privileges.

When I first entered the field over twenty years ago, only a handful of epigraphers were working on Mesoamerican writing. That handful included some of the field's truly great pioneers: Heinrich Berlin, Alfonso Caso, Tatiana Proskouriakoff, and J. Eric S. Thompson, all now deceased. The work of these early giants was anthropological; it was grounded in ethnohistoric, linguistic, and ethnographic knowledge of Indian culture, and guided by what was known of Mesoamerica in general.

Thanks to the Spanish documents of the sixteenth century, we have always known that Aztec picture-writing dealt with actual rulers and historic events. By 1949, Caso had also shown that the Mixtec codices referred to actual rulers, and by 1960 Proskouriakoff had shown that the same had been true of the Classic Maya (Caso 1949, Proskouriakoff 1960). Today there seems little doubt that all four writing systems contain a large amount of historic data, and this fact has determined the focus of most recent research.

The discovery that "real history" was involved has made Mesoamerican epigraphy so attractive that since 1975 we have seen a virtual population explosion in the field. Many of the new epigraphers are young, bright, energetic, and prolific. All know the agreed-upon corpus of translated glyphs, and all can work out dates in the prehispanic calendars. The only thing we don't see much of nowadays is the explicitly anthropological perspective that characterized Berlin, Caso, Proskouriakoff, Alberto Ruz Lhuillier, and Thompson.

While this book has taken shape slowly over the last two decades, it was the deaths of my teacher Tania Proskouriakoff in 1985 and my friend Henry Berlin in 1988 that provided me with the impetus for finishing it. Perhaps the major message of the book is this: the notion that Mesoamerican scribes were writing "history," however exciting that may be, has been taken so literally that much of the recent literature now conflicts with what we know about the role of writing in the archaic state.

In twentieth-century America, we have three separate words for "history," "myth," and "propaganda." History is supposed to be objective and truthful; the *Washington Post* claims to check a story with at least two independent sources before it is printed. Myth we associate with Thor, Aphrodite, and Paul Bunyan, beings who we know never existed. Propaganda we recognize when the Chinese government tells us that no students were killed in Tiananmen Square during the 1989 demonstrations.

This separation of propaganda, myth, and history is, however, a relatively recent occurrence. As used by most archaic states, writing contained an inseparable mixture of all three. Nowhere was this more true than in ancient Mesoamerica, where the native Indian languages did not even have separate words for the three types of messages. In Mesoamerica, as we shall see, the important dichotomy was between elite speech and commoner speech. Commoner speech was trivial, inelegant, and frequently untrue. Whatever issued from the mouth of a ruler or noble was, *by definition*, "truth." Since the events pictured on Mixtec codices and Maya stelae were commissioned by nobles, those events were automatically true whether they had occurred or not. This, then, was not the "history" of the *Washington Post*, but the "official history" of a ruling party. It was based on actual events, but it was manipulated to serve the goals of the ruler.

In the Petén forest of northern Guatemala, a young epigrapher stands before the stela of a Maya ruler posed on a captive. Assuming the captive to be an average 5'4" Indian, the ruler would have been fifteen feet tall. Sensibly, the epigrapher discounts this size disparity as an artistic exaggeration that emphasizes the ruler's importance. He then moves on to the hieroglyphic dates of the ruler's birth and death, which would have made him ninety-five years old when he died. For some reason it never occurs to the epigrapher that this, too, could be an exaggeration, assigning the ruler a life span twice that of the average prehispanic Indian in the tropical forest. In fact, since a Maya ruler's date of birth was usually not carved in stone until he had already acceded to power, he could backdate it as far as he chose—to justify his accession to a disputed throne, to link himself to a previous legitimate ruler, to take credit for a conquest that actually preceded his reign, or simply to appear more venerable. Aztec ethnohistory tells us that members of the elite fiddled with their birth dates as a matter of course, relying on diviners to tell them which day, thirteen-day period, or year would provide the "luckiest" official birthday. And some Maya monuments record events that supposedly happened more than a million years ago, antedating not only the peopling of the New World but even the appearance of anatomically modern man.

This, then, is not a book on hieroglyphic prefixes or suffixes, or what the man in the street calls "cracking the code." Rather, it is an attempt to redirect attention to the kind of anthropological framework pioneered by Berlin, Caso, Proskouriakoff, Ruz, and Thompson, and used more recently by scholars such as Henry Nicholson and Mary Elizabeth Smith.

I believe this can best be done by looking broadly at all four major writing systems, noting the pan-Mesoamerican patterns, and comparing these to the Colonial Spanish accounts of Mesoamerican Indian cultures, with their invaluable linguistic and political data. By so doing, I hope to keep faith with the five giants to whom this book is dedicated.

Occasionally, I pick up the *New York Times* and see a reporter asserting that epigraphers can now read the history of the Maya as we read the history of Europe. On the contrary, I would compare Maya epigraphy more to the study of Early Dynastic Egypt. There, history was so interwoven with legend that scholars are not even sure whether the first king to unite Upper and Lower Egypt (ca. 3100 B.C.) was Rosette Scorpion, Menes, Hor-Aha, or someone else (Emery 1961). Some scholars conclude that even though this unification was a historic event, it was part of a process that took far longer than one ruler's reign; therefore an individual like Menes should be thought of as a composite figure, not a single "great man." Propaganda, myth, and history were as inextricably intertwined in Mesoamerica as they were in Egypt.

Given their ideology, Mesoamerican commoners had no choice but to believe everything their rulers told them. I urge present and future Mesoamerican epigraphers not to feel bound by the same constraints.

ACKNOWLEDGMENTS

When I started this book more than twenty years ago, many friends encouraged me; and over the years, many of them have shared their ideas with me. I wish to thank Bob Adams, Dick Adams, Will Andrews, Wendy Ashmore, John Baines, Kathryn Bard, Ignacio Bernal, Mike Blake, Rich Blanton, Elizabeth Boone, Bob Carneiro, Pedro Carrasco, John Clark, Mike Coe, Geoff Conrad, George Cowgill, Dick Drennan, Manuel Esparza, Barb and Bill Fash, Gary Feinman, Willie Folan, Dick Ford, Jill and Peter Furst, Susan Gillespie, Gary Gossen, Elizabeth Graham, Dave Grove, John Henderson, Mary Hodge, Frank Hole, Chris Jones, Mark King, Steve Kowalewski, Richard Leventhal, Olga Linares, Walter Lippincott, Floyd Lounsbury, Scotty MacNeish, Tricia McAnany, Arthur Miller, Clara and René Millon, Linda Nicholas, Henry Nicholson, Lorenzo Ochoa, Sherry Ortner, John O'Shea, John Paddock, Jeff and Mary Parsons, David Pendergast, Steve Plog, Emily Rabin, Elsa Redmond, Colin Renfrew, Don and Pru Rice, Angeles Romero, Jerry Sabloff, Ed Schortman, Bob Sharer, Betsy Smith, Chuck Spencer, Ron Spores, Patricia Urban, Evon Vogt, Joe Whitecotton, William Woodcock, Henry Wright, Norman Yoffee, Bob and Judy Zeitlin, and Ezra Zubrow.

I also want to thank the talented artists who contributed so much to this volume: Kay Clahassey, John Klausmeyer, Lois Martin, Mark Orsen, and Margaret Van Bolt. Unless otherwise stated, all illustrations of Zapotec monuments by Orsen and Martin are original drawings, done in the field from the actual carved stones.

Grants from the National Endowment For the Humanities and the Ford Foundation enabled me to spend ten years (1972–1982) having the corpus of 600-plus Zapotec monuments drawn and photographed; they will be published separately (Marcus n.d.d). William J. Folan invited me to record the Maya monuments of Calakmul and other sites in

Campeche (1983–1984). Jeffrey Parsons provided me with the opportunity to study the Aztec monuments of Acalpixcan. Other funding for my epigraphic work from 1970 to 1990 was provided by the Bowditch Fund at Harvard University, Dumbarton Oaks, the American Association for University Women, and the University of Michigan.

Finally, I should acknowledge my intellectual debt to the five pioneers to whom this book is dedicated. All were unbelievably generous with their time and advice, and all are now gone. Truly, as a wise old archaeologist once told me, "The big guys are always the most generous; it's the little guys you have to watch out for."

MESOAMERICAN WRITING SYSTEMS

1 ✦ TRUTH, PROPAGANDA, AND NOBLE SPEECH

Two sets of great civilizations arose in prehispanic America. One, including the ancient Moche, Wari, and Tiwanaku, arose in the Andes. The other set, including the Zapotec, Maya, Mixtec, and Teotihuacanos, arose in Mesoamerica. When the Spaniards arrived in the sixteenth century, an Inca empire covered the Andes from Ecuador to Chile; an Aztec empire dominated Mesoamerica from the Huasteca to the Guatemalan province of Soconusco and beyond.

While there were interesting similarities and differences between these two areas of high civilizations, one of the differences most frequently discussed is the fact that one region developed writing, while the other did not. Andean civilization shows us that a powerful militaristic state could integrate multiple ethnic groups over a distance of 4,000 kilometers without any writing at all. All by itself, that fact enables us to disagree with V. Gordon Childe's inclusion of writing as one of the ten hallmarks of civilization (Childe 1946, 1950, 1951).

In fact, Mesoamerica gives us yet another case: the powerful early state centered at Teotihuacán in the Basin of Mexico, perhaps the New World's largest prehispanic city. While there are individual symbols in Teotihuacán art whose "meaning" can be inferred and understood (e.g., C. Millon 1973, Langley 1986, Berrin 1988, Berlo 1989), true writing as I define it in chapter 2 did not exist there. Thus one of Mesoamerica's most important early states did just fine without writing.

Given the fact that writing is not necessary for the operation of a major state, why did it arise in other Mesoamerican cultures? This book responds to that question by comparing Mesoamerica's four best-known prehispanic writing systems—those of the Aztec, Mixtec, Zapotec, and Maya. While there were differences in time, space, and content among these systems, the same answer emerges from a study of all four: writing was a political tool of Mesoamerica's complex societies. From the Zapotec "chiefdoms" or pre-state "rank societies" of 600–400 B.C., to the early Zapotec and Maya states of A.D. 100–900, to the Postclassic Mixtec and Aztec states of A.D. 1000–1530, writing was used to make public and permanent a whole series of messages that the hereditary leaders of society deemed important (Fig. 1.1).[1] And when we look at the subject matter of those messages and the way in which they were expressed, we learn a great deal about those leaders and the things they considered important. They make a contribution to our *anthropological understanding of the Mesoamerican state.*

Stages in Our Understanding of Mesoamerican Writing

Just as there are differences among the writing systems of Mesoamerica, there have been great differences in the traditions of those scholars who have studied them. Consider, for example, the advantage of those doing research on the Aztec. No group was more thoroughly described by the sixteenth-century Spaniards, who even learned Nahuatl and taught Spanish to the Aztec. An enormous wealth of ethnohistoric data was therefore available to guide the Aztec scholar, and in some cases Spanish and Nahuatl captions or glosses (in European writing) were added to pictographic documents in early Colonial times. Moreover, there was usually no question whether the figures depicted in Aztec documents were real people, or deities, or something in between; with the aid of Aztec informants, it became clear that some were rulers like Tizoc or Ahuitzotl, while others were gods like Tezcatlipoca or Huitzilopochtli. Nor was there a lengthy period of mystery about the Aztec calendric system, since there were Aztec priests alive to tell the Spaniards how it worked. Equally important from the perspective of this book is the fact that there were so many lines of evidence, so many documents from different towns, and so many checks and counterchecks from different sources that no Aztec ruler's text had to stand unchallenged as absolute truth.

In the Maya region, the situation was different. While there were also fabulous ethnohistoric documents available, somehow their direct relevance to the texts of the much earlier Classic Maya was rarely sensed. Perhaps it was because the Classic Maya were seen as a kind of "peaceful theocracy," the "Athenians of the New World," while the sixteenth-century Maya were considered much more secularized, warlike, and tainted by "Mexican influence." The result is that the interpretation of Maya writing went through several stages not seen among Nahuatl scholars.

Stage I, largely prior to the 1960s, was an era when the working out of Maya Long Count dates and many calendric signs moved far ahead of the interpretation of any other

---

[1]All dates assigned to Mesoamerican developmental stages are based on radiocarbon assays, left uncalibrated as recommended by the journal *Radiocarbon.*

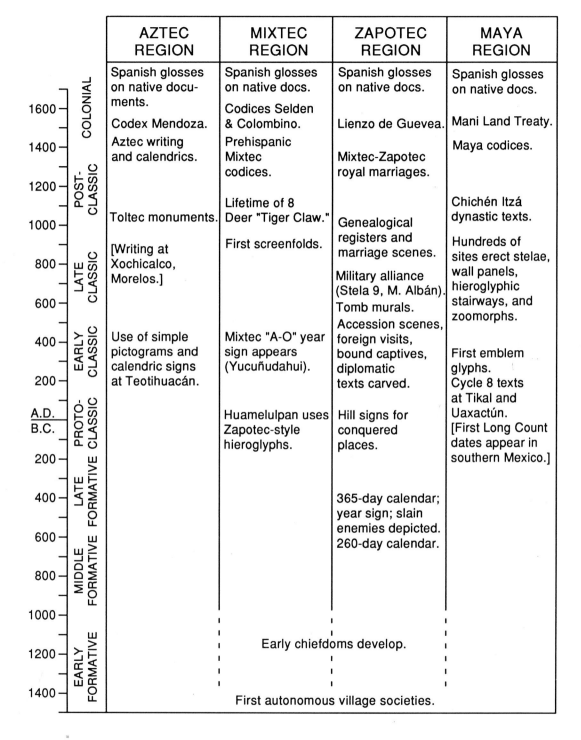

	AZTEC REGION	MIXTEC REGION	ZAPOTEC REGION	MAYA REGION
COLONIAL	Spanish glosses on native documents. Codex Mendoza. Aztec writing and calendrics.	Spanish glosses on native docs. Codices Selden & Colombino. Prehispanic Mixtec codices.	Spanish glosses on native docs. Lienzo de Guevea. Mixtec-Zapotec royal marriages.	Spanish glosses on native docs. Mani Land Treaty. Maya codices.
POST-CLASSIC	Toltec monuments. [Writing at Xochicalco, Morelos.]	Lifetime of 8 Deer "Tiger Claw." First screenfolds.	Genealogical registers and marriage scenes.	Chichén Itzá dynastic texts. Hundreds of sites erect stelae, wall panels, hieroglyphic stairways, and zoomorphs.
LATE CLASSIC			Military alliance (Stela 9, M. Albán). Tomb murals.	
EARLY CLASSIC	Use of simple pictograms and calendric signs at Teotihuacán.	Mixtec "A-O" year sign appears (Yucuñudahui).	Accession scenes, foreign visits, bound captives, diplomatic texts carved.	First emblem glyphs. Cycle 8 texts at Tikal and Uaxactún.
A.D. / B.C. PROTO-CLASSIC		Huamelulpan uses Zapotec-style hieroglyphs.	Hill signs for conquered places.	[First Long Count dates appear in southern Mexico.]
LATE FORMATIVE			365-day calendar; year sign; slain enemies depicted. 260-day calendar.	
MIDDLE FORMATIVE				
EARLY FORMATIVE		Early chiefdoms develop. First autonomous village societies.		

Left column time scale: 1600, 1400, 1200, 1000, 800, 600, 400, 200, A.D., B.C., 200, 400, 600, 800, 1000, 1200, 1400.

1.1. Chronological chart for the Aztec, Mixtec, Zapotec, and Maya regions, showing the dates and temporal stages (left column) associated with many of the important developments in Mesoamerican writing. (The developments shown in brackets took place in neighboring regions.)

glyphs. The result was that some scholars, such as the British archaeologist Sir J. Eric S. Thompson and the noted American archaeologist Sylvanus G. Morley, characterized the Classic Maya as "obsessed with time." Many assumed that Maya stelae dealt mainly with astronomical observations, legends, gods, and the supernatural; the individuals portrayed on monuments were assumed to be deities, priests, or perhaps astronomers. For many, the principal subject matter of the then-undeciphered inscriptions was thought to be "the worship of time."

We could perhaps sense the beginnings of *Stage II* when, in 1949, the brilliant Mexican anthropologist Alfonso Caso announced that the personages in certain Mixtec codices—a series of pictographic books on deer hide or bark paper—were actual rulers, their royal wives, offspring, and relatives who lived during the Postclassic era (Caso 1949). Certainly we leapt into Stage II in 1960 when archaeologist-epigrapher Tatiana Proskouriakoff announced that the personages shown in the Maya inscriptions of Piedras Negras were actual rulers (Proskouriakoff 1960). Slightly earlier, in 1958, Heinrich Berlin, an epigrapher who had emigrated to Mexico, proposed that one widespread kind of glyph was used to convey either the names of specific Maya cities or the ruling dynasties associated with those cities. Suddenly, the door to history had been thrown wide open; the Mixtec and Maya were writing about real lords and ladies and the things that had happened to them during the course of their lives. And *that* could be tied into real archaeological data.

By 1962, Thompson had already provided us with a catalogue of over 800 Maya hieroglyphs (Thompson 1962). Ripples of excitement were sweeping through Mesoamerican archaeology. Many epigraphers realized that, since it was now known that Maya inscriptions were concerned with real people, translations of those glyphs should follow rapidly—and so they did (Berlin 1959, 1963, 1965, 1968a, 1968b, 1973, 1977; Proskouriakoff 1961, 1963, 1964; Kelley 1962a, 1962b, 1965, 1968, 1976; Lounsbury 1973, 1974a, 1974b, 1976, 1980, 1982, 1984; Marcus 1974b, 1976a, 1976b, 1983b, 1987; Jones 1977; Jones and Satterthwaite 1982; Dütting 1978, 1979, 1985; Mathews and Schele 1974; Schele 1982; Houston and Mathews 1985; Schele and M. E. Miller 1986).

But a funny thing happened on the way to writing Mesoamerica's hieroglyphic history: the pendulum swung too far the other way. Gone was the notion that inscriptions were only about time, gods, astronomy, and Venus cycles. In its place was the notion that the Maya were writing real, true, accurate history, just like United Press International and the Associated Press. If the lord "Jaguar Breath" said that he had captured the ruler of Tikal on January 1, A.D. 735, he must have done so; "our Maya wouldn't lie." If a ruler's sarcophagus said that he lived to be eighty, then that's how old he was—even if the sutures in his skull and other osteological criteria showed him to be forty. Soon, Maya epigraphers were giving interviews to the press in which they claimed that the Maya were "a literate society," and that "we can now read the history of the Maya the same way we read the history of European royal families." They spoke of Classic rulers as if they had known them personally, referring to one as an "egotist" because of the number and size of his monuments, and to another as "extremely pious" because that's what they thought his inscriptions showed.

In this book I argue that the time has come for the pendulum to swing back part way, perhaps to the position taken by most Aztec specialists. Aztec epigraphers can point to a carved stone monument in which the ruler Tizoc showed himself taking fifteen captives, each from a different town. Had Tizoc been a Maya, and his inscriptions carved at Yaxchilán, we would hear some Maya epigraphers claiming that he was "a truly mighty warrior." Aztec ethnohistorians know better. They know that during Tizoc's reign he was trying to resubjugate towns that had been successfully conquered by previous rulers. During one of the battles in which he took captives, Tizoc, to use the vernacular, "got his clock cleaned": he lost at least 300 officers from his own army. Six years later, he died under mysterious circumstances—poisoned, according to one version, by military officers who wanted him replaced with the more aggressive Ahuitzotl.

By comparing Aztec, Mixtec, Zapotec, and Maya inscriptions, I hope to show some very fundamental similarities among them. The similarities are not in language, vocabulary, style, or medium, however; the similarities lie in the fact that for all these cultures, writing was a propaganda tool of the state. *None* of these societies was "literate"; in the words of Charles Dibble (1966:270), "literacy was not the province of all but rather of a select few." Only a tiny fraction of Mesoamerican society—hereditary nobles, trained in special schools restricted to the elite—ever learned to read. Literacy was one of those monopolies that distinguished the ruling class from commoners. Like the secret, ritual "Language of Zuyua" used by the Postclassic Yucatec to distinguish between nobles and pretenders (chapter 3), it was a monopoly jealously guarded.

The reasons for this monopoly are easy to find: Mesoamerican rulers also had a monopoly on truth. Every one of the four cultures discussed in this book made a distinction between "noble speech," which was invariably true, and "commoner speech," which was not. Only the true speech of the ruler was appropriate to carve in stone or paint in a codex.

It will come as no surprise to Aztec specialists to learn that certain Mixtec rulers had codices repainted so as to appear in genealogies into which they had not really been born. Aztec specialists, after all, know that during the reign of Itzcoatl, the Mexica burned all their former "histories" and rewrote them so that Itzcoatl and the Mexica would appear in a better light. Aztec documents claim that Xolotl ruled for 117 years and that Tezozomoc ruled for over 180 years (e.g., Dibble 1951:120; H. F. Cline 1966:83). Maya inscriptions were not restricted to the facts, either; one ruler of Palenque claimed to be the descendant of a woman who took office when she was over 800 years old, and who had given birth when she was over 700 years of age! This Palenque ruler likened his accession to the throne to hers, which had supposedly taken place 3,000 years before.

I hope in this book to give enough examples of such propaganda to move us toward a *Stage III* in the study of Mesoamerican writing. What I suggest, however, is not a simple pendulum swing away from history. I am not going to argue that Mesoamerican inscriptions are "all lies" or "pure propaganda," nor am I going to embrace the "deconstructionist" view that history does not exist (e.g., Hodder 1985, Shanks and Tilley 1987). What I argue is this. In our twentieth-century Western culture, we make a distinction among three categories we call "myth," "history," and "propaganda." For the cultures of ancient Mesoamerica—and many other non-Western cultures—*no such distinction was made*. In the true speech of their hereditary rulers, all three were combined.

To be sure, the word *propaganda* strikes many people as a modern concept, sometimes used by twentieth-century bureaucrats like Goebbels. *History* is considered to be a narrative of past events, described as accurately as possible, and placed in chronological order. *Myth* is something we identify with the cobwebbed corners of antiquity, like the legend of Theseus and the Minotaur. Be assured, however, that propaganda, myth, and history are *all* ancient; only the distinction among them is modern.

Myth

Myth is a form of poetry which transcends poetry in that it proclaims a truth; a form of reasoning which transcends reasoning in that it wants to bring about the truth it proclaims; a form of action, of ritual behavior, which does not find its fulfillment in the act but must proclaim and elaborate a poetic form of truth. (Frankfort and Frankfort 1977:8)

Because myth plays so large a role in non-Western societies, it has been intensively studied by anthropologists. For many scholars, myth is society's way of explaining those things for which there is no scientific or historical explanation—the origins of the world, the origins of one's ethnic group, the origins of one's social and political institutions, and the origins of one's beliefs. For most ancient Mesoamerican societies, myth provided the prologue to, and justification for, the present world order. Myth was not different in *kind* from history, only different in *time,* since it had occurred longer ago.

Like history, the narration of mythical events had a linear format in which episodes followed one another. However, in contrast to our view of history, it was believed that those episodes would repeat themselves, in the past and in the future. One of the ways in which our Western society differs most strongly from the ancient world is that we tend to treasure and immortalize the unique event, the one-of-a-kind occurrence. For the ancient Egyptians (e.g., Wilson 1951, Frankfort 1961) and the ancient Mesoamericans (e.g., Morley 1920, Thompson 1950, Proskouriakoff 1960, Caso 1967, Lounsbury 1982) the valued phenomena were those that recurred eternally—sunrise and sunset, Venus cycles, calendric rounds, anniversaries of rulers' inaugurations and deaths. Every effort was made to pretend that historic events had occurred on the anniversaries of mythical events, events linking the royal family to planetary cycles, celestial revolutions, calendric completions, and other phenomena associated with immortality. Major political acts or ceremonies were frequently delayed or sped up so that they might correspond to a predictable celestial phenomenon or the anniversary of a mythological event.

Since Mesoamerican peoples believed that what had happened in the past would recur at predictable times and places in the future, the maintenance of records combining myth and history became extremely important. The records were kept by specially educated priests, scribes, and members of the nobility; these were the only members of society who were in a position to predict what would happen in the future, to prophecy, and to engage in divination. Since the destiny of society rested in the hands of those who knew the past and could predict the future, the necessary information was too powerful to share with ordinary people. On the other hand, those who knew the body of information best were also in the best position to alter or amend it in the relentless struggle over the right to rule.

History

For most anthropologists and archaeologists, "history" for each world region begins with writing; what precedes the initial appearance of writing is "prehistory," and any accounts of events in that earlier era are referred to as "legends," "legendary history," or "ethnohistory."

True history is supposed to have a chronology, a sequence of events that happen one after another. We are delighted when early writing systems give dates, and even more delighted when those dates can be tied into our own calendar. In our subconscious, dates lend an air of authenticity and reliability to anyone's history, and this pleases us because our notion of history is that it should be a record of true events. We like to tell our students that many Mesoamerican calendars "were more accurate than the one used by the sixteenth-century Spanish conquerors." We rarely add, "and many of the dates given by the Indians were modified so that an important birth or inauguration would occur on the anniversary of a mythical event."

It is interesting to note that not all early writing seems to have arisen to record history. In Mesopotamia, for example, an overwhelming number of the earliest cuneiform tablets (up to ninety-five percent) appear to be records of economic transactions—allotments of grain, animals, oil, wool, and other commodities (Frankfort 1951:50; Kramer 1961:10, 1963:23–24). To be sure, economic affairs are no longer believed to be the *sole* subject matter of the Protoliterate and Early Dynastic tablets (Kramer 1961, 1963; Nissen 1988). Nevertheless, it would seem that the impetus for early cuneiform writing came from the need to keep permanent records of vast numbers of transactions carried out either by the temple or between individuals.

In Egypt, where the earliest writing was hieroglyphic rather than cuneiform, the subject matter is quite different. Some early Egyptian texts record the names of rulers in sequences, termed "king lists" (Wilson 1951, Emery 1961). Other inscriptions record the conquests and accomplishments of those rulers; such chronicles of royal deeds are sometimes referred to as "Egyptian history." However, most monuments reveal a very narrow range of subject matter, such as the major feats of a ruler and perhaps also those of his immediate relatives, predecessors, and successors. After a pharaoh's accession to the throne, he was proclaimed "King of Upper and Lower Egypt" and was shown on his monuments wearing the Double Crown of both territories. At that time, he might also acquire a new hieroglyphic title to signify his acquisition of a new office.

Indeed, one common characteristic of these early Egyptian texts was the use of titles that preceded the personal name of the ruler; many of those titles declared pharaoh's relationship to different deities. For example, pharaoh was said to be "Son of the Sun God." This close identification of the ruler with Egyptian deities meant that political decisions, as well as political offices and institutions, were conceived of as god-given, and when decision making is god-given, it removes all blame from the living pharaoh. One impetus for early writing in Egypt, therefore, seems to have been the desire of the state to proclaim the divinity of the pharaoh and the predestined order of society (Frankfort 1961:32, 48–51).

It is with such early Egyptian texts, rather than with Mesopotamian cuneiform tablets, that Mesoamerican writing finds its closest analogies. The Narmer Palette, thought to date to the origins of the state in Egypt, shows a lord grasping a prisoner (chapter 2); some of the earliest carvings of the emerging Zapotec state show prisoners (chapter 11). Murals from Egypt show rulers with their wives, their titles, and their list of accomplishments; Classic monuments from the Maya region show rulers with their wives, their titles, and their list of accomplishments (chapters 7, 8, 10, 11). Later Egyptian rulers sometimes defaced the monuments of their predecessors; later Aztec rulers sometimes burned the histories of theirs (chapter 5). Since we believe that the rulers depicted in both regions were real people who actually acceded to the throne, their monuments do give us a kind of "history." It is not, however, the kind of history that gets checked for accuracy by a managing editor.

Propaganda

Propaganda is a special type of speech, art, or writing whose goal is to influence the attitude of a specific target group of people (Ellul 1973). We may be fairly confident that verbal propaganda of some kind is as old as human speech itself. Rappaport (1979) has argued that lies are at least as old as language, which is why certain messages must be delivered in a sacred context in order to make them unquestionably true.

When Plains Indian orators said that the Ghost Dance would bring back the buffalo and drive the white man into the sea, it was a form of verbal propaganda. When the builders of Cerro Sechín in Peru or Monte Albán in Mexico set up hundreds of carvings of slain, mutilated, or dismembered enemies, it was a form of artistic propaganda. When the Maya ruler named Bird Jaguar described himself in his inscriptions as "The Captor of Jeweled Skull, Lord of Yaxchilán, and descendant of Shield Jaguar," it was a form of written propaganda. For complex societies such as those of later Mesoamerica, propaganda was the means by which ideology was disseminated to make political acts acceptable and intelligible to the masses of society. It provided a means for adapting mentally to past, current, and anticipated conditions.

Propaganda draws on history, but it simplifies history by focusing attention on idealized models and stereotypes. Propaganda is more forceful when it is direct and focused; hence it must reduce the number of facts, events, and details of history. Mesoamerica's ruling elite had a very selective memory, stressing only those events that could be used to reinforce the ideology they preferred.

For militaristic states, propaganda can be used "to maximize the power at home by subordinating groups and individuals, while reducing the material cost" (Lasswell, cited in Ellul 1973:x, n. 2). Before war, propaganda serves as a substitute for the physical violence of battle; during the war, propaganda can be an important supplement to the violence (Ellul 1973). Tenochtitlán coveted Tlatelolco's market, but the propaganda used to prepare their army for the actual conquest was the alleged insulting behavior of some Tlatelolcan women (Bray 1968:23).

In the course of this book, I will discuss Mesoamerican writing in terms of the typology of propaganda provided by theorists on the subject (Lerner 1951; Ellul 1965, 1973). The most easily recognized type is *vertical propaganda*, generated by the elite and aimed at influencing the attitude of commoners below them. Indeed, some historians might consider almost all political actions performed by the ruling elite to have a strong propaganda component. Diplomatic excursions, many ritual acts, and declarations of war might all serve the purposes of vertical propaganda. The rulers of Mesoamerican states, because of their monopoly on writing, controlled both the content of the message and one of its major vehicles.

When vertical propaganda was used to prepare the masses for war with a hated enemy, it could be called *agitation propaganda* (see chapter 11). When the message was aimed at stabilizing the current order, it could be called *integration propaganda*. While integration propaganda could be delivered vertically, it just as often belonged to a second major type of propaganda, called *horizontal propaganda* (Ellul 1973).

Horizontal propaganda takes place within a group organized on the same level—for example, within the ruling stratum of society rather than between the elite and commoners. Such a group may have a set of beliefs, principles, myths, and ideology that defines it or sets it apart from other groups within society. Many Mixtec pictorial manuscripts, for example, contain information about the genealogies of ruling families; those documents were kept by priests so that it would always be clear who would be the appropriate successor to the throne. Such painted books were not intended to influence commoners, since the latter were not going to vote for the next ruler anyway. Rather, the books were kept as a form of integration propaganda to settle disputes and keep all members of the elite aware of exactly where they stood in relation to the main line of royal succession.

The nature of integration propaganda is to maintain the current world order or social order. Groups not interested in maintaining that order might include usurpers, pretenders to the throne, or dynastic competitors who wished to be closer to the main line of royal descent. Their only hope of changing the order was through conquest, political assassination, or strategic marriage alliances, perhaps followed by official repainting of the manuscripts or alteration and destruction of stone monuments. As we shall see, all these strategies were carried out at one time or another.

The Integration of Propaganda, Myth, and History

Let us now look at the way in which prehispanic societies integrated three phenomena that we conceive to be different—*myth*, which we think of as a romantic and ancient falsehood; *history*, which we think of as true events set in a chronological framework; and *propaganda*, which we think of as a form of deliberate mind-control. A good way is to return to our earlier analogy with the Egyptian state.

The Egyptians drew the crucial line not between myth and history, but between the speech of the pharaoh and the speech of the common man. According to the Turin Papyrus, a king list of the second millennium B.C., the first actual king of the Egyptians had been Re, the sun. The sun delegated power to his son, pharaoh, initiating a line of rulers who would forever be seen as descending from a deity. Thus "kingship, the pivot of society, belonged to the basic order of existence and had been introduced at the time of creation" (Frankfort 1961:51).

As one of his duties, the original creator of Egyptian civilization had replaced all disorder and falsehood with something the Egyptians referred to as *ma'at*. The closest we can come to translating *ma'at* is "truth, order, and justice." The mouth of the pharaoh was the temple of *ma'at* (Frankfort and Frankfort 1977:14). He was incapable of speaking anything but truth; his commoner subjects, if they listened carefully to his words, could avoid the falsehoods that so abounded at their level of society.

The entrance of the pharaoh during ritual and the emergence of the sun at sunrise were referred to by the same Egyptian verb—*khay,* "to shine forth." At his inauguration to the throne, at every temple renovation, at every military victory, at every ritual, the pharaoh repeated the creator's divine replacement of lies and disorder with *ma'at.* As the Egyptian gods lived through *ma'at* given to them by the creator, so men lived through *ma'at* given to them by pharaoh. He spoke to them of events we would consider "historic" and linked them to events we would consider "mythical." Both were equally true because they issued from the temple of *ma'at.* Some of pharaoh's words were carved on stone and some were painted in colors on walls. It was believed that whatever was inscribed with writing would be eternally alive; writing converted an inanimate object into an animate one. Writing someone's name meant that that individual would live forever, and writing "bread" on a stone box placed in pharaoh's tomb meant that the container would always have bread.

While pharaoh ruled *as* the god in Egypt (Wilson 1951:45; Frankfort 1978:6), the kings of Mesopotamia ruled *for* the gods. This was similar to the situation in Mesoamerica where the Aztec ruler, upon his inauguration, was told:

> You are the substitute, you are the surrogate of Tloque Nahuaque (Lord of the Near, the Close), you are his seat (the throne from which he rules), you are his flute (the mouth through which he speaks), he speaks within you, he makes you his lips, his jaws, his ears. . . . He also makes you his fangs, his claws, for you are his wild beast, you are his eater-of-people, you are his judge. (Dibble and Anderson 1969:50; Sullivan 1980:228)

The deity thus spoke through the new ruler, his representative on earth. Like pharaoh, he was incapable of speaking falsehoods; the Aztec ruler's words were like precious jade and turquoise. His words were recited from *intlil, intlapal in huehuetque,* "the black ink, the red ink of the ancient ones," a reference to *imamox,* the sacred pictographic books (Sullivan 1980:227).

As in the case of the pharaoh, it was only the Mesoamerican *ruler's* words that were true enough to carve on stone, giving the stone life and making the words eternal. Often the texts were brief, perhaps with a scene added to impress both those who could read and those who could not. Lengthy details were not necessary; the observer was left with an emotional response, his attitude influenced by a message from someone through whom the god had spoken. Obviously, when the message was painted in the "black and red ink" of deer hide and bark paper manuscripts, the scribes knew it would not last as long as stone. Some books were therefore curated, to be copied over and over again, and many of those discovered at the time of the Spanish conquest are thought to have been copies of copies (Glass 1964, Glass and Robertson 1975).

One of the most remarkable (yet misunderstood) aspects of Mesoamerican writing is the fact that some systems—especially that of the Maya—included calendric records that were precise to the day (chapter 4). Because in our culture we use such dates to construct chronologies for our version of history, it is often assumed that the Maya were doing the same thing. Such is, however, not the case. One of the most important roles of the Maya calendar was not to fix recent dates accurately in time, but *to relate the actions of contemporary rulers to historic and mythological events.*

For the Indians of Mesoamerica, as for the ancient Egyptians, there was no dividing line between "mythical time" and "real time." Time cycled over and over again, so that acts performed by a deity in the distant past could be repeated by a ruler of long ago and would be repeated again by a future ruler, often on the anniversary of their original performance. There are Maya monuments, such as Stela F at Quiriguá, which refer to dates 90 million years in the past (or 91,683,930 Maya years); still other monuments, such as a series of wall panels at Palenque, speak of events that will occur 3,000 years in the future. In chapter 10 we will consider these Palenque texts in more detail, because they compare a living Maya ruler of the seventh century A.D. to a distinguished predecessor who allegedly lived 3,000 years before.

One way to explain what the Maya were doing is to draw an analogy from our own history. Abraham Lincoln was shot on April 14, 1865; John F. Kennedy was assassinated on November 22, 1963. Suppose that we were to "fudge" these dates and erect a monument in Washington, D.C., announcing that both presidents had been assassinated on the same day, exactly 100 years apart. Suppose that we were to add that because of this, Kennedy was the virtual reincarnation of Lincoln. Suppose that we went on to add that exactly 100 years before Lincoln's death, one of his supernatural ancestors had died—and that 100 years after Kennedy's death, in A.D. 2063, one of his descendants would also die in the same way. That would be similar to the kind of message the Maya were trying to send.

A Mesoamerican ruler's monuments were designed to place him in the most favorable light possible. To this purpose, the prehispanic calendars integrated propaganda, myth, and history. Out of myth, they pulled venerated individuals whose prestige could be used to enhance the legitimacy of a living ruler. That living ruler—a "historic" figure in our terms—was then shown to have accomplished something on an anniversary of his mythical predecessor. The horizontal propaganda for other nobles was: This is the legitimate heir to the throne. The vertical propaganda for the commoners was: Your king is the predestined reincarnation of a hero from mythic times.

The distinguished Mesopotamian epigrapher A. Leo Oppenheim, in speaking of a group of cuneiform documents, once announced that "nearly all the texts are as willfully unconcerned with the 'truth' as any other 'historical text' of the ancient Near East" (Oppenheim 1964:144). Indeed, he warned, "in all instances, we have to keep foremost in our mind that even strictly historiographic documents are literary works and that they manipulate the evidence, consciously or not, for specific political and artistic purposes" (ibid.).

In speaking of writing in the early literate period, another Near Eastern expert, Hans Nissen, states, "their usual aim was not to describe things exactly as they happened, but to describe them in such a way as to make them fit in with a specific view, follow a particular trend, or legitimate a certain course" (Nissen 1988:4). Oppenheim's and Nissen's warnings are as appropriate for Mesoamerica as they are for Mesopotamia, and Oppenheim's use of quotation marks around "historical" is a useful reminder.

Mesoamerican texts manipulated dates, life spans, astronomical cycles, and real events to put myth and history into a single chronological framework. Yet for us to call those texts "lies" also misses the point; whatever issued from the "temple of *ma'at,*" or its Mesoamerican equivalent, was a truth that banished disorder and falsehood.

A Theory of Mesoamerican Writing

At the start of this chapter I pointed out that a number of archaic states lacked writing. I then raised the question of why writing had arisen in so many of Mesoamerica's best-known high cultures.

In the course of this book, I will propose a new theory of Mesoamerican writing. The rudimentary outlines of that theory will be given in this introductory chapter, and we will then look at Mesoamerica's four major writing systems in more detail. After considering eight of the topics most often addressed by prehispanic texts, and looking at a series of examples from each of the four societies, we will add meat to our skeletal outline of the theory in chapter 12.

Our theory for Mesoamerican writing grows naturally out of the anthropological theory on chiefdoms and early states (Sahlins 1958, Service 1962, Fried 1967, Carneiro 1970). Both rank societies and stratified societies are characterized by intense competition for positions of leadership, which are significantly fewer than the number of elite individuals available to fill them. Chiefly societies are characterized by a high level of raiding among villages, and competition between chiefs and subchiefs. Early states were characterized by equally bitter conflicts over accession to the throne, with political assassination and even warfare documented. Male rulers tried to marry the highest-ranking women they could, even if it sometimes meant brother-sister marriage, as among the Egyptians, Hawaiians, or Mixtec.

In the theory proposed here, *Mesoamerican writing was both a tool and a by-product of this competition for prestige and leadership positions.* I believe it is no accident that the earliest Zapotec hieroglyphic texts are associated with depictions of slain enemies or captives, since they occur in an era of chiefly conflict that culminated in the building of a fortified capital city (Marcus 1974a, 1976b, 1980, 1989a, 1991).

In this book, we will see that Mesoamerican rulers used hieroglyphic inscriptions not only to identify their vanquished rivals, but also to define the limits of their political territory and the conquered places paying tribute to them. They further used writing to establish the importance of their royal ancestors; their genealogical right to rule; the date of their inauguration; their marriages to important spouses; the birth of their heirs; and the various honorific titles they could claim. We will also see that they rewrote history to their advantage; exaggerated their age; damaged or obliterated the records of some of their predecessors; inflated the length of their own reigns to cover the gaps left by those obliterations; claimed descent from, or a relationship to, mythical personages; altered genealogies to include themselves; and used a combination of conquest and political marriage to secure thrones for which they were never in the line of succession.

To be sure, these topics are many and varied, but they all relate directly or indirectly to one theme—propaganda used to help a particular chief or king obtain an important leadership position, hold on to that position, or increase the prestige of his position relative to others. In light of this theme, the origins and functions of Mesoamerican writing provide both an analogy to Egypt and a contrast to Mesopotamia. Mesoamerican nobles ruled either because of their links to mythical beings, their descent from elite ancestors, their ability to eliminate rivals militarily, or a combination of all three. Only an awareness that propaganda, myth, and history were inseparably combined in their inscriptions will bring us closer to an understanding of how their societies worked.

2 ◆ THE EVOLUTIONARY CONTEXT OF EARLY WRITING

Crucial to any discussion of Mesoamerican epigraphy is a definition of just what constitutes writing. My definition is more restrictive than that being used by some Mesoamerican scholars, and it is aimed at distinguishing between writing and complex iconography.

Some Mesoamericanists seem to be following the broader definition of Gelb (1974:12), for whom writing is "a system of human intercommunication by means of conventional visible marks." For me, this definition fails to achieve the distinction mentioned in the first paragraph. Petroglyphs, some mural paintings, calendric symbols, counting devices, and stylized motifs on Chavín, Olmec, or Moche pottery might be considered writing by this definition. If we know that a motif on a Pueblo Indian vessel represents "The Thunderbird," is that "writing"? No. And for this reason, even though there is some limited use of glyphic notations as possible names, captions, or labels at Teotihuacán (A. Miller 1973; C. Millon 1973, 1988; Langley 1986; R. Millon 1988; and Berlo 1989), I see less evidence for true writing in Teotihuacán art than some of the other scholars studying that culture (e.g., Caso 1967, Barthel 1982).

For me, complex iconography, whether produced by the Kwakiutl, the Maori, or the Olmec, is not writing. I prefer the definition of Diringer (1962:20), who defines writing as "the graphic counterpart of speech, the 'fixing' of spoken language in a permanent or semi-permanent form." Writing thus has a *format* and a *correspondence to spoken language*, which allow us to distinguish it from complex iconography.

Theoretical Stages for Early Writing

The same two authors mentioned above, Gelb and Diringer, have proposed universal "stages" through which writing passed as it evolved. In fairness, it should be noted that these proposals come from Old World epigraphers who had little, if any, knowledge of New World writing systems. Nevertheless, if their proposed stages are indeed universal, they should have some applicability to the New World as well.

Gelb's (1963, 1974) four stages through which writing has passed are as follows:

1. *Pictography*, in which pictures act as signs called pictograms.
2. *Logography*, in which a sign stands for a word and is called a logogram.
3. *Syllabary*, in which individual signs stand for one or more syllables.
4. *Alphabetic*, in which a sign stands for one or more phonemes (consonant or vowel).

As theoretical stages these entities are set up as ideal types, each of which is a pure system. In reality, however, no early New World writing system was 100 percent logographic (composed of only word signs), nor was there a system that was 100 percent syllabic, and so forth. Rather, early writing systems were *mixed* systems—partly pictographic, partly logographic, and partly syllabic. As one might expect, the relative percentage of each type of sign varied from writing system to writing system, and from one era to another within a single writing system. The earliest stages of some writing systems exhibited many elements of a pictorial nature, but as these systems evolved into logographic systems, they retained many signs from the previous stage. However, even some Old World systems such as Chinese are considered not to have passed through a pictographic stage (e.g., Laufer 1907). Additionally, there were always some signs that evolved out of arbitrary conventions. Each of Gelb's later stages actually retained legacies from earlier stages in its evolution; hence, to be accurate, we should speak of heterogeneous systems, such as logo-syllabic systems, pictographic-logographic-syllabic systems, and so forth.

Even from the beginnings of writing in Mesoamerica, we can state that the systems were mixed or heterogeneous; they never passed through the *pure stages* Gelb suggests. One general trend was that some writing systems came to rely more and more on phoneticism through time, but even those continued to be mixed systems which employed logograms, pictograms, determinatives, and so forth.

For Diringer (1962) there was a slightly different series of four stages through which early writing passed:

1. *Pictography* (defined above).
2. *Ideographic writing*: This is the first step in rendering a script capable of conveying abstractions and multiple associations. Thus, whereas in pictography a circle may stand for the sun, in an ideographic writing system it might also mean heat, light, a god associated with the sun, or the words "day" or "time." Also, animals may be ideographically depicted, using the head alone, or just a paw (whereby a part stands for the whole).

2a. *Analytical transitional scripts*: The basic units are words. This form of writing is intermediate between ideographic and pure phonetic writing.

3. *Phonetic scripts*: A sign stands for a sound. The convention of using symbols to represent syllables arose in many parts of the world at different times, but few scripts ever shed completely the ideograms of earlier stages.

4. *Alphabetic writing*: Individual letters represent single sounds, both vowels and consonants.

Once again, we find no evidence for "pure" systems exactly matching the ideal types given above. Certainly the four major Mesoamerican writing systems discussed in this book (Aztec, Mixtec, Zapotec, and Maya) were all heterogeneous systems—partly pictographic, partly logographic/ideographic, and partly phonetic. The only type of writing not represented in ancient Mesoamerica was the alphabetic type, which seems to have been a rare development frequently considered by Old World scholars to be the "highest" form of writing. Perhaps this ethnocentric view of alphabetic writing accounts for the demeaning view of New World writing expressed by Gelb:

> Would it not be surprising, somebody may ask, if the pre-Columbian Indians, who produced a culture frequently compared with the fully developed cultures of the ancient Near East, did not have a writing of the same stature as the systems found in the Orient? The answer I could give is that the Amerindian cultures cannot properly be compared with the cultures of the Near East. (Gelb 1974:57–58)

I suggest that the differences between Near Eastern and Mesoamerican writing that have lowered Gelb's opinion of the latter have more to do with the *functions of early writing in the two areas* than with the level of cultural achievement. Mesoamerican writing is better compared with Egyptian hieroglyphic writing, both in its format and in its function. Interestingly, Egyptian hieroglyphic writing has also been demeaned by various scholars because it, too, failed to develop into an alphabetic system. W. V. Davies (1987:35) has responded to these comments: "Such criticism, which is based essentially on the assumed superiority of alphabetic scripts over all others, is quite misplaced. It not only overrates the efficiency of alphabetic systems, it also seriously undervalues the merits of others."

By far the largest samples of early Near Eastern writing come from economic archives associated with temples (Falkenstein 1936; Frankfort 1951, 1961; Kramer 1961, 1963; Marcus 1970; Nissen 1988). Many of these texts deal with the internal administration of the temple. In addition to recording transactions on behalf of the temple, other texts reveal economic transactions between individuals, acting in their own interests. The sale of land was first recorded around 3000 B.C. on stone carvings called *kudurru* (Moortgat 1969, Diakonoff 1974). These texts on stone supplied data on "gifts" that were given as part of the sale: the recipients of these gifts, the name of the seller and purchaser, the location of the land, and the purchase price. At a later date, land sales were recorded on clay tablets, such as those from Fara at around 2500 B.C. (Postgate 1984:9).

Thus, in striking contrast to both Egypt and Mesoamerica, much early Sumerian writing served to document economic transactions made on behalf of the temple or on behalf of individuals. The earliest land deeds and sales were recorded on stone. Clay tablets, eventually to become much more numerous, continued to increase as (1) the number of individuals needing to keep this type of economic record increased; (2) the value of the written word increased; and (3) the transactions came to involve individuals from increasingly greater distances. Rather than pursuing the Mesopotamian writing system in detail here, we will select a couple of Old World examples that were more similar *in subject matter* to those of early Mesoamerican systems.

In addition to that of Mesopotamia, there were at least six other early Old World writing systems: Proto-Elamite, Proto-Indic, Cretan, Hittite, Egyptian, and Chinese. These seven Old World writing systems can all be classified as logographic-ideographic/syllabic systems. This type of writing was a mixture of word signs (logograms) and syllabic signs. The order of the written signs was determined by the order of the spoken words, meaning that there was a clear relationship between speech and writing in all seven cases. Given that there is no such thing as a "pure" logographic system (i.e., a writing system composed entirely of signs that stand for whole words), we would expect to see some signs that functioned as parts of words or syllables, and had phonetic value independent of meaning.

For some scholars interested in the evolution of writing systems, the initial use of the "rebus principle," an early form of phoneticism, is considered a revolution. (A well-known example of the rebus principle, already given by M. D. Coe [1962:98, 1984:84], has a human eye, a carpenter's saw, an ant, and a blooming rose, combined to be read as "I-saw-Aunt-Rose" [Fig. 2.1]). The rebus principle was often employed in Mesoamerica when the intended word was difficult to depict in writing; in that situation, a sign which was easy to draw and which resembled the desired item in sound value (homophone or homonym) was selected (Morley 1922:116; Thompson 1950).

As in the case of early Mesoamerican hieroglyphic inscriptions (and in striking contrast to economic texts recorded by the early Sumerians), the functions of early Egyptian writing were to commemorate the deeds of rulers and legitimize their divine right to rule. One of the earliest examples of this was the stone cosmetic palette from Upper Egypt, known as the Narmer Palette, whose carved subject matter is an event worthy of commemoration (e.g., Frankfort 1951, 1978).

While there are various interpretations of this famous slate palette (e.g., Frankfort 1951, Emery 1961, Bard 1981, W. V. Davies 1987), many scholars interpret it as showing the conquest of Lower Egypt by a ruler, Narmer, from Upper Egypt. The name *Nar-mer* (*nr* = catfish + *mr* = a chisel) is given in a rectangle, or *serekh*, above the ruler's head

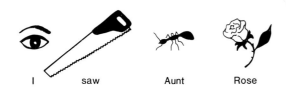

I	saw	Aunt	Rose

2.1. A well-known example of rebus writing is "I saw Aunt Rose." By depicting an eye, carpenter's saw, ant, and flower, a complete sentence based on homonyms can be constructed.

(Fig. 2.2). Lower Egypt is indicated by a stand of papyrus native to that area, growing out of the sign for "land." Above the papyrus is the falcon, associated with rulership and Narmer. The ruler is shown larger than life, a giant towering above others, with his right arm carrying a mace and his left hand grasping a kneeling captive's hair. The pose assumed by Narmer becomes part of standard royal iconography (W. V. Davies 1987:39). Narmer is also shown wearing the headdress and tunic typical of a ruler. In a lower register, below his feet, are two sprawling captives. The rigid, erect stance of the giant ruler can be contrasted with the awkward posture, small size, and skimpy attire of the slain or captive commoners and the decapitated corpses (Fig. 2.3).

The Narmer Palette also resembles early Mesoamerican monuments in that it records an event of political, religious, and symbolic importance which may or may not have actually happened. The immediate political significance of the Narmer Palette is that the unification of Upper and Lower Egypt had been achieved by an individual who began a dynastic sequence of rulers. Following Narmer, later rulers claimed the right to administer and control the resources of both Upper and Lower Egypt. Was this "event" historically true, and could it really be attributed to the actions of a single individual? Or should this "unification" of Upper and Lower Egypt be attributed to long-term historical processes that were merely foreshortened by an artist or a scribe? The resolution of this question (which cannot be achieved here) is of secondary concern. My purpose in illustrating it is to call attention to a non-alphabetic, hieroglyphic writing system, used by an Old World civilization to disseminate propaganda that legitimizes the claims of many rulers who followed a legendary hero. This function is very similar to that served by the Zapotec and Maya hieroglyphic writing systems of the New World, and it points out the fact that neither an alphabetic script nor Mesopotamian cuneiform writing can be used fairly as the standard by which all ancient writing systems must be judged.

Rather than comparing Mesoamerican writing to Mesopotamian writing systems, I find it more productive to mention a number of similarities shared by Egyptian and Mesoamerican writing, with Maya writing being particularly similar to Egyptian in several respects.

Egyptian hieroglyphic writing seems to have made its appearance some time during the Late Predynastic era, ca. 3300–3200 B.C., when Egypt was divided into at least two prominent chiefdoms (cf. Kemp 1989). This use of writing predates the unification of Upper and Lower Egypt; it occurs on portable objects and is used as short labels and captions to designate people and places.

The content of early texts on stone was "history," the association of a ruler with an important event (such as taking office, or the taking of captives), the acquisition of titles, and the linking of a ruler to a divine origin or to earlier rulers (real or fictional). These texts accompanied and complemented pictorial scenes that portrayed the ruler, a pattern analogous to the way the Zapotec and Maya used texts to accompany depictions of their

2.2.One side of the Narmer Palette—an
elaborately carved stone cosmetic palette from
Upper Egypt—depicts the ruler "Nar-Mer." His
hieroglyphic name (catfish = *nar*; chisel = *mer*)
is given in the rectangle at the top, between the
bulls' heads. In the middle register, Narmer wears
the White Crown of Upper Egypt, holds a weapon
in his right hand, and grasps the hair of a
skimpily clad captive with his left. The captive is
thought to symbolize Lower Egypt, and the two
hieroglyphs to the right of his head (a harpoon
and water sign) are thought also to refer to the
Nile delta of Lower Egypt. The signs above the
captive (a hawk, grasping a cord tied to the nose
of a man occupying "the land of the papyrus")
also point to Lower Egypt. In the lowest register
are two nude captives whose names (or
hometowns) are indicated by hieroglyphs near
their faces. This side of the palette is believed by
some to record the conquest of Lower Egypt by
Upper Egypt, an event that led to the unification
of those two regions around 3100 B.C. (Redrawn
from Emery 1961: fig. 4.)

2.3. On the opposite side of the Narmer Palette, the name "Nar-Mer" is given twice: in the top register between the bulls' heads, and in the second register in front of the ruler (second figure from the left). Narmer, here wearing the Red Crown of Lower Egypt, is shown with his assistants, who carry water jars and wooden standards. They set out to view a battlefield where 10 nude captives, arms bound with rope, lie with their severed heads between their legs. These 10 corpses symbolize the many who died; the hieroglyphic signs above them have been interpreted as representing a place in Lower Egypt. In the third register from the top, we see a circle (actually the depression where the cosmetic pigment was ground) defined by the long intertwined necks of animals; this intertwining is thought by some to symbolize the unification of Upper and Lower Egypt. In the bottom register is a bull (believed to represent Narmer himself) battering his way through a walled town and taking a nude prisoner. (Redrawn from Emery 1961: fig. 4.)

rulers. Some early Egyptian texts feature king lists that attempt to establish an unbroken genealogy back to fictional rulers. These king lists supply a divine origin for the reigning ruler, by linking him to the first few kings, some of whom were actually gods. Such divine prologues and the use of remote ancestors to establish the right to rule were also used by all Mesoamerican groups.

Egyptian hieroglyphs were used for more than 3,500 years, with the most recent text carved in stone in A.D. 394, just about 100 years after the first dated Maya hieroglyphic monument was carved at Tikal. This long span of time enables us to evaluate how Egyptian hieroglyphic writing changed over the centuries, something we are also in a position to do with the Zapotec and Maya writing systems.

The Egyptian hieroglyphic system was a mixed system, utilizing pictograms, logograms, ideograms, phonograms, and determinatives (Fig. 2.4). Some Egyptologists describe the Egyptian writing system as emerging "ready-made" (W. V. Davies 1987:40)—that is, not having passed through the developmental stages envisioned by Gelb and Diringer, a characterization that could also be made of the Maya. Also like the Maya system, Egyptian hieroglyphic writing had a repertoire of 700–1,000 signs during most eras (W. V. Davies 1987:11). A beginning Egyptian schoolboy might master 450 characters, but a competent scribe could handle 1,000 or more (Watterson 1981).

The earliest Egyptian texts employed the column as the basic organizing principle. The order of reading was indicated by the direction the human and animal heads were facing; if the heads were facing left, the text was read from left to right, from top to bottom. Maya writing employed the same principle, whereby the head and animal glyphs also faced the direction in which the text was read.

Egyptian writing was displayed on temples, tombs, pyramids (*mr*), stone obelisks (*thn*), stone stelae, wooden coffins, stone and wooden sarcophagi, and stone figurines. It was used as part of a public display on huge stone sculptures that often depicted the ruler as greater than life-size. The hieroglyphs were usually painted colorfully, and their arrangement followed important aesthetic considerations. When possible, hieroglyphic signs were positioned symmetrically, yet also spaced to avoid leaving any large gaps or blank spaces. These same considerations characterize Maya writing, which displays a strong interest in monumental public display, symmetry, balance, and a desire to fill in all blank spaces.

The Egyptians considered their writing sacred, and in fact called it "writing of the divine words" or simply "divine words." The Egyptians believed that the carving of a ruler's name gave that name and person eternal life; the mutilation or chiseling out of that name denied that individual an existence in the afterlife. As W. V. Davies (1987:17) has noted, on several occasions the names of dead rulers were systematically destroyed or removed from stone monuments on the orders of his angry successor. He goes on to say that even gods were not immune from this; an example would be Akhenaten's order that

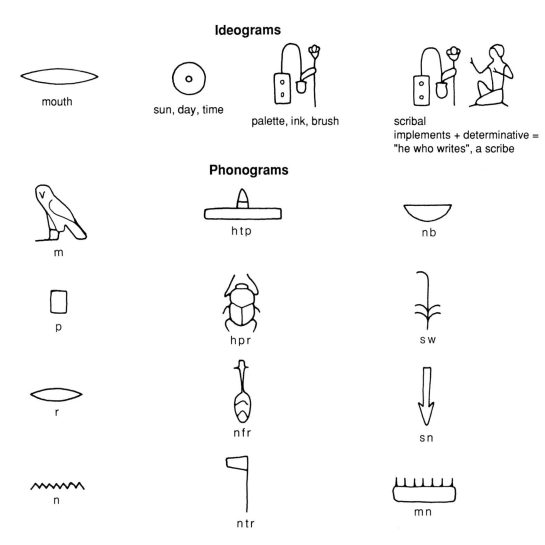

Ideograms

mouth

sun, day, time

palette, ink, brush

scribal
implements + determinative =
"he who writes", a scribe

Phonograms

m

p

r

n

htp

hpr

nfr

ntr

nb

sw

sn

mn

2.4. Egyptian hieroglyphs. In the top row are examples of *ideograms.* Below are examples of *phonograms* that correspond to 1, 2, or 3 consonants (uniconsonantal, biconsonantal, and triconsonantal signs). Note that vowels were not written. (Redrawn from Watterson 1981.)

the name of Amun be removed from all the monuments of the land. The monument of one person could thus be usurped by another, with the name of the new owner added in the very place of the former owner (see chapter 5). W. V. Davies (1987:19) gives as an example a carving of Amenophis (ca. 1400–1350 B.C.) that was usurped by Ramses II and Merenptah, later rulers who merely inserted their names and made no other changes in the sculpture.

Another Egyptian belief was that the carving of a name on a stone statue gave life to that formerly inanimate object. Similar ideas seem to have characterized the use and

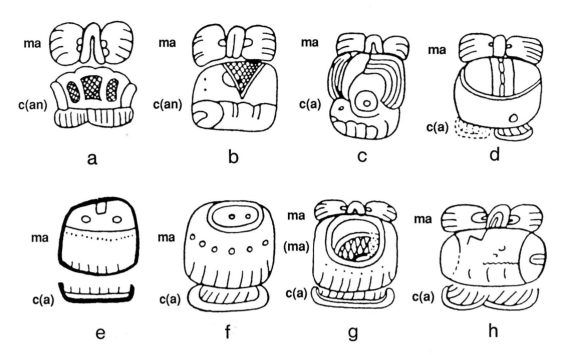

2.5. Maya hieroglyphs. A convenient example of writing a consonant + vowel + consonant (CVC) is the Maya month named *Mac*. This month could be written in at least five different ways, combining logographic and phonetic elements, as follows:

a, b, by using the *ma* superfix and a main sign that may have been pronounced *can* or *chan*.

c, by using the *ma* superfix and the "fish" or *ca* main sign.

d, h, by using the *ma* superfix and the "comb" or *ca* subfix (with the main sign serving as a logograph).

e, f, by using the *ma* main sign with the "comb" or *ca* subfix.

g, by using the *ma* superfix and the *ma* main sign with the "comb" or *ca* subfix. (Redrawn from Thompson 1950: fig. 18.)

function of Mesoamerican writing, particularly when used on stone and when placed in tombs.

One contrast we should note between Egyptian and Maya writing is the fact that Egyptian phonograms do not incorporate any vowels; rather, they utilize twenty-six uniconsonantal signs, perhaps eighty biconsonantal signs, and about forty-five triconsonantal signs (Fig. 2.4). Maya writing employs a syllabary whereby many syllables include a consonant + a vowel (CV), or a consonant + vowel + consonant (CVC) (Fig. 2.5).

As we learn more about the functions of early Egyptian writing (e.g., Bard 1981, Baines 1989)—the display of power on monumental stone sculptures, the establishment of the divine right to rule, the dissemination of propaganda, and the achievement of militaristic goals—we are finding that these functions are similar to those of early Mesoamerican writing, and that Egyptian hieroglyphic writing thus constitutes a much more appropriate analogy to Mesoamerican texts than does Sumerian writing.

Counting and Record Keeping

Two activities that theorists have often confused with writing are counting and record keeping. The invention of the abacus in China, the system of clay tokens used in the early Near East, and the development of the *kipu* in Peru were of great significance in maintaining accurate economic records, but they are not examples of writing, nor do they necessarily reveal the motives, causes, or conditions that led to the evolution of writing.

As we know from the case of the *kipu* in Peru, the presence of a sophisticated record-keeping system does not inevitably lead to writing. There was a time when civilizations were defined as such only if writing was present, and the Inca of Peru have often been cited either as a prominent exception or as a society that could not be classified as a civilization.

In some respects, we can compare and contrast the Inca with ancient Mesopotamia. Both states evolved a system of record keeping to keep track of economic transactions. However, the Inca never evolved a writing system. The Mesopotamian state not only had a system of record keeping (clay envelopes, or *bullae*, with clay tokens inside supplying the specific number of items being exchanged), but also integrated this counting system with their writing system. Once this wedding of two systems had taken place, the tokens themselves became less and less important, while the written word became more and more so (Schmandt-Besserat 1977, 1980). The written word reduced ambiguity and increased specificity. Rather than having a token stand for an item, words could be used with greater precision and clarity. The room for error was reduced.

The case of ancient Mesopotamia appears to be special because of the close association of record-keeping tokens and writing. The state seems to have taken over the accounting and record-keeping skills that were originally developed for the purpose of administering the economy of the temple and a growing bureaucracy. The writing that evolved was not a skill shared or learned by commoners, but rather was confined to a group of scribes and nobles who were educated in special schools. This brings us to the question of "literacy."

The Concept of Literacy

As in many cultures, literacy was not the province of all but rather of a select few.
—Dibble (1966:270)

In the ancient world a relatively small number of individuals, often restricted to members of the nobility, were educated and trained to be the scribes, the record keepers, and the specialized personnel in charge of the state's affairs. Not only were reading and writing skills restricted to a small segment of society, so also were the written records themselves. Books were often kept by religious personnel, to be consulted only by authorized persons. This inaccessibility of written records contrasts sharply with our modern egalitarian concepts, particularly in the United States, where our public libraries and public educational system throw open their doors to all children and adults.

Highly restricted access to knowledge, books, and education in most ancient civilizations, including those of Mesoamerica, makes the use of the term "literacy" inappropriate. Even the Maya should not be called a "literate civilization," not only because a very small segment of society controlled access to writing, but also because their goal was never that the society as a whole become literate. Among those ancient societies in which access to books was restricted to a special class, writing was considered sacred, and often said to have been a "gift from the gods." In the case of ancient Egypt, for example, the baboon-headed deity Thoth was considered the inventor of writing. In ancient China, either Fu Hsi (the inventor of commerce) or Ts'ang Chieh (the four-eyed dragon) was considered the inventor of writing. Writing was thus *given* to man by supernatural or divine beings. Ancient civilizations had a vested interest in asserting that writing had not changed or evolved.

It is thus not surprising that sacred powers accrued to those individuals who controlled knowledge of reading, writing, and books. This information was not to be shared, but rather jealously guarded within inegalitarian systems of government. Knowledge was passed from the divine world to the nobles, who, in turn, could interpret and convey to the commoners the necessary message. Since the nobles were descended from the divine and could interact directly with them, they mediated between the commoners and the "givers of knowledge."

In our modern Western world, writing is conceived of as a skill everyone needs. One of the goals of modern societies is to achieve a literacy rate of 100 percent. In most ancient societies, such a goal was totally undesirable; the segment of society that controlled writing wanted to keep it in the hands of the few.

A Definition of Mesoamerican Writing

Of the four theoretical stages in the evolution of writing outlined by Gelb and Diringer, at least three are evident in Mesoamerica. What we observe on stone monuments and paper manuscripts in Mesoamerica are *logographic-syllabic systems* that also retain a number of *pictographic elements.* Thus, we can speak of all four major Mesoamerican writing systems—Aztec, Mixtec, Zapotec, and Maya—as *heterogeneous systems,* partly pictographic, partly logographic, and partly syllabic (or phonetic). The only type of writing not represented in Mesoamerica was the alphabetic system, which we have seen is a very rare development. Worldwide, logosyllabic systems have evolved at least eleven times (if we count the seven Old World cases and the four Mesoamerican cases as separate writing systems). The Greeks and Romans had a true alphabet in which separate letters were assigned to vowels as well as consonants; some scholars consider these to be the only two groups to have developed true alphabets, since the other candidates—Egyptian, Aramaic, or Hebrew, for example—developed a form of "consonantal writing," that is, a writing without vowels. In Aramaic and Hebrew the vowels may be indicated with diacritical marks, while in ancient Egyptian hieroglyphic writing they were not indicated at all (Gardiner 1957; Watterson 1981, 1985; W. V. Davies 1987).

The data so far presented allow us to provide a definition of early writing that distinguishes it from complex iconography. Following that definition, given below, we will proceed directly to early Mesoamerican writing.

1. Writing is recognizable by its format. Even when we are unable to read or interpret certain examples of writing, we are able to infer that a certain text is writing by its organization.

2. More than ninety percent of all early writing has a linear format, either in *rows* (as in the case of Mesopotamia) or *columns* (as in the case of China and the Maya region).

3. This linear format implies the order of reading, either left to right, or right to left; and from top to bottom, or bottom to top.

4. Some relationship to the spoken language is evident.

5. A limited set of conventionalized signs can be combined according to specific rules; in other words, the system has a grammar.

Early Mesoamerican texts typically display a minimum of three or four (and in some cases as many as fifty) individual signs called *hieroglyphs,* arranged in one or more columns. The column seems to be the organizing principle of early Mesoamerican writing, especially on those monuments found from the Valley of Oaxaca east through the Isthmus of Tehuantepec to the Maya region (Fig. 2.6). The earliest texts are characterized by single columns; double columns occur later. Very characteristic of Classic Maya writing were paired columns that were read together, from left to right and from top to bottom.

The later Postclassic writing of the Mixtec and Aztec did not often use the column as a major organizing principle. These later writing systems can be considered "labeling" or "caption" scripts. That is, the hieroglyphic signs provide captions—the names and titles of the protagonists portrayed in the scene; the names of items or objects depicted; the names of places visited; and the dates of events, such as births, marriages, conquests, deaths, dedicatory dates of various buildings, calendric rituals, and accessions to the throne. Mixtec and Aztec books did not tend to display "pure texts" (that is, long columns of hieroglyphs used in isolation and unaccompanied by scenes or depictions), which were utilized on earlier Formative and Classic monuments. Rather, the Aztec and Mixtec seem to have used hieroglyphic elements as a kind of labeling system, specifying dates, names, places, titles, and events. The captions served to reduce ambiguity and eliminate confusion, aiding us in distinguishing between different rulers depicted in the same scene, or in identifying which towns were subjugated.

Ironically, while the Zapotec and Maya writing systems were the earliest two of the four systems discussed here, they were more capable of rendering a wider range of in-

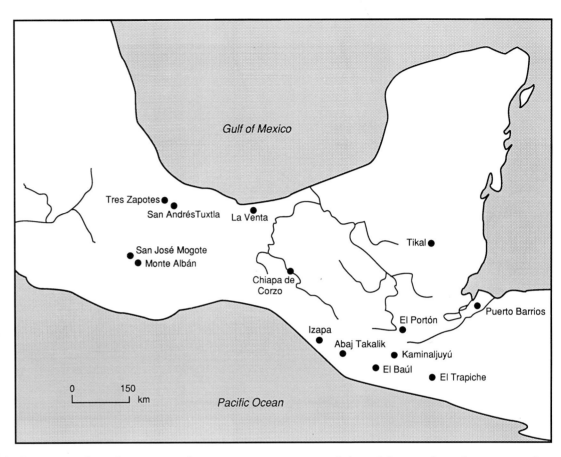

2.6. The locations of some of Mesoamerica's earliest examples of actual hieroglyphic texts or calendric inscriptions. (Redrawn from Marcus 1976b: fig. 1.)

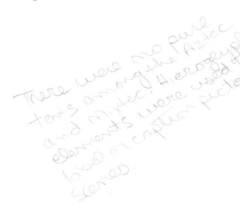

There were no pure texts among the Aztec and Mixtec. Hieroglyphic elements were used to label or caption pictorial scenes

formation than the Aztec and Mixtec manuscripts, and they did so without having to rely on artistic scenes and iconographic conventions to convey so much of the information. Whereas the Classic Maya scribe could use a pure hieroglyphic text to state that a ruler had been born, married, acceded to the throne, conquered a rival, captured a prisoner, and died, the painter of a Postclassic Mixtec codex might have to use a whole series of captioned drawings to show that many events.

Four Mesoamerican Writing Systems

As a culture area, Mesoamerica includes central and southern Mexico, Guatemala, Belize, El Salvador, and much of Honduras. Not all of Mesoamerica, however, shows evidence of prehispanic writing. From north to south—which is the order in which we will discuss them in this volume—there were four major systems. These were (1) the Aztec system, focused in the Basin of Mexico, which spread with the Aztec empire;

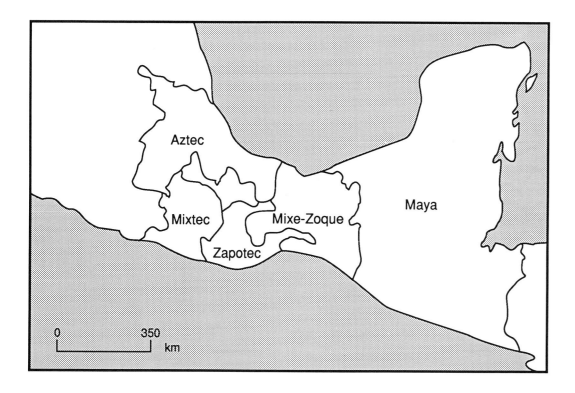

2.7. Mexico in A.D. 1519, showing the approximate linguistic boundaries of the Aztec, Mixtec, Zapotec, and Maya. Also shown is the Mixe-Zoque region, where some of the early texts of Figure 2.6 were found.

(2) the Mixtec system, based in southern Puebla and northern Oaxaca; (3) the Zapotec system, concentrated in the area running from the Valley of Oaxaca to the Isthmus of Tehuantepec; and (4) the Maya system, which covered the whole area from eastern Chiapas and Tabasco to western Honduras (Fig. 2.7).

In this volume we will compare the way the Aztec, Mixtec, Zapotec, and Maya states used writing to address a whole range of topics, such as royal marriage, descent and the ancestors, accession to the throne, territorial boundaries, warfare, and so on. It should be stated at the outset, however, that there are several obstacles to this comparison.

One of these obstacles is a lack of contemporaneity. The Zapotec and Maya texts we will consider are generally older, dating to before A.D. 900. The Aztec and Mixtec texts we will consider are generally more recent, dating from A.D. 1100 to the first century of the Spanish conquest (A.D. 1519–1619) (see Fig. 1.1).

A second obstacle is the difference in the medium employed by the scribe. The Zapotec and Maya writing systems are known primarily from carved stone monuments, while the Aztec and Mixtec systems are known primarily from painted books made of cloth, bark paper, or animal hide. These different media resulted in different kinds of texts. We should stress that these differences should not be taken to mean that the Aztec and

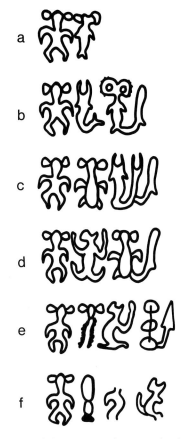

2.8. Much of the content of Easter Island script is genealogical. The names of important ancestors, such as the first six chiefs, were often written on small tablets. On this tablet, the six chiefs are given as: *a*, Heke; *b*, Tua-ma-Heke; *c*, Hotu-ma-Tua; *d*, Tupa-Hotu; *e*, Ororoine; and *f*, Pea-Motuha-Koro. In some oral histories that have been collected, the names of the six chiefs are given in a different order. These discrepancies have been explained as different versions of the early history of Easter Island given by local groups who wished to differentiate themselves (e.g. the "Short Ears" vs. the "Long Ears"). Significantly, Easter Island texts reveal two strategies used to legitimize new chiefs: frequent battles took place between chiefs, and their genealogies were manipulated. (Redrawn from Butinov 1962:8.)

Mixtec did not have stone monuments, or that the Zapotec and Maya did not use painted books. They did, but the bulk of the texts *that have survived to be studied* are primarily carved in one case, painted in the other.

Finally, a major obstacle to any comparison is the great difference in quantity of texts from one system to another. There are a few thousand Maya monuments, featuring hundreds of glyphs, many of which are repeated scores of times so that their meaning is relatively clear. On the other hand, there are so few Zapotec monuments with lengthy texts that an estimated 35 percent of the glyphs occur only once. The Spaniards knew the Aztec so well that we can use their sixteenth-century writings to help translate Aztec texts; the Spaniards knew much less about the Zapotec and Mixtec. The disparities in information are so great that there has been a temptation on the part of some epigraphers to interpret calendric and non-calendric signs as if they were just like those of the Aztec. As we shall see—especially in chapter 4—this is a mistake.

THE EARLIEST MESOAMERICAN WRITING: AN EVOLUTIONARY PERSPECTIVE

It is now clear that writing began in Mesoamerica among pre-state societies. Those societies, dating to the period 700–400 B.C., had evidence of *ranking*, or hereditary social inequality, but had not yet developed the true social stratification and four-level decision-making hierarchy characteristic of states (Wright and Johnson 1975, Wright 1977). They had the characteristics some anthropologists (e.g., Service 1962, 1975; Carneiro 1970, 1981; Kirch 1984) have referred to as *chiefdoms*—societies with individuals of elite status, but no kings living in palaces, no state religion with standardized temples, no urban centers, and no standing armies (although raiding and captive taking were known).

If we were to look for comparison to another part of the world where writing emerges in a pre-state society, we could cite the case of Easter Island, where fairly elaborate genealogical records "in script" were maintained for generations (Barthel 1956, Butinov and Knorozov 1957, Butinov 1962). Whether all investigators would consider their script to be "writing" is open to discussion, but the society on Easter Island would seem to qualify as a chiefdom (Fig. 2.8).

Why might writing first appear at a chiefdom level? There are several possible explanations. First, in those chiefdoms documented in the ethnographic or ethnohistoric record, chiefs often used their large labor force to create monumental works of art, architecture, and defense, and used elaborate feasting and gift giving to keep elites in other areas happy, thereby ensuring a flow of the exotic items needed to enhance their own status. From these actions we might conclude that chiefs had less institutionalized power than they wanted or needed, and therefore relied heavily on propaganda to make a case for their special powers and privileges (Marcus 1974a, 1991). This propaganda included monuments stressing their genealogical right to rule, their special relationship to the supernatural, the important captives they had taken in combat, and so forth.

Chiefs were also interested in controlling access to esoteric knowledge. In Mesoamerica, one of the most esoteric bodies of knowledge was that associated with the 260-day ritual calendar, which is fully explained in chapter 4. This calendar, consisting of 20 day names and 13 numbers, was used to name individuals, predict the future, and, to some extent, determine the course of history. The "luck" associated with each of the 20 day names and its associated number was used to decide when battles should be started, when long-distance expeditions should be mounted, whether or not it was appropriate for a particular individual to marry another, and so forth. This belief in predestination meant that some of the decision-making burden was taken out of the hands of the chief and his staff (deflecting potential blame away from the chief if things were to go wrong). The chief also had access to special interpretive powers and mnemonic skills developed by the religious personnel in charge of the calendar. Given that the 260-day calendar was an important component of all Mesoamerican writing systems, that it can be traced back to before 500 B.C., and that it had a geographic distribution from at least as far north as Hidalgo, Mexico, and as far south and east as Honduras, it is no surprise that it shows up on some of the widely scattered earliest monuments.

Let me hasten to add, however, that the need to keep track of the sacred 260-day calendar is insufficient to explain the origins of writing in Mesoamerica. The calendar merely provides the temporal framework into which writing—the text—is set. Early texts deal with the prowess of a chief or ruler, his involvement in a particular "historic" event (which may or may not have occurred), and his genealogical links to important ancestors or supernatural forces. These texts serve to place the ruler in a favorable light, serving to legitimize his claims to special privileges.

It seems almost certain that the use of the 260-day calendar pre-dated the first appearance of writing. However, it was not until chiefs wanted to record their accomplishments that we see actual writing; from then on the two go hand-in-hand, with the calendric system providing the name of the chief or the day on which he did something of significance.

Early texts often include the depiction of a chief or ruler, a date or dates drawn from one or another calendar, and a short text linking him to a specific event, a specific ancestor, or a supernatural being. Thus the use of Mesoamerican writing must be understood as merely one device—out of many—that could be employed by a chief to legitimize his position and powers. Perhaps by creating sufficient propaganda about his military prowess, his genealogical ties, or his links to the supernatural, a chief could convince his enemies and his own population of his power in spite of the fact that it was not yet fully institutionalized (Marcus 1974a:83).

Virtually all the earliest stone monuments with writing occur in southern Mexico, specifically in Oaxaca, Chiapas, and Veracruz (Marcus 1976b:49, 64). Ironically, some of these monuments occur in areas that did not go on, in later times, to develop more elaborate writing systems. The first two cultures to show such later elaborate development were the Zapotec (500 B.C.—A.D. 100) and the Maya (A.D. 250—400). As far as we can tell, both areas seem to have developed in at least partial contact, clearly aware of each other (to judge by the archaeological ceramics they exchanged during these periods). It is likely that writing developed over a much larger area, but outside of southern Mesoamerica we simply do not have many early texts preserved for analysis.

Neither the Zapotec nor the Maya case seems to be one of simple borrowing, because there are significant differences between Maya and Zapotec writing. While both share the pan-Mesoamerican characteristic of placing events within a chronological framework, and both overlap substantially in general subject matter, the repertoire of hieroglyphs is different. Not only are the individual hieroglyphs (or "main signs") different, so also are the affixes attached to them, especially in their frequency and distribution. These differences indicate different phonetic and grammatical structures and different degrees of phoneticism. One of the reasons for these differences may be the fact that the Zapotec language is a member of the Otomanguean language family, while Maya belongs to the family of Mayance languages. Otomanguean languages are considered by some to be members of the oldest language family within Mesoamerica, while the Mayance language family is considered to have diversified more recently (Swadesh 1967).

If a close relationship existed between the Zapotec spoken language and Zapotec writing, and a similar situation obtained for the Maya spoken language and Maya writing—and if both systems developed somewhat independently—we would expect Zapotec writing to differ significantly from Maya writing, reflecting the fact that the two languages are mutually unintelligible. This is one explanation for the significant differences between Zapotec and Maya writing. Another important difference that emerged was that Maya writing developed a much greater capacity to employ phonetic elements. Once this phoneticism became an important component, we would expect even less similarity between the two systems, particularly in their respective use of affixes.

There are at least three different explanations for the similarities and differences between Zapotec and Maya writing. Either (1) they represent parallel developments by two groups partially in contact; (2) they have a common origin, but later diverged, evolving their special characteristics independently; or (3) one group developed the writing system, and the other group simply borrowed it. At present, we cannot rule out any of these alternatives, although the case for simple borrowing would seem to be the weakest, because there are already such striking contrasts between the earliest Zapotec and Maya glyphs.

The other two principal writing systems of Mesoamerica—Mixtec and Aztec—may represent cases of divergent development, although one could argue that some borrowing was also involved. Mixtec writing owes some (but certainly not all) of its features to Zapotec writing, its forerunner in the region. Since both the Mixtec and Zapotec languages are members of the Otomanguean language family, we might expect some of the similarities they share to reflect their linguistic relationship (Marcus 1983c, 1983o). But Caso (1965b:955) has suggested that the Toltec culture of A.D. 1000–1200 also had a significant impact on Mixtec calendrics, and presumably on their writing as well. Since the Toltec spoke a Nahua language belonging to the Utoaztecan family, this could account for some of the similarities between Mixtec and Aztec writing during the late prehispanic era.

The origins of Aztec writing are not fully known. Some scholars suggest that the Aztec borrowed elements of their writing system from their forerunners in the Basin of Mexico (perhaps the Toltec, who in turn may have borrowed some elements from the earlier Teotihuacanos). One problem with this explanation is that the Toltec and the Teotihuacanos both lacked fully developed writing systems—in fact, some would say that they had a calendric and iconographic system rather than a true writing system. What these central Mexican populations do share are elements (such as day names and numerical coefficients) drawn from the 260-day calendar, which have great antiquity not only in the Basin of Mexico but throughout Mesoamerica (see chapter 4). An alternative explanation for the origins of Aztec writing is that the Aztec borrowed elements from other highland groups, such as the Mixtec of Puebla and Oaxaca, or the descendants of the Xochicalcans of western Morelos (Sáenz 1961, 1962, 1968; Berlo 1989).

A SAMPLE OF THE EARLIEST MESOAMERICAN TEXTS

Our earliest examples of hieroglyphic texts—all simple ones, in which only two or three glyphs are set in sequence—come from 700 to 400 B.C. and fall in the period of pre-state cultures known as the Middle Formative period (Fig. 1.1). Our sample is very small, and it is unlikely that these texts in stone were the first to be carved. Almost certainly future excavations will turn up earlier examples, although how much earlier is unknown. As of 1991, the area producing the earliest texts was southern Mexico, from the Valley of Oaxaca across the Isthmus of Tehuantepec to the Olmec region of southern Veracruz-Tabasco.

The early texts discussed in this chapter all seem to have dates in the 260-day ritual calendar, described in detail in chapter 4. In that chapter, we will move on to the Late Formative period (Fig. 1.1) and consider our oldest known examples of dates in the so-called "Long Count" calendar.

Monument 3, San José Mogote, Valley of Oaxaca

During the Rosario phase (700–500 B.C.), the Valley of Oaxaca had reached the level of development known as a "complex" or "maximal" chiefdom (Carneiro 1981, 1988;

Wright 1984; Flannery and Marcus 1990; Marcus 1991). Such societies are characterized by hereditary differences in rank, based on the degree of kinship to the chief, but lack the division into class-endogamous upper and lower strata seen in states. In the Rosario phase, the northern Valley of Oaxaca was occupied by a chiefdom whose paramount center was the sixty- to seventy-hectare village of San José Mogote, located fifteen kilometers north of the mountain where the later city of Monte Albán would arise. San José Mogote integrated a network of at least eighteen to twenty other villages, and perhaps more. Its chiefly elite practiced cranial deformation; wore jade ornaments; did their ritual bloodletting with obsidian knives chipped to resemble a stingray spine; lived in multiroom adobe houses, rather than the thatched huts of lower-status people; and ate from fine gray vessels decorated with white "resist" or "negative" paint.

As Carneiro (1981, 1987, 1988) points out, maximal chiefdoms often exist in an endemic state of raiding or low-level "warfare" with rival chiefdoms. Such was evidently the case in the Rosario phase, especially at San José Mogote, which lay immediately to the east of the main route through the mountains to the Valleys of Nochixtlán and Tilantongo in the Mixtec highlands. The first village in the Valley of Oaxaca to show hints of fortification walls lies along that route, only five kilometers west of San José Mogote (Kowalewski et al. 1989, vol. 1). At some point in the Rosario phase, the main temple at San José Mogote (atop Structure 28 on Mound 1) was burned so severely that its sand floor was reduced to silica slag. Traditionally in Oaxaca, the burning of a rival chief's main temple was one of the initial goals of a raid.

It was in the context of such chiefly hostilities that Monument 3 at San José Mogote was carved. This carved stone (Fig. 2.9) was discovered *in situ*, laid on a bed of leveling slabs and serving as the threshold for a corridor between two large public buildings of the Rosario phase (Marcus 1976b, 1980, 1991; Flannery and Marcus 1983b:57–58, 1990:42–52). Its stratigraphic context suggests a date of perhaps 600 B.C.

Monument 3 depicts a nude man sprawled awkwardly on the ground, his eyes closed, a complex scroll covering his chest to suggest the removal of his heart. A ribbon of blood runs from his chest to the edge of the stone, ending in two stylized drops that continue down the east side of the monument. This stone would appear to be one of our first depictions of a sacrificial victim, presumably a captive taken in raiding. By placing the stone flat as the threshold of a corridor, the occupants of the site guaranteed that anyone entering the corridor would tread on the captive. This symbol or "visual pun" of captor treading on captive was used by the later Zapotec and Maya (see chapter 11).

Between the feet of the figure in Monument 3 is the short hieroglyphic phrase "1 Earthquake"—an ornate dot for the number "1" below the glyph for "Earthquake," the seventeenth day name in the Zapotec 260-day calendar (chapter 4). While this was a date, in this context it probably served as the calendric name of the sacrificed individual, since it was Zapotec practice to take personal names from the calendar (see chapter 7). When

2.9.A slain captive is shown here on Monument 3 from San José Mogote, Oaxaca, dating to ca. 600–500 B.C. The victim has an elaborate scroll on his chest, symbolizing blood flowing from the opening where his heart had been removed. The chest scroll may be a pun, since the Zapotec word *gui* can mean "that which is sacrificed" as well as "flower." The two dots and triangles that extend over the edge of the stone (on the left) symbolize drops of blood. The hieroglyphic name "1 Earthquake" appears between the victim's feet. (Drawing by Mark Orsen.)

used as a date, a Zapotec day name was usually enclosed in a cartouche; when used as the name of a person, as in Monument 3, it was usually without a cartouche.

This early text appeared in the context of raiding and prisoner sacrifice between rival chiefdoms. During the next phase in the Valley of Oaxaca, known as Monte Albán Ia (500–300 B.C.), San José Mogote declined in importance and was replaced by the city of Monte Albán as the largest political center in the valley. By 150 B.C. there were quite a few fortified sites in the Valley of Oaxaca, including Monte Albán itself, which lay on a 400-meter-high hill and had three kilometers of defensive walls (Blanton 1978). Raiding and warfare thus seem to have increased as the Zapotec state formed.

Appropriately, one of the first public buildings erected at Monte Albán during Period Ia was a massive display of slain enemies (see Fig. 11.33 in chapter 11). This display, which may originally have included more than 300 carved stones set in a single wall of Building L, constitutes one of the most dramatic early examples of vertical propaganda in ancient Mesoamerica. Like the *tzompantli* (or "skull racks") of the terminal Classic Maya and the much later Aztec and the "prisoner staircases" of the Classic Maya, this wall at Monte Albán let rival polities know exactly what would happen to them if they went against the will of Monte Albán (Marcus 1974a, 1976b, 1980, 1983d, 1991).

The individual carvings on Building L at Monte Albán and Monument 3 at San José Mogote share the awkward position, the nudity, the closed eyes, and the open mouth, and some have flowery scrolls which indicate genital mutilation (see Fig. 11.34 in chapter 11). Paddock (1966a:118) has pointed out that "groin scrolls" may be a triple tone pun in Zapotec: the word for "sexual organ" was *gui*, plus a possessive prefix pronounced *sh*; the word for "flower" was also *gui*, but with a different tone; and the word for "that which is offered in sacrifice" was still another tonal variant of *gui* (Córdova ([1578a] 1942:367v). Such scrolls do not constitute writing, but they remind us that Mesoamerican writing featured a great deal of punning and rebus-writing that cannot be understood without reference to the spoken language.

Stelae 12 and 13, Monte Albán

At the southern end of the gallery of slain enemies on Building L at Monte Albán (see above) were two stelae, numbered 12 and 13 (Fig. 2.10). Their *in situ* position associates them with the 300-plus slain figures and places them in the same period, 500–300 B.C. (Caso 1928:95, 1947:8).

In contrast to the human figures, however, Stelae 12 and 13 constitute a two-column "pure text" of approximately eight separate hieroglyphs. In this and all subsequent discussions of hieroglyphic texts, we will use the standard Mesoamerican system for designating glyph positions. Columns receive letters (A, B, C, and D) beginning on the left, while rows within a column receive numbers (1, 2, 3, 4) beginning at the top. Thus, for example, the second glyph from the top in the second column would be B2.

JURCID

A   B

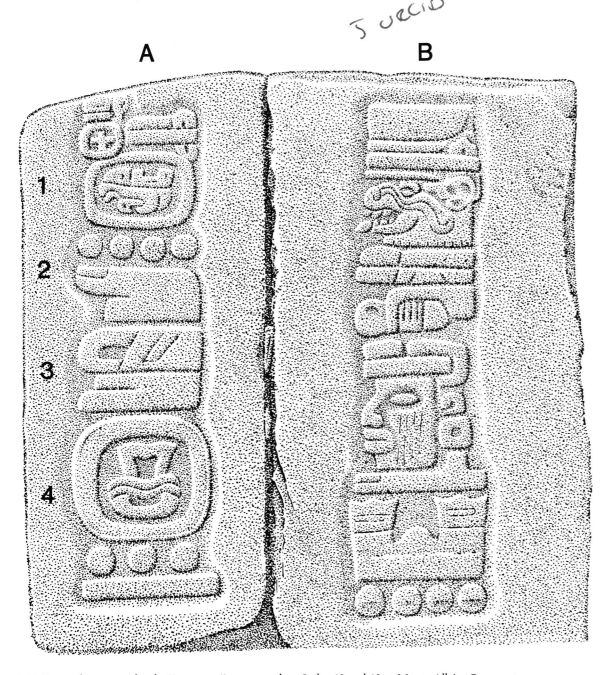

2.10. Our earliest example of a ''pure text'' was carved on Stelae 12 and 13 at Monte Albán, Oaxaca at approximately 500–400 B.C. Both calendric and non-calendric information is given. (Drawing by Mark Orsen.)

Although we cannot read Stelae 12 and 13 as we can some later texts, we can see that they contain calendric information. The calendric signs consist of *numbers* (dots for "1," horizontal bars for "5") and *day names* (depictions of animals or other items from the Zapotec calendar, usually within cartouches). Since the calendar is described in detail in chapter 4, we will keep our discussion here simple. The significant point to make about Stelae 12 and 13 is this: in addition to the 260-day ritual calendar (which we already saw on Monument 3 at San José Mogote), these stelae reveal evidence for the 365-day calendar. This evidence includes the glyph at B4, a sign which (on other Monte Albán monuments) often takes a number higher than 13. (Day signs in the 260-day calendar could take numbers only as high as 13, but month signs in the 365-day calendar could take numbers as high as 19; see chapter 4.)

Both calendric and non-calendric glyphs occur in this important early text, which probably had something to do with the battle or battles in which the more than 300 enemies were slain or sacrificed. Of the four calendric glyphs, some appear to be day signs (such as A4) while others (such as B4) are apparently month signs; one glyph (A1) is Caso's "year sign" with its associated "year bearer" (Caso 1928:46–47; see chapter 4).

On Stelae 12 and 13, non-calendric glyphs are sandwiched between calendric ones; the non-calendric glyphs in blocks A3 and B3 seem to be the subjects of phrases or clauses. Note that A2 and B2 are parts of hands or "hand compounds," some of which function as verbs. There are other Mesoamerican writing systems (e.g., Maya and Aztec) in which hands are also used as verbs or parts of verbs. (This use of "hands" as verbs contrasts with the Zapotec use of "thumb" and "finger" glyphs as ordinal numbers; see chapter 4 and Fig. 4.2).

Although Stelae 12 and 13 present a single text, the order of reading is still not agreed upon. According to one view, Column A (1–4) should be read first and then Column B (1–4). This reading of two parallel texts would be as follows:

A1 Year sign (with year bearer inside the cartouche)
A2 Hand with thumb prominent (possible verb)
A3 Non-calendric compound glyph
A4 Possible day sign in cartouche, to be read as 8 Water
B1 Jaguar glyph, with 2 bars apparently representing the number 10; this sign could be a year bearer, a month sign, or a personal name
B2 Hand grasping an object (a possible verb)
B3 Profile head with a finger used as subfix; possible personal name or statement of birth order, e.g., "second son" (see also Fig. 4.2a)
B4 Calendric glyph; in other texts, this sign is associated with numbers larger than 13, making it an excellent candidate for a month sign

Given our limited sample of pure texts at this time period it has been difficult to "prove" these readings, a fact which indicates that the study of Zapotec writing is still not very advanced.

These two stelae from Monte Albán provide our most ancient evidence for a year bearer, the year sign, and the possible use of the months that comprised the 365-day calendar. The lack of a pictorial scene on either stela qualifies the two as our oldest unambiguous examples of "pure writing." Stelae 12 and 13 also provide our oldest evidence for the use of columns, the organizing principle for most later Mesoamerican writing.

Further evidence for writing is found on 20 or so of the "slain enemy" slabs from Building L, which are contemporaneous with Stelae 12 and 13. The short texts (or "captions") usually include from two to six hieroglyphs (Fig. 2.11). While some glyphs in the captions differ (and might thus represent the names of the victims), other glyphs recur in several captions, and may constitute labels such as "slain in battle." The key hieroglyph among the latter may be a conventionalized depiction of an *atlatl*, or spearthrower fingerboard (Fig. 2.12).

Monument 13, La Venta, Tabasco

Other important chiefdoms of Formative Mesoamerica were those of the Olmec region of southern Veracruz and Tabasco (Drucker 1952; Drucker, Heizer, and Squier 1959; M. D. Coe 1965, 1968; M. D. Coe and Diehl 1980; Sharer and Grove 1989). In the secondary literature, one frequently sees these people credited with "inventing Mesoamerican writing" or "inventing the calendar." Hard archaeological evidence does not as yet confirm such an achievement for the Olmec. During their early florescence (1200–900 B.C.) the Olmec produced spectacular stone sculptures, but none have texts. Not until the Middle Formative do we see an Olmec monument with a column of glyphs, and it is probably no earlier than Stelae 12 and 13 of Monte Albán (see above). Ironically, our earliest examples of stone monuments with "Long Count" dates do not (so far) antedate 36 B.C., a date by which the Olmec chiefdoms of San Lorenzo, La Venta, and Tres Zapotes had already declined. Of course, future discoveries might one day change all this.

In Figure 2.13 we see Monument 13 of La Venta, discovered in 1943 by Drucker and Wedel (Drucker, Heizer, and Squier 1959). This is a carved columnar basalt slab which depicts a standing figure, carrying the pennant-like object that has given the stone its nickname "the Ambassador Monument" (Drucker, Heizer, and Squier 1959:40–43; M. D. Coe 1968:148). It was found upright in a drift sand layer (Level a), the uppermost stratum of Mound A-2 in Complex A at La Venta. This may place Monument 13 in stratigraphic Phase IV of La Venta. Based on the radiocarbon dates from the site, we must tentatively assign the monument to the period 500–400 B.C., making it roughly coeval with Monte Albán Ia; a later date cannot be ruled out since many scholars believe the

2.11. Slain enemy from Monte Albán, Oaxaca, with groin scroll indicating sexual mutilation. Note also his closed eye, open mouth, large earplug, and two short columns of glyphs—one on his chest which may include his name, and the other near his face. The last glyph in that column (near his mouth) may mean "defeated" (see Fig. 2.12). This enemy may have been a high-status combatant, judging from his jade (?) earplug and his hairstyle, which is one often associated with successful warriors. (Drawing by Mark Orsen.)

2.12. Four versions of a Zapotec hieroglyph that may mean "defeated" or "conquered." The glyph appears to be derived from the fingerboard of the spearthrower, or *atlatl*. (Redrawn by John Klausmeyer from field drawings by Marcus, 1972).

monument is in a secondary context. Although no clear calendric glyphs (days, months, year bearers, and so forth) or numbers (bars and dots) appear on Monument 13, there are three apparent hieroglyphs in a column which appear to the right of the standing figure. The last hieroglyph seems to be the head of a bird, perhaps constituting part of the name of the individual depicted. To the left we see a footprint in isolation; this is our first glimpse of a sign that later became a common convention in Mesoamerica for "travel" or "journey."

This monument is crucial for those who maintain that the Olmec invented writing. Three hieroglyphs is admittedly slim evidence, but they do constitute a column, which is the format for later Mesoamerican writing. There are, however, no corresponding calendric hieroglyphs or numbers on any other Olmec stone monument of this period.

SUMMARY AND CONCLUSIONS

True writing, featuring two to four hieroglyphs in a column, first appeared in southern Mexico in the Middle Formative period. It appeared in the context of chiefdoms, flamboyant and aggressive pre-state societies in which raiding and status competition were endemic. The first monuments with writing show elite individuals, or the captives slain or sacrificed by them. Some individuals are shown with dates from the 260-day calendar, perhaps their calendric names. By 400 B.C., both the 260-day ritual calendar and the 365-day solar calendar seem to have been in use, and both calendars almost certainly existed long before they were carved in stone. At this early stage, we still have no evidence for the Long Count calendar made famous by the later Maya.

From the very beginning, it seems likely that writing was a propaganda tool of the hereditary elite—either horizontal propaganda aimed at competing chiefs, vertical propaganda aimed at their subjects, or a combination of the two. Moreover, some of the themes seen in the earliest monuments with writing are ones that went on to be developed by later Mesoamerican states. Included were victory in battle; the sacrifice of prisoners; the placing of political events in a dated context; the naming of important persons for the day on which they were born; and the depiction of travel by human footprints.

2.13. Monument 13 from La Venta, Mexico. The short text of three hieroglyphs on the right includes no obvious calendric information. The third sign appears to be a bird head and may be part of the individual's name. Behind the figure of the "ambassador" is a footprint, a well-known Mesoamerican pictorial convention for "travel." (Redrawn from Marcus 1976b: fig. 4.)

3 ♦ MESOAMERICA'S FOUR MAJOR WRITING SYSTEMS: THE ETHNOHISTORIC BACKGROUND

In chapter 2 we learned that Mesoamerican writing arose in the context of Middle Formative chiefdoms in what is today southern Mexico. Its first appearance was on stone monuments whose function was the strategic placement of political propaganda. As early as 400 B.C., events were dated in both the 260-day ritual calendar and the 365-day calendar. In general, however, this early writing was little more than the caption for a pictorial scene that conveyed much of the desired information.

Writing on stone was to achieve its greatest elaboration during the Classic period (A.D. 250–900) in the lowland Maya region. By the end of that period, there is also evidence from Mexico, Guatemala, Belize, Honduras, and El Salvador that *codices*, or books with painting on lime sizing, were in existence. Such books—whether painted on bark paper or deer hide—went on to become our greatest source of written texts for the later Mixtec and Aztec of A.D. 900–1521. Indeed, such codices (many of them copies of earlier hieroglyphic or pictorial manuscripts) continued to be painted into the early Colonial era, often at the request of the Spaniards, who made use of the data in adjudicating disputes (Fig. 1.1).

It was those conquering Spaniards who gave us our most detailed look at the way writing functioned within Mesoamerican society. While our greatest interest here is in prehispanic writing, no pre-Conquest period provides us with the richness of detail that we gain from eyewitness Spanish descriptions of native rulers, priests, and scribes during the sixteenth century. Therefore, in this chapter we will examine Spanish descriptions of the Aztec, Mixtec, Zapotec, and Maya—the cultures responsible for Mesoamerica's four major writing systems.

Our format (which also will be followed in later chapters) is to cover these cultures from north to south, beginning with the Aztec. This is not the order in which the ancient writing systems appeared (see chapter 2), but it allows us to begin with the culture the Spaniards contacted first, and for which we have the most detailed data.

We shall see that several essential points emerge from the ethnohistoric sources. One of the most important is the extent to which the ability to read and write was a monopoly of the elite. It was a skill taught in special schools attended almost exclusively by members of the upper stratum, and the documents and texts themselves concerned governmental and religious affairs. We have seen that Mesoamerican Indians distinguished between "noble speech," which was by definition true, and "commoner speech," which was full of errors. Writing was the visible form of noble speech.

AZTEC WRITING

The Mexica, or Aztec, rose to prominence late in Mesoamerican prehistory. They were one of a number of ethnic groups in the Basin of Mexico speaking Nahuatl, a Utoaztecan language that had evolved from the Nahua[1] tongue of the earlier Toltec state (see Fig. 3.1). Tenochtitlán, the Mexica capital, formed a political alliance for a time with the rival cities of Texcoco and Tlacopan (Tacuba) to create an ephemeral Aztec empire, but during much of their history these towns and their subjects were in competition with each other. Most towns kept paper or deer hide books that contained pictures and rebus writing related to the Nahuatl language. Many towns recorded their own self-promoting view of history. The Aztec referred to their own writing by using the metaphor *in tlilli, in tlapalli,* "the black, the red," a reference to the two main colors of paint employed by their scribes.

Like all major Mesoamerican states for which we have ethnohistoric data, the Mexica were divided into two class-endogamous social strata (Gibson 1964, Bray 1968, P. Carrasco 1971). The upper stratum consisted of the ruler (*tlatoani*), the major nobility (*tecuhtin*), and the minor nobility (*pipiltin*). The lower stratum consisted of commoners (*macehualtin*), landless peasants (*mayeques* or *tlalmaitl*), and slaves (*tlacotin*). Aztec society was one of Mesoamerica's most bureaucratic, with a wide range of personnel carrying out the orders of the ruler, advising and counseling him in his decision making, selecting beneficent days from the calendar system for the performance of various activities, and writing (and even expunging and rewriting) the "official" history of the Mexica (see chapter 5).

[1]The term Nahua was used by the Aztec to refer to all ethnic groups who spoke a dialect of *Nahuatlatolli* ("legitimate language"), the official language of the Aztec empire. The Toltec, Tlaxcaltec, Chalca, Cholultec, and even some geographically distant groups in modern El Salvador and Nicaragua were speakers of the "greater Nahua" language.

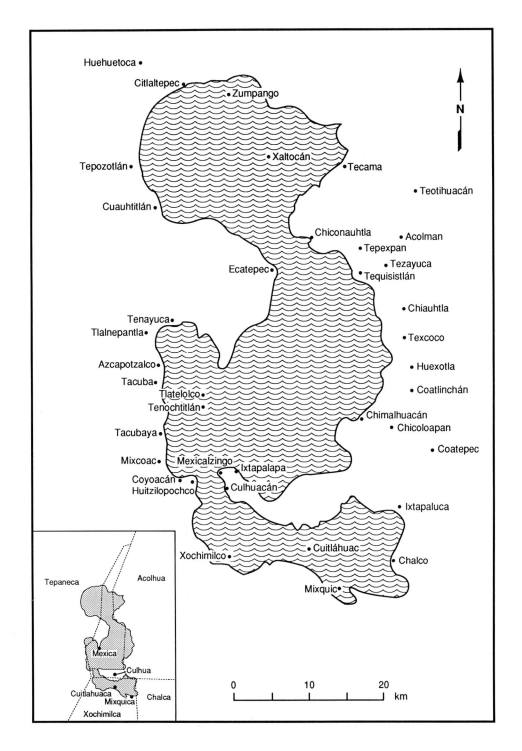

3.1. Map of the Basin of Mexico, showing places prominent during the sixteenth century A.D. The map (lower left) shows the location of ethnic groups, most of whom spoke Nahuatl; the exception would be the Otomí speakers who lived in Tecama and other towns, after having been displaced by the Mexica from their island capital of Xaltocán. (Redrawn with modifications from Gibson 1964: endpapers.)

Some hint of the importance of writing, speech, and words within Aztec society can be seen in the fact that the Nahuatl terms for ruler, scribe, chronicler, poet, and ambassador were all derived from *tlatoa* ("to speak") or *tlatolli* ("speech"). The occupants of these posts were all valued for their ability to use words, whether written or spoken.

For example, while we have translated *tlatoani* as "ruler," it should be more accurately translated as "speaker." The *tlatoani* spoke on behalf of his people, representing them especially in external affairs or foreign relations, those involving other city-states and other ethnic and political groups (e.g., Gibson 1964; Bray 1972; van Zantwijk 1985:68). Complementing the functions of the *tlatoani* was another (usually male) individual, the *cihuacoatl* (literally, "snake woman"), who seems to have had the primary role of overseeing the internal affairs of the state. The post of *cihuacoatl* was filled by individuals in a separate descent line from those who could reach the level of *tlatoani* (P. Carrasco 1984:70).

Recording the words of the *tlatoani* and other important government personnel was the *tlatolicuiloani*, "the historian or chronicler, or he that writes the words that others say" (Molina [1571] 1944:141r). Additionally, the important position of ambassador was also derived from *tlatolli*, because he was a person who, through his words, represented the ruler and the Aztec people when he was outside their territory. The ambassador "had a way with words" in his joint role as diplomat, trader, and spy. Finally, and not surprisingly, the term for poet (*tlatollaliani*, "poet," "composer of verses," or something similar) was also derived from *tlatolli*.

Several sixteenth-century Spanish chroniclers, such as Fray Bernardino de Sahagún[2] (whose research and writings span the years from 1547 to 1585) and Fray Diego Durán[3] (whose principal writings were completed from 1576 to 1581), make it clear that Nahuatl speakers placed high value on oral tradition and on the power of words to accomplish important tasks. Durán ([1581] 1964:50) tells us that "there were great orators and speechmakers who on any occasion could talk at length and beautifully and most delicately, filling their addresses with profound and remarkable metaphors." In Book 10 of the Florentine Codex, Sahagún tells us that "one of noble lineage speaks eloquently," that "the good noblewoman is of elegant speech," and that what the esteemed noble "says, mentions, repeats, composes, is all wholesome, good, honorable" (Dibble and Anderson 1961:16). Some of this eloquent speech could be converted to writing, and Sahagún tells us that a *tlamatini*—a wise man—is "exemplary. He possesses writings; he owns books" (Dibble and Anderson 1961:29).

[2]Sahagún's writings include the *Historia General de las Cosas de Nueva España* ([1569–79] 1950–1969) and the *Códices Matritenses* (see Ballesteros Gaibrois 1964).

[3]Durán's writings include the *Book of the Gods and Rites* (ca. 1576–1579), *The Ancient Calendar* (1579), and *The History of the Indies* (1580–1581).

This brings us to the Aztecs' own view of the scribe who wrote the books (Fig. 3.2)—eloquently described in Nahuatl in the sixteenth century at the request of Sahagún, and translated as follows by Dibble and Anderson:

THE SCRIBE

The scribe: writings, ink are his special skills. He is a craftsman, an artist, a user of charcoal, a drawer with charcoal; a painter who dissolves colors, grinds pigments, uses colors.

The good scribe is honest, circumspect, far-sighted, pensive; a judge of colors, an applier of the colors, who makes shadows, forms feet, face, hair. He paints, applies color, makes shadows, draws gardens, paints flowers, creates works of art.

The bad scribe is dull, detestable, irritating—a fraud, a cheat. He paints without luster, ruins colors, blurs them, paints askew—acts impetuously, hastily, without reflection. (Dibble and Anderson 1961:28)

Aztec scribes came largely from the children of the upper stratum of society and learned their trade in the *calmecac*, one of two types of schools for which we have

3.2. Almost all Mesoamerican depictions of scribes show them as male. However, for the Aztec we also have an example of a female scribe (at right). This young woman served as scribe for the ruler Huitzilihuitl, and is said to have borne him children. An example of a more typical male Aztec scribe is shown at left, seated on a mat. (The man was redrawn from the Codex Mendoza [Corona Núñez 1964, 1: Lámina LXXI] and the woman from the Codex Telleriano-Remensis [Corona Núñez 1964, 1: Lámina III].)

sixteenth-century documentation. The *calmecac* (literally, "row of houses") was a set of priestly residences associated with the temples of Tenochtitlán (Fig. 3.3). Children of nobles were brought here by their parents to receive an education in the priesthood. Chroniclers differ on whether children entered the *calmecac* at the age of four (Torquemada 1723:22) or fifteen (Clavigero 1945, 2:199–200). Apparently, some promising commoner children could be enrolled by parents who wanted them to enter the priesthood, but they appear to have been a very small minority. In the Florentine Codex, Sahagún (Anderson and Dibble 1952:59) makes clear the association of the *calmecac* with the education of the well-born members of society.

The *calmecac* curriculum apparently included astrology, star lore, divination and the calendars, hieroglyphic writing, and "life's history" (*nemiliz tlacuilolli*); it is here that

3.3. Aztec depictions of "schools" or private educational institutions. At the top is a young man, 15 years of age, whose footprints lead him to a *tlamacazqui*, a man who both teaches at the *calmecac* ("row of houses") and serves in the temple. Below is a similar scene in which another 15-year-old is walking toward a *teachcauh*, a man who teaches at the *cuicacalli* ("house of song"). Note the distinctive roof of each type of structure. The *calmecac* (above) features painted and tenoned marine shells; it was dedicated to Quetzalcoatl, the deity associated with learning and knowledge. The *cuicacalli* (below) displays double trapezoidal tenons and was dedicated to Huitzilopochtli, the deity of war. (Redrawn from the Codex Mendoza and Corona Núñez 1964, 1: Lámina LXII.)

future scribes (not to mention priests and diviners) were started on their career trajectory. All nobles, including future rulers, received their education in one of the six or more *calmecac* located in Tenochtitlán. Following some years of education there, all those entering administration, law, or other important governmental positions would share a working knowledge of those subjects, including the use and role of the hieroglyphic writing. For example, in discussing the students in the *calmecac*, Sahagún stated:

> Carefully were they taught the songs which they called the gods' songs [*teucuicatl*]. They were inscribed in the books. And well were all taught the reckoning of the days [*tonalpohualli*], the book of dreams [*temjcamatl*], and the book of years [*xiuhamatl*]. (Anderson and Dibble 1952:65)

The other educational institution in Aztec society was the *telpochcalli* ("youths' houses"). These schools evidently served the needs of the lower-ranking members of the upper stratum, the children of minor nobles. Parents of a newborn child would promise to place their son or daughter in the school at the age of fifteen, according to Clavigero (1945, 2:199–200). While most male youths were trained for war or military service (Anderson and Dibble 1952:49), there was some religious instruction, as well as lessons in etiquette or proper behavior.

The girls sent to the *telpochcalli* were kept segregated from the boys. Old women instructed the girls in activities such as weaving and other skills deemed appropriate, so that girls could become good wives and mothers (Torquemada 1723, Clavigero 1945). Education at these "youths' houses" was apparently less demanding than at the more elite *calmecac* (Torquemada 1723:220–221). Some exceptional commoners were allowed to attend, and ultimately some of them were able to achieve greater status through success in war. For example, greater status came to those able to capture human victims for sacrifices. Such individuals became known as "captors" or *yaqui tlamani*. When the victim was to be sacrificed at one of the important festivals, the captor was required to fast and keep vigil over him.

Participation in warfare contributed to both advancement in social standing as well as to involvement in the ritual and religious activities of the city (P. Carrasco 1971:357). Those Mexica warriors, commoner or noble, who succeeded in capturing four captives from the fiercest "enemy towns," acquired membership in the war councils, and these captors constituted a pool of potential candidates for a series of important military offices (see chapter 11).

It is interesting to consider how these two schools—*calmecac* and *telpochcalli*—resulted in a "career tracking" of noble children. All were taught etiquette, but only those attending the more elite *calmecac* really learned the sacred lore and hieroglyphic writing; many attending the *telpochcalli* became military officers. Save for an exceptional few who made it to the *calmecac*, Aztec commoners did not know how to read, nor did the minor nobles who attended the *telpochcalli*. So much for society-wide literacy in Mesoamerica's best-known state.

The Content of Aztec Writing

Much of what we know about Aztec writing we owe to the Franciscan friar Sahagún, who during the years 1558–1560 began one of the first analyses of the codices or "ancient picture writings" of Nahuatl scribes. He was aided in his studies by ten Aztec nobles from Tepepolco, Hidalgo, and four *gramáticos*—native scribes who had been educated at the Colegio de Santa Cruz in Tlatelolco, where Sahagún himself taught Latin (Edmonson 1974, Nicholson 1974). In his prologue to Book II of his *Historia General de las Cosas de Nueva España*, Sahagún (1956, 1:106) says:

> All the things discussed [here in this book] they gave to me in pictures which was the writing they used in ancient times, and the gramáticos [educated scribes] rendered them into their own language, writing the explanation as a caption at the foot of the picture.

Thus these Spanish-educated Aztec scribes—some trilingual in Nahuatl, Spanish, and Latin—were essential to Sahagún's research, adding captions in Spanish (or Nahuatl written in Latin characters) to the indigenous-style pictorial documents.

Nahuatl speakers distinguished between *tecpillatolli*, the "lordly" and courteous speech of the upper-stratum nobles, and *macehuallatolli*, the "rustic" speech of the commoners. They also distinguished between *tlatollotl*, "spoken words," and *tlacuilolli*, "written texts." Another expression derived from *tlatolli* (or "speech") was *huehuetlatolli*, "ancient speech," often translated by the Spaniards as "ancient history." This was not history as we know it, however, but rather the words of the ancestors, the telling of the great deeds that took place in the past that served to link the ancients to their noble descendants.

The distinction between oratory and writing was underscored in two other Aztec expressions, both of which used the term *nemiliz*, "life." *Nemiliz tlatollotl* was translated by the Spaniards as an oral "chronicle, history, or legend" (Molina [1571] 1944:67v). *Nemiliz tlacuilolli*, on the other hand, was considered to be a written "chronicle, history, or legend." Both Spanish Colonial translations reflect the fact that the Aztec did *not* have terms to distinguish between the categories "history" and "legend" as the Spaniards did. Ancient legends were as true for the Aztec as recent history; they were part of a continuum of events leading up to the present day, establishing precedents and justifying current policies.

It is true that the Aztec could speak of writing being "true" or "false," but these terms were not used to distinguish history from legend. "False writing" was *iztlaca tla-*

cuilolli (from *iztlaca*, "fabricated") or *tlatlapiquicuilolli* (from *tlatlapiqui*, "to lie frequently"), and was used to describe documents whose version of history did not suit the speaker. "True writing" was referred to as *neltiliz tlacuilolli* (from *nelli*, "true") or *melauaca tlacuilolli*. Texts we would call "myth" or "legend" were considered just as "true" as history if they suited the speaker.

The primary Nahuatl term for "book" was *amatl*, their term for "paper" from the bark of the native fig tree. From this the scribe could produce a very long, continuous strip of paper which could be folded as a fan or screen is folded, rather than cut into individual pages (Fig. 3.4). The paper might be given a sizing of lime to provide a nice white background and smooth surface for painting. Such screenfolds, codices, or books could also be made of deer or other animal hide. On these different media the Aztec scribe recorded his government's official history, myth, and propaganda.

Based on the root word *amatl*, the Aztec classified documents according to their subject matter. A book containing "history" was called *nemilizamatl* ("life's book"). The year-by-year account of events was called the *xiuhamatl* ("year book"). Lineage and genealogical data were contained in *tlacamecayoamatl* ("*abolorio de linage o de generación*," according to Molina [1571] 1944:115v). A book that revealed property and territorial boundaries was called *quaxochamatl*. In the sixteenth century the *quaxochamatl* were used as land deeds, presented in Spanish Colonial courts of law so that communities might retain rights to particular pieces of land. Referring to the leader of a *calpulli* (residential landholding unit), Zorita says (ca. A.D. 1570–1580):

He has pictures on which are shown all the parcels, and the boundaries, and where and with whose fields the lots meet, and who cultivates what field, and what land

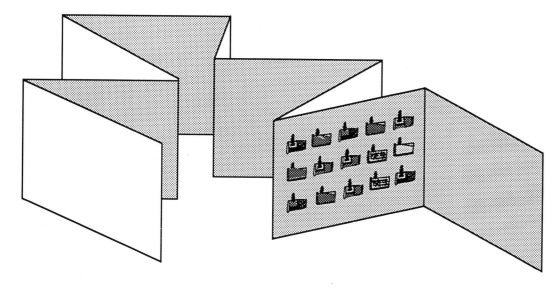

3.4. Genealogical, calendric, and mythical information were kept in codices or screenfolds— long strips of hide or paper folded accordion-fashion. Usually both sides (the obverse and reverse) were covered with a thin sizing of lime, which provided a smooth white surface ideal for painting and writing. Painting on this surface utilized the same skills and techniques employed in painting murals on white plastered walls of rooms and tombs.

each one has. The paintings also show which lands are vacant, and which have been given to Spaniards, and by and to whom and when they were given. The Indians continually alter these pictures according to the changes worked by time, and they understand perfectly what these pictures show. (Keen 1963:110)

One of the significant points of this quotation is Zorita's comment that the Indians continually "altered" their texts, a point to which we will return in our chapter on "rewriting history" (see chapter 5).

The records of tribute payers by region and town, and the kinds and quantities of goods paid, were kept in the *tlacalaquilamatl* ("tribute book"). Information regarding marriage ceremonies was written in the *tenamicamatl*. A book recording dreams, prophecies, and acts of divination was called *temicamatl*. A list of names that could be used by parents with newborn infants was given in the *tocaamatl*. The book recording the dates upon which the feasts were to be held was called the *ilhuiamatl* (from *ilhuichiua*, "to celebrate a fiesta," according to Molina [1571] 1944:37v). Some communities had so many books that they were kept in a "library" called *amoxpialoyan* or *amoxcalli*, literally "house of books."

While oratorical ability was and continued to be of great importance for the Aztec ruler, once a system of writing had been developed he and his official governmental personnel had a new tool that enabled them to store information, expand record keeping, and open up new forms of communication. Just as this new form of record keeping could be used to document past events in a complete and accurate manner, so too did it present an opportunity (1) to rearrange the order of past events recorded in the "year books"; (2) to create more time depth for ruling dynasties that lacked sufficient antiquity; and (3) to sanctify a series of political moves by giving them precedents from legendary times. In later chapters we will see some examples of these manipulations of the written word.

Technical Aspects of Aztec Writing

Like other Mesoamerican writing systems, Aztec writing was a mixed system, containing pictographic, phonetic, and logographic or ideographic elements. The percentage of each type of sign or element was what varied through time. For example, the writing system might be characterized as 70 percent pictographic, 20 percent logographic, and 10 percent phonetic at one time; and it might be 50 percent pictographic, 30 percent logographic, and 20 percent phonetic at another. There was an increase in the number of phonetic elements used by Aztec scribes following the Spanish conquest, leading one to wonder how large a role phoneticism would have played had the Spaniards not arrived. Were phonetic components already increasing at the expense of pictographic, ideographic, and logographic signs prior to European contact, or was their increase the result of Spanish influence?

Aztec writing, perhaps to a greater extent than the more ancient Zapotec, Maya, and Mixtec writing systems, seems to have included a high percentage of pictograms. However, we must keep in mind that the pictograms have been more fully studied and interpreted, with far less attention having been devoted to the study of the logograms and phonetic components. Perhaps this accounts for the perception on the part of some scholars that the Aztec writing system was one of the least evolved in Mesoamerica. Almost certainly, some of the complexity of Aztec writing has been underemphasized in the literature. For the pre-Conquest period, there is only a moderately sized corpus of carved stones with Aztec hieroglyphic writing available for study. Most (if not all) of the Aztec codices are copies of earlier books, or even specially solicited documents prepared for the Spanish conquerors during the sixteenth century (or later). Thus, the study of Aztec writing seems to suffer from a lack of texts preserved from the prehispanic era, relative to the number of codices and other late documents available from Colonial times. However, we must also keep in mind the short span in which it may have developed.

Aztec pictograms are actually drawings of a whole range of objects—men, women, children, plants, animals, mountains, smoke, and so forth. Many of these items could be depicted easily without recourse to a set of logograms or phonograms (Fig. 3.5). However, to convey more abstract concepts (such as speech, song, sacrificial blood, capture, the end of the 52-year cycle, or war), the Aztec developed logograms or ideograms, whereby each grapheme stood for a concept or idea. Characteristic of Aztec writing was the close integration of pictograms and ideograms on the same page of a codex, and often in the same sign; these picto-ideographic signs may be considered hieroglyphic compounds.

Some scholars have characterized Aztec writing as primarily a picto-ideographic or pictographic/logographic system (e.g., Tozzer 1912; Dibble 1940, 1955, 1966, 1971; Prem 1970), with a limited amount of phoneticism. However, increasing evidence for phoneticism has been shown by ongoing research on Aztec place names, proper names, and titles (e.g., Nowotny 1959a, 1963, 1967; Prem 1967; Dibble 1971; Nicholson 1973). Today, most disagreements about the nature of Aztec script revolve around the following question: what was the extent of phoneticism *prior* to the arrival of the Spaniards?

Phoneticism usually refers to the fact that a sign is used for its sound value. Unlike pictograms or logograms, such signs (or phonograms) were not selected for their semantic meaning, value, or content. Logically, then, such phonetic signs would only be understood by someone who actually spoke Nahuatl. Thus, the use of phonograms contrasted with the use of pictograms and logograms, which in most cases could be understood just as easily by non-Nahuatl speakers.

The Stone of Tizoc

As a concrete example of the way the Aztec combined pictographic, ideographic, and phonetic writing, let us now turn to a carved stone monument we know to be of pre-

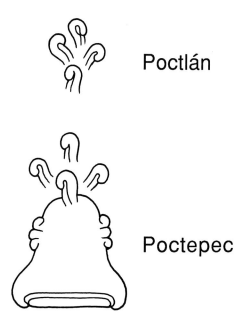

Poctlán

Poctepec

3.5. In Aztec place signs, not all components of a name were included. For example, in the pictographic place sign for Poctlán—"Place of Smoke"—only four smoke scrolls (*poc [tli]*) were painted; the suffix *tlan* (place of) was not given. In the case of Poctepec (below)—where the smoke scrolls appear above the "hill sign" (*tepetl*)—both parts of the name "Smoke Hill" were given. (Redrawn from Peñafiel 1885:164.)

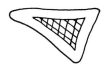
Matlatzinco

Tochpan

Tlatelolco

Colhuacán

3.6. Aztec place signs for Matlatzinco (from *matlatl*, "net"); Tochpan (from *toch[tli]*, "rabbit"); Tlatelolco (from *tlatelli*, "artificial mound"); and Colhuacán (from *coltic*, "curved," "hook"). Note that these place signs do not provide all the components of the place names. As we saw in Figure 3.5, word endings (suffixes) were often deemed unnecessary to convey the place name. Evidently, an educated person would know from the context *which* place was intended and would be able to distinguish between two places with similar names. (Redrawn from the Stone of Tizoc; see Orozco y Berra 1877, Nicholson 1973.)

Ahuilizapan

Teotitlán

3.7. Two examples of Aztec place signs—Ahuilizapan and Teotitlán—that can be considered logograms or ideograms. (Redrawn from the Stone of Tizoc; see Orozco y Berra 1877, Nicholson 1973.)

Conquest date. This is the Stone of Tizoc, a monument giving the names of fifteen places alleged to have been conquered or subjugated by Tizoc (A.D. 1481–1486), the seventh Mexica ruler of Tenochtitlán (see chapters 5, 7, 10, and 11).

1. Pictographic Writing

Some of the places purportedly conquered by Tizoc are indicated by pictograms—simple drawings of an object that suggest the place name. Examples include (1) the drawing of a net (*matlatl*) to suggest the place name Matlatzinco; (2) a rabbit (*tochtli*) to indicate Tochpan; (3) a mound (*tlatelli*) with a round shape (*ololtic*) that stands for Tlatelolco; and (4) a curved (*coltic*) mountaintop that represents Colhuacán (Fig. 3.6).

In these four examples, the object depicted supplies us only with the *root word* of the place name; the *endings*, or suffixes, are not given. Thus, the *matlatl* (net) is sufficient to suggest the place name Matlatzinco, even though the suffix *-tzinco* (small) is not depicted. The rabbit or *tochtli* supplies the root *toch*, but the suffix *pan* is not given; the mound (*tlatelli*) that has a rounded (*ololtic*) form gives us *tlatelol*, but the locative suffix *-co* is not indicated. Finally, the curved (*coltic*) mountaintop supplies us only with the *col* in Colhuacán. It is evident from these examples that a knowledgeable Nahuatl speaker would be able to supply the missing suffixes. Given the context of the monument—a list of places conquered during the reign of Tizoc—a simple picture was sufficient in these four cases to indicate the names with little chance of error.

2. Ideographic Writing

On the same Stone of Tizoc we can also locate some examples of ideographic writing—signs that have ideas or abstract concepts associated with them.

For example, the place sign for Ahuilizapan depicts a swimmer in a water-filled canal (Fig. 3.7). The swimmer with arms uplifted apparently served as an ideograph for "in glee" or "merriment," which is *ahauializpan* in Nahuatl (Molina [1571] 1944:3r). The water-filled canal may also be an ideograph, in this case standing for "irrigation"; the Nahuatl verb *ahuilia* means "to irrigate" (Molina [1571] 1944:3r), while *ahuililiztli* is "irrigation." When combined, these two terms—"*ahuililiztli*" and "*ahauializpan*"—provide us with most of the sounds needed to generate "Ahuilizapan." The last two syllables of the place name are supplied and/or reinforced by the canal itself, which is *apantli* in Nahuatl. Thus, the place name Ahuilizapan is a hybrid, combining a pictograph of a canal with what seem to be two ideographs: water-filled canal = "irrigation," and a man with arms uplifted = "in glee," "merriment."

Another place name that includes an ideograph is Teotitlán. The disk of the sun suggests the sun deity Tonatiuh, and by extension any deity or *teotl* (Molina [1571] 1944:101r). In this case, therefore, the sun disk serves as an ideograph for "deity" in general. Below the sun disk is a hill sign on its side; this hill stands for "place of." Thus, Teotitlán ("place of the deity") appears to combine two ideographs: sun disk = "deity"; and hill = "place of" (Fig. 3.7).

3. Phonetic Writing

The place name Acolhuacán on the Stone of Tizoc seems to include a phonetic element, in this case reinforcing a sign that is a pictograph (Fig. 3.8). The arm (*acolli*) that provides the initial two syllables—*acol*—serves as a pictograph. The water sign (*atl*), visible on the right, was often used by the Aztec scribes to express the initial sound "*a*" (Dibble 1966:272). Thus, this water sign appears to function as a redundant phonetic indicator, reinforcing the initial "*a*" sound.

While the first two syllables (*acol*) are supplied, the latter two (*huacan*) are omitted, presumably because a Nahuatl speaker knowledgeable in Mexica history and geography could supply them. Another place, such as Acolman, might theoretically have been the one indicated, but given the historical context a knowledgeable Aztec noble of that time would not have been confused.

MIXTEC WRITING

Like the Aztec whom we have already discussed, the Mixtec (Fig. 3.9) had a society divided into two class-endogamous strata. The upper stratum consisted of the ruler and his family (*iya, yya tnuhu* [from *yya*, "lord," and *tnuhu*, "lineage"] and the hereditary nobility, *tay toho*). The lower stratum consisted of commoners, landless tenant farmers (*tay situndayu*), servants, and slaves. There were numerous terms for specific groups of commoners, such as *tay ñuu* ("townsmen"), *tay yucu* ("hill people"), and *tay sicaquai* ("people who walk with humility") (Alvarado [1593] 1962; Reyes [1593] 1976; Spores 1965:977–985, 1967:9–14, 1983:228).

Sixteenth-century Mixtec also had terms for individuals with professions such as merchant (*tay cuica*) or priest (*tay saque* or *ñaha niñe*). Of special interest here are those people designated as *tay huisi*, "artisans" or "craftsmen" (*tay* = people; *huisi* = a trade or craft); *tay huisi taca*, "painters"; and *tay toatutu*, "paper or book designers" (Arana and Swadesh 1965:128). Terms closely associated with the scribe were "to paint" (*coco/saco, huisa*, or *tacu*); "to write" (*casi, coco/saco, taa*); "written" (*ndudzu*); and "to read" (*cahi, cahui*) (Alvarado [1593] 1962).

Acolhuacán

3.8. The Aztec place sign for Acolhuacán ("Place of the Acolhua [ethnic group]," or "Place of the Big-Shouldered" in Pomar [1582] 1941) employs a phonetic element. *Atl*, "water," is used here for its sound value, supplying the initial "*a*." The addition of the sign *atl* also helps to reduce ambiguity, because the depiction more closely resembles an arm or hand (*maitl*) than a shoulder (*acolli*), although "shoulder" is intended. By reinforcing the "*a*" sound to begin the place name, the scribe tells the reader that the word begins with *acol(li)*. (Redrawn from the Stone of Tizoc; see Orozco y Berra 1877, Nicholson 1973.)

3.9. Mixtec speakers occupy the area to the west of the dashed line, in what is today western Oaxaca and southern Puebla. To the east lie the Zapotec (Fig. 3.17) and the Cuicatec. (Redrawn from Smith 1973a: map 3.)

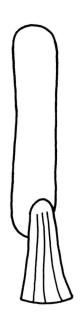

3.10. A Mixtec scribe (at right) and his brush (enlarged at left). Such a brush was used to paint polychrome codices or screenfolds, as well as murals in tombs. (Redrawn from the Codex Vindobonensis, folio 48b; Caso 1977: Lámina XI.)

The Mixtec scribe was referred to as *huisi tacu*[4] ("he whose craft is to write"). He was the individual charged with painting the colorful books, or codices, for which the Mixtec were famous (Fig. 3.10). The skills used by the codex painter seem to have been very similar to those utilized by the painter of a tomb mural, who also had to lay out his design on a fresh surface of lime sizing. Reconstructions indicate that the scribe first drew outlines of the figures with red paint. Later, he filled in the areas with a flat color, and finally, his last step was to outline the figures with black paint. Charcoal or soot was usually used as the black paint, while the reds were iron compounds, and the other colors were probably also of mineral origin. Thus, like the Nahuatl scribe whose writing was metaphorically termed "the red, the black," the Mixtec scribe relied heavily on red for initial layouts and guidelines indicating the order in which scenes were to be read, and relied on black for the final outlining.

Although we know less about Mixtec schools than Aztec schools, it is likely that the education of nobles included calendric training as well as astrological knowledge. The scribe's job necessitated that he know everything from mixing paints, to making the lime

[4]*Huisicara* would refer to the best scribe or painter; *huijca dzicudusa tacuta*, to the scribe or painter with the better hand; and *huisica nootacuta*, to "he who puts the colors on best" (in murals or codices) (Reyes [1593] 1976:11).

sizing with which pages were surfaced, to altering documents to suit a new ruler. Page layouts—the integration of scenes and captions, as well as reading order—were also very important, and must have been worked out carefully in advance. The sixteenth-century Mixtec books that have survived are almost all considered to be copies of earlier books, often preserving genealogical and dynastic sequences which go back several centuries.

The Content of Mixtec Writing

Mixtec writing is known mainly from paper, hide, or cloth books and "maps," and it is not known exactly when the Mixtec style crystallized. Earlier stone monuments at places like Huamelulpan in the Mixteca Alta (Caso and Gamio 1961, Gaxiola 1976, Marcus 1983f), dated to the time of Christ, display writing in a style similar to that on Zapotec monuments in the Valley of Oaxaca (Fig. 1.1). The later Classic or early Postclassic writing style on Ñuiñe monuments from the Mixteca Baja (Moser 1977) is also different from that displayed in the Mixtec codices, most of which are thought to date to A.D. 1100–1600.

The sixteenth-century Mixtec referred to their codices as *tonindeye*, "the history of lineages," or *naandeye*, "remembrances of the past" (Caso 1949, 1977, 1979). Pages of an individual codex were called *tutu ñuhu*, "sacred paper," or *ñee ñuhu*, "sacred hide," depending on the raw material. Genealogical documents were kept to establish royal succession and the right to rule, and *lienzos*—indigenous painted "maps" on cloth—were used to establish the lands belonging to a ruler.

In the Colonial period, such documents were brought to Spanish courtrooms as written evidence to support the territorial claims of the Indians. As will be seen in a later chapter, documents were also repainted in order to link rulers to important ancestors to whom they may, or may not, have been closely related. In codices that are principally genealogical, the ruler's "calendric name" (taken from the day of his birth in the 260-day calendar [described in chapter 4]) and "nickname" (which distinguishes him from others born on the same day) are given. So also are the year in which he was born; the names of his royal parents and the places where they reigned; the names of his brothers and sisters; and the names of the royal spouses his siblings married. In addition to these genealogical data, there may be data on battles fought, rituals performed, and pilgrimages made (e.g., Selden Roll [Burland 1955], Códice Gómez de Orozco [Caso 1954]; Caso 1949, 1950, 1977, 1979).

On other documents, however, such as the reverse side of the Codex Vindobonensis, there may be a "celestial prologue" in which recent dynasties were linked to a "primordial couple"—a divine man and woman who lived "at the highest levels of the sky," and who were nameless because they predated the 260-day calendar (e.g., Lehmann and Smital 1929, Caso 1950, Furst 1978). This "prologue in the sky" served to legitimize the Mixtec ruler's right to the throne by linking him to his divine ancestors, and was just as important as the more recent genealogical information.

Most importantly from the standpoint of this book, these Mixtec codices united history, cosmology, and propaganda. For example, in the Codex Vindobonensis, a "history" of recent Mixtec rulers is presented on one side, while the other side gives the mythical origin of the ruling lineage stretching far back into legendary time. Propaganda, myth, and history are so interwoven in such documents that it is often impossible to separate them.

Another common theme in Mixtec codices is the royal marriage alliance, which often linked two dynastic houses and increased the size and prestige of the political unit administered by the couple. The Mixtec themselves referred to this administrative and political unit as *yuvui tayu*, a metaphor that refers to "the place of the mat." The mat on which the ruler sat was a symbol of authority, one sometimes mistakenly translated as "throne" by the Spaniards.

The Mixtec sometimes made "maps," called *taniño*, which represented the territory controlled by a ruler; these maps included a ring of landmarks (hills, rivers) that defined its political boundaries (see chapter 6). Often such "maps" were on large pieces of cloth, called *dzoo cuisi* ("white [cotton] cloth") or *dzoo yadzi* ("maguey-fiber cloth") depending on their raw material. The Spaniards called these *lienzos*, and many of the examples we have were painted after the Conquest for the purpose of settling land disputes between communities.

Technical Aspects of Mixtec Writing

Thanks to the careful work of many past and present scholars (e.g., Nuttall 1902; Clark 1912; Long 1926; Spinden 1935; Caso 1949, 1950, 1951, 1954, 1956, 1960, 1961, 1964a, 1964b, 1964c, 1965b, 1966a, 1966b, 1977, 1979; Nowotny 1961; Smith 1963, 1966, 1973a, 1973b, 1983a, 1983b, 1983c; Troike 1974, 1978; Furst 1978; Rabin 1981; Jansen 1982; King 1988, 1990; and Pohl and Byland 1990), many of the pictorial conventions utilized in Mixtec writing are now well understood.

In most Mixtec codices the text and accompanying scenes are meant to be read in *boustrophedon* fashion (Fig. 3.11). This is a Greek term meaning "as the ox plows" and refers to a style in which each line zigs from left to right, then zags from right to left, then zigs left to right, and so on. Examples of Mixtec books read in this fashion would be the codices Colombino, Selden, Bodley, Vindobonensis, Nuttall, and Becker I.

Less frequently encountered is a two-register format, in which there is usually a red line that divides a page into two zones (e.g., in the Codex Becker II). Indeed, in both formats, boustrophedon and two-register, there are usually red guidelines to help the reader follow the correct order of the text. Finally, there is still a third format, known principally from the Colonial era, in which husband-wife pairs are shown in a long column. An example would be the 1580 Mapa de Teozacoalco (see Fig. 9.3 in chapter 9). The Mixtec referred to each column of text as *yucu*.

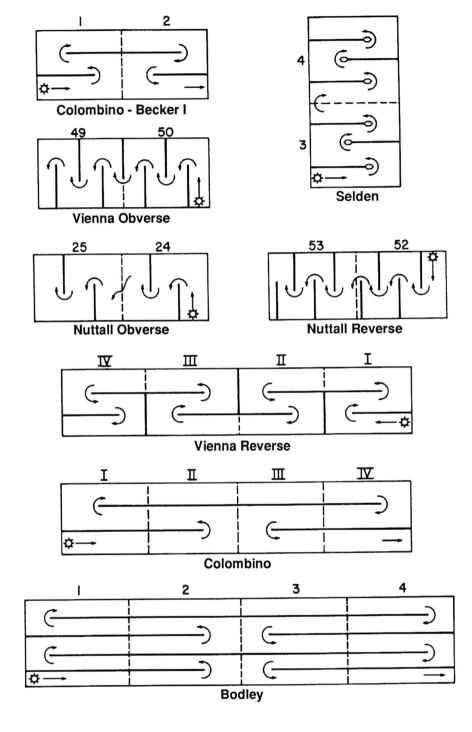

3.11. The Mixtec codices were meant to be read in *boustrophedon* fashion, a term meaning "as the ox plows" or in a zigzag way. Boustrophedon layout had a long antecedent history among the Mixtecs' neighbors, the Zapotec, who from A.D. 600 to 900 had carved genealogical registers that were meant to be read in a manner very similar to that of the Codex Selden (upper right). (Redrawn from Smith 1973a: fig. 1.)

Parenthetically, we should mention that most of these late prehispanic/early Colonial Mixtec styles of writing have precedents in earlier stone monuments from the neighboring Zapotec region. As we will see in chapters 8 and 9, some Zapotec monuments of the period A.D. 300–1000 had multiple registers; some had columns naming royal husbands or wives; and some seem intended to be read in boustrophedon style (Marcus 1980, 1983k). Since the Zapotec and Mixtec are linguistically related and shared a common border for millennia, these similarities are not surprising.

As Caso (1949, 1950, 1960, 1964a, 1977, 1979) and his student and successor M. E. Smith (1963, 1973a) have emphasized, the Mixtec were concerned primarily with writing (and "rewriting") genealogical and dynastic history. We have reason to believe that many codices were kept by the priests of various royal houses in order to establish rights to succession and territory. Codices emphasized the perspective and self-interest of the Mixtec city-state in which they were painted; when various towns' versions of "history" were in conflict, they were often deliberately repainted. As Smith once put it, "Every codex is in a sense a 'local yokel' codex," telling us only what its own community wanted us to hear.

As we have already indicated, codices often record the life-crisis history of a ruler, his parents, his siblings, and his offspring. Because we might have trouble recognizing individual rulers from the conventionalized, cartoon-like drawings in the codices, their names are given in hieroglyphic signs—first their calendric name from the 260-day calendar, then a nickname to distinguish them from others with the same day name. Important events in the life of a ruler included birth, marriage, and conquest, and we will now look at some of the pictorial conventions for these.

The pictorial convention for birth was to attach to the human figure a small (usually red) band which has been identified as an umbilical cord (Spinden 1935:432). This umbilical cord is often used to link the offspring with the year sign of his birth (Fig. 3.12); alternatively, it may link the offspring to his mother (e.g., Bodley 6-I and Codex Nuttall 16, 27). In some cases, the umbilical cord ends in a small circle which has been interpreted as the afterbirth (Smith 1973a:32). The royal offspring is rarely depicted as an infant, or unclothed; usually, both the parents and the offspring are shown as adults. Furthermore, it is significant that elderly Mixtec adults are not usually depicted as aging individuals with wrinkles. In most codices, Mixtec royalty are shown as unchanging adults from infancy to old age. This fact reveals that while the codices do relate the deeds of real men and women, their depictions are *not* intended as portraits of the newborn, the young, middle-aged, or elderly.

The birth of a royal Mixtec infant is shown in some codices by placing his figure below, or close to, his parents. In some codices (such as the back of the Codex Vindobonensis or in the Codex Nuttall) the offspring resulting from a marriage are shown immediately following the marriage scene. Year signs with their dates of birth often accompany the offspring.

3.12. One of the pictographic conventions for "birth" in the Mixtec codices was to show the newborn still linked to its mother by an umbilical cord. At the top, we see a woman giving birth to a son; the woman is named 4 Death, her son is 13 Dog, and his birth occurred in A.D. 1037. Below is a woman named 3 Flint "Feathered Serpent" (her calendric name appears below her; her nickname runs parallel to her right hand). This woman is shown giving birth to a daughter, also named 3 Flint. The daughter's name is given to the left of the Mixtec "A-O" year sign. (Redrawn from Codex Nuttall 27, 16.)

Mixtec expressions for royal birth were often rather elegant metaphors. They included *yosiñenanaya,* "the lord becomes a face"; *yotuvui nanaya,* "the lord appears with a face"; and *yocoocoodzicaya,* "the lord leaves to arrive at his house." One non-metaphorical expression for "was born" would be *nicacuya,* from the verb *cacu,* "to be born."

Mixtec royal marriage was usually conveyed by depicting the man (*yya*) and woman (*yyadzehe*), seated and facing each other. The royal woman usually has her hair braided with ribbons and wears a skirt with a very loose blouse. The man may wear a loincloth or a long gown with a tassel. In various codices the couple is shown on a woven mat (a symbol of authority) or sitting on place signs. Occasionally, the bride is shown offering to the groom a pottery vessel filled with foaming chocolate or pulque. From Reyes ([1593] 1976:34, 76) we know the Mixtec had several idiomatic expressions for marriage, such as "the nobility join hands"; "there is a royal celebration of the mat" (Nahuatl *petlatl;* Molina [1571] 1944:81r); and "the nobles begin to drink pulque." Some of these expressions correspond to motifs employed in royal marriage scenes. (See chapter 8 for a more detailed discussion of royal Mixtec marriages.)

The Mixtec scribe conveyed "conquest" by showing a place sign with an arrow thrust into it. Alvarado ([1593] 1962) in his sixteenth-century Mixtec dictionary gives *chihi nduvua ñuhu ñaha,* an expression meaning "to put an arrow into the lands of another." This means that the pictorial convention we see in the codices has a definite analogue in the Mixtec language (Smith 1973a:33; Caso 1977, 1979). Another expression for "to fight" or "to battle" was *sami ñuu,* "to burn the town." In some codices, red flames were attached to the place sign of the town being conquered, indicating that the place was burned at the time of its defeat (see chapter 11).

Some of the pictorial conventions we have reviewed (e.g., royal marriage, conquest) have a partial or complete counterpart in the spoken language. Another important device in Mixtec writing, however, was the *rebus principle,* whereby a word that cannot easily be written is represented by a word or words that have the same sound and can easily be written. An example of such a rebus in English would be the use of pictures of a "bee" + a "leaf" to = "belief" (Fig. 3.13).

To write the place name for the town the Aztec called Teozacoalco, Mixtec scribes employed this rebus principle (Fig. 3.14). The Mixtec name for Teozacoalco was Chiyocanu (Reyes [1593] 1976:89), which can be translated "great foundation, base, or platform." However, the same word can also mean "bent foundation, base, or platform" (Caso 1949:11–13, 1977:23; Smith 1973a:57–58). Since "great" is a difficult word to write, the Mixtec scribes elected to use the homophone "bent." Figure 3.14a shows the place sign for Chiyocanu, composed of a small man in the act of bending a frieze or platform foundation that has blue and red geometric decorations. In Figure 3.14b the platform supports a temple with two streams (of blood?) and an apparent cacao bean on its roof; there is also a prominent flower at the right, at the base of the steps leading up to the temple. The

belief

3.13. An example of a difficult-to-write abstract noun is the word "belief," which can be conveyed by using the rebus principle (bee + leaf = belief).

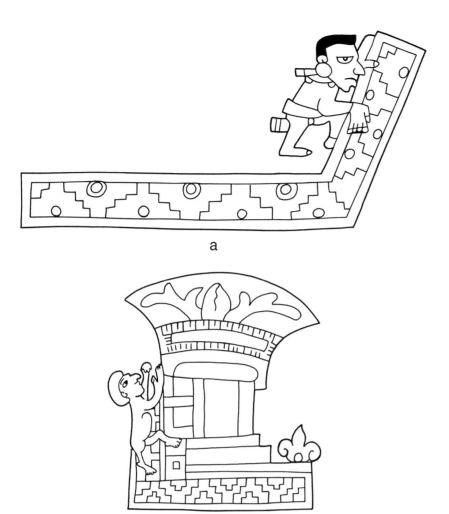

a

b

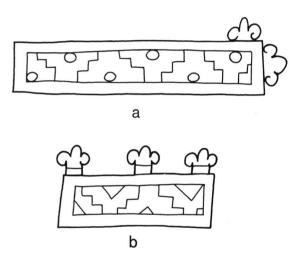

a

b

3.14. The rebus principle was often used to represent the place name of Teozacoalco, a dynastic seat in the Mixteca Alta (see Fig. 3.9). Although this place is best known by its Nahuatl name, we must turn to its Mixtec name (Chiyocanu) to understand the rebus. Chiyocanu meant "great platform," but since "bent platform" had virtually the same sound in Mixtec, the scribe used a small man in the act of "bending" a platform to represent the place name (*a*). Below, at *b*, we see a different version in which the little man is also apparently bending the platform; but additional elements are included, such as the decorated roof and a flower to the right of the temple. Perhaps these additions reduced even further any ambiguity about the identification of the place as Chiyocanu. (*a* was redrawn from Codex Bodley 15; see Corona Núñez 1964, 2: Lámina XV. *b* was redrawn from the Mapa de Teozacoalco of 1580; see Caso 1949.)

3.15. The place name of Teozacoalco could evidently also be depicted by showing flowers above a platform to indicate the associated hillslope Yuhitaini. (*a*, redrawn from Codex Bodley 18; Corona Núñez 1964, 2: Lámina XVIII. *b*, redrawn from Codex Selden 13; Corona Núñez 1964, 2: Lámina XIII.)

3.16. This example of the Yanhuitlán place sign was also based on the rebus principle. The Mixtec name for Yanhuitlán—Yodzo Cahi, meaning "wide plain" or "broad valley"—was difficult to depict. Because the word *yodzo* could mean both "large feather" and "plain" or "valley" depending on the tone, a wide feather platform was used to depict the place. Sitting atop the place sign in this version are two individuals who were ruling Yanhuitlán at the time of the Spanish conquest: at the left is Lord 8 Death, and at the right is his wife 1 Flower "Jaguar Quechquemitl." (The *quechquemitl* was a poncho-like garment worn by Indian women, and was frequently used in female nicknames.) (Redrawn from Codex Bodley 19; Corona Núñez 1964, 2: Lámina XIX.)

little man shown in the act of bending the platform creates *chiyocanu,* while the additional details probably reduce ambiguity.

In most depictions of Teozacoalco the little man bending the platform is shown, but sometimes it was apparently sufficient to use flowers above a geometrically decorated platform, as in Figure 3.15. That is because in the description of Teozacoalco, it is stated that the town is on a slope named Yuhitaini (Martínez Gracida 1883; Smith 1973a:58). Since *ita* means "flower," the Mixtec may have used it as part of the expression *yuu-ita-ini,* recorded by the Spaniards as Yuhitaini (Smith 1973a:58).

Another example of rebus writing would be the toponym for Yanhuitlán, whose Mixtec name was Yodzo Cahi. Since Mixtec is a tone language, *yodzo* can mean "plain" or "valley" with one tone, but given another tone it can mean "large feathers." The Mixtec scribe therefore painted a rectangle of large feathers forming a mat or platform as a tone pun for "plain" (Fig. 3.16). Since one of the meanings of *cahi* is "wide," Yodzo Cahi may have meant "wide plain" or "broad valley."

When we look at the place sign for Yanhuitlán as given in the Codex Bodley (Fig. 3.16), the feather mat representing *yodzo* is clear; but we also see a bird with darts or spear points depicted, as well as an open mouth with teeth in the center of the feather mat. Smith (1973a:63) suggests a number of possible explanations for these unexpected elements, one of which is that another name for Yanhuitlán was Yodzo Dzaa, "Plain of the Bird." Therefore, in some cases Mixtec scribes may have reduced the ambiguity of their rebus writing by giving alternative names for a place, or adding the names of nearby landmarks. This would have been particularly important when two places had similar names.

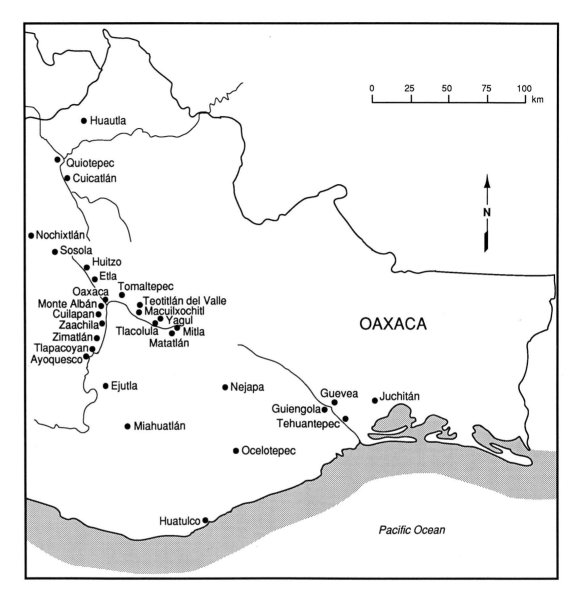

3.17. Map of the Zapotec region in the present-day Mexican state of Oaxaca, showing important places mentioned in the text. Also shown are two Mixtec towns (Nochixtlán and Sosola), two Cuicatec places (Cuicatlán and Quiotepec), and a Mazatec town (Huautla). (Redrawn from Flannery and Marcus 1983a: endpapers.)

As in the other Mesoamerican states discussed earlier, Zapotec society was divided into class-endogamous upper and lower strata (see Fig. 3.17 for a map of the Zapotec region). The upper stratum included the royal family and other hereditary nobility, with the Zapotec lord referred to as *coqui* and his wife as *xonaxi*. Suffixes of various kinds were used to distinguish persons such as a *coquitào* ("great lord" or "king") or a *coquihualao* (prince). Minor nobles might be referred to as *xoana*, a title thought by the Colonial Spaniards to be equivalent to their term *hidalgo* (Córdova [1578a] 1942:219r; Marcus 1978; Flannery and Marcus 1983a).

Within the upper stratum of Zapotec society there were numerous distinctions in rank, but these distinctions did not constitute separate classes. They were merely distinctions of rank among major and minor nobles, all of whom could intermarry, and all of whom were regarded as distinct from commoners. For example, Córdova ([1578a] 1942:246r) lists at least three terms for different elite lineages, as follows:

1. *tija coqui*, the lineage of the *"señores grandes,"* or greatest hereditary lords.
2. *tija joana*, a lineage of lesser nobles "like those called *caballeros* in Spain."
3. *tija joanahuini*, a lineage of still lesser nobles (*huini* = a diminutive), "like those called *hidalgos* in Spain."

Commoners were referred to as coming from the *tija peniqueche* (*peni* = people; *queche* = town), the lineage of *populares o labradores* (working-class townspeople). This lower stratum of society consisted of free commoners, servants, and slaves. Terms of respect among commoners included *golaba*, "lord's solicitor," and *peni coxana*, "male household head." There were also numerous terms for occupations, such as diviner or "interpreter of dreams" (*peni cobeepecala*), teacher (*hueyococete*), or master craftsman (*copeeche*).

Zapotec lords, like their Aztec and Mixtec counterparts, used the courtly speech on which Zapotec writing was based, while members of the lower stratum used more rustic "commoner speech." The sixteenth-century Zapotec referred to noble speech as *tichaquihui* (from *ticha*, "speech" + *quihui*, "palace") or *quelanaquihui* (from *lana*, "word" + *quihui*, "palace"). Their nobles might also use *ticha nayacha*, "elegant speech," or *ticha nataa*, "exquisite speech" (Córdova [1578a] 1942).

We do not have terms for the Zapotec stonecarvers who produced the hieroglyphic monuments of 600 B.C.–A.D. 900. The scribes who produced the books of the sixteenth century, however, were called *huezeequichi* (from *huezee*, "person [who paints or writes]" + *quichi*, "paper"). So strongly had writing shifted from stone monuments to books by this time that almost all verbs for writing include the word for paper: *tozeeayyequichi* ("to put a picture or glyph on paper") and *tozeeaquichi* ("to put on paper") are typical.

The phrase for "writing" itself was *ticha yye caaquichi*, "picture or glyph message written on paper." The individual glyph was referred to as *yye lana* (from *yye*, "picture" + *lana*, "word"). Like their Aztec contemporaries, the sixteenth-century Zapotec distinguished between "true writing" (*tichanaliy, nayaa,* or *nayati*) and "false writing" (*tichanaxihui, ticha huenilachi,* or *yanaliy*).

We have only minimal information on how Zapotec scribes were educated. According to the Spanish friar Juan de Córdova ([1578a] 1942), the Zapotec had different types of schools. Some were called *yoho toatoceteni* (from *yoho*, "house" + *tococetea*, "to teach each other") or *yoho huecete* (from *huecete*, "passive learning"). Most intriguing were a series of schools said to be "like those of Salamanca" in the sixteenth century. These were called *quechetoatoceteni quechenoo quelahuecete* (combining *queche*, "town," with the terms we saw earlier for "to teach each other" and "passive learning"). Which of these schools would have been appropriate for future scribes is an unanswered question.

The Content of Zapotec Writing

Because Zapotec writing has such a long history—from at least 600 B.C. to the end of the Colonial period—it provides us with more evidence of change through time than any other Mesoamerican writing system. Zapotec writing was closely linked to the sociopolitical order, and as that order changed, the content of Zapotec texts changed. We can watch its focus shift as Zapotec society evolved from a maximal chiefdom (600–200 B.C.) to an expansionist militaristic state (200 B.C.–A.D. 300), to a mature state with diplomatic skills (A.D. 300–700), through a period of balkanization (A.D. 700–1000), to a series of small states trying to resist Aztec aggression (after A.D. 1400).

As we saw in chapter 2, some of the earliest stone monuments from the Valley of Oaxaca depict nude enemies slain in combat or sacrificed after battle. A few are supplied with animal names, and the largest prisoner display is accompanied by a text with what may be the dates of historic events. Militaristic themes continued into the Terminal Formative or Protoclassic (Fig. 1.1), at which time there were glyphs of places conquered or subjugated by the Zapotec state centered at Monte Albán (Marcus 1976c, 1980, 1983e).

By the time of Monte Albán's apogee in the Classic period, state monuments seem to deal with the taking of prisoners, diplomacy, and foreign relations (Marcus 1976c, 1980, 1983g). Following the collapse of Monte Albán's hegemony around A.D. 700–900, the portrayal of named royal persons, their births, marriages, ancestors, and offspring became a dominant theme. Royal ancestors—already seen on funerary urns and tomb murals during the Classic—were shown with their descendants on monuments whose texts were clearly meant to be read in boustrophedon style, like the later Mixtec codices (Marcus 1980, 1983k). Often these monuments were laid out in horizontal bands or registers, called *pelayye* or *nezayye* (from *neza*, "road" + *yye*, "picture, glyph"). This concern with establishing the genealogies and life crises of hereditary nobles carried on into the sixteenth century and provides a plausible prototype for the paper, hide, and cloth books of that period.

Unfortunately, we have no large corpus of Zapotec codices comparable to that for the Mixtec. We know that such "books" existed, for there are sixteenth-century Zapotec terms for them. Indeed, during the early Colonial period there were so many native documents that they were kept in a library called a *lichi quichi*. Those codices written on paper from indigenous plants were called *quiychipeyo* or *quichiyagapeo* (from *quiychi*, "paper" + *yaga*, "tree or plant"). Those copied onto paper imported from Spain were called *quiychiyati Castilla*. Some books had a paper cover (*piahuilao quichi*); others had a wooden cover (*piahuilao yaga*). One piece of paper or page of a book was termed *tobilagaquichi, lagaquichiyati,* or *lagaquichinatiba.*

The Zapotec classified their books by shape and by subject matter. While they had codices of the usual screenfold style, they also had scrolls that were rolled rather than folded (*pillaa tooquitiquiuña*). There were "account books" (*quichi xigaba* or *quichi caaticha xigaba*) that may have been tribute records, and "genealogical books" (*quiychi tija colaca,* from *tija,* "genealogy"). The latter were probably similar to the Mixtec codices, and it is a shame that virtually none have survived.

In addition, the Zapotec also made large territorial maps (called *lienzos* by the Spaniards), although most of the examples that have survived are post-Conquest. Two of the best known are the *lienzos* of Guevea and Huilotepec (Seler 1906, 1908; Marcus 1983l, 1984; Paddock 1983a; Whitecotton 1990).

Technical Aspects of Zapotec Writing

The study of Zapotec writing is still in its infancy. Most scholarly attention so far has been directed to the calendric inscriptions, although there are ongoing efforts to interpret the non-calendric subject matter of the texts (Caso 1928, 1947; Marcus 1976b, 1980, 1983e, 1983g, 1983j, 1983k, 1984, n.d.d). Much of the recent progress has been in the identification of proper nouns, such as personal names and place names. The meanings of some events, verbs, and other grammatical elements have been deduced, but not "deciphered" in the sense that the text can be read, pronounced, or understood as it would have been by the original Zapotec stonecarver or scribe. True decipherment involves a demonstration of proof for both the meaning and the phonetic rendering. Just as with Maya writing (discussed below), sometimes we are reasonably confident of the meaning of a Zapotec text, but not of the pronunciation.

Between 100 and 300 different Zapotec signs or glyphic elements have been classified. This is approximately one-tenth to one-third the number of Maya hieroglyphs known. However, the actual number of known Zapotec monuments is an even smaller percentage of the number of Maya monuments. What makes the analysis of Zapotec writing so difficult is that many glyphs occur only once in our corpus of inscriptions. Since context is one of the main clues to decipherment, this infrequency of occurrence puts the Zapotec epigrapher at a real disadvantage compared to his or her Maya counterpart.

Like Maya, Mixtec, and Aztec writing, Zapotec writing is a heterogeneous system that uses a mixture of pictographic, logographic, ideographic, and phonetic elements. The exact percentage of each type of sign has not been quantified precisely for Zapotec, or for that matter, for any of Mesoamerica's writing systems.

3.18. These two sixteenth-century Zapotec nobles apparently had the same name and title. In both cases, the head of an eagle is attached by a black line to a seated man. The eagle head was used by the scribe to stand for the noble's personal name *Biciyatuo* (*Biciatao*), which can be translated "Great Eagle." The second term —*Rigula*, "elder"— is not depicted hieroglyphically, although the shield and spear may relate to military successes that contributed to the individual's status as an elder. (The two men depicted on the left are redrawn from Copy A of the Lienzo de Guevea; the pictograms on the right are redrawn from Copy B of the Lienzo de Guevea. See Seler 1906, 1908, 1902–1923.)

Progress is being made in classifying and interpreting the meaning of the Zapotec hieroglyphic signs (Marcus 1980, 1983j, n.d.d). So far, the identification of pictographic, logographic, and ideographic elements has been easier than isolating phonetic signs. Zapotec place names and personal nicknames frequently incorporate pictographic elements, while calendric signs tend to be either pictographic or logographic.

In Figure 3.18, we see pictographic signs used in the personal names of two men whose glosses are *Biciyatuo,* or "Great Eagle"; the head of an eagle is depicted in both cases. Pictographic signs were also used in place names such as "Hill of the Spindle Whorl" (*Tani Guie Bigoce*) and "Hill of the Fierce Feline" (*Tani Guebeche*); a spindle and whorl were shown above a hill in the first case, and the head of a feline above a hill in the second (Fig. 3.19).

We also have examples of the same place sign written two ways, pictographically and logographically. For example, on the right in Figure 3.20 we see the pictographic sign for a place called "Hill of Lightning" (*Tani Guie Cociyo*), shown as a billowing cloud with zigzag lines of lightning above a hill. On the left in Figure 3.20 is a logographic or ideographic sign for "Hill of Lightning," in which "lightning" is represented by what appears to be a fierce feline. In Figure 3.21 is an example of a personal name incorporating a logogram; the name *Logobicha* or "Face of the Sun" (from *lao* = face + *copiycha* = sun) is indicated by the circular disk that stands for the sun. The serpent head near the disk may be an additional part of this individual's name, but it is not expressed in the gloss added nearby.

Other Zapotec personal names utilized pictographic elements, logographic elements, or some combination of the two. For example, the name *Xilacache Guiebisuño* ("Yellow Feather Rattle") was expressed by a rattle with stone pebbles inside (*guie* = stone + *pizoono* = rattle) and feathers (*xilla* = feathers + *nagache* = yellow) (Fig. 3.22). The name *Picezuño* was also represented as a rattle (Fig. 3.22). The name of a nobleman named *Xuana bechecha* ("Lord Fierce Animal") was shown by combining the pictogram of a carnivore (*beche*) with a flint knife and the sign for blood (Fig. 3.23). *Xuana Nece,* another noble, had his name depicted as a serpent head. Finally, in the last example—that of *Pisialo* ("Eagle Face" or "Eagle Eye")—we have a case in which the accompanying gloss, which refers to an eagle, does not match the associated pictogram (Fig. 3.23).

Like the Aztec and Mixtec, the Zapotec used logograms for most calendric units. For example, in Figure 3.24 we see examples of the Zapotec year sign, year bearer, and bar-and-dot numerals.

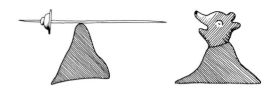

3.19. Two examples of Zapotec place signs that employ pictograms. On the left is "Hill of the Spindle Whorl" (*Tani Guie Bigoce*) and at right is "Hill of the Fierce Feline" (*Tani Guebeche*). (Redrawn from the Lienzo de Guevea, Copy A; Seler 1906, 1908, 1902–1923.)

3.20. Two ways the Zapotec depicted "Hill of Lightning" (*Tani Guie Cociyo*). On the left is the logographic method, in which a descending feline was used to suggest lightning. At right is the pictographic method, in which lightning itself is shown. (Figure at left redrawn from Copy A of the Lienzo de Guevea, that on the right redrawn from Copy B of the Lienzo de Guevea. See Seler 1908, 1902–1923.)

3.21. The Zapotec name *Logobicha* ("Face of the Sun") could be expressed logographically by using the sun disk, as shown in both names here. The serpent head may have served as an additional name or nickname, which is not given in the Spanish gloss. (Figure at left redrawn from Copy A of the Lienzo de Guevea, that on the right redrawn from Copy B of the Lienzo de Guevea. See Seler 1908, 1902–1923.)

3.22. Zapotec depictions of the name *Xilacache Guiebisuño* ("Yellow Feather Rattle") appropriately combine a rattle with feathers. In the lower figure, the name *Picezuño* (a shorter version of *guiebisuño*) is also indicated by a rattle. (Figures at left redrawn from Copy A of the Lienzo de Guevea, those on the right from Copy B of the Lienzo de Guevea; see Seler 1908, 1902–1923.)

3.23. The names of three sixteenth-century Zapotec nobles are given here. At the top is the name *Xuana bechecha* (from *xoana* = noble + *beche* = fierce animal). Behind his head we see an animal, a flint knife, and blood. The knife and blood may reinforce the idea that this animal is ferocious enough to kill a man. The second figure, below, is glossed as *Xuana nece* (noble + snake?). *Nece* seems to be derived from a word for snake (*ce* or *zee* in Zapotec), and is therefore depicted by a serpent. At the bottom, the third individual's name is written as *Pisialo* ("Eagle Face" or "Eagle Eye"). However, the associated pictogram is not the head of an eagle, as we might have expected. In Copy A of the Lienzo de Guevea (at left), it appears to be a deer's head, while in Copy B of the same lienzo (at right) it appears to be that of a serpent. (Redrawn from Seler 1908, 1902–1923.)

3.24. Zapotec logograms could include year signs, year bearers, and numerical coefficients. Each of these glyphic compounds combines a year sign (at top), the year bearer in a cartouche, and the number of the day sign below. (Redrawn from Caso 1928, 1965a.)

Ancient Maya society—despite occasional claims that inflate its system of stratification—had the same division into two class-endogamous strata seen among the Aztec, Mixtec, and Zapotec (Roys 1965; Marcus 1983b, n.d.a, n.d.b; see Fig. 3.25 for a map of the Maya region). Members of the upper stratum, consisting of the royal family and the major and minor nobles, were called *almehen*. Members of the lower stratum were referred to as *yalba uinic* (? + man) and *pach kah uinic* (townsmen). Some confusion in the literature has resulted from the fact that sixteenth-century Spaniards did not always specify whether certain intermediate-level posts were filled by minor nobles or respected commoners.

The hereditary ruler in Yucatec Maya was called *halach uinic* (literally "true man"). Given the lack of separation of church and state in Mesoamerican civilizations, the Spaniards translated *halach uinic* as both "governor" and "bishop" (Martínez Hernández [1585?] 1929:(176r)369). A more general term for "king, monarch, emperor, prince, or great lord" was *ahau*.

Hierarchically below the hereditary rulers were *batabob* (singular *batab*), sometimes relatives of the ruler or lower-ranking nobles who administered dependencies below the ruler's capital city. Below the *batabob* were *ah cuch cabob* (ward leaders, tribute collectors) and various specialists such as the *ah kulelob* (diviners, prognosticators).

Sixteenth-century sources also make it clear that Maya society was not "literate" in our sense. Knowledge of hieroglyphic writing, just as we have seen among the Aztec, was restricted to certain members of the nobility and the priesthood. These people were educated differently from commoners, and the fact that knowledge of writing was shared by only a limited number of people made it easier for the Spaniards to wipe it out. One of the most tragic losses for Maya epigraphers was the burning of twenty-seven hieroglyphic books at Mani, Yucatán, in 1562 by Diego de Landa, who considered the books to be "words of the devil." The Spaniards also hanged many of the Maya priests and nobles who could read the codices, resulting in a loss of knowledge felt keenly by the Maya themselves, who expressed it thus:

> There is no great teaching. Heaven and earth are truly lost to them; they have lost all shame. Then the territorial rulers of the towns, the rulers of the towns, the prophets of the towns, the priests of the Maya are hanged. Understanding is lost; wisdom is lost. (Roys 1967:151)

Education of the Maya Elite

As in the case of the Aztec, the children of Maya nobles were educated in special schools, where they were given esoteric knowledge unavailable to commoners. Writing

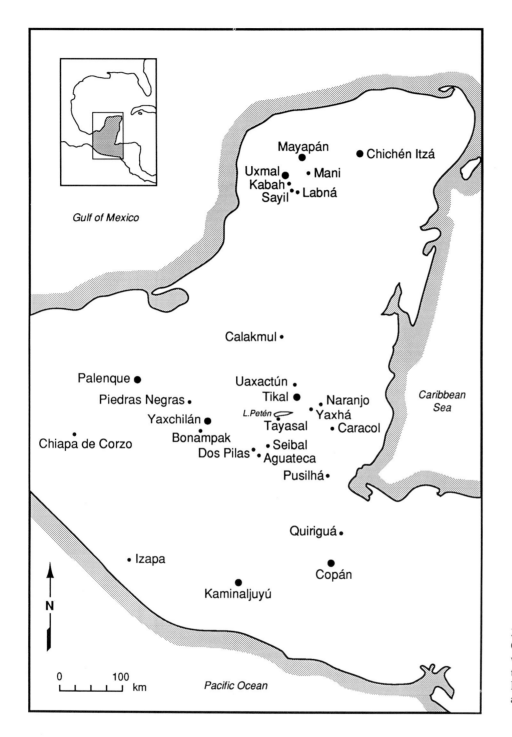

3.25. The Maya region of southern Mexico, Guatemala, Belize, western El Salvador and western Honduras, showing places mentioned in the text. (Redrawn with modifications from Morley and Brainerd 1956; and Morley, Brainerd, and Sharer 1983: fig. 1.1.)

3.26. The founder of the Xiu lineage at Mani in northern Yucatán is shown here with a pair of glyphs on his left thigh. In his left hand he holds a simplified version of the "manikin scepter," a short staff held by Classic Maya rulers. (For additional information on this Xiu founder, see chapter 9.) (Redrawn from Morley and Brainerd 1956: plate 22.)

was one of those esoteric skills, and we have several examples that indicate how strong the association of hieroglyphs was with the elite. We are told that at the fall of the city of Mayapán (ca. A.D. 1450), the Maya ruler Ah Kin Chel "wrote on the fleshy part of his left arm certain letters of great importance in order to be esteemed" (see Landa [1566] in Tozzer 1941:8; Spinden 1913:fig. 10; Roys 1967:68, n.2). This use of hieroglyphs recalls another document, the Xiu Genealogy, which portrays the legendary founding of the Xiu dynasty of Maya rulers at Mani. In that scene, the legendary progenitor of the Xiu dynastic line is shown with a hieroglyph painted or tattooed on his thigh (Fig. 3.26). Both these examples are interesting because, in the sculpture and murals of the much earlier Late Classic period (A.D. 600–900), we find several individuals shown with hieroglyphs carved or painted on various parts of their body (see chapter 11). Still other individuals have hieroglyphs in their headdress or on ornaments; for example, the royal woman in Figure 8.24 of chapter 8 wears her hieroglyphic name in her headdress. What the sixteenth-century examples from Yucatán suggest is that earlier Classic depictions may reflect the actual wearing of glyphs by rulers, rather than captions added by the artist or sculptor.

The sixteenth-century documents give us one other example of the way the Maya elite used esoteric language (whether written or spoken) to reinforce the gap between themselves and commoners. Apparently, in the sixteenth-century provinces of Yucatán there was a perennial problem with *batabob* who had acquired their posts under false pretenses. In order to identify pretenders or usurpers, the *halach uinic* gave each of his *batabob* an oral exam every twenty years to see whether he was a true member of the elite. Both the exam and the answers were given in a special language, called the "Language of Zuyua" (Brinton 1882, Roys 1933). Knowledge of this special language was possessed only by the elite, handed down from father to son, and jealously guarded from others not in that hereditary line.

Both the questions and the answers were metaphorical in nature, and resembled riddles. For example, in the sixth question as given in the Chilam Balam of Chumayel, a sixteenth-century document, a *batab* would be asked to "go and get the branch of the *pochote* tree [*Ceiba schottii*], and a cord of three strands, and a living liana [vine]. This will be my food for tomorrow." The correct answers were that (1) the *pochote* tree was a lizard; (2) the cord of three strands was the tail of an iguana; and (3) the living liana was the entrails of a peccary. Only someone indoctrinated by an elite father would know the correct responses.

Perhaps the most fascinating aspect of the exam was that the Language of Zuyua was apparently not Maya, and may even have been Nahua—the language of the Toltec or Chontal who immigrated to Yucatán around A.D. 900–1000 (see chapter 10). Brinton (1882:110) has argued that Zuyua was a mythical place associated with the Seven Caves of Chicomoztoc, the legendary place of origin of Nahua speakers. The Toltec or Chontal presence in Postclassic Yucatán left a number of Nahua words in Yucatec Maya, and many of those words were associated with political power and social standing (Roys 1967:192). One legacy of the Toltec elite who penetrated the highest levels of Yucatec society may therefore be this special ritual Language of Zuyua, which was part of the esoteric knowledge monopolized by those Maya educated to be nobles (Roys 1933, 1967).

This possibility is reinforced by the genealogy of the Xiu family, late rulers of the Yucatec Maya. Landa ([1566], Tozzer 1941) tells us that the Xiu family traced its origins back to "West Zuyua." In the Xiu family tree, two members have the name Ah Cuat Xiu. Cuat is a variant spelling of *coatl* ("snake"), a Nahua word that may be used either as a name or as a title. Furthermore, in the *Relaciones de Yucatán* (1898–1900, 1:161) we learn of a town near Mani where the people "were subject to a lord whom they called Tutul Xiu, a Mexican name, who, they say, was a foreigner. He came from the west, and having come to this province the prominent people agreed by communal consent to have him as their ruler."

In our discussion of Mixtec calendars (chapter 4), we will learn that an archaic form of Mixtec was used as a "ritual language" for the 260-day almanac. The *iya* dialect was spoken by the Mixtec elite as their special language. The use of the Language of Zuyua by the Yucatec Maya provides a second example of an esoteric tongue, known only to the elite, which was used for ritual purposes. The fact that an exam in Zuyua could be used to disqualify *batabob* who were not true nobles reinforces a point made earlier: certain forms of esoteric communication, whether spoken or written, were used by Mesoamerican elites to maintain the gulf between the two class-endogamous social strata. The situation is somewhat analogous to Europe's Middle Ages, when only a small percentage of society could use ritual Latin and illuminate biblical manuscripts.

The Maya Scribe

Two Maya verbs can be translated "to write." One of them, *dzib* or *ts'ib*, is a key root, leading to a number of very important words. The scribe was *ah ts'ib*, literally "he who writes," while the term for "notary," "writer," or "historian" was *ah ts'ib hu'un*, "he who writes on paper." Two other expressions, *ah ts'ib u bel mak* and *ah ts'ibul*, have also sometimes been translated as "historian."

The second Maya verb for "to write" is *wooh*, which also means "to paint." Thus, a scribe or painter could also be called *ah wooh*. As a noun, *wooh* means "letter," "character," "symbol," or "individual hieroglyph." This word (spelled *uooh*) appears in a copy of the Chilam Balam of Chumayel, as part of the name *Ah Uooh-puc*. This man, *Ah Uooh-puc*, had "a glyph (*uooh*) written on the palm of his hand. Then a glyph was written below his throat, was also written on the sole of his foot and written within the ball of the thumb of Ah Uooh-puc" (Roys 1967:68).

It would be interesting to study all the contexts in which these two words, *ts'ib* and *wooh*, were used. When a stonecarver was entering a hieroglyphic text on a Maya stela, which of the two verbs would have been employed? Apparently *ts'ib*. When a scribe was writing a text in a deer hide or paper book, which verb would he have employed? Apparently *uooh*. I suspect that *uooh* and *ts'ib* were appropriate in different contexts, but at present this dichotomy remains to be fully demonstrated.

Both the *ah wooh* and *ah ts'ib* were expected to place their writing in a specified order. For this action the Maya used the term *tsol*, which means "row," "order," or "succession" (Barrera Vásquez et al. 1980). Significantly, in Maya culture such diverse phenomena as a dictionary, a vocabulary, a ceremony, a narration, a battle, an orator, an interpreter, and writing were all seen as having an "order," the result being that the words for those phenomena all incorporate the term *tsol*. The term for "writing in order," or "dictating" what someone else would write down, is *tsol ts'ib*—which suggests that such messages were written exactly as dictated.

Finally, the sixteenth-century Maya verb "to read," *xochun*, emphasized the calendric component of many Maya texts, since it was formed from *xoc* ("to count") and *hun* ("book"). This use of the verb *xoc* is important, because it suggests that many books embedded the events they covered in a calendric framework.

The Content of Maya Writing

As was the case with the Zapotec, the Maya present us with a tradition of writing that was more than 1,000 years long, and includes both stone monuments and paper books. While the use of hieroglyphic writing in the Maya region is not as early nor as long as in the Valley of Oaxaca, the corpus of Maya stone monuments is many times larger. The study of Maya writing is much farther along than the study of Zapotec writing, in part because there are many more occurrences of each glyph (hundreds more occurrences, in some cases), which greatly increases the pace of decipherment.

From the earlier periods of Maya archaeology, such as the Classic period (A.D. 250–900), the evidence for writing consists mainly of stone monuments and painted polychrome pottery. There are a few thousand stone monuments known at this writing, and approximately 1,000 different hieroglyphs have been classified. This huge corpus of monuments dwarfs the number of Maya paper books or codices, which understandably have not survived well in the tropical lowlands of Mexico, Belize, Guatemala, El Salvador, and Honduras. Fragments of Classic period books have been found at Uaxactún in Guatemala, Altun Ha in Belize, Copán in Honduras, and El Mirador in Chiapas, Mexico, among other places. At present, the El Mirador Codex is a lump of coalesced lime sizing, since all the paper sandwiched between the sizing has long since disintegrated. With future laser or x-ray breakthroughs, it is hoped that some of the content can be gleaned from this codex.

We saw in the case of the Zapotec that the subject matter of monuments changed over time as the sociopolitical order evolved. The Classic Maya present us with an even more complex case, for they had several different types of monuments in use at any one time, and each type appears to have featured a specific subject matter.

Let us therefore look briefly at the subject matter of stelae, lintels, wall panels, hieroglyphic staircases, zoomorphs, tomb murals, and polychrome pottery vessels. The principal dichotomy is between one ruler's personal history and an entire site's history (encompassing far longer spans of time and including the reigns of several rulers). Texts on stelae, lintels, polychrome pots, and tomb murals tend to emphasize the reign of one ruler; huge wall panels and hieroglyphic staircases tend to cover multiple reigns during the history of the site (Marcus 1976a, 1987).

Stelae

The free-standing monoliths we call *stelae* usually recorded a 5, 10, or 20-year segment of one ruler's reign (Figs. 3.27, 3.28). They were usually set up in an orderly fashion in front of a prominent public building. Typically, following a ruler's accession to the throne, an initial stela would be carved and set up to honor that event. Later, at regular temporal intervals, one or more stelae would be set up to document other events that took place during the ruler's reign—possibly his marriage, his "capturing" of other lords, his taking of captives, his conquests, or a number of important religious and political rites he had performed (Proskouriakoff 1960, 1963, 1964, 1973; Berlin 1977; Marcus 1976a, 1983b). Long after the events (i.e., retroactively), the ruler might supply the date of his birth, the names of his parents, and information about events that had taken place prior to his inauguration. This retroactive presentation of birthdates, childhood rites, and kinship data gave any new ruler the opportunity to select, alter, and fabricate data; there were no monuments to contradict him, because his first monuments had been erected *after* he took office.

Maya stelae are often truly monumental pieces of stone sculpture, sometimes depicting the ruler as greater than lifesize, a practice similar to that known from ancient Egypt (Marcus 1987:60). The Maya ruler is usually the only individual depicted, but may occasionally be accompanied by members of his immediate family. Their size and public placement make it clear that stelae are mostly concerned with vertical propaganda.

Lintels

Unlike stelae, carved lintels tend to depict scenes of private ritual, such as bloodletting rites carried out by members of royal families. As befits their more private content, they

3.27. Example of a Maya temple with two stelae set up in front of it. Here, at Structure K-5 at Piedras Negras, Guatemala, the second ruler in the dynastic sequence erected his last two monuments around A.D. 682. (See chapter 10 for more information on this ruler's accession to the throne.) (Redrawn from Proskouriakoff 1946.)

3.28. Example of a hieroglyphic staircase (left), a free-standing stela (center), and a zoomorph (lower right). Pictured is Structure 26 at Copán, Honduras, whose stairway (when fully intact in A.D. 750–760) once bore the longest-known Maya text, a dynastic sequence conveyed in more than 2,000 hieroglyphs. (Redrawn from Proskouriakoff 1946.)

3.29. Example of a carved wall panel (center), door jambs (left and right), and lintel (above) in a Maya temple. The Temple of the Cross at Palenque, Mexico, was one of a triad of temples supposedly built and dedicated by the ruler "Snake Jaguar" in A.D. 690. (Redrawn from Proskouriakoff 1946.)

were often placed in the rooms of palaces and temples where their restricted access makes it clear they communicated horizontal propaganda (Fig. 3.29).

In addition to royal autosacrifice, lintels may depict high-level conferences among members of the elite. They may also show the taking of a prisoner or sacrificial victim. The invocation of the spirit of a deceased royal ancestor is still another theme deemed appropriate for display on a lintel, but in a place where only nobles were likely to see it.

Zoomorphs

Zoomorphic sculptures, often carved in the round on multi-ton boulders, depicted supernatural beings or fantastic creatures that were often composites of several animals. Some creatures on zoomorphs may even represent "animated" versions of such great natural forces as "earth" and "sky."

Zoomorphs were on public display like stelae, their vertical propaganda serving to link the current ruler to a divine ancestor or fantastic creature. Often the ruler himself, or one of those ancestors, was depicted in the mouth of the zoomorphic creature, perhaps a way of showing his descent from a powerful supernatural. (A similar concept was depicted in Classic period stone monuments among the Zapotec, where beings from the "Jaws of the Sky" overlooked current rulers.)

One Classic Maya site particularly famous for its zoomorphs is Quiriguá, situated in southeastern Guatemala (Sharer 1978, 1990). In Figure 3.28 we see a zoomorph from Copán, a city politically linked to Quiriguá at various times in its past.

Wall Panels and Hieroglyphic Staircases

Many wall panels (Fig. 3.29) and hieroglyphic staircases (Fig. 3.28) are inscribed with long texts that contain a chronologically ordered sequence of the events that supposedly took place during the reigns of several different rulers. Good examples include the wall panels in temples at Palenque (see Maudslay 1889–1902; Berlin 1963, 1965; Kubler 1969, 1972, 1974; Lounsbury 1980; Morley, Brainerd, and Sharer 1983: fig. 11.39) and the Hieroglyphic Staircase at Copán (Gordon 1902, Morley 1920). Both wall panels and hieroglyphic staircases contrast with stelae in not restricting themselves to events that took place during the reign of one ruler. However, they differ in their placement on sites, with hieroglyphic stairways clearly intended for public (*vertical*) propaganda and wall panels intended for less public (*horizontal*) propaganda.

Wall panels and hieroglyphic stairways have proved important in showing gaps in succession between Maya rulers (chapter 10). They do not *explain* those gaps, however, since growing evidence suggests that Maya rulers did not necessarily want us to know exactly what took place during such interruptions in the dynastic sequence.

With the political changes taking place around A.D. 900, monument carving ceased at many sites in northern Guatemala. For the later stages of Maya archaeology, as is the case in so many areas of Mesoamerica, our study of writing deals increasingly with paper books rather than stone monuments. And here we suffer from the tragic loss of many perishable documents, such as the twenty-seven codices deliberately burned by the Spaniards.

The most completely preserved prehispanic codices from northern Yucatán—the Codex Dresden, the Codex Madrid, and the Codex Paris (named for the cities where they now reside)—give us some idea of the information that has been lost. These three codices have been interpreted as ritual almanacs, divinatory horoscopes, and astronomical prognosticators.

At one time, every major town in Yucatán must have had its own books. One class of sacred document was called the Book of Chilam Balam (from *chilam*, "prophet," and *balam*, which can mean "jaguar" or "priest"). Among the postconquest texts that escaped burning by Spanish priests were the Books of Chilam Balam of the towns of Chumayel, Tizimín, Tekax, Nah, Oxkutzcab, Mani, Ixil, and Kaua (Barrera Vásquez 1939; Brinton 1882; Roys 1933, 1946, 1949, 1967; Edmonson 1982, 1986). Royalty, nobles, and priests used these sacred books to understand the past and to predict the future.

The Maya of the southern highlands of Guatemala also kept books. One of the most famous is the postconquest Popol Vuh, "The Book of the Mat" (from *vuh*, "book," and *pop*, "mat," which we have already seen used as a symbol of authority). This document eloquently presents the origin myth and "history" of the Quiché Maya. However, it is a very late manuscript, having apparently been written (in European script) in the sixteenth century in the Quiché capital of Utatlán. Another highland Guatemalan book, Annals of the Cakchiquel, is an equally late history of the Cakchiquel Indians.

The Maya revered their ancient documents, which were painted on paper (*huun*) produced by pounding the native fig tree or *kopo'* (*Ficus* spp.) with a bark beater. This bark paper was then sized with lime, as were highland Mexican codices. Obviously, the Spaniards examined a lot of these before burning them; Sánchez de Aguilar ([1639] 1900:95) tells us that "in these [books] they painted in colors the count of their years, the wars, epidemics, hurricanes, inundations, famines, and other events."

Avendaño, writing in 1696, tells us of Maya "books of prophecies" that showed

not only the count of the said days and months and years, but also the ages [*katuns*] and prophecies which their idols and images announced to them, or, to speak more accurately, the devil by means of the worship which they pay to him in the form of some stones. These ages are 13 in number; each age has its separate idol and its priest, with a separate prophecy of its events. (Avendaño 1696b)

So well had Avendaño studied Maya documents that when he was shown a mask set in a stone column at Tayasal, the Itzá Maya capital of the Petén district of northern Guatemala, he instantly identified it as a supernatural being named *Ah-Cocah-mut*.

> I came to recognize it, since I had already read about it in their old papers and had seen it in their *Anahtes*, which they use, which are books of the barks of trees, polished and covered with lime, in which by painted figures and characters, they have foretold their future events. (Avendaño 1696a, folio 29r; cf. Roys 1933:153, n.5)

Unfortunately, since the Spaniards had already equated Maya supernatural beings with Satan, many of the documents they found were doomed to destruction.

Technical Aspects of Maya Writing

During the course of his career, Sir Eric Thompson isolated and catalogued over 800 Maya glyphs. These were divided into "main signs" and "affixes" (prefixes, superfixes, postfixes, subfixes, and infixes; see Fig. 3.30). In 1962 Thompson published *A Catalog of Maya Hieroglyphs*, which continues to be an important sourcebook on the distribution and frequency of glyphs. However, as new monuments are found and further analysis is

a

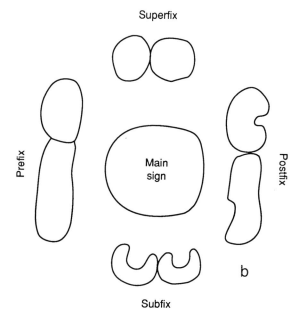

b

3.30. Example of a Maya hieroglyph, showing the use of affixes surrounding the main sign. At *a* is the Palenque emblem glyph; at *b* is a diagram that labels all the elements seen in *a*. (Redrawn from Marcus 1976a: fig. 1.3.)

undertaken on previously known but eroded texts, it is becoming increasingly difficult to fit all the new glyphs into Thompson's system, particularly in the category of "head variants" or "portrait" glyphs (Thompson 1962).

As with the other three writing systems discussed earlier, Maya writing is heterogeneous—a mixture of pictographic, logographic, ideographic, and phonetic elements. Compared to Aztec, Mixtec, and Zapotec writing, however, Maya writing appears to have employed more phonetic elements, and to have employed them in many more contexts than simply in nouns. If we were to place all four Mesoamerican writing systems on a continuum, with an absence of phoneticism on the far left and complete phoneticism on the far right, most scholars would place Maya well to the right of the other three because of its seemingly greater percentage of phonetic elements. However, one caution seems in order: since we still do not read or understand the Zapotec, Mixtec, and Nahuatl systems as fully as that of the Maya, we may be underestimating the degree of phoneticism in the other three systems.

Examples of Pictographic Writing

Some of the earliest signs in ancient Maya writing are pictograms. In fact, early personal names are often made up of pictograms, and some continue this pattern throughout the Classic. For example, the use of the jaguar (*bahlam, bahlum*) in names is known for the entire Classic period; other names include birds (such as the macaw, *mo*) and bat (*suts, zotz*) (Fig. 3.31). During the Late Classic (A.D. 600–900), the Maya stonecarver sometimes expressed the same name pictographically, logographically, and phonetically.

Examples of Logographic Writing

Logograms and ideograms are very frequent signs in Maya writing. Examples include signs for the sun (*kin*), moon (*u*), earth (*cab*), sky (*caan*), wind (*ik*), and darkness (*akbal*) (Fig. 3.32). Other logograms include calendric signs (for day and month names, see chapter 4), as well as signs for numbers. A finger could stand for "1"; a crossed-hatched, four-petaled flower could stand for "zero" or "completion" (see Fig. 3.32e, f). Some words were expressed logographically in one text and phonetically in another, and sometimes they were expressed both ways in the same text.

Examples of Phonetic Writing

For over 100 years, Maya epigraphers have been using Landa's 1566 "alphabet" as an aid to decipherment (Fig. 3.33). To produce this so-called alphabet, Landa pronounced

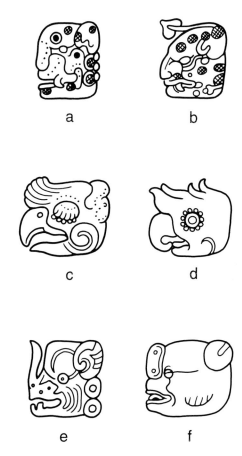

3.31. Examples of Classic Maya pictograms used as parts of rulers' names. *a, b,* jaguar heads; *c, d,* macaws; *e, f,* bats. (Redrawn from Thompson 1962.)

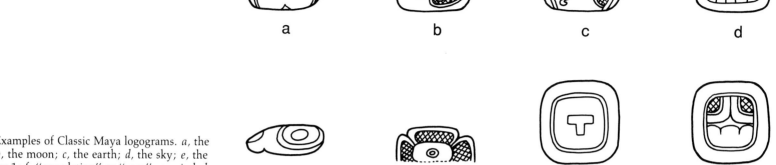

3.32. Examples of Classic Maya logograms. *a*, the sun; *b*, the moon; *c*, the earth; *d*, the sky; *e*, the number 1; *f*, "completion" or "zero"; *g*, wind; *h*, darkness. (Redrawn from Thompson 1950, 1962.)

out loud the letters of the Spanish alphabet (pronounced *ah, bay, say, day,* and so on) while a Maya scribe listened and drew the hieroglyph that most closely matched the sound. To be sure, the Maya had no alphabet in our sense, but Landa's list continues to be useful to epigraphers today. For example, Landa's *ene* (the Spanish pronunciation of the letter "n") elicited a drawing of the Maya subfix for the final "n" or "ne" sound. In such words as *kin* ("sun," "day," "time"), *lakin* ("east"), *chikin* ("west"), and *Yaxkin* (a month name meaning "new sun"), we see the Maya "n(e)" sign used as a suffix to reinforce the final "n" sound, even though this final "n" sign is optional (see Figs. 3.34—3.36).

During the 1950s and 1960s, Knorozov (1955, 1958a, 1958b, 1967), Thompson (1950, 1962), Kelley (1962a, 1968), and Barthel (1969) continued to assign sounds to signs. During the last 20 years, more progress has been made in determining the percentage of signs that can be read phonetically (e.g., Dütting 1965, 1970, 1972, 1976, 1978, 1979; Kelley 1976; Lounsbury 1984; Justeson and Campbell 1984; Bricker 1986; Stuart and Houston 1989).

The "principle of glyph substitution," whereby one element—main sign or affix—stands in for another without altering the meaning, was noted early on by Thompson (1944, 1950, 1962). Thompson emphasized that much of the phonetic content in Maya writing was evident in affixes that functioned as adjectives, adverbs, and verb tenses. Examples of affixes that can now be read phonetically (Knorozov 1967) include *u*, "his, hers, its" (Fig. 3.37a); an affix pronounced *ah*, meaning "he" (Fig. 3.37b); and a series of affixes pronounced *yax*, "new, green, fresh, precious" (Fig. 3.37c, d), which we have already seen used in Figure 3.36 to modify *kin* (Thompson 1950).

3.33. Landa's "alphabet." By speaking each letter of the Spanish alphabet (for example, a, b, c, pronounced *ah, bay, say*), Diego de Landa elicited these hieroglyphs from his Yucatec Maya informants in the sixteenth century A.D. Thompson (1950), Knorozov (1967), Lounsbury (1973, 1974a), Bricker (1986), and others have successfully utilized this "alphabet" to reconstruct many phonetic and syllabic elements in Classic Maya writing. (Redrawn from Tozzer 1941:170.)

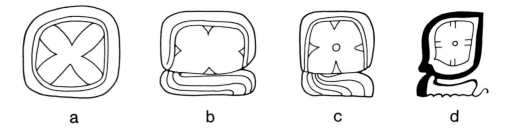

3.34. Examples of a Classic Maya sign: *kin*, meaning "sun," "sunlight," "day," and "time." These meanings can be expressed by using a logogram (*a*), or by attaching a phonetic suffix to the logogram (*b, c, d*). *b, c,* and *d* include a subfix, the terminal consonant *n(e)*. This subfix, which resembles a curved tail, is the same sign Landa's Yucatec informants drew for the Spanish letter "n" (pronounced *ene*) many centuries later (see Fig. 3.33). (Redrawn from Thompson 1950.)

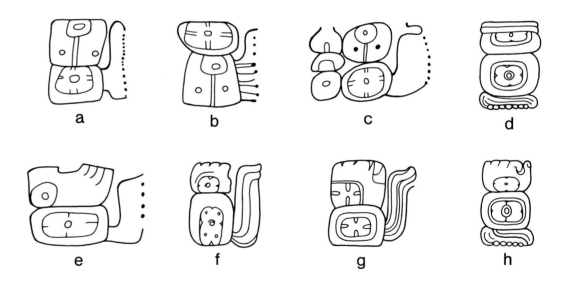

3.35. Examples of phonetic renderings of "east" and "west" in the Maya writing system. The top row shows four ways to express "east" (*lakin*), while the second row shows four variants of "west" (*chikin*). At *a*, we can read *la* + *kin* + *n(e)*; at *b*, *kin* + *la* + *n(e)*; at *c*, *ti* + *la* + *kin* + *n(e)*; and at *d*, *la* (?) + *kin* + *n(e)*. At *e, f, g,* and *h*, we can read *chi* + *kin* + *n(e)*. (Redrawn from Thompson 1950.)

3.36. Maya hieroglyphic writing reveals great versatility and flexibility, especially in its substitution patterns. All of the hieroglyphic compounds in the upper row can be read as *Yaxkin*; thus, *Yaxkin* could be written by combining and substituting different logograms and phonograms. All of the hieroglyphic compounds in the lower row show the month *Yax*. Although all the compounds in the lower row include a prefix pronounced *yax*, the main signs functioned as logograms and were not pronounced. (Redrawn from Thompson 1950.)

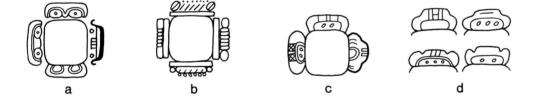

a   b   c   d

3.37. Examples of affixes in Classic Maya writing. At *a* we see the signs for *u*, "his, hers, its" (third person singular, possessive). At *b* are the signs for *ah*, "he." At *c* and *d* are seven examples of the prefix *yax*, "new," "fresh," "green." Compare *c* and *d* with examples in Figure 3.36. (Redrawn from Thompson 1962.)

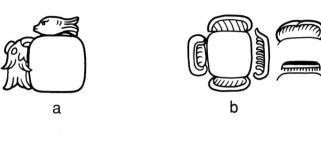

a   b

3.38. Substitution of phonetic elements was an important feature of Maya hieroglyphic writing from A.D. 250 to 1000. The fish affix (*cay*), two examples of which are shown at *a*, could substitute for any of the six examples of the "comb" (*ca*) shown at *b*. (Redrawn from Thompson 1962.)

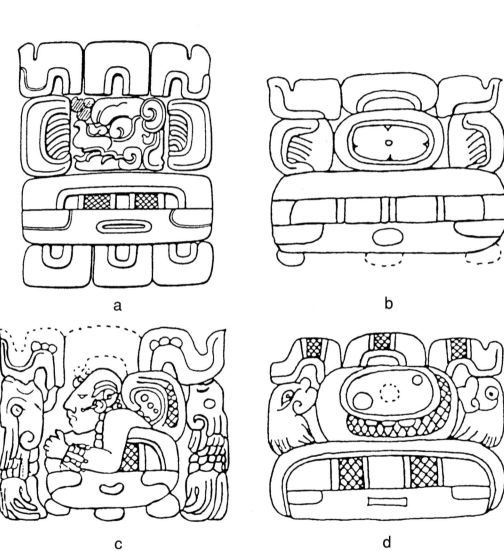

a   b

3.39. Thompson (1944) demonstrated the "principle of substitution," in which one Maya sign could stand for another. One of his examples was the Initial Series Introductory Glyph, where he showed that the comb affixes (*ca*) (at *a* and *b*) occupied the same positions that the fish affixes did (see *c* and *d*). (Redrawn from Thompson 1950: fig. 23.)

c   d

Thompson (1944, 1950) noted that the initial sound *ca* could be expressed either by using a fish (*cay*) or a comb (*ca*) as an affix (Fig. 3.38a, b). As an example, Thompson used the Maya Initial Series Introductory Glyph, where the comb and fish signs can substitute for each other (Fig. 3.39). Today, we also have examples of a "past tense indicator" (third person singular) that was pronounced *(a)h* or *h(a)* (see Fig. 3.40). A final example of Maya phonetic writing comes from the sixteenth century, when Landa elicited the phrase "I do not want" from his Yucatec informants (Fig. 3.41).

As we have seen, Landa's "alphabet" has proved to be a boon for today's epigraphers. However, there are still many signs in the Classic Maya inscriptions that are not similar in form to any of the elements in Landa's list and whose meaning as well as pronunciation remain to be discovered.

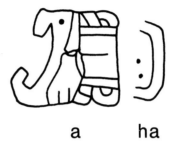

a   ha

3.40. Landa's sixteenth-century Yucatec informants drew the Maya "past tense indicator" when he asked them to show him how to write *ha*. (This suffix is well-known from Classic Maya texts; see chapter 11 for examples of *chu* + *ca* + *ha* ["was captured"] written with the same *ha* suffix.) In the example shown here, the word *achah* is written by using a turtle (*ac*) to supply the initial *a* sound, and the *ha* suffix is used to supply the final sound. (Redrawn from Tozzer 1941:170.)

ma   i   n   ka   ti

3.41. This phrase was the result when Landa asked a Yucatec informant to write a complete sentence. Using phonetic elements that corresponded to the "alphabet" given in Figure 3.33, his informant wrote the Maya phrase, *ma inkati*, "I do not want" or "I do not wish." These signs, with their Spanish captions, have helped twentieth-century epigraphers in their efforts to attach sounds to similar signs used by the Classic Maya. (For example, compare this sixteenth-century *ma* sign with that given in Figure 2.5 from Classic texts of A.D. 500–900.)

4 ◆ NOT ONE CALENDAR, BUT MANY

In an earlier chapter we noted that one of Mesoamerican writing's earliest roles was to present real or mythical persons, places, and events in a calendric framework. In this chapter we look in detail at some of the calendars used for that framework.

Each of the four ethnic groups we consider—Aztec, Mixtec, Zapotec, and Maya—had two principal calendars. Their details are known from sixteenth-century dictionaries and documents as well as prehispanic codices. One was a secular calendar of 365 days, composed of 18 months of 20 days (18 x 20 = 360) plus 5 additional days, which roughly approximates our year. The other was a sacred calendar or "divinatory almanac" of 260 days, composed of 13 numerical coefficients and 20 day signs (13 x 20 = 260). These two calendars could be combined to form a 52-year cycle analogous to our century; that was the length of time it took for the two calendars, running concurrently, to come back to the identical day and month positions on which they had simultaneously begun.

The fact that many widely separated groups from northern Mexico to Honduras, all speaking different languages, had similar calendric structures suggests that the calendars were of great antiquity. Both calendars go back to at least 400 B.C. in the Valley of Oaxaca (chapter 2), and both may already have been ancient at that time. They may have diffused rapidly throughout Mesoamerica prior to their first appearance in stone.

Even though the calendars kept their basic *structure* during this diffusion, the names of individual days had begun to diverge; in addition, many groups chose to begin their years in different months. It is because of these facts that the chapter title "Not One Calendar, But Many" was chosen. It is designed as a cautionary note, drawing attention to one of the most common errors in Mesoamerican epigraphy: the notion that there is just one "Mesoamerican calendar," of which each ethnic variant is but a direct translation.

[handwritten margin notes:] Not to trace them to an actual historical event, but rather to associate them with a mythological creature, or story.

there are both

Remember, Spanish and pre-hispanic codices.

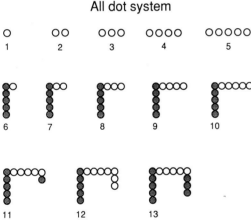

Bar and dot system

O 1	OO 2	OOO 3	OOOO 4	▭ 5
O 6	OO 7	OOO 8	OOOO 9	10
O 11	OO 12	OOO 13		

All dot system

O 1	OO 2	OOO 3	OOOO 4	OOOOO 5
6	7	8	9	10
11	12	13		

4.1. The Zapotec and Maya wrote their numerals in the bar-and-dot system (dot = 1, bar = 5) shown above. The Mixtec and Aztec (after A.D. 1300) usually used the "all dot" system, shown below.

Time and again, well-meaning epigraphers have lined up the days of the Aztec calendar (which is one of the best known, and therefore often used as a prototype) and tried to show that the day names of the Mixtec, Maya, or Zapotec calendar were the same. Such investigators assume that if the Aztec had a day named Xochitl (flower), everyone must; if the Aztec had a day named Cuauhtli (eagle), everyone must. Unfortunately, it is not that simple. While preserving a certain underlying structure, Mesoamerica's various calendars had evolved different sets of day names by the time we first see them carved or painted. In fact, as we shall see below, some scholars have even argued that different Nahuatl-speaking towns within the Basin of Mexico had different calendars.

In addition to sharing basic calendric structures, all Mesoamerican peoples made use of a vigesimal system for counting. The vigesimal system is based on multiples of 20, in contrast to the decimal system we employ. Mesoamerican groups used two principal elements to express numerals: the *dot*, with the numerical value of 1, and the *bar*, which had the value of 5. All four ethnic groups[1] we are studying employed both elements. However, from 600 B.C. to A.D. 900 the Zapotec and Maya typically used both bars and dots to express numbers between 5 and 13, while from A.D. 1300 to 1550 the Mixtec and Aztec typically used only dots for numbers 1 through 13 (Fig. 4.1).

In addition to the bar and dot, a thumb (or other digit) was occasionally used to represent a number. This practice is known for the Zapotec, Maya, and Aztec (see Fig. 4.2). In the case of the Maya and Aztec, a thumb or finger stood for the cardinal number "1" (Kingsborough 1831; Caso 1928; Clark 1938; Thompson 1950:137). In contrast, the Zapotec usually used the thumb to stand for the ordinal number "first" (Marcus 83d:93). According to Córdova ([1578b] 1886:213), the Zapotec used the terms for all the fingers of their right and left hands to express ordinal numbers when referring to the birth order of sons. Thus, the term *yobi* was used by the Zapotec to designate both "right thumb" and "first-born son"; the term *tini* was used for "right index finger" and "second-born son"; the term *texi* was used for "right third finger" and "third-born son"; and so forth.

In the case of the Aztec, not only was a digit used to indicate the cardinal number 1, but other objects were used to indicate the number 20 and multiples of 20. A flag was used as a symbol for 20, an upright feather for 400, and a bag or pouch for 8,000 (Fig. 4.3). In Figure 4.4 we see how those numbers were attached to tributary goods, thus specifying the amount exacted from a region.

In this chapter we proceed, as throughout the book, from north to south. We look first at the Nahuatl calendars of the Aztec region, then those of the Mixtec, then the Zapotec, and finally the much-cited Maya calendar. Before detailing the nature of each ethnic group's calendars, however, we will first review some of the principal sources for

---

[1] Bars also were used occasionally by the ancient occupants of Teotihuacán, Xochicalco, Tenango, and other towns and cities whose ethnic affiliation and language are not known.

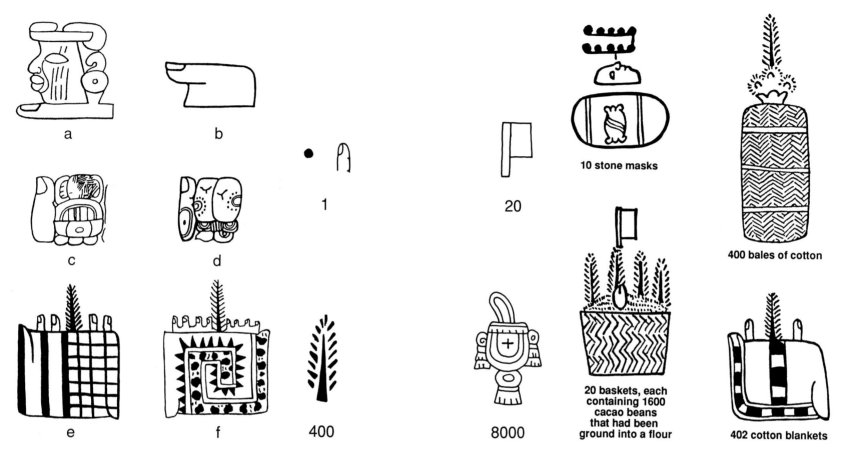

4.2. A human thumb or other digit was sometimes used as a number by the Zapotec, Maya, and Aztec. At *a* and *b* are Zapotec examples that functioned as ordinal numbers (*a*, "second"; *b*, "first"). At *c* and *d* are Maya examples of a finger used as the cardinal number "one" (*c*, 1 *katun* [7,200 days]; *d*, 1 *baktun* [144,000 days]). At *e* and *f* are Aztec examples (*e*, 4 fingers + feather = 404 decorated mantles; *f*, 8 fingers + feather = 408 mantles with a feline motif [feather = 400; see Fig. 4.3]).

4.3. Examples of Aztec numbers. To write 1, a dot or finger was used; for 20, a flag; for 400, a feather; and for 8,000, a copal pouch.

4.4. In their tribute lists, the Aztec attached numbers to particular items in order to indicate quantities. For example, a tribute payment of 10 stone masks was indicated by drawing 10 dots, a mask in profile, and the sign for "stone." For 400 bales of cotton, they used a feather (= 400) above the sign for "cotton," and placed both above a huge basket. For 20 basketloads of cacao, they used a flag (= 20); for the actual number of cacao beans in each basket, they used 4 feathers (4 × 400 = 1,600). For 402 blankets, they used 2 fingers (= 2) and a feather (= 400).

reconstructing them. If the reader is not interested in a review of these sources, he or she can skip ahead to the section called "Nahuatl Calendars."

SOURCES FOR RECONSTRUCTING MESOAMERICAN CALENDARS

Sources for the Nahuatl Calendars

Nahuatl calendric data are available in a variety of sources, including prehispanic and early Colonial codices; carved stones and portable objects; and early accounts written by the Spaniards themselves or by Indians trained by Spaniards to write in Nahuatl using Latin characters.

One of the important prehispanic divinatory books that provides valuable calendric data is the Codex Borbonicus, a source of primary data on both the 260-day and 365-day calendars (Paso y Troncoso 1898, Hamy 1899, Bowditch 1900, Seler 1904–1909, de Jonghe 1906, Kubler and Gibson 1951, Apenes 1954, Lizardi Ramos 1954, Caso 1967). This codex enabled the Aztec priests to plan all the religious festivals to be celebrated during the year. Books II and IV of Sahagún's *History of the Things of New Spain* provide the written description of the ceremonies whose timing and performance were structured by the Nahuatl calendar presented in the Codex Borbonicus. Fixed ceremonies were geared to the 365-day calendar, while *ad hoc* rites were linked to the 260-day calendar. The 18 rituals celebrated at the end of each month of the 365-day calendar were by far the most important calendric ceremonies, and many of these were related to the agricultural cycle (first planting, first harvest, first rains, and so forth).

Another important source is the Tonalamatl de Aubin (Seler 1900–1901) apparently painted by a scribe who copied several parts of the Codex Borbonicus. Other essentially indigenous-style codices include the Codex Telleriano-Remensis, probably painted in A.D. 1554, and the Codex Ríos (Vaticanus A), painted between A.D. 1566 and 1589.

Additional sources include Cristóbal del Castillo (1908), a Texcocan noble writing in A.D. 1596; Boturini (1746); Durán (1867–1880); Orozco y Berra (1880); Serna (1900); Gómez de Orozco (1945); the Tovar Calendar (Kubler and Gibson 1951); the Calendario Mexicano (1919); Motolinía (1903); Sahagún (1938); Seler (1901–1902, 1902–1903, 1904); Veytia (1907); Caso (1939); Kirchhoff (1950, 1956); Jiménez Moreno (1961); and Nicholson (1971, 1978a).

Sources for the Mixtec Calendars

Calendric studies for the Mixtec have relied on a series of sixteenth-century documents, such as El Mapa de Teozacoalco (Caso 1949); the Códice de Yanhuitlán (Jiménez

Moreno and Mateos Higuera 1940); the Mapa de Xochitepec (Caso 1958b); the Codex Muro (Smith 1973b); and Codex 36 in the National Museum of Mexico, as well as eight famous manuscripts painted in pre-Conquest style (Códices Nuttall, Vienna, Colombino, Bodley, Selden, Becker I, Becker II, and Sánchez Solís).

Volumes IV and V of the *Relaciones Geográficas* (Paso y Troncoso 1905)—with data collected between 1579 and 1581—and Volumes I and II of the *Revista Mexicana de Estudios Históricos* (1927–1928) have been utilized by Caso (1928) to reconstruct the Mixtec calendars. Jiménez Moreno and Mateos Higuera (1940) used the Codex Sierra (León 1933), and Dahlgren de Jordán (1954) used the Lienzo de Natívitas. An important series of articles by Caso (1949, 1951, 1955, 1956, 1965b) also deals with the Mixtec calendar.

The most important sixteenth-century sources on the Mixtec language— *Arte en lengua mixteca* by Fray Antonio de los Reyes and *Vocabulario en lengua mixteca* by Fray Francisco de Alvarado—were both published in 1593, and they, too, supply vocabulary and essential data on the Mixtec calendar (see Alvarado [1593] 1962, and Reyes [1593] 1976).

Among the carved bones in Tomb 7 at Monte Albán are several with examples of Mixtec day signs and year signs (see Caso 1932a, 1932b; Marcus 1983n:284). Carved stones from the much earlier Classic era (A.D. 200–900) are also important (Caso 1938, 1956; Spores 1967).

Sources for the Zapotec Calendars

Important sixteenth-century sources include two works—a dictionary and grammar—by Fray Juan de Córdova (1578a, 1578b). The other key sixteenth-century source is the *Relaciones Geográficas* (Paso y Troncoso 1905, vol. IV). For the earlier Classic era we turn to studies of the carved stone monuments from archaeological sites in the Valley of Oaxaca, particularly the texts at Monte Albán (Caso 1928, 1947, 1965a; Marcus 1976b, 1976c, 1980, 1983d, 1983k). Other important studies include those of Seler (1904, 1908, 1902–1923), Leigh (1966), Paddock (1966b), and Caso (1967).

Sources for the Maya Calendars

The literature on Maya calendars is so vast that we cannot do it justice here, but a few sources can be featured. First and foremost is Bishop Diego de Landa's *Historia de las cosas de Yucatán*, written around 1566 (see Tozzer 1941). Landa gives a good description of the calendar, along with some of the associated ceremonies. Significantly, his description was illustrated with drawings of the hieroglyphs for the 20 days and 18 months of the 365-day calendar (see Figs. 4.5 and 4.6).

Three indigenous precolombian codices—the Dresden, Paris, and Madrid (Tro-Cortesianus)—have been basic tools in understanding the use and structure of Maya cal-

4.5. Sixteenth-century Yucatec Maya drawings of the 20 days. (Redrawn from Landa [1566] in Tozzer 1941:134.)

Pop Uo Zip Zotz

Tzec Xul Yaxkin Mol

Chen Yax Zac Ceh

Mac Kankin Muan Pax

Kayab Cumku

4.6. Sixteenth-century Yucatec Maya drawings of the 18 Maya months. (Redrawn from Landa [1566] in Tozzer 1941:151–166.)

endars (Förstemann 1880, 1902; Thompson 1972). Ernst Förstemann's early calendric work enabled others (such as Goodman, see below) to understand Classic period inscriptions carved on stone.

Other essential sources include the books of Chilam Balam, Colonial manuscripts written in Yucatec Maya using Latin characters. The most important of these books—the versions from Chumayel, Mani, and Tizimín—include chronicles of indigenous Maya myth and history set within the framework of the Maya calendar, as well as prophecies for individual years and 20-year periods, or *katunob* (see Martínez Hernández 1927; Roys 1922, 1933, 1949, 1967; Barrera Vásquez 1943, 1949; Gates 1931a; Edmonson 1982, 1986).

One of the first epigraphers to utilize Classic inscriptions of the period A.D. 250–900 to reconstruct the Maya calendars was J. Thompson Goodman. His work entitled *The Archaic Maya Inscriptions* appeared as an appendix in Alfred P. Maudslay's *Biologia Centrali-Americana*, published in 1897. While J. Eric S. Thompson (1950:30) has discovered some details which demonstrate that Goodman made free use of Förstemann's earlier work, most scholars have credited Förstemann with calendric contributions derived from codices (particularly the Dresden Codex), while crediting Goodman with calendric discoveries made from studying Classic period stone monuments.

Goodman was the first to advocate a correlation of the Maya and Julian calendars that involved the adding of 584,283 days to a Maya date to reach the equivalent Julian date. Goodman's 1905 correlation has stood the test of time—it endures today as one of the most popular correlations, and with some modifications by Martínez and Thompson it is now called the Goodman-Martínez-Thompson (or GMT) correlation (Thompson 1950:303–305).

Other important works include those by Bowditch (1901, 1910), Spinden (1913, 1924), Gates (1931b, 1931c), Long (1919, 1923a, 1923b, 1925, 1931), Teeple (1925a, 1925b, 1926, 1928, 1930), Beyer (1931, 1936a, 1936b, 1937), Ludendorff (1931, 1933, 1934, 1938, 1940, 1942), Satterthwaite (1965), Lounsbury (1978), and Edmonson (1988).

Last but not least come two of the most indefatigable and brilliant contributors to our knowledge of the Maya calendars—Sylvanus G. Morley and J. Eric S. Thompson, whose books have endured as classics on this topic (see particularly Morley 1915, 1920, 1937–1938, 1946; Thompson 1950).

Let us now turn to the actual working and use of the calendars by the Aztec, Mixtec, Zapotec, and Maya.

NAHUATL CALENDARS

The Nahuatl calendar of 365 days was referred to as *xiuitl* or *xihuitl* (a word meaning "year," but also "comet," "blue-green stone," and "plant"). The sacred round of 260 days was called the *tonalpohualli*, from *tonal* ("sun," "heat," "day") and *pohualli* ("count"). *Tonal* is derived from the Nahuatl term *tona* or "life force." *Tonal* provides an interesting analogy to the Zapotec, whose term for the 260-day calendar, *piye*, is also derived from their word for "life force," *pèe* (Marcus 1978:174; Marcus, Flannery, and Spores 1983:37).

As stated above, most scholars have emphasized only one of many Nahuatl calendars; there were apparently significant variations among Basin of Mexico communities. Most reconstructions of "the Nahuatl calendar" refer to the Tenochca or Mexica calendar of A.D. 1521. Because it was employed at the Aztec capital at the time of the Spanish conquest, this calendar is the best known and has come to be considered *the* Nahuatl calendar (and even, by some, *the* Mesoamerican calendar).

The degree of variation among Nahuatl calendars at the time of the Spanish conquest is still a matter for debate. Kirchhoff (1950, 1954/1955:259) argued for significant variation among calendars, even between those employed by the "sister cities" of Tenochtitlán and Tlatelolco. Other scholars (e.g., Jiménez Moreno 1961, Caso 1967, C. N. Davies 1973, Nicholson 1978a) acknowledge some variation but think that the differences were not as great as Kirchhoff had indicated; they suggest a "wait and see" approach until more of the documents can be carefully restudied. Significantly, Nicholson (1978a:291) believes that some of the calendric differences among Nahuatl communities might be due to the "well-known penchant of the native annalists to rearrange their community's past events to conform to various political advocatory positions and religious preconceptions (and Kirchhoff himself often clearly recognized this tendency)." We will return to the significance of such calendric differences at the end of this chapter.

The 260-Day Calendar

The Mexica *tonalpohualli* of Tenochtitlán was composed of 20 distinct day names and the set of numbers from 1 to 13. Each day was represented by a day name with a number (sometimes called a numerical coefficient) attached to it. This combination of 13 numerical coefficients and 20 day names resulted in 260 differently designated days (Figs. 4.7 and 4.8).

In Table 4.1, day names are given in the column on the left; they are to be combined with the numbers on the right as we proceed down the columns. Thus 1 Cipactli is followed by 2 Ehecatl, then by 3 Calli, then by 4 Cuetzpallin, and so on. The last day of the 260-day calendar (i.e., 13 Xochitl) is to be found on the last line of the final column. Then the next 260-day cycle begins with 1 Cipactli again.

Because the *tonalpohualli* was a sacred calendar, used for many ritual purposes, it carried with it a great deal of cosmological baggage. Specifically, it was associated with 13 levels of an upper world (or "heaven") and 9 levels of a lower world (or "hell") in which the Aztec believed (see Figs. 4.9, 4.10).

Cipactli (Crocodile)   Ehecatl (Wind)

Calli (House)   Cuetzpallin (Lizard)

Coatl (Serpent)   Miquiztli (Death)

Mazatl (Deer)   Tochtli (Rabbit)

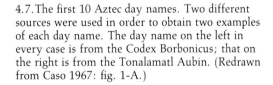

4.7. The first 10 Aztec day names. Two different sources were used in order to obtain two examples of each day name. The day name on the left in every case is from the Codex Borbonicus; that on the right is from the Tonalamatl Aubin. (Redrawn from Caso 1967: fig. 1-A.)

Atl (Water)   Itzcuintli (Dog)

Ozomatli (Monkey)

Malinalli (Grass)

Acatl (Reed)

Ocelotl (Jaguar)

Cuauhtli (Eagle)

Cozcacuauhtli (Vulture)

Ollin (Movement)

Tecpatl (Flint Knife)

Quiahuitl (Rain)

Xochitl (Flower)

4.8. The last 10 Aztec day names. Sources as in Figure 4.7. (Redrawn from Caso 1967: fig. 1-B.)

Table 4.1 The *Tonalpohualli* of Tenochtitlán

Day Names	Day Numbers												
Cipactli (Crocodile)	1	8	2	9	3	10	4	11	5	12	6	13	7
Ehecatl (Wind)	2	9	3	10	4	11	5	12	6	13	7	1	8
Calli (House)	3	10	4	11	5	12	6	13	7	1	8	2	9
Cuetzpallin (Lizard)	4	11	5	12	6	13	7	1	8	2	9	3	10
Coatl (Serpent)	5	12	6	13	7	1	8	2	9	3	10	4	11
Miquiztli (Death)	6	13	7	1	8	2	9	3	10	4	11	5	12
Mazatl (Deer)	7	1	8	2	9	3	10	4	11	5	12	6	13
Tochtli (Rabbit)	8	2	9	3	10	4	11	5	12	6	13	7	1
Atl (Water)	9	3	10	4	11	5	12	6	13	7	1	8	2
Itzcuintli (Dog)	10	4	11	5	12	6	13	7	1	8	2	9	3
Ozomatli (Monkey)	11	5	12	6	13	7	1	8	2	9	3	10	4
Malinalli (Grass)	12	6	13	7	1	8	2	9	3	10	4	11	5
Acatl (Reed)	13	7	1	8	2	9	3	10	4	11	5	12	6
Ocelotl (Jaguar)	1	8	2	9	3	10	4	11	5	12	6	13	7
Cuauhtli (Eagle)	2	9	3	10	4	11	5	12	6	13	7	1	8
Cozcacuauhtli (Vulture)	3	10	4	11	5	12	6	13	7	1	8	2	9
Ollin (Motion)	4	11	5	12	6	13	7	1	8	2	9	3	10
Tecpatl (Flint)	5	12	6	13	7	1	8	2	9	3	10	4	11
Quiahuitl (Rain)	6	13	7	1	8	2	9	3	10	4	11	5	12
Xochitl (Flower)	7	1	8	2	9	3	10	4	11	5	12	6	13

Table 4.2 Lords of the Days and Their Winged Companions

Lord of the Day	Winged Companion
Xiuhtecuhtli (fire lord)	Blue hummingbird
Tlaltecuhtli (earth lord)	Green hummingbird
Chalchiutlicue (water goddess)	Turtle Dove
Tonatiuh (sun deity)	Quail
Tlazolteotl (goddess of love)	Eagle
Mictlantecuhtli (underworld lord)	Screech owl
Centeotl (maize deity)	Butterfly
Tlaloc (rain deity)	Falcon
Quetzalcoatl (feathered serpent)	Turkey
Tezcatlipoca (smoking mirror)	Horned owl
Chalmecatecuhtli (lord of sacrifice)	Macaw (?)
Tlahuizcalpantecuhtli (lord of dawn)	Quetzal
Citlalinicue (celestial goddess)	Parrot (?)

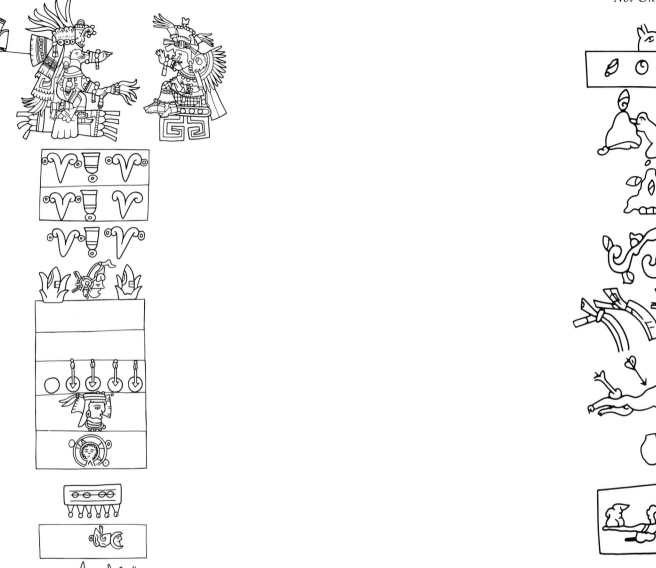

4.9. The Aztec levels of heaven, 13 in all, beginning at the bottom with "earth" shown as an agricultural field. At the highest level we see the divine couple Tonatecuhtli and Tonacacihuatl. (Redrawn from the Codex Vaticanus A; see Nicholson 1971: fig. 7.)

4.10. The Aztec levels of the underworld were 9 in all, including "earth." Since "earth" was already shown in Figure 4.9, we see here only the 8 levels below it. (Redrawn from the Codex Vaticanus A; see Nicholson 1971: fig. 7.)

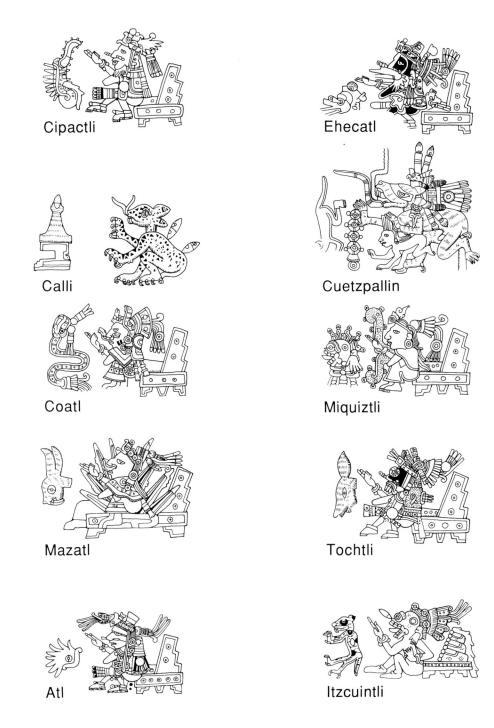

Cipactli

Ehecatl

Calli

Cuetzpallin

Coatl

Miquiztli

Mazatl

Tochtli

4.11. Among the Aztec, each day of the ritual calendar was associated with a "patron." Here we see the first 10. On the left in each case is the day sign, and on the right is the patron "Lord of the Day." (Redrawn from Caso 1967: fig. 10a.)

Atl

Itzcuintli

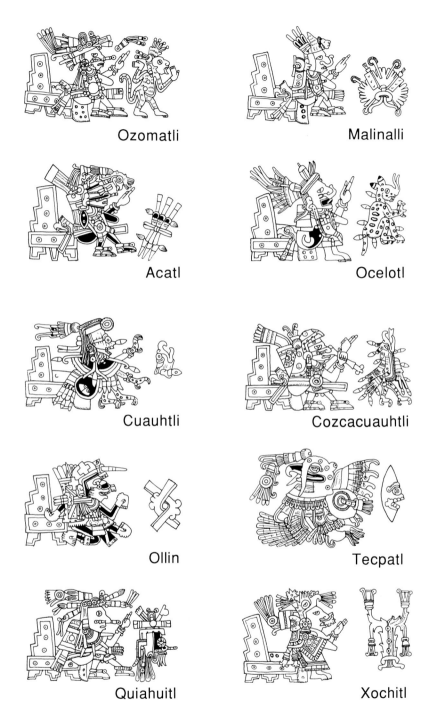

Ozomatli

Malinalli

Acatl

Ocelotl

Cuauhtli

Cozcacuauhtli

Ollin

Tecpatl

Quiahuitl

Xochitl

4.12. Here we see the last 10 days of the Aztec ritual calendar. On the right in each case is the day sign, and on the left is the patron "Lord of the Day." (Redrawn from Caso 1967: fig. 10b.)

Because of its relationship with the 13 levels of heaven, each of the days of the *tonalpohualli* was associated with a "Lord of the Day" (Figs. 4.11, 4.12) and each of these "Lords of the Day" had a "winged companion" flying in the heavens (see Table 4.2; also see Paso y Troncoso 1898, Seler 1900–1901, Caso 1967).

As for the 9 levels of the lower world, they were represented by 9 "Lords of the Night," some of whom were the same supernatural beings given in Table 4.2 as Lords of the Day. The Lords of the Night were (1) Xiuhtecuhtli (lord of fire), (2) Itztli or Tecpatl (obsidian or flint), (3) Piltzintecuhtli (lord of princes, or the sun), (4) Centeotl (maize deity), (5) Mictlantecuhtli (underworld lord), (6) Chalchiutlicue (water goddess), (7) Tlazolteotl (love goddess), (8) Tepeyolohtli ("heart of the mountain" or jaguar), and (9) Tlaloc (rain deity).

In addition to the lords of the day and night, each of the 20 day names of the *tonalpohualli* had a "patron" or "protector," as shown in Table 4.3.

As if the above associations with the supernatural were not complex enough, each 13-day period of the *tonalpohualli* that began with a day whose numerical coefficient was "1" had its own patron(s) as well. Unfortunately, we have lost the indigenous term used by the Aztec for these 13-day units, and are therefore forced to refer to them by the Spanish term *trecena*. Their patrons are given in Table 4.4.

Table 4.3 Patrons of the Day Signs of the *Tonalpohualli*

Day Sign	Patron
Cipactli (Crocodile)	Tonacatecuhtli
Ehecatl (Wind)	Quetzalcoatl
Calli (House)	Tepeyolohtli
Cuetzpallin (Lizard)	Huehuecoyotl
Coatl (Serpent)	Chalchiutlicue
Miquiztli (Death)	Teccistecatl
Mazatl (Deer)	Tlaloc
Tochtli (Rabbit)	Mayahuel
Atl (Water)	Xiuhtecuhtli
Itzcuintli (Dog)	Mictlantecuhtli
Ozomatli (Monkey)	Xochipilli
Malinalli (Twisted Grass)	Patecatl
Acatl (Reed)	Itzlacoliuhqui or Tezcatlipoca
Ocelotl (Jaguar)	Tlazolteotl
Cuauhtli (Eagle)	Xipe Totec
Cozcacuauhtli (Vulture)	Itzpapalotl
Ollin (Movement)	Xolotl
Tecpatl (Flint)	Chalchiuhtotolin or Tezcatlipoca
Quiahuitl (Rain)	Chantico or Tonatiuh
Xochitl (Flower)	Xochiquetzal

Table 4.4 The *Trecenas* of the *Tonalpohualli* and Their Patrons

Beginning Date of Trecena	Patron(s)
1 Cipactli	Tonacatecuhtli and Tonacacihuatl
1 Ocelotl	Quetzalcoatl
1 Mazatl	Tepeyolohtli and Quetzalcoatl
1 Xochitl	Huehuecoyotl and Ixnextli
1 Acatl	Chalchiutlicue and Tlazolteotl
1 Miquiztli	Tonatiuh and Tlamatzincatl
1 Quiahuitl	Tlaloc and Chicomecoatl
1 Malinalli	Mayahuel and Xochipilli
1 Coatl	Tlahuizcalpantecuhtli
1 Tecpatl	Tonatiuh and Mictlantecuhtli
1 Ozomatli	Patecatl and Eagle-Feline
1 Cuetzpallin	Ixtlacoliuhqui
1 Ollin	Ixcuina and Tezcatlipoca
1 Itzcuintli	Xipe-Totec and Quetzalcoatl
1 Calli	Itzpapalotl and Tamoanchan
1 Cozcacuauhtli	Xolotl and 4 Ollin
1 Atl	Chalchiutototl
1 Ehecatl	Chantico and Ce Acatl
1 Cuauhtli	Xochiquetzal and Tezcatlipoca
1 Tochtli	Iztapaltotec and Xiuhtecuhtli

The Importance of the Tonalpohualli

Every day of the 260-day calendar had an associated "fate": lucky, unlucky, or neutral. Since every day name, day number, combination of day number and day name, and position within a 13-day period was associated with a different fate, it was the task of the diviners or *tonalpouhque* to ascertain which would hold sway, especially if some of the fates were at odds with others (Molina [1571] 1944:150r). The sorting out of one's fortune required consultations with those specialists, to determine whether an event planned for a particular day should actually take place at that time, or if a new day should be selected.

One case in which the diviner played a critical role was that of a child born on an unlucky day. Often the *tonalpouhqui* would recommend that the child be named after a luckier day within the same *trecena* or 13-day period. This was an important decision made on behalf of the child by the *tonalpouhqui* and his parents, because the fate associated with one's calendric name and designated birthday was believed to affect the rest of one's life.

In addition to the naming of one's child, many other events of social and political importance were scheduled on the basis of the *tonalpohualli*. Merchants awaited lucky days for their expeditions' departure and return; marriages and other ceremonies were held on days of good fortune. To all who sought him, the *tonalpouhqui* offered help and advice in selecting the appropriate days for particular rituals; he eased the wary through all critical rites of passage.

The *tonalpohualli* and those who manipulated it reinforced the Aztec notion of predestination. This notion both justified the Aztec system of social ranking and partly absolved the ruler of any mistakes. Predestination meant that those who had power, privilege, and rights were preordained to have them; those who lacked those rights were not to complain, because they were predestined to lack them. Since the fates in the calendar determined when it was a good day to go to war or carry out some other activity, the calendar and its *tonalpouhque* also took the decision making out of the hands of the ruler, effectively protecting him from blame. If the battle was lost, the explanation was that the fates had determined it; it was predestined. But those who interpreted the fates of the 260-day calendar could clearly manipulate the outcome. Since the various fates of a particular day or *trecena* were frequently at odds—some favorable, some not—the *tonalpouhqui* had the opportunity to determine the exact day on which an event would take place by deciding which fate took priority. With such a decision making structure and a belief in predestination, there was built-in protection for those who made incorrect decisions. When correct decisions were made, credit or praise might be given to human individuals, but more often than not the supernatural entities were applauded for helping man.

The Good, the Bad, and the Neutral

The associated fates of the calendric numbers are given by Sahagún (Books 4 and 5; see Dibble and Anderson 1957) as follows: 1 = variable, 2 = neutral, 3 = good, 4 = bad, 5 = bad, 6 = bad, 7 = good, 8 = bad, 9 = bad, 10 = good, 11 = good, 12 = good, and 13 = good. Another source (Durán 1880, 2:259) provides us with the fates associated with the day names: Cipactli (good), Ehecatl (bad), Calli (good), Cuetzpallin (good), Coatl (bad), Miquiztli (bad), Mazatl (good), Tochtli (neutral), Atl (bad), Itzcuintli (good), Ozomatli (neutral), Malinalli (bad), Acatl (neutral), Ocelotl (neutral), Cuauhtli (neutral), Cozcacuauhtli (good), Ollin (neutral), Tecpatl (bad), Quiahuitl (bad), and Xochitl (neutral).

There is some disagreement as to whether the day number, the day name, or the combination of the two played the biggest role in determining the fate of a particular day. Sahagún assigns the largest role to the number, while Durán places it on the day name (Caso 1967:28–29). Still another source (Serna 1900) places most of the weight on the day sign, but clearly indicates that the number also had an impact on a particular day's fortune. Each *trecena* also had its associated luck, as seen in the Codex Borbonicus (Paso y Troncoso 1898:21ff). Apparently, the fate of each *trecena* was determined by the day on which it began, as follows: 1 Cipactli (good), 1 Ocelotl (bad), 1 Mazatl (neutral), 1 Xochitl (bad or neutral), 1 Acatl (bad), 1 Miquiztli (neutral), 1 Quiahuitl (bad), 1 Malinalli (bad), 1 Coatl (good), 1 Tecpatl (good), 1 Ozomatli (good), 1 Cuetzpallin (good), 1 Ollin (neutral), 1 Itzcuintli (good), 1 Calli (bad), 1 Cozcacuauhtli (good), 1 Atl (bad), 1 Ehecatl (bad), 1 Cuauhtli (bad), and 1 Tochtli (good) (Caso 1967).

As for the fates associated with the 9 Lords of the Night, it was as follows: Xiuhtecuhtli (good), Iztli or Tecpatl (bad), Piltzintecuhtli (good), Centeotl (neutral), Mictlantecuhtli (bad), Chalchiutlicue (neutral), Tlazolteotl (bad), Tepeyolohtli (good), and Tlaloc (neutral).

The 365-Day Calendar

The Nahuatl *xiuitl*, or year of 365 days, consisted of 18 "months" of 20 days (18 x 20 = 360) plus 5 additional days. These 18 "months" (*meztlipohualli* or "count of the moons or months") and 5 extra days (*nemontemi*) are known from the work of Paso y Troncoso (1898) and Seler (1902–1923), and can be matched with their equivalents in the Spanish year A.D. 1521.

As we will see below, one of the significant differences among ethnic groups was the month in which each began the year. For example, the Tlaxcalans began their year in the month Atemoztli; people in Teotitlán and Tecciztlán began theirs in the month Tlacaxipehualiztli; those in Meztitlán in the month Panquetzaliztli; and those in Texcoco in the month Cuauhuitlehua (which corresponds to the Mexica month of Atlcahualo).

Table 4.5   The Eighteen *Meztli* ("Months")

Meztli	*Dates in the Year A.D. 1521*
Izcalli[a]	January 24–February 12
Atlcahualo[b]	February 13–March 4
Tlacaxipehualiztli[c]	March 5–March 24
Tozoztontli	March 25–April 13
Hueytozoztli	April 14–May 3
Toxcatl[d]	May 4–May 23
Etzalcualiztli	May 24–June 12
Tecuilhuitontli	June 13–July 2
Hueytecuilhuitl	July 3–July 22
Tlaxochimaco[e]	July 23–August 11
Xocotlhuetzi[f]	August 12–August 31
Ochpaniztli[g]	September 1–September 20
Teotleco[h]	September 21–October 10
Tepeilhuitl[i]	October 11–October 30
Quecholli	October 31–November 19
Panquetzaliztli	November 20–December 9
Atemoztli	December 10–December 29
Tititl	December 30–January 18
"Nemontemi" (5 extra days)	January 19–January 23

[a]Also known as Izcalami, Xochiteca (Meztitlán), or Xochilhuitl.
[b]Also known as Cuahuitlehua (in Texcoco), Xilomanaliztli (Tlaxcala), and Cihuailhuitl "fiesta of the women" (Teotitlán).
[c]In Tlaxcala this month was known as Coailhuitl.
[d]Other names are Popochtli (Meztitlán), Tepopochtli (Teotitlán), and Tepopochhuiliztli.
[e]Other names are Miccailhuitontli (Texcoco), Miccailhuitl (Meztitlán), Miccailhuitzintli (Tlaxcala), and Nexochimaco (Tlatelolco).
[f]Also known as Hueymiccailhuitl (Texcoco) or Hueymiccailhuitzintli.
[g]Also known as Huechpaniliztli (Meztitlán) or Tenahuatiliztli (Teotitlán).
[h]Also known as Pachtontli (Texcoco), Pachtli (Meztitlán), Teteoeco (Texcoco), Teotleco (Tlatelolco), and Ecoztli (Teotitlán).
[i]Also known as Hueypachtli (Texcoco) and Pilahuana.

The 52-Year Cycle

Rather than a century of 100 years as we have, the Aztec had a period called a *xiuhmolpilli*, equivalent to 52 of our years. The two calendars that we have seen up to this point—the 260-day *tonalpohualli* and the 365-day *xiuitl*—ran concurrently. At the end of the year of 365 days, one whole 260-day *tonalpohualli* had been completed, plus 105 days of the next. The day name had advanced 5 positions, while the day number had advanced 1 position (i.e., 105 days divided by 20 day names, leaving 5; and 105 days divided by 13 numbers, leaving 1). If the day name advances 5 positions every year, at the end of 4 years we return to the same day name, but it carries a different numerical coefficient which is 4 numbers higher. Since only 4 of the day names could coincide with

Table 4.6 Year Bearers and Their Associated Colors and Animals

Year Bearer	World Direction	Color	Animal
Acatl	East	Yellow	Eagle
Tecpatl	North	Red	Jaguar/Puma
Calli	West	White	Serpent
Tochtli	South	Blue	Rabbit

any month position (e.g., the first day of the year, or the last day of the year), and since there were only 13 different numbers that could combine with those day names, it follows that the Aztecs could run through 52 (4 x 13) different *xiuitl* before the two calendars coincided again.

Each of the four day names that coincided with the first day of the year—Acatl (reed), Tecpatl (flint), Calli (house), and Tochtli (rabbit)—was called a "year bearer" (Dibble and Anderson 1957:137–139, Caso 1967). The Aztec recognized four world directions and four quarters, each associated with a color (Seler 1904–1909, Caso 1967, Nicholson 1971). Each year bearer was linked to one of these directions, its associated color, and an animal, as shown in Table 4.6.

Thus, the *xiuhmolpilli* was the product of 52 *xiuitl* and 73 *tonalpohualli*, for a total of 18,980 days. The Aztec regarded each *xiuhmolpilli* as a "bundle" of 52 *xiuitl* and used that as the unit by which they kept their archives of political and dynastic information. Unfortunately, these annals are not always easy to interpret. Most obviously, they are difficult because although important events are usually dated to a specific year, the 52-year cycle to which those events belonged is not specified. A further problem is that we have reason to believe that *xiuitl* and *xiuhmolpilli* were not always synchronized from one Aztec town to another.

There is evidence that various ethnic groups within the Nahuatl-speaking area were aware of the fact that other groups had different "bundles" of years, since different groups celebrated their "New Fire" ceremonies at different times. Such ceremonies took place at the end of each 52-year cycle and helped to ensure the beginning of the next. Emphasizing this diversity, López Austin (1973:99) says that some Nahuatl groups claimed "*our* years are tied, *toxiuh molpilia*," to differentiate their *xiuhmolpilli* from those of other groups.

López Austin also states (1973:101) that different ethnic groups (or even segments of the *same* ethnic group) had different lucky and unlucky periods. For example, the day 1 Rabbit was bad for the Mexica, and 1 Flint was bad for the Toltec; 1 Reed was an unfavorable day for the lower-class members of Mexica society, but a favorable day for the nobles. The suggestion that some days were lucky for upper stratum members and unlucky for lower stratum members is important, because it shows how the calendar could be manipulated to reinforce the gulf between commoner and noble.

Regional Variation in Nahuatl Calendars

According to Paso y Troncoso (1898) and the Codex Borbonicus, the people in Tenochtitlán began their year in the month Izcalli (see Table 4.7). Various sources, however, suggest that this starting point was not standardized even within the Basin of Mexico (Paso y Troncoso 1898, Kirchhoff 1950, Jiménez Moreno 1961). For example, Seler (1902–1903, 1904, 1902–1923) and de Jonghe (1906) concluded that the year actually began in the month Toxcatl; Nuttall (1904) opted for the month of Tlacaxipehualiztli; and Sahagún

Table 4.7   Correlation of Calendric Systems

Group	Month in which Year Begins	Year Bearer	Years Added to Mexica Calendar
Mexica	Izcalli	11 Tecpatl	—
Texcocano	Tititl	4 Tecpatl	20 years
Cuitlahuaca	Atlcahualo	5 Tecpatl	32 years
Colhua I	Quecholli	9 Tecpatl	28 years
Colhua II	Tlacaxipehualiztli	12 Tecpatl	12 years
Matlatzinca	Hueytozoztli	13 Tecpatl	24 years
Cuauhtitlán	Toxcatl	7 Tecpatl	4 years
Meztitlán	Panquetzaliztli	3 Tecpatl	8 years
Chalca (?)	Tecuilhuitontli	8 Tecpatl	16 years

(1938) for Atlcahualo. These different starting points resulted in several calendars, each utilized by a different ethnic group.

Kirchhoff (1950) suggested that there were 13 different calendric systems in use simultaneously by 13 different groups in and around the Basin of Mexico. As part of his evidence, Kirchhoff was able to demonstrate that the discrepancies among the dates for the founding of Tenochtitlán could be resolved if the documents actually were referring to the same date *in different calendars*. Soon thereafter, in 1951, Jiménez Moreno presented a paper showing the existence of at least three different calendric traditions he called Acolhua or Huexotzinca, Mexica, and Mixtec. Still later, Jiménez Moreno (1961:146) published seven other calendric systems, including the Matlatzinca, Chalca, Cuitlahuaca, Colhua I and II, Cuauhtitlán, and Meztitlán.

Such differences among ethnic groups meant that the year designated 1 Acatl (reed) by the Mexica would be designated 7 Acatl by the Texcocanos, 3 Acatl by the Matlatzinca, 8 Acatl by the Cuitlahuaca, 12 Acatl by the Colhua, and so forth (see Tables 4.8–4.9). This lack of concordance among different calendars means that some correlations linking European calendars with indigenous dates in the codices need careful rechecking. Such correlations should always be based on dates in documents whose specific provenience and ethnic group are not in doubt.

We have seen that there are several suggestions as to when the year began for different Nahuatl-speaking groups, and that there is still a lack of agreement among scholars (Kirchhoff 1950, 1954–1955; Jiménez Moreno 1961; López Austin 1973; Castillo Farreras 1974:184; Nicholson 1978a). While most of these suggestions involve different 365-day years, Kirchhoff (1950; see also Jiménez Moreno 1961) has also suggested that different 260-day *tonalpohualli* were in simultaneous use in Central Mexico, complicating the situation still further.

We also have data indicating that the transition from one 52-year cycle to the next was celebrated at different times by different ethnic groups. For example, the Chichimec

Table 4.8   Year Bearers for a 52-year Period (A.D. 1415–1466) in Different Calendars (Part I)

Years A.D.	Mexica	Texcocano	Matlatzinca	Cuitlahuaca
A.D. 1415	1 Acatl	7 Acatl	3 Acatl	8 Acatl
A.D. 1416	2 Tecpatl	8 Tecpatl	4 Tecpatl	9 Tecpatl
A.D. 1417	3 Calli	9 Calli	5 Calli	10 Calli
A.D. 1418	4 Tochtli	10 Tochtli	6 Tochtli	11 Tochtli
A.D. 1419	5 Acatl	11 Acatl	7 Acatl	12 Acatl
A.D. 1420	6 Tecpatl	12 Tecpatl	8 Tecpatl	13 Tecpatl
A.D. 1421	7 Calli	13 Calli	9 Calli	1 Calli
A.D. 1422	8 Tochtli	1 Tochtli	10 Tochtli	2 Tochtli
A.D. 1423	9 Acatl	2 Acatl	11 Acatl	3 Acatl
A.D. 1424	10 Tecpatl	3 Tecpatl	12 Tecpatl	4 Tecpatl
A.D. 1425	11 Calli	4 Calli	13 Calli	5 Calli
A.D. 1426	12 Tochtli	5 Tochtli	1 Tochtli	6 Tochtli
A.D. 1427	13 Acatl	6 Acatl	2 Acatl	7 Acatl
A.D. 1428	1 Tecpatl	7 Tecpatl	3 Tecpatl	8 Tecpatl
A.D. 1429	2 Calli	8 Calli	4 Calli	9 Calli
A.D. 1430	3 Tochtli	9 Tochtli	5 Tochtli	10 Tochtli
A.D. 1431	4 Acatl	10 Acatl	6 Acatl	11 Acatl
A.D. 1432	5 Tecpatl	11 Tecpatl	7 Tecpatl	12 Tecpatl
A.D. 1433	6 Calli	12 Calli	8 Calli	13 Calli
A.D. 1434	7 Tochtli	13 Tochtli	9 Tochtli	1 Tochtli
A.D. 1435	8 Acatl	1 Acatl	10 Acatl	2 Acatl
A.D. 1436	9 Tecpatl	2 Tecpatl	11 Tecpatl	3 Tecpatl
A.D. 1437	10 Calli	3 Calli	12 Calli	4 Calli
A.D. 1438	11 Tochtli	4 Tochtli	13 Tochtli	5 Tochtli
A.D. 1439	12 Acatl	5 Acatl	1 Acatl	6 Acatl
A.D. 1440	13 Tecpatl	6 Tecpatl	2 Tecpatl	7 Tecpatl
A.D. 1441	1 Calli	7 Calli	3 Calli	8 Calli
A.D. 1442	2 Tochtli	8 Tochtli	4 Tochtli	9 Tochtli
A.D. 1443	3 Acatl	9 Acatl	5 Acatl	10 Acatl
A.D. 1444	4 Tecpatl	10 Tecpatl	6 Tecpatl	11 Tecpatl
A.D. 1445	5 Calli	11 Calli	7 Calli	12 Calli
A.D. 1446	6 Tochtli	12 Tochtli	8 Tochtli	13 Tochtli
A.D. 1447	7 Acatl	13 Acatl	9 Acatl	1 Acatl
A.D. 1448	8 Tecpatl	1 Tecpatl	10 Tecpatl	2 Tecpatl
A.D. 1449	9 Calli	2 Calli	11 Calli	3 Calli
A.D. 1450	10 Tochtli	3 Tochtli	12 Tochtli	4 Tochtli
A.D. 1451	11 Acatl	4 Acatl	13 Acatl	5 Acatl
A.D. 1452	12 Tecpatl	5 Tecpatl	1 Tecpatl	6 Tecpatl
A.D. 1453	13 Calli	6 Calli	2 Calli	7 Calli
A.D. 1454	1 Tochtli	7 Tochtli	3 Tochtli	8 Tochtli
A.D. 1455	2 Acatl	8 Acatl	4 Acatl	9 Acatl
A.D. 1456	3 Tecpatl	9 Tecpatl	5 Tecpatl	10 Tecpatl
A.D. 1457	4 Calli	10 Calli	6 Calli	11 Calli
A.D. 1458	5 Tochtli	11 Tochtli	7 Tochtli	12 Tochtli
A.D. 1459	6 Acatl	12 Acatl	8 Acatl	13 Acatl
A.D. 1460	7 Tecpatl	13 Tecpatl	9 Tecpatl	1 Tecpatl
A.D. 1461	8 Calli	1 Calli	10 Calli	2 Calli
A.D. 1462	9 Tochtli	2 Tochtli	11 Tochtli	3 Tochtli
A.D. 1463	10 Acatl	3 Acatl	12 Acatl	4 Acatl
A.D. 1464	11 Tecpatl	4 Tecpatl	13 Tecpatl	5 Tecpatl
A.D. 1465	12 Calli	5 Calli	1 Calli	6 Calli
A.D. 1466	13 Tochtli	6 Tochtli	2 Tochtli	7 Tochtli

Years A.D.	Colhua I	Colhua II	Cuauhtitlán	Meztitlán
A.D. 1415	12 Acatl	2 Acatl	10 Acatl	6 Acatl
A.D. 1416	13 Tecpatl	3 Tecpatl	11 Tecpatl	7 Tecpatl
A.D. 1417	1 Calli	4 Calli	12 Calli	8 Calli
A.D. 1418	2 Tochtli	5 Tochtli	13 Tochtli	9 Tochtli
A.D. 1419	3 Acatl	6 Acatl	1 Acatl	10 Acatl
A.D. 1420	4 Tecpatl	7 Tecpatl	2 Tecpatl	11 Tecpatl
A.D. 1421	5 Calli	8 Calli	3 Calli	12 Calli
A.D. 1422	6 Tochtli	9 Tochtli	4 Tochtli	13 Tochtli
A.D. 1423	7 Acatl	10 Acatl	5 Acatl	1 Acatl
A.D. 1424	8 Tecpatl	11 Tecpatl	6 Tecpatl	2 Tecpatl
A.D. 1425	9 Calli	12 Calli	7 Calli	3 Calli
A.D. 1426	10 Tochtli	13 Tochtli	8 Tochtli	4 Tochtli
A.D. 1427	11 Acatl	1 Acatl	9 Acatl	5 Acatl
A.D. 1428	12 Tecpatl	2 Tecpatl	10 Tecpatl	6 Tecpatl
A.D. 1429	13 Calli	3 Calli	11 Calli	7 Calli
A.D. 1430	1 Tochtli	4 Tochtli	12 Tochtli	8 Tochtli
A.D. 1431	2 Acatl	5 Acatl	13 Acatl	9 Acatl
A.D. 1432	3 Tecpatl	6 Tecpatl	1 Tecpatl	10 Tecpatl
A.D. 1433	4 Calli	7 Calli	2 Calli	11 Calli
A.D. 1434	5 Tochtli	8 Tochtli	3 Tochtli	12 Tochtli
A.D. 1435	6 Acatl	9 Acatl	4 Acatl	13 Acatl
A.D. 1436	7 Tecpatl	10 Tecpatl	5 Tecpatl	1 Tecpatl
A.D. 1437	8 Calli	11 Calli	6 Calli	2 Calli
A.D. 1438	9 Tochtli	12 Tochtli	7 Tochtli	3 Tochtli
A.D. 1439	10 Acatl	13 Acatl	8 Acatl	4 Acatl
A.D. 1440	11 Tecpatl	1 Tecpatl	9 Tecpatl	5 Tecpatl
A.D. 1441	12 Calli	2 Calli	10 Calli	6 Calli
A.D. 1442	13 Tochtli	3 Tochtli	11 Tochtli	7 Tochtli
A.D. 1443	1 Acatl	4 Acatl	12 Acatl	8 Acatl
A.D. 1444	2 Tecpatl	5 Tecpatl	13 Tecpatl	9 Tecpatl
A.D. 1445	3 Calli	6 Calli	1 Calli	10 Calli
A.D. 1446	4 Tochtli	7 Tochtli	2 Tochtli	11 Tochtli
A.D. 1447	5 Acatl	8 Acatl	3 Acatl	12 Acatl
A.D. 1448	6 Tecpatl	9 Tecpatl	4 Tecpatl	13 Tecpatl
A.D. 1449	7 Calli	10 Calli	5 Calli	1 Calli
A.D. 1450	8 Tochtli	11 Tochtli	6 Tochtli	2 Tochtli
A.D. 1451	9 Acatl	12 Acatl	7 Acatl	3 Acatl
A.D. 1452	10 Tecpatl	13 Tecpatl	8 Tecpatl	4 Tecpatl
A.D. 1453	11 Calli	1 Calli	9 Calli	5 Calli
A.D. 1454	12 Tochtli	2 Tochtli	10 Tochtli	6 Tochtli
A.D. 1455	13 Acatl	3 Acatl	11 Acatl	7 Acatl
A.D. 1456	1 Tecpatl	4 Tecpatl	12 Tecpatl	8 Tecpatl
A.D. 1457	2 Calli	5 Calli	13 Calli	9 Calli
A.D. 1458	3 Tochtli	6 Tochtli	1 Tochtli	10 Tochtli
A.D. 1459	4 Acatl	7 Acatl	2 Acatl	11 Acatl
A.D. 1460	5 Tecpatl	8 Tecpatl	3 Tecpatl	12 Tecpatl
A.D. 1461	6 Calli	9 Calli	4 Calli	13 Calli
A.D. 1462	7 Tochtli	10 Tochtli	5 Tochtli	1 Tochtli
A.D. 1463	8 Acatl	11 Acatl	6 Acatl	2 Acatl
A.D. 1464	9 Tecpatl	12 Tecpatl	7 Tecpatl	3 Tecpatl
A.D. 1465	10 Calli	13 Calli	8 Calli	4 Calli
A.D. 1466	11 Tochtli	1 Tochtli	9 Tochtli	5 Tochtli

celebrated their New Fire ceremony on 9 Tecpatl, while the Acolhua performed theirs on 1 Tecpatl; the Totomihuaque on 7 Acatl; and the Tepaneca, Culhuaque, and Mexica on 2 Acatl (López Austin 1973:99). In addition to the implications for the calendar itself, such variation indicates that each ethnic group was able to emphasize its own distinctiveness and identity by celebrating its New Fire ceremonies on different days.

Much of this rich diversity, apparently actively cultivated and maintained by different ethnic groups, has too often been ignored. Its political and ethnic significance is that calendric knowledge, the timing of New Fire rituals and fiestas, as well as the keeping of local history, were handled at the level of the ethnic group. Even after many of these groups were incorporated into the Aztec state, each still attempted to maintain its past, its history, its rites, and its very identity as a separate group.

THE MIXTEC CALENDARS

Like the Aztec, the Mixtec had two calendars, one of 365 days and one of 260 days. The 365-day year was called *cuiya*, while the name of the 260-day calendar remains unknown. Of the two, the 260-day ritual calendar is perhaps the more interesting, for it displays a characteristic seen also among the Zapotec: the use of a "ritual vocabulary" that differs from normal Mixtec.

When the 260-day cycle was combined with the 365-day *cuiya*, the result was a 52-year unit called *eedziya, eedzini,* or *eetoto.* (The first part of the Mixtec word "*ee*" refers to the number "1," while *dziya* or *dzini* means "crown" or "garland.") By combining the 260-day and 365-day calendars, the Mixtec obtained 18,980 differently named days.

The *cuiya* began on March 16 according to one source (Ríos 1900), and on March 12 according to another (Burgoa [1674] 1934b). Still a third view is that of Jiménez Moreno and Mateos Higuera (1940), who see the Mixtec year beginning at the same time as the Nahuatl year, sometime in November or December.

The Mixtec 260-day calendar had the typical pattern of 20 day names and 13 numbers. However, unlike the Aztec—who used everyday Nahuatl words for day names and numbers—the Mixtec had a special vocabulary for both. Dahlgren de Jordán (1954:367) suspects that this special vocabulary may represent an archaic form of Mixtec that was preserved for ritual use by priests. (This would be analogous to the preservation of Latin or Medieval English for modern Christian ritual.) From the Mixtec words written in Latin characters on post-Conquest documents and dictionaries, ethnohistorians have been able to reconstruct this special Mixtec vocabulary for calendric signs and their associated numerical coefficients (León 1933, Caso 1956). This special vocabulary is given in Tables 4.10 and 4.11.

The Mixtec special vocabulary numbers—given in Table 4.11 as they appear in Colonial documents—are superficially confusing, because it looks as if the same sounds were used for several numbers. For example, *ca* is given for 1, 2, and 12; *co* is given for 1, 2, and 3; and *si* is given for 10 and 13. However, it should be remembered that Mixtec is a tone language (Pike 1945, 1948), and the Spaniards did not always hear or write down tonal differences. Since the Mixtec language has three tones, words such as *ca*—which look the same in the Latin alphabet—may have been given different tones and used for three different numbers in *spoken* Mixtec (Smith 1973a:27).

Evolution of the Mixtec Calendar

It will be apparent from Table 4.10 that the Mixtec shared many day names with the Aztec. However, many of the similarities are believed to be the result of convergence in relatively late prehispanic times, when Nahua speakers were people of great influence. The early history of calendars in what is today the Mixtec region gives a somewhat different picture.

Table 4.10 Special Vocabulary Used for Mixtec Day Signs

Day Sign	Normal Mixtec	Special Vocabulary	Translation of Day Name
Crocodile	Coo yechi	Quehui	Day
Wind	Tachi	Chi	Wind
House	Huahi	Cuau	House
Lizard	(Ti)Yechi	Cuu	—
Serpent	Coo	Yo	Serpent
Death	Ndeye, Sihi	Mahua	—
Deer	Idzu	Cuaa	Deer
Rabbit	Idzo	Xayu	Rabbit
Water	Nduta	Tuta	Water
Coyote	Ina	Ua	Coyote (?)
Monkey	Codzo	Ñuu	—
Grass	Yucu	Cuañe	Grass
Reed	Ndoo	Huiyo	Reed
Feline ("Tiger")[a]	Cuiñe	Vidzu	Feline
Eagle	Yaha	Xayacu	Eagle
Vulture	(Ti)Sii	Cuij	Turkey
Motion	Tnaa, Nehe	Qhi	—
Flint	Yuchi	Cuxi	Flint
Rain	Dzahui	Co	Rain
Flower	Ita	Uaco	—

[a]Mixtec specialists usually refer to this day as "Tiger" (a translation of Spanish *tigre*). However, since there are no tigers in the New World, the feline referred to must have been a jaguar or puma.

Table 4.11 Special Vocabulary Used for Mixtec Numbers in 260-Day Calendar

Number	Normal Mixtec	Special Vocabulary	Special Vocabulary
1	ee	ca, co	gau
2	uvui	ca, co, cu	co
3	uni	co	ga
4	qmi	qui	—
5	hoho	q	q
6	iño	ñu	ñu
7	usa	sa	xa
8	una	na	na
9	ee	q	que
10	usi	si	xi
11	usi ee	si i	xi
12	usi uvui	ca	ca
13	usi uni	si	—

Sources: Normal Mixtec, Reyes ([1593] 1976) and Alvarado ([1593] 1962); Special Vocabulary (3d column), Lienzo Natívitas (see Caso 1967, Smith 1973a); Special Vocabulary (4th column), Codex Sierra (see León 1933).

For example, consider the carved inscriptions on stone monuments from the site of San Martín Huamelulpan in northern Oaxaca, believed to date between 200 B.C. and A.D. 300 (Fig. 4.13). Although this site today falls within the Mixteca Alta, or upland Mixtec-speaking area, its hieroglyphs are well within the style of the Zapotec calendar of the Valley of Oaxaca (Caso and Gamio 1961, Gaxiola 1976, Marcus 1983f:125). Not only are the day names and cartouches in Zapotec style, the numbers also follow the Zapotec convention in using a dot for 1 and a bar for 5.

The first hint of divergence from the Zapotec prototype comes from a tomb at Yucuñudahui, a mountaintop ceremonial center in the Nochixtlán-Yanhuitlán Valley of the

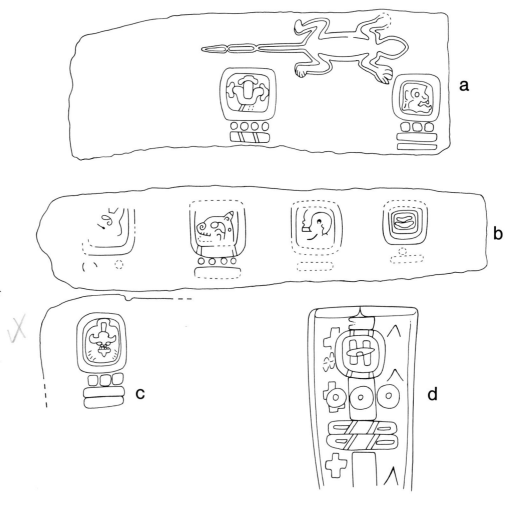

4.13. This group of monuments from Huamelulpan, located in the Mixteca Alta of Oaxaca, shows the use of bar-and-dot numeration and day signs. At this early date (Protoclassic times), the occupants of the Mixteca were using numbers and day signs similar to those of their Protoclassic (and earlier) Zapotec neighbors, rather than the "all dot" system and day signs they used in Postclassic times. At *a* we see a lizard and the glyphs for 9 Reed or Flower and 13 Monkey from a monument in the southeast corner of Building C. The three uneroded day signs at *b* are 9 Jaguar, 5 Monkey, and possibly 6 Water, from the east face of the same monument shown in *a*. At *c* we see 13 Bat (?) from a monument found immediately below the one shown in *a* and *b*. At *d* is a stone (now removed from the site) that seems to record the name "13 Flint Knife." (Redrawn from Caso and Gamio 1961; Gaxiola 1976; Moser 1977; Marcus 1983f: fig. 4.26.)

Mixteca Alta. In this Classic period tomb, thought to date to A.D. 300–500, were three carved stones that show both "Zapotec" and "Mixtec" elements. For example, the calendric glyphs themselves are considered "Zapotec in style" by Bernal (1965:803) and continue the use of bar-and-dot numerals; however, the stones also use an early form of the Mixtec "year sign," which resembles an interlocking "A" and "O" (Fig. 4.14). The Yucuñudahui tomb appears to catch the moment of Mixtec divergence from Zapotec-style writing.

Even more substantial changes in Mixtec writing, however, took place with the decline of Zapotec civilization (A.D. 700–900) and the rise of the Toltec state centered at Tula, Hidalgo (A.D. 900–1100). Caso believed that the prestigious, Nahua-speaking Toltec had an acculturating effect on the Mixtec, which extended to modifications in their calendar (Fig. 4.15). "If our hypothesis is correct," he wrote, "the Mixtec adopted the Toltec cal-

4.14. Two early examples of the Mixtec "A-O" year sign are given on this stone from Tomb 1 at Yucuñudahui in the Nochixtlán Valley of Oaxaca. This small slab of limestone measures only half a meter on a side, and like similar slabs placed in tombs (see chapters 8 and 9), it was obviously meant to be read from close up. At the upper left is a year sign with the number 3 below it; below it is an incomplete day sign that might have been 7, 8, or 9 Flower. On the upper right is another year sign, and below it an incomplete day sign with the number 7. This sculpture was probably carved between A.D. 300 and 500. (Redrawn from Caso 1938: fig. 68.)

Crocodile	**Wind**	**House**	**Lizard**
Serpent	**Death**	**Deer**	**Rabbit**
Water	**Dog**	**Monkey**	**Grass**
Reed	**Tiger**	**Eagle**	**Vulture**
Motion	**Flint**	**Rain**	**Flower**

4.15. The 20 Mixtec day names as depicted in prehispanic codices. As Caso (1967), Smith (1973a), and other authors have noted, these depictions of Postclassic Mixtec day names are similar, but not identical, to Aztec day names. (We have here followed most Mixtec specialists in giving the fourteenth day name as "Tiger," even though there are no tigers in the New World. The Aztec version of this feline, Ocelotl [Fig. 4.8], indicates that it is a jaguar; earlier versions on stone monuments, without spots, could even be pumas.) (Redrawn from Smith 1973a: chart I.)

Year "11 House"   Year "5 House"   Year "7 Flint"   Year "4 House"   Year "8 House"

endar at the end of the tenth century, and from then on the Mixtec glyphs were closely related to the Mexican [glyphs], and years were named Reed, Flint, House and Rabbit" (Caso 1956:488; see Fig. 4.16). Postclassic Mixtec codices of the period A.D. 1000–1500 also show that the bar had been dropped as a symbol for 5 and replaced by five dots, as in Aztec writing. Since the Toltec also had an acculturating effect on the later, Nahuatl-speaking Aztec, this could account for much of the similarity between Aztec and Mixtec calendars.

Future researchers will undoubtedly be able to trace more completely the evolution of the Mixtec calendar from a "Zapotec-influenced" to a "Toltec-influenced" system. At the moment, we face the problem of a half-millennium gap between the carved stone monuments of Huamelulpan and Yucuñudahui (200 B.C.—A.D. 500) and the painted screenfold manuscripts of the Postclassic and Colonial periods (A.D. 1000–1600). Until that gap is filled, we can only speculate on the rate and direction of change in Mixtec calendrics.

ZAPOTEC CALENDARS

Like the Aztec and Mixtec, the Zapotec had two calendars: a ritual 260-day calendar called *piye*[2] and a secular 365-day calendar called *yza*. According to the Codex Vaticanus 3738 (p. 34), the sixteenth-century Zapotec *yza* began on March 16.

Although the sixteenth-century Zapotec counted months (*peo*), the principal subdivisions of the *yza* were two units called *cociy* (from *cociyo*, "lightning").[3] One *cociy* was a dry season (*cociycobaa*) and the other a rainy season (*cociyquiye*).

The sixteenth-century Zapotec considered the *piye* to be a count of sacred time. Hence, the phoneme *pi* (from *pèe*, "vital force") was attached as a prefix to indicate that

4.16. Examples of Mixtec year dates. Note the so-called "A-O" year sign, the associated year bearer, and the number. (Redrawn from Caso 1965b, 1967; Smith 1973a.)

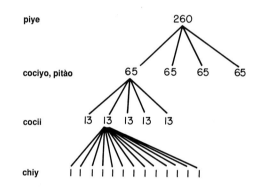

4.17. The Zapotec 260-day calendar was called the *piye*. It was divided into 4 units of 65 days, each of which in turn was divided into 5 units of 13 days. Individual days were called *chiy*. (Redrawn from Marcus and Flannery 1978: fig. 3.)

[2]Córdova ([1578a] 1942) spelled this word *pije*, but made it clear that he was using the Latin *j* (pronounced *y*).

[3]Once again, although Córdova ([1578a] 1942) spelled the word *cocij*, he was using the Latin *j* (pronounced *y*).

Table 4.12   The Four *Cociyo* Comprising the 260-Day Calendar

Cociyo named Quiachilla		*Cociyo named* Quialana		*Cociyo named* Quiagoloo		*Cociyo named* Quiaguiloo	
First *Cocii*	(1) Quiachilla	First *Cocii*	(1) Quelana	First *Cocii*	(1) Quiagoloo	First *Cocii*	(1) Quiaguiloo
	(2) Pillaa		(2) Pechina		(2) Peolapiya		(2) Pexoo
	(3) Pelaala		(3) Pelapa		(3) Peolaa		(3) Pelopa
	(4) Nelachi		(4) Calequeca		(4) Lache		(4) Lappe
	(5) Peciguiy		(5) Petella		(5) Qualanna		(5) Pelloo
	(6) Quelana		(6) Qualoo		(6) Pillalao		(6) Quachiylla
	(7) Pillachina		(7) Pillapiya		(7) Nixoo		(7) Pillaa
	(8) Nelaba		(8) Nelaa		(8) Neloppa		(8) Nelala
	(9) Pelaqueca		(9) Pillache		(9) Pelape		(9) Qualachi
	(10) Pillatela		(10) Pillannaa		(10) Pillaloo		(10) Pillazee
	(11) Neloo		(11) Nelloo		(11) Nichilla		(11) Nalaana
	(12) Piñopiya		(12) Piñaxoo		(12) Pinniy		(12) Piñochiyña
	(13) Piciguiy		(13) Pizopa		(13) Pizeela		(13) Pecelaba
Second *Cocii*	(1) Quiagueche	Second *Cocii*	(1) Quegappe	Second *Cocii*	(1) Quiagueche	Second *Cocii*	(1) Quianica
	(2) Palannaa		(2) Peoloo		(2) Pazeecato		(2) Petella
	(3) Peoloo		(3) Peochiylla		(3) Peolana		(3) Peoloo
	(4) Calaxoo		(4) Calaa		(4) Calachina		(4) Calapiya
	(5) Pellopa		(5) Pelaala		(5) Pelapa		(5) Pellaa
	(6) Qualappe		(6) Quelaache		(6) Qualanica		(6) Qualache
	(7) Pillalao		(7) Pillazi		(7) Pillatela		(7) Pillana
	(8) Nichiylla		(8) Nelaana		(8) Neloo		(8) Neloo
	(9) Peolaa		(9) Pichina		(9) Pelapiya		(9) Pelaxoo
	(10) Pillaala		(10) Qualapa		(10) Pillaa		(10) Pillopa
	(11) Lachi		(11) Pillanica		(11) Pillaache		(11) Lappe
	(12) Piñaze		(12) Piñatela		(12) Piñona		(12) Piñoloo
	(13) Pecelana		(13) Peceloo		(13) Peceloo		(13) Pecechiylla
Third *Cocii*	(1) Quiachina	Third *Cocii*	(1) Quicuiya	Third *Cocii*	(1) Quixoo	Third *Cocii*	(1) Quiguiy
	(2) Pelapa		(2) Pelaa		(2) Pelopa		(2) Pelaala
	(3) Peolaqueca		(3) Pellache		(3) Peolape		(3) Pillache
	(4) Calatella		(4) Calannaa		(4) Caloo		(4) Calaciy
	(5) Pelloo		(5) Pelloo		(5) Pechiylla		(5) Pelana
	(6) Qualapiya		(6) Qualaxoo		(6) Piliaa		(6) Qualachina
	(7) Pillaa		(7) Pilopa		(7) Pillaala		(7) Pillalapa
	(8) Lache		(8) Lape		(8) Nalache		(8) Calequeca
	(9) Pelannaa		(9) Pelloo		(9) Pecee		(9) Coatela
	(10) Neloo		(10) Pillachilla		(10) Pillalana		(10) Pillalo
	(11) Nixoo		(11) Laa		(11) Pillachina		(11) Calapiya
	(12) Piñopa		(12) Piñela		(12) Calalaba		(12) Piniy
	(13) Pizaape		(13) Piciquichi		(13) Pinipueca		(13) Pinieche

Table 4.12 *continued*

Cociyo named Quiachilla		Cociyo named Quialana		Cociyo named Quiagoloo		Cociyo named Quiaguiloo	
Fourth Cocii	(1) Quialao	*Fourth Cocii*	(1) Quiacee	*Fourth Cocii*	(1) Quiatella	*Fourth Cocii*	(1) Quiaquiñaa
	(2) Pichiylla		(2) Palalannaa		(2) Peolaa		(2) Peoloo
	(3) Peolao		(3) Peochina		(3) Peolapiya		(3) Peolaxoo
	(4) Laala		(4) Calalaa		(4) Calaa		(4) Calopa
	(5) Peolache		(5) Pelaqueca		(5) Pelaache		(5) Pelappe
	(6) Qualaze		(6) Coatella		(6) Qualannaa		(6) Pillalao
	(7) Pillalaana		(7) Pillaloo		(7) Pillaloo		(7) Nichilla
	(8) Nichina		(8) Calapiya		(8) Nixoo		(8) Laa
	(9) Peolapa		(9) Qualaa		(9) Peloppa		(9) Peolaala
	(10) Pillanica		(10) Pillaache		(10) Lappe		(10) Pillachi
	(11) Netella		(11) Piñannaa		(11) Piñoloo		(11) Calaziye
	(12) Peñeloo		(12) Piñaloo		(12) Piñochiylla		(12) Piñolana
	(13) Pizopiya		(13) Picixoo		(13) Quiciguiy		(13) Pecehiyna
Fifth Cocii	(1) Quiaguiy	*Fifth Cocii*	(1) Quiegopaa	*Fifth Cocii*	(1) Quiaquela	*Fifth Cocii*	(1) Quielapa
	(2) Pelache		(2) Peolape		(2) Pelachi		(2) Pelaqueca
	(3) Pelaana		(3) Caloo		(3) Peoziy		(3) Calatella
	(4) Calaloo		(4) Calachilla		(4) Calalana		(4) Pelloo
	(5) Pexoo		(5) Pellaa		(5) Pechina		(5) Pelapiya
	(6) Qualopa		(6) Qualaala		(6) Qualapa		(6) Pillaa
	(7) Pillape		(7) Pillachi		(7) Piniqueca		(7) Pillaache
	(8) Neloo		(8) Calaciy		(8) Netella		(8) Piñonaa
	(9) Pichiylla		(9) Pillalana		(9) Pelloo		(9) Peloo
	(10) Pillaa		(10) Pillachina		(10) Pillapiya		(10) Pillaxoo
	(11) Laala		(11) Calalapa		(11) Nellaa		(11) Loppa
	(12) Piniychi		(12) Piñaqueca		(12) Peceeche		(12) Piñappe
	(13) Picici		(13) Picitella		(13) Pecennaa		(13) Quiciloo

the calendar in question was "alive" and therefore sacred. Given its sacred character, ritual diviners called *colaniy* used it for their calculations during the sixteenth century.

The term *cociy(o)* was incorporated not only into words referring to the dry and rainy seasons, but also into the divisions of the 260-day *piye*. Four *cociyo*, each consisting of 65-days, comprised the *piye* (Córdova [1578b] 1886:202; Marcus 1983d:91). A second term used for these four 65-day units was *pitào*, "great spirit." Each of these *cociyo* or *pitào* was divided into five equal units, called *cocii*, consisting of 13 days. Making up these five 13-day units were individual days, each called *chiy* (Marcus and Flannery 1978: fig. 3; Marcus 1983d:91). Each *chiy*, or day, of the *piye* had its own name and number, usually that of an animal or natural force. A *chiy* began at midday and ran until noon of the next day (Córdova [1578b] 1886:212). Each of the *chiy* had its own corresponding fortune— neutral, benevolent, or malevolent. In Figure 4.17 we see the *piye* divided into four *cociyo* or *pitào*, five *cocii*, and 260 *chiy*.

Day names and numbers were used by the sixteenth-century *colaniy* to name the newborn children of individuals who consulted them, as well as to determine whether certain days would be benevolent for marriage, inaugurations, and political events. The sixteenth-century friar Juan de Córdova ([1578b] 1886:202) informs us that the Zapotec of his era regarded the *cociyo* or *pitào* as "the cause of all events." They made numerous offerings to the four *cociyo*, including autosacrifices such as extracting blood from the ear lobes, thighs, tongue tip, and other fleshy parts of their bodies.

The four *cociyo* were named after the day on which they began, each of which is given in Table 4.12. Note that the name for each day represents *the fusion of a number and day name*; such fusion may indicate great antiquity for the Zapotec 260-day calendar (Caso 1928).

The 20 day names used in the *piye* were given by Córdova ([1578b] 1886:204–212) as follows:

Table 4.13   The Zapotec *Piye*: Day Names Only

Zapotec Day Name	Possible Translation (Depending on Tone)
Chilla, Chiylla	crocodile, reptilian monster, divining bean
Laa, Quiy, Guiy	live coal, fire, wind?
Guela, Ela	night
Gueche, Quichi, Achi	frog, iguana
Zee, Ziy, Cee, Ziye	misfortune, serpent, young corn
Lana, Laana	soot, rabbit
China, Chiyña	deer
Lapa, Laba	divide into pieces, crown, garland
Niça, Queça	water
Tela, Tella	face down, dog
Loo, Goloo	monkey
Piya	twisted, turned
Quiy, Laa, Niy	reed
Gueche, Eche, Ache	fierce animal, jaguar
Naa, Na, Ñaa	mother
Guiloo, Loo	raven, crow, owl, eye
Xòo	earthquake
Opa, Gopa, Oppa	dew, vapor from the earth, stone
Appe, Ape	clouded, cloudy
Lao, Loo	eye, face

Table 4.14 The Zapotec *Piye*, Showing Fusion of Numbers and Day Names

Day Names	Fusion of Numbers + Day Names
Chilla, Chiylla	Quiachilla
Laa, Quiy, Guiy	Pillaa
Guela, Ela	Pelaala
Gueche, Quichi, Achi	Nelachi
Zee, Ziy, Ziye, Cee	Peciguiy
Lana, Laana	Quelana
China, Chiyña	Pillachina
Lapa, Laba	Nelaba
Niça, Queça	Pelaqueca
Tela, Tella	Pillatela
Loo, Goloo	Neloo
Piya	Piñopiya
Quiy, Laa, Niy	Piciguiy
Gueche, Eche, Ache	Quiaqueche
Naa, Na, Ñaa	Palannaa
Guiloo, Loo	Peoloo
Xòo	Calaxoo
Opa, Gopa, Oppa	Pellopa
Appe, Ape	Qualappe
Lao, Loo	Pillalao

Matching up ethnohistorically documented, sixteenth-century day names in the Zapotec *piye* with the hieroglyphic day signs on more ancient carved stones in the Valley of Oaxaca has been a challenging task (Caso 1928; Marcus 1976b, n.d.d). That is why Caso, quite cautiously, assigned letters of the alphabet (A, B, C, etc.) to the calendric glyphs, rather than words such as "deer," "crocodile," etc. Among other problems: there are more than 20 calendric glyphs in the prehispanic corpus, suggesting that the Zapotec calendar may have changed several times prior to the sixteenth-century version recorded by Córdova. Different towns may even have had different calendars, as we saw among the Aztec. And finally, as we will see among the Maya, there are different versions for the same day name.

Among the Aztec, Mixtec, and Maya, sixteenth-century documents provide us with invaluable glosses written in Latin characters adjacent to the indigenous drawings of the day and month signs; unfortunately, no such documentation is yet available for the Zapotec. On some Aztec codices and Mixtec carved bones, the day names of the calendar are given in chronological order. Texts giving the 20 day signs in order are so far unknown for the Zapotec, which makes our task more difficult. We have provided only a few tentative identifications so far (Figs. 4.18–4.24) and will be making a few more in the future (Marcus n.d.d).

In Figures 4.18–4.23 we see animal day signs that seem to correspond to the first day Chilla (reptilian monster or crocodile), the fifth day Zee (serpent), the seventh day China (deer), the tenth day Tela or Tella (dog), the eleventh day Loo (monkey), and the fourteenth day Gueche (fierce animal, puma, jaguar). More difficult to analyze are day signs that are neither animal representations nor pictograms, but arbitrary conventions called logograms or ideograms (see Figs. 4.19b, c; 4.22a, b; 4.23a; 4.24).

The Zapotec 260-day calendar continues to be one of the least mentioned in the extensive literature on Mesoamerican calendars. This is particularly ironic, because all available data suggest that the Zapotec *piye* was one of the most ancient of the four principal calendric systems we have discussed, and may have served as a prototype for the better-known Maya, Mixtec, and Aztec systems. However, precisely because it is so old, it has had more of an opportunity to change over time.

The Zapotec year sign designating the *yza* or 365-day calendar is known, but we are less certain about the year bearers (Fig. 4.25). Indeed, it appears that the Zapotec utilized different year bearers at different times in their past. Such a change over time is also documented for the Maya from Classic to Postclassic to Colonial times (Thompson 1950:127). During one period the Zapotec, like the Quiché Maya and Cuicatec, appear to have used the second, seventh, twelfth, and seventeenth days as year bearers. In contrast, the Aztec, Mixtec, Chuh, Jacaltec, Tzeltal, and Classic Maya (among others) used the third, eighth, thirteenth, and eighteenth days as year bearers. In the sixteenth century, the Yucatec Maya used the fourth, ninth, fourteenth, and nineteenth days as theirs.

4.18. Examples of Zapotec day signs from the *piye*. At *a* is the first day, called *Chiylla* or *Chilla* in Zapotec (Crocodile or Reptilian Monster). It is depicted as a two-headed creature (in this case, with the number 13 below it). At *b* are five examples of what appears to be an owl; this sign may refer to the sixteenth day (Owl) or the third day (Night). At *c* are two examples of the fifth day, one that could mean Misfortune or Snake (the Zapotec word *zee* or *ziy* can mean "snake," "misfortune," and "young maize"). (Drawn by Mark Orsen and John Klausmeyer from the original monuments.)

4.19. More Zapotec day signs. At *a* are four examples of a skull, which may correspond to the sixth day (Death). At *b* are three examples of a sign that appears to depict a flower, with the third example being similar to the sign for Reed in other writing systems. At *c* are three examples of a sign that may depict a precious stone, such as jade. Interestingly, *b* and *c* do not correspond to any of the Zapotec day names given in sixteenth-century sources; this lack of fit suggests either that changes in day names took place over time, or that different versions of the day signs were utilized. (Drawn by Mark Orsen and John Klausmeyer from the original monuments.)

4.20. More Zapotec day signs. At *a* is a day that depicts a head facing down; this sign is probably the tenth day, since "head facing down" was a homonym for "dog" (Tela or Tella). At *b* we see three examples of animal heads. The one on the left is probably a deer, corresponding to the seventh day (China); the next two signs could depict deer or rabbits, the latter being one meaning of the sixth day name. (It is often difficult to distinguish the depictions of deer and rabbit from Dog, the tenth day.) At *c* are three examples of an animal with whiskers, too generalized to identify with confidence. At *d* are two examples of the eleventh day (Monkey). (Drawn by Mark Orsen and John Klausmeyer from the original monuments.)

4.21. More Zapotec day signs. At *a* are four examples of the Deer sign, which corresponds to the seventh day. At *b* are two signs that probably correspond to the ninth day, Niça (Water). At *c* are two signs that may also be variants of the day sign Water. (Drawn by Mark Orsen and John Klausmeyer from the original monuments.)

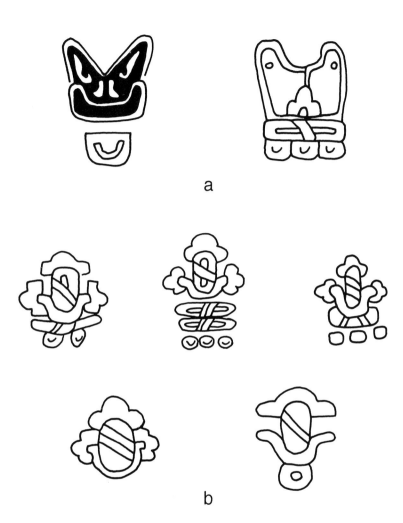

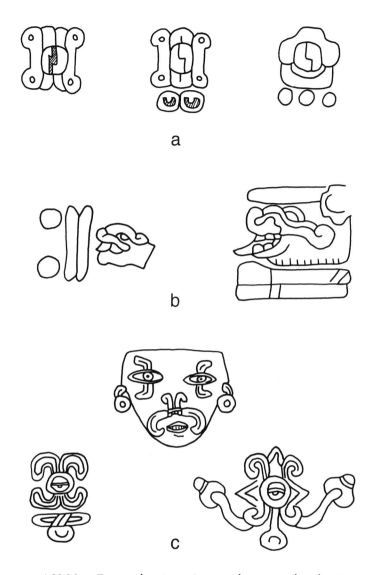

4.22. More Zapotec day signs. At *a* are two examples of the twentieth day, which means Eye or Face. (Superficially—and *only* superficially—this Zapotec glyph resembles the twentieth day sign for the Maya, *Ahau* or "Lord.") At *b* are five examples of Caso's Glyph J, which may correspond to the thirteenth day, Reed. (Drawn by Mark Orsen and John Klausmeyer.)

4.23. More Zapotec day signs. At *a* are three examples of a sign that may depict a knot or bone (Caso's Glyph A). At *b* we have two animal signs that may correspond to the fourteenth day, Jaguar or "Fierce Feline." At *c* are three versions of the seventeenth day, Xòo (Earthquake). (Drawn by Mark Orsen and John Klausmeyer.)

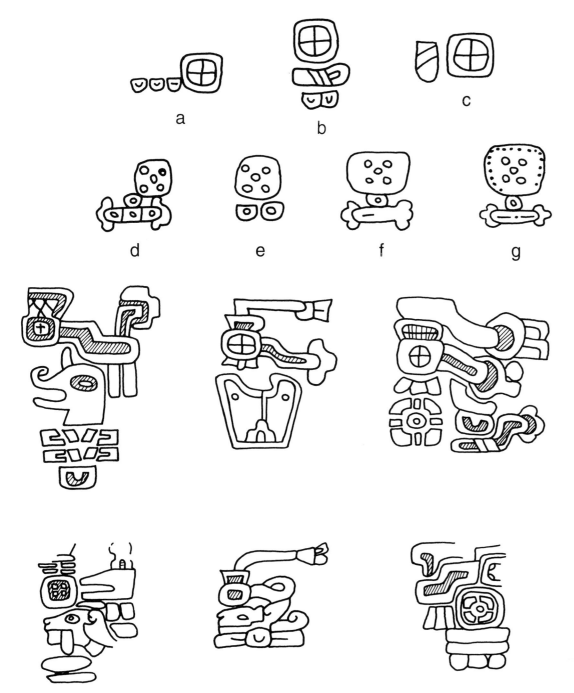

a b c

d e f g

4.24. More Zapotec day signs. At *a–c* are three examples of a sign that might correspond to the eighth day. At *d–g* are four examples of a day sign that might have evolved out of the *atlatl* glyph we saw used during Middle Formative times with slain captives and subjugated places (see Fig. 2.12). At this later time period, the sign may correspond to Fire, the second day, a symbol also used to suggest conquest. (Drawn by Mark Orsen and John Klausmeyer.)

4.25. Examples of the various Zapotec year signs and associated year bearers. Since not all of these year bearers were used during the same time period, we are led to the conclusion that the Zapotec year bearers changed through time. (Drawn by Mark Orsen and John Klausmeyer.)

Like the other indigenous Mesoamerican states we have examined, the Maya had a sacred calendar of 260 days and a longer unit, sometimes called a "Vague Year," of 365 days. During the Classic and Postclassic periods (A.D. 250–1500) the Maya combined the 260-day Sacred Round and the 365-day Vague Year to produce a Calendar Round cycle. Although these cycles were important, what the Maya are most famous for is their Initial Series or "Long Count" dating, a reckoning of dates from a starting point in the fourth millennium B.C. Of all the indigenous calendric cycles, the 260-day Sacred Round has proved to be the most resistant to the Conquest, partly because it did not interfere with the Spaniards' use of B.C. and A.D. Among contemporary Maya groups such as the Ixil, Mam, Tzutujil, Chuh, Jacaltec, Quiché, Tzotzil, Tzeltal, and Yucatec Maya, partial knowledge of the day names, meanings, and uses of the 260-day calendar has persisted (e.g., La Farge and Byers 1931, Lincoln 1942, Vogt 1969, Gossen 1974, Tedlock 1982).

The 260-Day Calendar

Since no Maya term for the 260-day ritual calendar or Sacred Round has been collected, early Maya epigraphers coined the term *tzolkin*, from *tzol* ("count of days, weeks, and nights") and *kin* ("sun, day, or time"). Forty years ago, however, Thompson (1950:97) argued that this artificial word "should be dropped, for an erroneous term masquerading as the true one is worse than none at all." We shall therefore not use the term in this book.

The 260-day calendar resulted from the familiar combination of 20 day signs and 13 numerical coefficients, each with its own "fate." The names of the 20 day signs are known from several groups speaking different Maya languages, such as the Yucatec, Tzotzil, Chuh, Pokomchi, Quiché, Ixil, and Jacaltec. Some of our data come from twentieth-century groups, while data on other groups come from sixteenth- and seventeenth-century accounts and word lists. Not surprisingly, there are differences among these lists of day signs, and particularly between highland and lowland Maya languages. Some of the highland Maya languages (for example, Quiché and Ixil) designate the twentieth day as Hunahpu (Ximénez [1722] 1929–31, Brinton 1885, Burkitt 1930–1931, Lincoln 1942), while at least one lowland Maya group (Yucatec) and two highland groups (the Chuh and Jacaltec) refer to the same day as Ahau (Landa [1566] in Tozzer 1941, Burkitt 1930–1931, La Farge and Byers 1931). The term Ahau can be translated "lord" or "ruler," while Hunahpu ("he of the blowgun") is also sometimes translated "lord" or "ruler."

One might conclude from this example that highland day signs are merely translations of lowland day signs, or vice versa. This may be plausible in some cases, but in others it seems less likely. For example, the sixteenth day sign is Cib in Yucatec; Chabin in Chuh,

Tzotzil, and Jacaltec; and Ah Mac in Ixil, Pokomchi, and Quiché. The terms have different meanings, with Cib referring to "wax," while Chabin may be derived from *cab*, "beehive," "honey," or "earth." Ah Mac can mean "sinner," or refer to a type of insect. Thus, in the case of the sixteenth day sign, it does not seem that highland and lowland Maya peoples simply translated the term while preserving its original meaning. Rather, it appears that the origins of Ah Mac are distinct from those of Chabin or Cib (Fig. 4.26).

The Fate of the Day Signs

When we turn to the specific fates (good, bad, or neutral) of Maya day signs, we find a great deal of variation from one language to another. It is not clear whether this variation is ancient or of recent origin, and we have no way at present to decide. Two lowland sixteenth-century sources that provide the fates of the day signs (the Chilam Balams of Kaua and Tizimín, both written in Yucatec) can be compared with four twentieth-century highland Maya sources (Quiché, Chuh, Jacaltec, Ixil) as we have in Table 4.15.

Table 4.15 Variation in the Fate of the Day Signs among Maya Groups, Based on 16th-Century and 20th-Century Sources

Day Sign	Yucatec (Kaua)	Yucatec (Tizimin)	Quiché	Chuh	Santa Eulalia	Jacaltec	Ixil
Imix	B	B	B	G	G	G	G
Ik	B	B	G	B	B	G	G
Akbal	B	B	B	G	G	G	B
Kan	G	B	B	G	N	B	B
Chicchan	B	G	B	B	G	—	GS
Cimi	B	G	B	G	G	BG	G
Manik	B	N	G	B	B	B	G
Lamat	B	B	G	G	G	N	G
Muluc	G	B	B	G	B	B	B
Oc	B	G	B	B	B	B	B
Chuen	G	B	B	B	G	B	G
Eb	G	B	G	G	B	GS	G
Ben	N	B	G	G	G	GS	G
Ix	B	B	G	B	B	G	G
Men	G	N	G	B	G	B	G
Cib	B	N	B	B	B	B	G
Caban	G	N	B	B	B	G	GS
Etznab	G	G	B	G	G	G	G
Cauac	N	N	N	G	G	G	G
Ahau	G	N	N	G	G	G	G

Source: Thompson 1950:90.
B = Bad, G = Good, N = Neutral, GS = Good day for special rite, BG = One informant regards that day as bad, whereas another informant (speaking the same language) regards it as good.

Imix **Ik** **Akbal**

Kan **Chicchan** **Cimi**

Manik **Lamat** **Muluc**

Oc **Chuen** **Eb**

Ben **Ix** **Men**

Cib **Caban** **Etznab**

Cauac **Ahau**

4.26. Classic Maya day signs. Two examples of each day are given. (Redrawn from Thompson 1950.)

Pop   **Uo**   **Zip**

Zotz   **Tzec**   **Xul**

Yaxkin   **Mol**   **Chen**

Yax   **Zac**   **Ceh**

Mac   **Kankin**   **Muan**

Pax   **Kayab**   **Cumku**

Uayeb

4.27. Classic Maya month signs. Two examples of the first 18 months are given, as well as three examples of the 19th month (Uayeb). (Redrawn from Thompson 1950.)

Even very recent ethnography reveals the difficulty of categorizing days as good, bad, or neutral. For example, among the modern Quiché of the Guatemala highlands who continue to use the 260-day calendar, Tedlock (1982:98) says that her informants "in the same community, when asked to separate the days as 'good' or 'bad,' often contradict one another and even themselves." Thompson (1950:88) also noted that there are cases in which a day is lucky in one Quiché town and unlucky in another town of the same dialect. Thus, to some extent, the "fates" of the day signs are difficult to pin down; each day sign appears to have a variety of associations, some of which are good, bad, or neutral. In prehispanic times, it was the task of the diviner to select a particular association out of the range of possibilities, making order out of confusion.

The Fates of the Numerical Coefficients

It is probable that the numerical coefficients of ancient Maya days had good, bad, or neutral fates just as those of other prehispanic states. We do not have many data from the sixteenth century on this topic, but some modern highland Maya groups still seem to regard day numbers as significant. Even in the case of such likely prehispanic survivals, it appears that the *combination* of day name plus number had more to do with a day's "luck" than did either component alone.

For the Quiché speakers of Momostenango (Tedlock 1982:107) and Chichicastenango (Bunzel 1952:283) in the Guatemalan highlands, the day numbers do appear to carry special meaning in isolation. The low numbers (from 1 to 3) are considered gentle; the middle numbers (7–9) considered indifferent; and the high numbers (11–13) are considered violent.

Were the Days Considered to Be Supernatural Entities?

There is good evidence that the sixteenth-century Maya considered every day to be alive, because it moved and had a life of its own. La Farge and Byers (1931:172–173) state that "strictly speaking these names are not the names of days, but of 'men' who control days. . . . These twenty men have charge of their respective days." Furthermore, in referring to the day 5 Ahau, the Yucatec Maya in the Chilam Balam of Tizimin (Edmonson 1982) used the expression *ah, ho Ahau*, ("he, 5 Ahau"). In referring to the days in general, one passage in the Chilam Balam of Chumayel (Roys 1967:118) notes, "Then they [the days] went to consider and spoke as follows. . . . Then they went to the center of heaven and joined hands." Thus, the days were animate; they moved and behaved in known and predictable ways.

In reviewing the sixteenth-century data on the nature of the 260-day calendar, one finds convincing evidence that the days were animate, feeling beings. However, unlike

Thompson (1950:96), I find myself less convinced of the "divinity of the days"—an expression by which he meant that "the days were originally gods, and it has been suggested that they were always regarded as such." Rather, ethnographic data on the twentieth-century Maya (La Farge and Byers 1931:172–173; Lincoln 1942:112,123; Tedlock 1982:107) suggest that the 20 day names were probably the names of supernaturals or revered ancestors—perhaps royal ancestors—rather than deities.

As in the case of the Aztec, Mixtec, and Zapotec, the 260-day calendar was used by the Maya as a divinatory almanac whose days wielded great influence over the daily lives of both nobles and commoners. The fates associated with each day aided them in their decision making, determining the best day to plant the maize crop, when a battle should be started, when a marriage should take place, and whether the two individuals to be married were well-matched. This system of predestination affected every individual, beginning with one's birth date. As we have seen in other Mesoamerican groups, one of the effects of this system was that decision making was taken out of the hands of the individual and left inherent in the calendar. It also meant, however, that the interpreters of the calendric system were influential people, since they had to resolve the conflicting fates of number and day combinations in cases where one was good and the other bad.

The 365-Day Year

The Maya *haab*, or 365-day year, had the usual Mesoamerican division into 18 months of 20 days each. As in the case of the Aztec, each month had a patron associated with it; in Table 4.16 we give the patrons associated with the 18 "months" of the *haab* in Yucatán according to sixteenth-century friar Diego de Landa ([1566] in Tozzer 1941). As we show, some of the patrons are often planets, animals, or natural forces. Following the 360-day period comprised of these 18 units came a final period of 5 days, called Uayeb. This 5-day period was considered dangerous or unfortunate (see Fig. 4.27).

Table 4.16 gives the month names of the *haab* in Yucatec Maya of the sixteenth century. Hieroglyphic data suggest that many of these months were the same during the Classic period. However, "month" names varied from region to region during the Postclassic period, particularly if we compare the highlands with the lowlands. In Table 4.17, we compare *haab* month names from 6 different regions, compiled from several sources.

Each of these months contained 20 days, numbered from 0 through 19. Even though we usually give these designations as cardinal numbers, it is clear from various sixteenth-century sources (such as the Chilam Balams and the Motul dictionary) that ordinal numbers were actually employed. For example, the first day of the month Pop is expressed *tu hunte Pop* (literally, "on its *first* of Pop").

Table 4.16 The 18 "Months" of the Yucatec *Haab* and Their Patrons

Month Name	Patron
Pop	Jaguar
Uo	Jaguar of the underworld
Zip	Monster head
Zotz'	Composite *Xoc* fish
Zec	Sky or earth signs
Xul	Youthful head
Yaxkin	Old sun
Mol	Old person
Ch'en	Moon
Yax	Venus
Zac	Frog
Ceh	Sky
Mac	Head with headdress
Kankin	Fantastic creature
Muan	Head
Pax	Night sun
Kayab	Young moon or earth
Cumku	Fantastic reptile

Source: Landa ([1566] Tozzer 1941).

Table 4.17   Comparison of Highland and Lowland Maya Month Names

Yucatec	Chol	Tzotzil	Kanhobal	Ixil	Cakchiquel
Pop	—	Nichilkin	Nabich	Metchki	Likinka
Uo	Icat	Hum Uinicil	Moo	Mu	Nabei Tokik
Zip	Chaccat	Xchibal Uinicil	Bak	Zilki	Rucac Tokik
Zotz'	—	Yoxchibal Uinicil	Canal	Tchotzcho	Nabei Pach
Zec	Cazeu	Ixchanibal Uinicil	Cuhem	Xetki	Rucam Pach
Xul	Chichin	Pom	Huachsicin	Tzicinki	Tzikin Kih
Yaxkin	Ianguca	Yaxkin	Yaxacil	Yaxki	Cakam
Mol	Mol	Mux	Mol	Mol	Ibotan
Ch'en	Zihora	Tzun	Khek Sihom	Petzetzki	Katic
Yax	Yax	Batzul	Yax Sihom	Avaxki	Izcal
Zac	Zac	Zizac Chaikin	Sah Sihom	Huiki	Pariche
Ceh	Chac	Muctazac	Khak Sihom	Kohki	Tacaxepual
Mac	Chantemat	Moc	Mac	Chentemac	Nabe Tumuzuz
Kankin	Uniu	Olalti	Oneu	Ochki	Rucab Tumuzuz
Muan	Muhan	Ulol	Sivil	Muen	Cibixik
Pax	Ahkiku	Okin Ahaul	Tap	Pactzi	Uchum
Kayab	Kanazi	Uch	Uex	Talcho	Nabei Mam
Cumku	Olh	Elech	Sakmai	Nimcho	Rucab Mam
Uayeb	Mahi Ikaba	—	—	Oki	—

Sources: Yucatec, Chilam Balam books (e.g., Roys 1933, 1967; Edmonson 1982, 1986; Landa [1566] Tozzer 1941); Chol, Gates 1931c, Thompson 1932; Tzotzil, Pineda 1845, Starr 1902, Becerra 1933, Schulz 1942, Barbachano 1946, Guiteras Holmes 1946, Vogt 1969; Kanhobal, La Farge 1947:168, Table 2; Termer 1930: 391; Ixil, Lincoln 1942; Cakchiquel, Hernández Spina 1854; La Farge 1934, 1947; Carmack 1973.

The Integration of the 260-Day and 365-Day Calendars

In an earlier section, we saw that the Aztec allowed the 260-day and 365-day calendars to run concurrently, producing a cycle that repeated after 52 years of 365 days and 73 sacred rounds of 260 days. The Maya had a similar cycle. For example, the first day of a Maya year might be designated "2 Ik 0 Pop," where the "2 Ik" refers to a day in the 260-day calendar and "0 Pop" refers to a month position in the 365-day *haab* or "Vague Year." As in the case of the Aztec calendar, it would be 18,980 days (or 52 years of 365 days) before the day 2 Ik in the 260-day calendar again coincided with the position 0 Pop in the 365-day calendar.

The Maya ''Long Count'' or ''Initial Series''

Some time prior to 36 B.C., the Indians of southern Mesoamerica had developed a way of recording specific dates to the exact day in a system integrating the 260- and 365-day calendars. To do this, they selected a starting point for the 365-day calendar that works out to August 11, 3114 B.C., expressed by the ancient Maya as 13.0.0.0.0 [4 Ahau 8 Cumku]. It is not known why this base date was selected. Some scholars feel it was a mythical date, such as the creation of the present world; others argue that it was the end of 13 full cycles and the beginning of a new 400-year cycle.

By the first century B.C. some Mesoamerican Indians had developed the mathematical concept of zero or ''completion,'' which allowed them to reckon in large numbers by position-value notation, much as we reckon large numbers in columns of tens, hundreds, thousands, and so on.

The position-value notation was based on five units of time (see Table 4.18). The smallest unit of the calendar was the individual day, called *kin*. The second smallest unit consisted of 20 days and was called the *uinal* or ''month.'' Since the Maya had a vigesimal system of numeration, one might expect 400 to be the third-order unit. However, so as to correspond more closely to the actual solar year, the third-order unit, or *tun* (plural, *tunob*), was composed of 360 days—the familiar 18 ''months'' of 20 days each. The fourth-order unit was a period of 20 *tunob*, called a *katun*. Finally, the fifth or largest unit was composed of 20 *katunob* (400 *tuns*) and was called a *baktun* (plural, *baktunob*).

Following the Initial Series Introductory Glyph were five units of time presented in descending order, as shown in Table 4.18.

Early in the history of Maya epigraphy, scholars usually argued that the *kin*, or day, was the basis for all calculations into the past and future from the starting date in 3114 B.C. (Spinden 1924:8–9; Morley 1915:37, 1938, 5:274). Now, however, the view that the 360-day year or *tun* was the basis for all calculations—a position supported by Goodman (1897), Teeple (1930), and Thompson (1950:141), among others—has come to be favored by most scholars. There are several lines of information that can be used to support this view. First, in the Classic Maya inscriptions of A.D. 300–900, the symbolic forms of the hieroglyphs for all units of time larger than a year employ the so-called *cauac* glyph or *tun* sign; none employ the *kin* hieroglyph. Second, the principal element of the standard glyph that introduces the Initial Series is the *tun* sign. Third, in the various books of the sixteenth-century Chilam Balam, time is expressed in *katuns* (units of nearly 20 years) or *haabs* (units of 365-day years), rather than in days. Fourth, the only Maya name we have for a unit of time larger than the *tun* is the *katun*—possibly derived from the term *kaltun* (20 + year) (Thompson 1950:141).

As we have seen, Maya Long Count dates have sometimes been called ''Initial Series'' dates by Maudslay (1889–1902) and others (Morley 1915, Thompson 1950), because they

Table 4.18   Components of an Initial Series or Long Count Date

Unit		Number of Days
baktun	=	144,000 days
katun	=	7,200 days
tun	=	360 days
uinal	=	20 days
kin	=	1 day

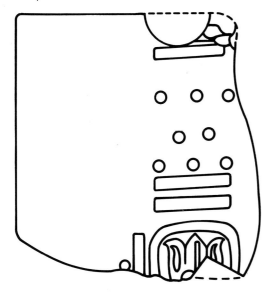

4.28. Stela 2, Chiapa de Corzo, Chiapas. The Long Count date corresponds to December 9, 36 B.C. (Redrawn from Lee 1969: fig. 60; Marcus 1976b: fig. 6.)

begin or initiate the text. The Initial Series date may correspond to the dedicatory date of the monument, and sometimes it places a specific event (such as a ruler's birth, accession to the throne, and so forth) in time.

At the moment, our oldest stone monument with an exact-day date—known as a "Long Count" date—is Stela 2 of Chiapa de Corzo, Chiapas (Fig. 4.28). If we assume the same base date of 3114 B.C. used by the later Maya, Stela 2's date (7.16.3.2.13) works out to December 9, 36 B.C. Our next oldest Long Count date is carved on Stela C at Tres Zapotes, Veracruz (Fig. 4.29). This date—7.16.6.16.18 [6 Etznab]—corresponds to September 3, 32 B.C. Stela C at Tres Zapotes gives us our first example of an Initial Series Introductory Glyph, the hieroglyph which signals that a Long Count date will follow (Stirling 1940). It is possible that Stela 2 at Chiapa de Corzo also had an Initial Series Introductory Glyph, but that damaged monument lacks the first part of the Long Count date.

While the Maya carried Long Count dating to its highest level of development, the oldest actual Long Count monument so far known from the Classic Maya lowlands is several centuries younger than those at Chiapa de Corzo, Tres Zapotes, and those from the Pacific piedmont of Guatemala. That monument is Stela 29 at Tikal, on whose back is a date corresponding to July 8, A.D. 292 (Fig. 4.30).

MESOAMERICAN CALENDARS: A SUMMARY

All four of the Mesoamerican groups we have studied used two calendars. One of these, the 365-day calendar, reflected the solar year and was composed of 18 "months" of 20 days plus an "orphan" period of 5 extra days. The other, a 260-day ritual calendar, resulted from the combining of 13 numbers with 20 day names. The day names, the numbers, and the combinations of the two were widely considered to have good fates, bad fates, or neutral fates associated with them. So important were these fates that when a noble was born on an unlucky day, diviners were consulted to pick a more propitious day as his official day of birth. Often, the noble would be named for the day selected—"1 Tiger," "3 Earthquake," "8 Deer," "13 Flower," and so on.

Both the 260-day and 365-day calendars are mentioned in hieroglyphic inscriptions between 600 and 400 B.C., and they are probably more ancient than that. The day name "1 Earthquake" of the Zapotec 260-day calendar appears on a monument dating to 600–500 B.C. in the Valley of Oaxaca. Apparent "months" in the 365-day calendar appear at Monte Albán in the same valley no more than 100 years later. Our earliest example of a Long Count date (combining the two calendars and using a starting point) comes from Chiapa de Corzo, Chiapas, and dates to 36 B.C. Our first example of a Long Count date from the lowland Classic Maya area comes from Tikal and works out to A.D. 292.

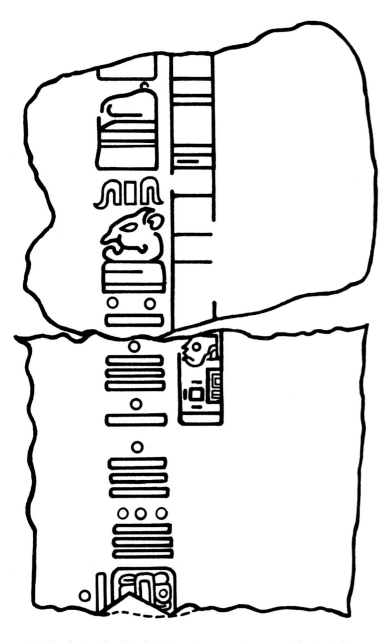

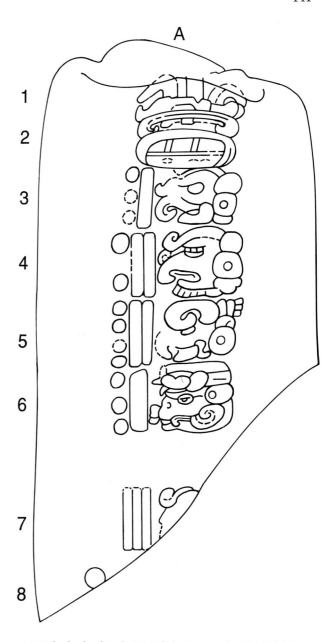

4.29. The back side of Stela C, Tres Zapotes, Veracruz. This Initial Series Long Count date corresponds to September 3, 32 B.C. (Redrawn from Marcus 1976b: fig. 7.)

4.30. The back of Stela 29, Tikal, Guatemala. This Initial Series Long Count date (8.12.14.8.15 13 Men [3 Zip]) corresponds to July 8, A.D. 292. (Redrawn from Shook 1960; Marcus 1976b: fig. 10.)

Despite the fact that the Aztec, Mixtec, Zapotec, and Maya all had 260-day and 365-day calendars, these were most emphatically not the same calendar translated into four tongues. Even within the Aztec culture of the Basin of Mexico, scholars have pointed to differences from town to town in the months or days on which the year began or ended, as well as differences in the years that began or ended the 52-year cycle that combined the two calendars.

Attempts to use the Aztec calendar as the prototype for all Mesoamerican calendars are probably doomed to failure. There was not one calendar, but many, and we do not even know whether the ultimate starting date for each calendar was the same from region to region. Furthermore, in addition to differences between language groups, there appear to be differences *within* language groups as to whether certain days were lucky, unlucky, or neutral. There were also differences in the "fates" of numbers and days for upper and lower stratum individuals; what was a bad day for a commoner could be a good day for a noble, and vice versa.

While calendric diversity may initially have been the result of nonadaptive drift as ethnic and linguistic groups diverged, the diversity eventually came to be emphasized as a way of preserving ethnic identity. Thus, certain Basin of Mexico towns deliberately held their New Fire ceremonies on different days. Even within towns, the gulf between nobles and commoners was reinforced by having the fates of certain days considered different for the two different social strata.

One of our most important points, however, is this: because cultures like the Maya could calculate dates that were accurate to the day, scholars and laymen alike have often assumed that their goal was to record accurate "history." As we will see in later chapters, this is not the case. We will see cases of rulers with implausible reigns of 80 years and life spans of 95 years, royal women who were said to have given birth at age 700, and ancestors who supposedly were alive before humans entered the New World. To believe these ages and dates would be to miss the point. The calendar was a tool of the ruling class to be manipulated for propaganda purposes, by linking actual rulers to renowned mythical ancestors, selecting names that ensured good fortune for rulers, and removing blame for nobles' bad decisions by attributing it to the inevitability of fate. If an important "historic" event took place on an inauspicious day, the rulers did not hesitate to move it to a more favorable date.

5 ◆ REWRITING HISTORY

This chapter elaborates the point made at the end of chapter 4: Mesoamerican rulers were not attempting to write truthful and objective history, but to communicate official propaganda. Their writings have historic content, but it is a manipulated history in which the facts are altered to meet successive rulers' changing political and ideological needs. Past events were fabricated to suit current policies, conquests were exaggerated, lies were told about genealogical relationships, and secondary centers claimed independence from primary centers even when such control had never been relinquished.

The clearest expression of this historical revisionism can be found in cases where stone monuments were defaced, recarved, or reset, and where hide or paper books were painted over, resurfaced with lime, or rewritten.

We give examples below from the Aztec, Mixtec, and Maya. To make the point that such revisionism was commonplace throughout the ancient world—even after the invention of history as we know it—let us begin with an example from the Old World.

An Egyptian Example

One of the classic examples of rewriting history comes to us from ancient Egypt, and took place during the reigns of five successive pharaohs known to us as Amenhotep III, Akhenaten, Tutankhamun, Ay, and Horemheb (ca. 1450–1300 B.C.). In my brief summary of the sequence, I follow Leslie White (1948) in attributing the events to cultural processes rather than to the "genius" of individual rulers.

Amenhotep III ruled at Thebes and built temples to its patron god Amun ("The Hidden One") and to the old sun god Re. During his reign, however, the priests of Amun became an increasing threat to his power. Underwritten by taxes, tribute from temple lands, and gold from mines in the Sudan, these priests unified to become a powerful economic force in Egypt.

Amenhotep III's son and successor, Amenhotep IV, hit on a strategy for curtailing the threat of these increasingly powerful priests: he inaugurated, at the state level, the worship of Aten ("The Sun Disc"), a new form of Re. To dramatize the move, he changed his name from Amenhotep ("Amun is Satisfied") to Akhenaten ("Effective for the Sun Disc") and moved his capital from Thebes to a new city which he named Akhetaten ("Horizon of the Sun Disc"). By the sixth year of his reign, ca. 1372 B.C., he had closed the temples of all the other gods, including Amun, taking away the lands and all sources of revenue for the priests who had posed a threat (White 1948, Aldred 1973:11–15; Wilson 1975:207–218):

> Everywhere, in temples, tombs, statuary, and casual inscriptions, the hieroglyphs for "Amun" and representations of the god were chiseled out; objects sacred to him were likewise defaced. People who bore names compounded with "Amun" [with Amun comprising part of their name] were obliged to change them. (Redford 1987:176)

Akhenaten instructed workmen to place coats of plaster over his former name and replace it with his new one. They were also instructed to remove the plural word "gods" from all monuments. From now on there would only be one god, Aten, instead of polytheism, and all revenues would be diverted to Akhenaten in the name of the Sun Disc.

Needless to say, the disenfranchised priests smarted under this regime, which ended with Akhenaten's death some seventeen years later. His successor Tutankhaten ("Beloved in Life is Aten") was a mere boy of nine when he ascended the throne, to be confronted instantly by the angry priests of Thebes. Realizing that he needed their support to retain the throne, Tutankhaten changed his name to Tutankhamun ("Beloved in Life is Amun") and moved his capital back to Thebes, ending Egypt's brief phase of solar monotheism. Tutankhamun died nine years later and was succeeded by Ay, a former member of Akhenaten's court. Ay ruled but a short time and was succeeded by a man named Horemheb.

Horemheb, a military man who had served under both Akhenaten and Tutankhamun, was a faithful follower of Amun. He had never left Thebes, nor had he ever converted to the cult of Aten. He thus had the full support of the priests of Amun, who carried out his coronation themselves. Horemheb set about restoring the temples of Amun and returning the temple lands and other sources of revenue to the priests; he destroyed the temple of Aten at Akhetaten and had its building blocks carried 300 miles to Thebes to enlarge the temple of Amun.

Most interestingly, in an effort to erase the heresy of Aten worship, Horemheb tried to have all references to Akhenaten, Tutankhamun, and Ay chiseled out of public monuments. For example, on a sandstone block from a dismantled structure of Tutankhamun's at Karnak, the name of Tutankhamun had been carefully removed (Fig. 5.1). The name

5.1. Sandstone block from a dismantled structure attributed to Tutankhamun, Karnak, Egypt. The double cartouche at left once contained Tutankhamun's name. After his death, those inscriptions were carefully removed and replaced with the name of his successor, Ay. Later, Ay's name was removed almost beyond detection when political power fell into Horemheb's hands. As Redford (1984:206) has noted, such alterations—made on behalf of the reigning pharaoh at the expense of deceased predecessors—were characteristic of ancient Egypt. (Photograph courtesy of Donald Redford.)

of his successor Ay was then carved in those spaces; later that name, too, was almost completely removed when Horemheb came to power and inserted his own name. By so doing Horemheb sought to make it appear that he was the direct successor of Amenhotep III, which of course was not the case. History had been rewritten so that it would appear that there had never been a challenge to Amun, and that three rulers had never existed. Redford (1987:206) has also noted that "such accommodation of the reigning pharaoh at the expense of deceased ancestors on standing monuments is characteristic of ancient Egypt."

The Rewriting of Aztec History

One of our clearest cases of rewriting history comes from the Basin of Mexico and involves two protagonists, Itzcoatl and Tlacaelel. Itzcoatl, the fourth ruler of the Mexica, reigned from ca. A.D. 1428 to 1440. Tlacaelel was a *cihuacoatl* or "snake woman" who served not only Itzcoatl but the later rulers Motecuhzoma I, Axayacatl, and Ahuitzotl. During the reign of Itzcoatl, according to the Códice Matritense de la Real Academia de Historia (Paso y Troncoso 1907, 8:192), there was a massive "book burning" of all previous Aztec history, followed by an equally massive rewriting:

> They preserved their history, but it was burned at the time that Itzcoatl reigned in Mexico. The Aztecs decided it, saying, "It is not wise that all the people should know the paintings. The commoners would be driven to ruin and there would be trouble, because these paintings contain many lies, for many in the pictures have been hailed as gods."

These burned texts, of course, contained the deeds of previous rulers, their genealogies, and their relations with neighboring peoples. To understand why Itzcoatl wanted them burned, we must consider the history of the Mexica people before, during, and after Itzcoatl's reign. Before him, the Mexica were subjects of the Tepaneca; during his reign, they won their independence by force of arms and set about rewriting their origins; after him, they became the dominant force in all of central Mexico.

The story, in brief, is as follows: prior to establishing Tenochtitlán (ca. A.D. 1325–1345), the Mexica were but lowly subjects of the earlier Culhua state. During the reigns of the first three Mexica rulers—Acamapichtli (ca. A.D. 1376–1396), Huitzilihuitl (ca. A.D. 1397–1417), and Chimalpopoca (ca. A.D. 1417–1428)—the Mexica were still not one of the more important ethnic groups within the Basin of Mexico. Other, more powerful groups (especially the Tepaneca, Culhuaque, and the Acolhuaque) had formed alliances and confederations, enabling them to subjugate other peoples in their desire for labor and goods. Three lakeside cities (Azcapotzalco, Coatlinchán, and Culhuacán) may have formed one of the first temporary triple alliances, with the Tepaneca capital of Azcapotzalco finally taking over the preeminent role.

With Acamapichtli as their leader, the Mexica aided the Tepaneca of Azcapotzalco in their military campaigns against the Xochimilca, Cuitlahuaca, and Mixquica. The territories of these peoples lay to the south and east of Tenochtitlán. Another campaign led them to the north, to destroy the Otomí center of Xaltocán. The Mexica carried out these conquests while under political allegiance to the Tepaneca, and several of the areas needed to be reconquered during the reign of Huitzilihuitl. During the short reign of the Mexica ruler Chimalpopoca, the Azcapotzalco ruler Tezozomoc was able to incorporate much of the Acolhua territory.

The death of Tezozomoc in A.D. 1426 was followed by a crisis for the Tepaneca. The new Tepaneca ruler, Maxtla of Azcapotzalco, had Chimalpopoca murdered, and in anger the Mexica allied themselves with the Acolhua in hopes of overthrowing Azcapotzalco. This alliance with the great Acolhua leader Nezahualcoyotl of Texcoco gave the Mexica new power. Nezahualcoyotl himself was eager for the alliance because he wished to avenge the killing of his father by the Tepaneca in A.D. 1418. Thus there were two main reasons for the Mexica-Acolhua alliance against Azcapotzalco: (1) revenge for the deaths of Chimalpopoca and Nezahualcoyotl's father, and (2) a chance at last for the Mexica to collect tribute, labor, and lands for their own purposes instead of fighting other ethnic groups on behalf of Azcapotzalco.

Itzcoatl became the new ruler of the Mexica in A.D. 1428 with his people still dominated by the Tepaneca, but they were joined in their revolt by the Acolhua. The story of how the Mexica achieved their independence by overthrowing the yoke of Azcapotzalco exists in different versions, each having been recorded by a different ethnic group with different propaganda goals.

Itzcoatl was aided in his campaign by his two nephews, half-brothers named Tlacaelel and Motecuhzoma I. These half-brothers were the offspring of the same father, Huitzilihuitl II, but by different mothers—Tlacaelel's mother was Cacamacihuatzin from Teocalhuiyacan, while Motecuhzoma's was Miyahuaxiuhtzin from Cuernavaca. These half-brothers were both said to have been born not only in the same year in the Aztec calendar (10 Rabbit, or A.D. 1398), but also on the same day; since this coincidence is very unlikely, it may well be another case of the Aztecs' rewriting of past events. In Durán's version, Tlacaelel is given much of the credit for the eventual Mexica victory over Azcapotzalco, and is called "the greatest warrior, the bravest and mightiest, that the Aztec nation has ever had—the most cunning man ever produced by Mexico" (Durán [1581] 1964:52).

Following the defeat of Azcapotzalco, the ruler Itzcoatl, his military commander Tlacaelel, and perhaps other leaders met to discuss the writing of the "official version" of the Mexica victory over the Tepaneca. In addition to recording the defeat of Azcapotzalco, the Mexica needed to create some appropriate ancient history for the period prior to the reigns of Acamapichtli, Huitzilihuitl, and Chimalpopoca. For this early "history," they turned to officials knowledgeable in oral traditions, and to scribes who had been keeping records.

While the now-defeated Azcapotzalcans had been keeping records of their own, those records naturally had recorded the glories of the Tepaneca state and presented their own view of their defeat at the hands of the Mexica. If only we could turn to those Azcapotzalcan books, we could compare the same events from different points of view; unfortunately, none have survived. One way we *can* obtain a different perspective on the Mexica conquest of Azcapotzalco is to consult Alva Ixtlilxochitl (1952, 1975, 1977), who used Texcocan codices to write the Acolhua version of those events.

In the official Mexica version of the conquest of Azcapotzalco, the Mexica did not acknowledge the substantial aid they had received from their allies, the Acolhua of Texcoco; in fact, they neglected to mention that they had had any help. To legitimize their new prominence, the Mexica also needed to establish that they had had a glorious and worthy heritage; thus, they decided to claim descent from the last great civilization, that of the Toltec. They also decided to elevate their patron deity of war, Huitzilopochtli, to a level above that of the other deities populating the cosmos. Through this device, new acclaim could go both to Huitzilopochtli and to the warriors who had fought on his behalf; it was made to appear that the sacred mission of these warriors had been to procure sacrificial captives who could provide a fresh supply of blood to nourish Tonatiuh, the sun. Thus Huitzilopochtli became closely associated with Tonatiuh, the former taking care of the warriors who procured captives for the latter's sustenance. The Mexica version of this human sacrifice also emphasized the need to procure captives from places not too distant from Tenochtitlán. To feed Huitzilopochtli, Tlacaelel suggested that the Mexica situate their market for captives near the capital:

> This market, say I, Tlacaelel, let it be situated in Tlaxcala, Huexotzinco, Cholula, Atlixco, Tliuhquitepec, and Tecoac. For if we situate it farther away, in such places as Yopitzinco or Michoacan or in the region of the Huaxteca, all of which are already under our domination, their remoteness would be more than our armies could endure. They are too far, and besides, the flesh of those barbaric people is not to the liking of our god. They are like old and stale tortillas, because, as I say, they speak strange languages and are barbarians. For this reason it is more convenient that our fair and markets be in the six cities that I have mentioned. . . . Our god will feed himself with them as though he were eating warm tortillas, warm and tasty, straight out of the oven. . . . And this war should be of such a nature that we do not endeavor to destroy the others totally. War must always continue, so that each time and whenever we wish and our god wishes to eat and feast, we may go there as one who goes to market to buy something to eat . . . organized to obtain victims to offer our god Huitzilopochtli. (Durán [1581] 1967; chapter 28)

The Mexica also created a series of new titles to be awarded to those who had fought against Azcapotzalco, especially those who were cousins, nephews, and other close relatives of Itzcoatl. Apart from giving titles to such heroes, Itzcoatl had stone statues carved of them in order to perpetuate their memory, and he had historians and painters inscribe the events of their lives in books, using fine brushes and bright colors. In this way, their fame "would grow and magnify like the brightness of the sun throughout all the nations" (Durán [1581] 1964:70). Itzcoatl also took on the additional title *colhuatecuhtli*, "Lord of the Colhua."

In addition to creating an official history of the Mexica struggle for independence, assigning a series of new titles for warriors and nobles who had fought, and dispensing parcels of land as a reward for victory, the Mexica changed the rules of succession to the throne (P. Carrasco 1984:74). Prior to the reign of Itzcoatl, the Mexica had practiced father-to-son succession, but the rulers' mothers had tended to be non-Tenochca women. Beginning with the marriage of Itzcoatl's son to the daughter of Motecuhzoma Ilhuicamina (A.D. 1440–1469), all rulers of Tenochtitlán, the Mexica capital, had to be sons of Tenochca women. High offices in Tenochtitlán henceforth followed collateral succession, with the Tenochca rulers preferring agnates as wives.

The Mexica also narrowed the recruitment pool of rulers by creating a council of four lords from whom the new *tlatoani* had to be chosen. The titles of these four lords were Tlacochcalcatl ("Head of the House of Darts"), Tlacatecal ("Man-slasher"), Ezhuacatl ("Blood-shedder"), and Tlilancalqui ("Lord of the House of Blackness"). No one, according to Durán ([1581] 1964:72), could be given one of these titles unless he was the son or brother of a ruler. The new *tlatoani* would be chosen from this council, thus ensuring that all future rulers would tend to come from the same small group of royal candidates, while at the same time allowing for selection on the basis of talent.

To summarize: the reign of Itzcoatl was one of rapid and spectacular political change, including the Mexica's rise to prominence as an independent polity and the extensive revision of their system of government. Itzcoatl thought that the Mexica's historical archives were no longer appropriate to their new-found prominence, so he burned them and wrote a new history that was more in line with current needs. Only because we have independent documents from other ethnic groups, such as the Acolhua, can we see the full scope of his revisions.

Mixtec Examples

We have now seen two examples, one from Egypt and one from the Aztec, where the records of earlier rulers' deeds were destroyed by later rulers, either by defacing monuments or burning books. Two alternative approaches, used often by the Mixtec, were (1) to alter the written record when making new copies, or (2) to cover up previous records with a fresh layer of lime sizing and then repaint the new surface. The second method produces what is called a palimpsest, from the Latin *palimpsestus*, "scraped again." This refers to a document from which earlier writing has been scraped off (usually incompletely) to make room for a new text.

In 1950, Alfonso Caso discovered that the Mixtec document called the Codex Selden contained several palimpsests:

> During a trip to Oxford in June of 1950, we discovered upon examining the back of the Codex Selden, which was covered with a white priming, that vestiges of previous painting could be seen in the small cracks.
>
> . . . [V]estiges of underpainting can clearly be seen on the reverse sides of pages 12 and 14; underpainting can also be noticed on the reverse side of page 11, where, according to Burland, it would be discovered more readily than in other parts, because of the fineness of the white priming covering the whole page. (Caso 1964a:62)

After careful examination it was shown that vestiges of old underpainting appeared on the obverse side as well as the reverse side. It appears that "the painter erased these old paintings as well as he was able before applying the stucco layer on which he was to paint" (Caso 1964a:65).

While it is usually not possible to determine what these Mixtec palimpsests said before they were altered, most authorities believe that later rulers wanted either to erase the sections where earlier rulers were mentioned, or to insert themselves into royal genealogies to which they really did not belong. Direct-line descent was extremely important for Mixtec royal succession (Dahlgren de Jordán 1954; Spores 1967), and the rival lords who competed for a city-state fought not only with weapons but with rewritten genealogies.

At the orders of a Mixtec ruler, scribes could also simply copy a codex, making changes and additions as they did so. Many codices were kept by the priests in order to establish a ruler's territorial rights and genealogical entitlements, but deliberate alterations could be made when an old painted manuscript faded and needed to be copied.

For example, at least two different scribes were responsible for painting the Codex Vindobonensis (Caso 1950, Smith 1973a, Furst 1978, Jansen 1982). The obverse is concerned with the mythological birth of the ruling dynasties at Apoala, and was painted by a careful, sure-handed scribe. The reverse deals with historical and dynastic data concerning the genealogies of Tilantongo; this side was painted by a scribe who was apparently hurried while recopying the historical data from an older book. Thus, the two sides differ in thematic content as well as authorship. The historical side appears to have been completed first, while the mythological and divine origin of the ruling dynasties (called by Caso [1950, 1977, 1979] "the prologue in the sky") was added later by a different scribe, perhaps to provide necessary cosmological-ideological support for the rulers of those dynasties.

We have looked briefly at the burning or repainting of books by the Aztec and Mixtec. When we move to the Maya and Zapotec, who made great use of stone monuments for political purposes, we see a set of strategies more like those of Akhenaten and Horemheb. Both these southern Mesoamerican peoples buried, sawed, moved, defaced, or covered up monuments whose messages were no longer deemed appropriate. This practice is well documented at Monte Albán in Oaxaca, where the Zapotec reused or plastered over stone monuments in the process of new construction (Caso 1938, 1947, 1965a; Marcus 1974a, 1976c, 1983d, 1983e). Such behavior may have a long history in Mesoamerica; even at Gulf Coast Olmec sites of 1200–900 B.C., M. D. Coe and Diehl (1980) and Grove (1981) have presented evidence for the deliberate defacement of stone monuments. Grove (1981:159), in fact, states that the

> destruction of monuments was not a one-time act. It was, rather, something which apparently took place regularly. With a few exceptions, every portrait monument in the [Olmec] heartland was mutilated. This means that monuments personifying each and every ruler over a long time-span were destroyed.

As for the lowland Maya, we have evidence for widespread burying of earlier stone monuments from Early Classic times onward (for example, see Jones and Satterthwaite 1982:117; Marcus 1987, n.d.b). Satterthwaite (1958:68) documents several cases of stelae (free-standing stone monuments) that were reset, sometimes upside down, after the upper half had been removed. An example would be Stela 4 at Tikal (Jones and Satterthwaite 1982:13), which was found standing, but had been reset upside down. Maya monuments could be reused as building material, re-erected in a new location, or reshaped to serve as an altar (e.g., Uaxactún's Stela 10 and Uolantún's Stela 1). The practice may have been analogous to Horemheb's defacing of earlier monuments mentioning Akhenaten. However, as we shall see in chapter 11, the destruction of monuments at one site may correspond to a flurry of monument carving and stelae erection at another, indicating that some of the monumental destruction must be viewed within the context of the entire polity or region, rather than from the narrow perspective of one site, one lineage, or one ruler versus another.

SUMMARY AND RETROSPECT

We have looked briefly in chapter 3 at some of the state personnel who had access to writing, education, and decision making in Mesoamerican society. Some of these individuals were clearly instructed to rewrite history, whether by destroying old records (burning or resurfacing books, fracturing stone monuments, and so forth) or by creating new ones (carving new stones, painting new books, or inserting new data on still unused surfaces). In addition to writing and rewriting, Mesoamerican scribes probably recited texts like their Near Eastern counterparts, who carved the following text for an Akkadian king of ca. 2290 B.C.: "Let wise scribes read aloud thy stele" (I. Winter 1986:25). Maya history was sung in songs and recited from written texts by nobles (Sánchez de Aguilar [1639] 1900, Thompson 1972).

We now turn to a set of chapters (6–11) that treat specific themes concerned with the political manipulation of history. The themes range from territorial boundaries and indigenous map-making to the naming of nobles, the depiction of royal marriages and ancestors, the taking of office, and military conquest. To evaluate similarities and differences among the four writing systems, each chapter includes examples drawn from the Aztec, Mixtec, Zapotec, and Maya.

6 ✦ PLACE NAMES AND THE ESTABLISHMENT OF POLITICAL TERRITORIES

Among the earliest-encountered signs or hieroglyphs in ancient writing systems are *toponyms*, or names for geographic places. Often these glyphs referred to natural landmarks, plants, or animals native to a specific region. For example, the ancient Egyptians used a hieroglyph for papyrus to refer to the delta of Lower Egypt, while the lotus was used to refer to the Nile Valley of Upper Egypt.

Mesoamerican states also used "place signs," or glyphs with geographic referents, to define the limits of political territories. Such signs have been identified in the writing systems of the Aztec, Mixtec, Zapotec, and Maya by researchers such as Peñafiel (1885, 1897); Barlow and McAfee (1949); Caso (1949); Nowotny (1959a); Prem (1967); Nicholson (1973); Smith (1973a, 1983a); Berlin (1958); and Marcus (1974b, 1976a, 1980, 1984:48, n.d.d). They occur in many contexts, including lists of places and two-dimensional "maps."

When sixteenth-century highland Indians were ordered by the Spaniards to draw maps of a ruler's territory, they usually assigned east—the point where the sun rises—to the top. The ruler's capital city (or place of residence) was set in the middle of the map. This spot was then encircled (often at some distance) by a series of landmarks such as named mountains, rivers, springs, or water-filled sinkholes called *cenotes*. From this map-making tradition it is clear that many highland rulers conceived of their territories as delimited by a series of natural landmarks which were constant and changeless—not by human settlements, which inevitably came and went. Moreover, on such maps the named landmarks are those on the borders of the territory, not places close to the capital; it was the territorial limits that concerned most rulers.

In addition to naming the mountains and landmarks on the frontiers of their realm, ancient Mesoamericans listed conquered regions, tribute-paying places, or the names of

153

royal dynasties and patronymics associated with specific places or regions. As we shall see, the last category was particularly important among the northern and southern lowland Maya, who usually had no substantial mountains to use as landmarks.

By plotting the geographic distribution of ancient place signs, we are often able to reconstruct territorial units that can be compared to those defined on the basis of linguistic, archaeological, or sixteenth-century ethnohistoric data. At times, it has even been possible to reconstruct patterns of political allegiance, and to detect changes in the formation and dissolution of political hierarchies.

Nevertheless, we must never lose sight of the fact that these ancient maps and tribute lists included their share of propaganda. Each map represented the view of one ruler or one polity, and the claim that a given place had been conquered, owed tribute, or was a dependency may in fact have been disputed by a rival ruler.

A potential source of confusion in the interpretation of place names is a result of the fact that our Western concept of "place" does not correspond to that of the Mesoamerican Indian. For the Mesoamericans, the important unit was the population owing allegiance to a specific ruler—only partially corresponding to a fixed territorial unit. This unit included the ruler's residence, an area of land, and a series of dependent towns and villages. Mesoamericans did not view the dependent towns, villages, or hamlets as being separate from the ruler's territory (Marcus 1983a:208; 1984:60–61).

This fact has confused not only epigraphers and art historians, but even anthropologists such as Sanders and Nichols (1988). Ethnologists tend to associate a name with a village; archaeologists define "places" as sites with archaeological features, a surface scatter of sherds, or some other criterion. But when a scribe used the place glyph "Hill of the Vulture," he often was referring to a unit of towns, villages, hamlets, and fields belonging to a specific ruler, within whose territory the most prominent landmark was a mountain named "Hill of the Vulture." To complicate matters further, a ruler's territory was often composed of several sectors of land that did not even comprise a contiguous unit.

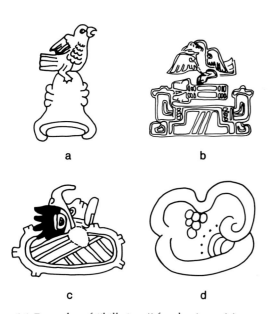

6.1. Examples of "hill signs" for the Aztec (*a*), Zapotec (*b*), Mixtec (*c*), and Maya (*d*). *a*, *b*, and *c* all represent "Hill of the Bird" (Tututepec or Tototepec in Nahuatl). *d* is the Maya sign for "stone" (*tun*), an "isolated hill" (*huitz*), and the phonogram *ku*. Hill signs could have various meanings, ranging from "place" to "hill," to "town," to "sacred spot on the landscape."

The Hill Sign

Three of the writing systems we will discuss—the Aztec, Mixtec, and Zapotec—were products of highland regions. All made extensive use of what has been called the "hill sign," although the style of depiction was different in each system (see Fig. 6.1). The hill sign was known as far back as 150 B.C.—A.D. 150 in the Zapotec area (Fig. 6.1b), and while it may have begun as the depiction of a "mountain" or "hill," in its later usage it became broad enough to mean "place."

The hill sign itself is a constant which does not vary. Resting on top of, or contained within, the hill sign is a second glyph (or cluster of glyphs) that gives the name of the hill, and this sign does vary from place to place. Although we are not always able to identify the specific place given (or locate its exact geographic position), we can definitely state that the entire compound is a place sign because of its overall structure and the presence of the hill sign.

In this chapter, we first compare the three highland systems employing the hill sign in their geographic referents. Next, we discuss the construction of lowland Maya place names. Unlike highland peoples such as the Zapotec, Mixtec, and Aztec, who could circumscribe their territories by reference to prominent hills, the lowland Maya most often designated specific places or boundaries by referring to natural landmarks such as rivers, *cenotes*, and swamps, or by referring to the names of royal lineages or dynasties. As an example of the latter, the Canul patronymic (or "lineage") provided the name for the province of Ah Canul in sixteenth-century Yucatán. The Chel and Cupul lineage groups also gave their names to territorial provinces located in the northern Maya lowlands. In other cases, the name of a prominent natural feature seems to have supplied the name of a political unit. Examples include Chakan, "Savanna"; Ecab, "Point of Land"; and Yaxhá, "Blue-green Water" (Roys 1957). The ancient Maya made offerings at sacred spots on the landscape, particularly on natural limestone promontories the Yucatec Maya still call *huitz* (Fig. 6.1d).

AZTEC PLACE NAMES AND TERRITORIAL BOUNDARIES

Rather than a politically unified, completely integrated polity, the Aztec empire was an impermanent alliance among three major cities: Tenochtitlán, Texcoco, and Tlacopan. These three cities administered a total of 489 towns scattered through 38 provinces and containing an estimated 15 million persons speaking many different languages (Barlow 1949a; Gibson 1964; C. N. Davies 1968, 1973, 1987; Bray 1972). While the heart of this tributary empire was the Basin of Mexico, outside it were a number of regions paying tribute to the Triple Alliance, as well as an equally impressive series of regions that had managed to remain autonomous. Because some of these unconquered, autonomous polities occurred as islands surrounded by conquered, tribute-paying polities, the limits of the empire were not contiguous (see Fig. 6.2).

Tribute was paid annually, semi-annually, or even every eighty days, depending on a variety of factors, especially the distance from the capital to the subject territory. Aztec scribes maintained a series of painted books specifying which places paid tribute, in which commodities, and in what amounts.

While many of the prehispanic books have been lost, still others were commissioned by the Spaniards in order to reveal the resources of tributary areas. The surviving corpus of documents is an excellent source of information on toponyms, on tribute-paying provinces, and on the maintenance of boundaries between the Triple Alliance and the unconquered hinterland.

156

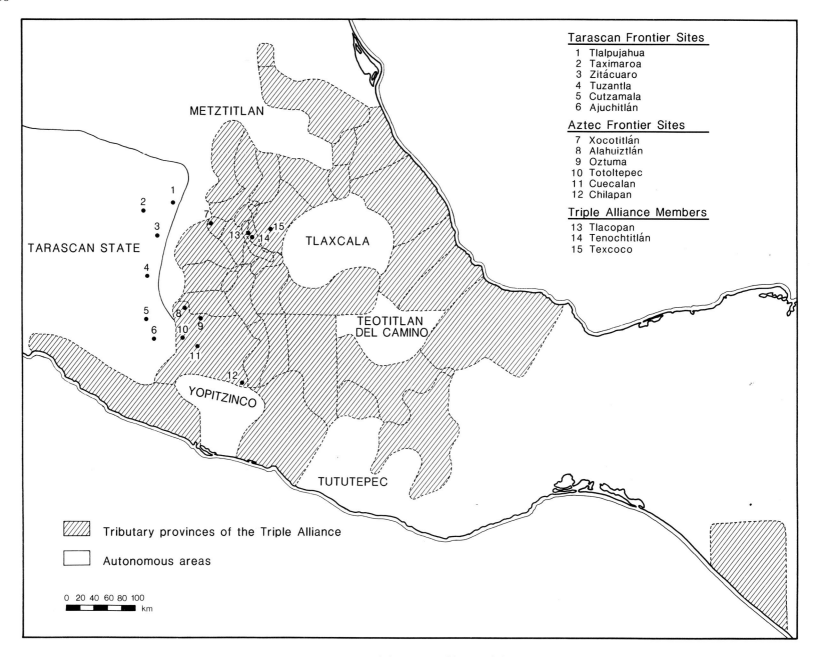

Tarascan Frontier Sites
1 Tlalpujahua
2 Taximaroa
3 Zitácuaro
4 Tuzantla
5 Cutzamala
6 Ajuchitlán

Aztec Frontier Sites
7 Xocotitlán
8 Alahuiztlán
9 Oztuma
10 Totoltepec
11 Cuecalan
12 Chilapan

Triple Alliance Members
13 Tlacopan
14 Tenochtitlán
15 Texcoco

METZTITLAN

TARASCAN STATE

TLAXCALA

TEOTITLAN DEL CAMINO

YOPITZINCO

TUTUTEPEC

Tributary provinces of the Triple Alliance

Autonomous areas

0 20 40 60 80 100
km

6.2. Reconstruction of the territorial limits of the Aztec tributary empire. To the west of the empire was a buffer zone that separated the Aztec domain from the fortified frontier of the Tarascans, a linguistic and cultural group whose powerful state successfully warded off Aztec control. (Adapted with modifications from Brand 1943, Barlow 1949a, and Marcus 1984.)

For example, Barlow (1949a), Berdan (1975), and C. N. Davies (1968, 1973) have studied the boundaries of the Aztec empire using the Matrícula de Tributos, the Codex Mendoza, and the Información de 1554 of Velasco y Quesada. Barlow (1949a:1–2) believed that each page of the Codex Mendoza represented one "province," arguing that (1) all the towns listed on a page were geographically contiguous; (2) all the towns on a page paid tribute as a unit; and (3) the first town on each page (usually in the upper left margin) was the head town responsible for collecting the tribute exacted from that region.

While Barlow (1949a) focused on those provinces that paid tribute to the Triple Alliance and were thus incorporated into the tributary empire, C. N. Davies (1968:11) concentrated on those areas *not* conquered by the Aztec. Combining the data amassed by Barlow on conquered, tribute-paying provinces with those collected by Davies on unconquered, non-tribute-paying provinces, we are in a position to establish some of the territorial boundaries that defined the limits of the Aztec empire (Fig. 6.2).

In our examination of the Aztec, we look first at examples of toponyms in Nahuatl, the language of the Aztec. Next, we examine Quauhtinchán, a tribute-paying polity falling within the empire. Finally, we examine the western frontier of the Aztec state with the Tarascans, an ethnic group who were never conquered, never paid tribute, and maintained a border fortified against the Aztec.

Nahuatl Toponyms

Sources that have been used to study the structure of Nahuatl toponyms include the "Stone of Tizoc"; many codices of the early Colonial period, such as the Matrícula de Tributos, the Codex Mendoza, and the Codex Boturini (Tira de la Peregrinación); and later sixteenth-century documents such as the Codex Vergara, the Telleriano-Remensis, the Matrícula de Huexotzinco, the Codex Azcatitlán, and the Codex Kingsborough (Kingsborough 1831–1848; Orozco y Berra 1877–1881; Peñafiel 1885; Clark 1938; Barlow 1949b; Nowotny 1959a, 1967; Corona Núñez 1964; Prem 1967; Bittmann Simons 1968).

As suggested above, one of the most frequently encountered components of Aztec place signs is the hill glyph, called *tepetl* in Nahuatl. It was employed by the Nahuatl scribe in at least three contexts. First, its use may indicate that the actual word *tepetl* (or an abbreviated form of it) was part of the place name, as in Tzinacantepec, "Hill of the Bats." Second, the glyph may refer to a town named after a nearby hill. Third, the hill sign may simply be there to indicate the presence of a place name—i.e., it should be translated "place of," rather than "hill." In the last case, the hill sign serves as a *determinative*, specifying the class of objects ("place names") to which the glyph belongs.

Tepetl could also function as a root in the formation of several other important Nahuatl words. For example, it forms part of the word *altepetl*, frequently defined as "town" or "populated place." Some scholars have translated *altepetl* literally as "water" + "hill," assuming that "those two elements" [were] "fundamental necessities for a community"

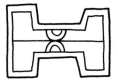

Tlachco

Tecuhtepec

Xaltepec

Chilapan

6.3. Aztec place signs for Tlachco ("In the Ballcourt"), Tecuhtepec ("Hill of the Ruler"), Xaltepec ("Sand Hill"), and Chilapan ("In the Canal [or River] of the Chile Peppers"). (Redrawn from Peñafiel 1885.)

(e.g., Karttunen 1983:9). Another meaning assigned to *altepetl* was "king" or "ruler," he who rules over the "populated place" (see Molina [1571] 1944:4r). Still other terms derived from *altepetl* are the expressions for "village" (*altepemaitl*), "the town's boundary" (*altepenauac*), and "lands that are held in common, lands that are shared" (*altepemilli*). Finally, *altepetlianca* could refer to the dependency of a city, town, or village, or the boundary of a city, town, or village (Molina [1571] 1977).

In the Nahuatl language, this concept of boundary was an important one. "To set up boundaries or limits" was expressed as *quaxochquetza*. "To set up boundary markers for a town" would be *altepequaxochquetza*, which can be divided into the two words *altepe(tl)* "town" and *quaxochquetza*, "to put up markers at the boundaries."

An analysis of Nahuatl toponyms reveals that either nouns or verbs could serve as the root or main sign of the hieroglyph. Four examples where a noun serves as the root of a toponym are (1) Tlachco ("In the Ballcourt"), where ballcourt (*tlach[tli]*) takes the locative suffix -*co*, "in"; (2) Tecuhtepec ("Hill of the Ruler"), where the ruler's headdress or headband (*tecuh[tli]*) and hill (*tepe[tl]*) take the locative suffix -*co*, which is here reduced to a "c" because it follows a vowel; (3) Xaltepec ("Sand Hill"), where sand (*xalli*) is shown in the shape of a hill; and (4) Chilapan ("In the Canal [or River] of the Chile Peppers") (Fig. 6.3).

Two examples of toponyms in which verbs serve as roots are (1) Chichipinaloyan ("Where It Drips or Sprinkles Frequently"), composed of *chichipi[ca]*, "to drip or sprinkle" and *lo*, indicating the passive voice, with the suffix -*yan*, "place where something is often done, or something often occurs"; and (2) Zoquianaloyan ("Where the Clay is Removed"), made up of *zoqui*, "to remove clay" and *lo*, the passive voice, also with the suffix -*yan*, "place where something is often done."

Nahuatl names often lose the final syllable or vowel, the result being that words composed of consonant + vowel + consonant + vowel (either CVCV or CVC + CVC) are converted into monosyllables (CVC). This morphological characteristic of Nahuatl place names facilitates the use of pictograms and signs serving as syllables (phonograms). For example, Dibble (1971:330) gives the example of *poc(tli)* "smoke" + *tlan(tli)* "near," which is read as Poctlán, "Near the Smoke." Since *tlan(tli)*, "near," is a homonym for "teeth," the glyph shows smoke + teeth. Use of such homonyms is necessary because there is no easy way to draw a picture of "near"; another example would be Atlán in Figure 6.4 where water + teeth gives us *at(l)* + *tlan*. Water (*atl*) was incorporated into many other Aztec place signs, often used as a pictogram or logogram (Fig. 6.4), and occasionally used as a phonogram (see Fig. 3.8).

The Boundaries of Quauhtinchán

Let us now look at the way the Aztec described the boundaries of Quauhtinchán, a prehispanic polity under Aztec hegemony in what is today the state of Puebla, south of

Acocolco Anenequilco Ameyalco

Atzacan Atlan Atepec

Atenco Auchpanco Atlapulac

Apancalecan Atotonilco Acocozpan

6.4. All these Aztec place names incorporate the sign for *atl*, "water": Acocolco (*atl*, water; *coltic*, curved; and *-co*, locative suffix); Anenequilco (*atl*, water; *nenenqui*, running; and *-co*, locative suffix); Ameyalco (*atl*, water; *ameyalatl*, spring; and *-co*, locative suffix); Atzacán (*atl*, water; *atzacua*, to enclose or seal off; and *can*, place of); Atlán (*atl*, water and *tlan*, teeth, meaning "near water"); Atepec (*atl*, water and *tepetl*, hill, meaning "a populated place that has water"); Atenco (*atl*, water; *tentli*, lip or edge of something; e.g., a riverbank); Auchpanco (*atl*, water; *ochpantli*, wide road [indicated by footprints]; *pan*, flag; and *-co*, locative suffix); Atlapulac (*atl*, water; *tlapolactia*, to submerge something); Apancalecan (*atl*, water; *apanatl*, water from canals; *cale*, houses; and *can*, place of, meaning "place where houses have water brought by canals"); Atotonilco (*atl*, water; *totonilli*, to heat [the depiction of a jar set on a stone hearth gives the place name of "hot springs"]); and Acocozpan (*atl*, water; *cuztic*, yellow; and *apantli*, "in the canal"). Note that some, but not all, elements of the place names are depicted; occasionally, as in the place signs for Atlán and Atepec, all elements are given. (Redrawn from Peñafiel 1885.)

Mexico City. The Historia Tolteca-Chichimeca or *Anales de Quauhtinchán* is a pictorial manuscript believed to have been painted there in the sixteenth century at the request of the Spaniards. Among its pages are indigenous-style maps to which the Spaniards ordered the addition of Nahuatl words and sentences written in Latin characters. One of the distinguishing features of these maps is that they provide the territorial limits of political or ethnic groups. They do so by placing hill signs around the periphery of the map, with each named place representing a specific landmark on the border or outer limits of the territory.

We will look specifically at two of a group of maps that define the boundaries of Quauhtinchán-Totomiuacán in the sixteenth century. For example, on pages 30v and 31r of the *Anales* is a map bearing a Nahuatl inscription that has been translated by Kirchhoff, Odena Güemes, and Reyes García as follows:

> Here is the town and its boundaries. Here [on this page] everything is painted. And here also are described the subdivisions that comprise the Totomiuaque, those who went away, those who went away to establish Ueuetlan [Huehuetlan]. They [the ethnic subdivisions] are the Tlaxichca, the Itzmauaque, the Xauetochca, and the Xillotzinca. (Kirchhoff, Odena Güemes, and Reyes García 1976:188–189)

By way of explanation, the Totomiuaque were one of the seven ethnic groups that supposedly left Chicomoztoc ("Place of Seven Caves," a mythical place of origin). The Totomiuaque, in turn, were themselves divided into seven subgroups—the Tlaxichca, the Itzmauaque, the Xauetochca, the Xillotzinca, "those who live in Axomolco," "those who live in Atenpan tlacpac," and "those who live in Acaxouayan."

Figure 6.5 shows the limits of the territory of one of these smaller ethnic groups, the Tlaxichca, whose name is depicted just to the right of center on the map. A mountain called Chiquiutepec ("Hill of the Basket," from *chiquiu(itl)*, "basket," and *tepe(tl)*, "hill") is given immediately to the left. (Today that mountain is still called El Chiquihuite; it lies near the present-day town of Totomihuacán.) Around the edges of the map are the thirty-two places on the boundary of Tlaxichca territory; the names of these places are given in the caption accompanying Figure 6.5.

Note that although pages 30v-31r (shown in Fig. 6.5) are considered to constitute a "map," the position of a few landmarks along the border does not correspond to geographical reality. We can see this lack of fit if we compare Figure 6.5 with Figure 6.6, another map from Kirchhoff, Odena Güemes, and Reyes García (1976: Mapa 7), which shows the actual geographic positions of the places used to define Tlaxichca territory. This lack of fit illustrates a point to which we will return frequently: it was not essential to indigenous mapmakers that their product always mirror geographic reality, and it would be a mistake for us to treat these "maps" as if they did. In fact, we do not even know for sure if the Tlaxichca actually controlled all the places they claimed on their frontier.

On pages 32v-33r of the *Anales de Quauhtinchán* occurs a map of the Totomiuaque-Quauhtinchantlaca territory (Fig. 6.7). As we saw before, the boundary is shown as a series of landmarks named with place glyphs. On page 33v there is a list of places given in Latin characters, once again beginning with Tepoxocho and proceeding counterclockwise in groups of five. This time, however, the list is somewhat different, as follows:

Tepoxocho	Tetliztacan	Centli pallancan
Couatepetl	Temallacayocan	Mitli ymancan
Atzontli	Chiyapolco	Uauauhtla [Atltzayanca]
Couatepetzintli	Acoltzinco	Ueitepetl matlalcueye
Tollocan	Totolquechco	Auatepetl
Malinallocan	Matlatlan	~~Amaliuhqui~~ [sic]
Atoyatl	Poyauhtecatl	Nacapauazqui
Atotonilco		
Tlequaztepetzinco	Napateuhctli	
Tzicatepec	Couatepetl	
	Quauhtepetl	
Zoyapetlayo yyacac[1]	Ocelotepetl	
Molcaxac		
Uillotepec	. . . .	
Atezcac		
Nepoualco		

It is worth noting that although the vast majority of the place glyphs on these two Aztec maps include the hill sign, a few do not. Some are evidently bodies of water, perhaps rivers; these begin with the term *atl*, "water," and are shown painted blue in the original. As we will see below, the Zapotec also used mountains and rivers as the major landmarks along their boundaries.

[1]This hill shows a head in profile with whiskers and a beard. Zoyapetlayo yyacac is the same mountain mentioned by the ruler Tezozomoc as having been used as a base of operations by the Aztec to conquer Quauhtinchán, Tepeaca, and Tecamachalco. Today this mountain is called Tentzón; it had religious as well as strategic military value for the Aztec (Kirchhoff, Odena Güemes, and Reyes García 1976: 196). On another map in the *Historia Tolteca-Chichimeca*, the Chichimec groups who were established in Quauhtinchán and Totomihuacán visit a cave located inside this same mountain. Contemporary residents in the region believe that inside the mountain of Tentzón a supernatural being still lives, one that is a giver of wealth.

6.5. Sixteenth-century indigenous-style map showing the territorial limits of the Tlaxichca ethnic group, as defined by named hills and places with water. Around the edges of these pages are 32 places which were on the border of Tlaxichca territory. Beginning at the upper left corner and proceeding counterclockwise are Couatepetl, Itztenenec, Quauhyaualolco, Centepetl, Tepoxocho, Couatepetl, Temomoztli, Atzontli, Tecolotl, Tecuicuilli, and Iztac cuixtla. Continuing counterclockwise we see Atlpatlauacan, Totolquetzale, Techimalli, Tecaxitl, Tochtepetl, Temalacayo, Tecpatepetl, Quauhyaualolco, Tenpatzacapan, Atlauimolco, Oztoyaualco, Chiltecpintla, Petlatzinco, Acatlán, Mazacholco, Chapolmetzco, Couacuitlachichiquilco, Tepipilolco, Iztocan, Epazouac, and Tecciztitlán, and we have returned to Couatepetl. At the center of the map we see the name of the place and ethnic group that controls this territory: on the left is the glyph for Tlaquimilolli, above the sign for Chiquiutepec, "Hill of the Basket"; on the right is the sign for the Tlaxichca ethnic group (derived from the bow and arrow). (Redrawn by John Klausmeyer from Kirchhoff, Odena Güemes, and Reyes García 1976: left half, folio 30v; right half, folio 31r.)

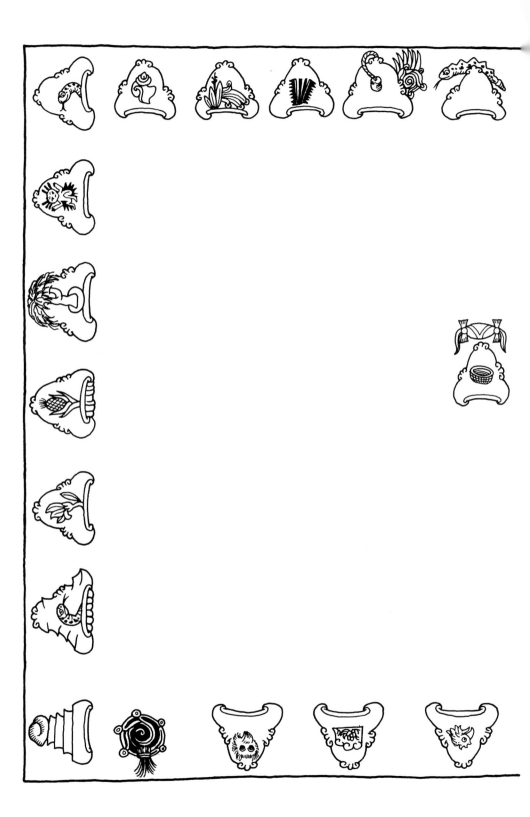

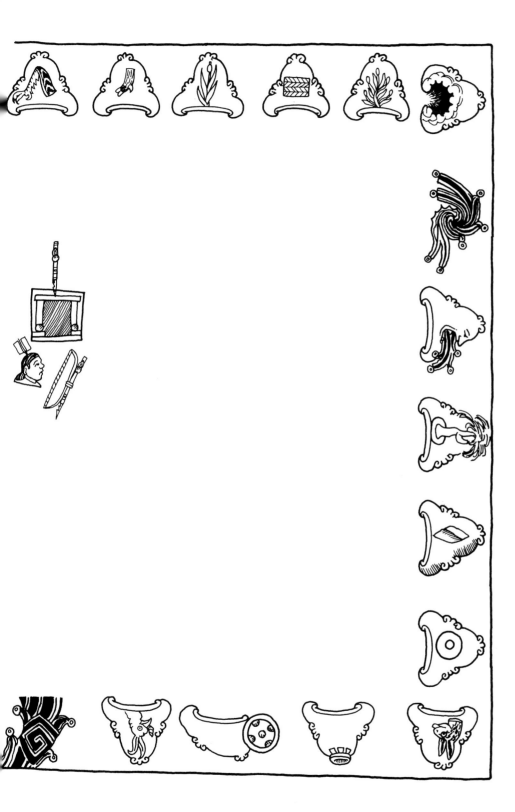

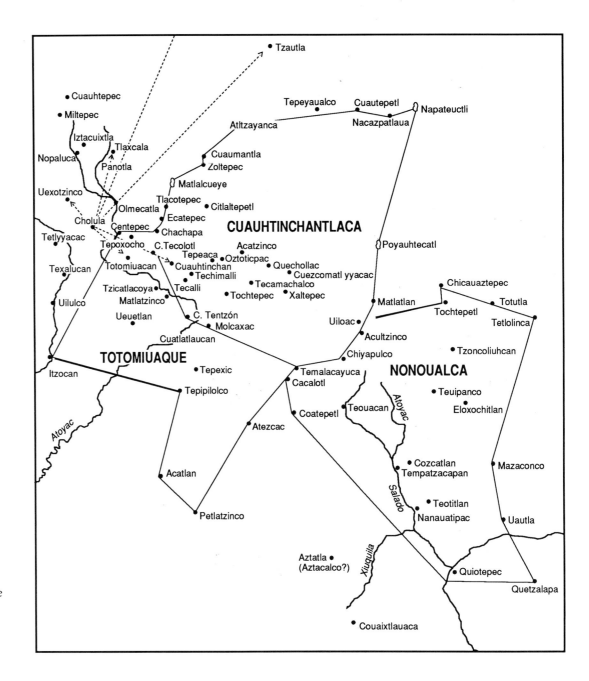

6.6. Western-style map showing the actual boundaries separating the territories claimed by three different ethnic groups, which includes many localities shown on the indigenous maps in Figs. 6.5 and 6.7. In the southern and eastern parts of Figure 6.6 we see many of the places mentioned in Figure 6.5, including Acatlán, Petlatzinco, Coatepetl, and Tochtepetl. In the north and west we see many of the places mentioned in Figure 6.7, including Matlalcueye, Tepoxocho, Atltzayanca, and Cuauhtepec (Quauhtepec). It is instructive to compare the actual spatial relationships of these places with the spatial relationships implied by the indigenous maps. (Redrawn from Kirchhoff, Odena Güemes, and Reyes García 1976: 259, Mapa 7.)

The Tarascan Frontier

Having looked at the definition of a territory within the Aztec empire, let us now turn to the way the Aztec defined their frontier with the Tarascans, a rival people whom they never subdued.

From both the Matrícula de Tributos and the Codex Mendoza we can obtain the names of tribute-paying places along part of the western frontier of the Aztec with the Tarascans. From north to south, these were Xocotitlán, Alahuiztlán, Oztuma, Totoltepec, Cueçalan, and Chilapan. From ethnohistoric records (e.g., the *Relaciones Geográficas de la Diócesis de Michoacán*), we know that the Aztecs and Tarascans each maintained a chain of forts along their respective frontiers (Armillas 1951, Gorenstein 1973, Marcus 1984). We also learn that the western frontier of the Aztec state was separated from the eastern frontier of the Tarascan state by a kind of "buffer zone" occupied by people speaking neither Nahuatl nor Tarascan (see Fig. 6.2). These buffer zone people included Otomí, Matlat-zinca, Mazahua, Chontal, Cuitlateco, and "Chichimec" (a term sometimes used by the Aztec to indicate "non-civilized" or semi-nomadic peoples living on the frontiers of civ-ilization). Some of the Tarascan military and administrative centers on their eastern fron-tier included Tlalpujahua, Taximaroa, Zitácuaro, Tuzantla, Cutzamala, and Ajuchitlán (Brand 1943, Armillas 1951).

Significantly, since these Tarascan frontier towns were located outside the area from which the Aztec could collect tribute, they were *not* mentioned in the Codex Mendoza and Matrícula de Tributos. Also not paying tribute, and therefore not mentioned, were some of the Aztec frontier towns that were obliged to maintain the local Aztec garrisons. For example, Totoltepec was exempt from tribute payments because it supported at least one local Aztec garrison and another at the fort of Oztuma.

From this we learn the following: if a prehispanic Aztec map shows a named locality on the frontier of a polity, it is likely to have been a tribute-paying dependency, or at least claimed as such. Enemy towns not paying tribute were not mentioned, nor (apparently) were subject towns exempt from tribute.

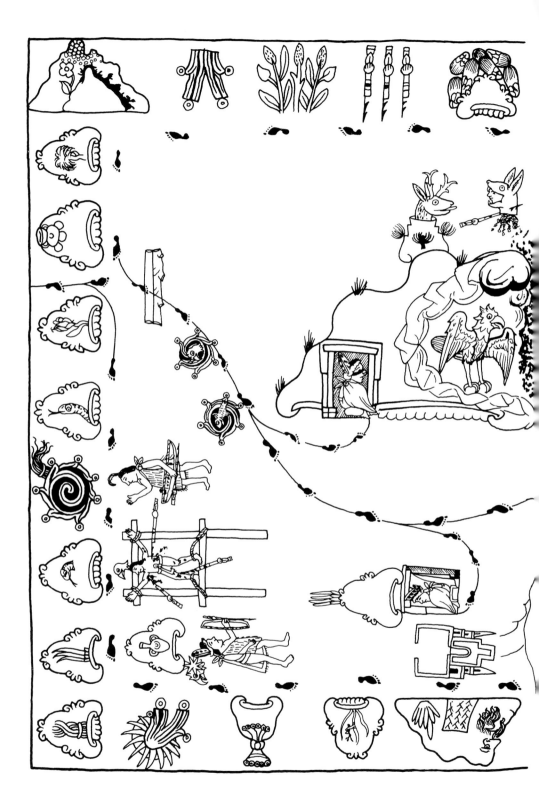

6.7. Indigenous-style map showing the boundaries of the Quauhtinchantlaca (Cuauhtinchantlaca) as defined by hill signs and "places with water" along the edges of these two pages. Beginning at the upper left corner and proceeding counterclockwise are Matlalcueye, Auatepec, Nacapauazqui, Tepoxochco, Couatepetl, Atzontli, Couatepetzintli, Tollocan, Malinalocan, Atoyatl, Tlequaztepetzinco, Tzicatepec, and Zoyapetlayo yyacac. Continuing counterclockwise we see Molcaxac, Uilotepec, Atezcac, Nepoualco, Tetl iztacan, Temalacayocan, Chiyapolco, Acoltzinco, Totolquechco, Matlatlán, Poyauhtecatl, Napateuhctli, Couatepec, Quauhtepec, Ocelotepec, an unidentified place, Centli ypalancan, Mitl ymancan, Uauautla, and Atltzayanca, and have returned to Matlalcueye. (Redrawn by John Klausmeyer from Kirchhoff, Odena Güemes, and Reyes García 1976: left half, folio 32v; right half, folio 33r.)

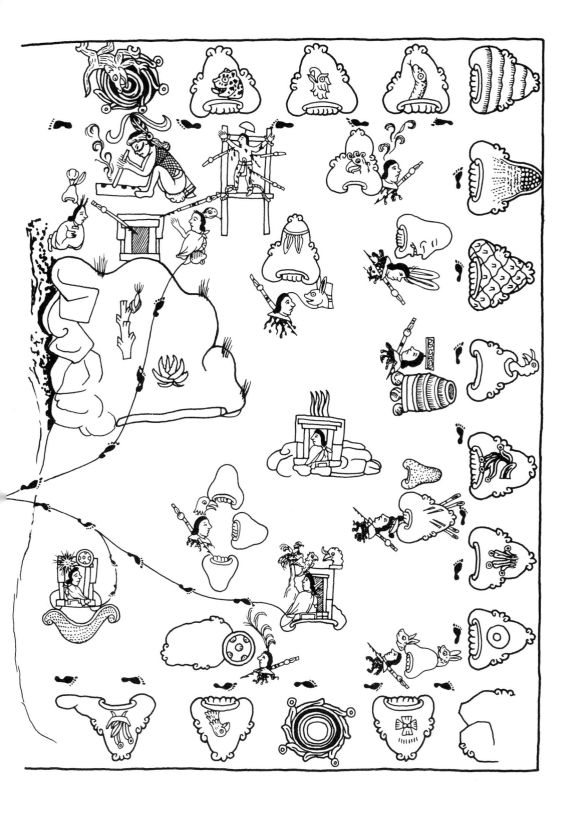

We move now from a Utoaztecan language (Nahuatl) to a pair of Otomanguean languages (Mixtec and Zapotec). The move is instructive, for it shows us certain universals in place-naming that crosscut language families. In Nahuatl, the qualifier precedes the noun, so that "Hill of the Bird" is Tototepec (*tototl* = bird + *tepetl* = hill) and "Hill of the Jaguar" is Ocelotepec (*ocelotl* + *tepetl*). In Mixtec and Zapotec, the qualifier follows the noun. Thus, "Hill of the Bird" in Mixtec would be Yucu Dzaa, from *yucu* (hill) + *dzaa* (bird); "Hill of the Jaguar" in Zapotec would be Tani Guebeche, from *tani* (hill) + *guebeche* (fierce carnivore). In all three hieroglyphic writing systems, however, the specifying element (e.g., "bird," "jaguar") is shown above the hill sign, indicating a convention that makes the word order of the spoken language irrelevant in some cases.

The Mixtec hill sign is a *pictogram*, or conventionalized picture of a hill (Fig. 6.8). It often has a bell-shaped form whose lower corners curl inward, forming scrolls to either side of a central base that is often scalloped (Fig. 6.8b). Other typical features of these Mixtec hills are their tiny bumps or rough spots which may indicate a stony surface (Fig. 6.8a, b). We have already seen similar bumps on the hill signs forming the periphery of the maps in the *Historia Tolteca-Chichimeca* (Figs. 6.5, 6.7).

In addition to hills, Mixtec place names often include other natural features such as rivers (*yuta* or *yucha*); plains, fields, or valleys (*yodzo*); or the term for "populated place" or town (*ñuu*). Again, Zapotec is quite similar to Mixtec, forming some place names from rivers (*guigo*), water (*nisa*), stone (*guie*), and town (*queche*) (Marcus 1983a).

The Mixtec sign for town (*ñuu*) is represented in the painted codices by a long, rectangular frieze decorated with multicolored geometric patterns, usually with the stepped pyramid design. Town signs are sometimes used interchangeably with hill signs (Smith 1973a:40), while in other place glyphs both signs occur. In some cases, it is clear that the geometric frieze was used because the Mixtec scribe needed to indicate that a town was present. In still other situations, the *ñuu* or *yucu* signs seem merely to indicate "place."

The Mixtec word "plain" or "valley" is represented in place glyphs as a rectangular mat of multicolored feathers tied together by bands. As in the Aztec case where teeth were used to represent the homonym "near," this feather mat is an example of letting an easily depicted word stand for one that sounds similar but is difficult to depict. In Mixtec, a tone language, the words for "plain" or "valley" (*yodzo*) and "large feather" (*yodzo*) are differentiated only by tone. Given the difficulty of depicting a plain or valley, the Mixtec scribe used large feathers to convey the word *yodzo*. This "tone pun" of *yodzo* was first noted by Caso (1949; see also Codex Bodley 17–18 in Corona Núñez 1964, vol. 2), and, as Smith (1973a:41) pointed out, it amounts to what Gelb (1963:102) has called a "phonetic transfer."

Another frequently encountered element of the Mixtec place sign is the glyph for "river" (*yuta*), often shown as a profile or cross-section of a river. (As we shall see below,

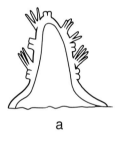
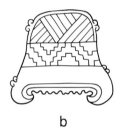

a   b

6.8. Examples of the Mixtec hill sign. At *a* is a hill with small bumpy protrusions, indicating stones; the longer, feather-like elements indicate that the place was conquered and burned. Like *a*, the figure at *b* shows a hill with small bumps indicating stones; but within the hill sign are mat and frieze motifs specifying the name of the place, which has yet to be identified.

this convention of showing a watercourse in cross-section was used by the Zapotec as early as 150 B.C.–A.D. 150 at Monte Albán.) Smith (1973a:41) shows that just as the sign for "river" is the most common geographic designation for water found in Mixtec town names, the Nahuatl equivalent *apan* is the most prevalent geographic designation for water found in the names of Nahuatl towns (see Fig. 6.4 for examples).

In addition to the terms *yucu, ñuu, yodzo,* and *yuta,* seventeen other geographic terms are frequently encountered in the names of Mixtec places that are not specifically towns (Smith 1973a:45). Such places include outlying dependencies, special ceremonial sites, and unoccupied places such as the natural landmarks on a polity's territorial boundaries.

For the Mixtec area we have several examples of "maps" (*mapas, lienzos*) depicting a town at the center of a territory, with its boundaries indicated around the periphery of the map by place signs. These include the Mapa de Teozacoalco, the Map of Amoltepec, the Map of Sinaxtla, the Lienzo de Jicayán, the Lienzos de Zacatepec 1 and 2, the Lienzo de Ocotepec, the two maps of Xoxocotlán (1718, 1771), the Lienzo de Tamazulapan, the Map of Xochitepec, the Lienzo de Natívitas, the Lienzo Seler II, the Codex Meixuiero-Lienzo Seler II, the Lienzo Ixtlán-Lienzo B or Lienzo de Coixtlahuaca, Map No. 36, Lienzo Córdova-Castellanos, and the 1870 Map of Ixcatlán. This long list of maps makes it clear that the ancient Mixtec, like the Aztec, viewed particular rulers (whose towns of residence were shown in the center) as controlling a territory delimited by named geographic landmarks on the periphery of a map. There are at least three different arrangements of the boundary signs: they may be arranged in an imperfect circle, a perfect circle, or a rectangle (Smith 1973a:166). However, the limits of a ruler's domain could, and did, change over time, necessitating either that changes be made to that map, or that an entirely new map be prepared.

We earlier mentioned east as a preferred prehispanic orientation. Most of the Mixtec maps listed above, however, are Colonial in age, and the group reveals no standard orientation. Of a sample of 11 early Colonial Mixtec maps, three place east at the top, three west, two northwest, one northeast, and another southeast. Significantly, *none* of the maps place true north at the top. Thus, even though these Mixtec maps were for the most part painted (or recopied) in the latter part of the sixteenth century, the hieroglyphic conventions, layout, and basic subject matter reflect a great deal of the indigenous pattern and world view, even though they sometimes include some non-indigenous elements.

Most of the Mixtec maps we have referred to were painted with the specific purpose of protecting the lands held by a native ruler, his family, and descendants; they were to be used in current or anticipated lawsuits in a Colonial Spanish court of law. In most cases, the ancient sizes of the territories controlled by the rulers exceeded the size of their town's landholdings at the time of litigation. In other words, following the conquest, over time most towns came to control less and less land, and most rulers came to have fewer and fewer subjects.

6.9. The place sign for Zacatepec, from the Lienzo de Zacatepec 1. Knowing that its Mixtec name was Yucu Satuta, meaning "Hill of 7 Water," enables us to make sense of the elements within the hill sign—7 dots below a sign for water. The purpose of the other details in the drawing is not clear. They include an "earth monster" at the base with open jaws above "stars" or "night's eyes"; four bald-headed men protruding from the sides of the narrow hill; and a double-headed bird and possible plant at the very top. (Redrawn from Smith 1973a: fig. 94.)

Despite the problems of Colonial acculturation, these maps provide us with an idea of the size of the territories controlled by particular rulers at specific times. We know through the ethnohistoric work of Caso (1949, 1966b), Spores (1967, 1983), and others that the city-state (*señorío, cacicazgo,* or "kingdom") was the principal unit of political, economic, and social control for the sixteenth-century Mixtec. These Colonial maps make it clear that surviving rulers still considered their domain to consist of a central town and a series of dependencies which owed tribute and corvée labor to them, and also to have been delimited by a series of hills, rivers, or other landmarks. The maps, some of which will be discussed below, also served to reinforce rulers' genealogies and tie them to royal ancestors at specific localities.

Let us now look at a few of these Mixtec maps, completed in the Colonial era for the purpose of protecting a noble's or community's landholdings, establishing the boundaries of that political or administrative unit, or documenting the association of a particular lineage, dynasty, or ruler with a town or administrative unit.

Zacatepec 1

During the early Colonial period, probably somewhere between A.D. 1540 and 1560, a *lienzo* we now call Zacatepec 1 (Smith 1973a: figs. 85–116) was drawn to establish the boundaries of the town of Santa María Zacatepec (Smith 1973a:93). This *lienzo* can be considered a genealogical as well as a cartographic document, since information on the ruler's ancestry runs from upper left to upper right. East is at the top of the map (see Smith 1973a: fig. 85).

Fifty place signs—representing the names of the town's boundaries—surround a large rectangle that encloses all but the top of the *lienzo*. As in many of the sixteenth-century Mixtec cartographic documents, Zacatepec's boundary sites all face inward toward the central town, Santa María Zacatepec. Unlike some other sixteenth-century documents, the map includes some places and towns outside Zacatepec's frontier, perhaps as reference points for the Spaniards.

While Zacatepec's boundary signs face inward, the signs for places outside its territory face outward. This inward vs. outward orientation of place signs reveals the Mixtec conception of a frontier, differentiating towns that owed allegiance to Zacatepec from those that did not.

The place sign for Zacatepec itself occurs within the top quarter of the large rectangle depicting the polity's boundaries (Fig. 6.9). The Mixtec name for Zacatepec was Yucu Satuta (in the Teposcolula dialect in the Mixteca Alta) and Yucu Chatuta (in the Zacatepec dialect in the Mixteca Costa). In both dialects the place name means "Hill of 7 Water," since *yucu* is hill, *sa* is the calendric number 7, and *tuta* refers to the day sign "Water." Appropriately enough, 7 dots and the sign for "Water" are located within the tall, narrow hill. As Smith (1973a:96) has noted, Caso had suggested an alternative translation, "Hill of the Poisonous Herb" (from the Mixtec *satu*, "poisonous herb"), but that translation seems to be in conflict with the glyph for 7 Water.

A second, smaller hill shown nearby gives the Nahuatl name for Zacatepec, "Hill of Zacatl." In prehispanic times, *zacatl* seems generally to have meant "weeds" or "thatch." However, the sixteenth-century Spaniards, searching for an appropriate fodder for their recently introduced Old World animals such as donkey, horse, cattle, sheep, and goat, apparently altered the meaning of *zacatl* to its present "coarse grass" (Marcus and Flannery 1978:69–72).

Among the fifty towns facing in toward Zacatepec, and apparently forming its boundary, are Putla, Santiago Yosotiche, Amusgos, Atoyac, Jicayán, Pinotepa de Don Luis, Chayucu, and Ixtayutla.

The Lienzo de Jicayán

Another *lienzo* that serves to establish the place names delimiting the borders of a territory controlled by a Mixtec town is that of Jicayán, drawn around A.D. 1550 (Smith 1973a:144). As in the case of the Lienzo de Zacatepec 1, the boundary place names face inward. In this case, fifty-two place signs encircle the Mixtec coastal town of Jicayán, which is depicted in the center of the cotton cloth. At a later date, glosses in Latin characters were added to aid the viewer in the identification of these place signs, most probably when this *lienzo* was used in a Spanish Colonial court of law. Moving from north to east, to south, to west around the irregular circle, the boundary places include Amusgos, Sayultepec, Atoyac, Pinotepa de Don Luis, Tlacamama, Ixcapa, and Cacahuatepec (see Fig. 6.10 and Smith 1973a:144).

A comparison of Zacatepec 1 and the Lienzo de Jicayán suggests that a frontier buffer zone separated the extended territories of the Zacatepec *señorío* (to the northeast) and the Jicayán *señorío* (to the southwest). In both cases, the territory controlled by the modern towns of Santa María Zacatepec and San Pedro Jicayán is much smaller than that administered by the rulers of these towns during the sixteenth century. Places that had formerly been *sujetos* (or dependencies) of Zacatepec and Jicayán are today independent towns and villages. Smith (1973a:163) suggests that the prehispanic place sign appears to have persisted longer in its function as a boundary marker than it did as the name of a town. This is a very interesting suggestion, as it strengthens our interpretation of the Zapotec place signs of Monte Albán II (see below) by stressing that the most long-lived toponyms were those for boundary landmarks, not for communities.

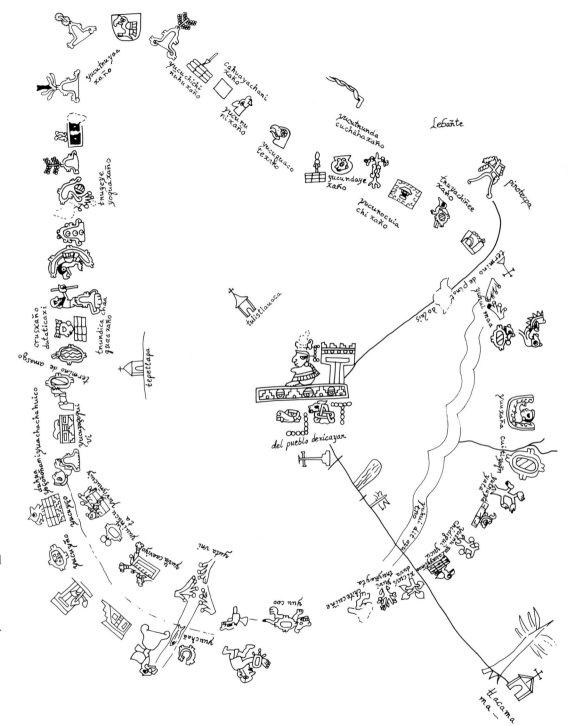

6.10. A coastal Mixtec map called the Lienzo de Jicayán. This map is one of several painted in the sixteenth century (but in prehispanic style) that continues the practice of using place signs to define territorial boundaries. A series of annotated glosses—labels added later, written in the Mixtec language using Latin characters—aid us in identifying the various localities. Encircled by 52 place signs, all of which face inward, is the ruler of Jicayán (Xicayan), who sits in front of a temple. Among the place signs on the periphery are hills, rivers, trees, plants, animals, and other objects. Many of the glosses use the word *yucu*, "hill," even when a hill sign is not depicted. (Redrawn from Smith 1973a:144.)

In the prehispanic era, the territorial boundaries of a Zapotec realm usually consisted of natural landmarks, such as named mountain peaks and rivers. Territorial maps indicating the limits of a Zapotec ruler's realm were drawn up by Zapotec nobles in response to demands made by sixteenth-century Spaniards, who required that the titles of land ownership be painted on paper to indicate which rulers and communities claimed which pieces of land. As a result of these demands, many *lienzos* or cartographic-genealogical documents were painted during this period by native artists. Unfortunately for us, very few of these Zapotec *lienzos* survive. The few that have survived show a pattern of named mountain peaks, rivers, and other natural landmarks.

An example of a Zapotec realm is given in the Lienzo de Guevea, a "map" initially completed in A.D. 1540 during the regime of viceroy Antonio de Mendoza. In both known copies of this map, A and B, the town of Santiago Guevea in the Isthmus of Tehuantepec is shown encircled by a ring of named boundary landmarks (Seler 1906, 1908; Marcus 1980, 1983l: fig. 8.34; Paddock 1983a; Whitecotton 1990). We will look first at Copy A (Fig. 6.11). Beginning at the bottom and proceeding counterclockwise, we see the following places:

Zapotec Gloss	*Place Sign*
Guietalaga	Stone or Cliff with a Leaf
Tani Guiexosa	Hill with Two Peaks
Tani Guiegoxio	Hill of Lightning
Nisa Quiegodaa	Water of the River of Petapa
Tani Quiebitao	Hill of the Sacred Spirit
Tani Guieguiña	Hill of the Stone Box
Tani Quiebiti	Hill of the Penca (= agave leaf)
Tani Quegohue	Dark/Shaded Hill
Tani Quechohuy	Burnt Hill
Nisa Guluga	Water of the Gourd Vessel
Guigo Liasa	River of Camalote Grass
Tani Guebeche	Hill of the Fierce Carnivore
Tani Quecheta	Stones that Are Opposed
Nisa Belote	Water of the Tadpole
Guigo Xanaya	River Beneath the Ground
Guigo Iloxi	River of Sand
Tani Quiape	Hill of the Chayote
Tani Guiebigoce	Hill of the Spindle Whorl

174

Chapter 6

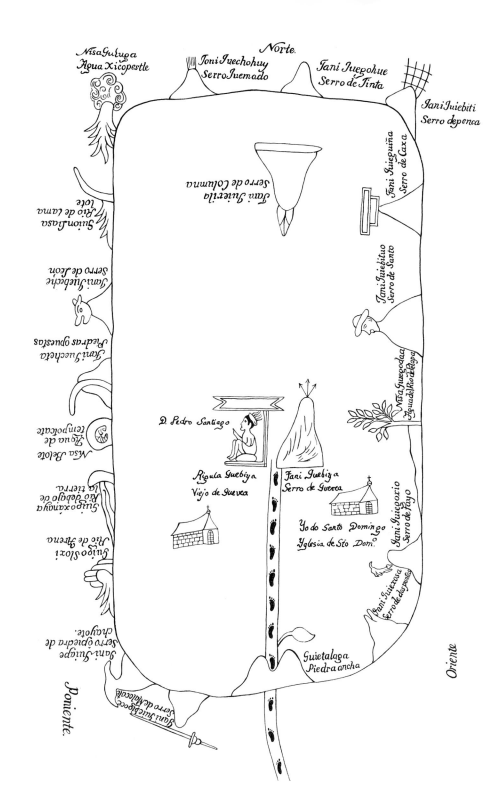

6.11. Sixteenth-century Zapotec map showing 18 named landmarks (hills and rivers) delimiting the polity of Guevea. (Redrawn from Seler 1906, 1908; see Marcus 1983l: fig. 8.34.)

This map uses four categories of natural landmarks: hills (*tani*), rivers (*guiego*), water (*nisa*), and cliffs (*guie*, "stone"). Significantly, however, two-thirds of the boundary markers are named mountain peaks. In Copy B of the same *lienzo* (Paddock 1983a), the eighteen landmarks delimiting the realm were referred to as *tepetl-mojón*—an expression that is half Nahuatl and half Spanish, meaning "hill/boundary marker."

To return to Copy A (Fig. 6.11), we see in the middle of the ring of boundary landmarks the labels *Tani Guebiya* ("Hill of Guevea") and *Serro de Guevea*, located below a naturalistic hill with three arrowheads. In front of the hill (and below a ruler sitting inside a structure) appear the phrases *Rigula Guebiya* and *Viejo de Guevea*. A road with footprints leading to the Hill of Guevea divides the town into two wards, each with its own church; *Yodo Santiago Guebiya* (*Yglesia de Santo Guevea*) occurs on the left, and *Yodo Santo Domingo* (*Yglesia de Santo Domingo*) on the right. Above each set of names is the depiction of a Spanish church. Today the word *yu'du'* is still used for "church" by the Zapotec of the Isthmus of Tehuantepec.

The "Viejo" (*rigula*, or "old man") sitting in the prehispanic-style structure at Guevea is labeled "Don Pedro Santiago." This is obviously his baptismal name; his Zapotec name is not given. This ruler of Guevea was in office in A.D. 1540, shown sitting at the center of the realm he administered. He had apparently descended from the line of Zapotec rulers who formerly administered the town of Zaachila in the Valley of Oaxaca.

The Lienzo de Guevea reveals a number of similarities to Mixtec *lienzos* such as the Lienzo de Zacatepec and the Lienzo de Jicayán. Both Zapotec and Mixtec were clearly interested in (1) showing the areal extent of the territory controlled by a central town; (2) linking a particular ruler or dynastic line to that centrally located town; and (3) depicting the borders of the town's territory as a set of named natural landmarks such as hills and rivers.

*Building J at Monte Albán: An Early Example of
Toponyms Used to Delimit a Tributary Territory*

The Zapotec custom of defining territorial limits by the use of hieroglyphically named mountains was, of course, much older than A.D. 1540. Some time between 150 B.C. and A.D. 150, during Period II at the site of Monte Albán in the Valley of Oaxaca, more than fifty carved slabs were set in Building J in the site's Main Plaza (Fig. 6.12). Carved on each slab is a hieroglyphic place name including (1) the Zapotec hill sign; (2) a glyph or set of glyphs defining that specific hill; and sometimes (3) a human head in a distinct regional headdress set upside down—presumably to indicate that the place had been subjugated.

By analogy with the documents we have seen so far, this set of slabs was probably a list of places on the boundary of the Zapotec state during Monte Albán II. It is unfortunate

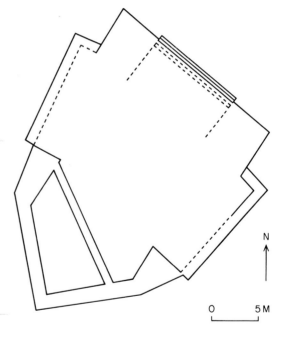

6.12. Plan of Structure J, Monte Albán, an arrowhead-shaped building constructed in the Main Plaza sometime between 150 B.C. and A.D. 150. (Redrawn and adapted from Caso 1938.)

176

Chapter 6

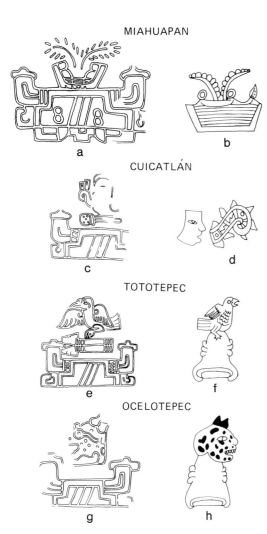

6.13. Examples of place signs from Structure J at Monte Albán (*a, c, e, g*) that can be matched with place signs from the later Codex Mendoza (*b, d, f, h*). The latter document is a sixteenth-century Aztec codex that lists places in Oaxaca which paid tribute to Tenochtitlán. (For other Structure J place signs that have been identified, see chapter 11, Figs. 11.36—11.38). (Redrawn from Marcus 1983e: fig. 4.15.)

that many slabs had fallen from their original positions and were reset by archaeologists in the 1930s. This means that many are out of position and that the slabs, as a group, cannot therefore be seen as a "map" of places to be matched up with real geography. Of course, as we have seen in the case of the Aztec, we cannot even assume that the prehispanic carvers desired such geographic accuracy.

Of the fifty places depicted, perhaps twenty can be "read" in the sense that we know what the hill was named (see chapter 11 for examples). Perhaps ten can be matched with actual places known today. At least four of the ten closely resemble the glyphs for places in the state of Oaxaca given in the Codex Mendoza (Barlow and McAfee 1949:10, 25), an Aztec tribute list. These include Slab 43, which shows maize tassels growing in an irrigation canal (Fig. 6.13a). This slab resembles the sign for Miahuapan (*miahuatl*, "maize tassels" + *apan*, "irrigation canal") in the Codex Mendoza (Fig. 6.13b). Miahuapan was an alternative name for Miahuatlán, a Zapotec town 85 kilometers south of Monte Albán, which has a major Monte Albán II site (Markman 1981).

A second example is that of Cuicatlán ("The Place of Song"), one of the most convincing matches between a Building J slab (Fig. 6.13c) and a place glyph in the Codex Mendoza (Fig. 6.13d). Significantly, recent archaeological work carried out by Spencer (1982) and Redmond (1983) has confirmed a Zapotec takeover of the Cuicatlán region during Monte Albán II. At one settlement in that region the Zapotec erected a skull-rack of slain enemies, and further north they fortified a mountaintop, closing off the main route from the Valley of Oaxaca to the Valley of Tehuacán. (For more information on Monte Albán's conquest of Cuicatlán, see the discussion on Zapotec warfare in chapter 11.)

A third identifiable place occurs on Slab 57 (Fig. 6.13e), which shows a bird perched atop two *atlatl* darts above a hill sign. Tototepec ("Hill of the Bird") also appears in the Codex Mendoza (Fig. 6.13f) and refers to Tututepec, a town on the Pacific coast 140 kilometers southwest of Monte Albán. Tututepec is known to have a major hilltop site during Monte Albán II.

Slab 23 shows a spotted feline above a hill sign (Fig. 6.13g). It is similar to the sign for Ocelotepec ("Hill of the Jaguar") as shown in the Codex Mendoza (Fig. 6.13h). Ocelotepec is a district in the mountains near Miahuatlán, approximately 140 kilometers southeast of Monte Albán. Its ancient name in Zapotec was Quiebeche, meaning "Hill of the Jaguar" (*quie*, "cliffs, stone, hill"; and *peche*, "fierce carnivore, jaguar, feline") (Marcus 1980, 1988). Unfortunately, this area is still archaeologically unknown.

All ten place signs that I have tentatively matched to specific places lie between 50 and 150 kilometers from Monte Albán (see chapter 11 for more examples). This distance suggests that the territorial boundaries of the Monte Albán II state extended well outside the Valley of Oaxaca proper. It also suggests that the use of named hills (not "towns") to delimit political territories had a 1,500-year history in southern Mexico.

As noted earlier, the lowland Maya landscape did not have many large mountain peaks that could be used as major landmarks; thus the "hill sign" was not as important for the Maya as it was for the Aztec, Mixtec, and Zapotec. The Classic Maya of the southern lowlands *did* have a hill sign (Fig. 6.1d), but it was used to indicate specific sacred places *within* a polity, and probably corresponded to the spoken word *huitz*, "isolated hill" (Stuart and Houston 1989). To designate larger units on the order of political realms and provinces, the southern lowland Maya used prominent geographic features such as rivers, lakes, and swamps.

The Maya of the northern lowlands used water-filled sinkholes or *cenotes* (*dz'onot*) as important landmarks, a practice understandable given the lack of rivers in that karstic plain. They also distinguished between a chain of low hills (*puuc*) and a single, low, isolated hill (*huitz*). For example, the "Puuc Hills" (an unfortunate redundancy) in the northwest sector of the Yucatán Peninsula served as a prehispanic landmark that at different times divided one sociopolitical jurisdiction from another.

Additional terms for places on the lowland Maya landscape included *ku*, "sacred" [place]; *kuna*, "temple" (from *ku*, "sacred," and *na*, "house"); *multun*, "artificial mound or pyramid, natural hill, or boundary marker"; *sak mul*, "white mountain of stone made by hand"; and *buktun*, "elevated places where houses and public buildings could be constructed" (Martínez Hernández [1585?] 1929; Barrera Vásquez et al. 1980).

The Sixteenth Century: Northern Lowlands

At the time the Spaniards arrived in the sixteenth century, northern Yucatán was divided into sixteen provinces, sometimes referred to as jurisdictions (*cuchcabalob*), city-states, or territorial units. Some of these sixteen provinces were named after geographic features, as in the case of Chakan ("savanna terrain," which is said to have abounded in that province). Others were named for the patronymic of the ruling family or lineage of that territory. For example, the province of Ah Canul took its title from the surname of the ruling Canul family, which was passed down in the male line (Fig. 6.14).

The Maya of the northern lowlands did not hold private property, but farmed areas considered to be "lands held in common." One sixteenth-century source, Gaspar Antonio Chi (Tozzer 1941:230), reported:

The lands were in common and so between the towns there were no boundaries or landmarks to divide them except between one province and another because of wars, and in the case of certain hollows and caves, plantations of fruit trees and cacao trees,

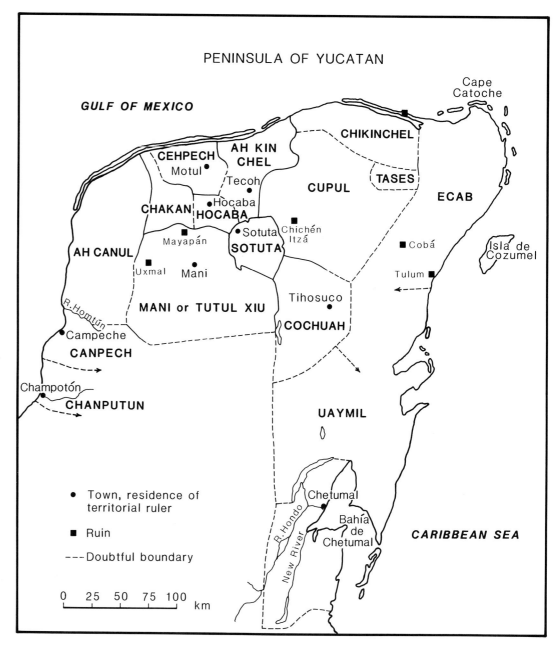

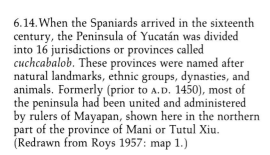

6.14. When the Spaniards arrived in the sixteenth century, the Peninsula of Yucatán was divided into 16 jurisdictions or provinces called *cuchcabalob*. These provinces were named after natural landmarks, ethnic groups, dynasties, and animals. Formerly (prior to A.D. 1450), most of the peninsula had been united and administered by rulers of Mayapan, shown here in the northern part of the province of Mani or Tutul Xiu. (Redrawn from Roys 1957: map 1.)

and certain lands which had been purchased for the purpose of improving them in some respect.

Thus, the most likely landmarks to be emphasized on Maya maps of that era are those dividing one province from another.

The Yucatec Maya referred to the maps they drew as *pepet dzibil* (from *pepet*, "circular," and *dzibil*, "painting" or "writing"). This term was an accurate description for the circular maps used to delimit the territory controlled by a particular ruling family. Such native maps usually placed east at the top, orienting the Maya world to the rising and setting sun. An excellent example of such a *pepet dzibil* comes from the Province of Mani, discussed below.

Mani

The province of Mani was sometimes referred to in the sixteenth-century documents as the "Tutul Xiu province." The term "Mani" refers to the capital or head town of the province, while "Tutul Xiu" refers to a male lord of Maya origin who claimed Toltec descent and who was a member of the Xiu lineage (Roys 1957:63). As we will see below, this use of both head towns and lineage names as geographic referents is relevant to our analysis of the "place names" or "emblem glyphs" used in the hieroglyphic inscriptions of the more ancient Classic period (A.D. 250–900).

The province (or *cuchcabal*) of Mani was divided diagonally from northwest to southeast by a range of low mountains, extending from Muna to a point southwest of Tzuccacab (Fig. 6.15). To the northeast of these mountains, low limestone ridges alternate with thin pockets of soil. To the southeast of this range the soil is thicker and more productive, but the water table during the sixteenth century was apparently far below the surface and virtually inaccessible. Nearly all sixteenth-century settlements were located to the east of the mountain range; however, the remains of huge earlier cities such as Uxmal, Kabah, Labná, and Sayil are packed into the zone west of the mountains, presumably to take advantage of the deeper soil there. Evidently these earlier, prehispanic centers had better ways to store water or gain access to subsurface water, perhaps because of superior manpower or political administration.

On August 15, 1557, the Maya territorial ruler (*halach uinic*) of the province of Mani met with various town governors (*batabob*) who were his subjects, to mark off town boundaries, "fixing the corners and placing crosses at the borders of the fields of the towns of their subjects, for each [town] separately" (Roys 1943:185). All the *batabob* were advised that they should come to the center of Mani, each bringing two *regidores* with him as witnesses for the "marking off of the borders of the forests, the borders of the lands"

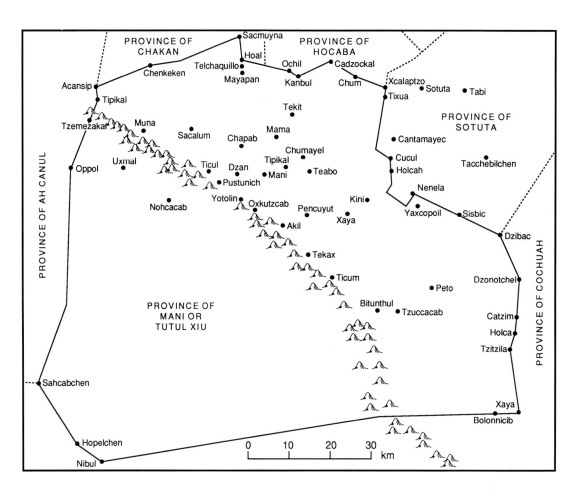

6.15. Details of the Province of Mani, showing the location of sites and settlements. Running diagonally from the northwest to the southeast are the hills the Maya called *puuc* ("chain of hills"). (Redrawn from Roys 1957: map 7.)

(ibid.). It is stated in the Mani Land Treaty (Stephens 1843, vol. 2; Roys 1943: figs. 1–3) that this was done because Maya nobles (1) wanted all their descendants, in both female and male lines, to know the boundaries of the territory controlled by the *halach uinic*; (2) wanted the *halach uinic* to continue to receive the tribute and attention due him; and (3) wanted to ensure that the borders of their forest lands were marked off accurately.

Let us start at the top of the indigenous-style Mani map (Fig. 6.16) and move east, then north, then west, then south—following the sequence given in the Land Treaty, which states that the *batabob* came from the east, north, west, and south. This is the same counterclockwise listing of directions that still prevails during native Maya rituals in the highlands of Chiapas (see Vogt 1969, Gossen 1974).[2]

[2]We saw this same counterclockwise reading order in the *Historia Tolteca-Chichimeca*.

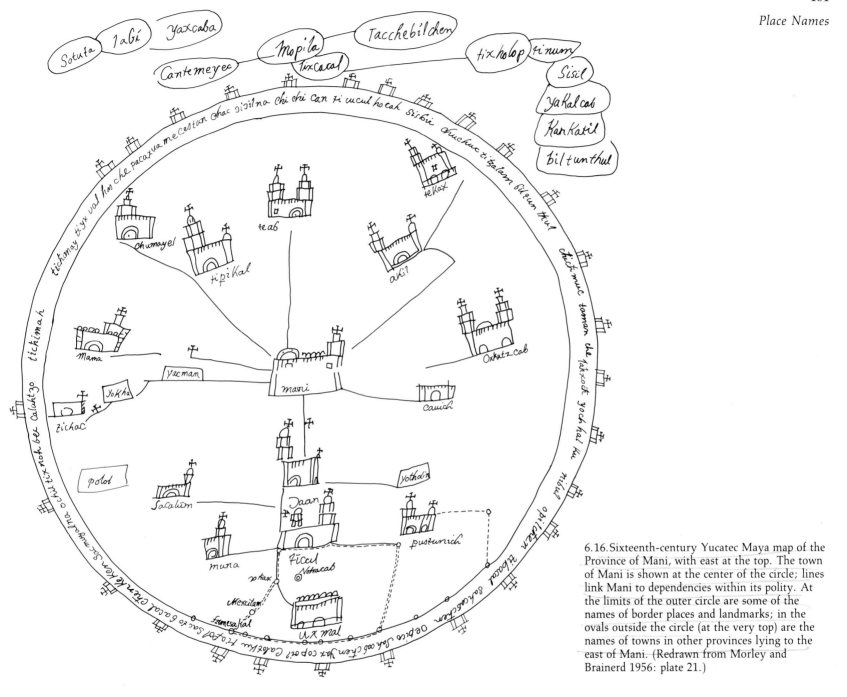

6.16. Sixteenth-century Yucatec Maya map of the Province of Mani, with east at the top. The town of Mani is shown at the center of the circle; lines link Mani to dependencies within its polity. At the limits of the outer circle are some of the names of border places and landmarks; in the ovals outside the circle (at the very top) are the names of towns in other provinces lying to the east of Mani. (Redrawn from Morley and Brainerd 1956: plate 21.)

Just as we saw in the Zapotec Lienzo de Guevea and the Mixtec Lienzos de Jicayán and Zacatepec, the provincial capital of Mani is shown at the center of the map and is ringed by a circle of named places along the frontier of its territory. Inside that circle are some of Mani's nearby subject communities, including Teabo, Tipikal, Chumayel, Mama, Yacman, Yokha, Tichac, Polol, Sacalum, Muna, Dzaan, Ticul, Nohcacab, Xkax, Mexcitam, Uxmal (the archaeological site), Pustunich, Yotholin, Cauich, Oxkutzcab, Akil, and Tekax. On the periphery of the circle—defining Mani's territorial borders—are more distant places like Nibul (to the southwest), Oppol and Tzemezakal (to the west), and Chum (to the northeast). We can work out the western, northern, and eastern boundaries with considerable confidence, but the southern boundary is more difficult to establish because today's maps do not include most of the place names given for the area between Nibul and Bitunthul. We can say only that the southern boundary of the province of Mani would have included places named Yochhalku, Tahxoch, Tamanche, and Chichmuc.

Finally, the indigenous map also gives us a series of towns, many of which fell outside Mani's sphere of control. It shows, for example, Sotuta, Tabi, Yaxcaba, Cantamayec, Mopila, Tixcacal(tuyu), and Tacchebilchen in the Province of Sotuta, and Tixholop and Tinum in the Province of Cochuah.

The Classic Period: Southern Lowlands

It is during the Classic Period in the southern lowlands (A.D. 250–900) that we first see the ancient Maya make use of hieroglyphs to designate place names. Unfortunately, the same glyphs used during the Classic did not continue in use after A.D. 900, nor do we have a set of ethnohistoric documents like the Land Treaty of Mani to aid us in translating them.

While most Maya epigraphers agree that certain hieroglyphs have a geographic referent, they do not agree on whether such glyphs stand for a *place,* or for the *royal family* that ruled the place. It was Heinrich Berlin (1958:111) who originally singled out this group of signs, referring to them as "emblem glyphs." He defined emblem glyphs as consisting of three parts: (1) a main sign, specific to a given Classic Maya city; (2) a superfix known as the "Ben-Ich" superfix; and (3) a prefix known as the "water-group" prefix (Fig. 3.30). The "Ben-Ich" superfix and the "water-group" prefix were considered to be the constant, unchanging elements that identify the compound as an emblem glyph, while the main sign could vary from site to site. Emblem glyphs are often the last hieroglyph to appear in a text, or the last one in a clause that includes a ruler's name or title. Hence, emblem glyphs were initially defined by Berlin on the basis of their tripartite structure and their position within Classic Maya clauses.

Berlin himself was appropriately cautious about the exact meaning of emblem glyphs, suggesting that they could be the names of tutelar deities, royal dynasties, cities, or geographic places. This was appropriate, since we have seen that for the sixteenth-century Maya of the northern lowlands, place names could be derived either from noble lineages or natural landmarks. Also in the sixteenth century, in the area of Lake Petén Itzá in the southern Maya lowlands, some polities were named after the *batab* (local lord) or *ahau* (supreme lord) administering them (Avendaño y Loyola 1696a, 1696b; Villagutierre Soto-Mayor 1701, 1933; Marcus n.d.c). If the Classic Maya of the southern lowlands followed similar customs, and also named districts, settlements, and polities after lords, lineages, or dynasties, we might expect some main signs of emblem glyphs to have been derived from dynastic names, while others might have been drawn from natural features of the landscape.

Prominent natural features in the southern lowlands include swamps, extensive *bajos* (low-lying areas that are seasonally flooded), some bodies of water (*ha*), a few major rivers, and numerous streams (*ukum*). Some ancient Maya places (e.g., Yaxhá, "blue-green water"; see Fig. 6.17) are known to incorporate "water" into their names. Additionally, if the so-called "water-group" affixes of emblem glyphs do have something to do with water (or "precious liquid" as Thompson [1950] originally suggested), it could mean that many places took their names from the swamps, *bajos, cenotes*, or prominent bodies of water that occur near most huge Classic Maya cities (Adams, Brown, and Culbert 1981:1462). However, some Maya epigraphers (e.g., Stuart 1988) now see the "water group" affixes as being linked to blood and genealogical descent rather than to water *per se*. This suggestion would tie in with Thompson's (1950) earlier work with the "water group" affixes, since many of their variable elements were read by him as "precious" (Fig. 6.18).

The other constant affix of the emblem glyph is the "Ben-Ich" superfix, which Lounsbury (1973) has interpreted as "ruler" or "lord of." Depending on how the "water group" prefix is interpreted, emblem glyphs could refer to the lord of a specific place on a *cenote* or body of water, or to a lord linked by blood descent to a major royal lineage. The fact that some major cities have more than one emblem glyph might suggest the latter, but the issue is not yet settled.

Of the hundreds of very large lowland Classic Maya sites, a relatively small percentage had their own emblem glyph(s). In the 1970s, the fact that not all sites had emblem glyphs suggested to me that the glyph probably referred to something larger than an individual city (Marcus 1974b, 1987). As I have stated in detail elsewhere (1976a, 1983b, 1984, 1987), I believe that each emblem glyph referred to a politically controlled unit that was much more geographically extensive than the individual "site" as defined by an archaeologist. That fact does not rule out the possibility that such a unit (realm, or province) might be referred to by the patronym of the royal lineage controlling it.

Given that approximately 40 Maya sites (out of the hundreds known) had their own emblem glyphs, and that many others did not have their own but did mention those of

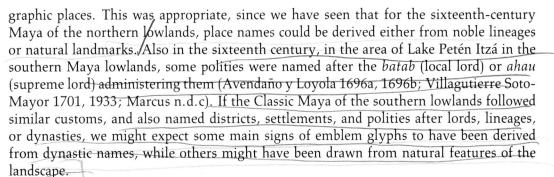

6.17. Two examples of the emblem glyph for Yaxá or Yaxhá. The prefix in both cases is the sign Thompson (1950, 1962) and others have read as *yax*, while the *a* or *ha* is the sound for the main sign, which was given in Landa's alphabet as "a," pronounced "ah." (See Figs. 3.36 and 3.37 for examples of *yax*, and Figs. 3.33, 3.40 for Landa's "a.") The upper emblem glyph includes the so-called "Ben-Ich" superfix (*ahpo* or *ahau*, meaning "lord of"); the lower glyph lacks this superfix. (Redrawn from Justeson 1975, Stuart 1985.)

a

b

c

6.18. Three examples of "water-group" prefixes that usually precede the main sign of an emblem glyph or place name. These signs have been interpreted as "precious" or "sacred" (Thompson 1950, 1962). (Redrawn from Marcus 1976a: fig.1.4.)

other sites, I decided to study their use and distribution for the period A.D. 250–900. What became apparent was that there were at least four kinds of Maya sites: (1) very large sites—the largest in their respective regions—which had their own emblem glyphs, and referred to each other; (2) large sites—often the second-largest in their respective regions—which had their own emblem glyphs, but referred only to larger sites within their own regions; (3) sites without their own emblem glyphs, which referred to larger sites with emblem glyphs; and (4) sites that neither had their own emblem glyphs, nor referred to other sites that did.

Given this patterning, it was possible to infer the existence of a settlement hierarchy, whereby very large sites commanded political allegiance from numerous smaller sites. The current state of our understanding is that each "primary" or "first-order" center controlled an extensive territory (Fig. 6.19), whose subunits were administered by second-, third-, and fourth-order sites (Marcus 1973, 1976a, 1983b, n.d.c).

Now let us return to the main sign, the element of the emblem glyph that varies from place to place. Some main signs are clearly animal heads (naturalistic, composite, or grotesque) while others are very abstract conventions, making it more difficult to suggest origins, meanings, and phonetic readings. The animal heads are interesting, since we know that many of the patronymics of the later Yucatec Maya were derived from animals such

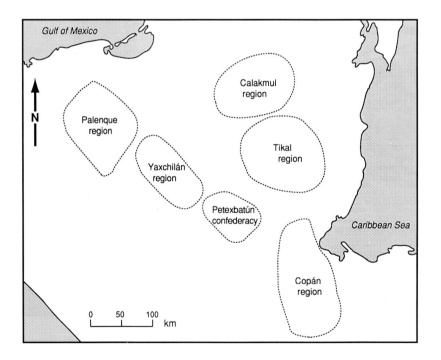

6.19. Maya administrative territories during part of the eighth century A.D. These polities were determined on the basis of the distribution and use of emblem glyphs. (Redrawn from Marcus 1983b.)

as *ba*, "gopher"; *balam*, "jaguar"; *coh*, "puma"; or *huh*, "iguana" (Roys 1940). Still other patronymics, such as *ceh*, "deer" and *pech*, "tick," might be combined into one word (Cehpech) and used for a large territorial unit or province in the northern lowlands.

The emblem glyph for the Classic period city of Copán was a leaf-nosed bat (*tzotz* or *suts'*) (Fig. 6.20). Sites within the Copán polity mentioned that emblem glyph, and were

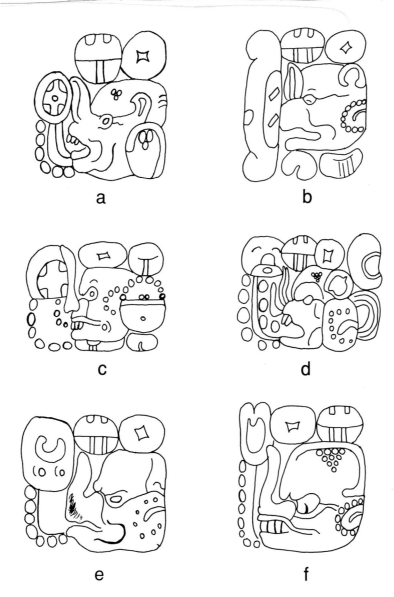

a   b

c   d

e   f

6.20. Six examples of the Copán emblem glyph, whose main sign is a leaf-nosed bat. All these examples include the "Ben-Ich" superfix; however, there is variable use of other elements. For example, at *b*, the *yax* (or precious) prefix substitutes for the "water-group" prefixes that include "beads of blood," as seen in *a, c, d, e,* and *f*. Copán's main sign (utilizing logograms for "bat" and "stone") may have been pronounced *sutstun* (or *sutsku,* if the "stone" logogram was read phonetically). (Redrawn from Thompson 1950: fig. 43 and Marcus 1976a: fig. 4.37.)

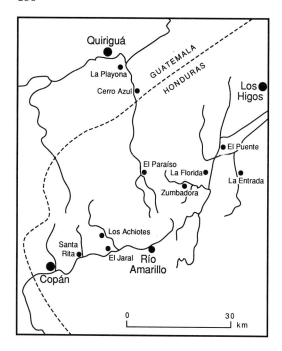

6.21. At different times during the seventh and eighth centuries A.D., the polity of Copán included secondary centers such as Quiriguá, Río Amarillo, and Los Higos; tertiary centers such as Pusilhá (farther to the north, and therefore not shown in this map) and El Paraíso; and quaternary centers such as Santa Rita and La Florida. (Redrawn from Morley 1920: fig. 57, Pahl 1977: fig. 1.)

hierarchically below Copán (Fig. 6.21). For example, sites such as Quiriguá, Río Amarillo, and Los Higos were secondary centers below Copán at various times (Marcus 1976a, Pahl 1977). Quiriguá eventually acquired its own emblem glyph (Fig. 6.22) after it successfully broke away from Copán in a "war of independence" in A.D. 738; Río Amarillo and Los Higos seem to have gained a measure of autonomy after A.D. 770 (see chapter 11).

The emblem glyph for the Classic city of Yaxhá has recently been phonetically transcribed as *yax* + *ha* (Fig. 6.17). Utilizing Landa's "alphabet" (Tozzer 1941), Thompson's 1950 study of the series of *yax* affixes used in the names of months such as Yaxkin, and Knorozov's (1955, 1967) phonetic transcriptions, Stuart (1985) has suggested that this place sign was actually pronounced "Yaxhá," the same way the nearby lake is still pronounced. Such name retention is very important, because it suggests that some places (such as Yaxhá) have kept the same name for 1,500 years, while others (such as Copán) have lost their prehispanic names.

One of Palenque's emblem glyphs appears to be a fusion of "bird" and "fish" elements (Fig. 6.23d). Other variants of the Palenque emblem include "bone" or "skull" elements (Fig. 6.23a, b). Since the Maya word *bak* can refer to a specific aquatic bird, or to "bone" in general, we may be dealing here with homonyms or phonetic transfers like those we saw in some Aztec and Mixtec place names. Interestingly, not far from the ruins of Palenque, Chol Maya informants gave Aulie (1961) a place name incorporating the word for "bone" (*bak*); that name was Bakte'el, "Forest of Bones." Since the language spoken by the occupants of ancient Palenque is assumed to have been Chol (Thompson 1954), the phonetic reading for at least this set of emblem glyphs at Palenque may be Bak or Bakan, "Place of Bones" (Fig. 6.23a, b; Fig. 6.24 a-e).

For the main sign of the Yaxchilán emblem glyph, the Classic Maya used a logograph standing for "sky" (Fig. 6.25). This sign can also be phonetically transcribed as *caan* or *chan* (Knorozov 1955; Thompson 1950; Marcus 1974b, 1983b; Houston 1984). The subfix (the affix which occurs below the main sign) appears to reinforce the final "n" sound, since it can be transcribed as *(a)n* or *n(a)*.

Maya main signs based on animals are often not very naturalistic depictions, so scientific identification of a particular genus or species is rarely possible. Some animal head glyphs even seem to be deliberate composites of fantastic creatures that never occurred in nature. Employing the principle of *pars pro toto* (where the part stands for the whole animal), various attributes of birds, fish, snakes, felines, and rodents might all be combined to create unreal animals (Marcus 1978, n.d.b). The head of one animal might be combined with the wing of another and the foot of another, producing a creature that had the powers and characteristics of all three animals but would never have been encountered in the real world. This fusion is one way to create the supernatural denizens of the world occupied by the divine ruling family.

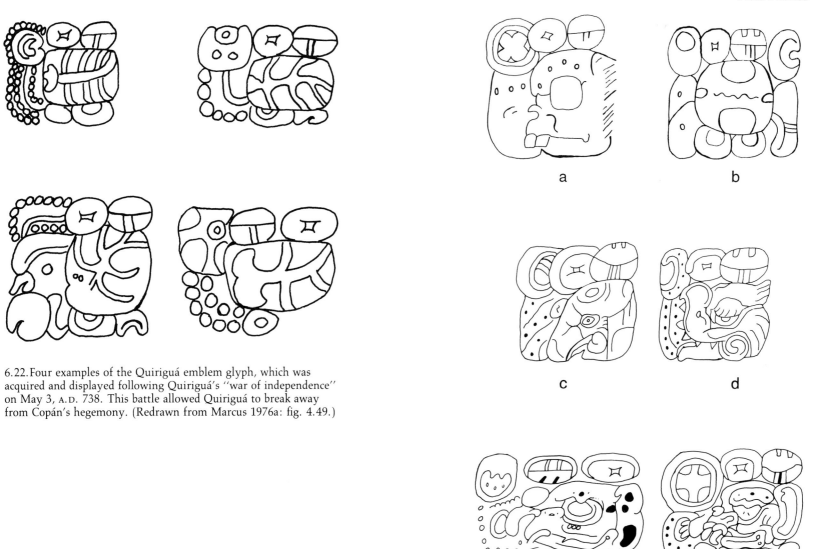

6.22. Four examples of the Quiriguá emblem glyph, which was acquired and displayed following Quiriguá's "war of independence" on May 3, A.D. 738. This battle allowed Quiriguá to break away from Copán's hegemony. (Redrawn from Marcus 1976a: fig. 4.49.)

a   b

c   d

e   f

6.23. Six examples of the Palenque emblem glyph. Palenque, like some other regional capitals, used a variety of different main signs: *a*, a skull; *b*, a bone; *c*, an animal head; *d*, a "fantastic creature" fusing fish and bird elements; and *e* and *f*, skull and animal "fantastic creatures." (Redrawn from Marcus 1976a: fig. 4.21.)

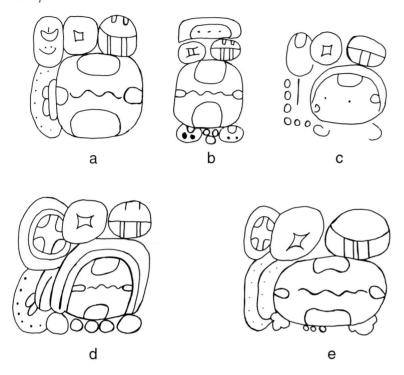

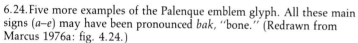

a

b

6.24. Five more examples of the Palenque emblem glyph. All these main signs (*a–e*) may have been pronounced *bak,* "bone." (Redrawn from Marcus 1976a: fig. 4.24.)

6.25. Three examples of the paired Yaxchilán emblem glyphs. Yaxchilán was unusual among Classic Maya sites in using a pair of emblem glyphs to stand for its political and territorial unit, rather than a single glyph. In this illustration, each row gives an example of that pair. The *a* row displays the "cleft-sky" main sign first and the *muluc* main sign second. More frequently this order of presentation was reversed, as seen in the *b* and *c* rows. The "cleft-sky" main sign may have been pronounced *caan,* "sky," or *caan-na,* "sky house." (Redrawn from Thompson 1950; Marcus 1976a: figs. 4.14, 4.15.)

c

There is reason to believe that all four of the cultures discussed in this book had similar ways of visualizing their territory. At the center of the territory was the place of residence of a ruler, usually a "capital" or "head town" but sometimes just a royal palace or residence. The most meaningful political unit, however, was the entire territory controlled by that one ruler, including not only his capital but all the secondary centers, tertiary centers, villages, hamlets, agricultural lands, and forested areas of his realm.

The limits of a ruler's territory were shown on indigenous maps as a ring of named landmarks, often mountains or bodies of water. These landmarks, which were given hieroglyphic names such as "Hill of the Bird" or "River of the Tadpoles," were chosen because they were more eternal and unchanging than human settlements.

Within the circle of named landmarks were dependent towns and villages, ritual localities, and other significant places. Highland cultures were more likely to name these after hills, while lowland cultures were more likely to name them after animals or bodies of water.

In some cases, the ruler's capital or "head town" was named for a natural feature of the landscape, but in other cases it was named for his lineage. Indeed, the two might be closely related. Occasionally entire polities might be named for an important ruler, his lineage, or some combination of landmark and lineage.

When a picture could stand for a landmark, as in "Hill of the Bird," it was used. When a difficult-to-depict term, such as "wide plain" or "valley," was involved in the place name, homonyms were used. The Mixtec, for example, might use "feathers" (*yodzo*) to indicate "valley" or "plain" (also written as *yodzo*, but with a different tone).

While we would like to be able to use today's maps to interpret prehispanic names, it is clear that prehispanic people did not share our view of accurate geography. Only occasionally did their placement of toponyms reflect true spatial relations in the sense that we demand of our maps. Mesoamerican cultures were unconcerned with the exact mileage between places and the exact placement of north and south. Their concern was to show all those places claimed as dependencies by a particular ruler whether those places had agreed to be subjugated or not, and as a result, maps produced by different polities give different pictures of the landscape. Like some maps produced in the 1990s by Iraq—which showed Kuwait as a province of Iraq—they were more concerned with propaganda than with geographic reality.

7 ✦ THE NAMING OF NOBLES

What's in a name? For Mesoamerican nobles, apparently quite a bit. Names were selected with great care, not only to reflect the desired qualities of a person, but also in the belief that the name itself would bestow those qualities. In the hieroglyphic texts from all regions of Mesoamerica, personal names are one of the most common entries.

While we do not know all the rules by which Mesoamerican rulers and nobles were named, there seem to have been a few widespread patterns: names were either taken from the 260-day ritual calendar (chapter 4) or drawn from animals, plants, or important objects. Some nobles had both, with their calendric name followed by a non-calendric nickname.

Some ethnic groups—especially the two speaking Otomanguean languages, the Mixtec and Zapotec—relied heavily on names taken from the 260-day calendar. Theoretically, one was named for the day on which he or she was born, but as we saw in chapter 4, some days were considered luckier than others. The parents of nobles born on unlucky days would consult diviners to select a more favorable day, the result being that not all days were equally represented as names. For example, the Mixtec wound up with many more male nobles named 1 Crocodile, 10 Reed, 3 Wind, 4 Motion, and 7 Flower than ever bore the names 2 Death, 4 Vulture, or 12 Flint (see Whallon, Appendix).

The high frequency with which certain calendric names appeared made it necessary to distinguish between persons with the same name. To cope with this situation, the Zapotec and Mixtec often had nicknames that were specific to an individual. For example, in the Codex Bodley the granddaughter of the Mixtec ruler 8 Deer "Tiger Claw" is shown being married to another 8 Deer, but his nickname was "Feathered Serpent" (see Fig. 7.1).

The Maya naming pattern was different from that of the Zapotec and Mixtec. Instead

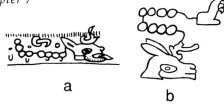

Chapter 7

7.1. Nobles with the same calendric name often differentiated themselves with nicknames. Here we see two Mixtec nobles named 8 Deer. The one named in *a* and *b* took the nickname "Tiger Claw"; the one shown in *c* and *d* took the nickname "Feathered Serpent." (*a* was redrawn from Codex Nuttall 26c; *b, c,* and *d* were redrawn from the Codex Bodley.)

of taking their names from the 260-day calendar, Maya nobles of all periods had names taken from animals and objects. Even though the Maya, like other Mesoamericans, believed that one's fate might be determined by one's birthdate, it is clear that few if any Maya nobles were known by calendric names. We do know that the days of the 260-day calendar were used by the Maya to determine when particular events (such as marriage, battles, or accession to the throne) should take place. Thus their calendar played a very important role in many events, but apparently not in the naming of rulers.

The Aztec situation was similar. While the 260-day calendar was important in many phases of their lives, we do not know most Aztec nobles by their calendric names. We know them primarily by their nicknames, titles, or secondary names, many of which featured animals, plants, or precious objects such as mirrors, feathers, turquoise, or jade. Several hereditary lords in the Basin of Mexico had names derived from the word *chimalli*, or "shield," as follows:

Name	Translation
Chimalpahin	"Swift-Running Shield"
Chimallaxochtzin	"Revered Flower Shield"
Chimalcuauhtli	"Eagle Shield"
Chimalman	"Resting Shield"
Chimalpopoca	"Smoking Shield"

These Nahuatl names are very interesting because some Classic Maya rulers, as we shall see, also incorporated the word "shield" into their names.

In addition to calendric names and nicknames, Mesoamerican rulers frequently acquired additional titles during their lifetime, particularly following events such as accession to the throne, victory in battle, or the taking of an important captive or sacrificial victim. The acquisition of these titles (such as "Captor of X") lengthened a ruler's name, and occasionally replaced his personal name. In some cases, it even becomes difficult to determine which hieroglyphs in a clause refer to the ruler's name and which to his titles.

Complicating our analysis of naming patterns still further is the fact that some rulers or nobles changed their names. These name changes sometimes make it difficult for us to determine if we are dealing with the same person or not. One case in which we can be confident that we are dealing with the same individual, before and after the name change, appears in the Codex Selden from the Mixtec area. It involves a female ruler who during her earliest years was known as 6 Monkey "Serpent Quechquemitl" (Fig. 7.2a, c). She kept this name until A.D. 1038, when she was involved in the defeat of two lords who had allegedly insulted her; following their defeat, 6 Monkey had them sacrificed. After the sacrifice, 6 Monkey is shown with a new nickname, "Warband Quechquemitl" (Spinden 1935; Smith 1973a:28). The new element in her nickname is a band of chevrons signifying "war." These chevrons were sometimes incorporated into her quechquemitl, replacing the

a

b

c

d

7.2. A female Mixtec ruler, 6 Monkey "Serpent Quechquemitl," acquired a new nickname ("War Quechquemitl") after defeating two rival lords. At *a*, we see her with a shield and spear; from her poncho-like overblouse we know that her nickname at this time is "Serpent Quechquemitl." At *c* she is shown seated, wearing her serpent garment. However, at *b*, she is shown with her "War Quechquemitl," decorated with chevrons. At *d*, she also wears her "War Quechquemitl," but her earlier nickname of "Serpent Quechquemitl" is given as a hieroglyphic sign behind her back. (Redrawn from the Codex Selden.)

head of the serpent used earlier (Fig. 7.2b, d). Sometimes her former nickname was placed behind her while she wore her new nickname on her clothing (see Fig. 7.2d).

The impetus for 6 Monkey's acquisition of a new nickname was apparently the defeat and sacrifice of the aforementioned rival lords. It is unusual for us to be able to document precisely when or under what circumstances a new nickname was acquired, since most nicknames seem to be present the first time we encounter an individual in the codices, and the name is usually retained throughout that individual's lifetime.

We will now discuss in more detail the naming patterns displayed by Aztec, Mixtec, Zapotec, and Maya nobles. Unfortunately, because prehispanic writing records only the names and feats of nobles, no comparable analysis of commoners' names can be undertaken.

THE NAMING OF AZTEC NOBLES

Although we know Aztec nobles almost entirely from their nicknames or secondary names, sixteenth-century ethnohistoric data indicate that both nobles and commoners did have primary names taken from the *tonalpohualli* or 260-day calendar. It may be the case that commoners continued to be known only by their calendric names, while rulers and nobles came to be known mainly by their more elegant nicknames and acquired titles. In the Florentine Codex, Sahagún discusses the birth and naming of a child on the first day of the year 1 Crocodile as follows: "Upon a good day sign hath he been born and created and come forth on earth; he hath arrived upon the earth on [the day sign] One Crocodile. Let him be bathed" (Dibble and Anderson 1957:3).

In this case, the child was named Ce Cipactli ("One Crocodile"), but this might not have been done had the day been less favorable: "And, on the other hand, if it were the wish [of the parents], perchance they passed over the days; perchance they settled upon still another day for him to be bathed. For One Crocodile bore with it all favorable day signs" (Dibble and Anderson 1957:3).

As we noted in chapter 4, when an infant was born on a day whose number or day sign was unfavorable, the *tonalpouhqui* or "soothsayer" would select a more propitious day, ideally within the same *trecena* or 13-day period as the actual birthdate.

In the paragraphs that follow we will look at the names of some rulers and nobles from the Mexica capital of Tenochtitlán and the cities of Texcoco, Huexotla, and Tlatelolco, all Nahuatl-speaking places. Birds such as the eagle, hawk, falcon, hummingbird, and quetzal were favored as names. Sometimes the attributes of two different objects or animals were combined to create a fantastic creature such as an "obsidian-backed serpent." We will also see that many rulers' names terminated in the honorific suffix *tzin*, which might be translated as "honored" or "revered." For example, Huetzin, Itzcoatzin, and Quinatzin all had such a suffix. *Tzin* was also attached to the names of revered females such as Coyolicatzin ("Cotton Flake"), the daughter of the Aztec ruler Ahuitzotl, who was given the Zapotec name Pelaxilla (also meaning "Cotton Flake") after she married the Zapotec ruler Cociyoeza (Marcus 1983l:302).

Tenochtitlán, the Mexica Capital

The rulers from Tenochtitlán we will consider are Acamapichtli (A.D. 1376–1396), Huitzilihuitl (1397–1417), Chimalpopoca (1417–1428), Itzcoatl (1428–1440), Motecuhzoma Ilhuicamina (1440–1469), Axayacatl (1469–1481), Tizoc (1481–1486), Ahuitzotl (1486–1502), Motecuhzoma Xocoyotzin (1502–1520), Cuitlahuac (1520), and Cuauhtemoc (1520–1525). All these Mexica rulers are depicted in the Códices Matritenses and in the

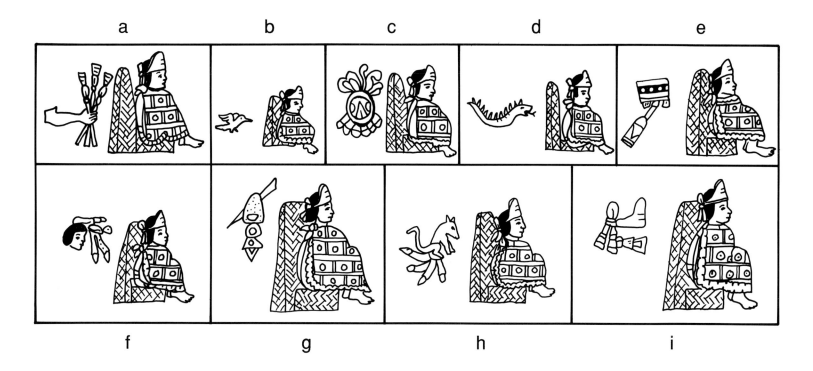

Florentine Codex in stereotyped fashion, either seated on a woven mat (*petlatl*), seated on a mat "throne" called an *icpalli*, or standing next to a jaguar pelt–covered cushion and high-backed throne. So stereotyped, in fact, are these figures that no individual could be recognized from the drawing; the scribe had to distinguish each ruler by drawing a hieroglyphic sign by his head (Dibble 1981:8–9). These associated glyphs can be called "name labels" or "captions," because they supply some of the pictographic counterparts of the personal name.

For example, the hieroglyph associated with the figure of Acamapichtli ("Handful of Reeds") shows a hand grasping reeds (Fig. 7.3a). The initial part of the name is conveyed by the depiction of "reeds," *aca(tl)*, while the second part is suggested by the "grasping hand," *mapichtli*. The glyph associated with Huitzilihuitl ("Hummingbird Feather") is a flying hummingbird, *huitzili(n)*, but the sign for "feather," *ihuitl*, is not given as a second, separate sign (Fig. 7.3b). Chimalpopoca ("Smoking Shield") has a name glyph which includes an ornate round shield with smoke rising from it. The term for "shield" is *chimal(li)*, while the term for "smoke" was *popoc(tli)* (Fig. 7.3c). The name sign for Itzcoatl ("Obsidian Serpent") is a snake with eleven obsidian blades along its back; this sign was derived from *itz(tli)*, "obsidian" and *coatl*, "serpent" (Fig. 7.3d).

7.3. Names of Tenochtitlán rulers. *a*, Acamapichtli; *b*, Huitzilihuitl; *c*, Chimalpopoca; *d*, Itzcoatl; *e*, Motecuhzoma Ilhuicamina; *f*, Axayacatl; *g*, Tizoc; *h*, Ahuitzotl; *i*, Motecuhzoma Xocoyotl. (Redrawn from Anderson and Dibble 1954.)

7.4. Names of Tenochtitlán rulers (continued). *a*, Cuauhtemoc; *b*, Motelchiuh; *c*, Xochiquen; *d*, Uanitl; *e*, Teuetzquiti; *f*, Cecepatic. (Redrawn from Anderson and Dibble 1954.)

Motecuhzoma means "He Who Grows Angry (like a) Lord." The first Motecuhzoma was sometimes called "The Elder" (*Ueue* or *Yeue*) to distinguish him from the second ruler of the same name. Motecuhzoma the Elder also carried the qualifying name of Ilhuicamina ("He who Shoots Arrows Against the Sky" or "He who Pierces the Sky with Arrows"). Shown behind the figure of Motecuhzoma in Figure 7.3e is an arrow piercing the sky symbol.

The names of the rulers that followed Motecuhzoma the Elder—Axayacatl, Tizoc, and Ahuitzotl—have been translated in various ways (van Zantwijk 1985, Hassig 1988, Gillespie 1989). Both the terms that comprise Axayacatl's name and the hieroglyphic signs used to depict it—a human head in profile and rivulets of water—can be translated "Water Face" (Figs. 7.3f). The term *axayacatl* is defined by Molina as "a water animal like a fly" (Molina [1571] 1944:10v).

The ruler Tizoc was sometimes associated with a sign showing a lower leg being pricked by spines; in other cases, an object other than a leg is shown being pricked by a sharp object (see Fig. 7.3g). The word *teço* is usually defined as "bleeder" (Molina [1571] 1944:92v); thus Tizoc is often translated as "Bleeder," "Bloodletter," or "He Who Has Made People Bleed."

Ahuitzotl's name sign includes an animal placed above the sign for water (Fig. 7.3h). His name is usually translated as "Water Creature" or "Otter," a definition also given in Molina ([1571] 1944:9v) as "cierto animalejo de agua como perrillo."

The ninth Mexica ruler, Motecuhzoma the Younger (Motecuhzoma Xocoyotl), is shown in Figure 7.3i, accompanied only by the depiction of a ruler's headdress. Evidently, the scribe who rendered this picture could not think of a way to convey the idea of "He Who Grows Angry," or find a suitable homonym. The tenth ruler, Cuitlahuac, is not depicted in this sequence of rulers from the Florentine Codex, probably because he ruled for only eighty days after the Spaniards arrived (Anderson and Dibble 1954:4).

The eleventh and last Aztec ruler was Cuauhtemoc, whose name meant "Descending Eagle" (*cuauh(tli)* = eagle + *temo* = to descend) and could be depicted quite literally (Fig. 7.4a). Mexica rulers baptized by the conquering Spaniards were known by Christian first names and Nahuatl last names, such as don Andrés Motelchiuh, don Pablo Xochiquen, don Diego Uanitl, don Diego Teuetzquiti, and don Cristóbal Cecepatic. Obviously, only their Nahuatl names could be given hieroglyphically in Colonial documents (Fig. 7.4b–f). For example, in Figure 7.4c we see a cloth with flowers (*xochitl*) painted on it, providing the initial syllables in the name [don Pablo] Xochiquen. [don Diego] Teuetzquiti's name meant "Something that Makes One Laugh." Cecepatic meant "Easily Frightened." (Some of these Colonial Nahuatl names seem to be so tongue-in-cheek, compared to prehispanic nicknames, that one wonders whether the informants were having a bit of fun at the Spaniards' expense.)

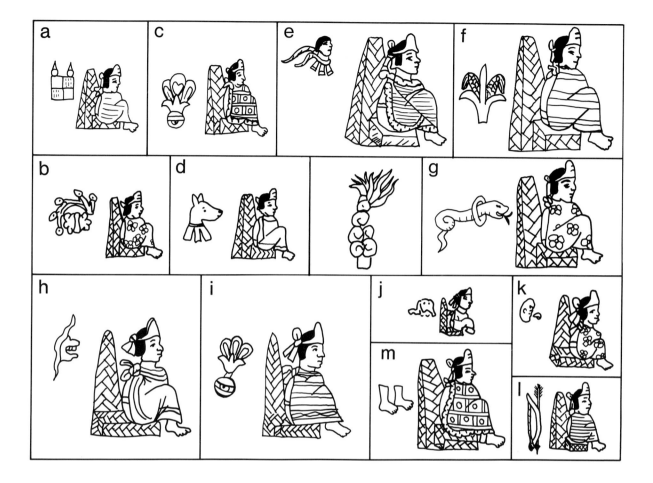

7.5. Names of Texcoco rulers. *a*, Tlaltecatzin; *b*, Techotlalatzin; *c*, Ixtlilxochitl; *d*, Nezahualcoyotl; *e*, Nezahualpilli; *f*, Cacamatzin; *g*, Coanacochtzin; *h*, Tecocoltzin; *i*, Ixtlilxochitl; *j*, Yoyontzin; *k*, Tetlaueuetzquititzin; *l*, [don Antonio] Tlauitoltzin; *m*, [don Hernando] Pimentel. (Redrawn from Anderson and Dibble 1954.)

Texcoco, a Member of the Triple Alliance

The name of the first Texcoco ruler, Tlaltecatzin, was shown in the Florentine Codex (Anderson and Dibble 1954) by a square divided into four parts with two elements above (Fig. 7.5a). The second ruler, Techotlalatzin, had a hieroglyphic name combining the water sign (*atl*) with the sign for stone (*tetl*) (Fig. 7.5b). The next ruler was Ixtlilxochitl the Elder, whose name sign included a flower (*xochitl*) (Fig. 7.5c). The fourth ruler was Nezahualcoyotl ("Fasting Coyote"), whose name was simply given as the head of a coyote (Fig. 7.5d).

The fifth ruler was Nezahualpilli, whose name "Hungry Prince/Lord" also incorporated the concept of "hungry" or "fasting." This concept was conveyed by placing three strips of skin or flesh at the neck of the coyote in "Nezahualcoyotl" (Fig. 7.5d) and below the human head in "Nezahualpilli" (Fig. 7.5e).

Cacamatzin was the ruler of Texcoco when the Spaniards arrived in the Basin of Mexico. His name sign (Fig. 7.5f) included a plant which we can identify as maize, since *cacamatl* means "small ears of corn" (Molina [1571] 1944:10v). Cacamatzin was followed by Coanacochtzin, the initial sounds of whose name was provided by the picture of a snake (*coatl*) (Fig. 7.5g). The eighth ruler, Tecocoltzin, had a name sign that included an open mouth (Fig. 7.5h); the ninth ruler was a second Ixtlilxochitl, whose name sign is identical to the first ruler with that name (Fig. 7.5i). The tenth ruler was Yoyontzin, whose name is difficult to translate (Fig. 7.5j), and the eleventh was Tetlaueuetzquititzin, whose name sign included an anthropomorphic blade or bean with associated speech scroll (Fig. 7.5k). The word *tetlaueuetzquiti* is defined as "clown" by Molina ([1571] 1944:110r).

Tlauitoltzin, the twelfth ruler, was baptized "don Antonio" by the Spaniards. His name combined the signs for bow and arrow (Fig. 7.5l). The last ruler depicted was don Hernando Pimentel, whose name was given as a pair of lower legs behind his throne (Fig. 7.5m). These feet must refer to his Nahuatl name, which was not given in Sahagún's accompanying text (Anderson and Dibble 1954:11).

Huexotla, a Subordinate Center

The sequence of "rulers" of Huexotla given in the Florentine Codex (Anderson and Dibble 1954) is interesting because the first five are referred to only as *tecuhtli*, "nobles," and are shown sitting on a bundle of reeds rather than "thrones" (see Fig. 7.6a–e). Not until Yaotzin took office are Huexotla's rulers shown seated on the high-backed woven mat "throne" associated in Aztec documents with kingship (Fig. 7.6f). The first two Huexotla *tecuhtin* have animal names in which the head stands for the whole animal. Some of the other rulers have names derived from plants, war, or homonyms for "to be in charge."

The first *tecuhtli*, Mazatzin (*mazatl* = deer; *tzin* = revered), has as his name sign a deer's head (Fig. 7.6a). The second, Tochin tecuhtli (*tochin* = rabbit; *tecuhtli* = lord), uses a rabbit's head (Fig. 7.6b). The third, Ayotzin tecuhtli, has a name sign derived from a plant (Fig. 7.6c), which is probably a squash (*ayotli*) (Molina [1571] 1944:3v). The name of the fourth ruler, Quatlauice tecuhtli, shows a set of feathers or a plant above a human head (Fig. 7.6d). The fifth ruler's name, Totomochtzin, is indicated by what are almost certainly dry maize leaves or *totomochtli*, "hojas secas de la mazorca de mayz" (Molina [1571] 1944:150v; see Fig. 7.6e).

Significantly, the first ruler to be seated on the woven mat throne has a name associated with war (*yao[yotl]*) (Fig. 7.6f). His name, Yaotzin tecuhtli ("Revered Warrior"), includes a face with war paint indicated by the use of black horizontal bands; below the

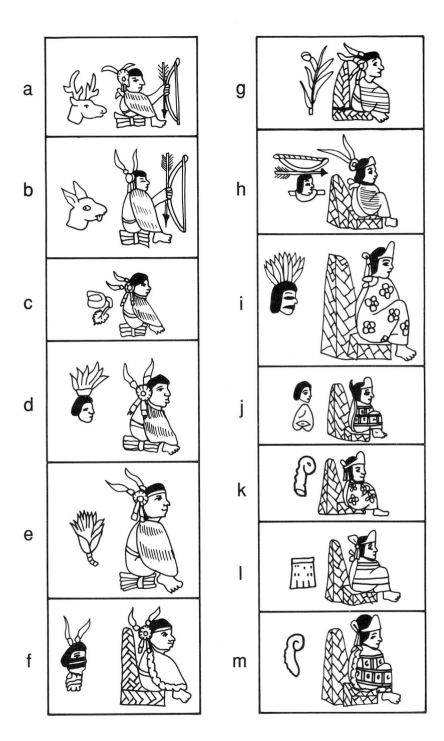

7.6. Names of Huexotla rulers. *a*, Mazatzin; *b*, Tochin tecuhtli; *c*, Ayotzin tecuhtli; *d*, Quatlauice tecuhtli; *e*, Totomochtzin; *f*, Yaotzin tecuhtli; *g*, Xilotzin tecuhtli; *h*, Itlacauhtzin; *i*, Tlazolyaotzin; *j*, Tzontemoctzin; *k*, Cuitlauatzin; *l*, Tzapocuetzin; *m*, Cuitlauatzin. (Redrawn from Anderson and Dibble 1954.)

head is the sign for stone (*tetl*). This was not the last time the word for war (*yao, yaoyotl*) was to be used as part of a Huexotla ruler's name (see Fig. 7.6i).

Following Yaotzin tecuhtli in office was Xilotzin tecuhtli, whose name sign (Fig. 7.6g) may depict a young maize plant (*xilotl*). The next ruler was Itlacauhtzin, whose name sign combines a bow and arrow and the head of a sacrificial victim (Fig. 7.6h). (The word *itlacauh(qui)* means "corrupted or damaged thing" [Molina [1571] 1944:43r]). Tlazo-lyaotzin's name sign, once again using *yao* (war), combines feathers and a face with war paint (Fig. 7.6i). Tzontemoctzin's name combines a human head and a possible hill sign (Fig. 7.6j). This name might be derived from *tzontepeua*, which means "to pull out hair from the head with the hand," with the *te* sound reinforced by the sign for "hill," *te(petl)*.

Surprising as it may seem to a Western scholar, two of the last three rulers of Huexotla include in their name signs a depiction of *cuitlatl*, "feces." This can be explained, however, as an attempt to provide a homonym for *cuitlauia*, "to be in charge of," "to take care of something." Since it was difficult for the Nahuatl scribe to provide a glyph for "to be in charge of," he painted the sign for excrement to generate the initial syllables *cuitla* in the name of the ruler Cuitlauatzin ("Revered Person in Charge"); the honorific suffix *tzin* was omitted (Fig. 7.6k, m). Finally, the name sign of the ruler Tzapocuetzin shows a rectangular object (Fig. 7.6l).

Tlatelolco, a Member of the Triple Alliance

The first ruler of Tlatelolco was Quaquapitzauac, shown seated on a woven mat throne in Figure 7.7a with his name sign (an animal head) behind him (see Anderson and Dibble 1954). The word *quaquaue* can be translated "animal with horns," while *pitzauac* refers to "thin or columnar-shaped" objects. The second ruler, Tlacateotl, received a composite sign that remains untranslated (Fig. 7.7b). The name of the third ruler, Quauhtlatoa, can be translated "Eagle That Speaks" (*cuauh[tli]* = eagle; *tlatoa* = speaker) and his name sign appropriately depicts the head of an eagle with three speech scrolls (Fig. 7.7c). The fourth ruler, Moquiuixtli, has a name sign using a star or eye (Fig. 7.7d).

Next we come to the later rulers, who were baptized by the Spaniards. Don Pedro Temilo has a composite name sign—a hand, a stone(?), and perhaps something else, with the "te" sound in Temilo possibly derived from *tetl*, "stone" (Fig. 7.7e). Don Martín Ecatl is depicted simply by the head and open mouth of the "wind god" Ehecatl (Fig. 7.7f). Don Juan Auelittoc's name sign is a human prisoner(?) (Fig. 7.7g).

Don Martín Tlacatecatl (Fig. 7.7h) has a name sign with an element on top of a human head; don Diego Uitznauatlailotlac (Fig. 7.7i) is given an arrow and the sign for blood (a circle plus a diamond). In Figure 7.7j we see don Alonso Quauhnochtli, whose composite name sign includes a cactus (*nochtli*) above the head of an eagle (*cuauhtli*).

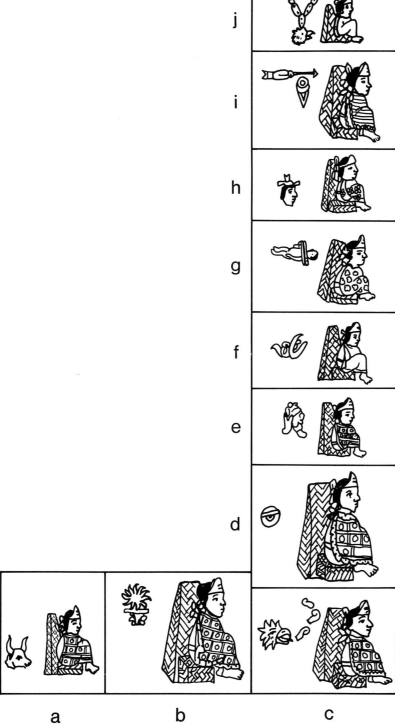

7.7. Names of Tlatelolco rulers. *a*, Quaquapitzauac; *b*, Tlacateotl; *c*, Quauhtlatoa; *d*, Moquiuixtli; *e*, [don Pedro] Temilo; *f*, [don Martín] Ecatl; *g*, [don Juan] Auelittoc; *h*, [don Martín] Tlacatecatl; *i*, [don Diego] Uitznauatlailotlac; *j*, [don Alonso] Quauhnochtli. (Redrawn from Anderson and Dibble 1954.)

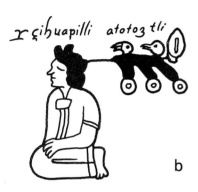

7.8. Examples of Aztec noblewomen's names. At *a*
is doña María Moyeztica from Ecatepec; her
hieroglyphic name (attached to her shoulder by a
line) illustrates the use of a pictogram as part of
her name. At *b* is *çihuapilli* ("noblewoman")
Atotoztli, whose hieroglyphic name (attached to
her head by a line) illustrates the possible use of
phoneticism. (Redrawn from Caso 1958a.)

Royal Aztec Women

Royal Aztec women were often given beautiful and elegant names such as Miahua-
xiuitl, "Maize Tassel/Flower" + "Turquoise Stone"; Quiauhxochitl, "Rain Flower";
Matlalxochitl, "Green Flower"; Atotoztli, "Water Parakeet"; and Malinalxochitl, "Prairie-
Grass Flower." The Spaniards baptized many noble women and gave them Christian first
names, but like their male counterparts many Aztec women maintained Nahuatl last
names as well. Such was the case with doña María Moyeztica, a woman depicted in the
Genealogía de los Príncipes Mexicanos (Cat. Boban 72), whose name was linked to the
town of Ecatepec (San Cristóbal Ecatepec), probably because she married a nobleman there.
In Figure 7.8, we see the names of doña María Moyeztica Ecatepec and another Aztec
noblewoman. The name glyph for Moyeztica (Fig. 7.8a) consists of the head of a bird
above a yellow ribbon being braided or unbraided; Caso (1958a:30) gives "unbraiding
something" as a possible translation for *moyeztica*.

The name of the second Aztec woman in Figure 7.8b, Atotoztli, is interesting because
it illustrates the possible use of phoneticism, a determinative, and the *pars pro toto* principle. Atotoztli is written with what appear to be the signs for (1) water; (2) a yellow
parrot; and (3) an obsidian blade. The sign for water, *atl*, supplies the first phoneme of
her name—"*a*" or "*at*." The two bird heads may provide the sounds *to(totl)* + *to(totl)*;
alternatively, however, the first bird head may simply serve as the determinative "bird,"
while the second bird head (which is painted yellow) may signify a specific type of bird—
toz(nene) or parrot, "papagayo que habla mucho" (Molina [1571] 1944:151r). The final
sign, which looks superficially like a feather (*ihuitl*), may in fact be an obsidian blade
(*iztli*); in the latter case, it would supply the final sound, *tli*, for "Atotoztli."

THE NAMING OF MIXTEC NOBLES

Because of the large number of proper names in the Mixtec codices, this ethnic group gives
us our largest sample of nobles who had a calendric name plus a nickname. The Mixtec
calendric name was given very early in life, and usually corresponded to a "lucky" day
from the 260-day calendar that fell on or near the individual's actual birthdate. The nickname was given later; for example, one ethnohistoric source (Herrera 1947:321) indicates
that a child would be given his or her nickname by a priest at the age of seven.

The codices also reveal that some nicknames were gender-specific. The hieroglyphic
sign for "ballcourt," for example, occurs only with men, while "quechquemitl" occurs
only with women (Fig. 7.9). Examples of men with "ballcourt" nicknames include 1 Crocodile "Eagle Ballcourt," 1 Lizard "Ballcourt," 4 Eagle "White Ballcourt," 5 Flower "Warband Ballcourt," 3 Rain "Ballcourt with Lines," and 11 Water "Smoking Ballcourt" (Fig.
7.9b). Some of the women whose names incorporate quechquemitl include 4 House "Eagle

Quechquemitl,'' 1 Flower ''Jaguar Quechquemitl,'' 6 Rabbit ''Sun Quechquemitl,'' and 6 Monkey ''Serpent (or Warband) Quechquemitl'' (Fig. 7.9a).

Although not restricted to women, the hieroglyphic signs for ''jewel'' and ''flower'' were very common components of women's nicknames (Fig. 7.10). In both men's and women's nicknames, animals such as butterflies, serpents, jaguars, ocelots, parrots, and eagles were featured. Often animals or objects were combined with an adjective, an adverb, or another noun to form compound nicknames such as ''Falling Eagle,'' ''Bloody Coyote,'' ''Blue Bird,'' ''Smoking Ballcourt,'' ''Eagle Ballcourt,'' ''Jeweled Heart,'' ''Parrot Hummingbird,'' ''Butterfly Creature,'' ''Jaguar with Bird Beak and Bee Tail,'' ''Sun Jewel,'' and ''Red Flower.''

Relative Frequencies of Day Names

Theoretically, there were 260 possible calendric names for Mixtec rulers and nobles—the number of days in the ritual calendar. Even a superficial examination of the codices, however, suggests that some names were much more common than others. Presumably this had to do with the fact that certain day names, certain numerical coefficients, and certain combinations of the two were considered unlucky, leading priests or diviners to suggest alternative names (chapter 4).

Rather than rely on superficial impressions, I decided that our sample of Mixtec calendric names was probably large enough to allow us to test whether in fact names were not chosen at random. I therefore undertook the collection of a list of 2,612 calendric names of Mixtec nobles, consisting of 1,661 men's names and 951 women's names. Taking note of the associated nicknames allowed me to guard against the possibility of recording the same person twice.

My list of 2,612 was compiled from a variety of sources, including codices, maps, and *lienzos* drawn from all three major divisions of Mixtec territory—the highlands (Mixteca Alta), lowlands (Mixteca Baja), and Pacific coastal plain (Mixteca Costa) (see Spores 1967 for a discussion of these subdivisions). My sources included the Códices Zouche-Nuttall, Bodley, Selden, Sánchez Solís (or Egerton), Becker I and II, Colombino, and Vienna (Vindobonensis). In addition to these codices, I consulted the Lienzos de Jicayán, Zacatepec, Filadelfia, and Atlatlahuca. Various maps, such as the Mapa de Teozacoalco in the *Relaciones Geográficas*, provided additional names. Other works consulted included Berlin (1947); Burland (1955, 1965); Caso (1949, 1950, 1951, 1954, 1960, 1961, 1964a, 1964b, 1964c, 1966a, 1966b, 1977, 1979); Clark (1912); Jiménez Moreno and Mateos Higuera (1940); Long (1926); Nowotny (1948, 1959b, 1961); Nuttall (1902); Parmenter (1966); Paso y Troncoso (1905–1906); Peñafiel (1900); Smith (1963, 1966, 1973a, 1973b, 1983a, 1983b); and Spinden (1935).

I then turned over my list of 2,612 day names to my colleague Robert Whallon, who subjected it to a statistical analysis designed to determine how far the selection of names

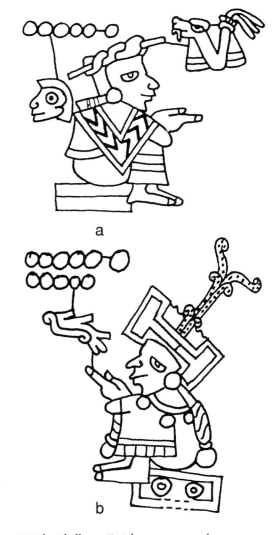

7.9. The ''ballcourt'' nickname was used exclusively by Mixtec noblemen, while the ''quechquemitl'' nickname was used exclusively by noblewomen. At *a*, we see once again the female ruler 6 Monkey ''War Quechquemitl''; in this case, her earlier nickname, ''Serpent Quechquemitl,'' is given as a pictogram (attached to the front of her hair by a line). At *b* is the male noble 11 Water ''Smoking Ballcourt,'' whose nickname is worn as a headdress. (Both redrawn from the Codex Selden.)

7.10. Examples of Mixtec noblewomen's names. *a*, *b*, two versions of 1 Flower "Parrot"; *c*, 3 Serpent "Garland of Cacao Flowers." (*a* and *b* were redrawn from the Codex Bodley; *c* was redrawn from the Codex Selden.)

deviated from the expected. Whallon's study appears as an appendix of this volume, and the reader can refer to it for details. Simply put, there were 20 possible day signs, 13 possible numerical coefficients, and 260 possible combinations that could be selected as names. Whallon's study shows that the selection of male names deviated significantly from what one would expect if men were always named for the day on which they were born. For example, male nobles seem to have favored the day names "Motion," "Wind," and "Reed," and avoided the day names "Vulture" and "Death." Furthermore, some *combinations* of day number and day name were favored over others, and it appears that some day *names* carried more weight than *numbers* (see Appendix for full results).

It is more difficult to test Mixtec nicknames for non-randomness, since we do not know how many possibilities there were. We can suggest, however, that Mixtec nobles (both male and female) seemed to prefer many of the same name components as their Aztec counterparts, including eagles, serpents, flint, obsidian, feathers, jade, turquoise, and colorful flowers. We do not know which culture influenced its neighbor in this regard, but given the much longer archaeological time depth of the Mixtec, it is possible that they (or some other pre-Mexica group, such as the Toltec or Xochicalcans) influenced the Aztec.

Names in the Relaciones Geográficas

Other sources of Mixtec nobles' names include (1) unpublished documents from the sixteenth and seventeenth centuries and (2) the *Relaciones Geográficas* (Paso y Troncoso 1905–1906). The latter is a set of sixteenth-century questionnaires filled out at the request of the Spanish crown. The Spaniards who wrote the *relaciones* often listed the ruler of a particular Mixtec town, referring to him (incorrectly) by the term *cacique*, a Carib loan word. There are problems with these nobles' names, however. In contrast to the codices, where we see the ruler's name written in hieroglyphs by a Mixtec scribe, the *relaciones* were written by Spaniards who did not necessarily have a good ear for the Mixtec language. They often included the Mixtec ruler's title—*yya*, or "hereditary lord"—as part of his name, and they sometimes gave what appears to be a day name from the 260-day calendar, but without any numerical coefficient. Finally, we do not always know whether the Spaniards are giving us the ruler's calendric name or his nickname.

In Table 7.1, we see a list of some of the Mixtec men mentioned in these documents and *relaciones*. In some cases, such as 6 Flower of Mitlatongo, we clearly have a calendric name. In other cases, such as "Eagle + Rubber" of Acatlán, we seem to have a nickname. In still other cases, such as "Lord Lizard" of Ayusuchiquilazala, we could have either a nickname, or a day name whose numerical coefficient was omitted by the Spanish scribe.

There are many fewer instances of royal women's names in the sixteenth-century *relaciones* and other documents from the Mixteca, but some examples are given in Table 7.2 below. One royal woman, Yaani, is described as the ruler of Tejupan. Several of the

Table 7.1   Names of Mixtec Noblemen Given in Various
Relaciones Geográficas and Other Documents

Name	Possible Meaning	Title and Town
Ocoñaña	20 Jaguars	"cacique of Teozacoalco"
Yacoñooy	1 Monkey	"cacique of Mitlatongo"
Yacocuuñi	1 Grass (?)	"cacique of Tamazola"
Ñucoy	6 Flower	"cacique of Mitlatongo"
Cusivizu	11 Jaguar (?)	"cacique of Putla"
Yyachihuyzu	Lord Wind Jaguar	"cacique of Zacatepec"
Yyazauy	Lord Rain	"cacique of Jicayán"
Yyasina	Lord Dog (?)	"cacique of Jicayán"
Yyaquisayo	5 Rabbit (?)	"lord of Cuyatepexi"
Yyaqhusisa	Lord Lizard	"cacique of Ayusuchiquilazala"
Tondiqhunav	4 Death	"cacique of Tlaxiaco and Mixtepec"
Yesa huyya	7 Reed (?)	"cacique of Tejupan"
Yaqhhuyneñe	4 Crocodile	"first cacique of Tilantongo"
Yaqhisi	4 Vulture/Death (?)	"cacique of Mitlatongo"
Yaq Cuaa	4 Deer	Tilantongo ruler
Guacosagua	7 Deer	Acatlán ruler (?)
Yaha ghuigu	Eagle + Rubber	Acatlán ruler (?)
Nuchi	6 Wind	Petlalzingo ruler (?)
Xaquaaho	7 House	Petlalzingo ruler (?)
Tetzateotl	Mirror Deity	Ycxitlán ruler (?)
Namahu	8 Death	Yanhuitlán ruler
Cuaqusiqui	11 Deer	Juxtlahuaca ruler (?)

Sources: Paso y Troncoso 1905–06; Spores 1967; Caso 1977, 1979.

Table 7.2.   Names of Mixtec Noblewomen Given in Various
Relaciones Geográficas and Other Documents

Name	Relationship to Male Ruler	Town
Yajimane	wife of Yacocuuni	"Born from a cliff"
María de Cocuahu (2 House)	wife of Diego Nugh (6 Motion)	Yanhuitlán
Cahuaco (1 Flower)	wife of Namahu (8 Death)	Yanhuitlán
Yaani or Yaanicuu	wife of Yesa Huyya (7 Reed)	Santa Catarina Tejupan

Sources: Paso y Troncoso 1905–06; Spores 1967; Caso 1977, 1979.

other women are known by both their prehispanic names and their Colonial Christian names (e.g., 2 House, later baptized "María").

Two of the individuals in Tables 7.1 and 7.2, the lord Namahu or "8 Death" and his wife Cahuaco or "1 Flower," were co-rulers of Yanhuitlán at the time of the Spanish conquest (Archivo General de la Nación, Ramo Civil, No. 516; Caso 1966b, 1977, 1979; Spores 1967:132–135; Smith 1973a). In the Codex Bodley (19-III) we see a lord named 8 Death "Tiger-Fire Serpent"—probably the same ruler, since he is shown as the husband of Lady 1 Flower "Jaguar Quechquemitl" (see Fig. 3.16). According to Caso (1949, 1966b:313), the man named 8 Death in the Codex Bodley was the son of the third ruler of the Fourth Dynasty of Tilantongo, a man named 10 Rain "Tlaloc-Sun." A brother of 8 Death, Yaq Cuaa ("4 Deer"), was ruler of Tilantongo at the time of the Spanish conquest; Yaq Cuaa was said to have ruled an extensive area that included Teposcolula, Tlaxiaco, Teozacoalco, and Atoyaquillo (Paso y Troncoso 1905, 4:73; Spores 1967:66). Apparently, 8 Death left Tilantongo when he married 1 Flower, because *she* (not he) was in direct line to inherit the title to Yanhuitlán. In the Codex Bodley, 8 Death and 1 Flower are shown as rulers of a place depicted as "Feather Carpet-Jawbone-Arrow Beak," a place Caso (1960, 1964c, 1966b) identified as the sign for Yanhuitlán (Fig. 3.16). Thus we have agreement between a 1580 document found in the National Archives of Mexico (Archivo General de la Nación, Ramo Civil, No. 516) and the Codex Bodley.

Of the four writing systems we are reviewing in this book, it would appear that the Mixtec displayed the greatest degree of continuity in naming patterns over time. For example, we see a much greater retention of calendric names there than elsewhere, as well as a closer correspondence between the names given in the prehispanic codices and those given in the sixteenth-century documents. Furthermore, both the codices and the sixteenth-century documents indicate that Mixtec nobles continued to be known by a numerical coefficient and day name in the 260-day calendar even after they had been given Christian first names.

THE NAMING OF ZAPOTEC NOBLES

Like the Mixtec, Zapotec nobles were named for days in the *piye* or 260-day calendar, with adjustments made when their actual birthdate was unfavorable. The diviners who made such adjustments were known as *peni huechiylla,* and the use of divining to determine a name was called *tochiyllaxiaaya* (from *tochiyllaya,* "to divine," and *xiaa,* "the sign" or "calendric name"). The sixteenth-century Zapotec had an expression, *xiaa xiaa,* which meant "name" and "birth" as well as "the sign under which each one was born and which was his fate" (Córdova [1578a] 1942:283v). This sixteenth-century definition emphasizes the close relationship among three elements—one's name, birthdate, and destiny—that we have seen in other Mesoamerican groups.

The oldest calendric name known so far from the Zapotec region is the name "1 Earthquake" on Monument 3 from San José Mogote (see Fig. 2.9), dating to approximately 600 B.C. (Marcus 1976b, 1980, 1983d). A much larger sample of names comes from the stone monuments carved at Monte Albán between 500 B.C. and A.D. 800, and produced at other Valley of Oaxaca sites between A.D. 300 and 1000 (Marcus 1976c; 1983g, i, k). Table 7.3 gives examples of calendric names of Zapotec nobles taken from Classic period monuments at Monte Albán or nearby Xoxocotlán (Fig. 9.14):

Table 7.3   Calendric Names of Zapotec Nobles on Stone Monuments from Monte Albán and Xoxocotlán

Calendric Name	Location
8 Deer	Front of Stela 4, Monte Albán
3 Flower	Side of Stela 8, Monte Albán
12 Death	Underside of Stela 8, Monte Albán
5 Precious Stone	Underside of Stela 8, Monte Albán
8 Flower	Front of Stela 9, Monte Albán
3 Water	Lápida 1 of National Museum of Anthropology, Mexico
6 Earthquake	Lápida 1 of National Museum of Anthropology, Mexico
11 Monkey	Lápida 1 of National Museum of Anthropology, Mexico
6 Flower	Lápida 1 of National Museum of Anthropology, Mexico
5 Lizard	Lintel 2 of Xoxocotlán
5 Monkey	Lintel 2 of Xoxocotlán
8 Earthquake	Lintel 2 of Xoxocotlán
8 Reed	Lintel 2 of Xoxocotlán
4 Jaguar	Lintel 2 of Xoxocotlán
6 Earthquake	Lintel 2 of Xoxocotlán
8 Water	Lintel 2 of Xoxocotlán
4 Jaguar	Lintel 2 of Xoxocotlán
1 Flower	Lintel 2 of Xoxocotlán
6 Winged Insect	Lintel 2 of Xoxocotlán
7 Owl	Lintel 2 of Xoxocotlán
2 Precious Stone	Lintel 2 of Xoxocotlán
2 Jaguar	Lintel 2 of Xoxocotlán
3 Deer	Lintel 2 of Xoxocotlán
12 Precious Stone	Lintel 2 of Xoxocotlán

Another source of calendric names are the painted murals in Classic tombs at Monte Albán (A.D. 200–700). Frequently, these murals show couples (a man and a woman) dressed as royalty or nobles. When the tombs were first discovered, these couples were thought to be "gods" and "goddesses"; however, they have calendric names associated with them. This fact makes it clear that they are humans, since Zapotec deities did not have calendric names, being eternal rather than having been born on a day of the 260-day calendar. Some royal Zapotec couples in the murals may be ancestors or relatives of the deceased (Marcus 1983g, h); some appear to be leaving the funeral by exiting the tomb.

7.11. Mural from Tomb 105, Monte Albán. In the upper register are the stylized "jaws of the sky" often associated with depictions of Zapotec nobles. Below are four individuals in procession, exiting the tomb. These two marital pairs were presumably relatives of the deceased. From left to right, we can transcribe their names as: a woman named 7 Glyph E + a combination of signs; a man named Glyph E + Glyph E + 2 Glyph J; a woman named 1 Water + Glyph J + 3 Hill; and a man named 3 Glyph A + Glyph E + Glyph J. (Redrawn from Caso 1938: Lámina IV.)

For example, in Tomb 105 at Monte Albán the murals show four royal couples in a procession, moving from right to left (Caso 1938: Láminas III, IV). The names of the paired men and women consist of from two to four glyphic elements, combined into hieroglyphic compounds (see Fig. 7.11). One part of each name is drawn from the *piye;* the other part has non-calendric hieroglyphic elements, and was probably a nickname. Just as we saw for some Mixtec men, these Zapotec men have nicknames that differ from those of women. The compound names for the two royal couples shown in Figure 7.11 are as follows:

Table 7.4   Names of Zapotec Nobles on Murals of Tomb 105 at Monte Albán

Men	Women
Glyph E + Glyph E + 2 Glyph J	7 Glyph E + "Serpent" glyph
3 Glyph A + Glyph E + Glyph J	1 Water + Glyph J + 3 Hill

Sixteenth-Century Zapotec Nobles

Sixteenth-century Zapotec nobles continued to receive calendric names from the *piye.* However, many were also given elegant nicknames by which they are better known. Such non-calendric names have survived either because they were considered more important during that era, or because they were the only names recorded by the Spaniards. For example, the great Zapotec ruler who battled the Aztec at Tehuantepec (Marcus 1983l) is known to us only as Cociyoeza, "Creator of Lightning." We do not know his calendric name.

The names of some sixteenth-century Zapotec rulers can be gleaned from the *Relaciones Geográficas* (Paso y Troncoso 1905), but as we saw in the case of the Mixtec, the names are distorted by Spanish ears. Just as the Spaniards often included the Mixtec term *yya,* "lord," in a ruler's name, they also often included the Zapotec terms *coqui,* "lord," or *coquihualao,* "prince"—or even terms such as *rigula,* "elder," or *xoana,* "minor noble." In some cases, the Spaniards seem to have written down a day name from the 260-day calendar, but omitted the numerical coefficient. Despite all these problems, in Table 7.5 we can offer a list of Zapotec nobles from various *relaciones.*

As will be clear from Table 7.5, many names given in sixteenth-century *relaciones* and *lienzos* are non-calendric nicknames. The same is true of the few Zapotec noble women for whom we have names. As shown in Table 7.6, their proper names were often preceded by correct or garbled forms of *xonaxi,* "princess" or "noble female."

Table 7.5   Names of Zapotec Noblemen Given in the *Relaciones Geográficas* and the Lienzo de Guevea

Name	Possible Meaning	Title and Town
Coqui gualaniza (Coquihualao Niça)	Prince 6 or 9 Water	Ruler of Mitla
Coquebila	Lord —	Ruler of Macuilxochitl
Coque cehuiyo	Lord —	Ruler of Tlacolula
Coquihuani	Lord —	Ruler of Talistaca
Coqui Bela	Lord Serpent or Reed	Ruler of Santa Cruz Ixtepec
Hoqui Bilalaol	Lord 7 or 10	Ruler of Ixtepexi
Hoqui Bilana	Lord —	Ruler of Ixtepexi
Coquil Huany	Lord —	Ruler of Chichicapa
Baaloo	?	Ruler of Macuilxochitl
Baalachi	?	Ruler of Macuilxochitl
Quiabelagayo	5 Flower	Ruler of Macuilxochitl
Gualao Tzotziquetz	Prince + Bat Quetzal	Ruler of Ixtepexic
Laxuugalapetz	?	Ruler of Ixtepexic
Cosio Solachi	Lightning	Ruler of Miahuatlán
Petela	Dog	Ruler of Ocelotepec
Meneyadela	?	Ruler of Coatlán
Cosichaguela	Lightning +	Ruler of Amatlán
Colaca	Serpent (?)	Ruler of Amatlán
Pichina Vedella	Deer +	Ruler of Miahuatlán
Pichana gobeche	?	Ruler of Chichicapa
Pichanato	?	Ruler of Chichicapa
Logobicha	Face of the Sun	Noble of Guevea
Xilacache Guiebisuño	Yellow-feathered Rattle	Noble of Guevea
Pieezuño	Gourd Rattle	Noble of Guevea
Cociyopii	Lightning-Wind	Ruler of all Zapotec
Cociyoeza	Lightning-Creator	Ruler of all Zapotec
(Xuana) Bechecha	(Noble) + Fierce Feline	Noble of Guevea
Bichiyatao	Great Eagle	Noble of Guevea

Sources: Paso y Troncoso 1905; Seler 1906, 1908; Marcus 1983l.

Table 7.6   Names of Zapotec Noblewomen in the *Relaciones Geográficas*

Name	Possible Translation	Town
Tonaji Belachina	Princess Deer	Coatlán
Xonaxi Quecuya	Princess (?)	Tlacolula, Mitla (?)
Pinopiaa	12 Twisted Grass (?)	Zaachila

Source: Paso y Troncoso 1905–06.

Only a few studies of sixteenth- and seventeenth-century Maya names have been undertaken, with the most noteworthy and systematic being that of Ralph Roys (1940). He was able to assemble the names of many occupants of Yucatán. Additional names from the highlands of Chiapas and Guatemala can be found in early Colonial documents. Even twentieth-century ethnographic studies show the survival of some ancient naming patterns (e.g., Tozzer 1907).

Sixteenth-century Yucatec Maya surnames were often composed of two or more parts. The first part was usually the mother's matronymic, while the second part was the father's patronymic. The mother's matronymic, inherited through the maternal line, was called the *naal* name (Roys 1940:37); the term *naal* was derived from *na*, "mother," and *al*, "offspring." The patronymic, on the other hand, was the surname that an individual inherited in the male line.

In addition to these two surnames, a man could have two personal names: a *paal kaba*, or "boy name," and a *coco kaba*, or "nickname." Boy names began with the prefix *ah*; examples include Ah Chac, Ah Tzab, Ah Dzacab, Ah Xoc, Ah Man, and Ah Cen. Examples of nicknames include Ah Xochil Ich ("He of the Owl Face/Owl Eye"), and Ah Na Itza ("He of the House of the Itzá"). The *ah* prefix could also be attached to place names to designate a birthplace, as in the case of Ah Motul, "he who is a native of Motul." Women's names, on the other hand, were often preceded by *ix*, and this prefix could also be used to indicate a birthplace. Ix Motul, for example, would mean "she who is a native of Motul."

Many Yucatec patronymics were names of well-known plants and animals. Included among the animals were the blue jay (*chel*), macaw (*moo', moo*), iguana (*huh*), wild turkey (*cutz*), serpent (*can* or *chan*), deer (*ceh*), opossum (*och*), coatimundi (*chic*), anteater (*chab*), armadillo (*wech*), peccary (*ac*), gopher (*ba, baa*), and turtle (*mac*). Included among the plants were the cherimoya fruit *Annona cherimola* (*pox*), the fig *Ficus cotinifolia* (*copo*), the West Indian cherry *Malpighia glabra* (*chi*), tobacco (*kutz*), the shrub *Jatropha aconitifolia* (*chay*), *Agave* sp. (*ci*), the chicozapote tree *Achras zapota* (*ya, yaa*), and the hogplum *Spondias* sp. (*ab*). In his early twentieth-century ethnography of the Lacandón Maya, Tozzer (1907:40–43) reported that every family still had an animal name which was passed from father to son.

As with the Mixtec and Zapotec, some Maya rulers were designated by their titles, such as *ahau*, "ruler," or *batab*, "local lord." In some cases, they might use only their title and patronymic. For example, Brinton (1882:195) gives the titles of three rulers—Ahau Pech, Ahau Chel, and Ahau Cocom—whose full "surnames" (matronymic + patronymic) were Naum Pech, Namox Chel, and Nachi Cocom.

Of these four names—patronymic, matronymic, "boy name," and nickname—the one that continued to be of fundamental importance following the Spanish conquest was the patronymic. Roys (1940:35), following Landa (in Tozzer 1941:99), says that people with the same patronymic regarded themselves as (1) members of the same "lineage," and (2) descendants from a common ancestor. Some patronymics had a very limited distribution (for example, they might be confined to a small province of northern Yucatán, or to an island such as Cozumel), while others were very widely distributed.

> They always call their sons and daughters by the name of the father and the mother, that of the father as the proper name, and that of the mother as the appellative name as follows. The son of Chel and Chan is called Na Chan Chel, which means the son of such and such people. (Landa [1566] in Tozzer 1941:98–99)

In the case cited by Landa, a man named Nachan Chel had (1) a *naal* name with the prefix *na*, "mother," followed by (2) the mother's matronymic (Chan), and (3) the father's patronymic (Chel). In another example, a man named Nachan Canche had a father named Namay Canche (the father's patronymic was Canche), and a mother named Ix Chan Pan (the mother's matronymic was Chan). Another famous ruler whose matronymic and patronymic are known to us is Nachi Cocom, whose matronymic is Chi and patronymic is Cocom.

Some patronymics served to specify social and territorial units. An example would be Couoh, a patronymic that referred to a territory including twelve villages on the shore of Lake Petén Itzá. Such patronymics lead us to wonder if, in certain cases, some of the apparent geographic referents in earlier Classic Maya hieroglyphs might also have been rulers' patronymics. Some patronymics became geographic and territorial labels, and the reverse may have been true as well. It is often difficult to determine whether the polity was named after an ancient ruler, or if the current ruler had taken his name from the political unit he administered.

The Names of Classic Maya Royalty

Proskouriakoff (1960) was the first to identify rulers' names in the lowland Maya hieroglyphic inscriptions of the Classic period (A.D. 250–900). She was able to identify the name glyph by its position in a text—it usually follows a verb and precedes a title and/or emblem glyph. This position is consistent with the typical word order in Maya hieroglyphic texts (verb + subject). Unlike the emblem glyph, which could be defined on the basis of two constant elements (the so-called "Ben-Ich" superfix and the "water-group" prefix), the name glyphs of Classic Maya rulers do not have two constants; however, they typically include a main sign with attached affixes. Thus, name glyphs are usually identified by their position in the text.

The main signs in the name glyphs of many Classic Maya rulers incorporate animal parts, such as the head, tail, or paw of a jaguar; the carapace of a turtle; the head of a bird; or the skull of some other animal. Other frequent components (some used as main signs, others as affixes) are a warrior's shield, the sky, the sun, or some other object.

When we look at the whole of the Maya lowlands, we see that the ruling dynasties at different Classic cities had different preferences for names. Let us look now at some of the rulers from Tikal, Yaxchilán, Palenque, and Copán whose names have been identified.

Tikal

Nearly every early Tikal ruler bears a name that incorporates at least some animal element, either in its living state or in its skeletal state. Some of the later rulers were more likely to incorporate symbolic elements as logograms.

The jaguar was one of the important animals used in Maya iconography, serving as the symbol for rulership and authority; the figure of a jaguar also served as a throne (Fig. 7.12a). Given the close association of jaguar symbolism with royal power and authority, it is not surprising that the jaguar (or parts of the animal) was incorporated into the names of ancient Maya rulers. For example, we can recognize a jaguar paw as part of the name of one of the earliest rulers at Tikal, an individual who reigned in about A.D. 320 (Fig. 7.12b). The jaguar paw was also incorporated into the names of other rulers from other sites (Fig. 7.12c, d).

Following the reign of Jaguar Paw at Tikal, there were at least two other rulers whose names incorporated parts of the jaguar (usually an ear or paw). Also common at Tikal are rulers' names that contain birds, bird-like creatures, or the skulls of different animals. In fact, many of the Tikal rulers' names actually seem to have been composite "fantastic creatures." These fantastic creatures were deemed appropriate names for royalty, perhaps because such creatures could never exist in nature.

A good example of a fantastic creature used as a name was the Tikal ruler dubbed "Kan Boar" by Proskouriakoff (personal communication, 1970). His hieroglyphic name combined the ear of a jaguar with the face of a peccary; his eye was filled with a non-animal element, the so-called "Kan cross." This ruler reigned from perhaps A.D. 457 to 488 (Fig. 7.13a).

Other rulers named for fantastic creatures include "Curl Nose" and "Jaguar Paw Skull" (Fig. 7.13 b, c). The former apparently reigned from A.D. 379 to 426, and the latter from perhaps A.D. 488 to 537 (Jones and Satterthwaite 1982). Jaguar Paw Skull's name glyph combines a skeletal jaw with a long-nosed head whose nose is actually the tail of a jaguar. Protruding from his head is another upside-down mandible, while his ear is also that of a jaguar. Thus this ruler's name combines skeletal elements with parts of a living jaguar, creating a unique or fantastic creature (see Fig. 7.13c).

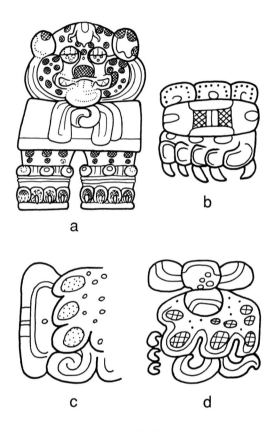

7.12. The jaguar, a symbol of power and authority, was an important part of many Maya rulers' names. At *a*, we see a jaguar used as a throne. At *b* is the name of an early Tikal ruler named Jaguar Paw; above the paw are glyphic elements that may have been read phonetically. At *c* and *d* are hieroglyphic names of other rulers that incorporate jaguar paws. (Redrawn from Jones and Satterthwaite 1982: fig. 11.17, table 6; J. Miller 1974: fig. 2; Marcus 1987: fig. 50.)

7.13. The names of Maya rulers at Tikal (and elsewhere) often featured the heads of fantastic beings, created by combining parts of different animals. At *a* is the name "Kan Boar," which places the Kan cross in an eye with three wide lashes, and combines it with the face of a peccary, the ear of a jaguar, and a comb (the phonetic sign for *ca*) in front of the jaguar's ear. At *b* is the name "Curl Nose," which combines a *yax* prefix, a knot superfix, a scroll at the nose, crossed-bands in the eye, and an unidentifiable animal head. At *c* is the name "Jaguar Paw Skull," which combines fleshless jaws, the tail and ear of a jaguar, scrolls, and a skull. At *d* is "Animal Skull," which combines fish and bird elements, and takes the phonetically rendered prefix of *ma* (kinah). At *e* is "Double Bird," which features one bird head above another. At *f* is the name "Shield Skull," which uses a shield as prefix in combination with the skull of an unidentified animal. (Redrawn from Jones and Satterthwaite 1982: table 6.)

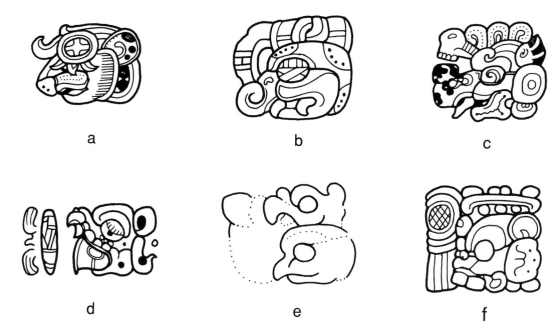

a

b

c

d

e

f

Following the reign of Jaguar Paw Skull were two rulers whose names incorporated the heads of fantastic animals. One has been called "Animal Skull" (Fig. 7.13d); he succeeded the ruler called "Double Bird," whose name sign includes one bird above another (Fig. 7.13e). Another ruler, the successor to "Animal Skull," was called "Shield Skull," because his name includes a shield and an animal skull as principal elements (Fig. 7.13f).

Two of the Tikal rulers whose names do not incorporate parts of animals have been called "Stormy Sky" and "Ruler A" (see Coggins 1975; Haviland 1977; Jones 1977, 1988; Jones and Satterthwaite 1982). Stormy Sky (who reigned from ca. A.D. 426 to 457) has a compound name that shows two arms uplifted above the main sign of "sky" (Fig. 7.14a). Ruler A has sometimes been called "Double Comb" because the main sign of his name appears to show two paired combs (Fig. 7.14b). Although the individual comb sign has

7.14. The names of two Tikal rulers. At *a* is "Stormy Sky" and at *b* "Double Comb" (Ruler A). (Redrawn from Jones and Satterthwaite 1982: table 6.)

a

b

often been read phonetically as *ca* (Thompson 1950, 1962), it is not at all clear that this double-comb sign was pronounced the same way. Nevertheless, this ruler's entire name has been read as *Ah Cacau* by Jones (1988); since the prefix to the main sign is often read as *ah*, Jones reads the entire hieroglyphic compound as *ah ca-ca-wa*.

Yaxchilán

Since the jaguar was the most powerful predator in the southern lowlands, it is not surprising to see it featured in the names of Maya rulers at such cities as Tikal and Calakmul. However, at no site was the jaguar more frequently a component of rulers' names than at Yaxchilán (Proskouriakoff 1963, 1964). There, at least five rulers bore such names as Lord Jaguar, Knotted-Eye Jaguar, Shield Jaguar, Bat Jaguar, and Bird Jaguar (Fig. 7.15a–h). At Yaxchilán the jaguar name appears to function as a patronymic, or lineage name, in contrast to other Classic Maya sites where it seems to have been used in personal names.

Copán

Did Maya rulers ever have calendric names? At least one ruler of Copán, the great Classic city in western Honduras, had the number 18 incorporated into his name. However, since numerical coefficients in the 260-day calendar can only go as high as 13, his name was not taken from that calendar. Furthermore, the main sign in his name does not correspond to any of the day signs in the 260-day calendar or any of the month signs in the 365-day calendar.

This famous ruler's glyphic name is usually given as (1) the number 18 (3 bars [15] + 3 dots [3] = 18); (2) a scroll, a "bone" affix or infix, or other prefix; (3) the head of an animal; and (4) a Kan cross below the animal's ear (Fig. 7.16). Initially, there was confusion about what species the animal head represented; some scholars called it a jaguar, others a dog. This uncertainty has led to the ruler being called "18 Jog," an artificial name constructed by combining the "j" of jaguar and the "og" of dog. However, in versions of the glyph where the full figure of the animal is seen (rather than just its head), it does not appear to be either a jaguar or a dog (see, for example, Maudslay 1889–1902, 1:plate 114b; Marcus 1976a: fig. 4.47).

Eventually, the "Jog" grapheme was identified by Proskouriakoff (1968) as a rodent. However, she too had difficulty deciding which animal was depicted. She was unsure whether the animal was "a paca, an agouti, or one of the larger gophers." Furthermore, she correctly noted that there is some confusion about which Maya term applied to each of those animals, "probably in part because the names differ locally and in part because they do not correspond to our zoological designations" (Proskouriakoff 1968:248). She suspected that both the Spanish word *tuza* and the Maya word *ba* might "designate various

7.15. Many rulers of Yaxchilán featured jaguars in their names. Because so many royal sons, grandsons, and great-grandsons at that site were designated by jaguar names, it is suspected that the jaguar glyph may have functioned as a lineage name. *a,* Lord Jaguar; *b,* Knotted-Eye Jaguar; *c, d,* Shield Jaguar; *e,* Bat Jaguar; *f, g,* and *h,* three examples of Bird Jaguar. (Redrawn from Marcus 1976a: fig. 4.16.)

burrowing rodents, including the agouti, which is said to burrow under the roots of trees, where it sleeps during the day" (Proskouriakoff 1968:249). In fact, there are good reasons for believing that *ba* is a generic term for a burrowing rodent.

One clue that the rodent in 18 Jog's name might have been pronounced *ba* is the fact that the same rodent is used in other contexts where the syllable *ba* may be called for. For example, it is used in the Quiriguá inscriptions in the so-called "battle glyph" (main sign 757 in Thompson 1962; Marcus 1976a: figs. 4.44–4.46), where it may have been part of the word *ba'te'el*, "to battle," or *yaltanba*, "to go to war." Both words include the syllable *ba*, which might have been reinforced by the rodent head. The "battle glyph" also has a prefix (T-333 in Thompson 1962) that might have reinforced this reading, because it may have been read *baat*, or "axe."

We should stress, however, that despite these clues we neither know this ruler's actual name nor how it was pronounced. His name seems to have included the syllable *ba*, as well as the logogram of the Kan cross and an 18 (or alternatively, it may have been the *sound* of the Maya word for 18, *waxaklahun*, that was desired). We can, however, say that despite the 3 bars and 3 dots, this was *not* a name drawn from the 260-day calendar.

Palenque

Ancient Maya scribes and stonecarvers at Palenque wrote the name of its most famous ruler, Lord Shield, in a variety of ways. The most frequently encountered way was to use the depiction of a shield (*pacal*) to express his name (Fig. 7.17a). The shield stood as a word or logogram and could also take a phonetic subfix (*la*) to reinforce the final "l" in *pacal* (Fig. 7.17b); this manner of expressing his name combines logography and phoneticism (Lounsbury 1974a, Bricker 1986). The same name could also be written and repeated in two different ways in the same hieroglyphic clause. For example, on the left in Figure 7.17c and 7.17e, we see the shield name expressed as a simple logogram; then, to the right, it is given phonetically as *pa-ca-la* and evidently pronounced *pacal* (Fig. 7.17d). Finally, the shield itself might be inserted into the eye of a bird, which takes the subfix *la* (Fig. 7.17f).

Royal Women's Names

When Classic Maya monument carvers wanted to indicate a woman's name, they used a particular prefix or main sign called the "feminine head glyph" (Fig. 7.18). This glyph may have served as a determinative, indicating that a woman's name was to follow; and it may have had a phonetic counterpart, either *ix* or *na* (Marcus 1976a:154–156). Occasionally, bar-and-dot numbers were included as parts of women's names, but the numbers were not attached to day names as we saw among the Mixtec and Zapotec. Rather,

7.16. Three examples of "18 Jog," the name of a Copán ruler who reigned from A.D. 695 to 738. "Jog" is an artificial name created by epigraphers, who could not decide whether the animal head was that of a jaguar or a dog. (Redrawn from Marcus 1976a: fig. 4.42.)

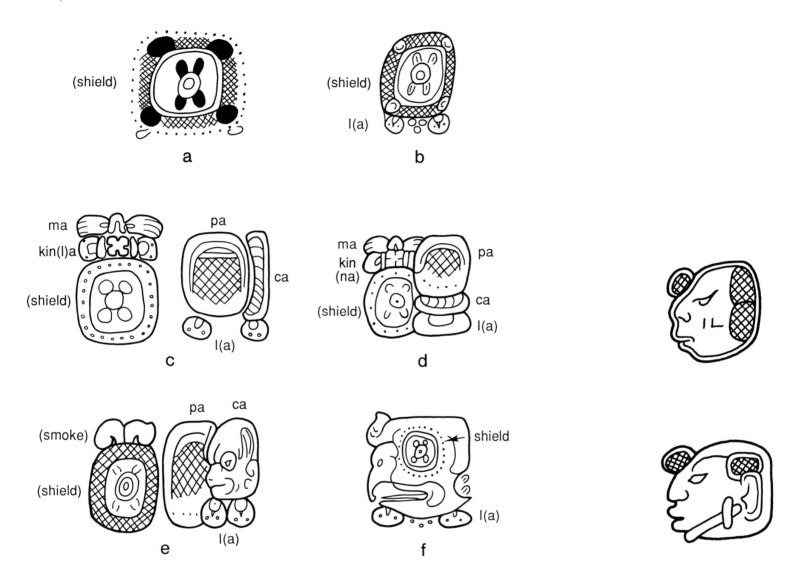

7.17. Six versions of the name Lord Shield (Pacal), the ruler buried in the Temple of the Inscriptions at Palenque. (Redrawn from Marcus 1976a: fig. 4.25.)

7.18. Two examples of the feminine head glyph, an identifier of royal Maya women's names. (Redrawn from Thompson 1962.)

they served as affixes (either prefixes or postfixes) to other signs. For example, the mother of Lord Scroll Squirrel, a ruler at the site of Naranjo, had the bar-and-dot number 6 as part of her name (Fig. 7.19a).

On Lintel 12 at Yaxchilán, we see a woman's name that combines the number "12" with other elements, some of them parts of jaguars (Fig. 7.19c). A Yaxchilán woman on Lintel 15 has the number 6 in her name, plus the glyph for *cauac* ("lightning") and the sign for *ik* ("spirit, wind, breath, life") (see Fig. 7.19b; Marcus 1987: fig. 47). This Lintel 15 name is similar to that of some later Zapotec rulers, like Cociyoeza and Cociyopii, whose names included elements such as "lightning" and "the breath of life."

Names of royal Maya women could also include animal components or skulls. Bird names were particularly favored, as they were by Aztec women. In Figure 7.20 we see examples of royal women from Palenque whose names were derived from birds. Still another royal woman, this time from Tikal, had a jaguar-pelt cushion as part of her name (Fig. 7.21).

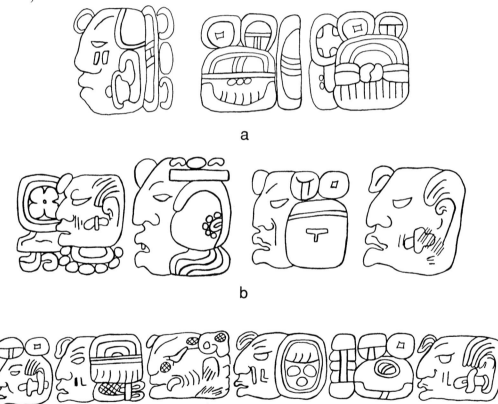

a

b

c

7.19. Names of royal Maya women. The row of glyphs at *a* refers to a woman from Tikal who married the lord of Naranjo, one of Tikal's subordinate centers. Her name is composed of a feminine head glyph with a postfix of 6 (left); a sky compound (center); and the Tikal emblem glyph (right). The row of glyphs at *b* refers to a Yaxchilán royal woman. Her name consists of a *kin* sign + a feminine head glyph; a second feminine head glyph with a 6 + *tun* sign; another feminine head glyph with an *ik* main sign; and a final feminine head glyph (far right). At *c* we see the even longer reference to another Yaxchilán royal woman. Her name is comprised of 12 + a feminine head glyph (far left); a feminine head glyph + phonetic elements; a jaguar head; a feminine head + jaguar paw sign; an untranslated glyph; and a final feminine head (far right). (Redrawn from Marcus 1976a: figs. 4.6, 5.8.)

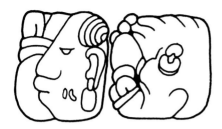

7.20. Palenque women with "fantastic names" derived by combining fish, bird, and other elements. (Redrawn from Maudslay 1889–1902.)

7.21. Two versions of the same Tikal noblewoman's name, one that incorporates a jaguar pelt covering a cushion. At *a* we see the feminine head glyph, followed by a jaguar cushion atop the head of a long-nosed animal. At *b* we see the longer version of the same name written as two separate glyphs. (Redrawn from Marcus 1976a: fig. 5.4.)

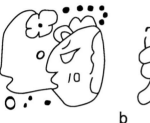

a   b

It is interesting to see how the Maya monument carver handled abstract concepts in women's names. For example, at Piedras Negras in Guatemala we have the name of a royal mother, "Lady Darkness," and her daughter, "Lady Sunlight" (Marcus 1976a: fig. 5.3, 1976b: figs. 12–13). The main elements (*akbal*, "darkness," and *kin*, "sunlight") function as logograms (Fig. 7.22).

THE NAMING OF RULERS AND NOBLES: A SUMMARY

Three of the cultures we have examined—the Aztec, Mixtec, and Zapotec—claimed, on the emic level, to name their children for the day in the 260-day ritual calendar on which they were born. As was so often the case, the etic reality was different. At least in the case of rulers and nobles, an effort was made to name the child for a day whose number and/or day sign were auspicious, and to avoid a day name considered unlucky. For that reason, a large sample of Mixtec male names (Appendix) shows significant deviation from the pattern that would have resulted had the emic rule really been followed. Because we lack a comparable sample of commoners' names, we do not know to what extent they also fudged their birthdays.

The avoidance of unlucky combinations of numbers and day names further reduced the list of possible names to the point where many nobles had the same calendric name. This, presumably, encouraged the custom of giving each noble a nickname that would distinguish him or her from others with the same calendric name. Zapotec rulers were given impressive nicknames such as "Creator of Lightning" and "Great Eagle." Mixtec rulers had nicknames such as "Tiger Claw" and "Fire Serpent." The Aztec created truly dramatic, often fantastic, nicknames such as "Obsidian-backed Serpent" and "Smoking Shield." In many cases we have only these special nicknames, while the calendric names have been lost.

The Maya, in contrast, seem to have been less interested in calendric names. They drew their names from plants, animals, ritual objects, or abstract concepts such as "darkness" or "stormy." Since abstract concepts are more difficult to depict in hieroglyphic writing, the Maya (like other Mesoamerican people) used such devices as rebus writing and phonetic elements to get across the name. The Maya also seem to have had names that were passed on for generations at the same site, such as the "jaguar" names at Yaxchilán. These may have functioned like the patronymics used by sixteenth-century Yucatec Maya.

While noble men often had nicknames containing references to ballcourts, war, shields, jaguars, coyotes, or lightning, noble women were more likely to be named for birds or flowers. Cottonflake, macaw, quetzal, and jade were common nicknames for women.

In constructing names, Mesoamerican nobles showed interest in creating "fantastic creatures" that had never existed in the real world. By so doing, nobles were able to associate themselves with the desired attributes of the sacred, the supernatural, and the powerful forces of nature. Such names served to widen the gap between the elite and the commoner, since the latter presumably did not have the right to acquire nicknames such as Lightning-Creator, Jaguar Paw Skull, Obsidian-backed Serpent, and Fierce Jaguar. Such names bestowed special qualities on the hereditary rulers, and were another device to signal the difference between upper and lower strata.

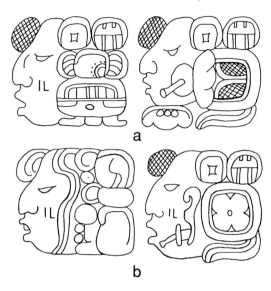

7.22. Names of a Maya mother and daughter from the back of Stela 3 at Piedras Negras. At *a* is the name of a royal woman named "Lady Darkness"; at *b* is the name of her daughter, "Lady Sunlight." Each name incorporates two feminine head glyphs. (Redrawn from Marcus 1976a: fig. 5.3.)

8 ✦ ROYAL MARRIAGES

Establishing genealogical links between ruling dynasties was an ancient practice of several Mesoamerican cultures. Frequently those links were established by royal marriages, unions that served as one component of a larger political and economic strategy. Arranged marriages could unite members of the same ethnic group (for example, a Mixtec nobleman with a Mixtec noblewoman), or members of two different ethnic groups (for example, a Zapotec lord with an Aztec princess).

Of all the marriages that took place in prehispanic societies, only those involving rulers or nobles were recorded by the scribes and monument carvers. And of all the royal and noble marriages that took place, surely only a small percentage were ever recorded. What were some of the factors that determined whether or not a royal marriage would be recorded?

Generally speaking, the recorded marriages were those that were sociopolitically advantageous. These included (1) marriages that established interethnic alliances; (2) marriages that established interdynastic alliances between prominent ruling houses; (3) marriages that integrated lower-order centers with regional capitals; (4) marriages that reaffirmed hierarchical relationships; and (5) marriages that established tributary relationships between centers. As we will see below, such alliances could unite political equals or unequals.

Although male nobles occupied many of the offices in Mesoamerica, noble women also played important roles as officeholders, marriage partners, and mothers. Furthermore, a nobleman's rank, office, and title were directly affected by the status of his mother and wife. For example, acquisition of new titles, new lands, additional manpower, and tribute-paying populations could be facilitated by a strategic marriage alliance.

One of the ancient mechanisms for establishing regional integration in Mesoamerica was that of sending out royal daughters from a higher-ranking center to a lower-ranking dependency. These higher-ranking females would marry local lords, thereby elevating the latter's status (and that of the local site), and just as importantly, raising the prestige of their offspring. This strategy apparently ensured some degree of loyalty, cooperation, and allegiance on the part of the lower-order community.

Types of Marriages

In this chapter we will employ a typology of strategic marriages derived from anthropological theory. This theory singles out three types of marriage, known as *isogamy*, *hypogamy*, and *hypergamy*. The frequency of each type, as reported in the indigenous written record (either in stone hieroglyphic inscriptions or in painted pictorial codices), is very significant. Among the four Mesoamerican groups discussed here, *reported* royal marriages most often took place between a woman of higher rank and a man of lower rank (hypogamy). Second in frequency were marriages between a man and a woman of equal rank (isogamy). Finally, the least frequently chronicled marriages were those uniting a woman of lower rank with a man of higher rank (hypergamy).

Although some readers might be surprised that marriages between a higher-ranking male and a lower-ranking female were the least likely to be recorded, we must keep in mind the original purpose of recording such information. If a male member of a prominent dynasty has married a woman of lower rank, there is no particular sociopolitical advantage for him to emphasize such a fact in writing. Rather, his desire to *de-emphasize* that fact partially accounts for such marriages being the least often reported. In such cases, even the name or true social position of the wife might be left out of a text.

Hypogamous and isogamous marriages were more frequently recorded because such marriages were far more advantageous for a male officeholder and his offspring. Since males appear to have largely controlled the written record and scribal tradition, the recording of marriages advantageous to women was an event less frequently commemorated in stone or codices. We have limited evidence that prehispanic women served as scribes, and no evidence at all that women controlled the written record. I know of just one instance in which a woman—evidently an Aztec noblewoman—was depicted as a scribe (see Fig. 3.1).

The "marrying down" of royal daughters was one of the mechanisms used by capital cities to guarantee the loyalty of subject towns that might otherwise have a greater tendency to secede. Hypogamous marriages also signaled the subordination of a ruler, a town, or a district among the Aztec, Mixtec, Zapotec, and Maya. In this chapter we will look at examples from each group.

Aztec royal marriages come under the heading of political strategy, not romance. Marriages between full siblings or between parent and child were forbidden, but otherwise there were few clear-cut rules that restricted marriage choices (Pomar [1582] 1941:26, Motolinía 1971:324–325). There is evidence for polygyny within the ruling stratum, allowing one ruler to effect marriage alliances with several different communities.

An Aztec wife of high rank might bring along a retinue of women—some noble, some commoner—who became additional secondary wives or concubines of the ruler (Ixtlilxochitl 1977:164; P. Carrasco 1984:44). A ruler who married sisters considered them "joint wives," although usually one main wife, or highest-ranking wife, was designated as the one who would provide the heirs. The offspring of the highest-ranking wives always had higher status than the children of concubines.

Aztec marriage ceremonies took place on days with "favorable" names such as Monkey, House, Crocodile, Reed, and Eagle. Depictions of marriage in the Aztec codices usually employed several conventions, some of which were shared by other groups like the Zapotec and Mixtec. In Aztec depictions of marriage (*nenamictiliztli*), one convention was to show a man and a woman seated on a woven mat, facing each other, having their clothing tied together.

We can turn to the Codex Mendoza (Clark 1938, vol. 3, folio 61) to see a depiction of an Aztec wedding (Fig. 8.1). Beginning at the bottom of the painting, we see that the bride is being carried to the groom's house on the back of a matchmaker (*amanteca*). Since this event took place at night, four women carrying lighted pine torches are shown accompanying the matchmaker and the bride; they light the dark trail. Footprints lead into a house, showing where the bride took her proper place on the mat. Also present in the house are four old people—two men seated on mat-covered cushions at the left, and two women kneeling at the right. All four of these witnesses are shown with speech scrolls in front of their mouths.

Shown above the heads of the bride and groom are a hearth and an incense burner where copal is offered. Below the couple are offerings of food and drink; in the basket is toasted maize, and in the pottery vessel to the right is *mole de guajolote* (turkey in a chocolate/chile sauce). In a jar, and in a shallow bowl or cup, is the fermented beverage pulque. Note that the facial paint worn by the bride while being married on the mat is different from that worn by her as she was being carried to the bridegroom's door by the matchmaker. The new design in facial paint indicates her married state. Also clearly shown is the fact that the bride's blouse is now tied to the upper garment of her husband. This tying together of the garments symbolized the new state of being united in marriage.

It is significant that the "names" of the royal women in Aztec marriage scenes are frequently not calendric names or nicknames, but *toponyms*. These toponyms may refer

8.1. An Aztec wedding scene. At the bottom, four women carry pine torches to light the path of the female matchmaker, shown carrying the bride on her back. Inside the building (above) are the groom and his parents. Footprints show that the bride entered the room and sat on the mat where she and the groom were to be married. The clothing of the bride and groom were then tied together, symbolic of the marital union. We see copal incense burned, food offered, and four old people offering advice to the newly married couple. (Redrawn from the Codex Mendoza in Clark 1938, vol. 3, folio 61; Corona Núñez 1964, 1: Lámina LXII.)

to (1) the woman's birthplace, (2) her palace, or (3) the lands associated with her (P. Carrasco 1984:44). The pattern of recording the bride's birthplace or possessions, rather than her own personal name, clearly demonstrates that the marriage was seen as an alliance linking the male ruler of one town to newly acquired lands or towns he or his offspring would one day control. Such use of a woman's birthplace, rather than her personal name, is also known for the Postclassic Zapotec and the Classic Maya (see below).

Interdynastic Hypogamy

Many Aztec royal marriages were used to link primary centers (for example, members of the Triple Alliance), or to connect one of those primary centers to one of its lower-order dependencies. In the latter case, the high-ranking ruler of a primary center would give his daughter to the lower-ranking ruler of a secondary center. Pedro Carrasco (1984:45) has called this type of marriage *interdynastic hypogamy.*

Interdynastic hypogamous marriages were part of a well-conceived long-term strategy, and they sometimes served as the solution to a pressing problem of disorganization or insubordination. Communities that posed a threat to the capital, subject towns that threatened to split off from their primary center and become independent (or worse still, form an alliance with a rival town) could be brought back under control through a hypogamous marriage, which raised their ruler's status and made him the in-law of a primary center's ruler. The flexibility of this system of marriage alliances was probably one of the main reasons that it was so widespread.

As was the case with many Mesoamerican cultures, the noble offspring of a hypogamous marriage would often emphasize the names and titles of his mother in his various stone monuments and codices, since she was the parent of more distinguished lineage. The scribes producing Aztec codices were particularly careful to supply the mother's name when she came from Tenochtitlán, the capital. The daughters of Tenochtitlán rulers were sent to marry local lords at such subject towns as Cuauhtitlán, Chalco, Cuitlahuac, Colhuacán, and Xaltocán; for example, there is evidence to show that at least four successive rulers of Xaltocán were married to women from Tenochtitlán.

Royal women from Tenochtitlán could also be used to establish a new second-order polity, or *tlahtocayotl.* In one case, Chimalpahin (1889:108) says that a daughter of the ruler Itzcoatl of Tenochtitlán was married to a lower-ranking man of Atotonilco, who as a result of this marriage became the ruler of a whole new province. In the writings of Alvarado Tezozomoc ([1609] 1949:112), we find another case of a new *tlahtocayotl* established as the direct result of the marriage of a Tenochtitlán ruler's daughter to a local lord. In addition, Motecuhzoma Ilhuicamina's daughter married a nobleman of Tepexic-mixtlán, making him the "lord" of his own *tlahtocayotl* or *señorío* (P. Carrasco 1984:53).

Indeed, there is reason to believe that interdynastic hypogamous marriages even characterized the relationship between Tenochtitlán and Texcoco, two members of the Triple Alliance that are generally seen as having been on the same hierarchical level. Several Texcocan rulers who succeeded their fathers on the throne were the sons of Tenochtitlán women. For example, Ixtlilxochitl (1977:164) says that the ruler Axayacatl of Tenochtitlán, along with other Aztec nobles, sent daughters to the ruler Nezahualpilli of Texcoco so that the latter could select a principal wife from among them and keep the others as secondary wives or concubines. As it turned out, the woman chosen as the principal wife was unable to bear children, so Nezahualpilli's seven sons were the offspring of other noble Tenochtitlán women; nevertheless, according to Pomar ([1582] 1941:25), those sons went on to rule Texcoco in succession. (It should be noted that Torquemada [(1615) 1969, 2:357] disputes Pomar's account).

Another example of a hypogamous marriage linking Tenochtitlán and Texcoco is that of Ixtlilxochitl, ruler of Texcoco. He married Matlalcihuatl, the daughter of Huitzilihuitl, ruler of Tenochtitlán from ca. A.D. 1397–1417. Ixtlilxochitl and Matlalcihuatl had two children—a son Nezahualcoyotl, and a daughter Tozquentzin. In Figure 8.2, behind the figure of Ixtlilxochitl is his concubine—Tecpaxochitl—who came from Azcapotzalco. She was the daughter of Tezozomoc, who had expected that his daughter would be Ixtlilxochitl's wife. Ixtlilxochitl, however, is reported to have rejected Tecpaxochitl as his wife, and it was this rejection that allegedly started the war between Ixtlilxochitl of Texcoco and Tezozomoc of Azcapotzalco (Dibble 1951:86). Nevertheless, Ixtlilxochitl and Tecpaxochitl had several children together, including Zihuaquequenotzin, Xiconocatzin, Chicuaquetzalli, Totoquetzalli, Yeitlamitzin, and Tilmatzin (all shown in Fig. 8.2f–l).

Since Texcoco received numerous hypogamous brides from Tenochtitlán, the notion that it sat on the same hierarchical level as Tenochtitlán probably should be reevaluated. The case could be made for a hierarchy in which Tenochtitlán sat alone at the top, with Texcoco hierarchically below it in the second tier, and smaller towns such as sixteenth-century Teotihuacán on the third level, owing allegiance to Texcoco. This hierarchy would accord well with the fact that when tribute was divided among members of the Triple Alliance, Tenochtitlán received two shares to every one for Texcoco and Tlacopan (Gibson 1964).

In this hierarchy, labor, goods, and allegiance moved upward while royal women moved downward. For example, Motolinía (1971:337, 394) describes the marriage alliances linking Texcoco to its fourteen subject towns. Each of these subject towns became the home of a "lord" after the local ruler was married to one of the daughters of the Texcoco ruler; after each marriage, the new son-in-law was granted a *tlahtocayotl* and the title "his lordship."

In the case of sixteenth-century Teotihuacán, already mentioned, Pedro Carrasco (1974) has shown the way in which noble brides from Texcoco enhanced the position of their Teotihuacán husbands. As part of their dowries, these brides contributed very sig-

oixtlilxochitl matlalcihuatl

8.2. The marriage between Ixtlilxochitl and Matlalcihuatl (daughter of Huitzilihuitl, the Tenochtitlán ruler) was recorded in the Codex Xolotl. *a*, Ixtlilxochitl; *b*, Matlalcihuatl; *c*, son Nezahualcoyotl; *d*, daughter Tozquentzin; *e*, Tecpaxochitl; *f*, Zihuaquequenotzin; *g*, Xiconocatzin; *h*, a son of Ixtlilxochitl whose name is not clear; *i*, Chicuaquetzalli; *j*, Totoquetzalli; *k*, Yeitlamitzin; *l*, Tilmatzin. Ixtlilxochitl apparently refused to accept Tecpaxochitl of Azcapotzalco as his principal wife, and this rejection started the war between Ixtlilxochitl and Tecpaxochitl's father, Tezozomoc. (Redrawn from Dibble 1951: Plancha VI.)

nificant landholdings called *ciuatlalli*, "woman's lands" [*cihua(tl)* = woman; *tlalli* = land] to the current and future lords of Teotihuacán. The son of the royal Texcocan woman and her Teotihuacán husband then became the successor to this lordship or *tlahtocayotl*.

MIXTEC ROYAL MARRIAGES

Like other Mesoamerican states, the Mixtec were stratum-endogamous: commoners married commoners, nobles married nobles. Most commoners could find suitable mates within their own community, and thus tended to be community-endogamous. On the other hand, rulers and nobles searched for eligible noble mates with whom they could forge advantageous marriage alliances, and hence tended to be community-exogamous. Often the search for suitable mates was extensive, reaching out to distant polities.

An important consideration in the marriage between a Mixtec lord and lady was planning for the inheritance of their titles and landholdings. These strategies have been described by the sixteenth-century Spaniards, using the borrowed Carib term *cacique*, or "hereditary lord," from which we also derive *cacica* ("female ruler") and *cacicazgo* ("the territory controlled by a *cacique*").

For example, following the Spanish conquest, the Mixtec ruler who had been baptized "Don Diego Nuqh" (formerly "6 Motion," *cacique* of Tamazola-Chachoapan) married "María Cocuahu" (formerly "2 House," *cacica* of Yanhuitlán); the couple decided that their first child would inherit the title to Tamazola-Chachoapan (the father's *cacicazgo*), while their second child would receive the title to Yanhuitlán (the mother's *cacicazgo*). As was common in the Mixtec highlands, the first child (a son) was reared in the town he was to inherit (Tamazola), while the second child (also a son) was taken to be reared in Yanhuitlán (Spores 1967:134; Spores 1974a; Archivo General de la Nación, A.D. 1572 document from Ramo Civil, No. 669, Expediente 1; A.D. 1580 document from Ramo Civil, No. 516, Inquisición 37–39).

Spores (1967:146, 1974, 1984) has amassed archival data indicating that decisions of succession and inheritance were made strictly on the basis of birth order. Caso (1964c:437–438) also states that it was customary in the Mixteca Alta for the first-born child to inherit the *cacicazgo* of the father, while the second-born inherited that of the mother. These statements are important, because some scholars in the past have assumed that males would always inherit the titles and lands of *cacicazgos,* and that primogeniture would have operated. This assumption may result from the fact that primogeniture seems to have been a special concern of the Spanish chroniclers, who had had such a custom for inheritance in Spain. The fact is that European-style primogeniture is not indigenous to most, if any, Mesoamerican groups.

Another misconception has resulted from the Spaniards' use of the term *linaje* when speaking of sixteenth-century native rulers. When Mixtec *caciques* referred to their "royal lineage," they were not referring to "patrilineages" or "matrilineages." They were referring to direct lines of ancestors through both mother and father (Spores 1984:70).

Regardless of how commoners reckoned their descent, Mixtec nobles (like Meso-american nobles in general) reckoned their descent bilaterally, so that both the mother's and father's bloodlines could be emphasized. If the mother and father were of equal rank and importance, both sets of rights, lands, and titles would be noted and recorded. However, when one line (for example, the mother's) had certain special rights, claims, lands, or titles, *that* line could be stressed at the expense of the other (Spores 1967). As we noted for the Aztec, the claims to titles, privileges, and lands by couples in hypogamous marriages featured the mother's title. Such marriages were common among the Mixtec, but so were isogamous marriages between partners equal in noble descent.

More names and family roles of Mixtec royal women are known than those of any other ethnic group, primarily since so many noble women are mentioned in the Mixtec codices. For this same reason, we have more royal marriage scenes for the Mixtec than for any other group. (The Zapotec would probably be in second place, with Maya and Aztec marriage scenes less frequently depicted). Although we have more noble marriages for the Mixtec than for any other group, it is still often difficult to determine which marriages were hypogamous, isogamous, or hypergamous because too few of the place names and dynastic seats have so far been identified. However, one clue to such differences in ranking between communities can be seen in the furniture depicted: that is, whether both bride and groom are seated on stools, thrones, or mats, or whether one is seated on a throne while the other is on a mat.

One of the purposes for the detailed marriage accounts given in the Mixtec codices was to document the fact that there were living claimants to particular titles, and that such claimants were the legitimate successors in a direct, unbroken line extending back to titled ancestors who had previously ruled the *cacicazgo* in question. We will next look at a few of the many royal marriage scenes in these codices, drawing on detailed studies by Spinden (1935), Caso (1949, 1950, 1954, 1960, 1964a, 1964b, 1966b, 1977, 1979), and Smith (1973a), among others.

Interpretation of marriage scenes in the codices is made somewhat less difficult by the fact that sixteenth-century Spanish descriptions of the Mixtec language (e.g., Alvarado [1593] 1962, Reyes [1593] 1976) give a number of indigenous expressions for marriage rituals which can be found in the pictorial documents. For example, one expression is *tnaha ndaha ya*, which means "to join hands" (*tnaha*, "to join"; *ndaha*, "hands" or "tribute"; *ya*, suffix used with nobles). Another marriage expression is *cuvui huico ya*, which indicates a "royal feast" or "celebration" (*cuvui*, "to happen" or "to be"; *huico*, "feast, celebration"; *yya*, suffix used with nobles). Still another expression, meaning "to sanctify or purify the kingdom or empire," is *ndoo sina ya* (*ndoo*, "to sanctify, purify"; *sina ya*, "royal kingdom, empire"). Finally, we can point to the phrase *nisiñe saha ya*, meaning "the royal vessel [of pulque = *ndedzi*] was placed before the noble man" (*ni*, past tense indicator; *sine*, "to be placed"; *saha*, "royal vessel"; *ya*, suffix used with nobles). As noted by Smith (1973a:30–31), this last idiomatic expression is reflected in a few marriage scenes, ones in which the bride is depicted in the act of giving a vessel of pulque or chocolate to the groom.

As in some Aztec marriage scenes already described, Mixtec scribes may show a man and woman seated, facing each other. The woman usually wears a skirt and a very large quechquemitl, while the man often wears a gown with fringe or tassels attached. Women may be shown with braided hair and interwoven ribbons, while men often have long straight hair (Smith 1973a:29). The couple may be seated on a low platform covered with jaguar (?) skins or woven straw mats, or before the entrance of a building presumed to be their palace. Sometimes they are shown with a vessel of chocolate or pulque; in other cases, marriage is shown as a "bathing scene." When a scene does not depict the actual marriage ceremony, but rather shows a couple that has already been married (for example, the parents of the bride), such a couple is shown facing the same direction, one seated behind the other.

In Figure 8.3, we see an example of a Mixtec marriage scene from the Codex Bodley. A woman named 13 Flower "Jade-Quetzal" (shown at *d*) is united with a man named 4 Crocodile "Serpent-Burning Copal" (at *c*). The groom is from Tilantongo, a place shown as a frieze containing black and white stepped frets (*a–b*). The names of the groom's parents are given above the frieze (at left), behind the seated figure of their son. Note that only their names are supplied; their actual depictions are not. The groom's father was the famous ruler 8 Deer "Tiger Claw," and his mother was 13 Serpent "Flowered Serpent" (Caso 1977, 1979; Smith 1973a:32). In this scene, the drawing of a road shows where the bridegroom 4 Crocodile is from (Tilantongo), and where he is going to live after his marriage (his bride's birthplace). Spores (1967) has indicated that the residence rule of the ancient Mixtec was ambilocal, meaning that the newly married couple could elect to stay in either the groom's or bride's *cacicazgo*.

In Figure 8.4, we see the union of the famous woman 6 Monkey "Serpent Quechquemitl" to 11 Wind "Bloody Tiger" (from Codex Selden 7-I). This type of wedding ceremony is sometimes called a "bathing scene" because the bride and groom are shown swimming in a river. Such marital baths were virtually the only context (other than as prisoner or when giving birth) in which a noble would be shown nude. The day of the wedding is given above as 7 Flower in the year 12 House (A.D. 1037 in Caso's chronology and A.D. 1089 in Rabin's chronology).

Another marriage ceremony featuring a bathing scene takes place between a groom named 12 Wind "Smoke Eyebrow" and his bride 3 Flint "Pearl Quechquemitl" in the Codex Nuttall (Fig. 8.5). In this bathing scene, two women are shown above, pouring water on the couple below. This wedding took place on the day 2 Eagle in the year 10 House, when 12 Wind was 32 years old. He was the second ruler of the first dynasty of Tejupan (or possibly Acatlán). This marriage united 12 Wind's *cacicazgo* with 3 Flint's, a place named "White Bundle of Flints." Since we are unable to determine the specific location of "White Bundle of Flints," we cannot tell if this was an isogamous or hypogamous marriage.

Another marriage scene from the Codex Selden (15-III) unites the male noble 3 Death "Gray Eagle" and the woman 3 Serpent "Garland of Cacao Flowers" (Fig. 8.6). She sits on a small throne, while he is seated on a cushioned stool; this distinction could indicate a difference in rank. The day and year of the wedding are given between the two seated figures—the day appears above and can be read as 9 Rabbit, while the "A-O" year sign (below) contains a flint and 5 dots, for the year 5 Flint. Caso, however, has suggested that this year date is a scribal error, and that the date should have been 6 Flint (A.D. 1408), not 5 Flint (A.D. 1368). He points out that the year A.D. 1368 is impossible, since the bride and groom were born after A.D. 1368 (Caso 1977, 1979). As for provenience, Smith (1983a) believes that the Codex Selden was painted in the Nochixtlán Valley.

The marriage of the famous Mixtec conqueror 8 Deer "Tiger Claw" to the woman 13 Serpent "Flowered Serpent" is shown in Figure 8.7. The wedding apparently took place in front of a building with an elaborate frieze at the top. The name of 8 Deer "Tiger Claw" is given below his cushion. Then we see the year and day of the wedding (year 13 Reed, day 12 Serpent); this corresponds to the year A.D. 1051 in Caso's chronology. The hieroglyphic name of the bride (13 Serpent) appears in front of her and below her out-stretched hands, which offer to her husband a vessel presumably containing pulque. In the Codex Nuttall from which this scene comes, the wedding is reported to have occurred on the day 12 Serpent; in other codices recording the same wedding, the day is given as 13 or 11 Serpent. Thus, both the 8 Deer-13 Serpent wedding and the 3 Death-3 Serpent wedding, already mentioned, indicate that scribal errors were not uncommon.

In Figure 8.8 we see another marriage (this time from Codex Nuttall 42) in which the couple is shown seated on individual cushions covered with the pelts of felines. On the left is the woman 9 Eagle "Garland of Cacao Flowers"; her nickname flows down behind her back, while her calendric name is placed in front of her face. She wears an elaborate headdress and prominent nose ornament. On the right is the groom 5 Crocodile "Rain Deity/Sun Disk." His name appears behind his back, which holds the "sun disk" symbol; he appears to wear a special mask. This wedding took place in the year 6 Flint, A.D. 992 in Caso's chronology (Caso 1977, 1979).

Two marriages involving the presentation of vessels filled with special beverages—pulque and/or foaming hot chocolate—are shown in Figures 8.9 and 8.10. In Figure 8.9, we see a woman named 10 Deer "Tiger-skin Quechquemitl" from a place called "White Flowers," seated on a platform. She is facing her new husband, 8 Wind "Flint Eagle," ruler of a place called "Hill of the Monkey." This wedding took place on the day 1 Eagle in the year 10 House (A.D. 805). Between the couple is a large tripod vessel with serpent-head feet, a typical "Mixtec polychrome" vessel in Postclassic style. The vessel contains a foaming liquid with flowers—usually a convention for hot chocolate, a beverage associated with noble weddings.

In Figure 8.10 we see a wedding scene with an apparent offering of pulque, a fermented beverage also associated with weddings. The large vessel of pulque seems to float between the bride and groom. This marriage ceremony united the nobleman 4 Wind "Fire Serpent" (at left) with a woman named 5 Lizard (at right), apparently his third wife. They both sit atop a large woven mat, a symbol associated with wedding ceremonies among Aztec, Mixtec, and Zapotec nobles. Since the woman also sits on a cushion, however, she may have been higher-ranking than her husband.

a   b   c   d

8.3. Mixtec marriage linking 4 Crocodile "Serpent-Burning Copal" (at *c*) and 13 Flower "Jade-Quetzal" (at *d*). The groom 4 Crocodile is from Tilantongo, the place with the black-and-white frieze (*a–b*). His parents were 8 Deer "Tiger Claw" (whose name glyph is above *b*) and 13 Serpent "Flowered Serpent" (whose name glyph is above *a*). (Redrawn from Codex Bodley 30; see Corona Núñez 1964, 2:65.)

8.4. This Mixtec royal "bathing scene" documents the marriage of 6 Monkey "Serpent Quechquemitl" (at right) and 11 Wind "Bloody Tiger" (at left). The date given above is 7 Flower in the year 12 House (A.D. 1037). (Redrawn from Codex Selden 7.)

8.5. The Mixtec marriage of 12 Wind "Smoke Eyebrow" (at left) and 3 Flint "Pearl Quechquemitl" (at right) conveyed in a bathing scene. Above are two women who pour water on the couple. This marriage united his polity (Tejupan) with hers ("White Bundle of Flints"). (Redrawn from Codex Nuttall 19.)

8.6. A Mixtec marriage scene uniting 3 Death "Gray Eagle" (at left) and 3 Serpent "Garland of Cacao Flowers" (at right) on the day 9 Rabbit in A.D. 1408. (Redrawn from Codex Selden 15.)

8.7. The marriage uniting Mixtec ruler 8 Deer "Tiger Claw" (at left) and 13 Serpent "Flowered Serpent" (at right) supposedly took place in A.D. 1051. She is presenting him with a foaming bowl, probably containing pulque (a fermented beverage) or hot chocolate. (Redrawn from Codex Nuttall 26.)

8.8. The marriage of 9 Eagle "Garland of Cacao Flowers" (at left) and 5 Crocodile "Rain Deity/ Sun Disk" (at right) took place in the year 6 Flint, or A.D. 992. This may be an example of a Mixtec isogamous marriage, since both sit on feline pelt-covered cushions. (Redrawn from Codex Nuttall 42.)

8.9. The marriage uniting 10 Deer ''Tiger-skin Quechquemitl'' (at left) with 8 Wind ''Flint Eagle'' (at right) in A.D. 805. Between them is a vessel that probably contained hot chocolate, since the flowers on top of the liquid seem to be cacao blossoms. (Redrawn from Codex Nuttall 5.)

8.10. A Mixtec marriage of A.D. 1073, uniting 4 Wind (at left) with 5 Lizard (at right), who was his third wife. The type of vessel shown between them usually indicates that pulque was the beverage exchanged. Note that while this marriage takes place atop a mat, the bride is also seated on a cushion, possibly indicating another case of hypogamy. (Redrawn from Codex Bodley 30.)

Zapotec royal marriages were commemorated in the Valley of Oaxaca at least as early as A.D. 500, but most of our examples come from stone monuments carved between A.D. 600 and 900. As in the case of the later Mixtec codices, Zapotec wedding scenes often show the couple's parents or other ancestors. The Zapotec often depict the couple seated on mats or on hill signs, sometimes exchanging vessels of foaming hot chocolate or pulque. Above the couple appears a motif that Caso (1928) has called "the jaws of the sky"; it includes a large, stylized maxilla with prominently displayed teeth. Descending from these celestial jaws are variable elements, such as a person carrying a long necklace, a bird, a plant, or what appear to be cords. Such jaws seem to be the opening to an upper world where the deceased nobles lived; this opening allows communication and gift-giving between living nobles and their ancestors.

While many Zapotec carved stones with wedding scenes and genealogical records are known, few have been found *in situ* by archaeologists. Those that have were in the antechambers of elaborate tombs at places like Lambityeco, Suchilquitongo, and Zaachila. These monuments were evidently intended to be read by a small number of elite individuals attending the funeral, rather than viewed by large crowds; the stones are small (less than 1 m²), with the hieroglyphs and scenes of such scale that they were clearly intended to be viewed from close up. These monuments therefore contrast with those from earlier periods (500 B.C.—A.D. 500) when Zapotec carved stones were truly monumental, set up in public places, and intended to be viewed from great distances, probably by larger numbers of people. This contrast is consistent with the difference between vertical propaganda, meant to be seen by multitudes, and horizontal propaganda, shown to a smaller group of nobles.

On a relatively simple Zapotec marriage slab (Fig. 8.11) we see a woman at left and a bearded man at right. Together they hold a rectangular object with a sign that might be interpreted as a "star" or "night's eye"; the meaning of the motif in this context is not clear. The couple is seated above a place name that includes the head of an animal.

The next marital slab (Fig. 8.12) supplies a more complete record, including the names of the couple. Between them is the sign for 10 Owl, apparently the calendric name of the woman seated at right. The name of the groom (at left) apparently includes "Death" (symbolized by the skull), and if the bar-and-dot number in the upper left corner is associated with the skull sign in front of his knees, his name might have been 7 Death. At the center of the stone, in the upper section, we see the frontal view of a probable ancestor who wears an elaborate headdress, earspools, and necklace. Both the bride and groom hold objects, evidently vessels with steaming liquid, perhaps hot chocolate.

A more elaborate marriage scene (Fig. 8.13) is shown on a carved stone reported to be from Matatlán, south of Mitla. Like others of its type, this slab is small (62 x 53 cm),

8.11. A Zapotec royal marriage scene uniting a woman (at left) and a man (at right) whose names were probably given in the destroyed portion of the monument above their heads. Both support with their hands a rectangular object containing a glyph that usually means "star" or "night's eye." They sit on a place sign that may feature a bat or feline. (Drawing by Mark Orsen.)

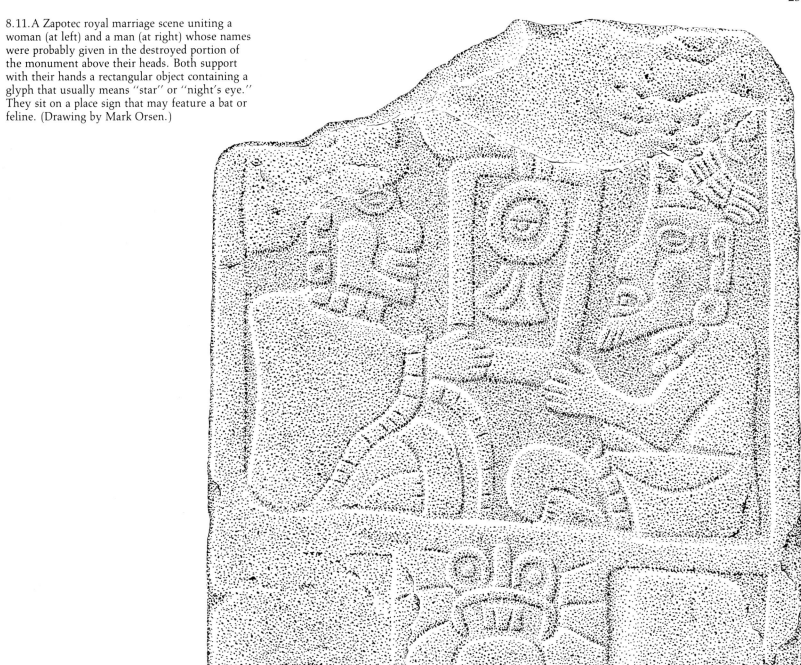

8.12. The marriage of a Zapotec nobleman (at left), possibly named 7 Skull (= Death), with Lady 10 Owl (at right). He emits a speech scroll and holds an unidentified object; she is shown offering a beverage to him (an act identical to that just seen in Mixtec royal marriages). In the center of the slab is the frontal view of a figure (probably a royal ancestor) who dominates the scene. (Drawing by Mark Orsen.)

8.13. This Zapotec marriage scene from Matatlán shows the groom at left and his bride at right. As we so often see in these "marriage slabs," (1) the groom emits a speech scroll, while the bride holds an object (in this case, a staff with leaves and a bird [?] head); (2) the bride and groom are seated facing each other; (3) their ancestors are shown below them (lower left and right corners); and (4) above them (at the center) are the "jaws of the sky," with something descending from them (in this case, a plant). (Drawing by Mark Orsen.)

and was intended to be read from close up; its original position was probably in a noble's tomb. At the top center is the celestial jaw with a plant of some kind descending from it. The principal couple is shown facing each other, each wearing an elaborate feather headdress. Atop the woman's feather headdress is the figure of a bird. The husband's name is given behind him; it appears to include an owl, another bird, and possibly a bar signifying the number 5. The woman is holding a staff with leaves like those on the plant shown descending from the celestial jaw; the head of the staff resembles the owl given as part of her husband's name. The bride's name is evidently given behind her. The couple's royal ancestors are shown below; we see the head of a man at lower left (below the feet of the husband) and the bust of a woman at lower right (behind the figure of the wife).

An unusual circular marriage slab, 43 centimeters in diameter, is shown in Figure 8.14. The stone was reported to have been found in a site at La Ciénaga, near Zimatlán in the southern Valley of Oaxaca (Caso 1928:113, citing Galindo y Villa). A bird is shown descending from the now-familiar celestial jaws. Arrayed around the bride and groom is a series of elements. Some of these elements are day signs with numbers associated (probably the names of the couple), but others are "floating" in the scene and difficult to interpret. We see, for example, signs and elements associated with the year bearer and death. The husband (at left) *may* have had the name 5 Owl, and the wife (at right) *may* have been called 5 Monkey. Both have speech scrolls in front of their mouths, and she appears to be offering something to him. They both sit atop a hill sign, suggesting that in this case both bride and groom were from the same polity or would co-rule that polity.

Among the more elaborate examples of Zapotec marriage scenes is one reported to have been found at Zaachila (Fig. 8.15). This carved stone measures only 38 × 60 cm, requiring that its text be read from very close up indeed. The monument is divided into two registers. On the left, in the upper register, we see the bride kneeling; she is shown with a speech scroll and faces the groom, who is seated on a mat. Both bride and groom hold pottery vessels, and between them we see a flowering plant. The woman's name appears behind her head, and might correspond to 3 Serpent or Water; the groom's name is 6 Earthquake (the bar for 5 appears above the day sign for "earthquake" and the dot for 1 occurs below it). Above the couple are the usual celestial jaws, with an ancestor (?) shown descending from them with a necklace of jade (?) beads in his hand; to either side of the celestial jaws we see conch shells. The marriage depicted in this upper register of the monument was evidently an event deemed important to record in a tomb antechamber (Marcus 1983k:193–195).

In contrast, the lower register of the same monument shows a couple from the more distant past. The noblewoman, on the left, is shown kneeling on a hill sign; to the right is a man with a speech scroll emanating from his mouth. Her name is 11 Monkey, and his is either 6 Flower or 8 Flower, depending on whether we include in his name the two dots located behind his back. This couple, shown in the lower register, appears to be ances-

8.14. On this circular Zapotec marriage slab from La Ciénaga, near Zimatlán, we see a couple seated together atop a "hill" or "place" sign. Above them is a stylized version of the "jaws of the sky," this time with a bird descending from it. The groom is seated at left, while the bride (at right) appears to be holding (or offering him) an object that cannot be identified. Both emit speech scrolls. Several calendric signs are associated with each figure, making it somewhat difficult to determine which glyphs supplied their names. For the groom's name we can choose among the signs 4 Glyph E, 7 Death, and 5 Owl. For the bride's name we can choose among 3 Death, 5 Monkey, and 2 Glyph E. (Drawing by Mark Orsen.)

8.15. This Zapotec marriage slab (attributed to Zaachila by Caso 1928) is divided into two registers, showing a marriage in the upper zone and ancestors in the lower. In the upper register, the "jaws of the sky" are elaborately depicted, with an ancestor descending from them with what appears to be a jade necklace. The bride (3 Serpent or Water) is shown at left and the groom (6 Earthquake) at right. Both hold pottery vessels; between them is a flowering plant. The ancestors in the lower register are seated on hill signs. The female ancestor (11 Monkey) is at left; the bearded male ancestor at right, with arms crossed, is named 6 (8?) Flower. The text accompanying these figures begins at the bottom, in the center. The first sign we see is the Zapotec year sign, followed by the year bearer, a verb, and a subject. Then follow the names of 13 individuals, running up the right margin of the slab, including the names of the bride and groom (at the upper right corner). To the left of the bride's and groom's names are two more calendric names (top margin, center), which because of their place in the sequence may be the names of their offspring. (Drawing by Mark Orsen.)

tors of one of the persons in the upper register; the man in the lower register is shown as bearded, with a lined, elderly face.

In addition to the two couples, this monument has a long text that begins at the bottom center of the stone and runs up the right edge until it ends at the top center. Thus, appropriately, it leads us from the bottom register (the more distant past) to the top register (the more recent past). The text begins with the Zapotec year sign, the year bearer, and the verb "to give one's hand in marriage," and is then followed by the calendric names of 13 individuals, many of them presumably ancestors or relatives of the couple in the upper register. In addition, the names of the bride and groom in the upper register—6 Earthquake and 3 Serpent or Water—are themselves given in the list, at the upper right corner of the stone. To the left of the bride's name are two more names, possibly (from their location in the sequence) those of the couple's children. This possibility reminds us that the stone was probably carved for a tomb following the death of one of the persons depicted, and that even the more recent marriage shown in the upper register may have occurred well before the stone was carved.

We can interpret this elaborately carved slab as a monument that not only sanctifies the more recent couple's marriage, but also acts as a "genealogical register" (chapter 9) listing the names of past relatives. Assuming that it was found in the antechamber of a tomb sacked by looters, it would be interesting to know in whose tomb (out of all the people listed) it was placed.

Zapotec marriage alliances were used not only to solidify political relations on the local level, but also to improve diplomatic relations with other ethnic groups. For example, the *Relación de Teozapotlán* (Mata [1580] 1905) asserts that "more than 300 years" before the Spanish conquest, a Mixtec woman married a Zapotec lord from Zaachila; it also mentions a later marriage between a Mixtec lord of Yanhuitlán and the sister-in-law of the ruler of Zaachila. These interethnic marriages may have been part of a strategy that brought surplus labor from the Mixtec highlands into the Valley of Oaxaca to work the lands of the western valley, which were relatively underpopulated at that time (see comments by Blanton in Marcus and Flannery 1983:221).

Perhaps the most famous royal marriage alliance recorded in Zapotec ethnohistory, however, was the one used to resolve the Zapotec-Aztec military conflict of A.D. 1494–1495 (Marcus 1983m). During this conflict, the Aztec army under Ahuitzotl is said to have sacked Mitla and Zaachila in the Valley of Oaxaca, and eventually to have laid siege to the Zapotec fortress of Guiengola in the Isthmus of Tehuantepec (Gay 1881; Marcus 1983l:301–304). The Zapotec troops under Cociyoeza defended this fortress successfully, while their Mixtec allies, led by the *cacique* of Achiutla, attacked the Aztec from the opposite bank of the Río Tehuantepec. After a 7-month siege in tropical heat, ambassadors from both sides arranged for a truce cemented by the marriage of the Zapotec ruler Cociyoeza to the Aztec princess Coyolicatzin, daughter of Ahuitzotl. This marriage converted

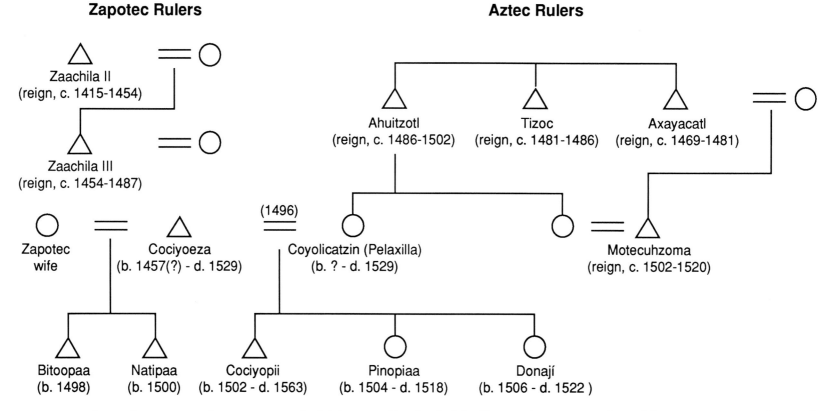

Zapotec Rulers

Zaachila II
(reign, c. 1415-1454)

Zaachila III
(reign, c. 1454-1487)

Zapotec
wife

Cociyoeza
(b. 1457(?) - d. 1529)

(1496)

Bitoopaa
(b. 1498)

Natipaa
(b. 1500)

Cociyopii
(b. 1502 - d. 1563)

Aztec Rulers

Ahuitzotl
(reign, c. 1486-1502)

Tizoc
(reign, c. 1481-1486)

Axayacatl
(reign, c. 1469-1481)

Coyolicatzin (Pelaxilla)
(b. ? - d. 1529)

Motecuhzoma
(reign, c. 1502-1520)

Pinopiaa
(b. 1504 - d. 1518)

Donají
(b. 1506 - d. 1522)

8.16. Diagram showing how one interethnic marriage alliance linked the Aztec and Zapotec royal houses in the fifteenth century A.D. To bring to an end the battle of Guiengola in the Isthmus of Tehuantepec, the Aztec ruler Ahuitzotl gave his daughter Coyolicatzin in marriage to the Zapotec ruler Cociyoeza. (Redrawn from Marcus 1983l: fig. 8.33.)

the highest-ranking lord of the Zapotec into a son-in-law of the Aztec emperor, thus ending hostilities (Fig. 8.16).

If we view this as a hypogamous marriage, it implies that the Aztec *tlatoani* outranked the Zapotec *coquitào*. This possibility is strengthened by the fact that Cociyoeza was succeeded on the throne not by his first-born son, but by his third son Cociyopii (A.D. 1502–1563), who was the offspring of his marriage to Coyolicatzin. Presumably because he was Ahuitzotl's grandson, Cociyopii seems to have reigned relatively untroubled by Aztec aggression (in contrast to his father, who had to fend off at least one assassination plot).

It is interesting that the marriage between Cociyoeza and Coyolicatzin, despite its political and military roots, was presented to the Zapotec people as a romantic love story. In one version (Gay 1881), Cociyoeza was said to have fallen in love with Coyolicatzin when he saw her bathing at the Charcos de la Marquesa, near Tehuantepec. This scenario recalls the "bathing scenes" in the Mixtec codices, when royal couples were shown bathing (Figs. 8.4–8.5). It is a further reminder that the emic portrayals of royal marriage in the monuments and codices might be quite different from the etic reality of political strategy.

Like the prehispanic Zapotec marriage stones and genealogical registers, which were intended to be read from bottom to top, the Zapotec marriage scenes and genealogical records painted in the years following the Spanish conquest were also read from bottom to top. For example, the Etla Genealogy, the Genealogy of Macuilxochitl, and the Yale Zapotec Genealogy are meant to be read this way (Whitecotton 1990). As we have noted elsewhere, some of the Mixtec codices also followed this pattern.

Each of the folios in the sixteenth-century Etla Genealogy shows an important "progenitor couple" in front of a structure that represents the founding of a lineage. Shown on the first folio, which bears a date of A.D. 1547, are the names of Etla's original or "founding lineage" ancestors— *Coqui Huedza Pillachi* ("Lord Creator 7 or 10 Lizard") and his wife *Xonaxi Quezayati Quecilaa* ("Princess White Flint Knife, 13 Wind or Reed") (Whitecotton 1990:51). Their son was *Pelao Piyobi Tonij* (shown in Fig. 8.17); *piyobi* refers to the fact that he was the first-born son (Córdova [1578b] 1886:213, Marcus 1983d:93). His wife's name is given at right as *Zayqueziña* (Fig. 8.17).

On the same folio, some of Pelao Piyobi Tonij's descendants are shown (see Fig. 8.18). His great-great-granddaughter was Quela Niça, 1 or 13 Water (*quela* = 1 or 13, *niça* =

8.17. During the sixteenth century A.D., the Etla Genealogy was painted in order to record the sequence of Zapotec nobles who had administered the Etla region of the Valley of Oaxaca. Noble progenitors, such as Pelao Piyobi Tonij and his wife Zayqueziña, are shown here in association with a temple or other structure. The Zapotec word *piyobi* means "first-born son." (Redrawn from Whitecotton 1990: fig. 3.2.)

8.18. In the Etla Genealogy, descendants of Pelao Piyobi Tonij and his wife Zayqueziña (see Fig. 8.17) are listed. Just like the Zapotec genealogical registers of A.D. 600 to 900, these genealogical records are meant to be read from bottom to top. Thus we see that Juan Lopa (lower left) married Quelaniça (lower right), and they had two offspring, a son and daughter. Their daughter, Anna, married Diego Hernández; their son, Thomás Méndez, married a woman named María. (Redrawn from Whitecotton 1990: fig. 3.4.)

8.19. Ancestors and descendants of Juan Lopa (see Fig. 8.18) are given in this sequence of married couples from the Etla Genealogy. Reading from bottom to top, we see the couple Texillai and y Lu; Juan Lopa and his wife Quelaniça; Diego Hernández and Anna Hernández; and finally Juan Pérez and Juana Pérez. As we move up in time, Zapotec personal names are replaced by baptismal names and Spanish surnames. (Redrawn from Whitecotton 1990: fig. 3.5.)

water), shown on the bottom at the right. She married a man baptized Juan Lopa by the Spaniards (shown at lower left). Their daughter, baptized Anna Hernández, is shown above them, connected to them by a black line. She married Diego Hernández (see White-cotton 1990 for discussion). They also had a son Thomás Méndez (shown to the right of his sister), who is shown facing his wife María Méndez.

A sequence of noble couples is also given on Folio 3 from the Etla Genealogy (see Fig. 8.19). All the husbands are shown at the left. Starting at the bottom, we see the couple Texillai and Y lu(?); they are the parents of Juan Lopa, who married Quelaniça. Above them is their daughter, Anna, who married Diego Hernández. Anna and Diego were the parents of Juan Pérez, who married Juana.

Although the Zapotec in the Etla arm of the Valley of Oaxaca adopted Spanish surnames during the sixteenth century, these surnames were not always passed along to their offspring. A similar pattern has been noted for Nahuatl speakers in colonial Culhuacán (S. Cline 1986:117–119). Interestingly, two of the prominent surnames in the Etla Genealogy—Hernández and Méndez—remain two of the dominant surnames in the Etla region today.

Like those of the Aztec and Mixtec, Zapotec noble marriages were designed to meet a variety of political and social needs, including the opportunity to gain strategic military and trading alliances. Arranged marriages could also ensure access to desired titles, lands, manpower, and tribute-payers. Clearly influencing the choice of a mate for the Zapotec noble was birth order. For example, marriage patterns during the earliest generations recorded in the Etla Genealogy suggest that first-born sons took first-born daughters as their wives, and that those women took the surnames of their husbands (Whitecotton 1990:54). Interethnic marriage alliances—linking Mixtec and Zapotec nobles—are revealed in the Genealogy of Macuilxochitl, which records fifteen generations, thirteen of them prior to the Spanish conquest (Whitecotton 1990). At the time of that conquest, some "Zapotec" nobles in the Valley of Oaxaca were actually the offspring of marriage alliances that had united the Zapotec with the Aztec and Mixtec (Marcus 1983l).

MAYA ROYAL MARRIAGES

Like the Mixtec, the Maya had a rich variety of expressions associated with marriage, many of them metaphoric. Expressions for "wedding" include *ok was* ("a handful of tamales"), *k'am nikte'* ("a communion of flowers"), and *machk'abil* ("to hold another's hand").

Some Classic Maya hieroglyphs can even be read as "wife" because they are based on the word *atan*, "married woman" (as in *atankil*, "to take a wife"). Two examples of hieroglyphs for *atan* are shown in Figure 8.20; one (at the top) is from the seventh century

8.20. Two examples of a Maya hieroglyphic sign that can be read *ya-tan*, "his wife." The upper example is from a seventh-century A.D. text and the lower example is from the thirteenth century A.D. (Redrawn from Bricker 1986:5 and Lounsbury 1984: fig. 10.)

A.D. and the other (at the bottom) is from the thirteenth century. Phonetically, each hieroglyphic compound can be read as *ya-tan(na)*, or *y-atan* ("his wife"). The prefix supplies the possessive "his" (*y[a]*); the main sign can be read as "wife" (*tan*); and the subfix serves to reinforce the final "n" sound, since it can be read as "*na*" (Berlin 1968a:19; Dütting 1970:204; Marcus 1974b, 1976a: fig. 1.2d; Lounsbury 1984: fig. 10e; Bricker 1986:5).

Royal marriage alliances were very important links between cities for the Classic Maya. Although there were isogamous marriages linking royal men to women of equal rank, many of the marriages considered worth commemorating in stone were hypogamous. Like the Aztec royal marriage alliances which linked Tenochtitlán with local lords at its dependencies, Maya royal marriages also linked the dynasties at regional capitals with local dynasties at secondary-level centers (Marcus 1973). Since we can often identify the names of hypogamous brides and their birthplaces, we are in a position to document intersite, as well as interdynastic, marriage alliances (Marcus 1973, 1976a).

Hypogamous Marriages

To ensure loyalty and achieve regional integration, rulers residing at the regional capitals sent their royal daughters, sisters, or other close female relatives to marry local lords at dependent centers.

Figure 8.21 gives an example of a hypogamous marriage. In this case, a royal woman from the regional capital of Tikal was united with a local lord at the dependency of Naranjo. Their offspring, named Scroll Squirrel, went on to become an important Naranjo ruler who attained far greater prominence than his father, partly as a result of his mother's ties to the Tikal royal dynasty (Marcus 1973:914). Apparently as a result of this important marriage alliance between a Tikal woman and the Naranjo lord, the site of Naranjo acquired its own emblem glyph and was elevated from tertiary level to secondary level in the administrative hierarchy.

We know that the Tikal dynasty was the highest-ranked in the region, so it is not surprising that all of Scroll Squirrel's monuments emphasize his relationship to his mother, a member of that dynasty. What *is* somewhat surprising is the fact that the name of Scroll Squirrel's father is not displayed at all on his son's monuments. Not only do Scroll Squirrel's monuments mention his mother, they also supply the names of his maternal grandparents. By mentioning those names, he can link himself directly to the royal dynasty of Tikal (Marcus 1973).

Scroll Squirrel's mother—Lady 6 Sky of Tikal—apparently arrived at Naranjo at a very young age (perhaps 11–14 years), presumably already promised to the local lord. They were eventually married, and a few years later, on January 6, A.D. 688, she gave birth to Scroll Squirrel. Lady 6 Sky's father should have been about the same age as the

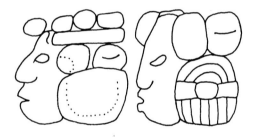

8.21. At the Maya site of Naranjo in Guatemala, an important series of stone monuments records information on a royal woman from Tikal. Her name ("Lady 6 Sky of Tikal") includes a postfix of the number 6, and ends with the Tikal emblem glyph. She is featured on her son's monuments because her bloodlines were bluer than those of his father, whose name remains unknown. (Redrawn from Marcus 1976a: fig. 5.7.)

251

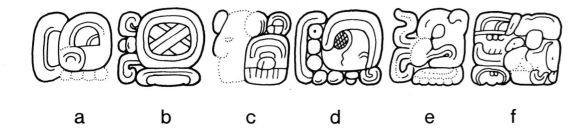

a   b   c   d   e   f

8.22. A Maya text from the site of Naranjo, Guatemala, recording the marriage of Scroll Squirrel (the son of "Lady 6 Sky of Tikal") with yet another woman from Tikal. At *a* is a "relationship" glyph; at *b*, the sign meaning "his wife"; at *c*, "woman of Tikal"; at *d*, the sign *u caban* (meaning "his land," "his people"); at *e*, "Scroll Squirrel"; and at *f*, the title *caan-na* or "sky lord" (of Naranjo). Since both his mother's marriage and his own were hypogamous, both marriages were featured in his monuments. (Drawn from a photograph of Stela 23 at Naranjo.)

then-reigning Tikal ruler "Double-Comb" (Jones 1977; Marcus 1974b; 1976a:167); in fact Double-Comb may have been her uncle or cousin (Closs 1985). Another important relative of hers was a ruler from the Dos Pilas dynasty, who apparently had been installed there by a Tikal ruler (Marcus 1976a).

Not only did Scroll Squirrel have a mother from Tikal, it also appears that he himself eventually married a woman from Tikal, thereby reconfirming the allegiance to Tikal initially established by his mother's marriage. The text that records Scroll Squirrel's marriage to a woman from Tikal is given on Stela 23 of Naranjo (Fig. 8.22).

Another apparent example of hypogamy involves a royal woman sent out from the regional capital of Calakmul to marry a local lord at the site of El Perú. This royal Calakmul woman was depicted on a stela set up at El Perú; that stela was paired with one depicting her husband (J. H. Miller 1974; Marcus 1976a: frontispiece; 1987: fig. 50). This pairing of stelae displaying a married couple, and the simultaneous dedication of the monuments, was a common pattern at Calakmul (Marcus 1987:135–147). In this case, the two stelae were dedicated in A.D. 692 and depict husband and wife facing each other.

In Figure 8.23 we see the stela depicting the elaborately attired El Perú husband, whose name was "Lord Jaguar"; a possible marriage bundle appears near his left foot. The Calakmul woman, like her husband, is elaborately attired, carrying a shield in her left hand and serpent staff in her right (Fig. 8.24). Her name is given in two places—in the two cartouches incorporated into her headdress, and in the text below her shield. Because she was from Calakmul and wished to show her close association with the ruling dynasty there, her stela refers to the accession of the Calakmul ruler "Jaguar Paw," who took office on April 6, A.D. 686. This Calakmul ruler may have been her brother.

A hypogamous marriage also linked the cities of Yaxchilán and Bonampak (Marcus 1974b, 1976a). A woman from the regional capital of Yaxchilán went to the dependency of Bonampak to marry the local lord (Fig. 8.25); she appears in stone monuments and inscriptions only at that dependency. Her name and title are given on Bonampak's Stela 2 (Fig. 8.26) and in the mural in Room 2 of the palace (Marcus 1976a:176–177). (In the Room 2 mural scene her name is abbreviated to what might almost be considered a label,

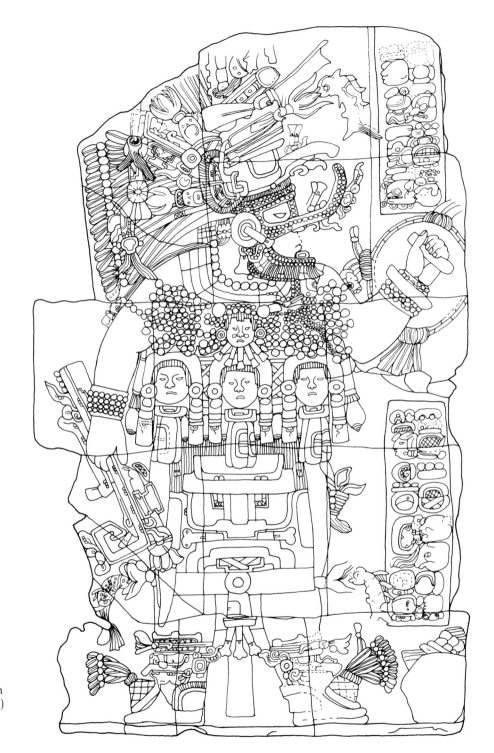

8.23. This magnificently attired ruler from a stela at the secondary site of El Perú, northern Guatemala, was involved in a hypogamous marriage. His wife was from the primary center of Calakmul (see Fig. 8.24), and their paired monuments were dedicated in A.D. 692. (Redrawn from J. Miller 1974: fig. 6; Marcus 1987: fig. 49.)

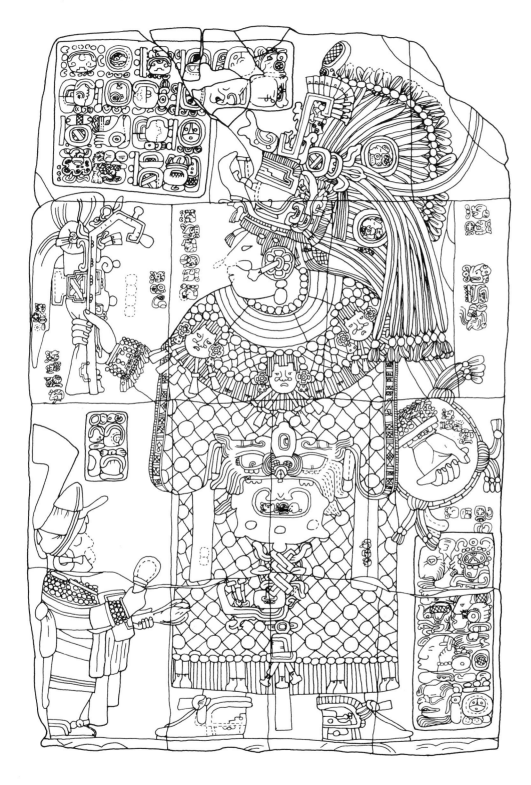

8.24. This royal Calakmul woman faces her husband from El Perú, who is depicted in Figure 8.23. Her name is given in the cartouches embedded in the feathers of her headdress, and repeated in the text next to her left leg. In the main text she mentions the accession to the throne of "Jaguar Paw," the current Calakmul ruler, who may have been her brother. (Redrawn from J. Miller 1974: fig. 2 and Marcus 1987: fig. 50.)

8.25. Another example of a Maya hypogamous marriage. In this case, a royal woman from the major center of Yaxchilán married the local ruler at Bonampak, one of Yaxchilán's dependencies. Here we see the feminine head glyph followed by the Yaxchilán emblem glyph, a compound that means "Woman from Yaxchilán." (Redrawn from Marcus 1976a: fig. 5.7.)

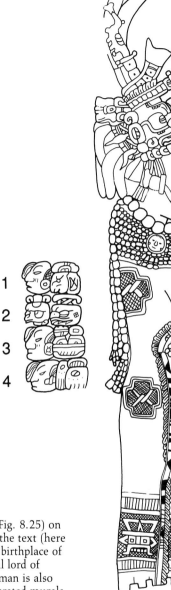

8.26. A depiction of the "Woman from Yaxchilán" (see Fig. 8.25) on Stela 2 at Bonampak. Her names and titles are given in the text (here shown behind her back); note that line 3 designates her birthplace of Yaxchilán. Her eighth-century A.D. marriage to the local lord of Bonampak elevated the status of the latter site. This woman is also depicted (and identified by name) in Room 2 of the celebrated murals of Bonampak, where she is shown as one of the witnesses to an arraignment of prisoners, following a battle in which Yaxchilán and Bonampak fought against a common enemy. (Redrawn from Mathews 1980: fig. 2.)

probably to be read as "*Ix* Yaxchilán" or "Woman from Yaxchilán.") The woman's husband, Chaan-Muan ("Sky-Bird"), is also depicted in both localities.

The text on Stela 2 at Bonampak also records the accession of "Sky-Bird" to the throne, which took place on 9.17.5.8.9 (6 Muluc 17 Yaxkin), a date that can be placed in A.D. 775 (Mathews 1980:61). His wife holds a vessel that may contain papers used in a bloodletting rite associated with his inauguration. This hypogamous woman may have been the sister of the Yaxchilán ruler called "Shield-Jaguar's Descendant."

Isogamous Marriages

Isogamous marriages were recorded, but not as frequently as hypogamous ones. They were sometimes used to link communities and dynasties on the same hierarchical level, that is, capitals with capitals, or secondary centers with secondary centers. For example, in the region of the so-called "Petexbatún Confederacy" it appears that isogamous marriages were combined with military alliances to effect a confederation of relatively equal secondary centers, who then were able to co-administer a larger polity (Marcus 1974b).

Some royal wives at Maya capitals seem to be from the capital itself (Fig. 8.27). In such cases, it was unnecessary to give their birthplaces or label them "Woman from _____." For example, some royal women at the capitals of Tikal, Palenque, and other major sites carry the emblem glyph of the capital, or are known only from their personal names, which do not include emblem glyphs.

A possible isogamous marriage linking Calakmul with Yaxchilán took place sometime between A.D. 705 and 708, involving a Calakmul woman and a Yaxchilán ruler (Schele and Freidel 1990:269). Shield Jaguar, ruler of Yaxchilán from A.D. 681–742, took as his second wife a woman who linked him directly to the powerful Calakmul dynasty (Fig. 8.28). Their offspring was the famous Bird Jaguar of Yaxchilán, who was born in A.D. 709. In A.D. 752, Bird Jaguar took office and ultimately went on to become a very powerful ruler, reported to have taken many captives and made many conquests (Proskouriakoff 1964). At the time of his mother's marriage to his father, however, I believe that that

a   b

8.27. The royal woman "Lady White Parrot of Palenque" is shown on both ends of the stone sarcophagus beneath the Temple of the Inscriptions at Palenque. She was evidently the mother of Lord Shield (Pacal), the ruler buried there. Note that her name (the top glyph in *a* and *b*) is followed by different variants of the Palenque emblem glyph (the lower glyph in *a* and *b*). (Redrawn from Ruz Lhuillier 1958; Marcus 1976a: fig. 4.27.)

8.28. The Maya text describing a royal Calakmul woman, commemorated at Yaxchilán after she became one of the wives of the Yaxchilán ruler. Although this may have been another hypogamous marriage, there are reasons for suspecting that it may actually have been an isogamous marriage. (Redrawn from Schele and Freidel 1990:269.)

particular marriage could have been considered isogamous, linking two roughly equal regional capitals.

Another possible isogamous marriage linked Copán and Palenque. The fifteenth ruler of Copán took office on February 18, A.D. 749. This ruler apparently took as his wife a woman from Palenque. On Stela 8 at Copán, the offspring of this marriage—Yax "Sun-at-Horizon"—mentions his mother from Palenque (Morley 1920: plate 32; Marcus 1976a). The occasion that prompted such mention of his mother's birthplace was his own accession to the throne on July 2, A.D. 763, when he became the sixteenth ruler of Copán (see Figs. 8.29, 8.30).

Sixteenth-Century Noble Marriages

Noble marriage alliances continued among the Postclassic and early Colonial Maya, but were recorded on cloth or paper rather than on stone monuments. It is very clear that marriage alliances linking nobles were still so important that Maya nobles did not follow the same marriage pattern as commoners.

For example, Roys (1965:667) notes that while it was rare for Yucatec Maya with the same patronymic (father's lineage name) to marry, there were exceptions among the nobility. For example, in A.D. 1557 the town of Calotmul was ruled by Ah Kukil Xiu. His daughter (baptized María Xiu by the Spaniards), under normal circumstances, would not have married anyone with the patronymic Xiu. However, to consolidate power she married Francisco de Montejo Xiu, the territorial ruler of Mani.

In Figure 8.31 we illustrate the Xiu Family Tree as given in the Mani Land Treaty (Roys 1943:73). The Xiu Family Tree shows that the founders of the family were Hun Uitzil Chac Tutul Xiu and his wife Ix (?) Ticul, a woman from the town of Ticul (Roys 1943:73). From the Xiu Family Tree we know that the first son of Ah Mochan Xiu[1] was Na-Cahun Xiu, and that the names of his younger brothers were Ah Ciyah Xiu, Ah Kukil Xiu, and Ah Cuate Xiu. In this case, only the first-born son had the prefix "*Na-*" added to his matronymic. Following matrimony the new husband gained the right to use his matronymic, to which the prefix "*Na-*" was added. Such a matronymic was his *naal* name (his mother's matronymic) and it always preceded his patronymic. An example would be the famous ruler of Mayapán, Nachi Cocom; his *naal* name, or matronymic, was "Chi," then followed by "Cocom," his patronymic (see chapter 7 and Roys 1940, 1943).

---

[1] *Ah Mochan Xiu is a composite name meaning "He of the Parrot-Snake and Plant"* [*Ah* = he; *Mo* = parrot; *chan* = snake, serpent; *Xiu* = from the Nahuatl word *xiuitl* meaning plant].

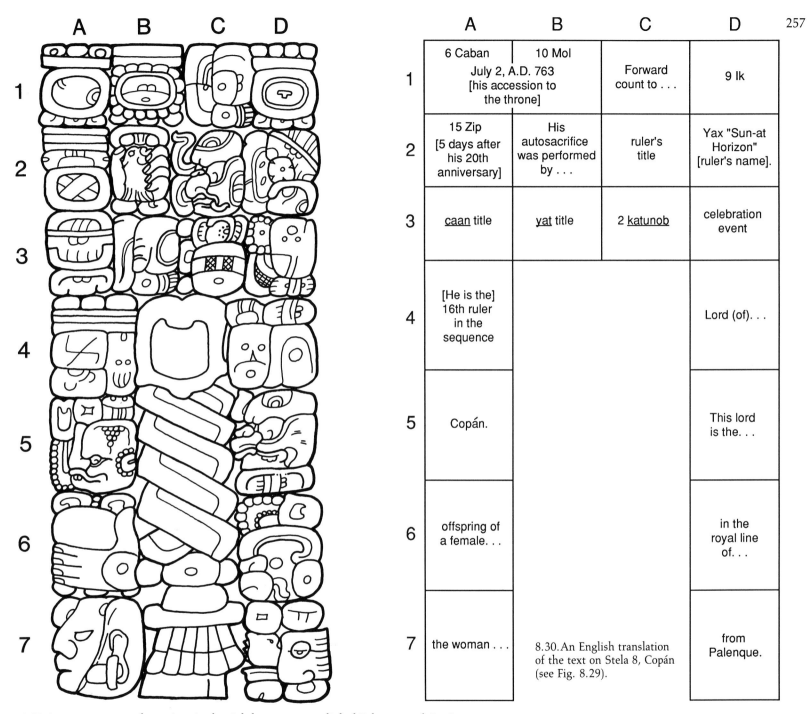

	A	B	C	D
1	6 Caban July 2, A.D. 763 [his accession to the throne]	10 Mol	Forward count to . . .	9 Ik
2	15 Zip [5 days after his 20th anniversary]	His autosacrifice was performed by . . .	ruler's title	Yax "Sun-at Horizon" [ruler's name].
3	caan title	yat title	2 katunob	celebration event
4	[He is the] 16th ruler in the sequence			Lord (of). . .
5	Copán.			This lord is the. . .
6	offspring of a female. . .			in the royal line of. . .
7	the woman . . .	8.30. An English translation of the text on Stela 8, Copán (see Fig. 8.29).		from Palenque.

8.29. An isogamous royal marriage in the eighth century A.D. linked Palenque and Copán.
Here, on Stela 8, the sixteenth Copán ruler (Yax "Sun-at-Horizon") refers to his mother as
the "Woman of Palenque." He features his mother's (not his father's) royal heritage and
birthplace on this monument, which marked the 20th anniversary of his accession to the
throne. (Redrawn from Morley 1920: plate 32; Schele and Freidel 1990:331.)

8.31. The genealogical tree of the Xiu dynasty of northern Yucatán, as drawn in the sixteenth century following the Spanish conquest. The founder of the Xiu lineage is shown at the bottom; rising from his loins is a tree on whose branches are circles containing the names of his descendants. (Adapted from Morley and Brainerd 1956: plate 22.)

Royal marriage alliances played an essential role in the overall political and economic strategies of the Aztec, Mixtec, Zapotec, and Maya. These marriages were arranged to achieve truces in warfare, to cement alliances between equals, and to ensure the loyalty of dependencies to capitals. Such marriage alliances can be detected as early as the stone monuments of the Classic period among the Zapotec and Maya; they continued to be recorded in Postclassic codices among the Mixtec and Aztec, and in the manuscripts of all four groups during the sixteenth and seventeenth centuries.

When we look at how such marriages were recorded in writing, where such marriages were commemorated, and in what frequency, we can see some interesting patterns. As we noted, there are three possible types of noble marriage: isogamous, hypogamous, and hypergamous. While we can assume that all three types were reasonably common, we now know that hypogamous marriages were the most likely to be recorded in monuments or codices, that isogamous marriages were less likely to be recorded, and that hypergamous unions were the least likely to be recorded.

Isogamous marriages, in which both spouses were of equal rank, are most often shown linking secondary centers to other secondary centers. However, as noted above, such isogamous marriage alliances could also link capitals.

Hypogamous marriages, in which the woman was of higher rank, were often used to link regional capitals to secondary centers. Royal women left the capital to marry a lesser lord at a secondary center, raising the status of that center; they also raised the status of the lesser lord's subsequent offspring, who usually (not surprisingly) went on to become the next ruler. Often, these hypogamous marriages were first mentioned long after they had taken place; the event prompting that mention was often the accession to the throne of the resultant offspring. Significantly, it was the secondary center receiving the hypogamous bride that was most likely to record that fact in writing; the donor site rarely deemed it worthwhile even to record the giving of the bride.

We know that hypergamous marriages, in which the groom outranked the bride, must have been much more common than the inscriptions and documents suggest, especially since polygyny was common. Yet much less effort was spent by scribes in recording hypergamous marriages. This is a further warning that Mesoamerica's epigraphic record is not an impartial, unbiased historical account of what happened, and how often it happened. Certain kinds of marriages were stressed for political and cultural reasons, while others went virtually unmentioned. As suggested in the introduction to this chapter, it seems evident that many of the marriages recorded in monuments or codices were the ones which politically benefited the *groom* and his *male offspring*. This is logical, since prehispanic writing was essentially in the hands of noble males and their scribes. Royal women were usually featured only when they were of higher rank—members of a royal dynasty through which their male offspring could claim special advantages.

9 ✦ EUHEMERISM AND ROYAL ANCESTORS

Sometime around 300 B.C., intrigued by the pantheon of gods his people worshiped, a Greek writer named Euhemerus presented an interesting explanation for the emergence of polytheistic mythology in general and Greek mythology in particular. He argued that the multitude of gods had arisen from the deification of dead heroes. This concept, named for its originator, is today known as euhemerism.

Euhemerism seeks to explain the origins of myth and the deities who populate it by tracing their development from real events and historical personages. Extraordinary men become folk heroes; some folk heroes become deified ancestors; some deified ancestors become more abstract deities.

While this framework may not explain all known pantheistic religions, it makes the important point that many pantheons grow by accretion. This was certainly true of the Aztec, who incorporated into their own pantheon the gods of the ethnic groups they conquered (van Zantwijk 1985). That fact should serve as a warning to those who try to trace the whole set of sixteenth-century Aztec deities out of earlier religions, such as that of Teotihuacán, or even out of Early Formative iconography (e.g., Covarrubias 1942, 1946).

In many societies, including those of Mesoamerica, the ancestors were important in religion and mythology (Marcus 1978). That was probably already true of the egalitarian societies of 1500—1000 B.C., and was certainly true of the ranked societies of the period 1000–500 B.C. (Flannery and Marcus 1976; Marcus 1989a). Ethnographic examples abound; among the Bwamba of Africa, for example, genealogical records may be telescoped or manipulated in order to provide certain individuals with rights or privileges based on their ancestors (E. Winter 1955).

With the emergence of stratification and the state, the ancestors of many elites were elevated from folk heroes to deified ancestors or actual deities, who could be communicated with only through their noble descendants or through full-time religious specialists. Divine descent depended on the ability of current rulers to present convincing links to supernatural ancestors.

In one of Mesoamerica's best-known examples, it appears that a Toltec ruler named Ce Acatl (One Reed) Topiltzin first took on the name of the deity Quetzalcoatl ("Feathered Serpent"), and then in later Nahua mythology virtually "became" Quetzalcoatl himself (Nicholson 1957, D. Carrasco 1982).

In the societies of Early Formative Mesoamerica, it is likely that everyone's ancestors were important; each household honored its own. As ranking gave way to stratification, however, the official state myth was that commoners had descended from other commoners, while rulers and nobles had descended from supernatural beings. By the Classic period, or after ca. A.D. 100–200, only the ancestors of nobles were important enough to be depicted in state art.

Mesoamerican elites used their divine ancestors as rationalization for the right to rule, as justification for a whole series of privileges not shared by commoners, and as explanation for skills (such as oratorical ability or literacy) that were in fact taught in special schools for young nobles.

Once the divinity of their ancestors was expressed in writing, it became both a boon and a danger to the ruling class. It was a boon because written texts were controlled by nobles and could be brought out to reaffirm "true history," showing how things "had always been." It was a potential danger because earlier records might contradict the current regime's version of history. In chapter 5 and elsewhere, we have already noted the ways in which history might be rewritten when necessary.

Propaganda Devices

In this chapter we sample data on the divinity of royal ancestors from the Aztec, Mixtec, Zapotec, and Maya. We will see that these societies implemented a number of propaganda devices to place their ancestors in the desired position.

One device was to establish kin relations between earthly nobles and the world's most important supernatural forces. While the elites were thought to have *no* kin ties to the commoner stratum, they often referred to gods or supernatural forces as "our mothers and fathers." Rulers invoked the names of at least three types of ancestors: (1) *near ancestors*, whose names and lives were easily known and remembered; (2) *distant ancestors*, whose lives were known only from oral sagas or the written record, and who were reported to have been descended from the gods; and (3) *mythical ancestors*, who were supernatural beings or natural forces that combined to give life to the distant ancestors.

A second device was to place the births and deeds of distant or mythical ancestors so far into the past that they exceeded society's collective memory. For example, the Mixtec began their "histories" at a time before the first humans had calendric names, and indeed before the calendar even existed (Caso 1950, 1977, 1979). As for the Aztec, Chimalpahin began their "history" in A.D. 50 (corresponding to the year 1 Rabbit) when the Aztec were said to have been living in their legendary homeland of Aztlán. In fact, A.D. 50 falls in the Protoclassic period (Fig. 1.1), a time when it is very unlikely that the Aztec even existed as a cultural or linguistic entity. Such a date was probably chosen because it was exactly 20 "bundles" of 52-year cycles (1,040 years) earlier than A.D. 1090, another year called 1 Rabbit, which is the date when Aztec legend says that their exodus from Aztlán began.

Be that as it may, the Aztec and Mixtec propagandists pale by comparison with the Maya (see below), who used their Long Count dating system to place some legendary events over half a billion years into the past!

There were several reasons why such mythological dates were carved in stone. One aim was to show that from time immemorial the world, the social order, and the gulf between nobles and commoners had remained the same. In other words, while social scientists believe that the state evolved, the Maya wished to show that it had always existed.

A second aim might have been to show that a particular ruler had been born, or acceded to the throne, on the exact anniversary of a similar event involving some mythical ancestor who lived thousands of years ago. As I will suggest in chapter 10, such claims might be even more strident when the ruler was a usurper, rather than someone in the direct line of succession.

A third propaganda device used by Mesoamerican peoples was to set significant events in the heavens, giving the nobility the proper celestial backdrop needed to emphasize their divine ancestry. Such a device has sometimes been called a "heavenly prologue" to a royal text or dynastic record (Caso 1949, 1950, 1977, 1979).

Still a fourth device, one that may go back as far as the iconography of the Formative period, was to depict deified ancestors by combining the attributes of powerful animals or great natural forces with those of men. An example would be the close association of Zapotec royalty with Cociyo, or "Lightning." Since such a powerful force (natural to us, but supernatural to the Zapotec) had existed from time immemorial, it reinforced the ruler's immortality.

Finally, a fifth device was the "performative reaffirmation rituals" often depicted in monumental art. These were rites which, when properly performed by members of the royal family, established communication between the living ruler and his divine ancestors. Such rituals included (1) invoking the name of the ancestor; (2) addressing the inner spirit or "life force" of the deceased; (3) offering royal blood which was flowing or "moving" (and thus still alive); and (4) burning copal (incense) to produce a long column of smoke, which was thought to turn into a sacred serpent in whose mouth the revered ancestor reappeared.

Among the Maya, this set of ritual activities constituted a "package" to be performed on certain anniversaries, such as on an ancestor's death, the birth of an heir, or a ruler's inauguration. It is unfortunate that the offering of noble or royal blood has been taken out of its social and political context by some epigraphers, whose own fascination with this act has led them to the conclusion that the Maya were "obsessed with bloodletting." This view seems somewhat ethnocentric. After all, no one considers the millions of Christians who drink a glass of wine, symbolic of the blood of Christ, to be "obsessed with blood," even if they drink it on every anniversary of his death. Our data suggest that royal Maya women performed their bloodletting far less often, on days corresponding to the fifth, tenth, or even twentieth anniversary of important events.

AZTEC ROYAL ANCESTORS

Mesoamerica's Nahuatl speakers have given us one of our best-known examples of euhemerism: the case of Quetzalcoatl. While all the details are surely not known, a Toltec ruler named 1 Reed (Ce Acatl) seems to have become a folk hero, then a deified ancestor, and finally merged with the divine feathered serpent, Quetzalcoatl (see Nicholson 1957, López Austin 1973, D. Carrasco 1982). A still unanswered question remains—How many members of the Aztec "pantheon" might actually have started out, far back in time, as human rulers?

In our discussion of Aztec royal ancestors, we will touch on four principal themes: (1) the "borrowing" of distinguished ancestors to legitimize and sanctify one's right to rule; (2) the use of a "kinship model" to link humans to the rest of the animal world, as well as the supernatural; (3) the way metamorphosis enabled dead humans to live on as flying creatures; and (4) the way priests served as mediators between living humans and their ancestors, communicating to the latter the needs of the former.

The "Borrowing" of Ancestors

Van Zantwijk (1985:177ff) has coined the expression "borrowing of ancestors" to describe how some Aztec rulers acquired the ancestors they needed to establish their legitimacy. Key to this process was the modification of codices on deer hide or paper. One example of this process is believed to have taken place just after A.D. 1427, when Itzcoatl, Nezahualcoyotl, Tlacaelel, and Motecuhzoma Ilhuicamina became dominant figures in a rebellion.

Following the death in A.D. 1426 of Tezozomoc (ruler of the Tepanec ethnic group and the town of Azcapotzalco), there were profound conflicts among ethnic groups in the Basin of Mexico. One of these conflicts involved the Mexica ethnic group, who felt they had been mistreated by the Tepaneca.

Prior to his death, Tezozomoc was called upon to select his successor from among his several sons, and he designated Quetzalayatzin (Tayauh). Another son, Maxtla, angry at being passed over, was successful in usurping the throne. He then continued the Tepanec mistreatment of the Mexica, imposing even heavier tribute demands on them.

The Mexica ruler at that time was Chimalpopoca. Chimalpopoca threw his support behind Quetzalayatzin, advising him to kill the usurper Maxtla. According to one account, a loyal dwarf from Maxtla's court overheard the plot against his master; after having been forewarned, Maxtla was able to eliminate both Chimalpopoca and Quetzalayatzin. Some accounts assert that Chimalpopoca committed suicide to avoid being murdered by Maxtla; still other versions have Chimalpopoca's successor, Itzcoatl, killing Chimalpopoca (C. N. Davies 1973, 1980).

Once in office, Itzcoatl was advised by two men, Motecuhzoma Ilhuicamina (who was to become his successor) and Motecuhzoma's younger brother, Tlacaelel. In some accounts, Tlacaelel played the major role in subsequent events, and is reported to have led Tenochtitlán—now allied with the Texcocans and their ruler, Nezahualcoyotl—against Azcapotzalco in a four-year war. Tlacaelel announced that all those who fought with him would be elevated in status if victorious. This new reward policy of Tlacaelel's meant a significant change: from that time on, the Aztec political and social hierarchy would not be based exclusively on descent, but would also take military achievement into account (van Zantwijk 1985:110).

Following the Mexica's victory over Azcapotzalco, Itzcoatl continued as ruler of Tenochtitlán. His adviser Tlacaelel acquired the title of *tlacochcalcatl* ("Lord of the House of the Darts"), and eventually became *cihuacoatl* ("Snake Woman"), principal adviser to Itzcoatl. Motecuhzoma Ilhuicamina became *tlacateccatl*, a high military officer equivalent to a general of the Aztec army; Nezahualcoyotl continued as ruler of the town of Texcoco and of the Acolhua ethnic group. All four men became members of the Imperial Council of Tenochtitlán. Seventeen other lords who had helped Itzcoatl in the war also received new titles, and lands were distributed to those who had been prominent in the victory.

Three of the four leaders—Itzcoatl, Tlacaelel, and Motecuhzoma Ilhuicamina—lacked the noble ancestors required by traditional Toltec rules to establish legitimate right to their offices. (Itzcoatl, for example, was the son of Acamapichtli and a "pretty slave girl" from Azcapotzalco [Corona Núñez 1964, 1:68], and therefore not descended from royalty on both sides). Although all four men supported the policy of reviving Toltec institutions, they also wanted to *exclude* all the descendants of Chimalpopoca (the recently deceased ruler), who were, in fact, the legitimate and direct heirs to the offices they held. The exclusion of Chimalpopoca's heirs from those offices was one of the motivations for burning the old Nahua books and records, and then for rewriting history (van Zantwijk 1985:19).

Toltec tradition required that "internal" rulers who administered domestic affairs— those who were to serve as *cihuacoatl*—must be able to trace their descent from the highest-ranked families through both their mother's and father's lines. The "external" ruler or *tlatoani*, who handled foreign relations, had to be related to the traditional line of rulers on one side (preferably his father's) and to prominent families in other communities on the other side (usually his mother's). This separation of powers set up the ideal division of labor, with the *cihuacoatl* administering affairs of the city and the *tlatoani* guiding the foreign policy of the expanding Aztec empire. In practice, however, this division of labor in policy and decision making was evidently not rigidly followed.

The benefits of having Tenochtitlán's *tlatoani* related to ruling families in neighboring city-states were many. The loyalty and cooperation of relatives could be counted on with greater confidence, and relatives would be less likely to withdraw from alliances that were mutually beneficial. Relatives of the *tlatoani* would have a vested interest in sustaining him in power, whether they were members of the same ethnic group or not.

In order to exclude the descendants of Chimalpopoca from office, a special plan of reform was required, and it began with the destruction of past genealogies and historical records that would have aided his descendants. The Florentine Codex describes how the burning was justified:

> The history of it [the Mexica and others] was saved, but it was burned when Itzcoatl ruled in Mexico. A council [meeting] of rulers of Mexico took place. They said: "It is not necessary for all the common people to know of the writings; government will be defamed, and this will only spread sorcery in the land; for it containeth many falsehoods." (Dibble and Anderson 1961:191; León Portilla 1961:90–91)

The burning of the ancient codices was also thought necessary because the Mexica ethnic group was not featured in any of them. To justify their right to dominate other ethnic groups, Itzcoatl and Tlacaelel had to create a fictional "glorious past" for the Mexica. The newly commissioned codices would feature the Mexica's pilgrimages, during which they established themselves as a "chosen people" who had the sacred right to rule, to conquer, to take captives, and to collect tribute from other peoples.

One of the "reforms" was a new requirement that exceptional military prowess would now be considered a prerequisite for access to the highest offices. Another change was that proof of community service would now be required (Clark 1938: folio 64–65; López Austin 1961:57; van Zantwijk 1985:113). Itzcoatl, Tlacaelel, Motecuhzoma Ilhuicamina, and Nezahualcoyotl could all demonstrate that they had done the required military and community service. Chimalpopoca's heirs, however, could be excluded on these grounds.

The second step in the rewriting of history was for the new Mexica rulers to "borrow" ancestors they had never had. How this was done by Itzcoatl is nicely shown in Figure 9.1, on a page from the Codex Telleriano-Remensis (Corona Núñez 1964, 1: Lámina V). This codex is thought to have been written in the Valley of Mexico sometime between

Chimalpopoca.

Itzcohuátl

1424 1425 1426 1427 1428 1429 1430 1431 1432 1433 1434 1435 1436 1437 1438 1439

9.1. The Aztec ruler Chimalpopoca was apparently assassinated by the Tepaneca of Azcapotzalco. According to the Codex Telleriano-Remensis, Chimalpopoca died in A.D. 1426, the Aztec year designated 12 Rabbit; here we see that date linked to the back of Chimalpopoca's throne by a black line. (According to another source, the Codex Mendoza, Chimalpopoca's death took place in 1427.) Chimalpopoca is shown as a mummy bundle on a woven mat throne; above his head is his hieroglyphic name (smoke + shield). A line connects the throne of Chimalpopoca to the throne occupied by Itzcoatl. Itzcoatl's father was Acamapichtli (not Chimalpopoca), and his mother was allegedly a slave girl from Azcapotzalco. The selection of Itzcoatl as the next Mexica ruler met with approval by the ruler of Texcoco, since the latter was married to Itzcoatl's sister, and his son (Nezahualcoyotl) had fought alongside Itzcoatl in their victories over Azcapotzalco and Tlatelolco. The defeated rulers of Azcapotzalco and Tlatelolco are shown in front of a temple to the right of Chimalpopoca, carrying shields and broadswords. (Even though they appear near Chimalpopoca, Itzcoatl was actually the victor in the battle against them.) (Redrawn from the Codex Telleriano-Remensis in Corona Núñez 1964, 2:269, Lámina V.)

1562 and 1563, on European paper; it is also believed to be a copy or synthesis from the lost Codex Huitzilopochtli (Glass and Robertson 1975).

In Figure 9.1 we see the dead ruler Chimalpopoca. We know that he is dead because he is shown as a mummy bundle tied up with cord. The hieroglyphs for his nickname, "Smoking Shield," are linked to his head by a line. Another line (behind the throne) links him to the hieroglyph for the year 12 Rabbit (A.D. 1426), the date of his death. Another line or cord leads from Chimalpopoca's royal mat throne, or *tlatoca icpalli,* to the mat throne of his successor, Itzcoatl. Itzcoatl's nickname, "Obsidian-backed Serpent," is given in a hieroglyphic sign linked to his head by a line.

Now, we have already seen that Itzcoatl was the offspring of Acamapichtli and a slave girl. Yet in this codex, Itzcoatl chose to link himself to Chimalpopoca by a line or cord (*mecatl*), which is the way Aztec scribes indicated continuity or *mecayotl,* "kinship." (Royal blood lines were expressed by the word *mecayotl,* derived from *mecatl,* "cord," and *yotl,* a suffix for abstract nouns.) Thus Itzcoatl "borrowed" Chimalpopoca as his ancestor in order to hide both his lack of proper ancestry and the fact that he was a usurper.

Also shown in Figure 9.1 (on the right) are the figures of Maxtla of Azcapotzalco, standing with a broadsword in his right hand and a shield in his left. He stands at the base of a temple. Maxtla's name sign ("Tied or Knotted Loincloth") is attached to his head by a short line. Behind Maxtla is Tlacateutl, ruler of Tlatelolco, who also carries weapons for fighting. His name sign consists of a sun disk above the sign for stone. The sun disk stands for "day," *tlaca(tli),* and provides the first part of his name; the second part, "lord" (*tecuhtli*), is indicated by the sign for "stone," *tetl.* The Mexica scribes wanted to show that Itzcoatl had defeated these two allied rulers from Azcapotzalco and Tlatelolco.

Establishing fictive kin relations with previous rulers was merely part of a broader cosmological model. Rulers and nobles were interested in documenting their kinship relations with all beings who occupied the world, whether they were genetically related or not.

This "all inclusive" kin model, according to van Zantwijk (1985:197), was applied to many political relationships. For example, Aztec historians and scribes tried to document distant kin relations between Tarascan ancestors and those of the Nahuatl, perhaps as a way of justifying expansion of the Aztec empire (José de Acosta [1590] 1962:325–326; Lafaye 1972:14).

Predictably, therefore, the Aztecs tried to incorporate the newly arrived Spaniards into their kinship structure by offering them female relatives in marriage (Díaz del Castillo [1560s] 1908–1916). Even prisoners of war were called the "sons" of their captors, and the ancestors of those beheaded enemies were adopted as the ancestors of the conquerors (van Zantwijk 1985:197).

Above all, it seems to have been important for the Aztec rulers to borrow ancestors who linked them to the Toltecs of Tula—or, even further back, to the rulers of Teoti-

Borrow ancestors if yours are not proper

huacán. Since Teotihuacán was seen as "the burial place of rulers," a connection to that site was particularly ennobling.

In summary: after the "reforms" of Tlacaelel, ascent to the position of Aztec ruler required both inherited and acquired status. One had, first of all, to be ethnically Mexica, which placed one in the dominant group according to recently rewritten history. Second, one had to be of noble birth, even if this required "borrowing" the appropriate ancestors. Third, one had to distinguish oneself through community service and military prowess.

Once having become *tlatoani*, the Aztec ruler was placed in a unique position: he could be deified. While both rulers and nobles were of high birth, only rulers could be deified after their death.

> Thus, the old men said, he [a ruler] who died became a god. They said, "He hath become a god," that is, he hath died. And thus [the ancients] deluded themselves so that those who were rulers would be obeyed. All were worshipped as gods when they died; some became the Sun; some the Moon, etc. (Dibble and Anderson 1961:192; Sullivan 1980:236)

This fifteenth-century Aztec case is a nice example of how writing was manipulated by the state. It begins with a set of emic rules—ancient Toltec rules—for accession to the throne. Candidates were supposed to be of noble lineage on both the father's and mother's side, and candidates for *tlatoani* had to have kin ties to other communities and ethnic groups. The etic reality is that usurpers could seize power by burning the old writings, and by commissioning new ones in which they were supplied with the necessary bloodlines. They could also add new criteria, such as military achievement, in order to exclude rivals from candidacy. Once in office, they had the potential to become royal ancestors, then deified royal ancestors, and ultimately gods.

Metamorphosis

Key to the transformation of a ruler into a god was the Aztec concept of metamorphosis. This process was not restricted to royalty or folk heroes, but was extended to warriors who died in battle, women who died in childbirth, and other persons. Often such persons metamorphosed into flying creatures, which enabled them to ascend to various levels of heaven. This concept also helped to explain the existence of certain flying animals, such as hummingbirds, butterflies, and moths, all of which were considered special by the Aztec.

A parallel was drawn between warriors who had died in combat and women who had died in childbirth; both were considered to be "those who had battled." Their inner spirits or "souls" were converted into flying creatures. They accompanied the sun on its journey along the east-west axis of the heavens. They were assigned to a quadrant of paradise.

270

Chapter 9

9.2. Women who died in childbirth were depicted with weaving implements such as battens and swords, wearing a headband of unspun cotton because their weaving had been left unfinished. At death they were transformed into deities, because they had died in the struggle to produce life. (Redrawn from the Codex Borgia; see Seler 1963: plate 47.)

Their deaths "while fighting for the state" were honored by giving them perpetual life: they were metamorphosed into creatures that flew forever in unchanging generations.

Specifically, warriors who died in battle became "companions of the sun" on its journey through the heavens in the "eastern paradise." After spending four years traveling with the sun, the warriors' inner spirits or "souls" either returned to earth as hummingbirds, who could live on wild honey, or returned as butterflies. Women who died in childbirth were turned into cihuapipiltin, deified women who occupied the "western paradise," where they also accompanied the sun on its journey through the western sky. When they returned to earth, their inner spirits or "souls" had been turned into moths. In Aztec pictorial manuscripts, women who died in childbirth were metaphorically portrayed as spinners who had woven nothing; they are represented in the Borgia Codex (Fig. 9.2) as Tlazolteteo-Ixcuiname, wearing headbands of unspun cotton from which the spindles are missing (Sullivan 1982:18–19, fig. 9). As for royal ancestors, they were seen as the repository of all the knowledge and wisdom necessary for their descendants on earth. "Ca yehuantin teteu in ipalnemoa," they told their descendants, "it is through the gods that all live" (Sahagún 1949:103).

The Evolution of the Aztec Pantheon

Because deceased rulers could metamorphose into deities, the number of "gods" mentioned in Aztec documents is greater than that for any other Mesoamerican people. It has been traditional to think of all Mesoamerican Indians as having pantheons, but when the evidence is examined closely, it is clear that most did not. Many of our misconceptions about Mesoamerican religion are a result of Spanish misconceptions, as well as our own expectations about the nature of state religions. For example, when the Indians invoked the inner spirits of natural forces, royal ancestors, and other phenomena, the Spaniards wrongly called all of them "gods." Only in the case of the Aztec is the concept of pantheon plausible, and that is almost certainly because their list of "gods" grew by accretion in at least two ways.

First, even if each generation of royal Aztec men and women produced some deified ancestors who metamorphosed into gods, that process alone would account for the growing multitude of gods. Second, the policy of the expansionist Aztec state was to tolerate the religious beliefs and gods of conquered peoples. The continual incorporation of these foreign gods, combined with those who were deified royal ancestors, led to the growth of a pantheon unlike any other in Mesoamerica. The Aztec case is an extremely interesting example of the effect social and political policy can have on religion.

Standing between this mass of deities and the Aztec people were the priests. While they could not metamorphose, they could stand in for deities by wearing masks, costumes, and special disguises. When so costumed, the priests were called in ixiptla in teteo, "substitutes of the gods." Close examination of many codex figures identified as "gods" reveals that they are, in fact, priests costumed as deities.

For example, at the A.D. 1487 sacrificial-inaugural rites at the Great Temple of Tenochtitlán, fifteen priests were costumed to represent the fifteen patron deities of the *calpulli* of that city (Alvarado Tezozomoc [1598] 1975). The captives destined for sacrifice were called "sons of the Sun," and each addressed his captor as "beloved father"—a further example of the Aztec expansion of the "kinship model" to link themselves to the ancestors and deities of their captives. As the sacrifices began, the ruler Ahuitzotl cut out the heart of the first victim. When he tired, the priest dressed as the god Huitzilopochtli took over, followed by the priest dressed as Tlalocanteuhctli; then the priest dressed as Quetzalcoatl-Tlahuizcalpantecuhtli; then the priest dressed as Opochtli; and finally the priest of Itzpapalotl. Through the process of *in ixiptla in teteo*, it was as if the gods themselves (some of whom were undoubtedly royal ancestors) had performed the sacrifices.

Aztec Written History and the Ancestors

Because the Aztec are much more fully documented than most Mesoamerican people, we can see the reverence with which they viewed the codices, or screenfold manuscripts, in which their "history" was preserved. Despite its writing and rewriting to serve the purposes of political propaganda—some of which we have documented here—the Aztec continued to believe that their pictorial manuscripts were a true legacy from revered ancestors whose noble birth made them incapable of deceit. I can think of no better example than the following poem from Alvarado Tezozomoc's *Crónica Mexicayotl*, thought to have been written in the early seventeenth century in the region of Tenochtitlán and Tlatelolco, but based on older sources (Alvarado Tezozomoc [1609] 1949:4–6):

> Thus they have come to tell it,
> thus they have come to record it in their narration,
> and for us they have painted it in their codices,
> the ancient men, the ancient women.
>
> They were our grandfathers, our grandmothers,
> our great-grandfathers, great-grandmothers,
> our great-great-grandfathers, our ancestors.
>
> Their account was repeated,
> they left it to us;
> they bequeathed it forever
> to us who live now,
> to us who come down from them.

Never will it be lost, never will it be forgotten,
that which they came to do,
that which they came to record in their paintings:
their renown, their history, their memory.

Thus in the future
never will it perish, never will it be forgotten,
always we will treasure it,
we, their children, their grandchildren,
brothers, great-grandchildren,
great-great-grandchildren, descendants,
we who carry their blood and their color,
we will tell it, we will pass it on
to those who do not yet live, who are yet to be born,
the children of the Mexicans, the children of the Tenochcans.

MIXTEC ROYAL ANCESTORS

In the early days of Mixtec epigraphy, most figures in the prehispanic codices were considered to be "gods" or "deities" (e.g., Seler 1902–1923, Lehmann 1905). In addition, one traditional approach to Mixtec religion had been to identify these supposed "deities" by trying to locate their counterparts in the Aztec pantheon. Using Nahuatl names for Mixtec "deities" was considered both appropriate and useful. For example, the Mixtec folk hero 9 Wind was considered a counterpart to the Aztec deity Quetzalcoatl-Ehecatl (Nicholson 1978b); 7 Rain was considered the Mixtec equivalent of Xipe Totec, "Our Lord, the Flayed One" (Furst 1978).

In 1949, Alfonso Caso published a path-breaking article which argued that most Mixtec codex figures were nobles—actual men and women who had lived and ruled in the Mixteca Alta (Caso 1949). Initially, he focused his attention on the Mapa de Teozacoalco and was able to demonstrate that the sequence of seated couples were different generations of married Mixtec nobles who ruled at Teozacoalco and Tilantongo.

In Figure 9.3 we see part of the third dynasty of Teozacoalco, which is read from bottom to top. The third dynasty begins with 2 Dog "Braided with Flints" and his wife 6 Reed "Plumed Serpent with Jewels." In this sequence of marital pairs, all of the husbands are on the left, their wives on the right. The third dynasty of Teozacoalco ends with a male who never married and left no offspring. A new dynasty, the fourth, was founded by a noble named Coyote "Stick in Hand" (baptized by the Spaniards "Felipe de Santiago"), who apparently came to Teozacoalco from Tilantongo. His marriage produced don Francisco de Mendoza (shown at the top), who was the reigning lord in A.D. 1580.

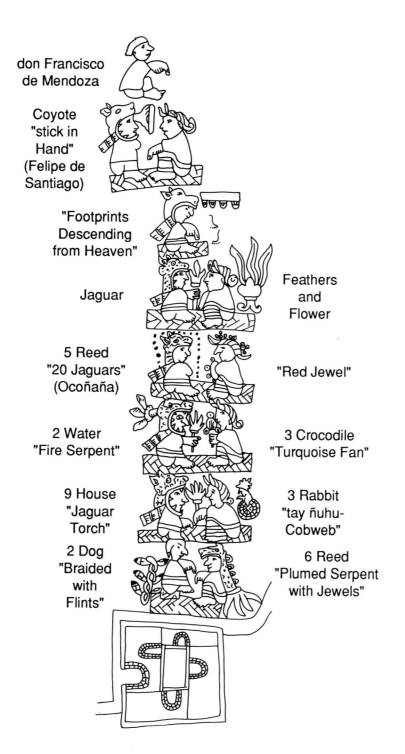

don Francisco
de Mendoza

Coyote
"stick in
Hand"
(Felipe de
Santiago)

"Footprints
Descending
from Heaven"

Jaguar

Feathers
and
Flower

5 Reed
"20 Jaguars"
(Ocoñaña)

"Red Jewel"

2 Water
"Fire Serpent"

3 Crocodile
"Turquoise Fan"

9 House
"Jaguar
Torch"

3 Rabbit
"tay ñuhu-
Cobweb"

2 Dog
"Braided
with
Flints"

6 Reed
"Plumed Serpent
with Jewels"

9.3. Mixtec genealogies of the early Colonial era usually show marital pairs arranged in a column, as we see here in the 1580 Mapa de Teozacoalco, with the earliest generation at the bottom and the most recent at the top. The third dynasty of Teozacoalco included 8 generations of royalty who reigned at that highland Mixtec town. (Redrawn from Caso 1949.)

Following Caso's breakthrough discovery of the noble marriages that had linked the dynasties of Teozacoalco and Tilantongo, there was an almost complete shift away from regarding all codex figures as gods, and from asserting that the subject matter was principally mythological. However, we must not go to the other extreme and assert that the content is entirely historical. For example, it is clear from such codices as the Vienna (Vindobonensis) that while one side (the reverse) of the deerhide screenfold is devoted to genealogical history and is full of dynastic history, the other side (the obverse) is largely mythological, dealing with supernatural beings who were consulted by several different generations of Mixtec nobles (e.g., Caso 1949, 1950, 1977, 1979; Smith 1973a:30–31; Furst 1978).

Depictions of Separate Descent for Nobles and Commoners

The Mixtec nobles claimed that their gods and rulers had had a single origin—both were born from trees growing beside the river at Apoala, a ritually and ideologically important place in the Mixtec sacred landscape. One of the sixteenth-century friars who wrote a grammar of Teposcolula recorded the following account:

> It was a common belief among the indigenous Mixtecos that the origin and beginnings of their false Gods and lords had been in Apoala, a town in the Mixteca, which in their language is called *yuta tnoho*, which is "river where the rulers come from," because they are said to have been split off from some trees that came out of that river that have distinct names. They also call that town *yuta tnuhu*, which is "River of the lineages," and this is the more appropriate name and the one that fits it best. (Reyes [1593] 1976:I)

There is an additional account by Burgoa ([1674] 1934b, 25:274) in which the Mixtec rulers, male and female, are said to have been born from two trees on the margins of the river in Apoala.

The actual depiction of the Mixtec nobles' birth from trees is shown on page 37b of the Codex Vienna, where a nude male figure emerges from the interior of a tree (Fig. 9.4). A nude female figure also appears above him and to the left, apparently having been born before him. Forty-nine other offspring of the tree birth are shown from page 37b to the bottom of page 35a (Furst 1978). At least three of the offspring of this tree birth are known to be lineage ancestors in other Mixtec genealogical and historical codices. One couple who appears in the list of offspring in the Codex Vienna—(nobleman) 1 Flower and (noblewoman) 13 Flower—is known from the Codex Bodley as the parents of human rulers. Their daughter, 9 Crocodile, married a man named 5 Wind "Descending Rain Deity." From the marriage of 9 Crocodile and 5 Wind proceeded members of the dynasty at Apoala and many nobles who married into other lineages. In fact, from the Codex

9.4. Codices and other documents reveal that Mixtec nobles and commoners had mythological explanations for their separate descent. Mixtec nobles (according to Reyes [1593] 1976, García [1607] 1981, and Burgoa [1674] 1934b) were born from trees on the banks of a river at the town of Apoala in the Mixteca Alta. This scene from the Codex Vienna depicts such a "tree birth." Flanking the tree are two men named 7 Eagle (left) and 7 Rain (right); they are among the offspring of the "original creator couple," a male and a female both named 1 Deer (Fig. 9.6). The two men hold cutting tools and have apparently opened the tree or removed its bark, thereby allowing hereditary rulers and nobles to be born. Over 40 noble offspring had already preceded the births shown in this scene. We see a man just emerging from the tree; above, left, is a woman whose birth has preceded his. (Redrawn from Codex Vindobonensis 37b; Furst 1978: fig. 38; Caso 1977: Lámina XIII.)

9.5. The birth of Mixtec commoners stood in contrast to the "tree birth" of hereditary nobles. Commoners (according to Reyes [1593] 1976) were *tay ñuhu*, "men of the earth." The "true" or "original" Mixtec—before the hereditary nobles came to rule in the Mixteca—are said to have been born from the earth, to have emerged from its center. They are often shown bald, with little bumps indicating that their heads and bodies were of stone. At *a* we see one of these little men coming out of the sign for "precious jewel" (Codex Selden). At *b*, one is shown emerging from a fissure in the earth (Codex Vienna). And at *c*, one appears to be going back into the earth (Codex Vienna). (Redrawn from Smith 1973b: fig. 5.)

Bodley we know that 1 Flower, 13 Flower, and 5 Wind were lineage ancestors whose descendants married into the lineages of Tilantongo and a town known as "Mountain that Opens/Bee" (Furst 1977:206–207). It is possible that other offspring shown in the Codex Vienna tree birth may have been lineage ancestors of other towns whose dynastic and genealogical codices were destroyed or lost.

Significantly, Reyes ([1593] 1976) not only tells us about the origins of Mixtec nobles, but also provides a second myth about the "first" or "original" people who emerged from the center of the earth. These *tay ñuhu* were said to have been non-Mixtec speakers. In addition, Reyes says that according to the Mixtec people, they had no laws until "laws were brought by the nobles."

Furthermore, prior to the birth of the "gods," remote ancestors, and nobles from trees at Apoala, the ground had given birth to small figures called *tay ñuhu*, or "men of the earth" (Fig. 9.5). Smith (1973b:68–71) has suggested that these *tay ñuhu* (mentioned in Reyes' 1593 *Arte en Lengua Mixteca*) corresponded to the *xolotls*—the small active figures often shown emerging, climbing, or ascending in the codices. Sometimes these *tay ñuhu* are shown emerging from or descending into clefts or openings in the earth's surface (see Fig. 9.5b, c).

In the Vienna Codex—in the first five pages leading up to the birth from the tree at Apoala—we see eight offspring of an original married couple named (male) 1 Deer and (female) 1 Deer. This 1 Deer couple has been considered a "creator couple," or the "creator gods," who lived at Apoala.

Interestingly, an origin myth about a couple named 1 Deer was also collected by Fray Gregorio García from Mixtec speakers in the town of Cuilapan in the Valley of Oaxaca (García [1607] 1981; Furst 1978:316). García mentions a codex from which his informant related the origin myth of the first members of the Apoala dynasty:

> In the year and in the day of obscurity and darkness, before there were days, or years, the world being in great darkness, that was all in chaos and confusion, the earth was covered with water; there was only mud and slime over the face of the earth. In that time, the Indians say, there appeared visibly a god who had as a name *un ciervo* (1 Deer), and for his surname (nickname) Culebra de León (Puma Serpent), and a very beautiful and lovely goddess whose name was 1 Deer, and who had for her nickname Culebra de Tigre (Jaguar Serpent). These two gods are said to have been first among the gods that the Indians had. (García [1607] 1981:327–328)

On page 51a of the Vienna Codex, the 1 Deer couple appears (Fig. 9.6). Despite the number "1" in the couple's names, all of this is depicted as taking place before any days or dates were used—in other words, so far back in time that it happened before the 260-day calendar was invented. The first actual date in the Vienna Codex does not appear until after the offspring of 1 Deer and 1 Deer have been given on page 50c.

The Ancestors of Nobles as Gods

In addition to discussing the origins of the Apoala royal dynasty, the myth recorded by García in Cuilapan reveals that offerings were made by the two sons of the 1 Deer couple to their parents, whom they describe as "gods, father and mother." This close identification of royal parents with gods is important for any understanding of the upper stratum of Mixtec society.

While Mixtec commoners had descended from "earth people," the upper stratum of society shared descent with the gods. Nobles were born from trees growing along the river at Apoala; when the first generation died, they became gods, and their offspring memorialized them by making offerings to them. The primordial offerings consisted of "*veleño polvido*," which may have been powdered tobacco placed in pottery incense burners (Furst 1978:9, 18). The two sons also honored their parents and the gods by performing autosacrifice, drawing drops of blood from their ears and tongues with flint or obsidian lancets, and then by scattering the blood on the limbs and branches of a willow tree. Offerings of blood and powdered tobacco were necessary rituals to invoke the spirits of their parents, the gods.

Metamorphosis as an Elite Ability

According to Reyes ([1593] 1976:328), the 1 Deer couple referred to above had two sons who were ingenious and knowledgeable in all the arts. The elder son, named 9 Wind "Serpent," amused himself by turning into an eagle that could fly in high places. The second son, named 9 Wind "Caves," could transform himself into a small serpent with wings, and could fly through the air with great agility. He could enter into cliffs and walls, making himself invisible. Those individuals who were below him could hear only the noise and clamor made by these two soaring creatures; they could not see them. The two sons "took these forms to make understood their power to transform themselves and to return to that which they had been before" (ibid.). As with Nahuatl speakers, flying was seen by the Mixtec as a special prerogative of the noble dead. Nobles could be metamorphosed after death into flying creatures that were unusual; they were special and divine, because they often were composite animals and "fantastic creatures" difficult to classify in any zoological scheme.

Mixtec pictorial manuscripts reinforce the notion that Mixtec elite had a divine descent they shared with the gods, which made them quite different from the lowly *tay ñuhu*, or "men of the earth." Two separate myths explain the origin of the elite and the gods on the one hand, and the commoners on the other hand. The elite were credited with

9.6. This Mixtec "creator" or "original" couple were the first individuals to bear names in the Codex Vienna. They precede the first date given in the codex; their marriage, as well as the births of their offspring, apparently took place "before time began." At left is the male named 1 Deer, whose left hand is believed to offer powdered tobacco; at right is the female named 1 Deer, who offers burning incense in her right hand. Both figures display fleshless jaws, which Furst (1978) has associated with fertility. Following this offering rite performed by the creator couple, we are introduced to their 47 progeny elsewhere in the codex. (Redrawn from the Codex Vindobonensis 51a; see Furst 1978: fig. 16.)

bringing the Mixtec people their language, their laws, the practice of autosacrifice or blood-letting, and the custom of making offerings in the name of one's ancestors. The myths, reinforced by manuscripts carefully preserved by priests, justified the rule of the elite by making it clear to the commoners that without nobles they would have had neither language nor laws.

As if further reinforcement were necessary, the Mixtec used a special vocabulary to label the parts of a noble's body (Reyes 1593 [1976]), making the point that nobles were as different from commoners as commoners were from lower animals. Some examples can be seen at left in Table 9.1.

Table 9.1 Body Parts of Mixtec Noble and Commoner

Body Part	Of a commoner	Of a noble
Head	*dzini*	*yayaya*
Face	*nuuu*	*nanaya*
Eyes	*tenuu*	*duchiya*
Ears	*tutnu*	*tnahaya*
Nose	*dzitni*	*dutuya*
Mouth	*yuhu*	*diyaya*
Teeth	*noho*	*yequeya*
Shoulders	*sata*	*yusaya*
Chest	*dica*	*yequendi yaya*
Stomach	*nuu ini*	*nuundiyaya*
Elbow	*sitendaha*	*catnundaya*
Hand	*daha*	*dayaya*
Feet	*saha*	*duhuaya*

Special Language of the Elite

We will see in chapter 10 that the ancient Maya employed a special, secret ritual language called "Zuyua," which helped maintain the gulf between nobles and commoners. The Mixtec elite were set apart from the commoners by their use of a special language called the *iya* dialect. Unfortunately, with the demise of the Mixtec upper stratum in the sixteenth century, much of the *iya* dialect was lost. Some words in that dialect were recorded by Reyes ([1593] 1976) under the page heading "On the reverential nouns and verbs that are used by the people with the great lords or when interacting with them." This heading indicates that those individuals who spoke directly with Mixtec lords had to employ a special reverential language, which reinforced their respective differences in status. A few surviving examples indicate that this language was replete with wonderful metaphorical expressions emphasizing elite-commoner differences. For example, while Mixtec commoners died, royalty did not; they merely "fainted" (King 1988). Commoner women held only milk in their breasts, while royal women had "honey" in theirs. Commoners urinated, but the royalty just "made dew."

ZAPOTEC ROYAL ANCESTORS

Royal ancestor worship was highly developed among the Zapotec, and because so much of their prehistory is known, we can see its components forming far back in time (Flannery and Marcus 1976, 1983b; Marcus 1978, 1989a). As long ago as 1150–850 B.C. one can see basic elements such as "earth" and "sky" depicted in stylized form on Oaxacan funerary ceramics (Marcus 1989a). "Sky" was often represented by Cociyo, "Lightning," the most powerful and revered force in the Zapotec cosmos. So important was lightning that sixteenth-century rulers such as Cociyoeza and Cociyopii had names derived from it. During the Classic period, after A.D. 200, urns of venerated royal ancestors often show them wearing a mask of Cociyo to indicate their association with sacred lightning (Fig. 9.7).

9.7. Zapotec nobles were buried with ceramic urns that often depict a human figure wearing the mask of Lightning (Cociyo). Here we see a figure seated on a low platform with hands on knees, wearing the chest ornament, mask with bifid tongue, and elaborate headdress usually associated with Lightning. Urns such as this have been found in tombs dating to approximately A.D. 200—500. (Drawing by Margaret Van Bolt; see Marcus 1983h: fig. 5.12.)

Other royal ancestors who had their names linked to powerful supernatural forces include Xòo, "Earthquake," and Pìy, "Wind" (Marcus 1983h, 1983p).

Associated with lightning were elements such as clouds, wind, rain, and hail. In fact, the Zapotec believed that royal ancestors ascended to heaven and became clouds, sometimes depicted as flying turtles. Their heavenly position allowed them to intercede with lightning on behalf of their descendants. They would only do so, however, if properly cared for and appropriately propitiated with sacrifices by their descendants.

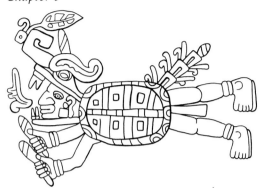

9.8. The Classic and Postclassic Zapotec depicted remote royal ancestors as flying figures. From a Late Postclassic tomb at Zaachila, we see this stucco-modeled flying figure, a man with a turtle carapace as the trunk of his body, with his head inside the jaws of a supernatural. The spear shaft in his body may indicate that he was killed in battle or sacrificed; he, in turn, holds a sacrificial knife in each hand, indicating that he is now prepared to perform the rite. (Redrawn from Caso 1966b:324.)

The Zapotec frequently depicted their "cloud ancestors" as flying turtles, such as one shown on a tomb wall at Zaachila (Fig. 9.8) or on the top of a genealogical register from Noriega (see below). This representation may be derived from a simile comparing the planoconvex carapace of a turtle and the shape of a cumulonimbus cloud, or it may have its origin in homonymic punning (Marcus n.d.d). Like the Aztec, the Zapotec also believed in metamorphosis, a process by which people could change into flying creatures; this is presumably how the ancestors reached the cloud layer of the sky. As early as 150 B.C.–A.D. 150, we have ceramic sculptures that show humans transformed into flying figures. For example, Figure 9.9 shows a caped flying figure with a Cociyo mask from the subfloor offering box of a Protoclassic temple at San José Mogote, Oaxaca (Marcus and Flannery n.d.). The figure carries an agricultural planting stick in one hand, and a bifid serpent tongue in the other (metaphoric of newly sprouted maize, since "serpent" and "new maize" are homonyms in Zapotec).

9.9. Already in the Protoclassic period, the Zapotec depicted the metamorphosis of nobles from human to supernatural by showing them as flying figures. In this case, the flying figure wears a cape and the mask of Lightning (Cociyo), holding a bifid tongue in his left hand and a possible dibble stick in his right. Cociyo—as the piercer of the clouds that contained rain—could have his name invoked by noble relatives to send rain, and was thus closely associated with agriculture. This figure was part of a scene placed in a stone offering box beneath a Zapotec temple at San José Mogote between 150 B.C. and A.D. 150. The stone slab on which the flying figure lies is the roof of a miniature tomb. (Drawing by John Klausmeyer.)

Classic Period Ancestors

Although Classic Zapotec funerary urns have often been described as "deities," there is increasing evidence to suggest that most are royal ancestors. For one thing, many are depicted with names taken from the 260-day calendar (Fig. 9.10); it is doubtful that any Zapotec deity had a calendric name, since their deities were eternal and therefore had no birthdays. In addition, close examination of many urns referred to as "Cociyo" reveals them to be depictions of human beings wearing the *mask* of Cociyo (e.g., Fig. 9.7). That kind of depiction presumably was a reference to the fact that royal ancestors were closely associated with lightning (Marcus 1983h).

The clearest epigraphic references to Zapotec royal ancestors can be found in royal tomb murals, lintels, and door stones of the Classic period (A.D. 200–600) and on marriage monuments and genealogical registers of the Late Classic and Early Postclassic (A.D. 600–900).

Some Classic tombs at Monte Albán contained a single adult (e.g., Tomb 104), a conjugal pair (e.g., Tomb 103), or several skeletons, the latter especially common in tombs with a cruciform plan. Not only did the cruciform tombs usually constitute veritable ossuaries, they also often showed evidence of having been reopened several times and of having had their wall murals resurfaced and repainted. Some of these tomb murals reveal the names of royal relatives and royal ancestors of the tomb occupants.

For example, the mural in Tomb 104 at Monte Albán refers to the ancestors of the tomb's occupants. Names and depictions of ancestors are often shown in association with the "jaws of the sky" motif (discussed in chapter 8), seen in this case at the top and center of the back wall of the tomb (Fig. 9.11). Offerings were probably made while a ritual specialist or relative invoked the spirit of a named ancestor; vessels containing food and beverages were typical of the offerings placed in niches built into the walls of the tomb. These niches seem to have acted as "openings" or "windows" through which the spirit of the deceased could be addressed, especially with offerings of burning incense, fresh blood, foaming chocolate, or fermented pulque.

One male ancestor is shown on a sidewall of Tomb 104 (Fig. 9.11, far right), wearing a Cociyo or "Lightning" headdress. He is shown holding an incense bag in his left hand, while his outstretched right hand is left empty. His name, 1 Cociyo, is given above the niche in front of him. This figure is probably a deceased ancestor, since he is shown facing inward, toward the central figure on the back wall. As we saw in chapter 7, tomb murals usually show living relatives exiting the tomb in a procession, and this clue is sometimes useful in distinguishing dead ancestors from living relatives.

For example, in the Classic-period mural of Tomb 105, which we already saw in chapter 7, royal couples are shown walking in procession toward the doorway to exit the tomb

9.10. Royal women with jade necklaces and prominent earplugs were sometimes depicted on pottery figures that were placed in their descendants' tombs. Their calendric names were also sometimes attached. In this case the woman's name is 13 Chilla, a date in the Zapotec *piye* or 260-day calendar. Classic period, ca. A.D. 200–500. (Drawing by Margaret Van Bolt; see Caso and Bernal 1952: fig. 43l and Marcus 1983h: fig. 5.11.)

9.11. Zapotec ancestors (both remote and near), as well as living relatives, were often shown in Classic tomb murals. In this mural from Tomb 104 at Monte Albán, we see a remote ancestor depicted on the back wall (at center) above the central offering niche. Above the anthropomorphic figure is the "jaws of the sky" motif, a symbol of divine descent. The side walls of the tomb (to the left and right of the central panel) reveal the names of the deceased's male relatives. (Redrawn from Caso 1938: Lámina I.)

(see Fig. 7.12). Both the north and south walls of that Zapotec tomb show more royal couples, below the "jaws of the sky" motif. All these nobles bear distinctive hieroglyphic names. In contrast to these living relatives, however, on the back wall of Tomb 105 and on the jambs flanking the entrance, we see the names of other royal couples who may be deceased ancestors. Painted on the south jamb, for example, are the name glyphs of a royal couple named 1 Deer and 2 Jaguar (Fig. 9.12), whose nearby depictions are somewhat eroded (Caso 1938: Lámina II-A). In general, Classic Zapotec tomb murals anticipate the later Mixtec codices, in which rulers' genealogies were expressed as a series of named ancestors, usually male/female pairs. They also anticipate the Zapotec "genealogical registers" and "marriage slabs" of the period A.D. 600–900, some of which we saw in chapter 8.

"Genealogical registers" were apparently an innovation of the Late Classic–Early Postclassic transition. They are small, well-made stone slabs meant to be seen and read from close up, for example, in the wall of a tomb antechamber. As their name implies, the slabs are divided into separate horizontal registers or zones (usually two or three) stacked one above the other, helping to indicate the order of reading. They deal with events that took place at different times in the past, with the events and figures in the top register

9.12. On the south jamb of Tomb 105 at Monte Albán were the names of this ancestral couple, named 1 Deer and 2 Jaguar. Such references to ancestral couples in Classic period Zapotec tombs anticipate the Postclassic Mixtec codices, which provide comparable dynastic data. (Redrawn from Caso 1938: Lámina II-A.)

usually the most recent, and the most distant ancestors appearing in the lowest register. Those placed in tombs presumably established the ancestors of the tomb's occupant.

Such a genealogical register is known from Noriega (Fig. 9.13), a site situated between Cuilapan and Zaachila. This register chronicles the early life of a noble named 2 Water. Divided into three registers, it shows his remote ancestors at the bottom. On the left is a man named 10 Water; to the right is a woman named 9 Serpent (Caso 1928). Between these ancestors is a hill sign with two crocodile heads attached to either side. Such a hill sign is similar to that depicted on Stela 1 at Monte Albán (see Fig. 10.11), a glyph that may have been the name of one of the hills making up Monte Albán. Above this place sign are the usual "jaws of the sky."

The middle register of this same monument was meant to be read from left to right. On the left, we see a newborn child named 2 Water with his mother; behind her is a tree not unlike those shown with some Maya royal ancestors (see Figs. 9.17–9.18). On the right the child, now old enough to sit up, is presented to his father. Moving now to the top register in boustrophedon fashion and reading from right to left, we see a still-older 2 Water being fitted with a headband by an unidentified person. His father watches from the left, his mother from the right. Above we see a flying turtle with the name 5 Death, possibly a "cloud ancestor." Clearly this monument supplies us with the near and remote ancestors of 2 Water, the person for whom the stone was presumably carved. Since he so clearly traces himself to a prominent mother, we would be justified in suspecting that he was the offspring of a hypogamous marriage between the local lord of Noriega and a royal woman from the more important site (possibly Monte Albán) depicted by the hill sign in the lower register.

Royal ancestors also appear in other contexts, such as the large lintel of Tomb 3 at Xoxocotlán, near Monte Albán (Saville 1899). This lintel lists fifteen ancestors (Marcus 1983i), each set in a compartment with a calendric name (Fig. 9.14). Each human head is shown bearded, a Zapotec convention making it clear that they are "elders" or "ancestors." From left to right, the fifteen compartments can be tentatively transcribed as follows: 5 Lizard, 5 Monkey, 8 Earthquake, 8 Reed, 4 Jaguar, 6 Earthquake, 8 Water, 4 Jaguar, 1 Flower, 6 Winged Insect, 7 Owl, 2 Precious Stone, 2 Jaguar, 3 Deer, and 12 Precious Stone. Presumably this lintel names the prominent male ancestors of the person buried in the tomb.

The size and context of the Zapotec genealogical registers are particularly interesting. All are small, and all of those found *in situ* during controlled excavation were in the antechambers of tombs. We may suggest that they constituted a permanent record in stone of a given ruler's royal ancestry, a record which could be consulted again and again whenever new offerings or additional deceased relatives were brought to the tomb. These records contained both named ancestors who had (presumably) died recently, and more distant ancestors, who may have lived so long ago as to be partly or completely mythical.

9.13. This Zapotec genealogical register from Noriega has as its major focus the early life of a Zapotec noble named 2 Water. The small slab (1 m × 60 cm)—divided into 3 zones or registers—is intended to be read from bottom to top in boustrophedon style. The lowest register depicts 2 Water's ancestors (possibly his grandparents), establishes their divine descent, and gives their place of origin (possibly one of the hills of Monte Albán). The middle register (beginning on the left) shows the newborn 2 Water with his mother; on the right, we see him being presented to his father. The upper register (read from right to left) shows a somewhat older 2 Water (at center) being fitted with a headband by an unknown individual, while his father (extreme left) and mother (extreme right) watch. Above 2 Water is the figure of a remote ancestor named 5 Death, who has been transformed into a flying turtle with the head of a supernatural. Such genealogical slabs were usually placed in the antechamber of a noble's tomb, to be read by other nobles attending his funeral (or the funerals of relatives who subsequently came to be buried in the same tomb). (Drawing by Mark Orsen; see Marcus 1980:64.)

286

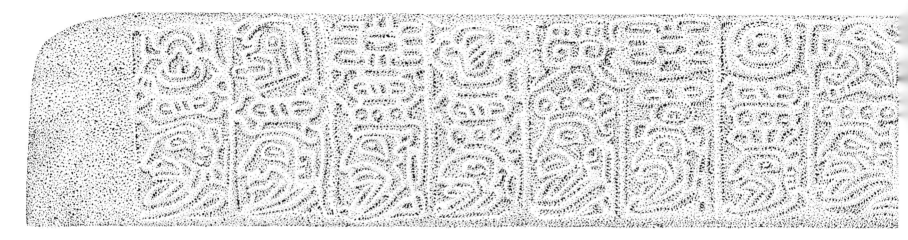

9.14. Lintel 2 from Tomb 3 at Xoxocotlán lists the
calendric names of 15 people, presumably
ancestors of the tomb's occupant. Each of the 15
compartments depicts a bearded, wrinkled head.
Above each head is a calendric name drawn from
the Zapotec 260-day calendar. Xoxocotlán, near
Monte Albán, reached its maximum size early in
the Classic period. (Drawing by Mark Orsen; see
Marcus 1983i: fig. 5.14.)

Sixteenth-Century Zapotec Ancestors

During the sixteenth century, Zapotec ancestors were referred to as *peniconiyto, nicoteteni,* or *nicotiniyto;* "ancestors in one's lineage" were *pixozecolatono* (Córdova [1578a] 1942:29v). Veneration of the ancestors continues today, particularly in the Isthmus of Tehuantepec, where one hears references to the *binigulaza, binnigola,* and *binizaa,* "old people of the clouds" (Marcus 1983p:348).

Unfortunately, the topic of royal ancestor worship was poorly understood by the sixteenth-century Spaniards. Their model of an "idolatrous" religion was based on ancient Greece and Rome, and they often mistook the images of deified royal ancestors for pagan gods. One reason the Zapotec have been described as having a "vast pantheon of gods" is that the Spaniards published long lists of supposed Zapotec "deities" from the towns they conquered. When one examines these lists with care, however, two features become apparent. The first is that the so-called "deities" are different in every town; the second is that many of the names the Spaniards collected for these "deities" contain the terms *coqui* ("male ruler" or "lord") and *xonaxi* ("female ruler" or "lady"). These terms denote *human* royalty or nobles, not gods. Clearly, the Spaniards were collecting the names of elite ancestors who were still venerated in the towns in which they had once ruled. This would explain why the names were different from one town to another, and why some names were derived from the 260-day calendar.

For example, according to Espíndola ([1580] 1905:134), a male-female pair named *Benelaba* and *Xonaxi Belachina* were revered by the Zapotec of Coatlán, who sacrificed dogs, turkeys, quail, and war captives to honor them. The male's name, *Benelaba,* can be translated "7 Rabbit," and *Xonaxi Belachina* can be translated "Lady 3 Deer." These are the calendric names of a revered royal couple who once lived and ruled in Coatlán, not the names of some "pagan gods."

Another example comes from Taliztaca (modern Tlalixtac de Cabrera in the Valley of Oaxaca). In the sixteenth century, Zapotec villagers there were sacrificing children, adults, quail and quail feathers, parrot feathers, and small dogs to *Coqui Huani*, "Lord Huani" (del Río [1580] 1905:179). Other towns venerated deceased royalty named *Coqui Bila* (in Macuilxochitl), *Coqui Cehuiyo* (in Tlacolula), and *Xonaxi Quecuya* (in Mitla). These deceased nobles were revered as semidivine, and they received sacrifices because they interceded with supernatural forces on behalf of their living descendants and communities.

This practice of interceding is clearly portrayed in the *relación* from Ocelotepec, a town in the mountainous region near Miahuatlán. The former ruler of the town was named Petela ("2 or 5 Dog"). When he died after a rule of 10 to 12 years, the Zapotec of Ocelotepec "commemorated him as a god, for having come from that [line of] people, and they sacrificed to him as a god" (Espíndola [1580] 1905:139). The Spanish vicar Bartolomé de Piza searched for and found Petela's remains "buried dry and embalmed, laid out in such a manner that all the bones were in place; he [de Piza] burned them publicly" to end such heathen practices. Six months later, Ocelotepec was hit by a plague in which more than 1,200 persons died. Immediately, the Zapotec nobles "went back to making sacrifices to Petela over the ashes of the bones which de Piza had burned, for he [Petela] was an intercessor with 'Bezelao,' whom they wanted to call off the plague." This *relación* makes it clear why we should be wary of the lists of Zapotec "deities" given to us by the sixteenth-century Spaniards. Petela was clearly a deified royal ancestor, as were Xonaxi Belachina, Coqui Huani, Coqui Bila, and others. "Bezelao" may have been a legitimate supernatural, although it is not clear how he was envisioned. Indeed, for almost no Zapotec "deity" can euhemerism be ruled out.

The Maya elite kept written records that linked them to their highly ranked ancestors and justified their special privileges. After the Conquest of the sixteenth century, for example, the Yucatec Maya nobles showed the Spaniards old deer hide manuscripts or newly prepared *probanzas* (proofs of nobility) with their genealogies. The *probanza* of the Xiu lineage began with a "family tree" (Fig. 8.31) and ended with the Mani Land Treaty (Fig. 6.16).

Each Maya noble lineage had its own patron deity (often a deified ancestor), and their ancestry was "discussed in their hieroglyphic books" (Roys 1943:35). As among the Mixtec, royal ancestors were often linked to sacred trees. A central "world tree" (usually a ceiba) might be conceived of as holding up the universe or penetrating the planes of heaven. There might be four other trees, each associated with one of the four world quarters. These trees were associated with different colors, birds, and other attributes (Landa [1566] in Tozzer 1941; Thompson 1934, 1950, 1970; Marcus 1973, 1983c).

Often a mythological founder was at the base of the tree, with the lineage issuing from him. Trees might also be associated with the perpetual life or apotheosis of a ruler. For example, behind the body (or issuing from the body) of the dead ruler "Lord Shield" (Pacal), shown on the sarcophagus lid in the Temple of the Inscriptions at Palenque, is a fantastic tree that links him to the heavens (see Morley, Brainerd, and Sharer 1983: fig. 4.23).

In the hieroglyphic inscriptions carved in stone after A.D. 250, the Maya mention three kinds of ancestors: (1) *near ancestors,* such as their immediate parents; (2) *distant ancestors,* who might extend back a hundred years or so; and (3) *remote, mythological ancestors,* who because of the Maya Long Count could be assigned absolutely astonishing dates. We will consider these in ascending order of age.

Near Ancestors

Figure 9.15 shows the near ancestors of a Tikal ruler whose reign began in A.D. 682 (Marcus 1976a: fig. 5.4, 1983b: fig. 6; Jones and Satterthwaite 1982). This ruler's hieroglyphic name has been given as "Double Comb"; his mother's name includes a Jaguar Cushion, while his father's name includes a Shield and Skull. There is at present no agreement as to how some of these names were pronounced.

Another example of near ancestors comes from a monument at Yaxchilán, where the parents of the ruler Bird Jaguar are given. At the top of Stela 11 (Fig. 9.16), we see the depiction of his parents; on the left is his mother, and on the right his father, "Shield

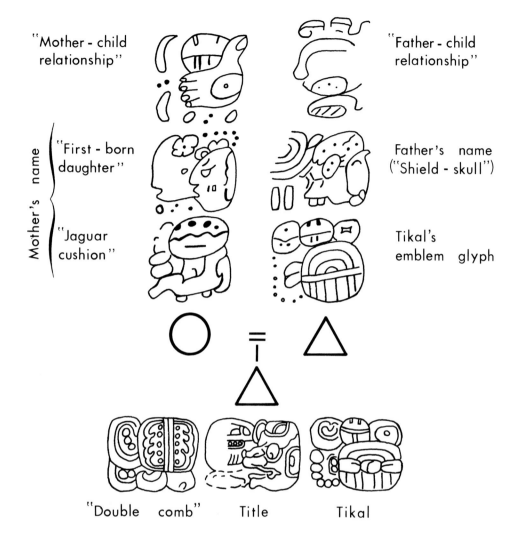

"Mother - child relationship"

"Father - child relationship"

Mother's name { "First - born daughter"

"Jaguar cushion"

Father's name ("Shield - skull")

Tikal's emblem glyph

"Double comb"   Title   Tikal

9.15. The immediate ancestors of a 7th century A.D. Maya ruler are given here. The Tikal ruler named "Double Comb"—inaugurated on May 6, 682—provided the names of his parents on his own monuments. (Redrawn from Marcus 1983b: fig. 6.)

Jaguar, Captor of Ahau" (Proskouriakoff 1963: fig. 2a). Shield Jaguar ruled Yaxchilán from A.D. 681 to 742; Bird Jaguar ruled from A.D. 752 to ca. 800.

Stela 11 was erected to commemorate the accession to power of Bird Jaguar on 9.16.1.0.0 (May 3, A.D. 752). Note, however, the fact that there was a ten-year gap between the end of Shield Jaguar's reign and the inauguration of his son (?) Bird Jaguar. This leads us to wonder who was ruling Yaxchilán during that decade (Proskouriakoff 1963:162). Was Bird Jaguar in fact the legitimate successor and direct descendant of Shield

9.16. An eighth-century Maya ruler, Bird Jaguar of Yaxchilán, included depictions of his parents on the top of one of his monuments (Stela 11). On the left is a depiction of his mother (her name and title are given in the text at far left); on the right is his father, Shield Jaguar, whose associated text (far right) gives his name and his honorific titles, "Captor of Ahau" and "Lord of Yaxchilán." At the time this stela was commissioned by Bird Jaguar, his father Shield Jaguar was deceased; the latter's monuments claim that he lived to the (improbably) ripe old age of 95. (Redrawn from Proskouriakoff 1964.)

Jaguar? Or was Bird Jaguar only *using* the depictions of Shield Jaguar and his wife because he was not really the preferred or legitimate successor (Marcus n.d.a)? Such questions remind us that even claims of "near" royal ancestors may not necessarily be rock-solid.

The near ancestors (parents) of Lord Shield (Pacal) of Palenque are apparently depicted on both ends of his stone sarcophagus (Fig. 9.17). This double depiction of both parents is unusual, but in the case of Lord Shield's father it may be significant. The fact is that we have no evidence to prove that Lord Shield's father ever ruled Palenque, so it is surprising that he is featured twice.

Distant Ancestors

On the sides of the stone sarcophagus of the same Lord Shield of Palenque (see above) were depictions of his distant ancestors, prominent royal men and women, some of whom had supposedly ruled before him (see Fig. 9.18 and Ruz Lhuillier 1954, 1958: figs. 13, 14; Berlin 1959; Marcus 1976a: figs. 4.26–4.28).

On Lintel 21 at Yaxchilán the same ruler discussed earlier, Bird Jaguar, cited more distant royal ancestors. Bird Jaguar also reused several lintels that had been carved hundreds of years before his reign. Such behavior—added to his need to demonstrate his military prowess by taking several captives—reinforces our suspicion (see above) that there might have been something in his background that made it necessary for him to use "overkill" in establishing his right to rule. In fact, in their determined invoking of the names of distant ancestors, Lord Shield of Palenque and Bird Jaguar of Yaxchilán reveal a greater need to legitimize themselves than we see in most Maya rulers.

Remote, Mythological Ancestors

Each member of the beautiful triad of temples at Palenque—the Temple of the Sun, the Temple of the Cross, and the Temple of the Foliated Cross—has a carved text referring to a "birth" that took place 3,000 years before the inscription was carved (Lounsbury 1980, 1985). These texts refer to three offspring whose mother was allegedly 754 years of age at the time of their births. Note that such a supernatural mother did not need the requisite nine months between births; all three supposedly took place within days or weeks of each other in the year 2360 B.C. (see Table 9.2). There is, of course, no evidence that Palenque was occupied at this date, which falls in the late Preceramic!

While some authors (e.g., Kelley 1965) have suggested that these dates refer to the births of the "gods" to whom each temple was dedicated (Fig. 9.19), it seems more likely—as Berlin (1963, 1965) has suggested—that the dates refer to the births of mythical royal ancestors from whom the later rulers of Palenque wanted to claim descent. As Berlin (1965:338) put it,

> One may ask if plain history may have been recorded on a tablet inside a shrine of a probable temple. This tablet was hardly meant to be seen by the general public. It may indicate mythological descent from divine ancestors in the remote past. Such a belief seems to have existed among the Mixtecs and Zapotecs. Even the Aztec rulers claimed a mythological descent from nebulous Quetzalcoatl.

Berlin's argument is strengthened by the fact that on each of these wall tablets from Palenque's triad of temples there are the names of other near and distant ancestors, in addition to the multiple births that took place in 2360 B.C.

These Palenque inscriptions underscore a point we have made elsewhere in this volume: myth and history were not separable in the Precolumbian world. Since every word that issued from a ruler's mouth was by definition true, no one would question his statement that he was descended from some divine being who lived 3,000 years ago. In chapter 10, we will give more details of the Maya female ancestor who supposedly gave birth at the age of 754 and took office at the age of 815 (Fig. 9.20)! If the ancient Maya were prepared to believe such statements, it posed no problem whatsoever to claim that Lord Shield (Pacal) of Palenque died at the age of eighty, in spite of the fact that his skeleton shows him to have been a man of only forty (Dávalos Hurtado and Romano Pacheco 1973).

In fact, the 3,000-year-old dates on the temple tablets at Palenque are not even close to being the oldest dates carved by the Maya. During the Classic period (and especially during the Late Classic of A.D. 600–900), there were Maya dates and calculations that

Table 9.2   Birth of the Three Ancestors Called GI, GII, and GIII at Palenque

Temple Name	Date	Ancestor/ Deity
Cross	Oct. 21 2360 B.C.	God I
Sun	Oct. 25 2360 B.C.	God III
Foliated Cross	Nov. 8 2360 B.C.	God II

Source: Berlin 1963.

9.17. The parents of the seventh-century A.D. Maya ruler Lord Shield (Pacal) are apparently depicted at the ends of his stone sarcophagus, which was placed in the Tomb of the Inscriptions at Palenque. In the upper panel (from the north side of the sarcophagus), we see at left a woman named "Lady White Parrot" and at right a man whose name is a fantastic animal—a bird with a Kan cross in its eye and the ear of a jaguar. Each name sits above the Palenque emblem glyph. In the lower panel (from the south side of the sarcophagus) we see the same two figures, but their positions are reversed and the Palenque emblem glyphs are somewhat different. These "immediate ancestors" are shown as parts of elaborately branching trees that emerge from the earth. The exceptional magnificence of Lord Shield's sarcophagus and tomb are fully in keeping with a ruler who may actually have been a usurper, since there is no evidence that his father or grandfather ever ruled Palenque. Such tremendous display of both horizontal propaganda (in the carving of his sarcophagus) and vertical propaganda (in the construction of the surrounding Temple of the Inscriptions) is consistent with someone whose claim to the throne was suspect, especially if he wanted to ensure that his offspring would have fewer problems succeeding him on the throne. (Redrawn from Ruz Lhuillier 1958: fig. 14.)

9.18.On the sides of Lord Shield's sarcophagus at Palenque, we see more distant male and female ancestors claimed by him. One of the male ancestors (at lower left) has a name similar to that of the deceased; he, too, was called Lord Shield (Pacal), and was supposedly the deceased's grandfather, but we have no evidence that he ever ruled Palenque (unless we follow Berlin [1977] in assuming that the grandfather's reign was followed by his grandson's, the latter claiming the 68-year combined reign as his own). All these ancestors are shown as associated with trees growing out of the earth; Ruz Lhuillier (1973) identified them as cacao, chicozapote, avocado, guayaba, coyol, and mamey. Like Aztec, Zapotec, and Mixtec nobles, Maya nobles were closely associated with trees. (Redrawn from Ruz Lhuillier 1958: fig. 13.)

9.19. This row of glyphs gives the names of three "gods" (possibly deified ancestors) commemorated by a triad of structures at Palenque—the Temples of the Cross, Foliated Cross, and Sun. All were commissioned by the ruler Snake Jaguar. At *a* is the glyph that refers to the entire triad. At *b*, we see the "god" from the Temple of the Cross; at *c*, the "god" from the Temple of the Foliated Cross; and at *d*, the "god" from the Temple of the Sun. The births of these three "gods" (all from the same mother) supposedly took place in the same year (2360 B.C.). (Redrawn from Marcus 1976a: fig. 4.35.)

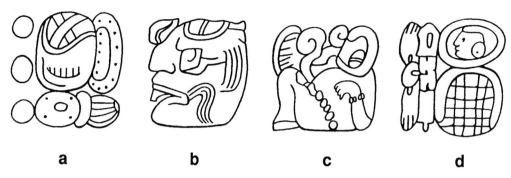

a   b   c   d

extended back preposterous distances into the past. Because of the great precision of the Long Count calendar, with its fixed datum and large units of time, the Maya were one of the few peoples who could specify *to the day* when a given mythological event happened, even if that event took place eons ago. These long calculations into the past (and sometimes even into the future) illustrate the fact that Maya scribes and nobles thought in terms of vast expanses of time, and wished to place contemporary events in that context.

Early in the twentieth century (Morley 1915:114–116; Long 1923a), Maya scholars successfully worked out a Long Count date found on Stela 10 at Tikal. The date they calculated corresponds to almost 5,000,000 years ago (Fig. 9.21). Other examples abound. From the Stone of Chiapa, a date extending back well over 2,000,000 years has been calculated (Thompson 1950). Morley (1915) and Thompson (1944) also found a date on Stela N at Copán that occurred more than 100,000 years ago (Morley 1915: fig. 58). On Stela F at Quiriguá, Guatemala (now designated Monument 6 in Sharer 1990), there is a date reaching back 91,683,930 *tunob*, or more than 90,000,000 years (Fig. 9.22a).

The record, however, is probably held by Stela D at Quiriguá (now designated Monument 4 in Sharer 1990), which has a dedicatory date of A.D. 766 (9.16.15.0.0 [7 Ahau 3 Pop]). At the glyph block designated C20 (see Fig. 9.22b) there is a unit of time called 13 *kinchiltunob*. The date recorded would be 400,000,000 years before Stela D was carved (Thompson 1950:316)! This is only one of a number of lengthy calculations at Quiriguá that reach well into the past.

While such impossibly early dates and amazingly large spans of time have been noted by a number of epigraphers (e.g., Morley 1915; Long 1919, 1923a; Thompson 1950:314–316; Berlin 1965; Kelley 1976; Lounsbury 1976, 1978, 1980, 1985), it has not always been clear what their function or meaning was. Before Proskouriakoff revealed that Maya monuments referred to actual rulers and noble individuals, some scholars viewed these associated dates as mystical, or as evidence that time itself was worshiped. Thompson (1950:315) suggested that the astronomers at Quiriguá might have been interested in

9.20. Snake Jaguar, the son of Lord Shield (Pacal), had to go to great lengths to establish his right to rule Palenque. One of his strategies was to say that he had taken office on the anniversary of the same day as a female ancestor, who supposedly was inaugurated thousands of years before.

at E5, 2 days, 11 months;
at F5, 7 *tunob*;
at E6, 1 *katun*;
at F6, 2 *baktunob*;
at E7, "was born";
at F7-E8, move forward to the accession of . . .
at F8, the name of a woman which includes a fantastic animal;
at E9, the day 9 Ik;
at F9, the month 0 Zac.

In English, this passage could be paraphrased, "at the age of 815, this revered female took office on the 13th of August in the year 2305 B.C." (Redrawn by John Klausmeyer from the Tablet of the Temple of the Cross; see Lounsbury 1980: fig. 1; Maudslay 1889–1902, 4: plate 75).

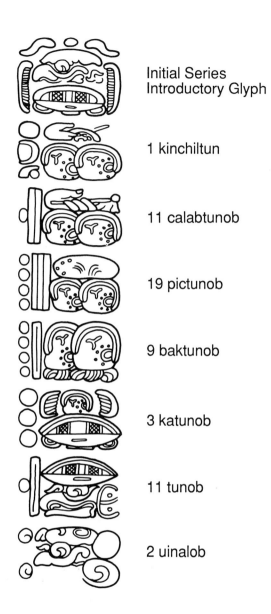

Initial Series
Introductory Glyph

1 kinchiltun

11 calabtunob

19 pictunob

9 baktunob

3 katunob

11 tunob

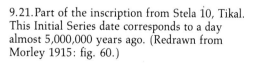

2 uinalob

9.21. Part of the inscription from Stela 10, Tikal. This Initial Series date corresponds to a day almost 5,000,000 years ago. (Redrawn from Morley 1915: fig. 60.)

13 Kinchiltunob   1 Ahau   13 Yaxkin

13 Kinchiltunob   7 Ahau   3 Pop

9.22. Quiriguá, Guatemala, has two monuments that record immense calendric calculations into the past. On Stela F (above) the calculation reached is over 90,000,000 years. On Stela D (below), it is more than 400,000,000 years. (Redrawn from Maudslay 1889–1902; Morley 1915; Thompson 1950.)

9.23. Above the figure of this Tikal ruler named "Stormy Sky" is the depiction of an ancestor, possibly "Curl Nose" (see Fig. 7.14; see also Jones and Satterthwaite 1982: table 6). In the crook of "Stormy Sky's" left arm is a head whose headdress includes a very early example of the Tikal emblem glyph (A.D. 445). (After Marcus 1976a: fig. 2.3; redrawn from W. R. Coe.)

taking the current date of a monument and casting back into the past until they found a "great period" or cycle that ended on the same day. However, he added:

> The desire to probe half a billion years into the past reveals a strange mental quirk. It was, perhaps, an attempt to grasp the intangible in order to show that infinity has no starting point. The Maya priest traveled 400 million years backward, but he was as far as ever from the beginning which still eluded him. (Thompson 1950:316)

Today, we would no longer see these ancient dates as the result of some Maya mental quirk. The Long Count simply allowed the Maya to date mythical events as easily as recent history. In a context in which Americans might say, "Long, long ago in a galaxy far, far away," the Maya could simply say, "on the 3rd of November in the year 1,250,486 B.C." Among other things, the Maya were eager to draw comparisons between ancient and present-day events—to show, for example, that a current ruler was just like a mythical one. They clearly felt that it was important to have a present-day birth fall on the anniversary of an ancient one, and to have a present-day inauguration fall on the anniversary of a truly ancient one. To show that a Classic ruler was the full counterpart of a mythical ruler, they could search back thousands of years in their calendar until they found just the right coincidence of great cycles.

History? Sure. Like Paul Bunyan is history. Like Gilgamesh. Like Adam and Eve, but with dates that were accurate to the day.

Remote Ancestors as Flying Figures

We have already seen that the Zapotec portrayed some remote royal ancestors as flying figures. There are possible analogies in the Maya region. Both early in the Maya sequence (Long Count Cycle 8) and later (in Cycle 10) there were "floating" or "flying" figures at the top of some stelae; these could represent remote ancestors (Marcus 1974b, 1976a). In Cycle 10 these figures are shown outlined in dots, in serpentine shapes, which may represent drops of blood and hence a consanguineal relationship with more recent rulers. Early versions of the flying figures (prior to A.D. 445) lack such dotted lines (Fig. 9.23). The Cycle 8 depictions of these figures occur at sites such as La Venta, Kaminaljuyú, Abaj Takalik, El Baúl, Nakbe, Tikal, Uolantún, and Uaxactún (Marcus 1976a:32).

With the emergence of the lowland Maya state by A.D. 514, the use of these flying figures almost dies out (Marcus 1976a). After A.D. 800, however, they reappear in some quantity. Stela 4 at Ucanal, dedicated at 10.1.0.0.0 or A.D. 849, has such a figure dressed as a warrior (Figs. 9.24, 9.25a). There are smaller versions on Stela 1 at Jimbal (Fig. 9.25b), and still others on Stelae 1 and 2 at Ixlú. Examples from Ucanal, Jimbal, Ixlú, and Seibal have the dotted outline already described (W. R. Coe 1967; Graham 1967; Marcus 1976a:42–43; Stuart 1988). Some epigraphers believe that through these dots, or "droplets," the Maya were trying to show remote ancestors who shared *k'ik'* (blood) or *k'ik'el*

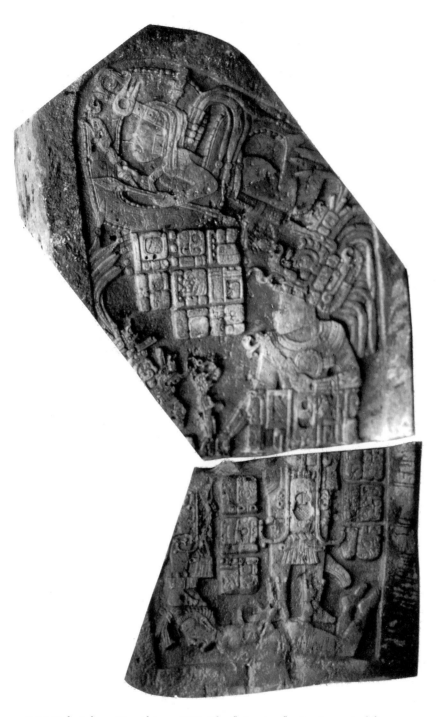

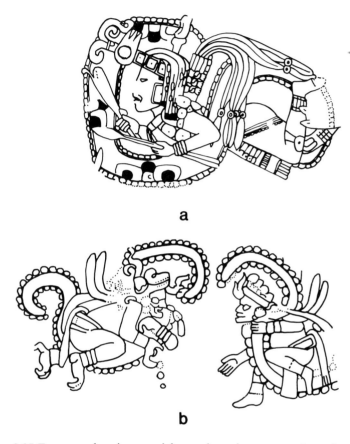

a

b

9.25. Two examples of ancestral figures from the upper portions of Maya stelae. *a*, the figure from the top of Stela 4, Ucanal (see Fig. 9.24). *b*, two figures from Stela 1 of Jimbal, a site near Tikal. The hieroglyphic names associated with the two Jimbal figures seem to refer to two long-dead rulers of Tikal, "Double Comb" and his successor. (Redrawn from Marcus 1976a: fig. 2.6; Jones and Satterthwaite 1982: fig. 78.)

9.24. Stela 4 from Ucanal (A.D. 849). The flying (or floating) ancestral figure at the top carries a weapon, and is encircled by feathers and dots. The living ruler stands below, stepping on the body of a captive. (Photo courtesy of Peabody Museum, Harvard University, Cambridge, Massachusetts, 1970.)

(semen) with the ruler shown on the stela, and thus were *etk'ik'elil*, "consanguineal kin." Similar droplets in the affixes associated with emblem glyphs (Affixes 36 and 37 of Thompson 1962) have been translated "of noble blood" or "descendant" by Dütting (1985), and "beloved offspring" by Barthel (1968).

Terms for some distant ancestors—such as *c'aa'na'*, "great-grandmother"—are similar to the terms for "sky dwellers," *c'aanal*. The carving of these possible remote ancestors high on the stela may be a way of showing that they dwelt in the sky (*ka'an*) or "on high" (*ka'nal*).

Invoking the Spirit of a Royal Ancestor

Like other Mesoamerican peoples, Maya rulers and nobles wished to communicate with their deceased ancestors. One of the most common rituals through which this was accomplished was bloodletting, and the frequency with which this act was depicted in art has helped contribute to the hyperbolic statement that the Maya were "obsessed with blood." The fact is that such rituals were not obsessive daily occurrences, but took place at designated intervals such as the fifth or twenty-fifth anniversary of a ruler's accession to the throne, the birth of an heir, or the twentieth anniversary of an ancestor's death.

The person often shown performing the bloodletting ritual was the wife of the reigning ruler. By performing that rite, she was able to invoke the image of an ancestral spirit, shown as a head emerging from the jaws of a fantastic serpent that rises out of a vessel filled with blood-spattered papers. The depiction of a serpent is appropriate, since in various Maya languages *kan*, "serpent," is a homophone of *ka'an*, "sky" or "celestial place," the abode of the ancestors (Marcus 1983b, Houston 1984).

At the site of Yaxchilán, Lintel 15 (Fig. 9.26) shows a royal woman seated at lower right, holding a basket containing (1) a stingray spine (for making the original perforation in her tongue); (2) the cord she used to pass through her tongue; and (3) the blood-spattered papers. On the left, ascending from another vessel filled with blood-spattered papers, is a fantastic serpent in whose mouth appears the face of a deceased ancestor.

Yaxchilán's Lintel 25 (Fig. 9.27) shows a similar scene, with the wife of the ruler Shield Jaguar holding a vessel with a stingray spine, blood-spattered papers, and a hieroglyph that refers to the act of bloodletting. Her ritual act has awakened the dormant spirit of a dead ancestor, apparently the lineage founder himself. He is dressed as a masked warrior and emanates from the upper mouth of a double-headed serpent, while another masked figure emerges from the lower end of the serpent. In the associated hieroglyphic text her husband's name "Shield Jaguar, Captor of Ahau" is mentioned, as is the special rite of conjuring up a deceased ancestor. The hieroglyphic sign that refers to this rite is a verb known as the "hand-grasping-fish" glyph (Thompson 1962:306; Glyph 714); its significance was first established by Proskouriakoff (1973:169–171). She thought of the resurrected figure as "a hero of the past or an ancestor of note, sanctified and invoked in

Bloodletting enables you to invoke the spirit of an ancestor.

9.26. Lintel 15, Structure 21, Yaxchilán. A rite of bloodletting has been performed by the Maya noblewoman (at lower right), apparently to commemorate the memory of an ancestor on the occasion of a temple dedication. The ancestor is visualized (at left) as a serpent who rises like billowing smoke from the blood-spattered papers the woman has deposited in the vessel below. In the jaws of this serpent we see the face of the deceased ancestor. This small lintel (sculptured area, 80 × 67 cm) provides an example of horizontal propaganda. It would have been seen only by a few, since it was set in the doorway of a temple and viewed when someone passed beneath the lintel. (Photo courtesy of the British Museum; see Marcus 1987: fig. 47.)

9.27. Lintel 25, Structure 23, Yaxchilán. A remote ancestor, one of the founders or early rulers of Yaxchilán, has just materialized as a fabulous double-headed serpent (shown at left). Inside the serpent's jaws we see a bust of the ancestral ruler, who holds a shield and spear and wears a mask. At lower right is the wife of the ruler Shield Jaguar, who has finished letting her blood, and now gazes on the image of the ancestor she has been able to conjure up. The occasion for this act of royal bloodletting seems to be have been her husband's accession to the throne. Once again we are dealing with horizontal propaganda, since the small scene was carved on the underside of a lintel in a temple. (Photo courtesy of the British Museum; see Marcus 1987: fig. 44.)

the ceremony depicted" (Proskouriakoff 1973:169). The occasion that prompts this blood-letting rite by Shield Jaguar's wife is her husband's accession to the throne. Note that both Yaxchilán lintels depicting the "serpent rite," or invocation of a deceased ancestral spirit, were set in the southeast doorway of different temples, commissioned by two different rulers when they took office.

There are other examples of royal bloodletting, of course. In Room 3 of the palace at Bonampak, one wall of the polychrome mural shows a whole family carrying out ritual bloodletting (Ruppert, Thompson, and Proskouriakoff 1955). A painted capstone from the Temple of the Owls at Chichén Itzá shows a "deified ancestor" issuing from the open jaws of a fantastic serpent (Morley, Brainerd, and Sharer 1983: fig. 13.28). Male members of the elite were not the only ones whose spirits were addressed by their descendants. On one famous polychrome funerary vessel from a tomb at Altar de Sacrificios (Adams 1963, 1971), a deceased lord dressed in serpent-skin pants and a belt with "death eyes" is shown dancing with a serpent over his head. This dancing figure offers apotheosis, or perpetual life, to the woman who was buried in the tomb in A.D. 754.

SUMMARY AND CONCLUSIONS

While the Mesoamerican states we have discussed were not uniform, we can isolate a few general principles. The divinity of one's royal ancestors was an important source of authority for the living Mesoamerican ruler. Living rulers controlled writing, and could charge their scribes to produce records linking them to the deeds and power of royal ancestors. Following metamorphosis into flying creatures, those ancestors had ascended to heaven and could then interact with powerful supernaturals such as the sun, lightning, thunder, or clouds. By linking himself with heaven and its denizens, the living ruler partook of the attributes of supernatural beings and powerful natural forces. Through the process of euhemerism, dead kings became heroes and eventually deities whose kin ties, real or imagined, to the living ruler were exploited to justify his actions.

Living rulers communicated with their divine ancestors through rituals of apotheosis. When these rituals were shown, either on stone monuments of the Classic or the pictorial manuscripts of the Postclassic, a whole series of fantastic images were used to capture the unearthly quality of the deceased ruler. He might materialize in the mouth of a fantastic serpent (Maya) or emerge from the fleshless jaws of the sky (Zapotec). He might appear disembodied, in a column of incense smoke, as a flying figure, or as a cloud depicted as a flying turtle; he might be tied to the living ruler by a cord (Aztec and Mixtec), or emerge from the interior of a fantastic genealogical tree (Mixtec).

Claimants to the throne might invoke the names of near, distant, or even mythical ancestors. When there was no gap in succession, and one's father or mother had been the previous ruler—in other words, when one's credentials were in order—it seems that near relatives were the ancestors principally invoked. However, when there were breaks in succession or when usurpers seized the throne, extraordinary efforts might have to be made to manipulate one's ancestry. A usurper might "borrow" a distinguished near relative (Aztec), or even argue that he was the descendant of an ancestor so remote as to have been mythological (Maya).

Mythical ancestors—and the mythical dates of their reigns—were the easiest aspects to manipulate, since no one could contest the assertions once they had been carved in stone or painted on deer hide. Usurpers or questionable candidates thus took great pains to commission extensive hieroglyphic texts, often going so far as to erase or destroy the texts of previous rulers. Since the ruler's speech was by definition true (chapter 1), no one was really in a position to question a text he had commissioned.

Scholars studying Precolumbian monuments have often interpreted specific rulers as "egotistical," "vain," "unusually pious," or "megalomaniacal" because of the number and magnificence of their monuments. As an anthropologist, I do not believe it is profitable to engage in such "paleopsychoanalysis" of individuals we cannot possibly know. It seems more likely to me that such cases of textual "overkill" were responses to uncertainty in the line of succession, either because of a gap in succession, a usurper's taking office, or competition between heirs to the throne. The claims of divine descent from supernatural beings, assertions of descent from mythical ancestors, and greater-than-lifesize stone monuments should be understood as forms of political propaganda, not the projections of ancient rulers' personalities.

10 ◆ ACCESSION TO THE THRONE

Every Mesoamerican state had rules concerning royal succession and the taking of lesser offices, but these rules differed from group to group. All coincided in restricting rulership to members of the hereditary nobility, but varied in the set of routes leading to the throne. Among the four groups discussed here, the Mixtec probably came the closest to maintaining the classic "first-born son of a first-born son" order of succession, while the Aztec were probably the most flexible about selecting a candidate on the basis of ability. In both systems, logical heirs sometimes died under suspicious circumstances, allowing a second-choice candidate to take office. Mixtec rulers occasionally married full siblings to ensure the bluest blood lines, while the other groups—perhaps bound by stricter incest taboos—did not. All groups reckoned descent in both male and female lines, but when a ruler's mother was of nobler lineage than his father, she was the one featured on his monuments.

When an individual was inaugurated as ruler, various rites took place. These rites varied from group to group, and sometimes from regime to regime. Some pre-inaugural and inaugural rites involved (1) the acquisition of a new title; (2) the taking of one or more captives for sacrifice; (3) one or more pilgrimages to sacred localities; (4) the insertion of a special nose ornament; (5) the taking of an "oral exam"; (6) rites of autosacrifice or bloodletting; and (7) the dedication of a new public building.

Among the Mixtec and Aztec, there is evidence for the presence of two separate sets of ceremonies related to office taking: first, a rite that involved the naming of the next ruler (sometimes while the current ruler was still alive), and second, a set of rites surrounding the official taking of office. In some cases, those two ceremonies were separated by a number of years; in other cases, by only a few months. During the interval between the naming ceremony and the office taking, the newly designated ruler often embarked

303

on military campaigns to secure captives who would be sacrificed at his inauguration, and/or made a number of pilgrimages to secure the support of local leaders, giving as well as receiving a series of gifts and offerings. This period of time served to prepare the ruler for his new job, as well as to reinforce past alliances and/or gain control of politically and economically important polities. Even Mesoamerican rulers, with all their power and prestige, often had to mollify competing factions of nobles, priests, or lower-order administrators before they could take office, especially when several potential candidates had been fighting for the throne. A great deal of propaganda was involved in these accessions to the throne, especially just before and after the inauguration.

Inaugurations often took place on days that were chosen by diviners for their auspicious character. There is reason to believe that the more questionable the candidate's right to rule, the more effort was devoted to making everything look auspicious. In this chapter we will see auspicious inauguration days selected in order to coincide with the supposed accession of an ancestor, whether real or mythical.

Days that bore the number 1 were considered particularly auspicious for both accession and royal marriage. For accession to the throne, the Aztec favored the day 1 Cipactli (Crocodile); the Mixtec also seem to have favored 1 Crocodile, although other days beginning with the number 1 were selected as well, such as 1 Wind, 1 Vulture, and 1 Motion. For the Maya, 1 Ahau, 1 Manik, and 9 Ik were some of the favored days. So few inauguration dates have been deciphered for the Zapotec that it has not been possible to note any special day preferences.

As we will see, one ruler at Palenque in the Maya lowlands selected 9 Ik for his accession so as to coincide with the accession of a mythical female ancestor who supposedly took office more than 3,000 years earlier, when she had reached 815 years of age; she had given birth to a child when she was 754 years old. This invocation of an ancient accession underscores the fact that some candidates to the throne believed they needed to draw a parallel between their accession and a venerated one that had taken place in the remote past. The two widely separated accessions were presented in the hieroglyphic texts as parallel events, clearly demonstrating the close integration of myth and history, of fact and propaganda.

Monuments relating to royal accession made use of a whole series of specific conventions. A convenient example is the depiction of the mat, which we have already described as a symbol for authority. The mat is one of the oldest iconographic motifs appearing on Formative ceramics in Mesoamerica, occurring as early as 1000 B.C. in Oaxaca (Fig. 10.1). What its precise meaning was at that early sociopolitical level, when social ranking was known but the state had not yet evolved, is not clear. However, during the subsequent Classic and Postclassic periods in Mesoamerica (A.D. 300–1520), the mat was utilized by several Mesoamerican groups as a symbol for power and authority. Among some groups, the mat constituted part of the metaphoric language and was an element in

10.1. Examples of the "mat" motif on Delfina Fine Gray pottery from San José Mogote in the Zapotec region, 1000 B.C. In later times, at least, this motif was a symbol of authority. (Dimensions of upper specimen, 20 × 8.5 cm.)

the system of iconographic signs or symbols; in other groups, it was only incorporated into the art, not into the metaphoric language of rulership.

Among the Aztec, the word "mat" was incorporated into the expressions "to govern" and "to hold office" (see discussion below under Prehispanic Aztec Rulership). In various Maya languages, "mat" (*pop*) was incorporated into the expressions for one kind of officeholder, a type of public building, and a verb meaning "to ennoble." The *ah hol pop*, "he at the head of the mat," was a government official in many towns in the Yucatán Peninsula who organized meetings in the *Popol Na* ("House of the Mat"), the municipal public building or "town hall." Like an Aztec ruler, the new Maya ruler was seated in office on the *ix pop ti balam*, "mat of the jaguar." The "seats" of nobles and lords were also called *pop*—a term that could also refer to the individual bulrush or cattail plants used to plait it. Like the Aztec scribes, those of the Maya used the mat as a symbol for "seated in office." One sixteenth-century Tzeltal dictionary also includes a term for "ennobled," *zbaopop*, which incorporates the word for "mat" (Ara [1571] in Ruz 1986:248).

Among the Zapotec and Mixtec, the term for "mat" was not included in expressions related to officeholding, but its absence in those linguistic expressions did not mean that it was absent from the iconography; in fact, the mat was an important iconographic symbol for both the Mixtec and Zapotec. What did vary among the four groups was the degree to which there was correspondence between language and iconography. Given this variation, we should not naively assume that all mat symbols had the same meaning in every group, nor that the same symbol corresponded to a similar expression in all four languages.

Mixtec expressions incorporating "mat," *yuvui*, seem to be more concerned with royal marriage than with taking office or governing, although it is also true that the married couple usually co-ruled their realm. Two Mixtec expressions for weddings—*yocuvuihuicoyuvuiya* and *huico yuvui*—incorporated the term for "mat" and can be translated "there was a royal celebration of the mat" (Reyes [1593] 1976:76, Arana and Swadesh 1965:138). In many Mixtec manuscripts the royal couple is shown on a mat, indicating that they are married and perhaps also indicating their co-administration of a polity. While floor mats are frequently depicted in the Mixtec codices, the use of the Aztec woven-mat "throne" was rarely used. It has therefore been argued that the woven-mat throne was an Aztec introduction (Smith 1983c:244).

The Zapotec term for "mat," *taha*, does not appear in any of the phrases for "to be seated in office" (Córdova [1578a] 1942:413v). Instead, the terms for "to govern" (such as *tozaalaoa ticha*, or *totogo tichaya*) incorporated the word for "speech," *ticha* (Córdova [1578a] 1942:207r). The importance of speech and oratorical ability for the Zapotec is also evident for the Aztec, whose term for "ruler," *tlatoani*, literally means "he who speaks."

Among some Mesoamerican peoples, achievement in battle became an increasingly important criterion for the selection of a ruler as time went on. Such achievement was never a substitute for noble status, but rather became an additional consideration, sometimes used to choose between more or less equally worthy claimants, or among several candidates each of whom was being pushed by a different faction. Maya rulers frequently took the title "Captor of X," and rulers of the Aztec and Mixtec also broadcast their conquests, often just before and after taking office. As early as the Classic period, Zapotec monuments suggest that prisoners of war were sacrificed at important rulers' inaugurations. These themes are discussed in more detail in our chapter on warfare (chapter 11).

Finally, we should stress that although each of these societies had rules for the selection and accession of rulers, the rules were not always followed. Some rulers died without heirs, and other heirs were poisoned or otherwise assassinated, sometimes by their own relatives. Candidates not in direct line to assume the throne, often seeking the support of dissidents or factions among the nobles, jockeyed for power and occasionally won out over the legitimate heir.

When a gap in succession occurred—for example, when no direct offspring or suitable close relative could be found—jockeying for power appears to have become particularly intense. Some claimants to the throne even seem to have been foreign to the polity, true outside usurpers. Often these usurpers, unlike those in the direct line of succession, had to expend more effort in legitimizing their claim to the throne by fabricating genealogical links to earlier rulers, mythical ancestors, or dynasties; they also probably had to expend more effort in currying the favor of a powerful faction. Some sought to impress by embarking on major building campaigns. In fact, I have suggested elsewhere that those with the least right to office were occasionally those individuals whose stone monuments or public buildings were the most numerous (Marcus 1974a, n.d.a). Often they commissioned hieroglyphic texts that associated them with mythical ancestors or employed hyperbolic and self-congratulatory language, particularly in regard to their success in battle or taking captives.

In this chapter we look at Aztec, Mixtec, Zapotec, and Maya royal accession as described by the sixteenth-century Spaniards. Then we turn to the prehispanic era to see to what extent those patterns can be seen in their stone monuments and hieroglyphic manuscripts. We will see how legitimate accession to the throne was documented, and the ways in which usurpers, or persons not in the direct line of succession, used propaganda to disguise any ambiguities about the legitimacy of their reign.

ROYAL ACCESSION AMONG THE AZTEC

As we saw in chapter 3, there were several Nahuatl-speaking ethnic groups living in the Basin of Mexico between A.D. 1200 and 1550, including the Tepaneca, Acolhua, Culhua, Xochimilca, Cuitlahuaca, Mixquica, Chalca, and Mexica. The history of the Mexica is most familiar to us, beginning with their settlement at Chapultepec and their subjugation at the hands of Culhuacán and Azcapotzalco, and ending with their independence and the founding of their twin cities, Tenochtitlán-Tlatelolco. However, the Mexica were but one of many ethnic groups that comprised Aztec society.

Several offices existed within the upper stratum of Aztec society. At the top of the ruling stratum were the supreme lord, the *huei tlatoani*, and many other lords, the *tlatoque* (plural of *tlatoani*). Prior to the arrival of the Spaniards, there were approximately fifty *tlatoque* in the Basin of Mexico, all supported by tribute and labor from their subjects. Some groups, such as the Mixquica, had just one *tlatoani*; others, such as the Chalca, had twenty-five.

There was perpetual competition for power among the *tlatoque*. One *tlatoani* might usurp the position of another and occupy both posts simultaneously. One *tlatoani* might subjugate another and let him remain in office while obligating him to meet a series of requirements. Or a conquering *tlatoani* might destroy another's office, reducing the town from the position of regional capital to that of dependency (Gibson 1964:34; Hodge 1984). This dynamic competition and jockeying for power characterized many Mesoamerican states for much of the period for which we have written records. A number of rulers achieved their position by conquest or usurpation, making it necessary for them to use propaganda to justify their position on the throne.

Of all the peoples we discuss in this book, the Aztec probably had the least rigid system of royal succession and the greatest social mobility. For example, commoners who were accomplished warriors could rise within the military to the point where they might be given grants of land, exempted from paying tribute, and allowed to attend sessions of the *tlatoani's* war council at the *quauhcalli* or "eagle's house" (Gibson 1964, Bray 1968, P. Carrasco 1971, van Zantwijk 1985; see chapter 11). A commoner warrior who took four captives in battle was given official rank, and his offspring might even be referred to as *pipiltin*, "minor nobles." However, his children's commoner heritage was never forgotten, and the honor their father had achieved by military prowess was not allowed to pass on hereditarily. Unlike real *pipiltin*, these "*pipiltin* by achievement" could only sell their land to true nobles; they could not have tenant farmers on their land; and they could not use feathers on their war costumes. These prerogatives were reserved for persons who were "*pipiltin* by birth," true hereditary nobles.

The *huei tlatoani*, or supreme ruler of the Mexica, was "elected"—a practice we cannot document for the Mixtec, Zapotec, or Maya. However, it should be emphasized that only hereditary nobles were candidates, and the "electorate" was not the general populace but a council of 100 nobles. In fact, from the time of Acamapichtli (A.D. 1372–1391) until the Spanish conquest, all Mexica rulers were chosen from a single family; however, the individual selected was not always a direct-line descendant.

The rules of succession varied from one Nahua ethnic group to another in the centuries leading up to the conquest. Among some groups, the oldest son of the previous ruler's principal wife was preferred, but his grandson (either his son's son or his daughter's son) might also be selected. Among other groups for example, the Mexica of Tenochtitlán—*brothers* often succeeded before sons. Once the council of nobles had made its selection, the candidate was presented to the populace for approval. The lords of the other members of the Aztec Triple Alliance—the *tlatoque* of Texcoco and Tlacopán—were also asked to approve the selection.

Election from among all noble candidates was supposed to result in the naming of the most able individual as the next *tlatoani.* However, as one can imagine, a number of factors entered into the decisions. Special interest groups and powerful factions played significant roles in determining the next ruler. For example, in A.D. 1416, even though there were far more experienced candidates than Chimalpopoca—he was only ten years old and had had no success in battle or experience in decision making—he was elected third *tlatoani* of the Mexica. One reason was that his mother was the daughter of Tezozomoc, ruler of Azcapotzalco, the town that was exacting tribute from the Mexica at that time. Thus the choice of Chimalpopoca was considered to be politically and economically advantageous; it was expected that since Tezozomoc's grandson would be the new Mexica ruler, tribute demands would be reduced.

When the first three Mexica rulers—Acamapichtli, Huitzilihuitl, and Chimalpopoca—were in office, they were the subjects of Azcapotzalco (Alvarado Tezozomoc [1609] 1949). However, with the fourth Mexica ruler, Itzcoatl, there was a major change; Itzcoatl was able to throw off the onerous yoke of Azcapotzalco. In gaining independence for the Mexica, Itzcoatl can be considered the founder of the Aztec empire. As a result of Itzcoatl's "reforms," enacted after A.D. 1428, new factors (in addition to genealogical proximity to the previous ruler) were involved in accession to the throne. The successor to office now had to display military prowess and achievement, and he had to be selected by a special inner council.

Rituals of Accession

The inauguration of the Aztec ruler took place on a day selected by a seer or diviner called the *tonalpouhqui.* As discussed in chapter 4, the *tonalpouhqui* was an expert at interpreting the 260-day calendar or *tonalpohualli.* For the performance of the inaugural rites, a beneficent day with good auguries was desired.

According to the Spanish chronicler Diego Durán (1951, 1:321–333), the day 1 Cipactli (Crocodile)—the first day of the 260-day calendar—was *always* chosen as the "coronation" or "office-taking" day. This statement is in agreement with Alva Ixtlilxochitl's (1952, 2:306) assertion that the two rulers named Motecuhzoma (Ilhuicamina and Xocoyotzin) were both "crowned" on the day 1 Cipactli. However, other ethnohistoric sources, such as the *Crónica Mexicayotl,* contradict these statements. They give inaugural dates other than 1 Cipactli for some, but not all, Aztec rulers (Alvarado Tezozomoc [1598] 1975).

One explanation for this apparent contradiction is that since each ethnohistoric source relied on informants from a different ethnic group, each of which may have employed a different calendric system, the inaugural dates which appear to be different may actually correspond to the same day (Nicholson 1961). The *Historia Tolteca-Chichimeca* (Kirchhoff, Odena Güemes, and Reyes García 1976), the Codex Xolotl (Dibble 1951), and other sources (e.g., Jiménez Moreno 1961) insist that there were several calendric traditions in the Basin of Mexico, some of which are designated by the name of the associated ethnic group—"Cuitlahuac," "Texcocan," "Mexica," "Matlatzinca," "Chalca," "Colhua I," and "Colhua II" (see chapter 4). Although most scholars today would agree that there *were* different calendric systems, most seem to feel that there were fewer than the thirteen different systems presented by Kirchhoff (1950, 1954/1955; Jiménez Moreno 1961).

According to Sahagún, the inauguration of the new *tlatoani* took place in the center of Tenochtitlán, at the Temple of Huitzilopochtli. The inauguree was dressed in a blue-green cape that bore a design of fleshless bones, and in the vestments of Huitzilopochtli, the hero who became deified in the likeness of the god Tezcatlipoca. Important speeches (*huehuetlatolli*) were delivered by the *tlatoque* and other nobles; those speeches served to link the new ruler with Tezcatlipoca.

As a result of the ceremony, the new ruler received the necessary powers from Tezcatlipoca, who had himself inherited them from his father, the "Old God" Huehueteotl, and from the "Fire God" Xiuhtecuhtli. To honor Xiuhtecuhtli, whose name can be translated "Turquoise Lord," the new ruler wore a turquoise diadem (*xiuhuitzolli*), a turquoise nose adornment (*yacaxiuitl* or *xiuhyacamitl*), and a turquoise-colored cape with turquoise stones knotted into it (*xiuhtilmatli*).

Prehispanic Aztec Rulership

Aztec authority and rulership were expressed by the metaphorical expression *in petlatl, in icpalli*, "the mat, the chair/throne." In the codices, the mat and woven-reed chair with backrest are used to convey these concepts; Aztec rulers are often shown seated on woven-reed "thrones" (such as the ones shown in Figures 7.3–7.7, 10.2).

In the Nahuatl language, the metaphor meaning "to govern" or "to hold office" was *petlapan, ycpalpan nica*, literally "on top of the mats" (Carochi [1645] 1910:188; Molina [1571] 1977:81r), and the ruler was referred to as "he who was on top of the mats." One of the other symbols for an Aztec ruler in office was a throne covered by a jaguar skin, the *oceloicpalli*. A mummy bundle set on a woven-mat throne stood for the death of a ruler; a living person seated on the same woven-mat throne depicted his successor (Dibble 1966:276) (see Fig. 9.1).

The ruler (*tlatoani*) and his rulership (*tlatocayotl*) were the topics of other metaphoric expressions. For example, the ruler was called the *iyollo altepetl*, "the heart of the city," addressed as *tlazotli*, "precious one," and compared to *chalchihuitl*, "jade"; *quetzalli*, "a quetzal feather"; and *teoxihuitl*, "turquoise" (Sullivan 1980:226–227). The ruler might also be regarded as a huge cypress tree or a silk cotton tree (*in ahuehuetl, in pochotl*) who created enough shade to protect all his people.

In addition to the Nahuatl metaphors and symbols of authority, a set of terms that included "quetzal feathers" or "precious green stones" was used to describe both the election and inauguration of the new ruler. Related Nahuatl terms included the following:

> *tlaixquetzalli*, "elected" (Molina [1571] 1977:123r);
> *tlaixquetzallotl*, "the inauguration" (Carochi [1645] 1910:216);
> *teixquetzaliztli*, "the election" (Molina [1571] 1977:49r); and
> *tlaixquetzaliztli*, "he who is elected for some cargo or office" (Molina [1571] 1977:123r).

Not surprisingly, there were many metaphors for the supreme ruler, *huei tlatoani* or *altepetl*, and his queen, *huei cihuatlatoani* (Carochi [1645] 1910:329). What is surprising is that there were so many metaphors for commoners. They might be called *cuitlapilli, atlapalli*, "the tail, the wing," from which Sullivan (1980:228) infers that the ruler was the "head" and the ruling class was the "body." Commoners were also referred to as *pacaloni, yacanaloni* ("one who is governed, one who is led"), or *in itconi, in mamaloni, in yecuexanco, in temamalhuazco* ("one who is carried, one who is carried on the back, one who is resting on one's lap, one who is in the cradle of one's arms")—all portraying the populace as helpless children dependent on the paternal ruler.

Let us now look at some specific accessions, beginning with that of the ruler Acamapichtli, as it was presented by the Aztecs in a pictographic document called the Codex Azcatitlán.

The Inauguration of Acamapichtli

Acamapichtli (A.D. 1376–1396) is generally regarded as the first *tlatoani*, or supreme ruler, of the Mexica. Like his successors, Huitzilihuitl and Chimalpopoca, Acamapichtli ruled at a time when the Mexica were still subjects of Azcapotzalco (see chapter 3). Because of this subject status, pictographic documents frequently emphasized the lowly Chichimec origin of the first three Mexica rulers by showing them seated on bundles of unwoven green reeds and wearing capes of animal hide (see Fig. 10.2). Such symbols of "primitiveness" were also used in depictions of the first five rulers of Huexotla (see Fig. 7.6a–e) and the first three rulers of Tenochtitlán. A similar device was to show one of the early Mexica rulers, such as Acamapichtli, dressed in a loincloth and carrying a weapon (Fig.

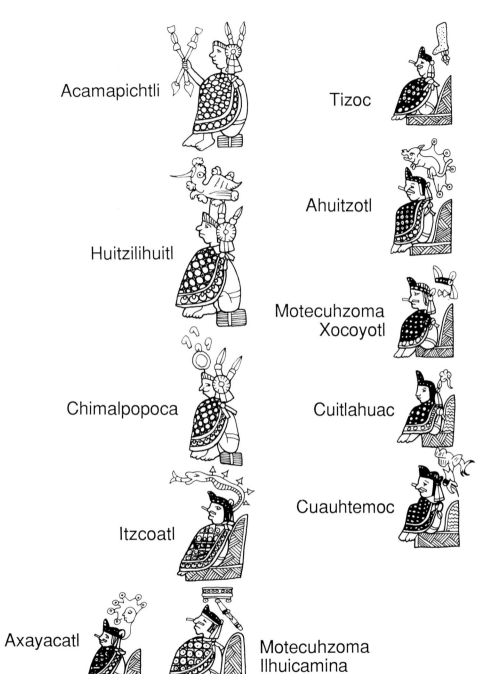

Acamapichtli

Huitzilihuitl

Chimalpopoca

Itzcoatl

Axayacatl

Motecuhzoma
Ilhuicamina

Tizoc

Ahuitzotl

Motecuhzoma
Xocoyotl

Cuitlahuac

Cuauhtemoc

10.2. Mexica rulers of Tenochtitlán. Note that the first three lords (Acamapichtli, Huitzilihuitl, and Chimalpopoca) sit on bundles of reeds; the fourth ruler, Itzcoatl, is the first to sit on a woven-mat "throne." Note also that Itzcoatl is the first of 8 rulers to wear a turquoise noseplug and royal headband. Rulers' name glyphs are usually drawn near the head of the figure. (Redrawn from Sahagún 1964: plate 39.)

10.3. The "first" or "founding" couple of the Mexica line of rulers. At left is Ilancueitl, and at right is her husband Acamapichtli. (Redrawn from *Fragment de l'Histoire des Anciens Mexicains* 1981: folio 8r.)

10.3). Almost certainly this display of primitive origins was an exaggeration—propaganda designed to contrast with the later glory of the Mexica.

Only with their fourth ruler, Itzcoatl, did the Mexica win their independence from Azcapotzalco. After this point, Mexica rulers were considered "civilized" and were shown seated on a woven-reed "throne" with a backrest (e.g., Figs. 7.3, 7.4). Sullivan (1980:234) has interpreted the earlier bundles of unwoven green reeds (*toloicpalli*) as symbols for "unconsolidated political power," while the later woven-reed thrones (*tepotzoicpalli*) represent symbols of "consolidated political power."

To return to Acamapichtli: despite his position as a subject of Azcapotzalco, he was revered and given partly legendary status as the first Mexica *tlatoani*. As so often happens with the founder of a line of rulers, there are so many versions of his life, his ancestors, his name, and the length of his reign that it is nearly impossible to straighten them out; perhaps we should not even expect to do so, knowing that his deeds and ancestry were rewritten at different times (e.g., van Zantwijk 1985, Gillespie 1989). Both the indigenous documents and the sixteenth-century Spanish sources give contradictory accounts of Acamapichtli's life, the result being that we can consider him a real historical figure, a symbolic lineage founder, or a combination of both.

One other ancestral figure was depicted in some—but not all—of the sixteenth-century documents that discuss Acamapichtli. This was a noble woman named Ilancueitl, "Old Woman's Skirt," who is shown with Acamapichtli in Figure 10.3. Ilancueitl is variously depicted as Acamapichtli's wife, his aunt, or a previous ruler under whom Acamapichtli had served as *cihuacoatl* or minister of internal affairs. In the Codex Mendoza (Clark 1938: folio 3r; Corona Núñez 1964, 1: Lámina II) Acamapichtli is shown serving as the *cihuacoatl* (internal governor) in the year 1 Flint (A.D. 1376). The title of "Snake Woman" or *cihuacoatl* appears above his head. Seven years later, in the year 8 Reed (A.D. 1383), he was selected to serve as *tlatoani*. Ilancueitl might have preceded Acamapichtli in this role. Part of the confusion comes from the fact that there were different women with the name Ilancueitl; for example, in one source (the Codex Xolotl) there are at least three women who bear that name (see Dibble 1951).

One of the women named Ilancueitl married Acamapichtli, son of Acolhua of Azcapotzalco. She is shown in the lower left part of Figure 10.4 (redrawn from the Codex Xolotl; for the original, see Dibble 1951: Plancha III, at E3). We know that Ilancueitl has moved to Tenochtitlán to marry Acamapichtli, because her footprints lead away from her birthplace, Culhuacán ("Hill with a Hook"), where her father Achitometl is shown seated on the throne. Above her we see her sister Atotoztli, whose footprints also show that she is leaving Culhuacán. At the upper left, Atotoztli is shown marrying Huetzin of Coatlinchán. With the marriage of his two daughters, Achitometl apparently gave each a dowry that included rights to special lands called *chinampas*, or "floating gardens"; these are shown immediately above the place sign for Culhuacán (Ixtlilxochitl 1891, 1952). The *chinampas* are divided into two sectors. On the left are the fields given to Atotoztli (note her hieroglyphic name among the fields); on the right are the fields given to Ilancueitl (whose hieroglyphic name is also shown among her fields). The marriage of Ilancueitl and Acamapichtli produced three offspring: Huitzilihuitl, Chalchiuhtlanetzin, and Xiuhtlanextzin.

The Códice Azcatitlán (Fig. 10.5) is the only pictographic document that shows the details of the accession of Acamapichtli (Barlow 1949b: Plancha XIII, 118). However, unlike most sources that discuss Acamapichtli, the Códice Azcatitlán does not include Ilancueitl.

The year of Acamapichtli's inauguration is given as 7 Rabbit (A.D. 1382). Acamapichtli is shown seated on an *oceloicpalli*, a stool with a cushion covered with jaguar skin (Fig. 10.5). We also see five individuals who supposedly participated in the inauguration. At the top center is Acacihtli ("Reed Rabbit"), seated on a high-backed chair; a black line connects his name sign, given on the left as "rabbit + plant," to his cape. Acacihtli was a member of the Tlacatecpan *calpulli* (a group of households that sometimes shared a common patron, ancestor, rights to use land, or ritual obligations) from the northeastern quadrant of Tenochtitlán. He was one of the two heads of that *calpulli*; the other head is

Atotoztli   Huetzin

10.4. The ruler Achitometl sits on his woven-mat throne in front of the place sign for Culhuacán ("Hill with a Hook"). Before him are his two daughters, Atotoztli and Ilancueitl. Footprints show them leaving their birthplace to marry the lords of other places. At lower left, we see Ilancueitl marrying Acamapichtli. At upper left, Atotoztli is shown marrying Huetzin of Coatlinchán. Each of Achitometl's daughters brought to her marriage the rights to *chinampa* lands, which are depicted above the place sign for Culhuacán. As indicated by the placement of each daughter's name glyph, Atotoztli's lands are on the left and Ilancueitl's are on the right. (Redrawn from the Codex Xolotl in Dibble 1951: Plancha III.)

Atotoztli

Achitometl

Ilancueitl

Acamapichtli   Ilancueitl

shown to the right. His personal name is not given, but the sign for (Tlaca)tecpan is. The sign includes a pennant or flag (*pan*), situated above an administrative building (*tecpan*). In this case, the pennant helps to distinguish the administrative building from a temple.

The other three men shown in Figure 10.5 are individuals who hold special paraphernalia associated with the rites of accession. On the right, we see a man who holds a large jade necklace; on the left is a man who holds up the royal cape. Immediately behind Acamapichtli is a standing figure who holds a staff of office in his right hand and a royal headdress in his left. To the right of Acamapichtli's stool is a hieroglyphic compound that includes the lower part of a leg (*icxitl, xotl*); an arrow (*mitl, chilatl*); and fire (*tletl*). This compound has been interpreted as "Chilatlexotl" by van Zantwijk (1985:102), who suggests that it is the ruler's personal name. He reinforced this suggestion by pointing out that "Chilatlexotl" could easily have been corrupted to "Xilechoz," a name for this ruler used in later documents written by the Spaniards (see *Relación de la Genealogía y Linaje de los Señores que han Señoreado Esta Tierra de la Nueva España* 1941:240–256). Van Zantwijk argues that "Acamapichtli" was a title taken on after inauguration, in order to draw a parallel between this Aztec *tlatoani* and an earlier Toltec ruler of the same name.

This accession scene is a good example of why Aztec writing cannot be considered history in our sense. To begin with, some of the people in the accession scene were not even contemporaries of Acamapichtli; for example, Acacihtli, regarded as one of the founders of Tenochtitlán and a participant in the Mexica migration, supposedly lived more than

10.5. Acamapichtli's inauguration in A.D. 1382. Acamapichtli is shown seated on a stool in the foreground, surrounded by five participants who carry all the new clothing and paraphernalia associated with his inauguration. This scene refutes the notion that scribes were writing history, since at least three of the people shown here (including the individual seated at top) could not have been in attendance—they lived 100 years or more before Acamapichtli. (Redrawn from the *Códice Azcatitlán* in Barlow 1949b: Plancha XIII.)

100 years before Acamapichtli's inauguration. Also, two antecedent Toltec lords—Huemac and Memexoch—are placed in the scene as well, apparently to link Acamapichtli to the Toltec imperial heritage. Like our own Mt. Rushmore, which juxtaposes several presidents whose lives did not even overlap, the scene makes an ideological statement rather than recording an actual meeting.

The Inauguration of Motecuhzoma Ilhuicamina in A.D. 1440

After having cried and mourned for the dead king Itzcoatl, the *cihuacoatl* Tlacaelel convened a meeting of the inner council and the rulers of Texcoco and Tlacopan to elect a new king. Tlacaelel is reported to have eloquently described the loss of their ruler Itzcoatl as follows: "[T]he mirror in which all see themselves is darkened. However, illustrious men, it is not suitable that the kingdom be left in darkness; may another sun emerge to light it" (Códice Ramírez 1944:78).

Motecuhzoma Ilhuicamina, "The Angry One" (also known as Motecuhzoma the Elder, or Motecuhzoma I), was selected ruler of the Mexica in A.D. 1440 (chapter 7). He was a nephew of the previous ruler, Itzcoatl; the son of a former ruler, Huitzilihuitl; and a relative of Tlacaelel. Since Motecuhzoma had served as the *tlacochcalcatl,* a high military official, during the war with Azcapotzalco, he was a member of the inner council at the time of his election to the throne. That membership was essential to his being named to the post of ruler, because as part of Itzcoatl's reforms the new ruler had to be selected from among the members of that inner council (Durán [1581] 1967, 2:125).

The Códice Ramírez (1944:78–79) provides a description of Motecuhzoma's inauguration. The newly elected ruler was taken with great pomp to the Temple of Huitzilopochtli, where he was clothed in royal garb and surrounded by all the noblemen who had been commanded to assemble in the courtyard. Motecuhzoma then performed rites of autosacrifice by piercing his ears and thighs with sharpened bones. The ruler's face was covered by a "fasting cape" decorated with bones. Days and nights of feasting and dancing followed. Many rulers and important officials from other cities attended and brought gifts.

As part of Motecuhzoma's inaugural rites, a new requirement for rulership had been introduced: the ruler himself had to go to war to obtain captives for sacrifice. Motecuhzoma had declared war on the Chalca—old enemies of the Mexica—and had fought bravely, taking many prisoners who were sacrificed on the day of his inauguration.

We should say a few words about the tradition of captive taking that followed Motecuhzoma's reign. Without question, the necessity to prove oneself in battle eliminated some candidates for *tlatoani.* It should not be imagined, however, that this was its sole purpose; it was also supposed to assure the Aztec that their next ruler would be able to add subjugated tribute-paying territory to the Aztecs' holdings. Nor should it be imagined that the battles in which these sacrificial victims were captured were tiny skirmishes, or "flower wars" fought only to procure captives, as has sometimes been suggested. In chapter 11 we will show that, whatever the emic rationalization for Mesoamerican warfare—imagined insults, the need for hearts to sacrifice, and so on—the etic reality was that hundreds of warriors died and foreign territory was seized. This was as true for the Maya, Mixtec, and Zapotec as it was for the Aztec.

The Mysterious Atotoztli, A.D. 1466–1472

Motecuhzoma I eventually died around A.D. 1468 or 1469 and was replaced by Axayacatl, then only nineteen years old (Fig. 10.6). There is some controversy about the beginning of Axayacatl's reign, and even the possibility of a gap in succession filled by a female "regent." Van Zantwijk (1985:188, 191) has argued that Motecuhzoma I did not actually live until 1469, but died earlier, leaving a six-year period between 1466 and 1472 during which a woman named Atotoztli was actually the Aztec ruler. (The *Relación de la Genealogía* [1941], in fact, suggests that Atotoztli ruled for more than 30 years.) One reason this reign is uncertain and poorly documented is the fact that some *tlacuilos* opted to leave a gap in the list of rulers, rather than be forced to mention the name of a female regent who filled in until a new male *tlatoani* could be chosen.

In the *Genealogía de los Príncipes Mexicanos* (Caso 1958a: Plate 1), Atotoztli is shown as the daughter of Motecuhzoma and the wife of Tezozomoc (see Fig. 10.7). Thick black lines link Tezozomoc to his father Itzcoatl (upper left), and connect Atotoztli to her father (upper right). Apparently Tezozomoc did not rule at this time, but served as an adviser to his wife Atotoztli, who did. She became *tlatoani* temporarily because her father lacked brothers, making the desired pattern of fraternal succession impossible. However, the pattern was resumed with the reigns of Atotoztli's and Tezozomoc's sons.

Significantly, the order in which their three sons appear in Figure 10.7—Tizoc, then Axayacatl, then Ahuitzotl (from left to right)—does not correspond to their birth order, nor does it correspond to the order in which each served as ruler (compare with dates in Fig. 10.6 and see discussion below). The youngest son (Axayacatl) served first, the middle son (Tizoc) served second, and the oldest (Ahuitzotl) served last.

The Sons of Tezozomoc and Atotoztli

With the death of Axayacatl in 1481, the selection of a successor was again of primary concern (Figs. 10.6, 10.7). All the leaders of subject cities were required to travel to the capital, Tenochtitlán. Old Tlacaelel, a long-term *cihuacoatl*, was apparently offered the post, but he refused because of his advanced age. Then the council turned to Axayacatl's older brother, Tizoc, who had been the *tlacochcalcatl* during the reign of Axayacatl, and selected him.

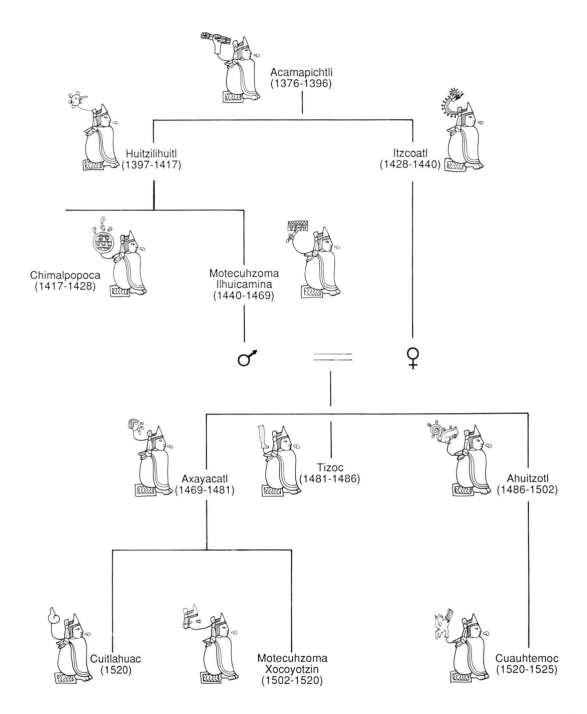

10.6. A reconstruction of the genealogical relationships among the 11 rulers of Tenochtitlán. (Adapted from P. Carrasco 1971, Hodge 1984.)

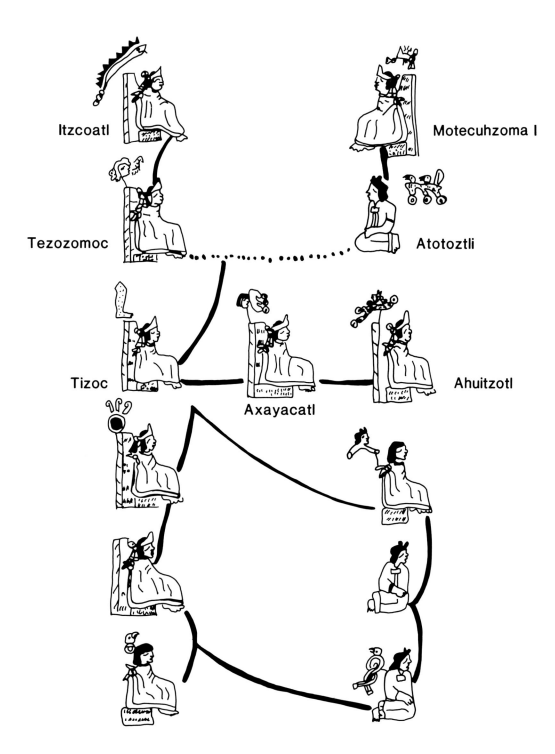

Itzcoatl

Motecuhzoma I

Tezozomoc

Atotoztli

Tizoc

Axayacatl

Ahuitzotl

10.7. Some of the later rulers of Tenochtitlán. Note that three women—including Atotoztli and María Moyeztica (lower right)—are also given. (We saw María Moyeztica earlier, in Fig. 7.8). (Redrawn from the Genealogía de los Príncipes Mexicanos 1958: plate 1.)

Like his immediate predecessors, Tizoc set out to secure sacrificial victims for his inaugural rites. (In chapter 11 we shall document the gap between Tizoc's claims in his stone monuments and the actual truth of his military "successes.") Tizoc's reign lasted from 1481 to 1486, possibly cut short because he was poisoned by his own nobles (Durán [1581] 1967, chapter 40); he was succeeded by his brother Ahuitzotl, whose military skills were such that he had no trouble obtaining sacrificial victims for his inauguration.

In 1502 came news of Ahuitzotl's death. Motecuhzoma Xocoyotzin, son of Axayacatl, was selected to be Ahuitzotl's successor. This new ruler set out to secure captives for his inauguration. Motecuhzoma Xocoyotzin was *tlatoani* when the Spaniards arrived in A.D. 1519 (Fig. 10.6).

While the Aztec rulers came relatively late in the Mesoamerican sequence, they display two patterns we see in earlier Mesoamerican peoples. The first was the need to show enough military skill to procure captives for one's own inauguration. We believe this pattern can be seen much earlier among the Zapotec and Maya (chapter 11). The second was the recruitment of royal women to serve as regents during a gap in succession between male rulers. We recognize this pattern much earlier in the Maya region (see below). Thus, although the Mexica may not have adopted these patterns until A.D. 1440 or so, when they did so they may have been borrowing the patterns of earlier peoples.

Since the Mixtec also had female rulers and inaugural sacrifices, they could have provided the Mexica with one model. However, still earlier Utoaztecan speakers, including the Toltec and perhaps even the Teotihuacanos, may have provided the Aztec with a model even closer at hand.

ROYAL ACCESSION AMONG THE MIXTEC

Unlike the Aztec, the Mixtec adhered much more strongly to birth order and displayed less flexibility in choosing their rulers. Often it was clear who the next ruler should be; nevertheless, since the approval of other nobles was considered important, it was customary that the heir to the throne solicit the support of other lords from nearby towns that had political and religious importance (Caso 1979:170). Furthermore, peregrinations to a number of powerful lords' towns were part of the preparations taken by the heir apparent before he was ready to take up the rulership of a *cacicazgo*. These pilgrimages involved the making of offerings at various localities—often caves and other sacred spots on the landscape—and consultations with real people or deities at politically important settlements.

Because the rules of Mixtec succession were clear, a successor to the current ruler was sometimes named years before the latter's death. This "naming of the successor" was a ceremony involving rites that confirmed and sanctified the heir's status. In the prehispanic era both the rite of naming the next ruler, and the inauguration itself, often took place on days beginning with the number 1. During the interval between those two ceremonies, the future ruler had time to consult with other lords, attend conferences, and embark on pilgrimages and conquests.

For the Mixtec, the day 1 Crocodile was ideal for accession to the throne, but other days carrying the coefficient of 1 were also favored for pre-inaugural rites. The day 1 Crocodile was the first day of the Mixtec 260-day calendar; probably not coincidentally, it corresponded to 1 Cipactli, the first day of the Aztec 260-day calendar. Since this day began the sacred calendar, it was an appropriate one to commence a new reign for both Mixtec and Aztec rulers. Accession dates were chosen specifically for their auspicious characteristics, so it is not surprising to see certain days occurring with higher frequency than others.

Examples of Accession

The Codex Nuttall provides us with an example of an accession that took place on the day bearing the coefficient 1: the Mixtec lord 8 Wind "Flint Eagle" supposedly took office on the day 1 Crocodile in the year 1 Reed, which was exactly 52 years to the day since his birthdate. In the codices Bodley and Vienna we see the Tilantongo ruler 5 Crocodile "Tlaloc Sun" (father of the famous conqueror 8 Deer "Tiger Claw") involved in at least two rites prior to his accession, both occurring on days with the number 1. On the day 1 Motion in the year A.D. 979, 5 Crocodile received a red jacket, a fan with yellow and green feathers, and two flint knives. Since he was just a ten-year-old boy in A.D. 979, this was probably a rite during which he was designated as being eligible to receive a *cacicazgo* (Caso 1977, 1979).

Eight years later, on the day 1 Crocodile in the year 1 Reed (A.D. 987), 5 Crocodile received the royal insignia of office. On that occasion he was officially named successor to the current ruler of Tilantongo, a man named Oconaña. The insignia consisted of a fan with quetzal feathers, a fan of gold, a breechclout with small gold beads and a fringe of feathers, a gold cup, a garland of flowers, and a red sleeveless embroidered jacket.

All these events evidently took place while the last ruler of the first dynasty of Tilantongo was still alive; Oconaña died in A.D. 992. It was not until two years after Oconaña's death, at the age of 25, that 5 Crocodile "Tlaloc Sun" finally became the official Lord of Tilantongo in the Mixteca Alta, on the day 4 Wind in the year 8 Rabbit.

In A.D. 1030, 5 Crocodile "Tlaloc Sun" died. At that time, 12 Motion "Bloody Tiger" became ruler of Tilantongo, since he was the oldest son of 5 Crocodile's principal wife. As for 8 Deer "Tiger Claw," he had to settle for becoming Lord of Tututepec on the Oaxaca coast, a title he apparently inherited from his mother.

In A.D. 1045, 8 Deer was approached in Tututepec by emissaries sent by a lord named 4 Tiger "Face of Night" (Caso 1979:321). According to the Codex Colombino, 8 Deer was challenged by 4 Tiger to play a ball game, which he won. Then 8 Deer was joined by his half-brother, 12 Motion "Bloody Tiger," and the two brothers conquered a place called "Hill of the Moon." From "Hill of the Moon" they took two prisoners (3 Crocodile and 1 Motion) and delivered them to 4 Tiger "Face of Night," so that the latter could sacrifice them. In addition, the Codex Colombino mentions five other places as having been conquered by these half-brothers; one of those places was Acatepec ("Hill of Reeds").

As the direct result of taking the ruler of Acatepec prisoner, 8 Deer "Tiger Claw" received a special honor, again on a day bearing the numerical coefficient of 1. On the day 1 Wind, 8 Deer was named a "great lord," *stoho*, and he is shown in three different codices undergoing the piercing of his nose for the insertion of a turquoise nose ornament. This insertion of a noseplug took place in the year 7 House (A.D. 1045 in Caso's chronology and A.D. 1097 in Emily Rabin's). Three depictions of this event from three different communities can be compared (see Figs. 10.8, 10.9, and 10.10); it was recorded in the Codex Nuttall, Codex Colombino, and Codex Bodley.

(Because the dates related to pre-accession and accession rites were selected, they often were days beginning with the number 1. Not only did 8 Deer's noseplug ceremony take place on a day with the coefficient of 1, so did that of another lord named 4 Wind "Fire-Serpent" [Codex Becker XV]. 4 Wind's nose-piercing rite occurred on the day 1 Vulture.)

The Codex Nuttall claims that 8 Deer's noseplug was inserted by a priest named 8 Death "Masked Vulture" (Fig. 10.8). The Codex Colombino shows 8 Deer having the noseplug inserted, but does not specify the name of the inserter (Fig. 10.9). The Codex Bodley shows Lord 4 Tiger "Fire Serpent" performing the rite (Fig. 10.10). According to the Codices Nuttall and Colombino, three days later, 8 Deer "Tiger Claw," accompanied by Lord 4 Tiger and their allies 1 Serpent and 8 Serpent, sacrificed quail. Then 8 Deer set out to conquer five places.

A few days later, 8 Deer's half-brother, 12 Motion, brought together 112 lords so that they could collectively conquer a place named "Xipe's Bundle." This was a town ruled by 12 Motion's brother-in-law, according to the Codices Nuttall and Colombino. (For additional evidence of important conquests by 8 Deer "Tiger Claw," see chapter 11 [see also Clark 1912; Caso 1979:172–173].)

With the death of his half-brother 12 Motion in A.D. 1048, 8 Deer "Tiger Claw" finally acceded to the prestigious throne of Tilantongo, but continued to rule Tututepec as well.

Gaps in the Succession to Office

In the prehispanic era, a direct lineal descendant of the royal couple usually inherited the title to their *cacicazgo*. When the royal couple failed to produce a direct lineal heir, a collateral relative had to be selected.

In the sixteenth century, several such cases are known for the Mixtec (see Spores 1967). Usually, this necessitated genealogical reversion to the grandparental generation, whence the most eligible surviving member of the dynasty could be traced. Sometimes the successful candidate was a cousin of the former ruler; sometimes it was a nephew or niece. In one case, a brother headed a new line of rulers (Spores 1967: fig. 3).

The Role of the Regent in Prehistory

We have already seen the case of a royal Aztec woman who served as regent while a new male heir was being selected. There is a similar case from the Mixtec dynasty of Tilantongo, involving the children of 8 Deer "Tiger Claw," whose exploits we mentioned above.

The appropriate heir to 8 Deer was his son 6 House "Tiger who Falls from the Sky," the oldest son of 8 Deer's first wife. However, when 8 Deer died in 1063, 6 House was only 3 years old and considered too young to take office. Therefore, 6 House's mother, 6 Eagle "Cobweb Tiger" (a daughter of the lord of Mitlatongo), seems to have served as his regent; by so doing, she prevented other young lords from seizing the throne. Other claimants included the sons of 8 Deer's other wives, men named 4 Dog and 4 Crocodile (Caso 1977:85).

We have stressed that in the Mixteca, there were first-born daughters who became rulers themselves. This case, however, involved a mother who held the position for her first-born son until he was old enough to rule. We will see similar cases from the Maya region.

10.8. In this figure and the next two (Figs. 10.9, 10.10), we see three different views of the same event, taken from three different codices. In A.D. 1045, according to Caso's chronology, the Mixtec ruler 8 Deer "Tiger Claw" became a "great lord" (*tecuhtli* [Nahuatl], *stoho* [Mixtec]), an event requiring him to have his septum perforated and a turquoise noseplug inserted. (This custom was also practiced among the Toltec and Aztec.) In this version from the Codex Nuttall, 8 Death "Masked Vulture" (on the left) performed the operation. The day is given as 1 Wind (above the figure of 8 Deer). On the far right we see the name sign "8 Deer," and at lower right is a "claw," the sign for his nickname "Tiger Claw." (Redrawn from Codex Nuttall 52.)

10.9. In this version from the Codex Colombino, 8 Deer "Tiger Claw" is shown having his noseplug inserted at a town whose name features plants, a step-fret frieze, and a jaguar pelt. The day 1 Wind appears at top center. Two figures, possibly priests, are dressed in elaborate attire for this rite. (Redrawn from Codex Colombino XIII.)

10.10. In this version from the Codex Bodley, 8 Deer is shown with his new turquoise noseplug already inserted; he wears a feline headdress and sits on a jaguar throne. The black-painted figure at right with the bone awl, evidently the person to be credited with inserting the noseplug, is a lord named 4 Tiger. (Redrawn from Codex Bodley 9.)

During the Classic apogee of Zapotec civilization (perhaps A.D. 200–700), stone monuments rarely showed accession to the throne. Other themes—the conquest of places, the capture of prisoners, royal marriage, and genealogical records—were far more frequently recorded.

Our one apparent record of Classic Zapotec royal accession, however, is spectacular. It involves a giant pyramidal platform, a set of offerings, and at least nine carved stone monuments depicting the ruler, a set of elite captives, and a series of noble visitors from Mesoamerica's largest Classic city.

The South Platform at Monte Albán, forming the south border of the Main Plaza, is one of the most impressive structures ever built at the site. Excavations by Acosta (1958–1959) suggest that the South Platform was built during Monte Albán IIIa (perhaps A.D. 300). It rises at least fifteen meters above the plaza and is more than 100 meters on a side. At least nine major stone monuments were set in the four corners of this building; they include Stelae 1–8 and the so-called "Estela Lisa" or "Plain Stela." In addition to carvings on the faces of eight of these stones, there are four that have "hidden scenes" carved on edges which cannot be seen under normal conditions (Marcus 1983j:175–181).

Analysis of this group of monuments suggests that the South Platform was dedicated at the time of inauguration of a ruler whose hieroglyphic name was probably 12 Jaguar. For the purposes of this inauguration, the ruler brought in six elite captives for sacrifice. Eight named persons from Teotihuacán visited him, bringing pouches of copal that were probably used in rituals at his accession. The relevant monuments are discussed in this chapter and chapter 11.

Let us begin with Stela 1 from the northeast corner of the platform, which shows the ruler seated on a cushion atop a massive throne supported by double heads of Cociyo, or "Lightning" (Fig. 10.11). He is dressed in the pelt of a jaguar and holds a decorated staff or lance in his left hand. His impressive headdress includes another depiction of Cociyo. The associated text is important, not only because of its length but also because of its content. The noncalendric portion of the text tells us of his divine descent (in the first column) and the sacrifices he has made at a temple (in the second column).

Now let us look at the hidden texts carved on the edges of Stelae 1, 7, 8, and the Estela Lisa, each of which was set into a corner of the platform (Fig. 10.12). All seem to relate to the same event—eight individuals leave a temple at Teotihuacán and arrive at the "Hill of 1 Jaguar" where a Zapotec lord welcomes them. These visitors wear a "Tassel Headdress" characteristic of Teotihuacán's ambassadors, men who carry copal bags instead of weapons (see C. Millon 1973, 1988). One group of Teotihuacanos is mentioned on Stelae 7 and 8, while another group is mentioned on Stela 1 and the Estela Lisa.

10.11. Stela 1, Monte Albán. This large monument (2 m × 2 m) was placed in the northeast corner of the South Platform to commemorate the inauguration of a Zapotec ruler probably named 12 Jaguar. The new ruler is shown seated on an immense throne, holding a decorated staff or lance. At right is a two-column text that records information on the date of this event, the ruler's inaugural ritual, and his genealogical past. (Drawing by Mark Orsen.)

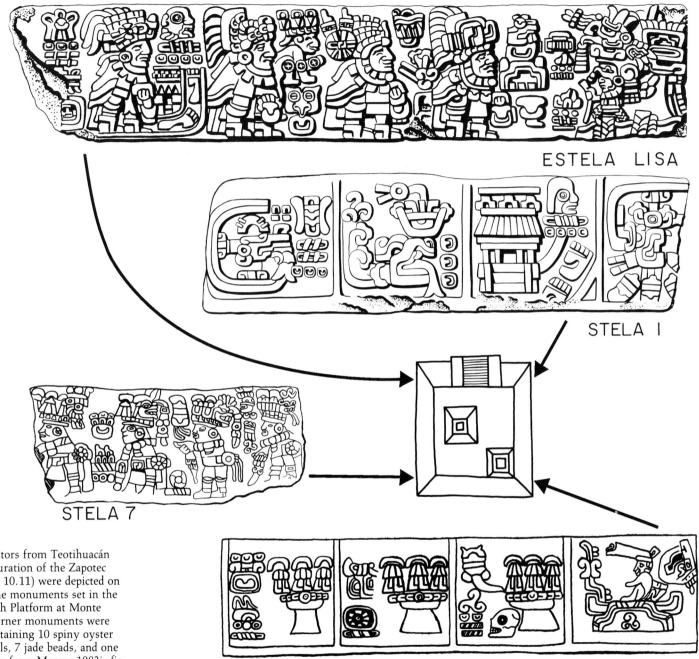

ESTELA LISA

STELA I

STELA 7

STELA 8

10.12. Distinguished visitors from Teotihuacán who attended the inauguration of the Zapotec ruler 12 Jaguar (see Fig. 10.11) were depicted on the hidden edges of stone monuments set in the four corners of the South Platform at Monte Albán. Beneath these corner monuments were offering boxes, each containing 10 spiny oyster shells, 10 tent olive shells, 7 jade beads, and one ceramic vessel. (Redrawn from Marcus 1983j: fig. 6.5.)

Beginning with Stela 1 and proceeding in counterclockwise fashion, we can retrace the steps that may have been taken by 12 Jaguar at his inauguration. Stela 1, in the northeast corner, depicts the ruler (see above); its underside, divided into four compartments, refers to Teotihuacán visitors named 13 Glyph A, 3 Serpent + Glyph C, and 9 Monkey. Moving on to the northwest corner we encounter the Estela Lisa, which depicts a procession of Teotihuacán visitors named 13 Glyph A, 9 Monkey, 1 Owl, and "Sacrificed Heart." Proceeding to the southwest corner, we find Stela 7, which shows Teotihuacán visitors named 3 "Maize Kernel" + 7 Glyph N, 5 Glyph D, and 12 Skull, each wearing a Tassel Headdress and carrying copal bags. Finally, in the southeast corner we come to Stela 8, divided into four compartments that again mention 3 "Maize Kernel" + 7 Glyph N, 5 Glyph D, and 12 Skull, each name shown in association with a Teotihuacán-style incense burner. It is likely that this visit by a small group of Teotihuacanos coincided with the dedication of the South Platform and the inauguration of the Zapotec ruler shown on Stela 1.

Also as part of this dedication, offering boxes were hidden under Stelae 1 and 7 and the Estela Lisa. Each contained a cache with two species of spiny oyster shells (5 *Spondylus princeps*, 5 *Spondylus calcifer*); 10 tent olive shells (*Oliva porphyria*); 7 jade beads; and a ceramic vessel in Monte Albán IIIa style.

Six large monuments in the South Platform—Stelae 2, 3, 5, 6, 7, and 8—depict bound captives, presumably nobles captured from enemy communities and brought to Monte Albán to be sacrificed at the ruler's inauguration. All these captives have their hands tied behind their backs with rope, and all stand on hill signs depicting their places of origin; many are dressed in elaborate animal costumes and/or feather headdresses. These stelae will be illustrated and described in chapter 11 under "Zapotec Warfare," but for the purposes of this chapter they should be considered part of the accession ritual associated with the South Platform.

Included in this group of monuments is Stela 4, which appears to show a Zapotec lord named 8 Deer conquering a place by driving a lance into it. This monument, too, is illustrated and discussed in chapter 11. We do not know the relationship of 8 Deer (not to be confused with the later Mixtec lord of the same name) to 12 Jaguar, the Zapotec ruler shown on Stela 1. Perhaps 8 Deer was a relative or an ancestor whose early conquests 12 Jaguar wanted to mention as analogous to his own.

What this group of South Platform monuments indicates is that during the Early Classic (Monte Albán IIIa), the Zapotec had many of the same inaugural rituals we see among the Classic Maya and the Postclassic Mixtec and Aztec. Accession to the throne involved conquests by the heir designate, the taking of captives for sacrifice, the making of offerings by the new ruler, the dedication of a temple or other new buildings, and visits by distinguished nobles from other communities. Interestingly enough, the scenes of the ruler and his noble captives seem to have been vertical propaganda, writ large and meant to be seen from afar. The much tinier scenes of Teotihuacán visitors, hidden on the edges of the same stones, were evidently horizontal propaganda aimed at other nobles, such as those placing items in the offering boxes.

Postclassic Zapotec Royal Accession

From the later periods of Zapotec civilization, we have documents that are partly historical and partly mythical. One of the best known is the Lienzo de Guevea, a nineteenth-century copy of an A.D. 1540 document from the Isthmus of Tehuantepec, part of which was discussed in chapter 6. To place the document in context we should discuss the movement of the Zapotec dynastic seat from the Valley of Oaxaca to the Isthmus.

The founder of the so-called Zaachila dynasty probably ruled from the end of the fourteenth century A.D. into the beginning of the fifteenth century. His personal name is no longer known, so he is referred to simply as "Zaachila I." He reportedly died sometime around A.D. 1415 (Burgoa 1670, 1674; Gay 1881; Bancroft 1882; Martínez Gracida 1888; Marcus 1983l, 1983m). In that same year his son, known only as Zaachila II, succeeded him. Upon the death of Zaachila II in A.D. 1454, his son Zaachila III acceded to the throne.

Beginning with the reign of Zaachila III, some scholars believe that Zapotec history begins to emerge somewhat from legend and become slightly more reliable. One reason for this is that the later Zapotec rulers are reported to have interacted with Aztec rulers, the details of whose reigns are much better known. For example, Zaachila III was on the throne when the Aztec ruler Tizoc died. Tizoc was succeeded by Ahuitzotl in A.D. 1486. In A.D. 1487, following the death of his father Zaachila III, the famous Zapotec ruler Cociyoeza ("Lightning Creator") acceded to the throne (Fig. 8.16).

Ahuitzotl was aggressive in his efforts to secure captives for his inauguration, and once in office he attempted to subjugate much of what is now the State of Oaxaca. According to the Codex Chimalpopoca, Ahuitzotl conquered Jaltepec and Tiltepec in the Mixteca between 1493 and 1495, and Juchitán and Tehuantepec in the Isthmus between 1496 and 1497. The Codex Telleriano-Remensis (Kingsborough 1831–1848, 5:153; Corona Núñez 1964, 1: Lámina XXII) claims that he conquered Mitla in the Valley of Oaxaca in 1494 and Zaachila itself in 1495. Alternatively, the Códice en Cruz gives 1496 for the conquest of Zaachila (see Dibble 1942:75, 146), while Ixtlilxochitl (1892, 2:271–289) gives 1492 for the same conquest. These differences among ethnohistoric documents may be partly a result of the different indigenous calendars that had evolved in the Basin of Mexico in the centuries immediately before the Spanish conquest (see chapter 4).

Cociyoeza was perhaps the most famous of all Zapotec rulers, in part because he was able to defend the Isthmus of Tehuantepec successfully against outside attackers with the aid of the Mixtec ruler of Achiutla. The famous battle of Guiengola was the focal point of this military success. This seven-month battle ended with a truce sealed by the marriage of the Zapotec ruler Cociyoeza to the daughter of the Aztec ruler Ahuitzotl (chapters 7, 8).

In A.D. 1518, at the age of sixteen, Cociyoeza's son Cociyopii ("Lightning-Wind/ Spirit") was named ruler of Tehuantepec, while his father remained in Zaachila as the supreme lord or *coquitào*. Cociyopii was the last of the great Zapotec rulers, and survived to be baptized Don Juan Cortés by the Spaniards. He died in A.D. 1563 at the age of sixty-one, the longest-lived Zapotec lord whose lifespan we can document. (In a recent study of 549 prehispanic skeletons from the Valley of Oaxaca, Hodges [1989] found only one or two whose age at death exceeded fifty-five.)

In the Lienzo de Guevea many of the aforementioned Zaachila rulers are shown, with their names written in Zapotec and Spanish in Latin characters (Fig. 10.13). At the bottom of the document we see the place sign for Zaachila (the label is "Sachila"), a hill sign inside a six-tiered pyramid that presumably represents the giant archaeological mound at Zaachila. Seated atop the place sign is a ruler in a red robe, red-peaked cap, and black beard, accompanied by the gloss *Yobicoxi chalachi*. Behind his head is a line leading to a serpent head. Above him is a similar figure whose associated gloss is *Rinicoxi chaleguesa*. These expressions in Zapotec correspond to "first ruler" and "second ruler," or "first-born son" and "second-born son." *Yobi* and *rini* were used by the Zapotec to record birth order or to count objects in sequence, based on the use of a hand where *yobi* meant "thumb," *tini* "second finger," and so on (see Córdova [1578b] 1886; Marcus 1983l:305).

We do not know whether these two figures correspond to Zaachila II and III, or whether they represent the first two sons of Cociyoeza. Those sons (Bitoopaa and Natipaa) did not rule at Zaachila, presumably because they were outranked by Cociyopii, whose mother was an Aztec princess (see Fig. 8.16).

The third person seen in the Lienzo de Guevea sequence is Cociyopii (glossed "Cosiobi"), who we know was the son of Cociyoeza and the Aztec princess Coyolicatzin. The fourth ruler shown is Cociyoeza (glossed as "Cosihuesa"), son of Zaachila III and father of Cociyopii. Above him is someone glossed "Penobiya" (which may mean "12 Twisted")—perhaps a reference to Pinopiaa, a daughter of Cociyoeza who died in Tehuantepec.

Footprints lead from the dynastic seat at Zaachila to a new place, designated by a fierce carnivore on a hill sign glossed "Tehuantepegue" (*te-cuan-tepetl*, "People-Eater Hill" [Paddock 1983a:310]). In front is the figure and gloss of "Cosiobi." Ethnohistoric sources confirm that, indeed, Cociyopii was named ruler of Tehuantepec in A.D. 1518. Cociyoeza is shown sitting above Cociyopii, as if legitimizing his son's right to rule. As

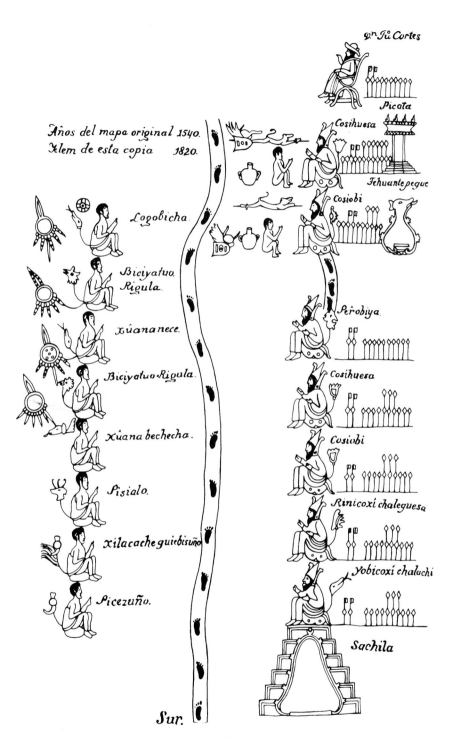

10.13. The original Lienzo de Guevea was painted in A.D. 1540 to establish the territory controlled by the Zapotec lord of Guevea in the Isthmus of Tehuantepec. As part of this record, scribes painted the sequence of Zapotec rulers whose original dynastic seat had been Zaachila (in the Valley of Oaxaca), until political and military pressures of the Postclassic era forced it to move to the Isthmus of Tehuantepec. As we have seen elsewhere in Mixtec and Zapotec genealogical records, such dynastic sequences are to be read from bottom to top. Beginning in the lower right corner, we see the place sign for "Sachila" (Zaachila)—a hill sign inside a six-tiered pyramid, evidently a reference to the huge archaeological mound at Zaachila. The first 5 individuals are associated with Zaachila; then we see footprints leading to a figure named "Cosiobi" (Cociyopii), who is associated with a hill sign with a feline head. This indicates that Cociyopii ruled "Tehuantepegue" (Tehuantepec). Above him is the figure of his father "Cosihuesa" (Cociyoeza, who was ruler at Zaachila), appearing here to legitimize his son's new dynastic seat in Tehuantepec. At the top is a figure seated in a Spanish armchair and wearing Spanish attire; he is labeled "Don Juan Cortes," a name we recognize from other documents as the baptismal name Cociyopii received from the Spaniards. On the far left are the names of other Zapotec nobles (discussed in chapter 3), and immediately in front of Cociyopii and Cociyoeza at Tehuantepec are offerings and gifts they received. (Redrawn from Seler 1908; see Marcus 1983l : fig. 8.35.)

part of Cociyopii's inauguration at Tehuantepec, both he and his father Cociyoeza are shown as having received a number of gifts, including meat, fermented beverages, feathers, and slaves. Finally, at the top of the dynastic list is an individual in Colonial Spanish clothing labeled "Don Juan Cortes." We know from ethnohistoric sources that Cociyopii was in fact baptized with this name in December of 1521.

MAYA ROYAL ACCESSION

We know a great deal about the rules and rituals of royal accession among the sixteenth- and seventeenth-century Maya because of the extensive ethnohistoric literature on that period. These data, in turn, can be used to inform our analyses of earlier accession texts and scenes from monuments of the Classic period.

Sixteenth- and Seventeenth-Century Data

Ethnohistoric sources tell us that during the late Postclassic and early Colonial period, *batabob* or local lords in Yucatán had to submit to a test or questionnaire to prove that they were qualified to rule. Another test was given at the end of every *katun*, or twenty-year period.

Even though these local lords had presumably inherited the right to rule, they also had to learn all the prophecies, rituals, and background information necessary to answer the questionnaire correctly. The previous incumbent—usually the *batab's* own father—was the person most likely to have supplied him with that crucial esoteric knowledge. Thus the right to rule combined hereditary eligibility with acquired competence. To make the exam more difficult, the questions were changed after each *katun*.

The Maya expressed the purpose of the oral exam as follows:

> This is the examination [demand for knowledge] which takes place in the *katun* which ends today. The time has arrived for examining the knowledge of the chiefs [local lords] of the towns, [to see] whether they know how the ruling men came, whether they have explained the coming of the chiefs, of the head-chiefs, whether they are of the lineage of rulers, whether they are of the lineage of chiefs, that they may prove it. (Roys 1967:89)

One of the key phrases in this quotation is "that they may prove it," referring to the fact that the rulers needed to learn the correct answers by maintaining access to privileged information. Since the questions were changed over time, a ruler had to be prepared for new questions if he were to be successful in his efforts to prove his right to rule each time he was interrogated.

Typical of such an exam was the one given in the province of Sotuta in Yucatán. All local lords were required to assemble at Mani during the month of Xul, to be tested by the supreme regional ruler or *halach uinic*. These *batabob* included some who bore the prestigious patronymics of (Tutul) Xiu and Itzá; even they had to prove themselves continuously.

An exam typically consisted of seven questions, phrased in the form of riddles and given in a special ritual language called "The Language of Zuyua (Suiua)." This language, which was apparently non-Maya, is discussed below. Obviously, the use of a special language that only hereditary nobles would have learned helped to weed out any impostors or usurpers.

Let us now look at some of the riddles, which are given in the Chilam Balam of Chumayel (Roys 1933, 1967). The second of the seven riddles was "Let them go and get the brains of the sky, so that the head-chief may see how large they are." The correct answer to this riddle was given in the Language of Zuyua as "I have brought copal," since "the brains of the sky" was a metaphor for copal gum (Roys 1967:90). Roys has suggested that copal (*Protium copal*), the primary incense burned by the Maya, produced thick clouds of smoke which may have reminded the Maya of the convolutions of the brain.

The seventh riddle was "Go and gather for me those things which plug the bottom of the *cenote*, two white ones, two yellow ones. I desire to eat them." The correct answer, in the Language of Zuyua, was "I have brought four *jícamas*, two yellow, two white" (Roys 1967:91). *Jícamas* (*Pachyrrhizus erosus*) can be shaped like huge plugs, are eaten raw, and come in yellow and white.

What can we say about the vehicle for this exam, the Language of Zuyua? There are hints that it may be Nahua-derived, perhaps a legacy from the Toltec or Chontal immigrations into Yucatán between A.D. 800–1000. Not only does "Zuyua" sound Nahua (from "Zuiven," the Nahua uppermost heaven, "abode of the creator Ometecuhtli"; see Fig. 4.9), but many of the answers in the exam, such as *jícama* (from Nahua *xicamatl*) are central Mexican as well (Marcus 1982b). This is perhaps not surprising, since the prestigious patronymic "Xiu" is itself a Toltec legacy (from Nahua *xiuitl*, "plant").

There are several opinions about the language of the exam. One holds that the Maya incorporated Nahua terms into the tests for their *batabob* after the Toltec had arrived in Yucatán. This could have happened because the Toltec elite gave Nahua words an aura of prestige; or perhaps the Maya nobles' ability to speak Nahua was a skill that could be used to distinguish them from commoners. Alternative opinions on the Language of Zuyua would see it either as a metaphoric language (Arzápalo 1986) or as Mixe-Zoque-derived (Stross 1983). One thing is clear: knowledge of the answers to the riddles could be controlled by the elite few.

Answers to the riddles could even be used by one Maya lineage to eliminate *batabob* from competing lineages. For example, the Xiu used their set of riddles to remove Itzá lords from the towns over which the Xiu had just recently gained control. Preempting accusations of favoritism, the Xiu used failure to pass the exam as justification for the removal of Itzá competitors from office. For all we know, the Classic Maya may have had similar tests, but we have no way of determining this at present.

The Terminology of Accession

The verb used by the Maya for accession to the throne, both in Classic and Postclassic times, was "to be seated." The fifteenth- and sixteenth-century Books of Chilam Balam refer to rulers being seated, being set "on high," and occupying the "jaguar-mat" (*ix-pop-ti-balam*). For example, Roys translates one passage from the Chilam Balam of Chumayel as follows:

> Then they began to declare him ruler. Then he was set in the seat of the rulers by them. . . . Then they began to take the prophecy of this ruler after it was declared. Then they began to set aloft the house on high for the ruler. Then began the construction of the stairway. Then he was set in the house on high in 13 Ahau, the sixth reign. (Roys 1967:75)

Just as there were seatings for new rulers, so were there seatings for units of time, such as the next *katun*. For example, *Buluc Ahau katun cumaan ti pop, cumaan ti dzaam, ti ualaac yahaulili* can be translated "*katun* 11 Ahau is set upon the mat, set upon the throne, when their ruler is set up" (Roys 1967:77). Also, the expression *nicte u kanche, culic tu dzam*, "the Plumeria flower is his chair, as he sits on his throne," could be used (Roys 1967:153).

During the twelfth to sixteenth centuries A.D., succession to office was often from father to son. Sometimes, however, sons were sent out to govern other towns within their father's territory, rather than to rule at the capital (e.g., *Relaciones de Yucatán*, 2:208). There were also cases, like the ones seen among the Aztec, where an heir was too young to reign. In this case, his mother or older brother might serve as regent until the heir was old enough:

> If when the lord died, his sons were not fit to govern, and if he had brothers, the oldest or the most forward of his brothers ruled, and they taught the heir their customs and their feasts, looking to the time when he should be a man himself. And though the heir was fit to rule, these brothers still held command to the end of their lives, and if there were no brothers, the priests and important people elected a man capable of ruling. (Landa [1566] in Tozzer 1941:100)

Classic Maya Accession

The stone monuments of Piedras Negras, a Classic Maya secondary center on the east bank of the Usumacinta River, offer us one of our best opportunities to study both the scenes that depict rulers acceding to the throne as well as the texts that record their inaugurations (Maler 1901–03). Specifically, the Piedras Negras stelae provide inscriptions that reveal a sequence of seven rulers who reigned there ca. A.D. 600–800.

Each ruler's set of monuments begins with a stela that depicts the "ascension motif." Associated with this motif are the date of his inauguration and a hieroglyphic expression, nicknamed the "toothache glyph" (see below), which refers to that event (Proskouriakoff 1960).

The ascension motif shows an individual dressed in elaborate garb, seated cross-legged upon a throne in a canopied doorway or niche; leading up to the throne are footprints and a ladder. Framing the niche is a band that includes a series of celestial and planetary signs. Above the niche is a celestial bird, and below it is a two-headed supernatural terrestrial. Thus each new ruler is shown seated in the doorway of his temple, close to the celestial realm (Fig. 10.14).

On one of these monuments—Stela 11 of Piedras Negras—a scene of human sacrifice is shown taking place at the base of the pyramid that supports the temple (Figs. 10.14 and 10.15). Although human sacrifice among the Maya may not have been on the same scale as that of the Aztec, it was apparently a requirement for inauguration rituals just as it was among the Aztec, Mixtec, and Zapotec.

At Piedras Negras, Ruler 1's monuments were set up on a platform in front of Structure R-9. He was inaugurated in A.D. 603 (Long Count date 9.8.10.6.16 [10 Cib 9 Mac]). Ruler 2's first seven monuments were aligned in front of Structure R-5 and his last two in front of Structure K-5 (Fig. 3.27). Ruler 3's monuments were set up in front of Structure J-4. Ruler 4's principal monuments were set up in front of Structure J-2. Ruler 5's were set up on a terrace in front of Structure O-13, while Ruler 6's and Ruler 7's monuments were set up in front of Structure O-13 (Fig. 10.16).

Rulers at Piedras Negras (Proskouriakoff 1960), Calakmul (Marcus 1987), and some other sites (Kelley 1962b, Marcus 1976a, Sharer 1990) attempted to arrange their monuments in groups. Such groups were often aligned in front of pyramidal platforms that had either been built or refurbished for them. In cases where the platform was a preexisting one, built originally by a previous ruler, the new lord either rededicated it or built a new temple on it, placing new dedicatory caches.

A ruler's age at inauguration varied considerably within a single site, as well as from site to site (Marcus 1976a, 1987). At Piedras Negras, Ruler 2 reportedly acceded to the throne at the age of twelve; Ruler 3 at twenty-two; Ruler 4 at twenty-eight; and Ruler 7 at thirty-one. The length of six rulers' reigns can be calculated as follows: 35, 47, 42, 28, 5, and 17 years (Proskouriakoff 1960).

However, only with Ruler 3 (on Stela 6) and Ruler 4 (on Stela 9 and Altar 2) do we encounter lords who recorded their birth dates on the same monument as their inauguration dates. For example, Ruler 2 first recorded his date of birth after he had already been on the throne for twenty years. Ruler 7 also did not record his birth date until he had

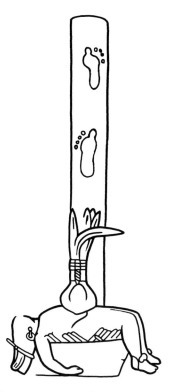

10.15. The inauguration of Maya rulers, like those of the Aztec, Mixtec, and Zapotec, could involve human sacrifice. Here, in this close-up view of the base of Stela 11 at Piedras Negras, we see a victim who was sacrificed as part of the new ruler's inaugural rites (see Fig. 10.14). (Redrawn from Spinden 1913.)

10.14. Maya stelae frequently used the "ascension motif" to indicate a ruler's accession to the throne. Stela 11 at Piedras Negras, Guatemala, shows the fourth ruler of that site in such a scene. He is seated cross-legged in the doorway of a temple, surrounded by planetary and celestial symbols. Above his head is a fantastic bird, evidently a supernatural. A ladder and footprints appear in front of the temple pyramid. At the base of the ladder is a sacrificial victim whose heart has been removed, and whose open wound issues blood (symbolized by a bundle of long feathers that rise up out of the victim's chest). This stela was carved in A.D. 731 to commemorate the reign of a new ruler, whose inaugural rites included human sacrifice. (Redrawn from Stuart 1988: fig. 5.26.)

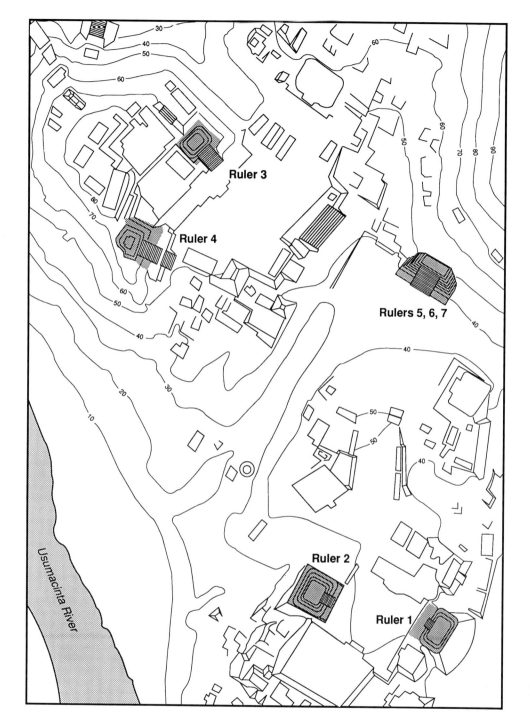

10.16. Each ruler at Piedras Negras erected all (or most of) his stelae in front of a structure he had either commissioned or rebuilt. Ruler 1 set his monuments in front of Structure R-9; Ruler 2, in front of Structure R-5; Ruler 3, in front of Structure J-4; Ruler 4, in front of Structure J-2; Ruler 5, on the terrace of Structure O-13; and Rulers 6 and 7, in front of Structure O-13. (Redrawn from Eldridge Johnson and Tatiana Proskouriakoff's 1939 map).

been on the throne for many years; and for Rulers 1, 5, and 6 no birth dates are given at all. What this means is that most rulers had an opportunity to tamper with their own dates of birth, projecting them backward in time to coincide with the anniversary of some mythical ancestor's birth, or simply to make themselves appear older and more venerable than they were.

Since the date of a Piedras Negras ruler's inauguration falls in the *hotun* (approximately a five-year period) before the monuments were carved—and since the scene on the front of the monument depicted the ascension motif—it appears that the inauguration itself was the motivation for carving and erecting these monuments (Proskouriakoff 1960: table 1). Each reign at Piedras Negras was marked by the setting up of a stela that depicted the ascension of a new ruler. Unfortunately for us, the Piedras Negras custom of depicting the ascension motif, in which footprints lead from the bottom of a pyramid to the ruler seated cross-legged on his throne, was not utilized at all Classic Maya sites. The Piedras Negras pattern of erecting monuments at the end of five-year periods was a boon for epigraphers like Proskouriakoff, allowing her to monitor change over very short periods of time. Other sites (such as Calakmul and Naranjo) typically commemorated ten-year and twenty-year periods, making our chronology less fine-grained.

As we noted earlier, eighth-century Piedras Negras was a secondary center below the capital of Yaxchilán. With the death of Ruler 4 of Piedras Negras, there seems to have been a dispute over succession, which required the visit of a representative from Yaxchilán (Marcus 1974b, 1976a:85–87, 1983b, 1987). Traveling downstream by canoe on the Usumacinta River, a lord named Bat Jaguar—a representative of the Yaxchilán ruler—held an audience at Piedras Negras in A.D. 757, just as Ruler 4 lay dying. When Ruler 4 died a short time later, a new ruler—apparently selected by the Yaxchilán representative—took office. Lintel 3 at Piedras Negras (see Marcus 1976a: fig. 4.18) shows the emissary Bat Jaguar holding an audience with Piedras Negras nobles and representatives from their dependencies. A few months after having been approved as successor, Ruler 5 took office (Proskouriakoff 1960:463). Note that Ruler 5 is one of those who never gives us his date of birth.

Inaugural Expressions

One of the earliest hieroglyphically recorded inaugural expressions is that on the Leyden Plaque (Fig. 10.17), a jade artifact found near Puerto Barrios, Guatemala. Its Initial Series date (8.14.3.1.12 [1 Eb 0 Yaxkin] or September 17, A.D. 320) records the "seating" of a Maya ruler, possibly a lord of Tikal (F. R. Morley and S. G. Morley 1938; Marcus 1976b:64–65, 1991:29). Significantly, the seating of the month and the seating in office of the new ruler use the same verb, shown at B9 and B10.

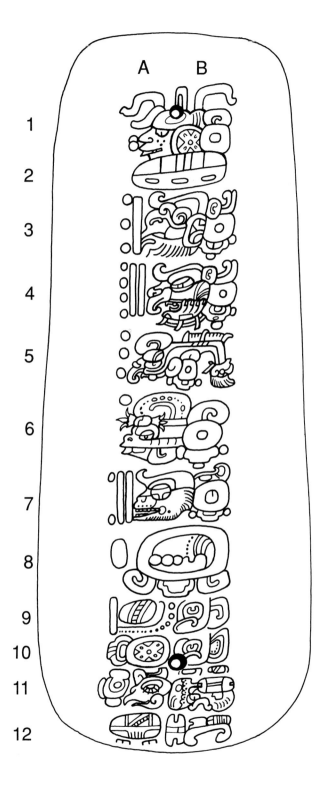

10.17. The accession of an early Maya ruler (possibly at Tikal) is recorded on the back of the Leyden Plaque, a jade artifact found at Puerto Barrios, Guatemala, in 1864 but now residing in Leyden, the Netherlands. The text gives an Initial Series date that corresponds to September 17, A.D. 320. At A1-B1 we see the Initial Series Introductory Glyph (with the patron of the Maya month named Yaxkin, a head with a *kin* sign in its ear). At A3-B3 we see 8 *baktunob*; at A4-B4, 14 *katunob*; at A5-B5, 3 *tunob*; at A6-B6, 1 *uinal*; at A7-B7, 12 *kinob*; and at A8-B8, the day 1 Eb. At A9 is the Fifth Lord of the Night; at B9, the verb "was seated"; and at A10, the month position, 0 Yaxkin. All preceding signs provide the number of days, months, years, units of 20 years, and units of 400 years since August 11, 3114 B.C., the Maya base date. At B10 is the beginning of the text that discusses what happened on September 17, A.D. 320. At B10 is the verb "was seated"; at A11, the personal name of the ruler, which includes a bird as the main sign; at B11, one of the ruler's titles; at A12, his "sky" title; and at B12, an emblem glyph that may refer to Tikal. (Redrawn from Shook 1960; see Marcus 1976b: fig. 11.)

As we have seen, accession to the throne at Piedras Negras was expressed by the "toothache glyph," so-called because it shows a bird's head tied up with cloth as if the bird were suffering from a toothache. Variants of the "toothache glyph" are shown in Figure 10.18 (Marcus 1976a: fig. 1.2b). However, as mentioned above, Piedras Negras was only a secondary administrative center. At regional capitals such as Palenque and Tikal, other hieroglyphic expressions corresponding to "was seated" were used (Fig. 10.19).

It is significant that rulers who acceded to the throne at secondary centers such as Piedras Negras and Naranjo utilized one set of inaugural expressions, while those who acceded to the throne at huge regional capitals were frequently or exclusively associated with other hieroglyphic expressions for inauguration. This allows us to detect the promotion of a city from lesser to greater importance. For example, early in Tikal's history (A.D. 300–450), that site used the inaugural expression we associate with secondary centers; later in its history (A.D. 550–800), it turned to the various hieroglyphic expressions used by regional capitals.

Still other hieroglyphs were sometimes used to indicate accession, or perhaps some similar event (Fig. 10.20). Such differences in inaugural expressions have been the subject of considerable discussion over the years (e.g., Proskouriakoff 1960:470; Berlin 1968b, 1977; Marcus 1974b, n.d.c; Schele and J. H. Miller 1983). Even today we are not sure whether all these inaugural expressions reflect different types of accession, different kinds of power, or different offices.

Accession at Palenque

Unlike Piedras Negras, Calakmul, and Quiriguá, the rulers of Palenque did not set up free-standing stelae every five, ten, or twenty years. Instead, they commissioned huge panels and slabs to be incorporated into the walls of particular temples and other structures. Such wall panels do not contain a thin slice of time, such as five, ten, or even twenty years; they typically cover spans far greater than any ruler's lifetime, sometimes even thousands of years.

For example, the principal tablet in the Temple of the Inscriptions at Palenque records the inauguration dates of seven rulers, two of them women (Kubler 1969, Mathews and Schele 1974). Some of those rulers are mentioned again in the tomb situated deep within the pyramid supporting that temple (see Figs. 9.17, 9.18). That tomb housed the body of a ruler called Lord Shield (Pacal), who reportedly was born on March 26, A.D. 603; took office on July 29, 615; and died on August 31, 683 (Ruz 1958, 1973, 1977; Berlin 1959, 1965, 1968b, 1977; Kubler 1969, 1974; Marcus 1974b, 1976a, n.d.a; Lounsbury 1974a, 1974b; Mathews and Schele 1974; Schele 1979; Barthel 1980). If his birth date were correct, he would have been eighty at the time of his death, and would have reigned at Palenque for sixty-eight years (Marcus 1976a:96).

10.18. Four examples of the so-called "toothache glyph," a Classic Maya hieroglyphic expression for "accession to the throne." (Redrawn from Marcus n.d.c)

10.19. Classic Maya hieroglyphic expressions for "seated in office," which was read phonetically as *chumaan* or *chumwan*. (Redrawn from Marcus n.d.c)

10.20. Other Classic Maya hieroglyphic expressions that relate to inauguration. These expressions seem to be variants of the "toothache" and "seating" glyphs, but there appear to be differences in meaning. (*a, b,* redrawn from Schele and J. Miller 1983: fig. 15; *c,* redrawn from Marcus 1976a: fig. 4.43; *d,* redrawn from Morley 1915: fig. 80a.)

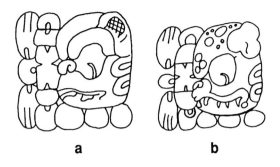

a   b

10.21. The Palenque ruler who succeeded Lord Shield (Pacal) in A.D. 684 was called Snake Jaguar. His name combines serpent and feline attributes. At *a*, we see the name without jaguar spots; at *b*, such spots are evident. (Redrawn from Marcus 1976a: fig. 4.22.)

One hundred and thirty-two days after Lord Shield's death, his successor Snake Jaguar took office at the age of forty-eight (Fig. 10.21). The buildings he commissioned include the beautiful temple triad—Temples of the Cross, Sun, and Foliated Cross—situated to the east of his predecessor's Temple of the Inscriptions.

The transfer of power from the deceased ruler Lord Shield to the living ruler Snake Jaguar is shown on a number of monuments at Palenque, including the three central wall panels in the Temples of the Cross, Sun, and Foliated Cross. In each case, Lord Shield is shown as much shorter in stature than his successor (Kubler 1969, 1974). This iconographic device was used to show that the successor was the more important person at the time of the carving. (A similar convention was employed in the monuments of Egypt).

Another transfer of power from a deceased ruler to a living ruler is depicted at Copán (Fig. 10.22). In this case, a ruler who reigned in the fifth century A.D. (second from left) is shown passing on the staff of office to his "successor" (whom he faces). The inaugural date given between them is 6 Caban 10 Mol, which corresponds to July 2, A.D. 763. Since at least 300 years separated these two rulers, the scene clearly must be understood as a metaphor and not as true history. This eighth-century Maya ruler's inauguration included rulers from previous eras, just as we saw earlier with Acamapichtli's inauguration (Fig. 10.5).

Other monuments at Palenque show a woman (sometimes alleged to be the mother of the next ruler, sometimes alleged to be his predecessor in office) passing on the headdress that symbolizes rulership. For example, on the Oval Tablet in the Palace, a woman named Lady White Parrot passes on the headdress to Lord Shield (Fig. 10.23). Lord Shield claims in his own texts that he reigned from A.D. 615 to 683, following Lady White Parrot's reign (A.D. 612–615). Significantly, however, we still lack inscriptions from the reign of Lady White Parrot, and this lack of corroboration for her reign makes us wonder if she ruled at all, if she constructed any buildings, if any monuments were dedicated to her— and if not, why not.

Falsifying Birth Dates and Life Spans

We saw that at Piedras Negras, a Maya secondary center, rulers were between twelve and thirty-one years of age when they acceded to the throne. At other Maya sites the average reign lasted about twenty years. The average reign of eleven Aztec rulers at Tenochtitlán was twelve years (see Fig. 10.6). All of this does not surprise us, given what we know about the life spans of Precolumbian Indians. For example, a study of 549 skeletons from the Valley of Oaxaca by Hodges (1989) lists only a dozen individuals whose age at death was over fifty, and only one or two considered over fifty-five.

10.22.An eighth-century A.D. inauguration scene from Copán, Honduras. The founder of the Copán royal dynasty (whose reign supposedly began ca. A.D. 430) is shown second from left, passing on his staff of office to the sixteenth ruler in the dynastic sequence (a man whose reign began in A.D. 763). Each ruler sits on his name sign. As in the Aztec case given in Figure 10.5, this scene cannot be considered "history" because it includes rulers whose reigns were separated by centuries. (Redrawn from Maudslay 1889–1902, 1: plate 92; Marcus 1976a: fig. 4.48.)

10.23. An accession scene on the Oval Tablet from the Palace (House E) at Palenque. A royal woman named Lady White Parrot is shown seated at left, holding a headdress. Seated on the two-headed jaguar throne (at right) is Lord Shield (Pacal) of Palenque. This scene may represent the passing of rulership from Lady White Parrot (alleged to be Lord Shield's mother) to Lord Shield himself. In his texts, Lord Shield claims that Lady White Parrot reigned from A.D. 612 to 615, while he took over the office in 615 and held it until his death in 683. (Redrawn from Maudslay 1889–1902, 4: plate 44.)

However, given that Palenque was a major capital, we are prepared to find greater ages alleged for some of its rulers. After all, one of the early rulers of Palenque (Kan Xul) was said to have been born in A.D. 490 and buried in A.D. 565, making him an improbable seventy-four years old. But nothing prepares us for the claims made by Lord Shield and some of his successors (see Table 10.1).

Table 10.1   Accession Ages and Length of Reigns Alleged for
Six Palenque Rulers

Name	Age at Accession	Length of Reign
Lord Shield (Pacal)	12 years	68 years
Snake Jaguar	48 years	18 years
Kan Toothache	57 years	18 years
Feathered Skull	43 years	?
Chac Bat	52 years	8+ years
Quetzal	?	19 years

To begin with, we find it surprising that four of Palenque's rulers would claim to have acceded to the throne when they were between forty-three and fifty-two years of age, a time by which most Maya were probably deceased. We find it even more surprising that their reigns would have put some of them into their seventies. Lord Shield, in fact, is said to have ruled for sixty-eight years, dying at the age of eighty. His alleged reign would have lasted three times longer than that of any other Palenque ruler.

Let us look at a few of the reasons why we should be suspicious of all this.

First of all, the Mexican archaeologist Alberto Ruz, who discovered Lord Shield's tomb, had the ruler's skeleton aged and sexed by physical anthropologists on two occasions, with identical results (Ruz Lhuillier 1973, 1977; Dávalos Hurtado and Romano Pacheco 1954, 1973). The skeleton is that of a man approximately forty years of age.

Second, consider the ancestors to whom Lord Shield's inscriptions link him. One, a man named Cauac-Uinal, is said to have been born in 9.1.10.0.0, a "round date" which makes us immediately suspicious that we are dealing with a date selected only because it was the completion of a *lahuntun*, or ten-year period.

Lord Shield goes on to associate himself with the royal woman already alluded to who reportedly gave birth when she was 754 years of age and acceded to the throne when she was 815 (Fig. 9.19). Lord Shield attempts to draw a parallel between this woman's reign and that of his mother's (Schele and Freidel 1990). He also likens this royal woman's birth to his own (Lounsbury 1976). It is clear that Lord Shield's goal was to establish his reign as a pivotal moment in Palenque's history, not to keep accurate count of his age (Berlin 1977).

Third, Lord Shield's birth date (and all other events of his early life) are recorded retroactively. In fact, the first monument giving the date of his birth was carved late in his reign, just twenty-four years before his death. His birth date of 9.8.9.13.0, another "round date," emphasizes the auspicious number 13. Berlin (1977:140)—one of the first epigraphers to express concern not only about the validity of Lord Shield's birth date, but also about those of other Palenque rulers—has pointed out that Lord Shield's accession date corresponds to the first appearance of Venus as Morning Star, a propitious day for the Maya. More recently, Dütting (1985:269) has pointed out that Lord Shield's alleged birth date coincides with the first appearance of Venus as the Evening Star, making us doubly suspicious. Berlin suggests that Lord Shield wanted to establish a close relationship with Venus, much as the later Toltec hero Quetzalcoatl did. Selecting such dates for his birth and accession made it easy for all subsequent Palenque rulers to remember and commemorate those dates, which they did.

Elsewhere (Marcus 1976a:96; n.d.a) I have suggested that Lord Shield's life history was falsified, perhaps because he was someone not actually in the direct line for the throne of Palenque. Note that there are no records for the first thirty-two years of his alleged reign, possibly because the throne was actually occupied by other rulers whose records he later destroyed. Perhaps one day, in the immense platform substructures supporting the temples dedicated by Lord Shield and his successors, we will find the monuments of earlier rulers to whom he had no genealogical ties.

In fact, one of Berlin's suggestions was that "Lord Shield" may have been the name of at least two Palenque lords, the second of whom took credit for the accomplishments of both. We do see the name of at least one other individual named "Lord Shield," carved on one side of the sarcophagus in the tomb within the Temple of the Inscriptions (see Fig. 9.18; Ruz Lhuillier 1958, 1973; Barthel 1980).

One further clue that Lord Shield might have been overcompensating for his lack of genealogical credentials lies in the massive building campaign he undertook after his accession. He went on to name himself "Builder of Five Pyramids," precisely the kind of monumental activity many usurpers have used to divert attention away from their questionable heritage. It is the kind of activity we might expect from someone who found it necessary to (1) falsify his birth date to associate himself with Venus; (2) claim mythical ancestors who lived 3,000 years in the past; (3) predict events that would happen 3,000 years in the future; and (4) appropriate the name of an earlier noble.

Whatever the case, Lord Shield succeeded in establishing himself as a kind of "lineage founder" at Palenque, the kind of pivotal role that Acamapichtli played in Aztec legendary history. All of Lord Shield's successors at Palenque (some of whom also probably falsified their birth dates) referred back to him to legitimize their right to rule. At least one of them—a man named Feathered Skull—also associated himself with a mythical female ancestor by choosing the same day (9 Ik) for his own accession as that of the mythical forebear.

In sum: the wall panels at Palenque are probably not, as some have alleged, "king lists" that place historic events in chronological order. They were the medium for a kind of horizontal propaganda in which rulers placed themselves in the best possible light, not merely establishing their credentials but fabricating them. After all, how could we doubt that some rulers at Palenque lived to be seventy-five or eighty when some of their ancestors had lived ten times longer?

Accession at Yaxchilán

We have seen that the Aztec used military prowess as a way of deciding between candidates for the throne. Inscriptions at the Maya capital of Yaxchilán indicate that as early as the eighth century, the same criterion may have been important. There, the ruler Shield Jaguar seems to have returned victorious from battle with an important noble captive just before his inauguration in A.D. 681. He acquired a new title in the process, perhaps a prerequisite for being selected over a number of royal competitors.

Shield Jaguar died in A.D. 742, supposedly when he was ninety-five years of age, and no one immediately succeeded him (Proskouriakoff 1963). Ten years later, he was succeeded by a ruler named Bird Jaguar. Bird Jaguar, who was inaugurated at forty-two, obviously had not been too young to rule at the time of Shield Jaguar's death. Who had ruled Yaxchilán during the intervening decade?

Like his predecessor, Bird Jaguar acquired several titles that reflect successful military exploits and the taking of important captives. For example, he was known as "Captor of Cauac" and "Captor of Jeweled Skull" (Proskouriakoff 1964). Not surprisingly, the texts and iconography of Yaxchilán record raids, battles, the taking of captives, and the sacrifice of prisoners. Militarism was a particularly important theme at the site, and seems to have been intimately linked to claimants' establishing themselves as frontrunners for the throne of Yaxchilán.

In chapter 11 we will see Stela 11 from Yaxchilán, which recorded the accession of Bird Jaguar on 9.16.1.0.0 (another suspicious "round date"). Also shown in the upper register was the previous ruler, Shield Jaguar, even though he had died 10 years before Bird Jaguar was "seated" (Fig. 9.16).

Anniversaries of Accessions

The anniversaries of rulers' accessions were important dates, commemorated at many sites on the occasion of a *katun* (ca. twentieth) anniversary, and occasionally on the

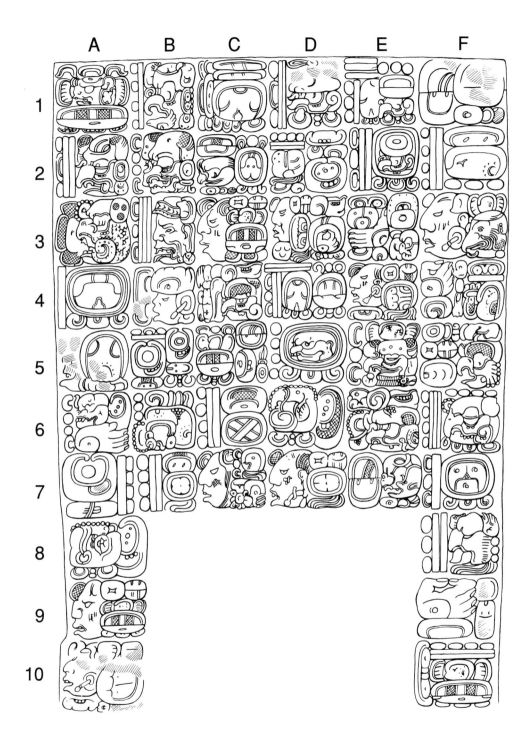

10.24. On the back of Stela 3 from Piedras Negras, the 25th anniversary of Ruler 3's inauguration to the throne is celebrated. When this stela was erected (in A.D. 711) the ruler was 46 years of age, his wife Lady Darkness was 37, and their daughter Lady Sunlight was 3. (Redrawn from Marcus 1976b: fig. 12.)

	A	B	C	D	E	F
1	Initial Series Introductory Glyph	9 baktuns [cycles]	0 kins 10 uinals	12 tuns	15 kins 8 uinals 3 tuns	Forward count to
2	12 katuns [units of 20 years]	2 tuns [years]	Forward count to / 1 Cib	14 Kankin	11 Imix	14 Yax
3	0 uinals [months]	16 kins [days]	Lady Katun	Lady Akbal [darkness]		Lady Katun [vulture substitute]
4	5 Cib	7th lord of the night	Ruler's title and name	10 kins 11 uinals 1 tun	Lady Akbal [darkness]	Completion of 5th haab
5	–	Moon age is 27 days	1 katun forward count to	4 Cimi	1 katun	25th anniversary of ruler's accession to the throne
6	2 lunations	Glyph X	14 Uo	Was born	Ruler's name	19 kins 4 uinals
7	29-day moon	14 Yaxkin	Lady	Lady Kin [sunlight]	Forward count to	6 Ahau
8	Was born					13 Muan
9	Lady Katun					Completion of
10	Lady Akbal [darkness]					14th katun [A.D. 711]

10.25. Glyph-by-glyph English translation of the text from the back of Stela 3, Piedras Negras (see Fig. 10.24). (Redrawn from Marcus 1976b: fig. 13.)

twenty-fifth anniversary (Marcus 1976b: fig. 12). For example, on the back of Stela 3 at Piedras Negras we read of a twenty-five-year anniversary (Figs. 10.24, 10.25). At least one Copán ruler, Yax "Sun-at Horizon," commemorated both his twentieth and twenty-fifth anniversaries (Morley 1920, 1937–1938). Occasionally, anniversaries even prompted the carving of more than one monument (Morley 1920, Marcus 1976a).

The Role of the Regent among the Classic Maya

We have already seen the case of an Aztec royal woman who served as regent in order to protect the office for her son until he was old enough to rule. While sixteenth-century documents from Yucatán describe male regents (often an older brother), evidence from Palenque, Naranjo, and other Classic-period Maya sites suggests that mothers of young rulers often served as regents during the Classic period. For example, Stela 33 from Piedras Negras shows Ruler 2 sitting on the throne at age twelve, accompanied by a woman who may well be his mother (Maler 1901–03; Proskouriakoff 1960:461).

ROYAL ACCESSION: A SUMMARY

Even though four different languages and writing systems were involved, there are some striking similarities in the way the Aztec, Mixtec, Zapotec, and Maya recorded the accessions of their rulers:

1. First, the candidate had to have the right bloodlines. The Mixtec were the least flexible about this, and the Aztec the most flexible. The Mixtec kept elaborate genealogies in order to determine birth order and distance from the main royal line; even so, we see codices which have been erased and repainted, presumably so that powerful usurpers could be added to genealogies in which they had never belonged.
2. To make sure that candidates were genuine nobles, the sixteenth-century Maya gave exams in a special ritual language unknown to commoners. However, the questions could also be biased in order to guarantee that certain lineages produced most of the *batabob*. The Mexica showed similar bias in creating a rule that mandated past public service as a criterion, making their Texcocan rivals ineligible to serve as *tlatoani*.
3. All groups wanted the accession to take place on an auspicious date, and it is likely that other inauguration dates and birth dates were "fudged" to make sure that all major dates were auspicious.
4. The dedication or refurbishment of a major temple or other public building might be arranged to coincide with the inauguration.

5. Ancestors—near, distant, and mythical—were invoked at the time of accession. Aztec documents show scenes containing persons who did not all live at the same time; Maya scribes often depicted a deceased ruler passing on the paraphernalia of office to his living successor; some texts link the new ruler to mythical ancestors who supposedly lived thousands of years before.

6. At various times and places, the new ruler was expected to prove himself as a warrior by leading a successful military campaign and bringing back captives to be sacrificed at his inauguration. We associate this with the Aztec, but it is clear that all groups did it, some of them long before the Mexica ever existed. For example, the Zapotec ruler 12 Jaguar, who evidently dedicated the South Platform at Monte Albán, brought back at least 6 elite captives; rulers at Maya sites, such as eighth-century Yaxchilán, often earned "captor" titles before acceding to the throne.

It used to be thought that Teotihuacán, the Classic predecessor for the Toltec and Aztec of central Mexico, was the capital of a peaceful theocracy in which such sacrifices played no role. That view is changing. Recent excavations at the Old Temple of Quetzalcoatl at Teotihuacán have revealed numerous sacrificial victims buried along the sides of the structure, as well as at the four corners of the building (Sugiyama 1989). It may have been the case that the sacrifice of war captives was part of the inaugural rites for a new Teotihuacán ruler.

7. Not every ruler was old enough to take captives; some were even too young to rule. When it happened that the candidate with the most important blood lines was still only a child, a regent might be named until such time as the heir to the throne was older. Often the regent was the child's own mother, but it could be a brother or other male relative.

8. The simultaneous inauguration of a new ruler and the dedication of a new temple is a practice we have seen in the South Platform at Monte Albán at ca. A.D. 300, at Kaminaljuyú in the Guatemala highlands by A.D. 400, throughout the Maya lowlands after A.D. 500, and among the Aztec ca. A.D. 1300.

9. While there were numerous rules for succession, it appears that almost all of them could be broken if conditions were right. This was done by manipulating writing—burning or repainting codices, breaking or defacing stone monuments, and providing new ones that falsified the facts of the case. Aztec nobles outside the royal line "borrowed" ancestors; Maya nobles outside the local dynasty selected accession dates that corresponded to ones used by a 3,000-year-old mythical ancestor. Even when the reigns of past rulers were "written in stone," such monuments could be destroyed, altered, or buried.

11 ◆ RAIDING AND WARFARE

From the moment that Mesoamerican societies reached a chiefdom level of development, raiding and intervillage conflict seem to have become widespread. This should surprise no one, since many anthropologists have argued that raiding is endemic among chiefly societies (e.g., Buck 1932:55; Vayda 1960, 1961, 1976; Goldman 1955, 1970:556; Carneiro 1981, 1987:246–247, 1988; Kirch 1984:195–197). In the case of Mesoamerica, sacrificed prisoners are depicted in art as early as 600 B.C. (Marcus 1974a, 1980, 1983d, 1991).

Raiding—which includes the burning of enemy villages and the slaughter of their defenders, but *not* the annexation of their land—characterized the latter half of the Formative and continued into the Classic and Postclassic periods. With the rise of states between 150 B.C. and A.D. 500, such raiding was joined by actual warfare, involving formal armies and bringing greater success at retaining land taken by conquest (Fig. 11.1).

While raiding and warfare were commonplace in Mesoamerica, true imperial expansion was much rarer, particularly on the scale displayed by the Aztec empire. More typical of most Mesoamerican cultures were numerous small-scale raids and skirmishes that occurred at irregular intervals. Only occasionally did archaic states embark on major campaigns of territorial expansion, attempting to consolidate dozens of subjugated ethnic groups into a large empire. We have perhaps overlooked the significance of small-scale raids, partly because it is more difficult to detect them archaeologically, and partly because we have used Aztec imperial expansion as the "ideal model" or standard by which we evaluate the impact of other kinds of military activity. To be honest, it is not always possible to distinguish between raiding and warfare in the archaeological record, and we will not consistently try to do so in this chapter.

One of the most interesting uses of writing by ancient Mesoamerican states can be found in the texts that report raiding and warfare. It was one of the themes in which

11.1. A large mural in the Temple of the Jaguars at Chichén Itzá records a major battle. In this detail of a section of the mural, we see a group of warriors wearing sandals and feather headdresses, brandishing shields and spears. Their target appears to be the village at upper right, where frightened women and children are emerging from their houses. Such scenes make it clear that Maya warfare involved much more than a handful of nobles, capturing a few rivals for sacrifice. (Redrawn from Tozzer 1957.)

messages were most likely to be filled with propaganda and exaggeration, not only in regard to the results of the fighting, but also in regard to the motives for going to battle.

The actual motives for Mesoamerican warfare included the elimination of rival candidates for a throne; revenge for alleged insults or previous defeats; the acquisition of new titles or territories; the acquisition of manpower in the form of captives; the suppression of rebellious subject communities; the enforcement of tribute payments (or conversely, the avoidance of tribute payments); the maintenance of borders between polities; and the breaking away of subject communities from higher-order centers and their onerous demands. The motives claimed publicly for such battles, however, might be as altruistic as ''we needed captives' hearts for sacrifice to keep our deity happy.'' Such claims were often only rationalizations, yet they seem to have convinced thousands of prehispanic commoners (and even a few twentieth-century epigraphers).

So self-serving were various rulers' reports of their victories that it is often difficult to evaluate how large the battle was and who actually won. With the advantage of long archaeological sequences, we can see that some Maya third-order centers were able to rise to second-order status following ''victories,'' and in a few cases, some even went on to become first-order centers (regional capitals). Conversely, some second-order centers declined in importance when their local populations emigrated following a defeat. Other second-order sites successfully fought battles for independence, freeing themselves from tribute obligations to a former overlord. Still other dependencies, like Bonampak (see below), apparently fought side-by-side with their capital, allowing the lord of the capital to claim that he took the first prisoner.

Occasionally a set of secondary-level dependencies formed confederacies, allowing them to assemble larger forces of warriors to repel primary centers or annex new territory. One example is the A.D. 1427 alliance of the Mexica of Tenochtitlán with the Acolhua of Texcoco to throw off the yoke of Azcapotzalco (which also headed a confederacy including Coatlinchán and Culhuacán). The alliance of several provincial Yucatec lords and their lineages (e.g., Cocom, Xiu) at the regional capital of Mayapán in the northern Maya lowlands is a second example; the earlier alliance of Dos Pilas, Aguateca, Tamarindito, and Seibal into a Petexbatún Confederacy in the southern Maya lowlands is a third. Often the most intense propaganda (as well as the most impressive defensive works) occurred at these secondary centers.

Unraveling the whole story of Mesoamerican warfare will be impossible without including a study of the way royal marriage alliance went hand-in-hand with truce and confederacy. Exchanges of brides cemented military alliances (Caso 1949, 1960, 1964a, 1964c, 1977, 1979; Spores 1974a; Marcus 1976a, 1980, 1983l:303; 1983m). One famous truce between the Aztec and Zapotec was sealed by the marriage of an Aztec princess to a Zapotec lord (see below, and chapter 8). In the Mixtec codices, we see victorious rulers marrying the widows, sisters, or daughters of the very rivals they had captured and sacrificed (Caso 1977:77).

11.2. Stela 21 from Izapa, Mexico, depicts the beheading of an elite individual from a chiefdom of the Protoclassic era (100 B.C.–A.D. 100). The fact that the decapitated victim also wears jade beads and earspools identifies him as someone of high rank. The equally elite warrior doing the killing (at right) is shown with an elaborate headdress, a feathered cape, large jade earspools, and a necklace of jade beads. In his left hand he holds a knife; in his right, he grasps the hair of his enemy's recently removed head. Flowing from both the head and the decapitated body is blood, symbolized by circular drops among long feathers. These symbols for blood continued to be used on stone monuments carved by the Maya from A.D. 200 to 1200. (Circles often represented jade beads or drops of blood; quetzal feathers could represent streams of flowing blood. Blood, jade, and quetzal feathers were all closely associated and considered precious.) In the background (at left) are two litter-bearers who carry a highly ranked witness to this rite of decapitation. Above the scene is a stylized set of symbols for "heaven" or "sky." (Redrawn from Norman 1973: plate 34.)

Captive Taking

In chiefdoms from Panama to Mexico, raiding was accompanied by the torture, mutilation, or sacrifice of prisoners taken in combat. As early as Middle Formative times in Oaxaca (see chapter 2), removal of the prisoner's heart was depicted in public art. From Protoclassic times on in Chiapas (Norman 1973, 1976), important enemies might be beheaded (see Fig. 11.2). When the early Zapotec state expanded into the Cuicatlán Cañada in the Protoclassic, it chose to display the skulls of some sixty-one enemies on a rack that anticipated the later Toltec and Aztec *tzompantlis* (Spencer 1982, Redmond and Spencer 1983:120).

While captives continued to be taken in later Mesoamerican warfare, the number actually sacrificed was probably only a tiny percentage of the number brought back to work as servants, farmers, slaves, and public laborers. Indeed, some states, including the Aztec, had such high labor needs for building public structures, canals, palaces, plazas, and defensive works that many foreign peoples were brought back alive. The Aztec even pacified rebellious border areas by butchering the adults and bringing the children back to Tenochtitlán to be raised as Aztecs; the border communities were then resettled with loyal subjects from the Basin of Mexico (Gibson 1964).

Usually, however, the scribes and stonecarvers did not choose to depict the hundreds of captives kept alive; they showed only those destined for sacrifice, especially captive rulers or members of the nobility. Often a monument will show one captive only, letting him stand for the whole conquered town or region. A codex will show "Lord X" having been taken captive and sacrificed, as if he were the only prisoner taken. Unfortunately, some archaeologists and epigraphers have chosen to take such scenes literally, suggesting that battles were fought just to obtain a few elite sacrificial victims. As Webster (n.d.) has recently argued, such ingenuous acceptance of prehispanic propaganda (as well as metaphoric and symbolic scenes) leads us to ignore the underlying political and economic reasons for warfare and its latent effect on the evolution of the whole sociopolitical system.

We should remember that of all the battles, skirmishes, and raids that took place in ancient Mesoamerica, only a small percentage were ever recorded in hieroglyphic or pictographic texts. Of all the prisoners taken in those battles, only a small percentage were ever depicted on monuments or in codices. Sometimes a prisoner stands for a single important noble; other prisoners stand for whole communities, tributary regions, or ethnic groups. We cannot calculate the number of prisoners taken in raiding from the small number shown in conventional Mesoamerican scenes, in which captives are shown being grasped by their hair, naked, stripped of elaborate headdresses and costumes, sprawling awkwardly, or squashed uncomfortably under the feet of a victorious lord.

It is virtually impossible to separate history from propaganda in texts that deal with Mesoamerican warfare. Prehispanic monuments do not usually tell us the motive for the battle, its scale and intensity, its duration, the actual number of casualties, the true number of prisoners, nor even the actual victor.

The Costuming of Warriors

Special military attire was a very important component of prehispanic warfare, both for noble officers and for those warriors who had fought bravely enough to be admitted to special military orders. Often the costumes worn by these orders consumed so many millions of feathers, jewels, resins, animal skins, and exotic tropical materials that those items were demanded and depicted as tribute from subjugated foreigners (Fig. 11.3). Such costumes were frequently shown on warriors (or rulers) in codices or monuments.

Although the best-known military orders were the ''eagle warriors'' or ''jaguar warriors'' of the Aztec state (Soustelle 1964:63), similar military attire was worn by nobles in much earlier states. As early as the Protoclassic, there were figurines in the Zapotec region showing men with headdresses like those of coyotes and other animals (Fig. 11.4). By Early Classic times (A.D. 200–500), Zapotec lords and their elite captives were shown on monuments in full-animal costumes or pelts in which only the mouth or lower part of the human face could be seen through the open mouth of the animal head (see below). Among Late Classic peoples (A.D. 600–900), the full feline (jaguar, ocelot, or puma) costume was the one most frequently worn during battles, but military dress could also include huge raptorial birds and a wide array of ophidian and saurian creatures. In some cases, animal heads were worn atop the head of the human warrior; when traveling along heavily wooded trails and through tall vegetation where only the headdresses would be visible, these warriors would appear from a distance as a column of tall, fantastic animals.

Sometimes when confronting bound captives, Maya rulers such as Bird Jaguar of Yaxchilán wore grotesque masks (see Fig. 11.5). In such contexts, the mask may have linked the ruler to a supernatural being (in this case, Lightning) or a particular ancestor. In contrast to the fabulously rich attire of animal skins and feathered garments worn by the victorious noble, the captive's attire was skimpy (just a breech clout) or non-existent, and he was sometimes shown with prominent holes in his ear lobes, where his jade earspools had been removed. Such a captive was often grimacing, with arms bound behind his back, in an awkward or anatomically impossible position (Marcus 1974a, 1976b, 1976c, 1980, n.d.c). The clues provided by the costuming of the figure on the monument help us to interpret the accompanying texts, which may be brief or sketchy. In many cases, the iconography and hieroglyphic text complement each other, rather than simply letting the text provide the caption for a self-evident scene.

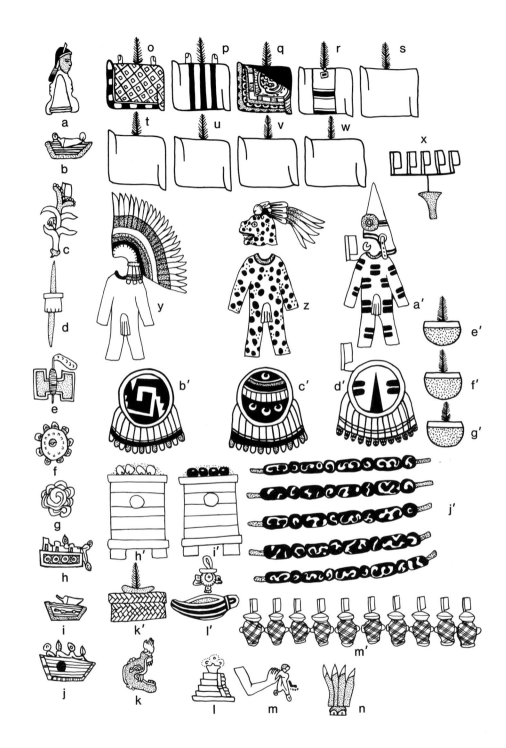

11.3. Conquered towns paid tribute to the Aztec in the form of feather headdresses and full-body military costumes (fifteenth and sixteenth-centuries A.D.). *a–n*, names of places conquered. *a*, Tepequacuilco, "Where the Face is Painted"; *b*, Chilapan, "In the Canal (or River) of the Chiles"; *c*, Ohuapan, "In the Green Stalks of Corn"; *d*, Huitzoco, "Place of the Weaving Tool"; *e*, Tlachmalacac, "Where Spindle Whorls are Made"; *f*, Yoallan, "Place of the Lord of the Night"; *g*, Cocolan, "Place of the Bramble Bushes"; *h*, Atenanco, "In the River of the Wall"; *i*, Chilacachapan, "In the Lake of the Chilacachtli" (an aquatic plant, *Azolla caroliniana*); *j*, Teloloapan, "In the River of the Round Stones"; *k*, Oztoma, "In the Cave"; *l*, Ychcateopan, "Cotton Temple"; *m*, Alahuiztlán, "In the Ford of the River"; *n*, Queçalan, "Place of the Precious Feathers." *o–m'*, tribute items received. *o*, 402 blankets (feather = 400, finger = 1) with this design; *p*, 402 blankets with these stripes; *q–w*, 400 of each of these kinds of cloth. *x*, 100 copper axes (each flag = 20); *y*, military garment with feather headdress; *z*, full feline military costume with feather headdress; *a'*, 20 full-body military costumes of this type. *b'*, *c'*, *d'*, three different kinds of shields; *e'*, *f'*, *g'*, 1200 gourds; *h'*, bin of corn and *chía* (sage); *i'*, bin of beans and *huauhtli* (amaranth); *j'*, 5 strands of beads called *chalchihuitl*; *k'*, 400 baskets of white (refined) copal (incense); *l'*, 8,000 units of unrefined copal, wrapped in palm leaves; and *m'*, 200 jars of honey. (Redrawn from Folio 37 of the Codex Mendoza; see Corona Núñez 1964, 1: Lámina XXXIX and Clark 1938.)

11.4. Protoclassic figurines from San José Mogote, Valley of Oaxaca (150 B.C.–A.D. 150). These small, mold-made figurines have human heads wearing large carnivore masks, with the human face emerging from the jaws of the carnivores. Superficially, at least, they resemble the "coyote warriors" depicted in the art of later periods. (Width of uppermost head, 1.7 cm.)

11.5. After taking over the throne of Yaxchilán, the ruler Bird Jaguar commissioned Stela 11, which shows one of the feats preceding his accession. Here Bird Jaguar, wearing the mask of Lightning, stands over three bound captives taken on June 4, A.D. 750. This captive-taking preceded his accession to the throne by almost two years (see chapter 10). In the upper register, a couple he claims as his parents are depicted. His "mother" is on the left and his "father" is on the right (see chapter 9). (Redrawn by John Klausmeyer from drawings by Proskouriakoff 1964.)

Selective Military Reporting

Nowhere is it clearer that scribes were not sworn to tell the truth, the whole truth, and nothing but the truth than in military reporting. Indigenous monuments and codices were highly selective, almost always proclaiming victories rather than defeats; naming important captives taken, rather than allies lost; and presenting new titles acquired after success, no matter how minimal that success was. Later in this chapter we will examine the case of an Aztec ruler whose own self-commissioned monument shows him taking fifteen prominent captives, each representing a subjugated town. Ethnohistoric documents reveal that some of his battles were actually fought by previous rulers, and that in at least one battle he lost 300 of his own warriors. So much for the notion that Mesoamerican writing is "history."

We have both ethnohistoric and epigraphic evidence to show that different rulers and ethnic groups altered the truth for their own purposes, either by omitting details or by lying about important facts, including the number of captives taken and who won or lost the battle. After all, each ethnic group and major city kept its own written records, and each presented its own local version of what had occurred. All these different and conflicting versions must be given "equal time" if we are ever to separate fact from propaganda. Indeed, the differences among such versions are often more informative than the points of agreement.

To be sure, in many cases it is not possible to separate fact from propaganda, nor should we lose sleep if we cannot do so. The general pattern of what various rulers wanted us to believe emerges quite clearly; the true facts about loss of life, autonomy, and goods, and the actual gains in captives, autonomy, and goods, are much more difficult to recover. That is, of course, exactly how the ancient Mesoamerican rulers wanted to keep it.

The message in all of this is that while military propaganda was all right for Mesoamerican commoners, it should not suffice as an explanation for Mesoamerican archaeologists and epigraphers. We should not believe that Aztec armies went to war "just to get a few prisoners for sacrifice." We should not believe that every boastful lord at a Maya secondary center really "conquered" or "overthrew" the regional capital. We need to understand that warfare was virtually endemic in Mesoamerican states, and in fact was often part of a long-term political strategy. Its effects must be read not just from rulers' claims in stone, but from an archaeological study of the changes in regional hierarchies, in territorial sizes and boundaries, in the expansion and destruction of monumental construction, and all that that implies about the land and labor controlled by each polity.

AZTEC RAIDS AND CONQUESTS

Sixteenth-century accounts from both Spaniards and Indians have made the Aztec seem to be Mesoamerica's most warlike people. In fact, growing evidence of warfare among peoples such as the Zapotec, Mixtec, and Maya make it unlikely that the Aztec were unique in this regard. What the Aztec have left us is an unusually detailed body of information on how their brand of warfare operated. Available information has also made it clear that there is only a partial fit between Aztec reality and Aztec propaganda. Sources of information include ethnohistoric accounts written by Indians and eyewitness accounts written by Spaniards. As for the use of writing by the Aztec state, we have codices that list the names of conquered towns, region by region; others that show warriors in battle or taking prisoners; and others that list the tribute demanded from regions subjugated by the Aztec.

Like those of other Mesoamerican states, Aztec armies reflected the same hierarchy seen in society. Officers were drawn from the hereditary elite, while soldiers were commoners who were drafted as needed. Valor in combat was important to both strata of society; we have already mentioned in chapter 10 that some rulers could not accede to the throne until they had taken a captive, while nobles who fought bravely could move up the hierarchy. There were also a series of military orders in which valiant commoners could earn membership. Among the most famous were the "jaguar warriors" and the "eagle warriors," who were entitled to special costumes depicting those animals. Such orders were, of course, not unique to the Basin of Mexico; as we have just seen in Figure 11.4, they may have been shown in figurines as far back as Monte Albán II (150 B.C.– A.D. 150) in the Valley of Oaxaca.

Nobles went into battle far better protected than commoners, with stronger shields, diverse weapons, and quilted cotton armor. In addition, persons of different rank wore different costumes. When the Aztec ruler (who was commander-in-chief) accompanied his army into battle, he wore a gold headdress with the feathers of blue cotinga and quetzal. His shirt was covered with cotinga feathers; he carried a blue skin drum fashioned on a frame and decorated with gold. Both rulers and noble warriors wore skirts made of quetzal feathers (Anderson and Dibble 1954:33). In addition, the noble officers were richly arrayed in brightly colored headdresses made from red spoonbill and green quetzal feathers, red shirts made of spoonbill feathers and gold strips, shields ringed with gold and quetzal feathers, necklaces of green stone and turquoise beads. Warriors who had been successful fighters were also easy to spot because of their special costumes. Commoner divisions did not wear uniforms and their shields were plain, while those of war captains bore special insignia.

Provisions for War

To be effective in warfare against other ethnic groups, the Aztec stockpiled weapons in very high numbers. These military goods were kept in permanent storehouses called *tlacochcalco,* and were handed out to soldiers just prior to their leaving for battle. Bernal Díaz del Castillo (1963:228) described the contents of Motecuhzoma the Younger's two military storehouses in A.D. 1519 as being "stocked with every sort of weapon," those destined for noble officers being richly adorned with gold and precious stones. The arms included large and small shields, *macanas* or wooden broadswords lined with inset obsidian blades (called *macuahuitl* in Nahuatl), stone knives, lances, bows and arrows, javelins, *atlatls* or spearthrowers, wooden and bone helmets, and quilted cotton armor decorated with colored feathers for the officers. Slings (*tematlatl*) and clubs were also important weapons (Carochi [1645] 1910:208); the slings were used to hurl specially prepared, rounded stones that also had been stored in preparation for battle (Díaz del Castillo [1560s] 1908–1916). Given a substantial need for them, Tenochtitlán exacted these round stones as part of their tribute from some regions (Durán [1581] 1967, 2:208; Díaz del Castillo [1560s] 1908–1916; Alvarado Tezozomoc [1598] 1975:441). Such weapons are depicted in the Códice Matritense de la Academia de la Historia (Ballesteros Gaibrois 1964) and are often held by warriors in battle (Sullivan 1972).

In order to feed its substantial army, the Aztec state used both its own farmlands and those of conquered peoples. Local land designated as *milchimalli* or *cacalomilli* was set aside for the growing of food to feed the soldiers (Clavigero 1787, 1:350; Torquemada 1975–1983, 4:334). Additional evidence for the considerable cost of maintaining warfare comes from several pages of the Codex Mendoza (Clark 1938; Corona Núñez 1964, 1: Láminas XIX–XXXVI), in which military costumes such as full-body jaguar suits, elaborate headdresses, mantles, capes, and helmets were exacted as tribute from several subject towns. In Figure 11.6 we see, in a column at the left, the names of seven towns required not only to provide bins of corn and beans to feed the Aztec army, but also to provide military garments (more than 2,800 ornate mantles; live eagles whose feathers were needed for headdresses and garment decoration; jaguar suits; full-head helmets; and elaborate shields).

Going to War

In preparation for war the Aztec ruler of Tenochtitlán, head of the Triple Alliance, would command his warriors to study the enemy city, paying particular attention to the roads so that they could decide where to enter. Then the ruler himself used a painted plan to study the roads to plan his strategy of attack (Anderson and Dibble 1954:51). The ruler of Tenochtitlán also would call upon the rulers of Texcoco and Tlacopan, presenting them

11.6. Military costumes and shields were among the items exacted as tribute from places conquered by the Aztec. Names of conquered places are given in the column at left: *a*, Xilotepec, "Hill of the Young Maize Plants"; *b*, Tlachco, "In the Ballcourt"; *c*, Tzayanalquilpa, "Plant growing in Canal"; *d*, Michmaloyan, "Place for Fishing"; *e*, Tepetitlan, "Between the Hills"; *f*, Acaxochitla (a type of flower, *Lobelia laxiflora*); *g*, Tecoçauhtla, "Where the Color Yellow is Abundant." Tribute included: *h*, 400 blankets with these designs; *i*, 408 of this type; *j*, 400 of this type; *k* and *l*, 800 with the feline pelt motif; *m*, 408 of this type; *n*, 400 of this type. Also exacted in tribute were live eagles (shown at *o*,) which were to be kept in the ruler's zoo; later, they supplied the feathers for military headdresses. At *p* and *r* are full-body military costumes; at *q* and *s* are shields. At *t* is a bin of maize (the Spanish gloss on the original document says "2 bins of corn and *chía*"). At *u* is a bin of beans (the Spanish gloss on the original document says "2 bins of beans and *huauhtli*"). (Redrawn from Folio 31 of the Codex Mendoza; see Corona Núñez 1964, 1: Lámina XXXIII and Clark 1938.)

with valuable capes and notifying them that they must declare war on the same city; then he ordered the commoners to present themselves for war.

When the moment arrived to go to war, a priest (dressed as a messenger of the god Huitzilopochtli) danced through the streets of Tenochtitlán with a rattle and shield, calling out the troops and warriors (Bray 1968:193). The war drum was sounded, and within an hour the army met at the main Aztec temple. There the warriors received their weapons and performed bloodletting rites, cutting their ears, tongues, and fleshy parts of their limbs to offer blood. At that time, diviners predicted the outcome of the combat (Díaz del Castillo [1560s] 1908–1916). Sometimes when the auguries were not good, these diviners advised against the army's advancing, and their advice was followed (Ixtlilxochitl 1977, 2:181); if the predictions were good, war ensued.

Priests led the battle, bearing images of appropriate Aztec deities upon their backs. These priests arrived one day before the warriors. When the enemy lands were reached, the priests brought forth "new fire" and blew shell trumpets and clay pipes. The blowing of the trumpets made such a noise that it ensured that the warriors would set forth together as a unit (Anderson and Dibble 1954:35). When the warriors arrived, they shot fiery arrows into the enemy's temples. The first captive taken in combat was slain on the spot, his chest opened with a flint knife. Victory was often acknowledged as soon as one side captured the opposing commander, or when the town's main temple had been set on fire. As we will see, these two symbols of victory were precisely those most often selected by Aztec scribes to depict the conquest and subjugation of a place. After the city was subdued, all captives were counted, as well as the number of warriors lost; then the amount of tribute due from the vanquished enemy was established.

Aztec Terms for Warfare

In the Nahuatl language, many of the key words that deal with warfare were derived from the related terms *yaotl*, "enemy," and *yaoyotl*, "war." For example, *xochiyaoyotl* meant "flower(y) war"; *yaocalli*, "fort"; *yaoquizqui*, "soldier"; *yaotlapixqui*, "scout"; *yaoquizcapatiotl*, "salary for soldiers"; *yaoitacatl*, "provisions for war"; *yaoquizque*, "squadron, army"; *yaochimalli*, "war shield"; *yaochiua*, "to make war"; *yaochiua*, "to make war on the enemies of my friends"; *yaochichiua*, "to be armed for war"; *yaoc niloti* or *yaocnitzinquica*, "to retreat or retire from war"; *yaoyaualoa*, "to surround or encircle the enemies in war"; *yaonotza*, "to call up for war"; and *yaoana*, "to take in war" (Molina [1571] 1944, 1977; Carochi [1645] 1910).

Some confusion has resulted from the fact that the term *tequitl* was used for "labor," "work," and "tribute" (Carochi [1645] 1910:228, 336). Thus, when we read in Nahuatl that one of the goals of war was to secure *tequitl*, we are often not able to decide whether tribute or labor was intended, or both. As we will see below, there was also a single term for labor and tribute in the Zapotec language—and, as in the case of the Aztec, gaining tribute and labor were motives for Zapotec warfare.

Iconographic Conventions for Warfare

Although scenes such as two lords battling with weapons are known, certain themes occur with even greater frequency. Among them are (1) the taking of a captive, and (2) the burning of a rival town, or at least the burning of its temple. Two metaphorical expressions for war also give us insight into the minds of Aztec military men. The terms are *in mitl in chimalli* ("arrow and shield") and *in atl in tlachinolli* ("water and conflagration/bonfire"), the latter probably a reference to the defenders' attempts to put out the fire of their burning temple (Garibay K. 1940:112–113). The image of the burning temple served to demoralize the enemy, an important part of the Aztec strategy. Not surprisingly, Aztec scribes often depicted conquered places by showing a collapsed temple roof, tilting forward with flames issuing from beneath it (see below). The roof is sometimes shown as thatched, while the pyramidal platform is stone masonry.

Nahuatl, however, made no distinction between "defeat" (in which a rival town was burned and left) and "conquest" (in which the Aztec actually stayed behind to lay claim to the land); both events were subsumed by the use of the term *pehua*. Thus the depiction of a toppled or burning temple only denoted the defeat of a particular place; it did not indicate whether that place ever regained its independence, or became a tribute-paying subject community. As C. N. Davies (1987:39) points out, "Certain triumphs listed as conquests, therefore, may amount to little more than raids in which the victims' temple is ravaged and prisoners are secured for sacrifice."

As for iconographic conventions of captive taking, there were several favored by Aztec scribes. These were as follows:

1. The noble captor, often richly attired in feather headdress, cotton armor, animal skin capes, or the like;
2. The prisoner, his hair usually held in the grasp of the captor, often shown bound with rope, and depicted as nude or in skimpy attire;
3. Facial paint appropriate for war;
4. Weapons held (for example, *macanas*, knives, spears, and shields);
5. Musical instruments (usually drums or shell trumpets, which as we have seen were used in battle).

After having integrated data from the depictions of warriors in the Aztec codices with descriptive texts written by the Indian and Spanish chroniclers, we can see that differences in clothing quickly conveyed the rank and status of all levels of military personnel. Those who knew which rank each garment was associated with could tell at a distance with whom they were dealing. For example, in Figure 11.7e we see an *otomitl* warrior. This term was derived from the word "Otomí," an ethnic group, but in this context *otomitl* referred to members of a military order above the level of the eagle and jaguar military orders. At 11.7f we see a *cuahchic* warrior (literally, "the shorn one"). This term was used for members of a military order above the level of the *otomitl*, and was given to those who had performed more than twenty brave deeds. At 11.7g we see a *tlacateccatl*, a military commander whose head was shorn except for one shock of hair above the left ear, left braided with a red ribbon. Such a commander wore a special mantle, as depicted in Figure 11.7g (Corona Núñez 1964, 1: Lámina LXV).

In contrast to honored captors, commoners wore maguey mantles and no sandals. Lower-level warriors also wore maguey-cloth breechclouts and body paint (Clavigero 1787, 1:366–367).

Advancement through Captive Taking

When a young man took a captive without help, he became a *telpochyahqui* and a *tlamani*, "captor." His face was painted with red ochre except for the temples, which were covered with yellow ochre. He was given a new outfit, an orange cape with a striped border and two breechclouts (Anderson and Dibble 1954:76). The Codex Mendoza depicts the mantle (called *tiyacauhtlatquitl*) that he was given, which bore a special flower design (Fig. 11.7a). As a reward for taking two captives, a young man was given an orange mantle with red trim (Fig. 11.7b). For taking three captives, he was given a special mantle and a feather tunic (Fig. 11.7c). For taking four captives, he was given the *ocelototec* war garment and a mantle of black and orange with a fancy border (Fig. 11.7d). If he took a fifth captive from one of three particularly "fierce" towns—Atlixco, Tliuhquitepec, or Huexotzinco—the warrior was named *cuauhyahcatl*, "great captain," and he received a blue lip plug, a headband with two tufts of eagle feathers, leather ear ornaments, a bright red cape, a leather cape, and a bichrome cape. Taking a second captive from one of those three very fierce towns led to a warrior's gaining a new title, that of *tlacochcatl*, "commanding general." Such a warrior would receive a yellow lip plug, a new series of capes, and black sandals. Still other successful warriors received elaborate headbands with feather tassels to tie into their hair, yellow or blue lip plugs, and other garments (see Fig. 11.8; Anderson and Dibble 1954:74, 77).

11.7. Different grades within the Aztec military hierarchy were determined by the number of captives taken. At *a* is a young man armed with shield and broadsword, taking his first captive; he was rewarded with a special blanket that bears a flower design. At *b*, dressed in military garb, is a man who has taken 2 captives; he received an orange blanket with white and red trim. At *c* is a warrior who has taken 3 captives; he received a blanket with a squash motif. At *d* is a warrior dressed in full feline attire, who has taken 4 captives; he received a blanket with a design featuring triangles of black and orange with a red and white trim. At *e* is an *otomitl* warrior who has taken 5 captives; at *f* is a warrior called *cuahchic*, who has taken captives from the fiercest towns, such as Huexotzinco. At *g* is the *tlacateccatl* or military commander, who wears an elaborate feather headdress and a rich red mantle edged with a black-and-white design. (Redrawn from Folio 64 of the Codex Mendoza; see Corona Núñez 1964, 1: Lámina LXV and Clark 1938.)

11.8. Aztec rulers gave presents to successful warriors. At the left in both scenes are Aztec rulers, seated on woven-mat thrones. In the upper scene, warriors receive headbands with feather tassels, ear plugs, lip plugs, and cloth. Below, warriors receive elaborately decorated cloth and knotted sashes. (Redrawn from Anderson and Dibble 1954: figs. 99, 100.)

The Depiction of Conquered Places

As an example of the way conquered places were depicted, let us consider some of the conquests claimed by Tizoc (A.D. 1481–1486), the seventh Mexica ruler. For Tizoc we are fortunate to have three perspectives and three kinds of records: (1) a stone monument he commissioned, (2) a copy of a prehispanic codex painted after the arrival of the Spaniards, and (3) ethnohistoric accounts of his battles and conquests.

Tizoc's conquests are given on the prehispanic "Stone of Tizoc" and in numerous posthispanic documents, including the Matrícula de Tributos and the Codex Mendoza. Most of the localities he supposedly conquered fall in the Toluca Valley west of the Basin of Mexico, and in the Huastec area of northeast Mexico.

For example, in the Codex Mendoza (Fig. 11.9) we see Tizoc seated on the woven mat, which (as we have seen in chapter 10) indicated authority. Tizoc was nicknamed "The Bloodletter," and in this case his hieroglyphic nickname is seen attached to his back by a black line; the glyph is a leg shown with prick marks resulting from the act of bloodletting. In front of Tizoc are three symbols that signify warfare—above is the *atlatl* (painted blue in the original); below is the shield (gold with turquoise trim around the edges); and behind the shield are spears or lances, poking out to either side.

This folio of the Codex Mendoza lists the places Tizoc claims to have conquered, while omitting any place he was unable to subdue. The conquered places, each shown with a burning temple, are as follows: Tonaliymoqueçayan, Toxico, Ecatepec, Çilan, Tecaxic, Tulucan, Yancuitlán, Tlapan, Atezcahuacan, Maçatlán, Xochiyetla, Tamapachco, Ecatlyquapechco, and Miquetlán.

Usually, the hieroglyphic signs that give the name of a conquered place appear to the left of the burning temple. However, in the case of Miquetlán (Fig. 11.9p) the principal sign (a dead person) appears below the burning temple, because that sign was too large and too long to appear to the left (Corona Núñez 1964, 1: Lámina XI).

Now let us look at the sculpture called the Stone of Tizoc, which was carved in the 1480s to commemorate Tizoc's inauguration (Fig. 11.10). It lists fifteen conquered places, some of which were in fact subjugated *prior* to Tizoc's accession to the throne. Ten have been identified as follows: Matlatzinco, Tochpan, Ahuilizapan, Colhuacán, Tetenanco or Tenanyocan, Xochimilco, Chalco, Acolman or Acolhuacán, Tlatelolco, and Cuetlaxtlán (Seler 1902–1923, vol. 2; Peñafiel 1910; Nicholson 1973:5). Note that there is only minimal overlap with the conquered places listed in the Codex Mendoza (Fig. 11.9).

Data That Contradict Tizoc's Claims

Now let us look at the ethnohistoric data on Tizoc's reign that give us a somewhat different version. These other sources indicate that Tizoc sometimes lost more men than

11.9. The Aztec ruler Tizoc (at *g*), who reigned from A.D. 1481 to 1486, has declared war (symbolized at *h* by a shield, *atlatl*, and spears). The places Tizoc reportedly conquered are shown as temples with flames issuing from below their toppled roofs. They are *a*, Tonaliymoqueçayan, "Where the Sun Rises"; *b*, Toxico, "Place of Toci" (a goddess); *c*, Ecatepec, "Hill of the Wind"; *d*, Çilan, "Place of Small Shells"; *e*, Tecaxic, "Place of Stone Boxes"; *f*, Tulucan, "In the Sloping Hill of the Matlatzinca"; *i*, Yancuitlán, "In the New Town"; *j*, Tlapan, "Place of the Dyers"; *k*, Atezcahuacan, "Place of the Small Lake"; *l*, Maçatlán, "Place of Deer"; *m*, Xochiyetla, "Place of Tobacco Flowers"; *n*, Tamapachco, (?); *o*, Ecatlyquapechco, "Where the Southern Wind Rises"; *p*, Miquetlán, "Place of the Dead." (Redrawn from Folio 12 of the Codex Mendoza; see Corona Núñez 1964, 1: Lámina XI and Clark 1938).

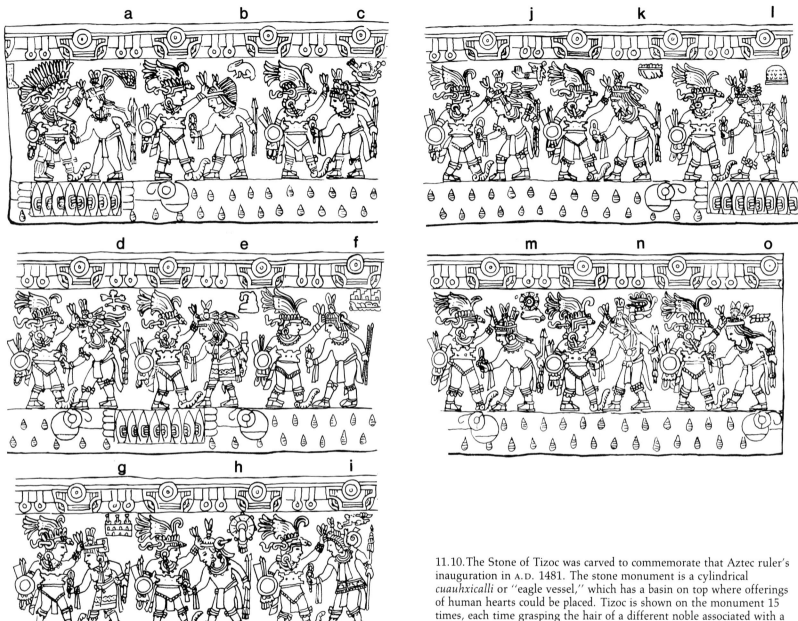

11.10. The Stone of Tizoc was carved to commemorate that Aztec ruler's inauguration in A.D. 1481. The stone monument is a cylindrical *cuauhxicalli* or "eagle vessel," which has a basin on top where offerings of human hearts could be placed. Tizoc is shown on the monument 15 times, each time grasping the hair of a different noble associated with a different place sign. Of those 15 places, the 10 identified with confidence are: *a*, Matlatzinco; *b*, Tochpan; *c*, Ahuilizapan; *e*, Colhuacán; *f*, Tetenanco; *g*, Xochimilco; *h*, Chalco; *j*, Acolman or Acolhuacán; *l*, Tlatelolco; *o*, Cuetlaxtlán. (Redrawn from Orozco y Berra 1877.)

he defeated—an aspect of his campaigns which is, of course, not mentioned on any of the monuments or manuscripts he himself commissioned.

From Durán ([1581] 1967), Herrera y Tordesillas ([1601] 1947), and the *Crónica Mexicana* (1975), we learn that Tizoc began by summoning men from various ethnic groups, including the Chalca, Chinampeca, and Matlatzinca. He then assembled these conscripts at Tetzontepec, eighty-five kilometers from Tenochtitlán, and proceeded to march to Metztitlán. The troops attacked Metztitlán, claiming "victory" after taking forty prisoners, most of whom were Huastec. In spite of this proclamation of victory, Tizoc had lost at least 300 of his own men and had to return to Tenochtitlán (Durán [1581] 1967, 2:303–304; Herrera y Tordesillas [1601] 1947, 6:212–213). (The figure of 300 is actually considered to be low; according to C. N. Davies [1987:73], it probably refers not to total losses, but only to nobles killed or captured, since Tizoc himself referred to the dead as "our sons, brothers and nephews.")

Significantly, even though Tizoc had lost more men than he captured, he emphasized the fact that he had taken the number necessary for his own inauguration (Acosta [1590] 1604, 2:493; *Crónica Mexicana* 1975, chaps. 57–58; Hassig 1988:193). Needless to say, no monument was carved to commemorate the fact that Tizoc had lost 300 men in battle, but that is the just the kind of information we need if we are to understand the relationship between "history" and propaganda in prehispanic society.

In fact, Tizoc's short reign is considered by some ethnohistorians to have been rather undistinguished in terms of military success, and this assessment is supported by data suggesting that there were revolts by several of the regions he claims to have subjugated. Durán, for example, says that Tizoc's reign was more noted for cowardice than audacity; Torquemada argues that while Tizoc was no hero, he was also no coward, since he had held the post of military commander (*tlacateccatl*) before becoming ruler. Whichever is the case, it seems that Tizoc's reign not only witnessed fewer military campaigns than those of other Aztec rulers, but also fewer successful campaigns, i.e., those in which more men were captured than lost. It is revealing that the Stone of Tizoc and the Codex Mendoza claim only successful conquests, while the ethnohistoric sources give us some information on losses, places not subjugated, and the number of Aztec warriors lost.

Thus, while the lists of conquered places from the Stone of Tizoc, the Codex Mendoza, and the ethnohistoric sources overlap, they definitely are *not* isomorphic. One sixteenth-century ethnohistoric source (Sahagún) even states that "no wars were made in [Tizoc's] reign" (Anderson and Dibble 1954:2). Since no line of evidence duplicates the others, the value of studying different accounts and of analyzing sources written on different media (stone, prehispanic codices, and Spanish manuscripts) should be apparent.

It seems clear to outsiders that Aztec warfare was motivated by competition for land, tribute, and goods. There were ethnic differences, however; the Tepaneca seem to have focused more on tribute, while the Mexica were more interested in gaining expanses of land (*Crónica X,* Barlow 1945). The Aztec, nevertheless, continued to claim that their wars were to avenge insults or to procure captives for sacrifice. A number of Mesoamerican peoples used this constant "need for captives" as the rationalization for warfare, and in some cases even seem to have convinced twentieth-century Mesoamericanists of its truth. Fortunately, most scholars remain skeptical (e.g., Vaillant 1950:208; Conrad and Demarest 1984).

Part of the reason so many scholars have emphasized the procurement of sacrificial victims is that they have been overly impressed by Aztec propaganda. They have focused attention on the Aztec practice of conducting "flowery wars" (*xochiyaotl*), which were explicit shows of power and propaganda. Such wars were not intended to be conquests, but rather a device to reestablish who was on top and who was not, a restatement of hierarchical relationships. In such cases, actual permanent conquest was not necessary to achieve the immediate end. Another benefit of the *xochiyaotl* was that it was usually easier and less expensive to bring captives from geographically close ethnic groups, rather than remote lands, as the Aztec empire expanded.

For example, the Mexica explanation for the "flowery wars" they carried out with Tlaxcala was that these battles provided a never-ending pool of sacrificial victims for Tenochtitlán. The truth, however, is that the Tlaxcalans were very powerful; true conquest would have required the Mexica to commit a very large army to fighting them, and most probably that army would have incurred heavy losses, if not actual defeat. So instead of all-out warfare, the Mexica decided to conduct less costly, smaller-scale battles with the Tlaxcalans. This strategy proved to be ideal for supplying Tenochtitlán with a steady stream of sacrificial victims, but not for subduing the Tlaxcalans.

The taking of captives was timed to coincide with particular Aztec festivals and rites. In chapter 10, we saw how the incumbent Aztec ruler was required to validate his election to *tlatoani* by bringing back a number of captives for sacrifice at his own inauguration. The time between the death of a former ruler and the inauguration of the next ruler was a critical period, during which the military prowess of the future ruler was closely scrutinized. Thus many Aztec military campaigns were timed to precede either inaugural rites (when the candidate needed to show his power) or occasions when a new temple was dedicated. (As an example of the latter, the *Anales de Cuauhtitlán* [1945:58] state that the Mexica ruler Ahuitzotl gave forty captives to Cuauhnahuac for the dedication of their temple.)

Aztec specialists (e.g., Hicks 1979; Isaac 1983a, 1983b; Hassig 1988) have, for the most part, been careful to separate the real reasons for Aztec warfare from the propaganda of sacrifice. The Aztec could not really conquer their more powerful contemporaries, such as the Tlaxcalans and the Tarascans. They nibbled away at the edges of those groups with *xochiyaotl* and reserved their most crushing conquests for weaker groups. Even in the case of smaller polities, such as Metztitlán in the time of Tizoc, the Aztec sometimes lost more of their own soldiers than they killed. These battles, however, could be claimed as victories if a sufficient number of enemy captives were taken—forty Huastec prisoners, for example, at a cost of 300 Aztec lives. The Aztec scribes do not give us the costs of these battles. They show us victorious rulers, naked and humiliated captives, hearts being sacrificed, and lists of tribute payments. Their role was not to record military history. Like the "spin doctors" hired by twentieth-century politicians, their job was to show us an unending series of victories in which nothing had ever gone wrong.

MIXTEC RAIDS AND CONQUESTS

While the Mixtec-speaking region of Oaxaca and southern Puebla has a long archaeological sequence (Spores 1972, 1974b), we know very little about Mixtec warfare before the Postclassic (A.D. 900–1530). Once we enter the period of the Mixtec codices, data on warfare become almost bewilderingly rich and detailed. Some of these codices are believed to have been painted and repainted in prehispanic times (e.g., the Nuttall, Colombino, Vindobonensis, and Bodley); others, such as the Codex Selden, are thought to have been painted (or completed) shortly after the arrival of the Spaniards; still others (e.g., the Mapa de Teozacoalco and Lienzo de Ocotepec) are thought to have been painted around A.D. 1580, at the request of the Spaniards, to show the extent of indigenous rulers' territories.

As in the case of the Aztec, we should remember that the Mixtec codices were a medium for state propaganda rather than objective history. As mentioned earlier in chapter 5, some manuscripts are palimpsests that show signs of having been altered or repainted by later rulers; some Mixtec nobles seem to have inserted themselves into genealogies to which they did not belong, claimed territories someone else conquered, or erased the record of a previous ruler. Smith (1963, 1973a, 1983b) and Caso (1964a, 1966a, 1977, 1979) have pointed to several cases where two versions of the same event are given in codices from two different regions, and it is clear that the scribes involved had different political perspectives and purposes. Each codex was written (or rewritten) to further the point of view of a particular royal family at the expense of others.

Judging by the codices, a great deal of Mixtec warfare consisted of conflicts between two rival lords, or hereditary rulers, within the Mixtec region. To be sure, there is evidence for at least two alliances between the Zapotec and Mixtec to fight the Aztec (see below); however, most of the time the Mixtec seem to have been fighting each other. One reason for going to war seems to have been competition over the throne of a particular polity, especially when the throne was vacant or the line of succession was ambiguous. The rationalization given by the attacker, however, was often some alleged insult, act of discourteous behavior, usurpation, or treacherous act by his adversary. In order to consolidate power, the victorious ruler often married the widow, sister, or daughter of the defeated ruler.

Because of the Mixtec system of measuring high rank by genealogical closeness to the main line of descent from a revered ancestor (Dahlgren de Jordán 1954; Spores 1967, 1984), some attackers were actually royal women. These women, who had genealogical reasons for believing that they outranked their male rivals, are portrayed in the codices as actually leading armies into battle (see below).

The Fit between Mixtec Language and Writing

Caso (1949, 1950, 1977, 1979) and Smith (1973a, 1973b) have given us a whole series of instances in which Mixtec picture writing reflected words, concepts, or metaphors in the spoken language. In this section we will consider a few of these.

In the Mixtec language, the expression *yecu tnañu* meant "war," with *tnañu* meaning "battle," and *yecu* meaning "enemy" (Alvarado [1593] 1962; Reyes [1593] 1976; Arana and Swadesh 1965). "Conquered," "battle," "*atlatl* dart," and "arrow" could all be expressed by the term *nduvua*; "to be seized" or "captured" was expressed as *tnee* (Arana and Swadesh 1965). Like the Aztec, the Mixtec depicted war by showing town conquests and the taking of captives. Mixtec warriors were shown carrying *atlatls*, shields, darts, swords, lances or spears, war clubs, bows and arrows, or occasionally blowguns (see Fig. 11.11).

"Conquest" in general, and "conquered town" in particular, were conveyed in the codices by showing an arrow thrust into a place sign (see Fig. 11.12a). This pictorial convention had a clear counterpart in one of the idiomatic expressions for "conquest": in Mixtec, the infinitive "to conquer" was *chihi nduvua ñuhu ñaha*, which literally meant "to put an arrow into the lands of another" (Smith 1973a). A shortened form of the expression (*chihi nduvua ñuhu*) meant "to battle."

Another idiomatic expression—*sami ñuu*, "to burn the town"—was also used to indicate conquest. The pictorial counterpart of that expression is also known from the codices. Occasionally, as seen in Figures 11.12b and 11.14, red flames were attached to a place sign to indicate that the town had been burned at the time of conquest. In still other cases, conquest was shown by depicting the victorious ruler grasping the hair of the defeated ruler (Fig. 11.13). This convention was very widespread in world prehistory, having

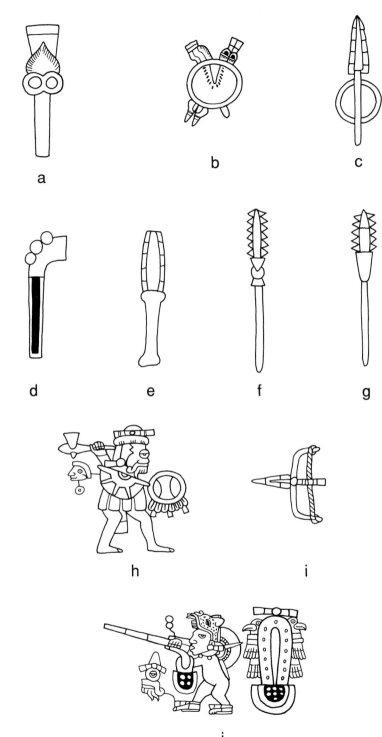

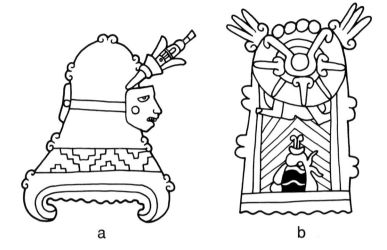

11.12. Mixtec conventions for conquered places. *a*, the spear thrust into the upper right side of this hill sign signifies "conquest." The place—"Hill of the Mask"—was conquered by 8 Deer "Tiger Claw" in the year 6 Flint (A.D. 1044). (Redrawn from Codex Nuttall 48.) *b*, a defeated place, signified by flames (which look like feathers) emerging from the sides. Two places—"Hill of the Moon" and the "Place of the Insect"—have been combined to form this place sign. These places were defeated in a two-day battle in A.D. 1038 by a female ruler named 6 Monkey "Serpent Quechquemitl." (Redrawn from Codex Selden 8-I.)

11.11. Weapons brandished by Mixtec warriors. *a*, atlatl (Codex Vindobonensis); *b*, shield, *atlatl*, and darts (Codex Vindobonensis); *c*, shield and spear (Codex Colombino); *d*, curved weapon (Codex Vindobonensis); *e*, short broadsword (Codex Selden); *f*, *g*, lances edged with obsidian blades (Codex Bodley); *h*, figure carrying a shield (left hand) and war hatchet (right hand) (Codex Selden); *i*, bow and arrow (Codex Bodley); and *j*, a figure using a blowgun. Behind *j* is a bag with captured birds hanging from the sides (Codex Bodley). (Redrawn from Caso 1977: Lámina VI.)

been utilized in Peru, in Egypt on the Narmer Palette (Emery 1961), and in Mesoamerica by the Aztec, Mixtec, and Maya.

One Mixtec expression for a person waging a military campaign was *tay caca yecu*, literally "a man who walks on the enemy" (from *tay* = man; *caca* = to walk; *yecu* = enemy). In the Mixtec codices, a road containing a pattern of red, white, and black chevrons indicates a "warpath," and persons standing on that warpath are usually shown carrying a weapon. Smith (1973a:33) has suggested that the chevron pattern may stand for the word *yecu*, indicating that the warrior depicted was walking on the enemy. Her interpretation is strengthened by the fact that two other Mesoamerican peoples, the Zapotec and the Maya, also used the image of "walking" or "stepping" on the enemy to symbolize conquest (see below). In Figure 11.14, the Mixtec ruler 8 Deer "Tiger Claw" is "on the warpath" (symbolized by the chevron-filled path); he holds a shield, spear, and *atlatl* darts. He has just captured the town of Acatepec ("Hill of the Moon"), whose ruler, 3 Crocodile, is shown as a prisoner with a rope around his neck. The convention of showing prisoners bound with ropes around their necks or arms was widespread in Mesoamerica, with examples known from all four cultures covered in this study.

Captives taken in battle were frequently shown nude and were sacrificed, with a flint knife used to open the chest of the victim (Fig. 11.15). Sometimes sacrificed figures were shown descending into the earth (as in the scene from Codex Bodley 36–35). Occasionally we see scenes of arrow sacrifice, as in the case of a victim from the Codex Nuttall (83d–84a), who was tied to a wooden scaffold and riddled with projectiles (Fig. 11.16). In the Mixtec codices, death was usually conveyed by showing a person with closed eyes, either seated or in a prone position. Occasionally, the corpse is shown as a mummy bundle (Fig. 11.17).

Some Examples of Conquests

Let us now look at some examples of Mixtec rulers who carried out extensive conquests. We will begin with a royal woman from the Nochixtlán Valley named 6 Monkey, and then look at the life of the famous male ruler from Tilantongo, 8 Deer "Tiger Claw." At the outset, we should say that the absolute dating of events in the codices is still undergoing revision by Emily Rabin (1981), and that any dates we give here should be considered tentative. We will use the correlation between Mixtec and Spanish calendars worked out by Caso (1951, 1955, 1965b, 1967, 1977, 1979), cautioning the reader that research by Rabin may eventually alter these dates. Some of her revisions move the dates fifty-two years forward. These revisions were deemed necessary by Rabin, since she noted that some individuals were having offspring at impossible ages, and others were dying at impossible ages. To bring these individuals back into "biological reality," she had to move some dates (and the associated individuals) into fifty-two-year cycles different from those assigned

11.13. A Mixtec ruler taking a captive. At right, 8 Deer "Tiger Claw" (armed with *atlatl* and shield) grasps the hair of 4 Wind (at left). This capture took place on the day 12 Monkey in the year 11 House (A.D. 1049 in Caso's scheme), four years after 8 Deer had received his turquoise noseplug (see chapter 10). (Redrawn from Codex Nuttall 83.)

11.14. A Mixtec ruler shown conquering a place. At right is 8 Deer "Tiger Claw," standing on the band of chevrons signifying "warpath"; he holds a spear, shield, and *atlatl* darts. At left is his enemy 3 Crocodile, shown with a rope around his neck, sitting in front of the "Hill of the Moon" (a place identified as Santa María Acatepec by Smith [1973a:68–70]). In addition to the spears thrust into both sides of the hill, flames emerge from the lower left side of the hill sign. (Redrawn from Codex Bodley 10-II.)

11.15. Death by heart removal. Here 12 Motion, half-brother of 8 Deer "Tiger Claw," is shown being murdered in a sweatbath in A.D. 1048 (appropriately enough, on the day "11 Death"). A sharp knife has been plunged into his chest; blood spurts out; his eyes are closed and his head is upside down, as he lies awkwardly on his back. (Redrawn from Codex Nuttall 81; a different version of this sacrifice is shown in the Codex Colombino.)

11.16. Death by arrow sacrifice. This Mixtec lord, named 6 House "Necklace of Flints," is shown dying by arrow sacrifice on a wooden scaffold in the Codex Nuttall. However, Codex Becker I (X) shows this same lord dying as the result of gladiatorial sacrifice. (Redrawn from Codex Nuttall 83.)

11.17. Dead Mixtec lords shown tied up as mummy bundles. These two lords (12 Vulture and 12 Lizard) had been sacrificed. (Redrawn from Codex Nuttall 20.)

by Caso. Until her complete argument and set of new dates are published, I have chosen to go with Caso's traditional chronology.

6 Monkey "Serpent Quechquemitl"

A powerful eleventh-century royal woman who enjoyed military success was 6 Monkey "Serpent Quechquemitl"[1]; her life has been described by Spinden (1935), Caso (1964a, 1977, 1979), and Smith (1973a). This woman was discussed at length in the Codex Selden, a manuscript painted in prehispanic style, but including dates as recent as A.D. 1556. The Codex Selden was concerned with the genealogy of rulers at a place called "Belching Mountain," believed by Smith (1983a) to be Magdalena Jaltepec in the Nochixtlán Valley of Oaxaca. In addition to being featured in the Codex Selden, Lady 6 Monkey's life is also discussed in at least four other codices—the Nuttall, Bodley, Colombino, and Becker I[2]—all painted in prehispanic style by scribes in other towns, who present their own different, local points of view.

Lady 6 Monkey had three older brothers named 1 Reed, 12 Water, and 3 Water, all of whom apparently were defeated in battle and sacrificed before they could accede to any throne. They were captured while trying to defend a place called "Skull Temple," and were sacrificed on the day 8 Vulture in the year 9 House (A.D. 1021) (see Fig. 11.18). Even following the death of her brothers—who, because of seniority, would have preceded her in gaining a title—it appears that 6 Monkey encountered some problems in being recognized as the rightful ruler of "Belching Mountain."

6 Monkey sought the advice of an old priest named 10 Lizard, who sent her to visit a second priest named 6 Vulture—this latter visit possibly involving a trip to a sacred cave (Figs. 11.19, 11.20). Then 6 Monkey and her future husband, 11 Wind "Bloody Tiger," made offerings in front of a priestess[3] named 9 Grass at "Skull Temple" (Fig. 11.21). Later, 11 Wind and 6 Monkey were married—as depicted in a bathing scene (Fig. 11.22)—and received numerous gifts from well-wishers.

During 6 Monkey's trip to her husband's town, a place called "Bundle of Xipe," she passed through places called "Hill of the Moon" and "Hill of the Insect"; in those towns, she and her two accompanying ambassadors were insulted by "cutting words"—shown in Figure 11.23 by speech scrolls tipped with sharp flint knives (Spinden 1935:435). These "cutting words" constitute a good example of agitation propaganda, used as justification for military action. 6 Monkey complained about the insults, and after having consulted

[1]Even though it has become conventional to use the Nahuatl term *quechquemitl* for this female poncho-like garment, it would be more appropriate to employ the Mixtec term *sighu*.

[2]Caso (1966a) and Troike (1974) have argued persuasively that the Colombino and Becker I are really two sections of the same manuscript.

[3]This may be a case of euhemerism, a process discussed in chapter 9, in which a royal ancestor becomes a folk hero and ultimately a deity.

again with the priestess 9 Grass of "Skull Temple," she declared war against those who had insulted her. Her decision to go to war is depicted by the shield and spear that the codex painter placed on the ground between 6 Monkey and 9 Grass (Fig. 11.24).

6 Monkey then sent her warriors out to battle. They successfully captured one noble each from places called "Hill of the Moon" and "Hill of the Insect" in a two-day battle, which took place on the days 3 Grass and 4 Reed in the year 13 Rabbit (A.D. 1038). It is worth noting that the scribe showed 6 Monkey dispatching only two warriors, who probably stood symbolically for a much larger army (Fig. 11.25). In Figure 11.26, 6 Monkey is shown grasping one of the captured nobles by the hair. One defeated noble—2 Crocodile—was sacrificed in "Belching Mountain," 6 Monkey's hometown (Fig. 11.27); the other was taken by her two ambassadors to her husband's town, "Bundle of Xipe," where he was sacrificed (Fig. 11.28).

Finally, 6 Monkey was named ruler by a priest named 2 Flower (Fig. 11.29), and she (along with her husband 11 Wind) was able to rule in peace (Fig. 11.30). She later bore two sons, both of whom ended up marrying daughters of the ruler 8 Deer "Tiger Claw" (see below).

8 Deer "Tiger Claw"

The story of Lady 6 Monkey gives what is probably a fairly typical picture of Mixtec warfare—a brief conflict over the right to accede to a throne. Although rationalized as revenge for an insult, the conflict probably had more to do with the need for one of several claimants to demonstrate military superiority in order to be granted the title.

Much less typical in the codices are conflicts affecting more than one small kingdom or district. Perhaps the most unusual case we have is that of the eleventh-century ruler 8 Deer "Tiger Claw" of Tilantongo (Clark 1912), who for a brief period actually succeeded in conquering so many places that he temporarily unified the Mixtec highlands and coast into a single large state.

Different views of 8 Deer's life were given in different codices (Clark 1938; Caso 1960, 1966a, 1979; Smith 1963, 1973a; Troike 1978). The Codex Nuttall gave the view from the highlands or Mixteca Alta, the region in which 8 Deer's birthplace of Tilantongo was situated. The Codex Colombino, probably painted in the vicinity of Tututepec, gave the view from the Pacific coast or "Mixteca de la Costa" of Oaxaca. (This Tututepec was probably the same "Hill of the Bird" which the earlier Zapotec of 150 B.C.–A.D. 150 had claimed as part of Monte Albán's territory; see Fig. 6.1 in chapter 6). Almost all of the Codex Colombino and Codex Becker I are devoted to detailing the events of 8 Deer's life, as is the reverse (back side) of the Codex Nuttall. (In contrast, in the Codex Selden 8 Deer is mentioned just once, as an "in-law" to 6 Monkey.) So great was 8 Deer's political impact that some codices were altered to enlarge the space devoted to him.

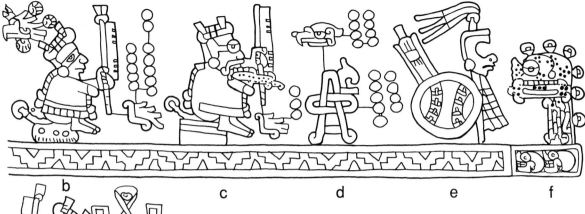

11.18. This is the first of a set of illustrations (Figs. 11.18–11.30) that depict events in the life of the Mixtec royal woman 6 Monkey "Serpent Quechquemitl." Our illustrations are taken from the Codex Selden, but 6 Monkey's life is also discussed in four other codices (Nuttall, Bodley, Becker I, and Colombino). We pick up her life here in A.D. 1021, when she was probably about 20 years old (her birth date is not given). Reading from bottom to top in boustrophedon fashion, we see at *a* her brother 1 Reed "Ballcourt-Astronomical Apparatus"; at *b* is her brother 12 Water "Eagle Down"; and at *c* is her brother 3 Water "Copal Breath." At *d* we see the day 8 Vulture (at top) in the year 9 House (below); this is A.D. 1021. At *e*, we see the symbols of battle: the shield, dart or spear, feathered staff, and military mask. At *f* is the "Place of the Skull" or "Skull Temple." This passage signifies that 6 Monkey's three brothers participated in a war defending "Place of the Skull." (Redrawn from Codex Selden 5d-6a.)

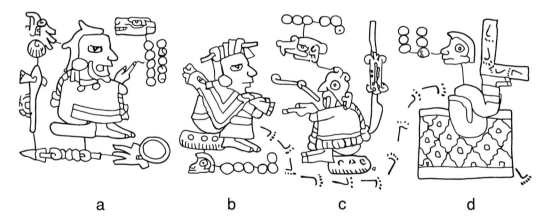

11.19. On the left is 6 Monkey, and at right is a priest named 10 Lizard "Dead Man's Hair–Jade Axe." Since her three older brothers had apparently lost their lives in the previous battle (see Fig. 11.18), 6 Monkey confers with this priest to discuss her rights of accession to the throne of "Belching Mountain," identified by Smith (1983a) as Magdalena Jaltepec in the Nochixtlán Valley of Oaxaca.

11.20. The priest 10 Lizard (at *a*) sends 6 Monkey (at *b*) to talk with another priest named 6 Vulture "Planting Stick" (at *c*). Footprints show that 6 Monkey also traveled to a sacred cave, which she entered (at *d*); this pilgrimage was apparently suggested to her by 6 Vulture.

a   b   c   d   e

11.21. A series of offerings (at *a*) were made by 6 Monkey (at *b*) and 11 Wind "Bloody Tiger" (at *c*) to a priestess named 9 Grass (at *d*) in "Skull Temple" (at *e*). The two apparently were seeking the priestess's blessing before their impending wedding.

11.22. The royal couple 11 Wind (lower left) and 6 Monkey (lower right) are shown in a "bathing scene," one of the conventions the Mixtec used for marriage ceremonies (see chapter 8). The wedding date is given above 6 Monkey's name as the day 7 Flower in the year 12 House (A.D. 1037). Some of their wedding gifts are shown at the top; most prominent are various types of clothing. (Redrawn from Codex Selden 7.)

a   b   c   d

11.23.6 Monkey sends out two ambassadors (note footprints). At *a* is the ambassador named 2 Flower, carrying 6 Monkey on his back. At *b* is the second ambassador, named 3 Crocodile. At *c* they pass through a place called "Hill of the Moon" and speak with a lord named 6 Lizard. At *d* they pass through a second place, called "Hill of the Insect," with its lord 2 Crocodile. These two lords (at *c* and *d*) insult her ambassadors; the insulting language is indicated by the flint knives attached to their speech scrolls, a depiction of "cutting" words. (Redrawn from Codex Selden 7.)

a   b   c   d

11.24.6 Monkey (shown at *d*) complains to the priestess 9 Grass (at *b*), who is seated in front of "Skull Temple" (at *a*), that she has been insulted and needs to go to war to avenge those insults. Depicted between 9 Grass and 6 Monkey (at *c*) are symbols of war (the shield and spear), above which we see a fire drill and a "new fire."

11.25. Sent out to fight for 6 Monkey are two warriors who carry shields in their right hands and obsidian-edged broadswords in their left hands. (Redrawn from Codex Selden 7.)

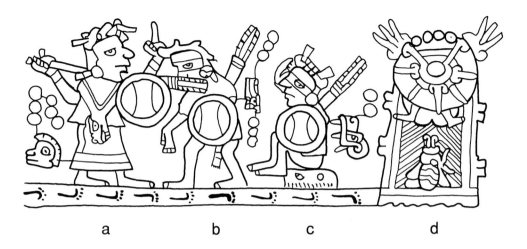

a   b   c   d

11.26.6 Monkey (at *a*) is shown grasping the hair of her enemy 6 Lizard (at *b*). At *c* is the seated lord 2 Crocodile. These are the two lords who had insulted her ambassadors (see Fig. 11.23). At *d* is the compound place name "Hill of the Moon" and "Hill of the Insect"; those two towns have been defeated or burned, as indicated by the flames shown at the upper corners (see also Fig. 11.12b).

11.27. Shown here is the sacrifice of one of the defeated lords seen in Figure 11.26. Lord 2 Crocodile—shown with closed eyes, nearly naked, and in an awkward position—has had his heart removed at "Belching Mountain" (6 Monkey's birthplace).

11.28. The other lord who had insulted 6 Monkey was taken to "Bundle of Xipe" (the birthplace of 6 Monkey's husband) for sacrifice. Here we see Lord 6 Crocodile, stretched on his back over a stone, with his chest open and a symbol (blood-and-heart) issuing from it, indicating that his heart has been removed. (Redrawn from Codex Selden 8.)

11.29. Following her successful war against the two lords who had insulted her, 6 Monkey is given a new name. A priest named 2 Flower (shown at left) performs a special rite for 6 Monkey (at right). For the first time she wears a "War Quechquemitl" featuring multicolored chevrons, like those on the warpath she had traveled. (Her former nickname, "Serpent Quechquemitl," appears behind her.) Thus 6 Monkey's military success resulted in her acquisition of a new nickname. (Redrawn from Codex Selden 8.)

11.30. Two days after sacrificing her enemies (on the day 6 Eagle in the year 13 Rabbit, or A.D. 1038), 6 Monkey is shown (at left) wearing her new "War Quechquemitl"; her former nickname, "Serpent Quechquemitl," appears above her face. In this scene, 6 Monkey and her husband 11 Wind (at right) have been installed as rulers at "Bundle of Xipe."

One of the most ironic aspects of 8 Deer "Tiger Claw's" life was that when it began, he was not even first in line to succeed his father. He was supposedly born on the day 8 Deer in the year 12 Reed (A.D. 1011) at Tilantongo, the home of one of the most prestigious lineages in the Mixteca Alta. He was the first-born son of Lady 11 Water "Blue Jewel Bird," the second wife of Lord 5 Crocodile. He was therefore outranked by his older half-brother, 12 Motion "Bloody Tiger," the son of his father's first wife and the logical successor to 5 Crocodile's title.

Unable to claim the throne of Tilantongo, 8 Deer looked for another venue. Caso (1977, 1979) has suggested that Lady 11 Water was from Tututepec, a Mixtec colony on the Pacific coast of Oaxaca. This made it logical for 8 Deer to assume rulership of Tututepec, a site of lesser prestige to which his mother's ties and his father's high rank entitled him. From his base on the Pacific coast, 8 Deer established an expansionist, militaristic state that attacked the Chatino Indians and the southern Zapotec, including those in the region of Miahuatlán and the Isthmus of Tehuantepec. Seventy-five to 100 place signs are listed in the Mixtec codices as the conquests of 8 Deer (Caso 1977, 1979). Many of these places were indicated by the now-familiar spear thrust into the place sign (see Fig. 11.12a).

In A.D. 1030, when 8 Deer was nineteen and his half-brother 12 Motion was thirty-seven, their father 5 Crocodile died. Following his father's death, 8 Deer embarked on a series of conquests of places such as "Hill of the Sky Tiger" and "River of the Mouth and Flames." He offered a human heart from a sacrificed captive to a priestess or deified ancestor named 9 Grass; consulted with nobles at Apoala in the Mixteca Alta; received important visitors sent from a lord named 4 Tiger at a place called Tula (perhaps the Toltec capital?); and took many important prisoners.

According to the Bodley and Colombino codices, one of the important places conquered by 8 Deer in A.D. 1044 was Acatepec, to the east of Tututepec. (Previously, in Figure 11.14, we saw 8 Deer's capture of Lord 3 Crocodile of Acatepec, shown with a rope around his neck.) Evidently this conquest was a major accomplishment for the thirty-three-year-old 8 Deer, for in the following year he received an honor recorded in at least four different codices: the placing of an ornament in his nose signifying that he was a "great lord" or "warrior" (Figs. 10.9, 10.10, 10.11). One version has 8 Deer traveling to Tula for this honor; Caso claims that he was given the Nahuatl title *tecuhtli*, "noble," by his Nahuatl-speaking neighbors.

In A.D. 1048, 8 Deer learned of the death of his half-brother 12 Motion "Bloody Tiger," who had succeeded 5 Crocodile on the throne of Tilantongo. 12 Motion had been killed as the result of a dispute over the title to "Bundle of Xipe" (a place already mentioned in the story of 6 Monkey). "Bundle of Xipe" had been ruled by 11 Wind, 12 Motion's brother-in-law. Following 11 Wind's death, 12 Motion had decided that *he* would be ruler of "Bundle of Xipe." This naturally angered his nephews, 10 Dog and 6 House, who (as 11 Wind's sons) had assumed that one of them would accede to the throne. In the ensuing battle, 12 Motion was killed (the Codex Nuttall version, given in Figure 11.15, shows him being sacrificed in a steam bath—perhaps he was ambushed there while he was temporarily without his weapons). Two days after his death his body was burned by priests, who carried out special rites involving the sacrifice of doves, burning of copal, and offering of cacao.

With the death of 12 Motion, 8 Deer finally was able to rule both Tututepec and Tilantongo. The death of his older half-brother provided the immediate opportunity; but all his highly successful military campaigns since the age of twelve, culminating with his defeat of Acatepec, had set the stage for his assumption of the Tilantongo throne. 8 Deer had showed that he had the necessary military experience and prowess.

8 Deer continued the war with "Bundle of Xipe," and after a long period of conflict he conquered it, gaining revenge on behalf of his half-brother. The two nephews, 10 Dog and 6 House, were taken prisoner and sacrificed. 8 Deer secured his claim to the throne of "Bundle of Xipe" by marrying Lady 13 Serpent, the only descendant who remained alive from the marriage of 11 Wind to 8 Deer's half-sister, 6 Lizard. Thus military con-

quest, followed by the sacrifice of rivals and a royal marriage alliance to ensure continued political control, had again proved an effective three-part strategy.

For more than a decade, 8 Deer "Tiger Claw" ruled the closest thing to a unified Mixtec state for which we have any evidence. His realm stretched from Tilantongo in the north to Tututepec in the south, and included scores of conquered towns. According to Caso (1950, 1977, 1979), 8 Deer married five times in all, and had at least eleven royal offspring.

Eventually, 8 Deer fell victim to his own insatiable desire for conquest. While attempting to subjugate the hometown of his second wife, Lady 6 Eagle "Tiger-Cobweb," he lost a battle to his allied rivals. 8 Deer was taken prisoner and sacrificed, supposedly in the year 12 Reed (A.D. 1063). This would have made him fifty-two years old exactly— which raises the question of whether the date is accurate, or whether the life span of this important ruler was adjusted to correspond exactly to a 52-year calendar round. In the Codex Bodley, 8 Deer is shown being sacrificed by persons named 9 Wind and 10 Jaguar, and in other codices his subsequent burial is witnessed by his brother-in-law and father-in-law.

Summary

The two eleventh-century Mixtec rulers whose conquests we have glimpsed—Lady 6 Monkey and Lord 8 Deer—illustrate the role that warfare played in royal succession. Both individuals were featured at length in several codices because of their ties to prominent dynasties, as well as their military successes (their ability to avenge alleged insults, deaths of relatives, and threats to their assumption of lordships). The hope of gaining title to a vacant throne, even when someone else was next in line to rule, was temptation enough for declaring war against another claimant. The military successes of several Mixtec rulers were then cemented by marital alliances. The key to victory in battle was not whether one was male or female, but whether one was powerful enough to assemble the necessary military personnel and factional support. As Spinden (1935:437) has noted, "we have already seen that Lady 6 Monkey could handle both martial and marital situations. We need not understand that she captured men with her own hands on the field of battle, but at least she led her soldiers into action." Warfare was one of the major themes featured by Mixtec scribes, who undoubtedly were instructed by rulers to repaint codex after codex to conform to the victor's view of his military prowess and legitimize his claim to the throne.

The ancient Zapotec have one of the longest histories of raiding, captive taking, human sacrifice, and warfare of any Mesoamerican people. Their carved stone monuments record the sacrifice of captives as far back as 600 B.C., even before the formation of the Zapotec state; and when the Spaniards arrived in A.D. 1519, the Zapotec were still at war. However, the Zapotec are also considered to have been skilled diplomats who knew how to negotiate behind the scenes—and, in several cases, to let their Mixtec allies do most of the fighting for them (Marcus 1983m:316).

The history of Zapotec conflict can be divided into several eras. The first of these is the Middle and Late Formative (850–150 B.C.), a time of chiefdom-level raiding and prisoner sacrifice epitomized by the stone carvings of Building L at Monte Albán (see below and chapter 2). By the end of this era, the Zapotec elite were perched on a 400-meter mountain and protected by nearly three kilometers of defensive wall.

The next era was a period of great military expansion during the Protoclassic (150 B.C.–A.D. 150), during which the Zapotec recorded the conquest of approximately 50 places, some of them outside the Valley of Oaxaca. After the transition to the Early Classic period (A.D. 200–500), the Zapotec were still carving monuments that showed their own nobles thrusting spears into conquered places, or depicted elite captives from other groups with their arms tied behind their backs.

Finally, late in the Postclassic period (A.D. 1000–1519), when Monte Albán had declined and the Zapotec were no longer consolidated under one urban capital, some Zapotec rulers engaged in another military expansion into the Isthmus of Tehuantepec. They also formed temporary alliances with certain Mixtec rulers in order to combat Aztec expansion into the Valley of Oaxaca and the Isthmus. This era is documented not on carved stones, but in ethnohistoric accounts and a handful of *lienzos*.

Ethnohistoric Descriptions of Zapotec Warfare

Sixteenth- and seventeenth-century documents, synthesized by Whitecotton and Whitecotton (1982), Whitecotton (1977, 1990), and Paddock (1982, 1983a, 1983b), describe the Zapotec as powerful and expansionist. However, the Zapotec really excelled at attacking and subduing neighboring peoples such as the Mixe and Chontal, who were organized on a much less sophisticated level (Burgoa [1670] 1934a, [1674] 1934b:412). Such warfare proceeded *a fuego y sangre* (Burgoa [1674] 1934b:189, 328, 341; Redmond 1983), a phrase that referred to setting communities on fire and massacring the inhabitants who resisted.

Motives for Zapotec battles included the exaction of tribute, the control of territorial frontiers, revenge for political insults, and as a by-product, the acquisition of prisoners for enslavement or sacrifice (Burgoa [1670] 1934a, [1674] 1934b). Significantly, the Zapotec—like the Aztec mentioned earlier in this chapter—described "labor," "tribute," "conquered land," and "prisoners destined to serve as a labor force" by the same terms, given as *china, chiyna,* or *quelachina* (Córdova [1578a] 1942). Many key militaristic terms were derived from *quelaye,* "battle" or "war," including *hueni quelaye,* "warrior"; *queche peni quelaye,* "battalion" or "army"; *tonia quelaye,* "to make war"; and *yoho quie queche quelaye,* "fort." Other important terms were *queche naxohui,* "subjugated town"; *tizohuia queche,* "town taken by force"; *tonixixobacia,* "to conquer," "to take land by force"; *china,* "conquered land"; and *huezaaquiqueche,* "conqueror" (Córdova [1578a] 1942).

Like the Aztec, the Zapotec are reported to have carried idols into battle to ensure victory (Burgoa [1674] 1934b:393). They also had titles for warriors of different rank (Córdova [1578a] 1942: 183, 211, 285, 292, 308, 384, 409), a practice that may have had its roots in the Protoclassic (see Fig. 11.4). There were also scouts and spies who gathered information in enemy territory (Córdova [1578a] 1942:186). Burgoa ([1674] 1934b), Córdova ([1578a] 1942), and Redmond (1983) have described the way the Zapotec trained civilian forces, constructed trenches and fortifications, and provisioned their armies.

Flannery and Marcus (1983a) have described Postclassic Zapotec warfare using information from the *Relaciones Geográficas* of the late sixteenth century (Paso y Troncoso 1905–1906). In virtually every case the scale of conflict was town versus town or *coqui* versus *coqui* (lord versus lord), never nation versus nation. Huitzo fought against the Mixtec of Teocuicuilco, the Zapotec of Coatlán, Miahuatlán, Chichicapa, and Nexapa, and the Aztec under Motecuhzoma (Zárate [1581] 1905:199). Tlacolula warred with the Mixe and with nearby Mitla (Canseco [1580] 1905:146). There were frequent alliances between towns that cross-cut ethnic boundaries, such as the Zapotec of Zaachila with the Mixtec of Achiutla; but no campaign, not even the Aztec wars, appears to have unified the Postclassic Zapotec into one nation and one army.

The Zapotec conducted auguries before an important combat, and are described as going into battle singing, playing the wooden drum, and carrying their principal idol (probably a deified royal ancestor) (Ximénez Ortiz [1579] 1905:18). The officers, who were members of the nobility, wore quilted armor and used cane shields, while the soldiers wore only loincloths. The weapons were bow and arrow, lance, club, shield, sling, and the broadsword edged with obsidian blades. Some of the arrowheads were tipped with a strong poison.

The first prisoner taken was sacrificed to the idol, while the rest were brought back to the victorious town (Ximénez Ortiz [1579] 1905:18). When a warrior captured a prisoner, "he tied the string of [the captive's] own bow around his genitals and thus led him back as a slave" (Espíndola [1580] 1905:128). Apart from the difficulty of escaping under such conditions, slaves rarely attempted to escape because if caught, "they would be cut into pieces" (Espíndola [1580] 1905:128). That is not to say that life was easy for docile slaves, since many of them were eaten following the battle. Some were kept for later sacrifice on particular religious holidays, or sold at markets for others to sacrifice. At Huitzo there was an annual festival at which one slave, taken in war, was selected to be sacrificed at a hilltop temple; the priests asked the idols to give them strength and courage in war, and later all those present ate the victim (Zárate [1581] 1905:198). The chest of the sacrificial victim was cut open "from nipple to nipple" with bifacially flaked stone knives (Espíndola [1580] 1905:127); the heart—the principal locus of *pèe*, the inner spirit that gives life—was removed; the idols were bathed with flowing blood (*tini*); and their bodies were quartered, cooked, and eaten (Ximénez Ortiz [1579] 1905:18).

The cosmological aspects of Zapotec warfare are unmistakable: the deified royal ancestor, whose influence on the supernatural was far beyond man's, had the power to give the warriors courage. And courage was a vital ingredient of this kind of warfare, where terror tactics and intimidation played as big a role as weaponry, and where soldiers entered battle knowing they had a good chance of being not merely defeated, but also eaten. Nevertheless the royal ancestors would not respond unless their images had received two of the most precious commodities that could be sacrificed: the heart and *tini* of a human being.

For defense against this kind of warfare, many Zapotec towns had fortifications. Usually the location was a high hill near the town, either naturally fortified by cliffs or artificially fortified by dry-laid stone masonry walls. Mitla is supposed to have had four of these (Canseco [1580] 1905:153), of which one has been archaeologically investigated. Yagul has another. Huitzo had a similar mountaintop fortress, from which its Zapotec name, meaning "military lookout," was derived. And Zaachila's defenders retired to a rocky hilltop "like the peak of a sombrero" near Quiané (Mata [1580] 1905:195). Such defensible hilltop sites had a long history in the Valley of Oaxaca; scores are known from Late Formative times onward (Elam 1989).

Yet with all their weaponry and terror tactics, the Zapotec are most famous not for their pitched battles, but for their strategy. It is clear that for the Zapotec, the whole battle plan for their campaign against the Aztec was to get the Mixtec to fight as many battles as possible for them, and ideally, to weaken both the Aztec and Mixtec. The nineteenth-century chronicler Gay (1881) states that the Zapotec ruler Zaachila III, after convincing the Mixtec lord of Achiutla to help him defend Huitzo, made a secret treaty with the Aztec to arrange a truce after the Mixtec had taken the brunt of the attack. And Zaachila III's successor Cociyoeza, after successfully defending Guiengola against the Aztec, "rewarded" his indispensable Mixtec allies with some of the most marginal land in the Isthmus of Tehuantepec. While all the facts are not yet in, future investigators may find this an interesting point of contrast between Mixtec and Zapotec warfare. While we should always take the romanticized stereotypes of the Colonial writers with a grain of salt, it is interesting that they invariably portray the Mixtec as "warlike, courageous mountain people" and the Zapotec as "devious, master diplomats, skilled at dissimulation" (Flannery and Marcus 1983a).

Raiding at the Chiefdom Level: 600—400 B.C.

Chiefdoms often exist in a state of endemic raiding and intervillage conflict, but lack the political institutions that make it possible for states to actually conquer and manipulate subjugated people (Carneiro 1981, 1987). Perhaps because of this very lack of institutionalized power, some chiefdoms have invested great energy in terror tactics and graphic displays of mutilated captives. Consider, for example, the carved monuments of Cerro Sechín on the north coast of Peru, which chronicle the disemboweling, decapitating, and dismembering of enemies, along with the taking of trophy heads (Figs. 11.31, 11.32).

The Zapotec equivalent of Cerro Sechín was the chronicle in stone of more than 300 enemies slain during the long transition from chiefdom to state. The earliest of these carved stones was Monument 3 at San José Mogote, already mentioned in chapter 2 (see Fig. 2.9). Because the stone served as the threshold for a corridor, anyone entering the corridor would tread on the prisoner's body. We have already seen that "walking on the enemy" was an important Mixtec metaphor, and similar metaphors were used at later Maya sites. For example, at Yaxchilán, Tamarindito, Dos Pilas, and other Maya sites, nude

11.31. In this impressive display of vertical propaganda from Cerro Sechín, Peru, enemies who had been decapitated, dismembered, and disemboweled were depicted on the walls of a public building. (Redrawn from Willey 1971: fig. 3–30.)

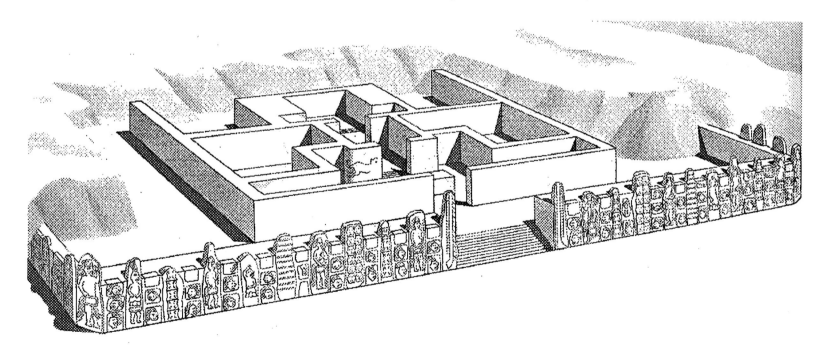

a

b

c

d

11.32. The stonecarvers of Cerro Sechín, Peru, depicted their slain enemies so graphically that no one could mistake them for "dancers" or "swimmers," as happened at Monte Albán in the Valley of Oaxaca. Mutilations included: *a,* plucking out the eyes; *b,* dismembering and beheading; *c,* cutting the victim in half; and *d,* pulling out the stomach, intestines, or other internal organs. (Photographs by the author.)

11.33. Here we see a surviving remnant of a gallery at Building L, Monte Albán, which once included more than 300-plus stone sculptures arranged in four rows. This gallery not only presents the single theme of slain enemies, but also reveals a carefully planned layout. The lowest row of victims features individuals whose hieroglyphic names could be read by persons standing close to the gallery; all those individuals face to the viewer's right. The second row shows corpses in a horizontal position. The third row shows victims facing to the viewer's left; the fourth row again shows horizontal corpses. When the gallery of 300+ stones was intact, it would have presented a very impressive display, similar to that on the walls at Cerro Sechín in Peru (Fig. 11.31). (Drawing by John Klausmeyer.)

or loincloth-clad prisoners were depicted on stairway risers and treads so that anyone ascending the staircase would symbolically step on their bodies (Marcus 1974a: plates 7,8). Obviously, this is a metaphor with considerable time depth.

Between 500 and 400 B.C., a far more impressive gallery of slain enemies was established on the east wall of Building L at Monte Albán. Monte Albán by this time was the largest site in the valley, and the political changes leading to the Zapotec state were quite advanced. However, perhaps because it did not as yet have all the institutionalized power it wanted, Monte Albán erected a display of terror tactics rivaling that of Cerro Sechín: Building L may once have held more than 300 carvings of corpses arranged in several tiers.

A surviving remnant of that gallery (Fig. 11.33) shows a lower row of figures facing north; above this is a row of figures lying horizontally; above this is a row of figures facing south; above this is another row of horizontal figures; and so on. Although the carved stones are set vertically, I believe that the figures are meant to be viewed as if they were

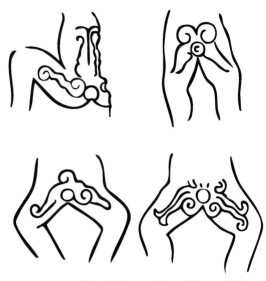

11.34. Some of the slain enemies at Monte Albán also show evidence of mutilation. Wavy lines and scrolls are used to symbolize blood flowing from the groin area, evidently symbolizing removal of the male organ. (Redrawn from Caso 1947: fig. 31.)

lying sprawled on the ground, just as the vertically set corpses at Cerro Sechín and the horizontally set monument at San José Mogote are meant to be viewed (Marcus 1976b:44, 1980:55, 1991; Flannery and Marcus 1983b:58, 1990:60). And when these carved stones were reused in other buildings, they were often placed in the staircases, so that anyone ascending those steps would tread on the bodies of the slain enemies.

Like slain prisoners in Mesoamerican art generally, the figures in Building L are naked, have their eyes closed, and are in awkward, even grotesque positions. Scrolls indicating genital mutilation occur on several (Fig. 11.34). Presumably because the lowest tier would be the easiest to see and read, it contains the most elaborate figures, often accompanied by necklaces, earspools, complicated hairdos, and hieroglyphic texts; the figures in the uppermost surviving row are the simplest. The earspools and necklaces may be intended to show that at least some slain enemies were members of the elite.

Of the short hieroglyphic texts accompanying the victims in the lowest tier, some seem to represent names, while others refer to the battle itself; one recurring glyph (Fig. 11.35a–d) may represent the fingerboard of an *atlatl* or spearthrower, one of Mesoamerica's oldest weapons. Associated with a victim's name, this glyph may suggest that he was killed in battle.

Given the lack of "place signs" in these texts, the slain enemies in Building L could depict people from within the Valley of Oaxaca. If that is so, it suggests that Monte Albán was able to establish itself as the capital of a Zapotec state only by eliminating a lot of competing chiefs who initially resisted its rise to power. In later periods, as we shall see, Monte Albán's might was such that it could list places 150 kilometers outside the Valley of Oaxaca as having been "conquered." This early display of military force, falling within Monte Albán's Period I, was probably a major propaganda statement designed to discourage the competing chiefs who initially resisted incorporation.

Wars of Expansion outside the Valley: 150 B.C.–A.D. 150

One of the major buildings erected at Monte Albán during the Protoclassic was Building J, an unusual structure with an arrowhead-shaped ground plan (Fig. 6.12). This building's unusual orientation (its stairway faces northeast) has led to its frequently being described as an astronomical observatory, although there is little evidence to support this interpretation (Marcus 1983e:106). As mentioned already in chapter 6, one of the most distinctive characteristics of this building is a set of fifty carved stones, which Caso (1938, 1947) believed to depict localities claimed as conquered by Monte Albán. In chapter 6 we suggested that, following the model of later Zapotec documents such as the Lienzo de Guevea, these fifty places represent landmarks that defined the outer limits of the territory claimed by Monte Albán during Period II (150 B.C.–A.D. 150).

While the majority of the "conquest slabs" on Building J cannot as yet be tied to a specific place, in this chapter I will discuss several of the more than twenty whose names can be read. Like the four slabs discussed in chapter 6, these stones usually feature (1) a "hill sign" meaning "the hill of" or "the place of"; (2) a glyph (or combination of glyphs) that specifies which "hill" or "place" is represented on that stone; and (3) a human head upside down below the hill sign, each head bearing a distinctive headdress which presumably reinforces the identification of the region mentioned.

As Caso (1947) has noted, all the inverted heads below the hill sign are facing the same direction, and all are drawn to the same scale. The majority of these heads have a specific pattern of lines crossing the face or eye, which may indicate facial painting or tattoos. The eyes of some are closed, while others lack a pupil; on the basis of these two characteristics, Caso (1947) concluded that the inverted human heads were depictions of dead rulers of the named places.

In 1976, I suggested that four of the fifty places could be identified by comparison with the *Matrícula de Tributos* and Codex Mendoza, sixteenth-century Aztec documents listing the places in Oaxaca that paid tribute to the Aztec (Marcus 1976c). First of all, the Aztec scribes of the Codex Mendoza also used the *tepetl*, or "hill sign," to indicate place names, and in several cases it is clear that the Aztec place name was simply a translation of the Zapotec place name. Second, the Aztec used a burning temple structure to indicate the conquest of a town—perhaps an analogy to the inverted, closed-eye heads of the Building J slabs. If all or most of the place names in the Codex Mendoza were Aztec translations of Zapotec names, might there be some which matched the hieroglyphs on Building J?

Initially, I was doubtful that very many of the places could be reliably identified. After all, it would require that some places retained the same name for 1,500 years, and then were hieroglyphically depicted in the Codex Mendoza in much the same way that they had been depicted during Monte Albán Period II. I felt it was worth the effort, however, because of the potential payoff in political and historical information. So far, I am reasonably confident that I have found at least five hieroglyphic place names on Building J that closely resemble hieroglyphic place names in the Codex Mendoza. The other twenty or so places that I have identified have not been linked to place names in the Codex Mendoza, but some are mentioned in other documents (Marcus n.d.d).

In the Codex Mendoza, eleven towns were assigned to the tributary province of Coyolapan (now Cuilapan), an important town in the Valley of Oaxaca (Barlow 1949a:118–119). Eleven place signs are depicted on the page of the Codex Mendoza devoted to that jurisdiction (Marcus 1976c). Another twenty-four were reconstructed by Barlow (1949a) from other sources, primarily the 1579–1581 *Relaciones Geográficas*. Four of the conquest slabs from Building J whose glyphs resemble place names in the Codex Mendoza are discussed at greater length in chapter 6.

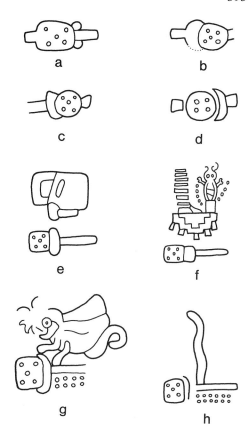

11.35. The first group of hieroglyphs (a–d) were used in association with enemies slain or captured in raids (ca. 500 B.C.) by the Zapotec at Monte Albán. The Zapotec continued to use the same glyph as a part of compound place names (e–h). In fact, it was used in 25 percent of the places shown as subjugated by Monte Albán between 150 B.C. and A.D. 150. Its probable meaning, "defeated in battle," was first used to characterize people taken in raids when Monte Albán was the head community of a very large chiefdom; later, it was used to characterize places subjugated by the Zapotec state. Appropriately enough, it is a hieroglyph that seems to have evolved out of a pictograph for the fingerboard of a spearthrower. (Field drawings by Lois Martin and Mark Orsen; redrawn by John Klausmeyer.)

One of the places identified as having been subjugated by Monte Albán is given on Lápida 47. The slab shows a human head with a feathered speech scroll emanating from its mouth (see Fig. 6.13c in chapter 6). It is similar to the glyph for Cuicatlán ("Place of Song" in Nahuatl) in the Codex Mendoza (Fig. 6.13d; Peñafiel 1885:101). The Cuicatlán Cañada runs north from the Valley of Oaxaca toward Tehuacán, and the present town of Cuicatlán lies eighty-five kilometers northeast of Oaxaca City.

Examples of other conquered places include present-day Sosola, "Place of the Pierced Face" (followed by the "battle" suffix) (Fig. 11.36a); "Hill of the Insect" (followed by the "battle" suffix) (Fig. 11.36b); Coyotepec, "Hill of the Coyote" (followed by the "battle" suffix) (Fig. 11.36c); "Smoke Hill" (followed by the "battle" suffix) (Fig. 11.36d); "Place of the Virile Member" (Fig. 11.37e); present-day Chiltepec, "Hill of the Chiles" (Fig. 11.37f); "Place of the Sacrificed Hearts" (followed by a hand grasping a tool) (Fig. 11.37g); "Place of the Maize Tassels" (Fig. 11.37h); "Place of the Stonecarver" (Fig. 11.38i); "Place of the Temple" (Fig. 11.38j); "Place of the Rabbit" (Fig. 11.38k); and "Place of the Heron" (Fig. 11.38l).

Because all the places on the Building J slabs that can be tentatively identified lie 50 to 150 kilometers outside the Valley of Oaxaca, I have suggested that they represent the frontiers of the Zapotec state (see chapter 6). Also, I have suggested that each region's identification could be confirmed if it were to yield convincing archaeological evidence for a Zapotec takeover during Monte Albán II.

So far, the best support for this suggestion comes from the Cuicatlán region, one of the few areas outside the valley that has witnessed extensive excavation. Work by Spencer and Redmond (1983) reveals that Cuicatlán had been an autonomous region prior to a military takeover by the Zapotec during Period II. During the period in question, the site of Quiotepec, located at a natural pass through a mountain ridge that seals off the northern Cañada from the Tehuacán Valley, expanded from two to forty hectares. The site became a fortified military installation with the construction of defensive walls and extensive settlement to either side of the natural pass. North of this fortified site there was no settlement for seven kilometers; beyond that "no man's land," the ceramic assemblage was closely tied to the Tehuacán Valley. To the south of Quiotepec, the pottery was like that of the Valley of Oaxaca.

Redmond and Spencer (1983) therefore concluded that Quiotepec marked the northern limits of Protoclassic and Classic Zapotec expansion. By controlling traffic through the natural pass, the Zapotec could claim the hot-country products of the Cañada for the Valley of Oaxaca. That this demand may have met with some resistance is suggested by Spencer and Redmond's discovery of sixty-one human skulls that seem to represent the remains of a toppled-over skull rack at a previously autonomous site burned by the Zapotec. Should future work show a similar Zapotec expansion at Tututepec, Miahuatlán, Ocelotepec, Sosola, Chiltepec, and other regions, we will have to conclude that Building J does indeed

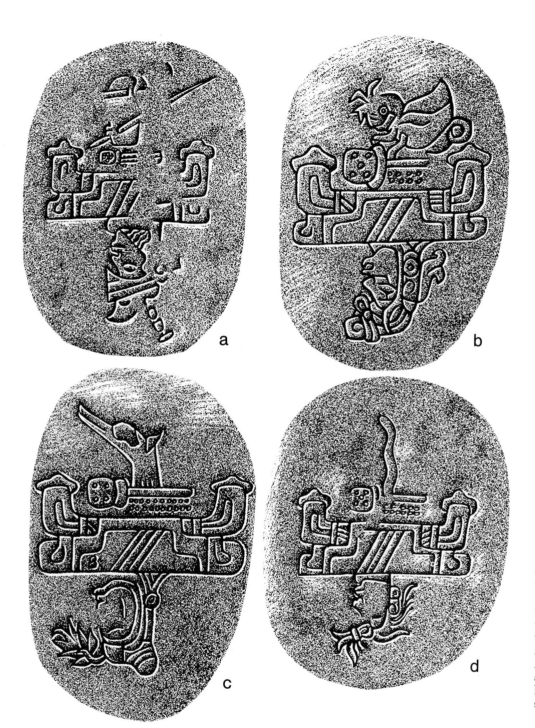

11.36. Among the places claimed as conquered by
Monte Albán during the Protoclassic were *a*,
"Place of the Pierced Face"; *b*, "Hill of the
[unidentified] Insect"; *c*, "Hill of the Coyote";
and *d*, "Smoke Hill." Note that all these slabs
show an inverted head with a distinctive headdress
or facial marks below the hill sign; these features
may have been characteristic of a particular town,
region, or ethnic group. Furthermore, many of
these place names are compound signs, similar to
those Aztec toponyms that consist of a hill sign
with a set of elements above it (chapter 6).
Among the names of conquered places on Monte
Albán's Structure J, compound signs often include
a hand grasping an object (Fig. 11.37g) or the
hieroglyph for "defeated in battle" used as a
suffix (*a–d*). (Drawings by Lois Martin.)

11.37. Other places claimed as conquered by Monte Albán during the Protoclassic were *e*, "Place of the Virile Member"; *f*, "Hill of the Chiles"; *g*, "Place of the Sacrificed Hearts"; and *h*, "Place of the Maize Tassels" (+ a suffix). The day on which *g* was conquered is probably given in the associated text. (Drawings by Lois Martin.)

11.38. Still other places claimed as conquered by Monte Albán during the Protoclassic were *i*, "Place of the Stonecarver" (or "Craft Specialist"); *j*, "Place of the Temple"; *k*, "Place of the Rabbit"; and *l*, "Place of the Heron." The day and year in which the place at *l* was conquered appear to be given. (Drawings by Lois Martin.)

record Zapotec subjugation of an area with a radius of 50 to 150 kilometers outside the Valley of Oaxaca.

Because the content of all fifty carved slabs from Building J seems to relate to subjugation or military conquest, I am skeptical of the notion that the building is an astronomical observatory. More likely, it was erected to commemorate the conquests claimed by Monte Albán; it may even have been a place where prisoners were detained for sacrifice, or returning warriors were rewarded. I cannot explain its unusual orientation, but since we know that the Maya used the position of certain bright heavenly bodies as auspicious signals for beginning warfare (Lounsbury 1982), it is possible that such bodies once influenced the orientation of military structures.

Classic Conquests and Elite Captives (A.D. 150–500)

In chapter 10 we discussed the accession to the throne of a major Zapotec ruler, 12 Jaguar, who is depicted on Stela 1 at Monte Albán. As part of his accession, the immense South Platform of the Main Plaza was dedicated; eight named visitors from Teotihuacán arrived at Monte Albán; and at least six elite captives were brought in for sacrifice.

In this chapter we look at the six captives, who are depicted on Stelae 2, 3, 5, 6, 7, and 8 of Monte Albán. All these stelae were set in the South Platform and most show elaborately costumed nobles with their arms tied behind their backs, standing on hill signs that depict their places of origin. Whether these captives came from places newly conquered by the Zapotec of Monte Albán IIIa (Early Classic), or whether they came from rebellious provinces already annexed, is not known.

Stela 2 (Fig. 11.39). On the front of this stela (Fig. 11.39a), found in the northeast corner of the platform, we see an individual dressed as a jaguar with his hands bound behind his back. Since this was a costume frequently worn by warriors in the "jaguar military order," this individual may have been a prominent military leader or rival lord dressed in his military garb. In the text to the right, in front of his chest, is his name glyph—a jaguar figure emerging from a cartouche. Immediately below are footprints, indicating travel, and the glyph for the day on which his arrival took place. Until we can securely identify the place sign on which this figure stands, we will not know if this captured noble was from a place within or outside the Valley of Oaxaca. On the back of this stela (Fig. 11.39b), we see an aborted carving which shows that the carver's "first try" at Stela 2 was a failure because of poor layout. Instead of discarding the stone, the scribe turned it upside down, reversed it, and did the carving successfully on the other side. It is a shame that we do not have more examples of this type so that we could gain greater insight into the planning for such monuments.

Stela 3 (Fig. 11.40). This stela, found next to Stela 2, also displays a bound captive dressed as an animal. (Caso [1928:82] suggested that the costume represents a coyote or

11.39a. A captive in puma or jaguar military costume is shown on the front of Stela 2 at Monte Albán. He has his arms bound behind his back, stands on a hill sign, and faces Stela 3, which shows another captive. The text (at right) includes four signs: (1) a year sign; (2) a sign that replicates the pictorial information at left, showing a puma or jaguar emerging from an opening; (3) footprints indicating that the feline-costumed person has traveled to his destination; and (4) a day sign ("3 Knot" or Caso's Glyph A). (See chapter 4 for the Zapotec day, month, and year signs.)

11.39b. On the back of Stela 2 we have an unusual opportunity to see the stonecarver's first effort with the same scene shown in Fig. 11.39a; it remained unfinished because once he had begun, he saw that the layout did not permit enough room for the planned text of four hieroglyphs. Note that because the hill sign spanned the entire width of the monument, there was insufficient room for the footprints between the second and fourth glyphs. Such errors in layout or omission must have been frequent, but such stones were probably more often discarded than reused. Since this stone evidently met all other specifications, it was decided to turn the stone upside down and carve the same scene on the other side. The architects of the South Platform then simply hid the unfinished side, letting it face inward against the fill of the platform so that no one would be the wiser. (Drawing by Mark Orsen.)

11.40. Another prominent captive was displayed on Stela 3 at Monte Albán. This figure has an elaborate headdress and full-body animal costume, but whether the costume represents a coyote, opossum, or some other creature is not agreed upon. Like the prisoner on Stela 2, this individual has his arms bound behind his back and is accompanied by a text that includes a footprint for "travel" or "journey." In contrast to Stela 2, there is an inverted year sign below the hill sign (probably giving the date of conquest of the place), and the captive is emitting a distinctive speech scroll. (Drawing by Mark Orsen.)

opossum.) His costume also carries an extremely elaborate feather headdress. As in the case of Stela 2, it would be important to know whether this, and other Oaxaca animal costumes, were associated with military orders like those we have described for the Aztec.

Stela 5 (Fig. 11.41). Although broken, this stela seems to depict a man with his hands behind his back, in a position similar to that of Stela 2. In this case we can see that his hieroglyphic text ends in a day sign, 6 Tella (6 Dog [since the Zapotec word for "head facing down" is a homophone for "dog"]). Given the format and the position, this would appear to be another depiction of a prisoner.

Stela 6 (Fig. 11.42). Located next to Stela 5, this stela also depicts a prisoner with arms bound behind his back. He has a prominent earspool, a necklace of jade (?) beads, and a speech scroll coming out of his mouth. Unlike Stelae 2 and 3, this captive does not wear an animal costume, and thus was perhaps not a member of a military order.

Stela 7 (see Caso 1928: fig. 42). Located in the southwest corner of the platform was this stela, which also depicts a prisoner with arms bound behind his back. The place sign on which he stands includes the rectangular sign for "sky," as well as a sine curve whose meaning is not known.

Stela 8 (Fig. 11.43). Located in the southeast corner of the platform, this stela depicts a scantily clad prisoner with arms tied behind his back. Unlike the other prisoners in the South Platform, most of whom are shown in elaborate costumes, this figure appears to wear only a loincloth. (However, he may have had a headdress which is now eroded.) Either this prisoner had been stripped of more elaborate clothing, or else he may have been a lower-ranking soldier from an enemy group. The hill sign on which he stands contains a human head above a mandible.

One other monument in the South Platform—Stela 4 (Fig. 11.44)—while not depicting a prisoner, continues the theme of conquest. This stela shows an elegantly dressed lord thrusting a lance into the hill sign of a place whose identity has not been securely identified. As we have seen in the later Mixtec codices, the thrusting of a lance into an enemy town was a metaphor for "conquest." The lord depicted on Stela 4 is named "8 Deer" (no relation to the Postclassic Mixtec ruler of the same name). He holds the lance in his left hand and another object in his right; below his name there is a footprint, indicating travel. We do not know the relationship of 8 Deer to the inaugurated ruler, 12 Jaguar. He could have been an important ancestor whose conquests were commemorated, or a lesser lord or general who fought beside the inauguree.

A Possible Military Alliance: A.D. 500—700

One of the most dramatic free-standing monuments ever erected at Monte Albán was Stela 9—a towering three-meter obelisk, carved on all four sides, originally set up in front of the massive stairway to the North Platform (Caso 1928). On the south side of the

11.41. Stela 5 in the South Platform of Monte Albán, although incomplete, seems to show another bound captive standing on a place name. The format would appear to be similar to that on Stela 2, since the captive's feet face to the right (toward Stela 6, which shows another captive); his hands are behind his back, suggesting that they are tied; and his text ends in a day sign (8 Tela). His hill sign shows a human head with a special hairdo often seen on prisoners, one that allows the hair to be grasped easily. (Drawing by Mark Orsen.)

11.42. Another captive is shown on Stela 6 at Monte Albán. Although he wears no animal costume, the prisoner is elaborately attired, with jade (?) necklace and earspools. Like the prisoner on Stela 3 (Fig. 11.40), this captive stands on a hill sign, has his arms bound behind his back, and emits a speech scroll. The text (at left) includes only three glyphs: a year sign with a year bearer of 10 Deer, followed by a verb, then a day sign. (Drawing by Mark Orsen.)

11.43. Still another bound captive is depicted on Stela 8 at Monte Albán. This individual does not appear as elaborately dressed as the other captives, but may have had an elaborate headdress that is now largely eroded. He stands on a hill sign that includes a face or mask resting above a mandible; such compound place names characterize Zapotec conquered places in both Protoclassic and Early Classic times. The text includes the sign for 3 Reed, which may be his name, followed by the "tied pouch" glyph for completion. (Drawing by Mark Orsen.)

11.44. Stela 4 at Monte Albán shows a warrior with a lance in his left hand and a smaller object in his right; the latter may be a doubled-over cord like those used to tie up prisoners. The lance thrust into the hill sign upon which he stands appears to be the same iconographic convention for "conquest" that was used later by the Mixtec in their Postclassic codices (see Fig. 11.12a). This lord's name is given as "8 Deer"; but since this carving dates to A.D. 300–500, he should not be confused with the famous Mixtec ruler 8 Deer "Tiger Claw," who lived during the eleventh century A.D. Below his name glyph is a footprint, indicating that he has journeyed to the place he has defeated—a place which unfortunately has not yet been identified. This lord of Monte Albán, whose military success was evidently of some importance to the ruler depicted on Stela 1, may have been the latter's relative or ancestor. (Drawing by Mark Orsen.)

monument is the frontal view of a Zapotec lord, apparently named 8 Flower (Fig. 11.45). On the east side of the stela we see two military men in quilted cotton armor and elaborate feather headdresses, emitting speech scrolls; both carry objects that appear to be doubled-over cords or cloth strips. The uppermost individual stands above an *atlatl* dart, part of the symbolism associated with embarking on a military campaign.

On the west side of the stela we see another individual, dressed similarly to those on the east side, and also shown with a speech scroll (Fig. 11.46). The individuals depicted on the east and west sides face toward the north (or back) side of the monument; in fact, they should probably be thought of as participants in the scene taking place on the back. On the north side, we see a scene in which one individual with a speech scroll (shown on the left) faces another. From the very rich accompanying text, it appears that a military alliance was effected between the two persons on the north side of the stela, with relevant calendric dates given, and that the figures depicted on the east and west sides of the obelisk were participants. Stylistically this stela dates to the Late Classic (A.D. 600–900), but it is unusual in its depiction of a ruler in frontal view (on the south side). I will have more to say about this monument elsewhere (Marcus n.d.d).

Carved monuments with hieroglyphic and iconographic elements strikingly similar to those of Stela 9 were found in 1961 at the coeval site of Xochicalco, a fortified hilltop center in western Morelos (Hirth 1989). Three tall stelae, also carved on all four sides, were ritually buried in a pit in Structure A (Sáenz 1962; Berlo 1989: fig. 15). These Xochicalcan monuments include calendric and noncalendric glyphs (including the "alliance" glyph) so similar to those of Late Classic Monte Albán that it seems unlikely the resemblances are coincidental. Future research could reveal that the military alliance involved, in some way, relations between Monte Albán and Xochicalco.

MAYA RAIDING AND CONQUEST

Like the Aztec, the Maya went to battle with shields, spears, spearthrowers, clubs, and lances (Fig. 11.47). Like Aztec and Mixtec lords, Maya nobles depicted themselves grasping captives by the hair. Like the Zapotec, they carved "prisoner galleries" and showed their rulers treading on the bodies of their captives. Like the Aztec, they witnessed struggles for autonomy between secondary centers and their capitals. And like the Zapotec, Mixtec, and Aztec, they built defensive works.

Given all the ethnohistoric, iconographic, and archaeological evidence for warfare available on the Maya, it amazes us today that early Mayanists such as Morley (1946), Thompson (1954), and others so successfully advanced an image of the Classic Maya as a "peaceful theocracy dominated by priests." No one working on the Aztec doubted the warlike character of that society, since it was abundantly clear in the ethnohistoric doc-

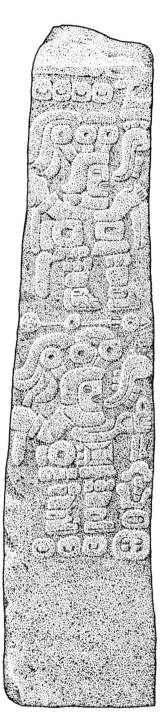

11.45. Stela 9 at Monte Albán—an unusual obelisk, carved on all four sides like many Maya stelae—was set up in the Main Plaza, in front of the North Platform, late in the Classic or epi-Classic period. It seems to record a military alliance involving the ruler 8 Flower, whose image appears on the south side. Moving counterclockwise to the east side, we see two other individuals, both similarly attired. Caso (1928) suggested that these might be priests carrying copal pouches; however, a more convincing case can be made that the two figures on the east side are military men in quilted cotton armor and standardized headdresses, separated by an *atlatl* dart that runs horizontally across the stela. Both men emit speech scrolls and carry identical items.

South

East

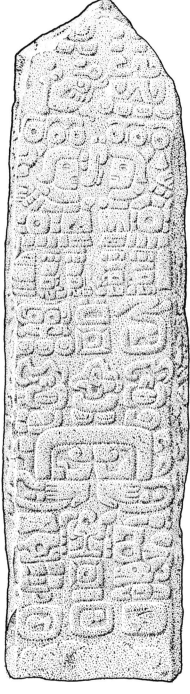

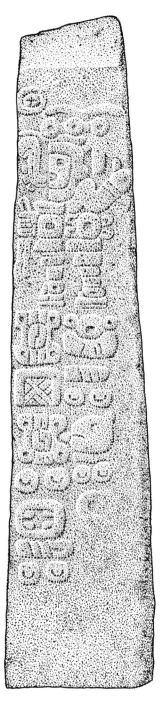

North

West

11.46. Continuing counterclockwise to the north side of Stela 9, we encounter a densely packed text. Near the top are two more warriors in quilted armor, whose names are given above them; the one on the left (whose name is probably 3 Jaguar) emits a speech scroll. Below the two figures are six hieroglyphs, several of which function as day names. Below the glyphs is a large sign that incorporates two open hands. This is the key glyph, since it refers to the alliance effected between these two military men. The date of this alliance is given below in a series of glyphs. (The final three signs at the bottom were never finished.) Moving on to the west side of the stela, we see yet another warrior who attended the rites associated with establishing the alliance. Below him is a series of day signs, perhaps names of the lords on whom he could count to fight beside him. While it seems likely that 8 Flower represented Monte Albán, we do not know where all the other lords mentioned were from. (Drawing by Mark Orsen.)

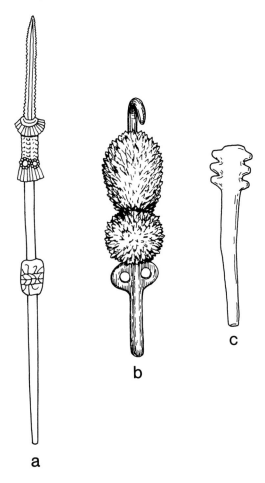

a

b

c

11.47. During the period from A.D. 250 to 900, the Maya used weapons similar to those employed in other regions of Mesoamerica. Here we see a lance or spear (*a*); an *atlatl* (*b*); and a club (*c*). (Redrawn from Morley and Brainerd 1956: fig. 6.)

uments used by all Aztec specialists. Somehow, most early Maya scholars refused to believe that the Classic Maya had been similar in this regard. Possibly they felt that most evidence for Maya warfare could be blamed on the influence of the Toltec (and other central Mexican peoples) who came into contact with the Postclassic Maya.

To keep intact their image of the peaceful theocratic Maya, many archaeologists and epigraphers had to ignore stone monuments and murals that showed warriors, military weapons, captive taking, human sacrifice, and fighting between men armed with spears and shields (Follett 1932). They also had to ignore the rich indigenous vocabulary of conflict recorded during the sixteenth and seventeenth centuries (e.g., Coronel 1620; Avendaño y Loyola 1696a, 1696b; Beltrán de Santa Rosa 1746; Pío Pérez 1898; Martínez Hernández [1585?] 1929; Morán 1935).

Depictions of lords dressed in military garb occur at countless Maya sites throughout northern and central Guatemala, Mexico, Belize, and beyond, especially from the fifth through eighth centuries A.D. On many free-standing stone monoliths, huge Maya rulers are shown standing on the bodies of small, scantily clad prisoners. The size disparity was used by Maya stonecarvers to emphasize the dichotomy between ruler and captive (Marcus 1974a).

True scenes of battle, the taking of captives, and the sacrifice of prisoners are less frequently depicted in Maya art, but well-publicized examples are present at western Maya cities such as Yaxchilán, Piedras Negras, La Pasadita, Palenque, and Bonampak (Fig. 11.48). Those sites are also noteworthy for stone lintels depicting the taking of prisoners, and for staircases in which stones with prisoner carvings are to be tread upon by persons ascending the steps. In addition to stone monuments displaying scenes of battle or prisoners, there are many hieroglyphic texts that record battles and the taking of captives, even when the accompanying scene does not depict such actions.

As more and more defensive works are found at Classic Maya sites (e.g., Lothrop 1924; Ruppert and Denison 1943; Webster 1976a, 1976b, 1977, 1978, 1979, n.d.; Rice and Rice 1981; Demarest 1990), as more and more texts on warfare are found (Marcus 1974b, 1976a, n.d.c; Riese 1984, 1988; Lounsbury 1982; Houston 1987; Fash 1988; Schele and Freidel 1990), and as murals of warfare like those of Bonampak are more fully studied (Ruppert, Thompson, and Proskouriakoff 1955; M. Miller 1986), the image of the peaceful theocratic Maya has waned (Sabloff 1990). It survives, however, in the minds of a few scholars who continue to believe that the Maya went to war only to take an occasional captive for sacrifice. The fact is that the Maya, like other Mesoamerican peoples, often let one or two prisoner depictions stand for a whole defeated town. Consider, for example, the naked prisoner shown on Stela 24 at Naranjo, who is labeled "Western Land" (Fig. 11.49c). Are we really to believe that a single captive was taken? More likely, he symbolized the fact that the "Western Land" had been subdued.

11.48. Lintel 1 from the Maya site of La Pasadita, Mexico. The ruler (at far right) is Bird Jaguar, lord of the major regional capital at Yaxchilán. He holds a lance in his right hand and a flexible shield in his left. The prisoner is kneeling (nude or nearly so, with rope around his neck and upper arms) and touches his left hand to his right shoulder—the Maya convention for subordinating oneself and paying homage to an individual in a superior position. The figure at far left is the local lord of La Pasadita, a subordinate site where this lintel was once set in a palace doorway, much like those known from Yaxchilán. This capture took place in A.D. 759 as the result of a joint effort by Yaxchilán and La Pasadita. Or did the ruler of Yaxchilán simply take credit for the capture? (Redrawn by John Klausmeyer from a drawing by Ian Graham.)

A few of today's Maya archaeologists, like the sixteenth-century Spaniards who preceded them, are both revolted and fascinated by human sacrifice. Thus we have rid ourselves of the notion that the Maya were "obsessed with time," only to see a new generation of scholars insist that they were "obsessed with bloodletting." Let us not attribute our own obsessions to the Maya. Ethnohistoric data suggest that only some special captives were destined for sacrifice; most ended up enslaved, serving in the houses of nobles or as common laborers. The Maya had many reasons for engaging in warfare, and captive sacrifice was usually the byproduct, not the underlying cause.

a

b

11.49. Maya glyphs for "earth" and "land." At *a* is a plant growing out of the sign for earth (*cab*). At *b* is the "maize deity" seated atop the sign for earth. At *c* is a bound captive from Stela 24 at Naranjo whose torso displays glyphs that mean "Western Land." (Drawings by John Klausmeyer.)

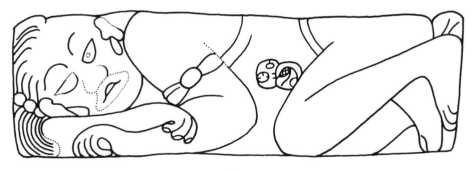

c

Landa ([1566] in Tozzer 1941:41) gives us a few insights into the reasons for Maya warfare:

> The reason they waged war with one another was to take their property from them and capture their children and wives, and because it was the custom among them to pledge what they possessed to each other; upon collection and payment they began to quarrel and attacked each other, and then the lord of that town armed his people against the other, and for that reason they waged war upon each other.

This statement makes it clear that taxation or tribute demands were a constant source of friction between the payer and the paid, with punishment including the loss of property, children, and wives. We can imagine that such conflicts might have been greatest between regional capitals and relatively powerful secondary centers, and that battles were fought to escape payment and achieve autonomy. Other ethnohistoric sources (Paso y Troncoso 1905–1906; Ciudad Real 1588; López de Cogolludo 1688; Noyes 1932; Roys 1957, 1962) indicate that boundary disputes, real or imagined insults, and acts of treachery or disloyalty were frequent causes of warfare.

Consider, for example, the reasons given for the breakup of Mayapán, a major Yucatec Maya city with perhaps 10,000 inhabitants during the mid-thirteenth through mid-fifteenth centuries (Landa [1566] in Tozzer 1941:32–36; Ciudad Real [1588] 1873, 2:470–471; López de Cogolludo 1688, 1867–1868, Book 2, Chap. 1; Noyes 1932:354–355). It is said to have been founded as a *mul tepal*, or jointly ruled confederacy of several Maya regional groups; chief among these were the Cocom and the Xiu.

During the period when the Cocom had the upper hand at Mayapán, they strengthened their position by bringing in "Mexican" warriors from Tabasco as mercenaries, perhaps rewarding them for their services with wives or land. Eventually, this led to complaints that the Cocom were using foreigners to tyrannize their own people. Members of the Xiu lineage therefore conspired to assassinate all the Cocom lords. Only one Cocom noble—a lord who happened to be away on a trading expedition to Ulúa, Honduras at the time—escaped assassination. As a result of this Xiu "disloyalty," Mayapán was abandoned in A.D. 1450.

Some eighty-six years later, in A.D. 1536, a member of the Xiu lineage (the great-grandson of the Xiu lord who had instigated the overthrow of Cocom rule at Mayapán) wanted to travel from his capital at Mani to make offerings at Chichén Itzá's Cenote of Sacrifice. To reach this sacred well, the Xiu lord and his retinue had to pass through the province of Nachi Cocom, a descendant of the Cocom lord who had been trading in Ulúa when all his relatives were killed at Mayapán. Nachi Cocom granted permission to the

Xiu lord, telling him that it was safe to pass through his province; he even wined and dined the forty Xiu pilgrims. However, on the fourth day of their stay, when they least expected it, Nachi Cocom ordered the massacre of the entire Xiu group. Thus their "dis-loyalty" was avenged eighty-six years after the fact.

Surprise and deception of this type were practiced in some Maya raiding, but often intimidation was more important than surprise. For example, some raids were preceded by loud, frightening noises designed to scatter the enemy, and in some cases the arrival of warriors was announced by beating on a turtle carapace drum with deer antler drum-sticks, blowing whistles, or sounding conch shell trumpets (Francisco de Cárdenas Valencia [1639] in Tozzer 1941:49).

Maya Military Vocabulary

Sixteenth- and seventeenth-century dictionaries (Morán 1935, Beltrán de Santa Rosa 1746, Pío Pérez 1898, Martínez Hernández [1585?] 1929, Barrera Vásquez et al. 1980) provide a rich vocabulary for Maya warfare. Many terms were derived from the word *katun*, which had a number of meanings, including "war," "conquer," "army," "battle," "battalion," and "soldier." Derived from *katun* were expressions such as *katun yah*, "to conquer land"; *katun chuc luum*, "to conquer land"; *ah katun*, "warrior"; *katun tah*, "to make war"; *katuntahil*, "to conquer by force"; and *cuch katun*, "to be defeated" or "to be killed in war."

"Enemy" could be expressed in a number of ways, too, either by referring to an individual lord or to a dynastic seat, town, or place. For example, *ah wal* referred to both the adversary and the enemy capital; *ah walah* meant "to be an enemy." The term *nup* meant "enemy" or "the state of enmity or hostility," and *nupankil* meant "conflict" or "war." Two other terms are important because they can be tied to earlier, Classic period hieroglyphs on monuments from Quiriguá and elsewhere (see below). These are *bateel*, "to make war" or "to fight," and *ah batelba*, "warrior."

The root word *mek*, "to be in charge," gave rise to several terms for two types of military captains: *ah mek nak katun* and *ah mek nak chuc*, the latter meaning "he who led the spy squadron." The term *ah chuc* meant both "spy" and "he who seizes, captures, or grasps," a perfect description for the dual role required for jungle warfare—the *ah chuc* first spied on an individual, then seized him as a prisoner. Below, we will see a related Classic period hieroglyphic expression that meant "was seized or captured." The meaning of this expression was determined by Proskouriakoff (1960:470, 1963:150–152, 1964: figs. 3, 4), while Knorozov (1958a:471, 1967:99) assigned it the phonetic rendering *chuc-ah*, "was captured" (Fig. 11.50). Both the meaning and the phonetic reading have been since confirmed by others (e.g., Kelley 1976; Marcus 1974b, 1976a). A verb derived from *chuc* was also used in Classic hieroglyphic texts to explain an accompanying scene in which a

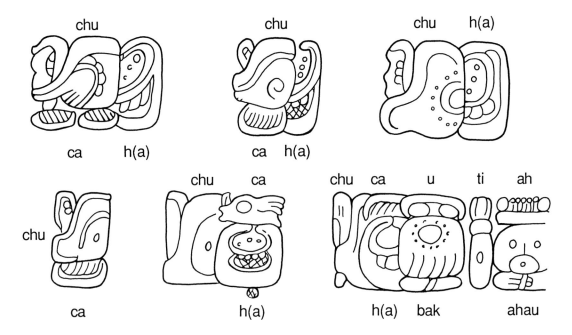

chu · chu · chu h(a)

ca h(a) · ca h(a) · ca h(a)

chu · chu ca · chu ca u ti ah

ca · h(a) · h(a) bak ahau

11.50. Six hieroglyphic expressions that phonetically express the verb *chuc-ah*, "was captured." This past tense verb usually followed the date of the monument on which it appeared (e.g., Lintel 8 at Yaxchilán [Fig. 11.52] and Lintel 1 at La Pasadita [Fig. 11.48].) Note that the fish (*cay*) in the lower row (central compound) stands in for the "comb" (*ca*), a well-known substitution originally noted by Thompson (1944, 1950). Also in the lower row (far right compound), we see the verb *chuc-ah* followed by the expression *u bak*, "his captive," followed in turn by the title *ahau*, "lord." (Redrawn from Proskouriakoff 1963, 1964.)

lord, using a spear and shield or grasping a captive's hair, was shown taking a prisoner in battle (e.g., Lintel 8 from Yaxchilán, discussed below).

Another Maya term for captive taking was *baksah*, "to seize," "to take captive," or "to be enslaved." In Classic period hieroglyphic inscriptions, the captive was usually referred to as *u bak*, "his captive" (see Fig. 11.51a–c, e); *ah bak*, "prisoner"; or *ah mak* "subject, person" (see below). Related terms included *bak*, "to grasp" or "to seize," and *bakal*, "to be tied up in rope." Both words—*bak* and *bakal*—have iconographic counterparts in Classic Maya art, where captives are shown being grasped by their hair, or with arms bound behind their backs with rope (see below).

Even the motivations for Maya warfare are sometimes suggested in sixteenth-century vocabularies. For example, *cuchpach kimsah* meant "killing those who committed treachery," while *pach luum* meant "to take possession of the land." (An analogous term was *tialtah*, which meant "to appropriate.")

Hieroglyphic Expressions for Warfare (A.D. 250–950)

On some carved stone monuments of the Classic Maya, both the pictorial scene and the hieroglyphic text give some of the same information about warfare; in such cases, the text acts as a kind of caption for the scene. In other cases, the text may record a battle not

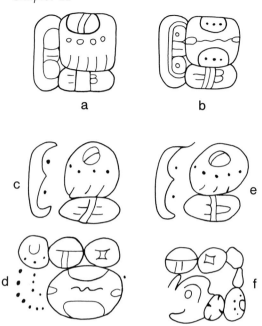

11.51. A captive, *bak,* is referred to in Classic Maya texts by a hieroglyph that often takes the prefix *u,* meaning "his" in such contexts. The expression *u bak,* "his captive," is recorded at *a, b, c,* and *e.* The captive at *c* is followed by the Palenque emblem glyph (at *d*); the captive at *e* is followed by what may be the emblem glyph for Copán (at *f*). Captives *c* and *e* were mentioned on carved bones from the tomb of the ruler "Double Comb" at Tikal (Burial 116 beneath Temple I). (Redrawn from Marcus 1976a: fig. 4.31.)

depicted in the accompanying scene, but which may have involved the same ruler shown on the monument. Examples of both types of monuments will be given below. There were a whole series of hieroglyphic expressions for warfare, captives, captors, and so on (Proskouriakoff 1960, 1963, 1964), some of which have been tied to actual Maya words and some of which so far have not been.

An example of a monument whose text serves as a caption for the accompanying scene would be Lintel 8 from Yaxchilán. This monument provided Proskouriakoff (1963) with the key opportunity to identify the verb "was captured." As seen in Figure 11.52, this lintel shows the Yaxchilán ruler Bird Jaguar (at far right) and a lesser lord (at far left) in the act of taking captives. Proskouriakoff (1963:150, 1964:188) isolated in glyph block A3 a hieroglyphic expression that she interpreted as a past tense verb meaning "was captured." This verb immediately followed the date of the capture—7 Imix 14 Tzec [Long Count date 9.16.4.1.1]—which corresponds to May 9, A.D. 755. This capture took place about three years after Bird Jaguar had acceded to the throne.

Carved on the thigh of each captive is a hieroglyph. Bird Jaguar's captive bears on his right thigh the glyph Proskouriakoff (1963:150) called "Jeweled Skull." In the accompanying text associated with Bird Jaguar, the verb "was captured" (in glyph block A3) is followed by the same name—"Jeweled Skull" (at A4); then we see the expression *u bak,* "his prisoner" (at B1); then the name "Bird Jaguar" (at B2); and finally, an emblem glyph identifying the latter as "Lord of Yaxchilán" (at B3). We can paraphrase this text as follows: "On May 9, A.D. 755, Jeweled Skull was captured, taken as the prisoner of Bird Jaguar, Lord of Yaxchilán."

The captive taken by the lesser lord bears a hieroglyph on his left thigh. That same glyph occurs in the text accompanying the lesser lord, who uses his right hand to grasp the captive. Proskouriakoff interpreted the centrally placed text as "captor of" + the captive's name; this became one of the titles of the lesser lord (Fig. 11.53c, d).

For an example of a battle mentioned in a text, but not reinforced by the accompanying scene, let us turn to a series of monuments from Quiriguá: Stelae E, F, and J, and Zoomorph G . These monuments have been studied by Kelley (1962b), Marcus (1974b, 1976a, n.d.c), Riese (1988), and Sharer (1978, 1990).

To understand these monuments, we have to consider their sociopolitical context. During the period from A.D. 550 to 738, Quiriguá was a secondary center in the realm controlled by Copán, a major regional capital in northwestern Honduras. We can presume that there were times when Quiriguá, like the towns described in the quotation from Landa above, squabbled with Copán over its subordinate status and the tribute and labor demands imposed on it. Finally, in 9.15.6.14.6 (6 Cimi 4 Tzec) or May 3, A.D. 738, Lord Cauac Sky of Quiriguá claimed to have defeated in battle the ruler 18 Jog of Copán. The defeat of 18 Jog was commemorated on at least four monuments at Quiriguá by Cauac Sky

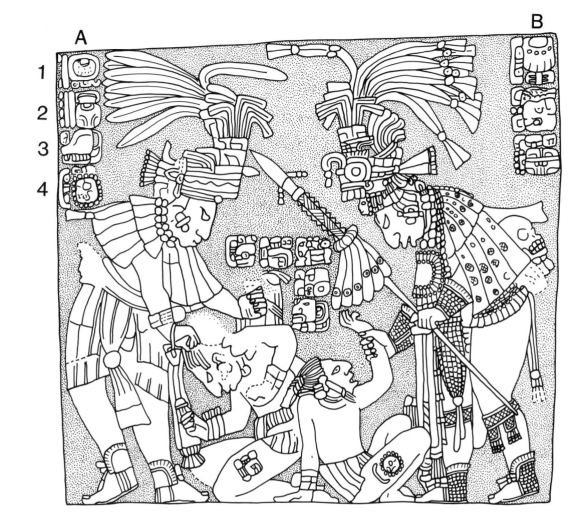

11.52. The Yaxchilán ruler named Bird Jaguar (at far right) is shown here on Lintel 8 taking a captive. A lesser lord (at far left) also takes a captive. The captives' names are shown on their thighs. In the short text at upper left, the name of one of the captives, "Jeweled Skull," appears at A4 following the verb "was captured" (at A3). Bird Jaguar acquired the title "Captor of Jeweled Skull" following this battle; the lesser lord also acquired a new title (see Fig. 11.53c, d). (Redrawn from Proskouriakoff 1964: fig. 1.)

(Morley 1920; Marcus 1976a:133; Riese 1988; Sharer 1978, 1990). These four monuments were erected anywhere from nineteen to thirty-nine years *after* the battle, to commemorate the Quiriguá ruler's claim of victory. Not surprisingly, this same battle is mentioned only once at Copán (on a disarticulated fragment from the Hieroglyphic Stairway). Indeed, even though the Hieroglyphic Stairway supposedly records the site's "history," it is surprising that Copán mentions the battle at all.

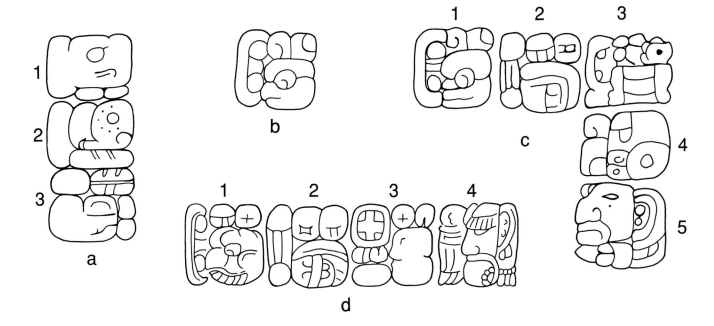

11.53. "Captor" expressions in Maya texts. *a*, the title of "captor" acquired by a Yaxchilán ruler, and conveyed in three hieroglyphic compounds on Lintel 2 at Bonampak. The glyph at *a1* is the "captor" glyph; at *a2* is the name of his captive, "Macaw"; at *a3* is a glyph meaning "Lord of Yaxchilán" (see also Fig. 11.59, B1–3, C1–4). *b*, another example of the "captor" glyph. *c* and *d*, phrases that refer to the title "captor of," followed by the name of the prisoner. This title was acquired by the lesser lord depicted on Lintels 8 and 6 of Yaxchilán; compare the second glyph in both *c2* and *d2* with the hieroglyph on the thigh of the captive kneeling at left in Figure 11.52.

As seen in Figure 11.54, the hieroglyphic expression corresponding to *batcaba* or *batelba*, "to do battle," is given. This correspondence between a sixteenth-century term and a Classic period hieroglyphic expression is important. More significant is the fact that the same battle is apparently recorded on the monuments of two different sites, increasing the likelihood that it actually took place.

However, it should be pointed out that there is no archaeological evidence to suggest that the large city of Copán was ever actually "conquered" or "overthrown." Thus, claims in the literature that Quiriguá "conquered" Copán are almost certainly exaggerations. Based on what we know ethnohistorically about Mesoamerican states, we are probably dealing here with a "war of independence." In such wars, discussed later in this chapter, secondary centers (such as Quiriguá) won their independence from major regional capitals (such as Copán) through a successful battle. Following its "victory" over Copán—in effect, its secession from the Copán state—Quiriguá went through a period of considerable expansion and monumental construction (Sharer 1978).

At least two other hieroglyphic expressions of warfare should be mentioned here. One—a compound combining a shield and a flint knife (Fig. 11.55)—seems to be a fairly direct reference to combat. The other is more subtle; it involves a heavenly body, believed to be either the planet Venus or a great star (Fig. 11.56), whose supernatural help was invoked for certain battles (Lounsbury 1982, M. Miller 1986).

11.54. Four examples of the verb *batcaba* or *batelba* ("to wield an axe," "to do battle"), used in the texts of Quiriguá to describe its "battle of independence" from Copán. This victory was allegedly achieved by the Quiriguá ruler Cauac Sky, who fought Lord 18 Jog of Copán on May 3, A.D. 738. However, it is interesting that this "victory" was not recorded in stone at Quiriguá until 20 years after the event. (Redrawn from Maudslay 1889–1902; Marcus 1976a: fig. 4.44.)

11.55. "Shield and knife" expressions also appear to denote Maya battles. On the left is the expression "his battle," with the prefix *u*, "his," followed by a knife above a shield (redrawn from Marcus 1976a: fig. 4.1). On the right is an expression that includes the shield and flint knife as a double superfix above the sign for "earth."

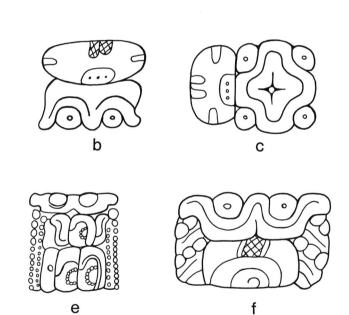

11.56. Classic Maya hieroglyphs associated with warfare. *a*, the Venus glyph; *b, c*, the "great star" glyph; *d*, the "star over earth" sign; *e*, the "star over triple *cauac*" sign; *f*, the "star over shell" sign. (Redrawn from Lounsbury 1982: fig. 3.)

Prisoner Galleries

Like the Zapotec before them, the Maya liked to depict captives as awkwardly positioned, scantily clad, grimacing figures, often sprawled at the feet of a ruler. One of the earliest such representations is that shown on the Leyden Plaque (Morley 1946; Marcus 1976b, 1991; Morley, Brainerd, and Sharer 1983: fig. 4.7), a jade artifact with a Long Count date of A.D. 320 (in other words, broadly contemporaneous with the bound captives on Stelae 2, 3, 5, 6, 7, and 8 at Monte Albán).

Another common Maya convention was to show the captive serving as a pedestal on which the ruler stands—perhaps the Maya equivalent of the Mixtec expression "to tread on the enemy." Such captives appear in the lowest panel or register of Maya stelae, like the examples from Naranjo seen in Figure 11.57 (Flannery and Marcus 1990: fig. 2.21). Prisoners might also be depicted on altars, or on natural outcrops such as those at Calakmul and Tikal, where many individuals would have stepped on their bodies (Morley 1933, Ruppert and Denison 1943, W. R. Coe 1967).

Perhaps the two most impressive uses of the captive theme, however, were in prisoner galleries and prisoner staircases. In prisoner galleries such as the one from Palenque, kneeling prisoners are shown with one hand touching the opposite shoulder, a gesture of submission (see Fig. 11.48). Because the prisoners are carved on vertical orthostats, the effect is not unlike that of the lowest row of the earlier gallery on Building L at Monte Albán.

In prisoner staircases, on the other hand, the carved slabs were set horizontally like those in the staircase of Building M at Monte Albán (Marcus 1974a: plates 7–9; Flannery and Marcus 1990: fig. 2.22). Prisoners were carved either on the risers or treads of stairs, usually lying full-length or kneeling, scantily clad, with arms bound behind their backs; thus, as one ascended the staircase, he trod metaphorically on the enemy. The accompanying hieroglyphic texts on such stairways might also give a kind of "site history," including the "conquests" of other sites or the "battles of independence" fought by former rulers (Marcus 1974b, 1976a, n.d.c).

Murals

While much of this book has used stone monuments and codices as sources of information, in the case of Maya warfare we find that murals painted in vivid colors were also deemed an appropriate medium to display scenes of conquest, militarism, and the taking of captives. Murals showing raids or battles are known from at least four sites in the Maya lowlands: Bonampak, Chichén Itzá, Chacmultún, and Mul-Chic (E. H. Thompson 1904; Ruppert, Thompson, and Proskouriakoff 1955; Tozzer 1957; Adams and Aldrich 1980; Barrera Rubio 1980; M. Miller 1986). In addition, the site of Cacaxtla in Tlaxcala has murals of warriors which many scholars believe were stylistically influenced by Classic

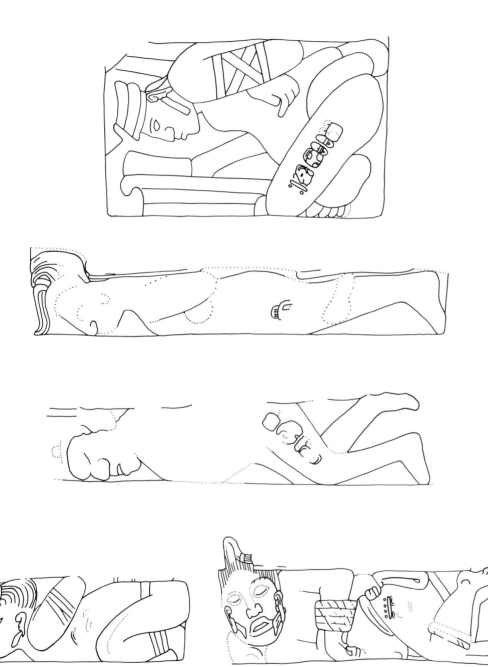

11.57. Captives from the lower registers of several stone monuments at Naranjo, Guatemala. The names of some of the captives are given on their thighs. (Redrawn from Graham and von Euw 1975.)

Maya artists (e.g., López de Molina and Molina 1976, López de Molina 1977, Foncerrada de Molina 1980, Kubler 1980).

One set of murals in particular, those from Bonampak (a site that oscillated between being a third-order and second-order center below the regional capital of Yaxchilán) were instrumental in eroding the notion of the "peaceful theocratic Maya." Discovered by Giles G. Healey in 1946 (Ruppert, Thompson, and Proskouriakoff 1955; Morley and Brainerd 1956; Morley, Brainerd, and Sharer 1983; Freidel 1986), the Bonampak murals portray a battle scene in which Maya lords are shown taking prisoners and later sacrificing them. Because this mural seems to document a real battle, Maya archaeologists found it increasingly difficult to ignore the iconographic, linguistic, and ethnohistoric data on such "Aztec-like" Maya behavior as raiding, warfare, militarism, and human sacrifice.

The Bonampak murals cover the walls of three rooms of a palace called Structure 1, and follow a clear chronological sequence beginning with Room 1. The scenes are thought to have been painted around A.D. 800, since the events commemorated by them probably took place between A.D. 790 and 796 (Ruppert, Thompson, and Proskouriakoff 1955). It is interesting that in contrast to the prisoner galleries and staircases—which were vertical propaganda carved in public places and clearly meant to be seen—the Bonampak murals were in a small palace to which access must have been very restricted indeed. They therefore probably qualify as horizontal propaganda.

The murals in Room 1 recount events that began before the battle, including the presentation of a young boy at a major ceremony attended by many nobles. This boy appears to be the heir designate to the throne of Bonampak, the one named to succeed his father; unfortunately, we do not know his name. Since these events took place as Bonampak's fortunes were waning and the site had become involved in military conflicts with other sites, we do not know the ultimate fate of the young boy; nor do we learn the name of the ruler who succeeded Chaan-Muan ("Sky Bird"), the reigning lord of Bonampak in A.D. 792. We do know that the new ruler's wife was an important woman from Yaxchilán (Marcus 1974b, 1976a:176–177, 1983b:466; Mathews 1980); in fact, there is some evidence to suggest that she was the sister of the reigning Yaxchilán ruler, a man named "Shield Jaguar's Descendant" (Proskouriakoff 1963, 1964; Mathews 1980; M. Miller 1986). This would mean that the subordinate center of Bonampak was ruled by a brother-in-law of the ruler at the capital of Yaxchilán, a familiar prehispanic arrangement (see chapter 8).

The mural in Room 2 (which covers the west, south, and east walls) depicts a raid that occurred between A.D. 792 and A.D. 796. This skirmish took place in the forest and featured hand-to-hand combat (Fig. 11.58). Although many men are shown poised to thrust a spear into a victim, no actual killing is shown. Rather, the victims are shown as surprised and unarmed, allowing the attackers to grab them by the hair or limbs. A surprise raid would have meant that the loss of life would be minimal, and that many captives could be taken alive as sacrificial victims, laborers, or servants.

11.58. This skirmish in the forest resulted in the taking of captives, ca. A.D. 795–796. The scene was painted on the wall of Room 2 in Structure 1 at Bonampak; it is just a small detail from the famous murals that cover the walls of three rooms of that small palace. (Redrawn from Ruppert, Thompson, and Proskouriakoff 1955: fig. 28.)

The date of the skirmish recorded in the Bonampak murals is uncertain. Owing to partial deterioration of that part of the mural, there are at least three alternative readings for the hieroglyphic date of the battle, two of which would place it in the dry season and one of which would place it in the rainy season. In a later section of this chapter, I will present data to suggest that the Maya usually went to battle in the dry season. If that occurred in this case, the two most likely dates are December 20, A.D. 795, or February 22, A.D. 796. Lounsbury (1982), however, prefers the alternative date August 2, A.D. 792, because he believes that that date corresponds to a day when Venus as the Evening Star was at its first stationary point, twenty-one days before inferior conjunction. As we have seen, there is some reason to believe that Venus (or some other bright heavenly body) might have been used as a "patron" or "protector" ensuring a successful battle. What the argument over the date boils down to is this: which was most important to the Maya, the logistic advantage of going to battle in the dry season, or the correct astronomical position of Venus?

The final Bonampak mural, in Room 3, shows the local royal family performing autosacrifice following the successful battle (Ruppert, Thompson, and Proskouriakoff 1955).

Lintels Associated with the Bonampak Murals

In addition to the raid shown in the Room 2 murals, each of the three doorways of the same palace at Bonampak has a carved stone lintel depicting a lord in the act of taking a captive.

On Lintel 1 the Bonampak ruler Chaan-Muan is shown taking a prisoner, grasping his victim's hair in his left hand (Mathews 1980). The accompanying hieroglyphic text records the date of the capture, followed by the verb "was captured," the name of the captive, then the name of the ruler (Ruppert, Thompson, and Proskouriakoff 1955; Mathews 1980).

On Lintel 2, the Yaxchilán ruler "Shield Jaguar's Descendant" is shown taking a prisoner; this capture precedes the one shown on Lintel 1 by only four days. Looking at the inscription (Fig. 11.59), we see at glyph block A1 the day 4 Lamat, and at A2 the month position 6 Cumku. Two alternative readings have been suggested for this Calendar Round—Mathews (1980) prefers 9.17.16.3.8 and Lounsbury (1982:164–165) prefers 9.15.3.8.8. The latter reading would place this captive taking on January 17, A.D. 735, in the dry season.

At glyph block A3 on Lintel 2 (Fig. 11.59) is the verb *chucah*, "was captured." At A4 is the name of the captive; at C2 is a glyph meaning "captor of," followed by the "macaw glyph" at C3; at C4 is the Yaxchilán emblem glyph. This honorific title—"Captor of Macaw"—was a frequent epithet used by "Shield Jaguar's Descendant" on his own

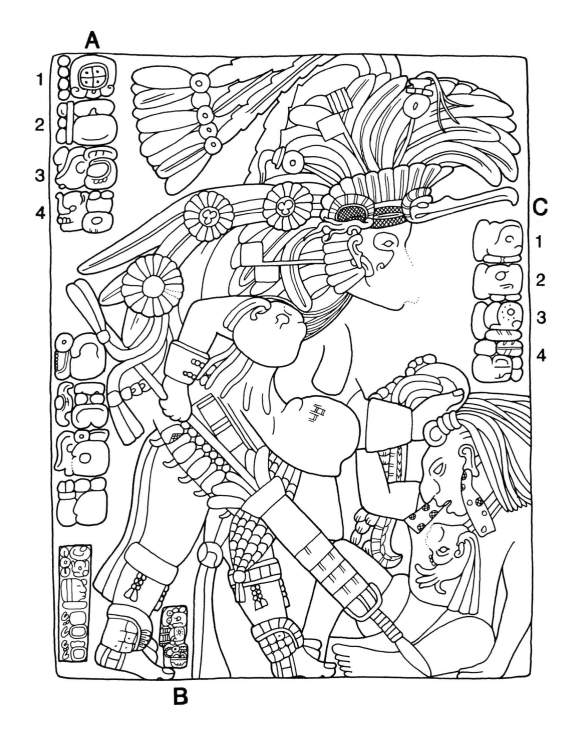

11.59. Lintel 2 at Bonampak features a Yaxchilán ruler called "Shield Jaguar's Descendant," shown here in the act of taking a captive. The captor holds a lance in his right hand and grasps the hair of the captive in his left; he has an elaborate headdress and wears a trophy head around his neck. In two places on this monument—B1–3 and C2–4—the Yaxchilán ruler is referred to as "Captor of Macaw, Lord of Yaxchilán." (Redrawn from Mathews 1980: fig. 6.)

monuments at Yaxchilán (Proskouriakoff 1964:196). Finally, in a short inscription near the right toe of "Shield Jaguar's Descendant," we see three glyph compounds in a column (at B), giving the honorific titles "Captor of Macaw" (B1–2) and "Lord of Yaxchilán" (at B3) (see Figs. 11.53a and 11.59).

Some interesting questions are raised by the presence of lords from Yaxchilán and Bonampak on the Bonampak palace lintels. First, it suggests that both Yaxchilán (the regional capital) and Bonampak (its dependency) were at war with a common enemy. The battle was so serious that the Lord of Yaxchilán ("Shield Jaguar's Descendant") evidently called on his brother-in-law, the lord of Bonampak (Chaan-Muan) for support. Since Bonampak was not autonomous—and its lord owed allegiance to the ruler of Yaxchilán—the latter could presumably have counted on the former's support even had they not been related by marriage.

Did "Shield Jaguar's Descendant" really take his captive four days before Chaan-Muan took his? Or did Maya protocol require that the ruler from the capital be given credit for the first prisoner captured? Assuming that the Bonampak ruler commissioned the building of his palace—along with its murals and Lintel 1 (Mathews 1980, M. Miller 1986)—then who was ultimately responsible for Lintel 2? Did the Yaxchilán ruler insist that the central doorway of his brother-in-law's palace have a lintel featuring his own captive taking, or did the Bonampak ruler commission the lintel to emphasize his strong ties to the regional capital?

Battles of Independence

In our discussion of the Aztec, we saw that the ruler Tizoc claimed "victory" in a battle that cost him perhaps 300 warriors, and might (from our perspective) have been considered a disaster. Tizoc considered it a "victory" because it yielded the forty captives he needed as sacrifices for his inauguration, and he commissioned the carving of a multi-ton stone monument that showed him taking captives. In spite of this outward display of military prowess many scholars consider Tizoc a weak ruler, and suspect that he was poisoned only a few years later so that the more aggressive Ahuitzotl could assume the throne (Bray 1968, Hassig 1988). This case shows us the gap between what rulers claimed in their military propaganda, and what they actually accomplished.

Much the same could probably be said of a number of "victories" or "conquests" recorded on Classic Maya monuments of the period A.D. 250–900. In particular, I am thinking here of secondary centers who claim to have defeated a major regional capital, or to have taken captive the lord of that capital. Often these "victories" are recorded only in the inscriptions at the secondary center, and there is no actual evidence from the capital to suggest an overthrow of that site.

What I suggest we are seeing are "wars of independence," battles fought by secondary centers in order to break away from a capital and achieve autonomy (Marcus 1976a, n.d.c). We have already seen, in an earlier passage from Landa, that there were continuous disputes between capitals and their dependencies over how much tribute (or "taxation") the latter owed the former. The lords at secondary sites, who controlled the manpower of an entire province, may at times have felt that they had the military strength to break away and keep their tribute for themselves. Such a situation was prototypically Mesoamerican: we see it in the Mexica revolt against Azcapotzalco, and the endemic warfare in the Mixtec codices.

In a war of independence, it is not necessary that the secondary center overthrow, sack, and burn the regional capital; after all, George Washington's troops did not sail to England and destroy King George's palace. All that is needed is for the secondary center to demonstrate that, on its own turf, it can defeat any force sent out from the capital to re-subjugate it. Since regional capitals like Tikal, Palenque, Copán, Seibal, and Yaxchilán had many secondary centers to worry about, they really could not afford to commit every warrior they had to keeping one very strong rebel in line.

Thus, when we see a Maya secondary center proclaiming *ts'oysah* ("victory") over a much larger city, we probably are only reading the propaganda of a province that has just won its autonomy from the capital. Unfortunately, some archaeologists working at secondary centers have leapt to the conclusion that their site once overthrew a Copán or Tikal, something for which there is no solid corroborating archaeological evidence. They should bear in mind that excavating a secondary center is nothing to be defensive about (no pun intended). The secondary-center level may very well be the most dynamic one in the entire Maya political system, the one at which most warfare and change took place.

We must also keep in mind that degrees of "control" and "autonomy" were relative. Many secondary centers were probably not under the absolute control of a regional capital even before their war of independence; and even after a successful battle, their autonomy was probably not absolute either. Secondary centers *needed* primary centers, because marriages to royal women from the capital raised the status of royal men at the dependency (see chapter 8).

Now let us look at a few possible "wars of independence." We have already mentioned the battle between Lord Cauac Sky of Quiriguá and Lord 18 Jog of Copán in A.D. 738. This battle allowed Quiriguá to win its independence from Copán, and touched off a flurry of expansion and monumental construction at Quiriguá; Copán, however, remained an important regional capital for at least 70 years afterward. This battle is mentioned on four monuments at Quiriguá, but only once at Copán (Morley 1920; Marcus 1976a:130, 138–140).

A second case involves a possible battle between Caracol and Tikal in A.D. 562 (9.6.8.4.2 [7 Ik 0 Zip]). The battle is alluded to on Altar 21 at Caracol (Fig. 11.60), but

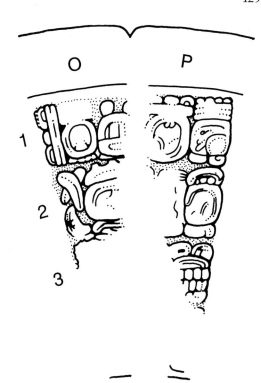

11.60. On the first of May, A.D. 562, Caracol allegedly broke away from the major capital of Tikal. This "war of independence" was recorded on Altar 21 at Caracol, but never mentioned at Tikal. Unfortunately, the passage on Altar 21 that discusses the "war" is very damaged. Nevertheless, at O2 we can see the "battle" glyph—similar to the hieroglyphic compound used by Quiriguá to describe its war of independence to throw off Copán's control (see Fig. 11.54). At P3 is the Tikal emblem glyph. Due to the damage suffered by the altar, some important glyphs (including, perhaps, the name of the Tikal ruler) are now lost. This altar was carved in A.D. 633 and centrally placed in the playing area of a ball court. It is interesting that Caracol's "war of independence" supposedly took place in A.D. 562, but was apparently not recorded in stone until more than 70 years had passed. By that time, it is unlikely that anyone involved in the "war" was still alive to dispute the claim. (Redrawn from Chase and Chase 1987: fig. 27.)

not mentioned at all at Tikal (Chase and Chase 1987:60). Caracol claimed victory and went on to achieve a substantial degree of autonomy, urban growth, and monumental construction thereafter. However, there is no evidence that the enormous city of Tikal was actually overthrown or conquered; it remained a major regional capital for at least the next 250 years. Significantly, the alleged victory was not mentioned at Caracol until seventy-one years after it took place, a lapse of time that virtually ensured that no one would be left alive who could dispute the claim.

A third example comes from the site of Dos Pilas, where a local lord claims on his monuments to have defeated Seibal in A.D. 735 (Lounsbury 1982, Houston and Mathews 1985, Demarest 1990). During this period, it appears that Seibal, Dos Pilas, and Aguateca were all secondary centers in the Petexbatún region. While the battle may have given Dos Pilas a measure of local autonomy, there is no evidence that Seibal itself was sacked and burned; in fact, less than 100 years later, Seibal became the capital of that region (Marcus 1973). One of the nice aspects of this case is that field archaeological data are present to supplement the epigraphic data: it appears that Dos Pilas was fortified with defensive walls and ditches (Demarest, personal communication), while Seibal, which was already in a defensible location, required no fortifications. Thus, a secondary center that invested in moats, walls, and other defensive works was able to defend itself against attack, and perhaps embark on some military campaigns as well.

In sum, we must keep Maya secondary centers' claims of conquest in perspective, just as we did with Tizoc's: their propaganda content is high. If we were really dealing with major defeats of cities like Copán, Seibal, and Tikal, we would expect to find evidence showing that Quiriguá, Dos Pilas, and Caracol went on to become the major capitals in those regions, while Copán, Seibal, and Tikal shrank to secondary status. What we really find, in each case, is that a subordinate lord proclaimed his independence from the capital in his region, then went on to undertake a flurry of monument carving and public construction. While the regional capital may temporarily have lost some of its labor and goods, it survived, and in some cases even regained control of these former dependencies later. In all likelihood, some lords at regional capitals just waited until a weaker lord took office at the secondary center before undertaking the task of re-annexing that dependency and its labor force.

The Timing of Maya Warfare

For agricultural peoples, the season of warfare makes a great deal of difference. The absence of too many warriors during planting or harvesting season could pose logistic problems. Consider, for example, the case of the Cherokee (Gearing 1958, 1962), a group featuring both endemic raiding and successful maize farming. The Cherokee selected winter—the non-agricultural season—as the appropriate time for raids. During the summer, which was the growing season for their crops, the Cherokee engaged in playing an indigenous ball game against rival villages. Since both activities are documented for the Maya as well, it would be interesting to know if the situations were analogous. I suggest that there is enough Long Count information available to indicate that the Maya favored the dry season for warfare. We also have a few inscriptions placing the Maya ball game in the rainy season, either preceding or following dry season skirmishes.

If we begin by looking first at the sixteenth-century ethnohistoric data, it appears that raiding between provinces was usually carried out during the dry season, from November to January, when most of the male population had little or no agricultural activity (Roys 1957:109–110). Herrera y Tordesillas ([1601] in Tozzer 1941:217) goes on to state:

> And so they never had peace, *especially when the cultivation was over,* and their greatest desire was to seize important men to sacrifice, because the greater the quality of the victim the more acceptable the service they did to god seemed to them. The number of people sacrificed was great. [emphasis mine]

Most Maya archaeologists have carefully noted the second part of Herrera y Tordesillas' statement—his remarks on taking important men as captives—but have ignored the equally important fact that the dry season was considered the ideal time for raiding.

One complication for the timing of Classic Maya warfare may have been the already-mentioned desire to choose the day of a battle so as to coincide with the appearance of Venus in one of its stationary or visible dates, apparently so that the bright planet could be invoked to aid the cause (Lounsbury 1982, M. Miller 1986). Whether this could push the timing of a raid into the rainy season is not certain. In fact, it is not even certain that the bright heavenly body used as a good omen was Venus, as opposed to some highly visible star. Such stars would probably not have been as visible during the overcast rainy season; so if the visibility of a bright star was essential to ensure victory, the dry season was the ideal time. Perhaps astronomical observations could be combined with agricultural logistics to select a day that was astrologically favorable and also occurred during the dry season.

While not all Classic Maya battles can be pinned down to the exact day (and some dates are abbreviated in such a way that several alternative readings are possible), there are many battles that can be interpreted as falling in the dry season (Table 11.1). Although it is clear that not all Maya warfare took place in the dry season, I suspect that it was the preferred time of year for raiding, and that when all the facts are in we will probably have more dry season dates than rainy season dates for battles. In the table below, battle dates are organized by the month in which they occur. We begin with November and go on until May, the end of the dry season.

The decision to wait until the dry season to undertake these military activities could mean that many men were required for these battles. After all, a small-scale raid involving

Table 11.1   Examples of Classic Maya Dry Season Battles and Related Events

Dry Season Date	*Yrs. A.D.*	*Event*
November		
Nov. 13	799	Palenque ruler accedes to throne after successful battle
Nov. 29	735	Dos Pilas lord claims "capture" of Seibal lord[a]
Nov. 30	735	Aguateca lord claims "capture" of Seibal lord
December		
Dec. 20	795	Bonampak battle[b]
Dec. 24	631	Caracol ruler "conquers" Naranjo (recorded at Caracol)
Dec. 27	631	Caracol attacks Naranjo (recorded at Naranjo)[c]
January		
Jan. 8	787	Yaxchilán lord (with help from Bonampak lord) takes captive
Jan. 16	378	Tikal's battle with Uaxactún
Jan. 17	735	Yaxchilán lord takes prisoner
Jan. 21	735	Bonampak lord takes prisoner
February		
Feb. 1	695	Naranjo battles Ucanal(?)
Feb. 10	752	Bird Jaguar of Yaxchilán takes prisoner
Feb. 12	724	Shield Jaguar of Yaxchilán prepares for battle; his wife brings him his helmet and shield
Feb. 22	796	Bonampak battle
March		
March 2	664	Dos Pilas lord captures Lord Macaw
March 4	636	Caracol battles with Naranjo
March 23	710	Naranjo's Scroll Squirrel attacks Yaxhá
March 29	781	Piedras Negras battle
April		
April 11	556	Caracol battles Tikal
May		
May 1	562	Caracol gains independence from Tikal as a result of battle
May 3	738	Quiriguá gains independence from Copán as a result of battle
May 4	627	Caracol has battle with Naranjo
May 5	755	Bird Jaguar of Yaxchilán takes captive

[a]Though the Seibal ruler was apparently taken captive, he was still alive for twelve years after that! (see also Lounsbury 1982).
[b]Alternative data and position for the Bonampak battle depicted in the murals of Room 2, Structure 1.
[c]After "victory," the Caracol ruler might have commissioned that such an inscription be carved at Naranjo itself.

only a few men could presumably have been mounted at any time without seriously in-
terfering with agricultural activities. The full decision making that must have preceded
Maya battles is impossible for us to reconstruct—especially since only successes are
claimed, and not the occasional bad decisions that resulted in loss of men and goods. The
taking of live captives is often featured in Maya art, but the number of captives who were
actually sacrificed may have been only a small percentage of the total. What the sacrifice
of an elite captive did was to dramatize the victory, like Julius Caesar's dragging of Ver-
cingetorix through the streets of Rome in a cage before executing him.

SUMMARY AND CONCLUSIONS

Raiding and captive taking are at least as old as the chiefdom stage of Formative Mesoamerica, and warfare seems to have been virtually endemic in all four of the major states
considered in this book. Indeed, contrary to popular belief, it would be hard to argue that
the Aztec were significantly more warlike than the Mixtec, Zapotec, and Maya. The Aztec
evidently did differ in the extent to which they actually annexed territory; the other three
states were more concerned with exacting tribute and obtaining manpower from defeated
neighbors than with maintaining armies of occupation.

Warfare was an instrument of foreign policy for all four states, and hieroglyphic
writing was a major propaganda tool. The taking of an important captive or captives was
a metaphor for victory; commissioned monuments show rulers grasping a prisoner by the
hair or claiming the title "Captor of X" (Fig. 11.52, 11.59). Defeats, or comrades taken
prisoner by the enemy, were rarely mentioned; one ruler, whom ethnohistoric sources
reveal to have lost 300 warriors in battle, commissioned a monument to show the fifteen
captives he took.

Sometimes secondary centers fought alongside their regional capitals in battle and
put up monuments side by side. In other cases, secondary centers claim to have captured
or defeated the ruler of a regional capital, but their claims are usually unsupported by
archaeological data. In such cases, what we are probably seeing are "wars of independence"
during which secondary centers won their independence from a regional capital. In some
cases, groups of secondary centers formed military alliances to shake off the yoke of a
capital. Many were re-subjugated, not always by conquest but sometimes by the device
of arranging the marriage of a royal woman from the capital to the lord of the secondary
center. Because of the volatility of this relationship, it is often at secondary centers that
we find the most elaborate defensive works.

While the underlying motives for war were the acquisition of tribute, material resources, and labor, many rulers relied on the "captive taking" theme as part of their vertical propaganda, claiming that their raids were aimed largely at taking prisoners for

sacrifice. Perhaps they felt that by linking their aggression to a sacred goal, such as dedicating a new temple by sacrificing captives to honor gods or divine ancestors, they would ensure support. Hence their monuments and codices show us a few captives being sacrificed, but not the hundreds of men who were kept as agricultural laborers or porters, nor the women kept as household slaves or textile workers.

As for the timing of battles, there is ethnohistoric evidence to suggest that the dry season—when manpower could be diverted from agriculture—was preferred. A list of twenty-three seasonal dates for Maya battles (assuming that they are accurate) would support this notion (see Table 11.1). However, Mesoamerican states also used auguries of different sorts to predict military success, and Maya monuments suggest that Venus or some other bright heavenly body was used as a sign. For logistic reasons, we can suspect that Maya astrologers tried to pick dates that did not fall during harvest times or periods of torrential summer rain; probably the timing of battles was determined by a combination of practical considerations, but rationalized through clever manipulation of astrology.

Finally, let us end on a more general question to be resolved by future research. Expansion of territorial and political control seems to have been one of the consequences of Mesoamerican warfare, but in neither the highlands nor the lowlands does that expansion seem to have been easy to maintain. Rather, there seem to have been cycles of conquest and expansion, followed by contraction and battles for independence, followed in turn by new cycles of expansion. Whether we are speaking of the Zapotec state centered at Monte Albán, the Maya state centered at Copán or Tikal, or the Toltec state centered at Tula, expansionist cycles seem to have lasted no more than 200 years in most cases. It would seem that the sociopolitical forces leading to fragmentation and balkanization were always present, and that at times they were strong enough to cause centralized systems to break down into their former autonomous components (Marcus 1989b:205–206, n.d.c). Is this an artifact of the archaeological record, or was territorial expansion in Mesoamerica impossible to sustain for more than a few hundred years?

12 ♦ AN ANTHROPOLOGICAL THEORY OF MESOAMERICAN WRITING

In chapter 1 I proposed a theory of Mesoamerican writing that is grounded in the research of anthropologists on chiefdoms and early states (Sahlins 1958; Service 1962, 1975; Fried 1967; Carneiro 1970, 1981). For years such anthropologists have expressed curiosity about the "engine of history," the driving force behind the evolution and development of complex society. No single answer has ever satisfied that curiosity, perhaps because there was always more than one engine in operation.

From the moment that rank societies or chiefdoms arose, however, surely one of those engines was the intense competition between elites that has been documented by anthropologists. Reinforced by mythologies that provide separate origins for low-status and high-status individuals, such competition led to endemic raiding between villages, and even to conflict among members of the same high-status families. As chiefdoms gave way to states, competition led to the falsification of genealogies; the acquisition of new land, titles, manpower, and tribute by force; the humiliation and sacrifice of rivals; the building of monumental works; and the obliteration of others' works.

In our theory, Mesoamerican hieroglyphic writing grew out of this competition for prestige and leadership, and almost immediately became one of the vehicles by which competition was escalated. As a political tool, writing reflected the level of development of the society in which it was embedded, and it changed as society changed. Mesoamerican writing did not appear until societies with leadership based on hereditary inequality already existed, and writing remained relatively simple until states had arisen.

This theory accounts for the timing of the first hieroglyphic texts. It explains why some of the earliest texts refer to slain enemies. It explains why "place signs" do not appear in serious numbers until there were actual states. It explains why hypogamous

435

marriages were recorded more often than hypergamous ones. It explains why some rulers claimed to have lived so long, and why some of their "ancestors" were assigned impossibly long lives. It explains why some monuments were huge and public, while others were small and private; and it explains why some monuments were defaced and some books were repainted. I believe that it even accounts for some texts, such as those in the Dresden Codex, which have traditionally been considered purely astronomical or ritual. Such texts were not pure science, but reference works that allowed the priests to link important births, battles, and inaugurations to celestial phenomena.

Of course, there are also questions our theory does not answer, such as why some other New World civilizations lacked writing. For example, I find it no surprise that both Monte Albán (in Mexico) and Cerro Sechín (in Peru) should erect major galleries of slain enemies at a comparable stage in their sociopolitical development. Why, then, did writing not arise in the Andes? Did something else serve as a vehicle for elite propaganda, playing the role that hieroglyphic texts served in Mesoamerica? If so, what was that "something else"?

In this chapter, as promised earlier, I will put some flesh on the bare bones of our theory. Toward the end of the chapter I look to the future of Mesoamerican epigraphy, and suggest some of the directions it might profitably take.

Four Major Systems: Similarities and Differences

Whenever one takes on a project of this size, there are always unexpected outcomes and serendipitous results. I began my research for this book with some trepidation, because so many good scholars had already worked on each of Mesoamerica's four major writing systems. I felt, nevertheless, that a comparison of all four systems might yield some new insights that the study of one system in isolation could not. Perhaps the biggest surprise was how similar in theme and function all four systems turned out to be.

At least four different languages were involved, four different cultures, four different civilizations. One writing system, that of the Maya, is almost as rich as the spoken language; another, that of the Aztec, has been described as "little more than pictures with short captions." The systems differ in the extent to which they use phoneticism, rebus writing, homophonics, puns, logograms, and so on. Yet every one of the four systems concentrates on giving us the names of rulers and nobles, the names and feats of their ancestors, and their important rites of passage—birth, death, marriage, accession to the throne, capture of enemies, and acquisition of new land and titles. In other words, the content is much more uniform than the differences in language, date, style, and medium would lead one to expect.

As an example of the unexpected rewards of looking at all four systems, let us use the case of the nine stelae set in the South Platform at Monte Albán (chapters 10 and 11).

Originally described by Caso (1928) more than sixty years ago, they were clearly important but had never been pulled together into a single explanatory framework. Even in my own more recent analyses—where some of the carvings seemed to depict Teotihuacán visitors and others showed bound captives (Marcus 1983g, 1983j)—they remained a group of nine unintegrated monuments.

As I began looking at the much richer data on the Aztec, Mixtec, and Maya, however, a pattern began to take shape. In all three cultures, whenever the way had been cleared for an ambitious lord to accede to the throne, many of the following steps were carried out. First, the candidate might visit important neighbors to make sure that they supported him. Second, he demonstrated his military skill by successfully leading his troops into battle and returning with noble captives for sacrifice at his inauguration. Third, he might erect or renovate an important temple (or other public building) to be dedicated at his inauguration. Fourth, on or after the occasion of his inauguration, he might commission an important stela that showed him on the throne, discussed his relationship to his ancestors, and listed his accomplishments.

As this pattern emerged from the Aztec, Mixtec, and Maya data, all nine of the South Platform stelae suddenly made sense as a set of monuments commissioned for the inauguration of an important Zapotec ruler. Stela 1, set in the northeast corner of the platform, shows him on his throne and discusses his divine descent. Stelae 2, 3, 5, 6, 7, and 8 show the captives to be sacrificed at his inauguration. The hidden edges of four stelae show distinguished visitors from Teotihuacán, coming in a procession to his inauguration; perhaps he had visited these important neighbors to elicit support prior to his accession, as was so often done. Under three of those scenes of visitors—set in the corners of the platform—were buried caches from the dedication of the building. In other words, the whole group of stelae in the South Platform comes together as a meaningful unit only when viewed in the context of Mesoamerica's three other major writing systems.

In addition to the similarities in theme and function displayed by our four major writing systems, however, we also find interesting differences. For example, at various times in prehistory the four cultures relied on different types of propaganda, often using different media.

In chapter 1 we distinguished two types of propaganda, vertical and horizontal. Vertical propaganda is hierarchic: the rulers attempt to influence the behavior of the ruled. Horizontal propaganda takes place on the same level: members of the elite attempt to influence other members of the elite. Both types of propaganda could be used either for agitation or integration; in the course of this book, we have seen both types of propaganda used both ways.

Vertical propaganda frequently involved grand public displays, which could be seen from a distance by noble and commoner alike. To begin by considering central Mexico, some of our earliest examples would be the giant carvings on the living rock at Chalcatzingo, Morelos (Grove 1984). The Aztec continued this pattern with cliff-carvings and giant three-dimensional monuments, visible from great distances. Some included larger-than-life figures of Aztec rulers, such as those of Motecuhzoma the Younger at Chapultepec (Nicholson 1961); others, like the reliefs of Acalpixcan (Marcus 1982a), included religious or cosmological themes. The multi-ton Stone of Tizoc, carved to honor Motecuhzoma's uncle on his inauguration, would be another example. While the Aztec monuments with cosmological themes probably had integration as one of their goals, those aimed at agitation are typified by the carved skull racks at Tenochtitlán; the latter created support for the continuing capture and sacrifice of the Aztecs' enemies. Cosmological themes reinforced the ideal world order to be attained, while the skull racks showed the kinds of military and ritual enforcement that would ensure that order.

Moving south in Mesoamerica, we see similar cases of vertical agitation propaganda among the Zapotec and their neighbors. The gallery of slain enemies on Building L at Monte Albán and the skull rack left by the conquering Zapotec at La Coyotera (near Cuicatlán) would be examples. We also see large stelae with bound captives; lists of conquered or tributary places; and rulers in military garb with lances in their hands. Stela 9 at Monte Albán—an obelisk carved on four sides and looming three meters above the Main Plaza—may be an example of vertical integration propaganda, the record of a military alliance between polities.

Vertical propaganda was not restricted to iconographic depictions on stone monuments. Although commoners were unable to read the hieroglyphic inscriptions, these texts were read to them by nobles who had been educated in special schools. Thompson (1972:5–14) notes that various sixteenth- and seventeenth-century sources (e.g., Avendaño y Loyola, Chi, Ciudad Real, Las Casas, Lizana, and López Medel) state that while only nobles could read, they did recite "history" to the commoners from texts and in song. Such reciting and singing allowed nobles to provide commoners with a particular version of "history."

The Maya produced vertical propaganda on a monumental scale. The staircase on Structure 26 at Copán is ten meters wide, has sixty-two steps, and features our longest-known text: 2,000 hieroglyphs. Copán also erected immense stelae in a huge open plaza. Not to be outdone, its former dependency, Quiriguá, celebrated its independence by erecting several stelae, one of which towered eight meters above the plaza. The later Maya of Chichén Itzá, perhaps influenced by immigrants from central Mexico, carved skull rack platforms that were almost as impressive as those of the Aztec.

Horizontal propaganda, on the other hand, employed smaller-scale media because it was intended only for the eyes of a select few—royal family members, nobles, priests, scribes. Here the medium was more likely to be a small wall panel in a palace or temple; the lintel over a palace doorway; a mural in a tomb or palace; the inner side of a tomb door stone; a small slab in a tomb antechamber; or a painted book, kept by priests in what amounted to a "royal archive" or "rare book room" as far as commoners were concerned.

A frequent topic of horizontal integration propaganda was royal genealogy. Among the Aztec and Mixtec such information appears most often in painted books, indicating that it was a relevant concern only for members of the nobility. To the south, the Zapotec typically placed such genealogical data on the lintels of royal tombs, in murals on the walls of the tomb chambers, or on small "genealogical registers" set in the antechamber. Still farther to the south, deep within the Temple of the Inscriptions at Palenque, the deceased ruler's alleged relatives were carved along the sides of his sarcophagus. Because of the restricted space, only a handful of nobles could ever have seen these carvings.

Also intended for elite eyes only were private rites, such as bloodletting by members of the royal family. Among the Maya these were often shown in small stone carvings or murals within palaces. Both the Maya and Mixtec also showed them in painted books. We know from ethnohistoric sources and artifacts for bloodletting that the Zapotec also engaged in such rites, but they were evidently so private as to almost never appear in public art; only the blood sacrifice of captive enemies was so publicly displayed.

Finally, there was horizontal agitation propaganda. A Mixtec example can be found in the pages of the Codex Selden which describe the royal woman 6 Monkey (chapter 11). There she is verbally insulted by two rival lords, their "cutting words" depicted by speech scrolls bearing flint knives; this scene could be used to justify her military campaign against them. And then there are the lintels in the palace of Bonampak, which show the lord of Yaxchilán and the lord of Bonampak taking captives. Was this agitation propaganda, designed to justify the military campaign? Or was it integration propaganda, designed to show that Yaxchilán and Bonampak were united by a common enemy?

Let us look now at some of the differences among Mesoamerican cultures that need to be explained by future research. What were the political conditions that led some societies, at various times, to put more effort into *horizontal* than *vertical* propaganda, and vice versa?

Looking at the Mixtec, we see far more investment in horizontal propaganda (codices) than vertical propaganda (huge public monuments). The Aztec, on the other hand, seem to have invested more energy than the Mixtec in huge public monuments for vertical propaganda. Could this have something to do with the differences in the way their rulers were chosen? Could the Aztec system—selection by 100 noble electors—have made the rewriting of genealogies less important? Could the small scale of most Mixtec polities have made monumental vertical propaganda less necessary?

The Zapotec and Maya seem to have divided their time between vertical and horizontal propaganda. The Zapotec could even combine the two varieties on one monument, as when Monte Albán showed a bound captive on the "public" face of Stela 7 and placed Teotihuacán visitors on the "hidden" edge.

But consider the following differences. The Maya showed royal marriage to the public, as in the case of the paired husband-wife stelae at Calakmul (Marcus 1987). The Zapotec usually showed it on small slabs set in tomb antechambers, where it would be seen only by noble relatives. The Maya made royal genealogy public, using enormous stelae; the Zapotec hid it on tomb lintels, tomb murals, and genealogical registers in tomb antechambers. The Zapotec put conquests, captives, slain enemies, and military alliances on carvings in very public places. While the Maya sometimes did this, they just as often hid scenes of warfare or captive taking in palace murals, lintels, or wall panels, where the public could not be expected to see it.

Why were some themes more appropriate for vertical propaganda in some cultures, and more appropriate for horizontal propaganda in others? Why did the Zapotec want conquests to be public and royal marriages to be reserved for elite viewing, while the Maya wanted royal marriages to be public and at least some conquests to be reserved for elite viewing? Are we dealing with significant cultural differences that need explanation, or only with sampling error?

Writing and the Calendar

Each of the Mesoamerican societies we have examined had at least two calendars. It is likely that both existed long before writing.

A 260-day calendar, composed of 20 day names and 13 numbers, was recorded in stone by 600 B.C. A 365-day calendar, featuring 18 months of 20 days, can be inferred from stone monuments of ca. 400 B.C. When combined, those two calendars resulted in a 52-year cycle of differently named days.

By 36 B.C., the two calendars had been combined with a starting point to produce a Long Count that textbooks tell us was "more accurate than the Julian calendar used by the conquering Spaniards in A.D. 1519." That statement is true, but it has also left readers with the erroneous impression that accuracy was the main goal of Mesoamerican calendars.

Yes, Maya priests could use the Long Count to record accurately when Venus had been the Morning Star or Evening Star, even centuries after the fact. But their goal in so doing might be to claim that the current ruler's accession took place when Venus was in the same position as it had occupied on the day a divine ancestor took office—a woman who ruled when she had reached the age of 815 years! Whenever possible, Mesoamerican scribes searched for anniversaries, selecting dates for future events that would fall on earlier occurrences of the same event. They also looked for dates that had favorable omens, days on which planetary bodies were visible or in alignment. If such coincidences and anniversaries could not be found, they were contrived to meet political goals. This maneuvering is more like astrology than accurate astronomy.

In particular, the 260-day sacred calendar was manipulated in that way. This sacred calendar was used by priests and diviners to select propitious dates for a ruler's inauguration, a temple dedication, a bloodletting rite, or the day when a raid should be carried out. Supposedly, nobles were named for the day on which they were born (chapter 7); but because some days were more auspicious than others, birth dates were often altered so that unlucky names would not follow a noble throughout his life. As an example of this, Whallon (Appendix) has shown that a sample of 1,661 Mixtec male nobles' names deviates significantly from the frequencies expected if every male were really named for his date of birth.

Why was the calendar first carved in stone? Recalling two early Zapotec examples from chapter 2, our answer is: to record the defeat of high-ranking enemies. In one case, the calendric name of a single victim is carved between his feet. In another case, the date on which more than 300 enemies were slain is recorded on paired stelae, and some of the victims have captions that may provide personal names.

Writing and Warfare

Having examined raiding and warfare in chapter 11, we will here only briefly consider its relationship to writing. Andean stonecarvers wanted to show the trophy heads and corpses of their enemies. Mesoamerican stonecarvers and scribes wanted to provide more information: they supplied the names of the victims and the places from which they came. For this purpose, they devised not only a way of recording calendric personal names and nicknames, but also a way of recording place names (chapter 6). In the highlands, this took the form of the so-called "hill signs" of the Zapotec, Mixtec, and Aztec; in the lowlands, it took the form of the Maya emblem glyph. It has long been argued that such emblem glyphs contain royal titles in addition to geographic referents, but that possibility only reinforces one of our main points: nobles and the territories they ruled were inseparable in Mesoamerica, so much so that many places took their names from a ruler or dynasty.

Under what conditions were place names first carved in stone? While earlier examples may one day be found, our largest early sample of hill signs comes from the Zapotec area between 150 B.C. and A.D. 150. By that time an actual state level of political organization had been reached, and that fact is probably significant. Ethnographic data suggest that while chiefdoms engage in a lot of raiding (with torture and mutilation of captives), they generally do not have the organization and manpower to annex defeated communities. States, on the other hand, can and do take conquered areas under their control, or force them to pay tribute. It may be that *standardized place signs only became common in Mesoamerican writing after states with the power to annex territory and/or exact tribute had arisen.* Chiefdoms would have less need for them, since their raiding was probably limited to burning a rival village or its temple, and killing or taking captive the rival chief.

In the later codices, place signs appear by the hundreds in tribute lists, or serve as pedestals for rulers; enemy places are shot with arrows or speared with lances. Maya rulers, shown as giants standing on tiny captives, took titles proclaiming themselves "Captor of X." Military propaganda made up an enormous part of later Mesoamerican writing, and claims of victory were often exaggerated.

As Westerners we have been taught that warfare is evil, a last resort when diplomacy fails. This attitude has blinded us to the fact that in Mesoamerica, warfare was as much a creator as a destroyer. Many of Mesoamerica's great civilizations, from the Zapotec of the first century A.D. to the Aztec of the fifteenth century, grew by subjugating their weaker neighbors. It is becoming increasingly clear that even the Classic Maya—once idealized as a "peaceful theocracy"—were no different. But because weak neighbors can grow stronger, many of the battles recorded on Maya stelae and wall panels were probably "wars of independence" that enabled subject provinces to break away from their capital. Thus, one of the earliest themes recorded in Mesoamerican writing was also one of its longest-lived.

Writing, Genealogy, and Marriage

Because there were always more nobles and royal family members than there were positions of leadership, competition for these positions was fierce. While rules of inheritance (such as birth order) provided some societies with a framework for succession, there were alternative routes for men and women of ambition. Some of these involved considerable propaganda, much of it ex post facto.

Genealogies in stone or on screenfold manuscripts were kept to determine whose ancestry most qualified him for the office. Rulers' texts refer to near ancestors, more distant ancestors, and finally to ancestors so remote that they are virtually mythological. By a process known as euhemerism (chapter 9), noble ancestors turned gradually into heroes, then semidivine intermediaries, and sometimes actual deities. While even a clever propagandist might not be able to deceive his contemporaries about his immediate ancestors, it is clear that some rulers "borrowed" more distant ancestors—including deified ancestors—to legitimize their claim to the throne. In fact, some of the most spectacular genealogical displays may have been the work of nobles who were not really in the direct line of succession.

Among the Maya, a ruler's first monument was usually set up *after* his accession to the throne. This fact gave him ample opportunity to backdate his own birth, expunge the records of his immediate predecessor, and extend his own lifetime of accomplishment back over several previous reigns. Such a process may account for the improbably long lifetimes and reigns of some rulers at Palenque, Yaxchilán, Quiriguá, and elsewhere (chapter 10).

Just as some Mixtec lords seem to have repainted codices, presumably to include themselves in genealogies where they did not belong, some Maya lords seem to have gone to suspiciously great lengths to legitimize themselves. They might erect monuments which drew parallels between their accession date and that of a remote ancestor who was supposedly inaugurated thousands of year before. Mixtec or Aztec rulers might trace their claim to a grandparent they shared with the legitimate heir, then concoct some way to erase the latter's descent line. Some lords whose claim to the throne was suspect might be particularly aggressive about going to battle, taking captives, and acquiring new manpower to build fabulous temples or pyramids. In terms of our theory, perhaps the best way to put it is to say that *writing was used both to keep genealogies and to falsify them when necessary.*

Competition was particularly intense when there was an unexpected gap in succession, or when the logical heir to the throne was still too young to rule. We have seen Aztec and Maya cases where a regent (often the heir's mother) ruled until the heir was old enough; and we have seen cases where the king's emissary helped to resolve a gap in succession at a secondary center. This, too, was recorded in writing.

In addition to moving themselves closer to the main line of descent by manipulating their ancestors, Mesoamerican rulers used strategic marriages to accomplish the same thing. In chapter 8 we discussed hypogamous marriage (higher-status noblewoman to lower-status nobleman); isogamous marriage (between equals); and hypergamous marriage (higher-status nobleman to lower-status noblewoman). We pointed out that although all three types of marriage must have been frequent, Mesoamerican noblemen were only concerned with recording hypogamous or isogamous marriages—those that would raise the status of their children or bring them new privileges. Clearly, if Mesoamerican nobles had simply been writing history, our sample would not be so skewed in favor of hypogamy.

We have seen Maya tertiary administrative centers become secondary centers following the marriage of their local lord to a royal woman from the capital. We have also seen Tenochtitlán, the Aztec capital, send royal women to marry the lords of secondary centers in order to keep them loyal to the capital. In one case, peace between Zapotec and Aztec was achieved by marrying an Aztec princess to the Zapotec king. Her son—rather than one of his sons by a Zapotec wife—became the next Zapotec ruler. All these cases are consistent with our hypothesis that *writing was used as the propaganda component of elite competition, whether through warfare, marriage, or manipulation of genealogy.*

The Next Stage of Mesoamerican Epigraphy

We have already seen Mesoamerican epigraphy pass through a number of stages. In the early decades of this century almost every impressive figure in a stela or codex was seen as a "god," almost every text seen as devoted to calendrics and astronomy, the product of cultures who "worshiped time." The revolution of the last four decades, whose early salvos were fired by Caso and Proskouriakoff, greatly changed our minds. Now the figures in the stelae and codices are "real people," and the dates refer to their births, deaths, marriages, conquests, and reigns. We hear that Mesoamerican scribes were writing history, "just like that of the European royal families." No wonder they needed a calendar "more accurate than the one used by the Spaniards."

Now it is time, if not for another revolution, at least for a pendulum swing in the other direction. In the next stage of Mesoamerican epigraphy we will have to concede that "history," in our terms, is not really what the scribes were writing. They *were* dealing with real people, real times, and real places, but what they were writing was a kind of political propaganda in which there was no line drawn between history and myth.

We have seen that for Mesoamerican cultures the important distinction was not between propaganda, myth, and history, but between *noble speech* and *commoner speech*. Noble speech, like the *ma'at* of the Egyptian pharaoh, was by definition true no matter how improbable. Commoner speech was confused, uninformed, full of falsehoods. Hieroglyphic writing, therefore, was the visible form of noble speech.

In the next stage of Mesoamerican epigraphy, we will not hear that Mesoamerican societies were "literate." Literacy was not even a goal; commoner speech was deliberately kept false because commoners were excluded from the special schools where nobles learned truth. Like the sixteenth-century *iya* dialect and "Language of Zuyua," writing was a skill used to maintain the gulf between ruler and ruled. Mesoamerican elites wanted to reinforce the differences between nobles and commoners; that was accomplished by a myth of separate origins.

In the next stage of Mesoamerican epigraphy, scholars will acknowledge the *potential* accuracy of dates in the Long Count system, without claiming that the system's *goal* was accuracy. After all, accuracy could hardly be the goal of a calendar that had royal ancestors giving birth at 754 years of age and taking office at 815. We should even be skeptical of prehispanic rulers who lived to eighty; in chapter 10 we saw at least one major discrepancy between the age at death according to osteology, and the age at death according to a scribe.

In the next stage, epigraphers will perhaps stop trying to treat the lesser-known calendars (such as that of the Zapotec) as if they were simply translations of better-known calendars (such as that of the Aztec). They may even stop trying to match isolated glyphs in one system with isolated glyphs in another system through superficial morphology. There are at least four different languages involved, each of which was embedded in a culture with its own analogies, homologies, puns, and ethnoscientific classification. In my opinion, the days of working on hieroglyphic writing without actually knowing the language and culture of the Mesoamerican peoples involved are almost over. Not quite, but almost. As Leach (1976:1) once put it, "Today, every detail of custom is seen as part of a complex; it is recognised that details, considered in isolation, are as meaningless as isolated letters of the alphabet."

In the next stage, epigraphers will treat records of conquest or capture not as textbook history ("Battle of Hastings, A.D. 1066"), but as self-serving attempts to show each ruler in the best light. They will not assume, when they see Lord Bird Jaguar holding a captive by the hair, that he and his captive were literally the only two warriors involved in the raid. They will be skeptical when a secondary center claims "victory" over a major capital, especially when the excavation of that capital shows no signs of its having been overthrown. They will interpret military texts in the light of the many miles of defensive walls at Monte Albán, Xochicalco, Tikal, Cucá, Tulum, Becán, and Mayapán, which suggest that hundreds of warriors fought in raids. And they will remember that the United States won its independence from England without burning London to the ground.

Finally, in the next stage we will not hear epigraphers claiming that they have "made field archaeologists irrelevant." By then they will have realized, as did Wilson in Egypt forty years ago, that hieroglyphic texts contain "distortions of the truth or . . . absolute untruths," despite the fact that in their ancient setting they were "sincere and consistent" (Wilson 1951:3). Wilson maintained that such material had to be tested "constantly against itself, against evidence known from other peoples and cultures, and against good common sense" (ibid.:4). And he knew that one of the few sources of "objective evidence" on prehistory, limited as it might be, was "the physical remains resulting from excavation" (ibid.).

Epigraphy and archaeology need each other. If a truly *objective* history is ever to emerge from prehispanic Mesoamerica, much of it will have to emerge at the point of a trowel.

APPENDIX • A STATISTICAL ANALYSIS
OF MIXTEC NOBLES' NAMES

ROBERT WHALLON

The data available for analysis consist of 1,661 names of Mixtec males and 951 names of Mixtec females. The names are binomial, consisting of a day number followed by a day name. There are 13 day numbers and 20 day names. Days, and thus people (since individuals in principle were named for the day on which they were born), were named as the two cycles of day numbers and day names proceeded sequentially throughout the Mixtec 260-day ritual calendar. This ritual calendar or "sacred almanac" has been described in chapter 4. The sources from which the names were taken are given in chapter 7.

In the present data, there are an average of 6.4 men named per day, with a standard error of 3.3, and a range from 0 to 19 names per day. For women, there are, on the average, 3.7 names per day, with a standard error of 2.2, and a range from 0 to 12. Men's and women's names are almost equally variable in these data, the coefficient of variation for men being 52.3 and that for women 60.5.

Lack of Cyclical Patterns of Naming

The first question investigated in the analysis of these data was whether there were any regular cycles of preferred naming throughout the 260-day calendar (for example, naming individuals by preference every 3rd day, etc.). Taking the frequencies of men's names throughout the calendar (Table A.1), a spectral analysis using a uniform window with a maximum lag of 20 (the length of the longer cycle composing the Mixtec calendar) showed that there were no significant cycles in the frequency of naming evident in these data (Fig. A.1). Similarly, for the frequencies of women's names, taken in sequence throughout the 260-day period (Table A.2), spectral analysis using the same parameters

447

Table A.1   Observed Frequencies of Mixtec Men's Names in 260-Day Calendar Sequence (significantly frequent names are indicated in bold type)

18	5	5	8	8	10	6	3	4	9	2	4	5	9	8	3	**18**	6	2	**14**
6	**16**	4	4	3	4	4	7	8	9	1	4	**14**	6	2	9	2	2	6	7
9	**19**	10	7	5	7	10	4	2	4	0	7	7	5	2	1	8	4	8	8
8	9	2	10	6	6	6	4	8	11	3	6	3	4	11	3	7	2	9	10
8	10	7	9	10	7	5	9	4	3	2	5	5	5	9	6	**14**	6	6	7
12	6	2	5	5	2	6	8	3	4	9	10	8	13	3	3	5	8	7	5
9	4	4	9	6	1	5	4	8	4	9	5	9	12	8	4	11	8	4	8
6	5	2	5	3	4	7	4	7	8	7	2	**16**	8	6	5	**14**	3	6	7
6	3	8	5	4	6	5	4	2	5	5	0	9	4	3	8	6	5	5	5
8	6	8	5	7	7	2	6	5	5	5	9	6	4	8	5	5	8	11	13
4	7	5	6	9	3	4	7	2	**14**	12	5	10	5	7	5	10	7	3	5
2	12	7	8	6	3	6	6	6	7	12	4	11	9	8	2	5	10	7	8
6	12	6	9	6	3	1	2	10	12	2	4	9	5	6	3	**16**	5	4	2

showed no detectable cyclical pattern of naming (Fig. A.2). These results confirm what seemed clear from visual inspection of the available data, and open the way to a consideration of possible differential importance, reflected in differential frequencies of use, of specific day names and day numbers in the naming of Mixtec men and women.

Men

One-way analysis of variance was used to test for the existence of patterns of preferential use of particular day names or day numbers in the naming of the Mixtec men represented in this set of data. Such analysis of the uses of the day names revealed highly significant differences among the day names in the extent to which they appear to have been either "favored" or "avoided" (Table A.3). Additionally, there is a strong and significant tendency for the frequencies of men's names that incorporate favored day names to be extremely variable from day number to day number. This is not true for avoided

ABSOLUTE TIME RANGE= 260 N= 260 OUT OF 260
         (UNIFORM WINDOW WITH MAXIMUM LAG= 20)

```
          +----+----+----+----+----+----+----+----+----+----+
0.        +            *                                     |
.02500    +*                                                 |
.05000    +                                                 *|
.07500    +                     *                            |
.10000    +                   *                              |
.12500    +*                                                 |
.15000    +                        *                         |
.17500    +                      *                           |
.20000    +                  *                               |
.22500    +   *                                              |
.25000    +                                    *             |
.27500    +      *                                           |
.30000    +                                       *          |
.32500    +               *                                  |
.35000    +      *                                           |
.37500    +                         *                        |
.40000    +                         *                        |
.42500    +           *                                      |
.45000    +                      *                           |
.47500    +          *                                       |
.50000    +     *                                            |
          +----+----+----+----+----+----+----+----+----+----+
         .30081         1.8943         3.4879    DENSITY
              1.0976         2.6911         4.2846
```

ACCEPTANCE INTERVALS ON LOG10 DENSITY   @.9500   @.9900
     UNDER MULTIVARIATE NORMAL   LOWER   .21651 -1   -.59527 -1
     EDF= 13.000   EIE= 20.000   UPPER   .71524   .86291
     USING APPROXIMATE NORMALITY   LOWER   -.32839 -1 -.13775
                                    UPPER   .63490   .73981

TESTS FOR FLAT SPECTRUM
     MEDIAN SPECTRUM STATISTIC= -.50066 -1   SIGNIF= .9601
     PYKE'S K-S STATISTICS (20 POINTS)= .31883 -1, -.52586 -1

FREQ	CYCLE	DENSITY	CUM %	LOG10 DENSITY
0.		1.4601	3.5	.16438
.0250	40.000	.30081	4.3	-.52171
.0500	20.000	4.2846	14.6	.63191
.0750	13.333	2.1125	19.8	.32481
.1000	10.000	2.0520	24.7	.31219
.1250	8.0000	.30567	25.5	-.51474
.1500	6.6667	2.4114	31.3	.38228
.1750	5.7143	2.2571	36.8	.35355
.2000	5.0000	1.9241	41.4	.28423
.2250	4.4444	.67404	43.1	-.17131
.2500	4.0000	3.6759	52.0	.56536
.2750	3.6364	.89169	54.1	-.49786 -1
.3000	3.3333	4.0798	64.0	.61064
.3250	3.0769	1.8378	68.5	.26430
.3500	2.8571	.85808	70.5	-.66470 -1
.3750	2.6667	2.7189	77.1	.43439
.4000	2.5000	2.7107	83.7	.43309
.4250	2.3529	1.6012	87.6	.20443
.4500	2.2222	2.5132	93.7	.40023
.4750	2.1053	1.5048	97.3	.17748
.5000	2.0000	1.1109	100.0	.45660 -1

Fig. A.1   Spectral analysis of Mixtec male names.

Table A.2   Observed Frequencies of Mixtec Women's Names in 260-Day Calendar Sequence (significantly frequent names are indicated in bold type)

4	1	4	5	4	4	2	5	4	4	5	5	2	3	3	4	2	3	2	**12**
1	4	6	2	2	3	8	2	4	3	2	3	1	4	4	8	3	6	3	5
3	0	7	2	2	7	4	2	8	3	1	5	6	7	3	3	1	4	2	2
3	4	1	2	5	5	1	2	5	1	3	**10**	5	4	6	0	1	4	4	3
2	8	5	2	4	4	4	1	5	4	5	4	5	4	2	6	2	7	4	1
7	2	3	2	7	3	0	**11**	2	0	0	6	4	4	3	4	4	3	2	3
2	8	4	2	4	1	8	3	6	2	6	7	4	2	6	3	2	8	5	5
6	2	2	1	2	1	3	2	4	3	7	2	3	3	4	2	1	6	0	2
3	5	1	6	6	2	4	2	1	3	4	2	2	1	8	6	2	5	1	3
3	2	6	2	6	5	3	4	5	2	6	3	3	7	4	4	4	9	2	4
3	4	5	2	**10**	2	1	8	3	4	4	7	2	2	8	2	3	3	1	4
5	4	2	4	3	4	3	1	2	3	6	1	1	1	5	6	4	4	2	2
2	2	2	0	**12**	2	4	4	0	0	3	3	7	3	3	4	4	4	5	9

day names, which tend to have relatively uniform low counts for all day numbers. The implication of these facts is that certain day names were not simply favored in general, but that it was certain specific *combinations* of day number and day name that were important.

Similarly, an analysis of variance of the uses of day numbers showed significant tendencies to favor certain day numbers and avoid others (Table A.4). Again there is a general tendency for the frequencies of names incorporating favored day numbers to be quite variable from day name to day name, although this is not strong enough to be accepted as statistically significant. In contrast, however, the avoided day numbers exhibit relatively uniform low counts across the day names with which they are combined. The implication again is that certain day numbers were not preferred uniformly, but that it is only certain combinations of day number with day name that are favored significantly.

The preference for certain combinations can be seen by inspecting the frequencies of male names tabulated by day name and day number (Table A.5). Names in which favored day names and day numbers are found indeed often do occur with higher frequency

ABSOLUTE TIME RANGE= 260 N= 260 OUT OF 260
(UNIFORM WINDOW WITH MAXIMUM LAG= 20)

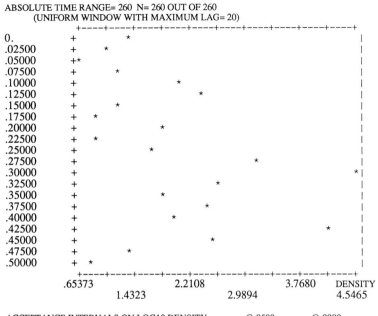

```
           .65373        2.2108         3.7680    DENSITY
                1.4323         2.9894          4.5465
```

ACCEPTANCE INTERVALS ON LOG10 DENSITY   @.9500   @.9900

		@.9500	@.9900
UNDER MULTIVARIATE NORMAL	LOWER	.21651 -1	-.59527 -1
EDF= 13.000 EIE= 20.000	UPPER	.71524	.86291
USING APPROXIMATE NORMALITY	LOWER	-.32839 -1	-.13775
	UPPER	.63490	.73981

TESTS FOR FLAT SPECTRUM
MEDIAN SPECTRUM STATISTIC= -.91442   SIGNIF= .3605
PYKE'S K-S STATISTICS (20 POINTS)= .40134 -1, -.14795

FREQ	CYCLE	DENSITY	CUM %	LOG10 DENSITY
0.		1.3960	3.4	.14490
.0250	40.000	1.1131	6.1	.46532 -1
.0500	20.000	.65373	7.7	-.18460
.0750	13.333	1.2064	10.6	.81503 -1
.1000	10.000	2.1176	15.8	.32584
.1250	8.0000	2.3995	21.6	.38012
.1500	6.6667	1.2286	24.6	.89425 -1
.1750	5.7143	.90799	26.8	-.41918 -1
.2000	5.0000	1.8230	31.2	.26078
.2250	4.4444	.89803	33.4	-.46709 -1
.2500	4.0000	1.7187	37.6	.23521
.2750	3.6364	3.1682	45.3	.50082
.3000	3.3333	4.5465	56.3	.65768
.3250	3.0769	2.6210	62.7	.41846
.3500	2.8571	1.8443	67.2	.26582
.3750	2.6667	2.4462	73.1	.38850
.4000	2.5000	1.9960	78.0	.30016
.4250	2.3529	4.1949	88.2	.62272
.4500	2.2222	2.5932	94.5	.41384
.4750	2.1053	1.3829	97.9	.14080
.5000	2.0000	.88403	100.0	-.53531 -1

Fig. A.2   Spectral analysis of Mixtec female names.

Table A.3   Analysis of Variance of Mixtec Men's Names by Day Name

N= 260 OUT OF 260

SOURCE	DF	SUM OF SQRS.	MEAN SQR.	F-STATISTIC	SIGNIF.
BETWEEN	19	513.00	27.000	2.7287	.0002
WITHIN	240	2374.8	9.8949		
TOTAL	259	2887.8	(RANDOM EFFECTS STATISTICS)		

ETA= .4215   ETA-SQR.= .1776   (VAR. COMP= 1.3158 %VAR. AMONG= 11.74)

EQUALITY OF VARIANCES: DF= 19, 24686   F= 1.8797   .0115

DAY-NAME	N	MEAN	VARIANCE	STD. DEV.
CROCODILE	13	7.8462	15.474	3.9337
WIND	13	8.7692	23.526	4.8503
HOUSE	13	5.3846	6.5897	2.5670
LIZARD	13	6.9231	4.0769	2.0191
SERPENT	13	6.0000	4.5000	2.1213
DEATH	13	4.8462	6.4744	2.5445
DEER	13	5.1538	4.9744	2.2303
RABBIT	13	5.2308	4.3590	2.0878
WATER	13	5.3077	7.3974	2.7198
DOG	13	7.3077	12.397	3.5210
MONKEY	13	5.3077	17.064	4.1309
GRASS	13	5.0000	7.0000	2.6458
REED	13	8.6154	13.256	3.6409
TIGER	13	6.8462	9.4744	3.0780
EAGLE	13	6.2308	8.3590	2.8912
VULTURE	13	4.3846	5.2564	2.2927
MOTION	13	9.3077	24.564	4.9562
FLINT	13	5.6923	6.2308	2.4962
RAIN	13	6.0000	6.1667	2.4833
FLOWER	13	7.6154	10.756	3.2797
GRAND	260	6.3885	11.150	3.3391

than other names, but such higher frequencies are strikingly irregular for any of these day names or day numbers. One might expect here that it would be the combinations of favored day names with favored day numbers that would exhibit the highest frequencies, but, in fact, not even these combinations are regularly characterized by relatively high

Table A.4   Analysis of Variance of Mixtec Men's Names by Day Number

N= 260 OUT OF 260

SOURCE	DF	SUM OF SQRS.	MEAN SQR.	F-STATISTIC	SIGNIF.
BETWEEN	12	525.12	43.760	4.5748	.0000
WITHIN	247	2362.6	9.5654		
TOTAL	259	2887.8	(RANDOM EFFECTS STATISTICS)		

ETA= .4264   ETA-SQR.= .1818   (VAR. COMP= 1.7097 %VAR. AMONG= 15.16)

EQUALITY OF VARIANCES: DF= 12, 39220.   F= 2.1928   .0097

DAY-NO.	N	MEAN	VARIANCE	STD. DEV.
(1)	20	7.4000	15.095	3.8852
(2)	20	6.1500	8.8711	2.9784
(3)	20	6.8000	17.221	4.1498
(4)	20	8.3000	12.642	3.5556
(5)	20	6.1000	9.4632	3.0762
(6)	20	5.7000	8.9579	2.9930
(7)	20	8.0000	6.7368	2.5955
(8)	20	6.5000	5.0000	2.2361
(9)	20	5.5500	11.103	3.3321
(10)	20	9.0000	13.474	3.6707
(11)	20	4.2500	2.6184	1.6182
(12)	20	4.8000	7.7474	2.7834
(13)	20	4.5000	5.4211	2.3283
GRAND	260	6.3885	11.150	3.3391

counts. Rather, it appears to be only *selected combinations* that are more frequently cho-sen for men's names.

To identify these apparently important or significant combinations of day name and day number, we can examine the frequency distribution of the counts of all names (Fig. A.3). We see that these counts are very close to being normally distributed, but that there is a slight tendency for them to be negatively skewed (i.e., to have several particularly high counts extending to the right, more than one would expect if the distribution of counts were perfectly random, or "normal"). There is a slight break in this distribution at 13 and a slight peak at 14, with another break at 15, followed by six instances of fre-quencies ranging from 16 to 19. In a normal curve fitted to these data, only 2.4 percent,

Table A.5 Mixtec Men's Names—Observed Frequencies by Day Number and Day Name (significantly frequent names are indicated in bold type)

	1	2	3	4	5	6	7	8	9	10	11	12	13
Crocodile	**18**	9	8	9	6	4	6	6	8	12	6	8	2
Wind	12	5	**19**	10	4	3	7	12	**16**	9	6	5	6
House	8	7	5	10	7	4	8	5	6	4	2	2	2
Lizard	5	5	8	8	7	9	9	5	6	9	4	10	5
Serpent	5	3	7	6	8	5	10	6	4	9	6	3	6
Death	6	2	4	7	3	10	7	7	1	6	3	3	4
Deer	4	6	6	7	2	6	6	10	5	5	5	4	1
Rabbit	2	7	4	8	4	6	6	3	4	9	4	4	7
Water	2	10	8	8	3	7	5	6	4	2	4	8	2
Dog	5	14	12	9	11	4	8	5	7	9	4	3	4
Monkey	9	5	12	2	1	3	9	7	5	12	2	0	2
Grass	5	5	0	5	4	4	6	10	2	9	4	4	7
Reed	7	5	9	9	10	9	**14**	3	8	**16**	6	11	5
Tiger	9	5	5	12	4	5	5	6	4	13	8	4	9
Eagle	8	8	2	9	8	3	7	6	2	11	3	6	8
Vulture	5	2	3	1	6	4	8	5	3	9	3	3	5
Motion	**14**	5	5	**18**	8	**14**	11	6	10	**16**	2	7	5
Flint	8	3	8	10	6	4	6	8	5	7	5	2	2
Rain	9	7	6	11	7	2	8	6	4	5	3	4	6
Flower	7	10	5	7	13	8	**14**	8	7	8	5	5	2

or about six, of the counts should be greater than 13, and only 0.5 percent, or roughly one count, should be greater than 15. In fact, we observe eleven counts above 13 and six above 15, about twice and six times the expected numbers, respectively. It seems reasonable, given the significant results of the analyses of variance previously obtained, to set these particularly high counts off as indicating combinations of day names and day numbers that were in some way distinctly favored or preferred.

When we do this, we find, as expected, that a large proportion (8 out of 11) of these particularly common names are composed of a favored day name and a favored day number (Table A.5). Of the three names that are not such combinations (2 Dog, 6 Motion, and 9 Wind), the day name of the combination is, in every case, a favored one, implying perhaps that day names have some greater importance over day numbers in significant names.

At least one significant name is found for each day name and each day number indicated by the analyses of variance as favored. The high variances are evident in all cases, however, in the great variation from high-count to low-count names, and in the fact that,

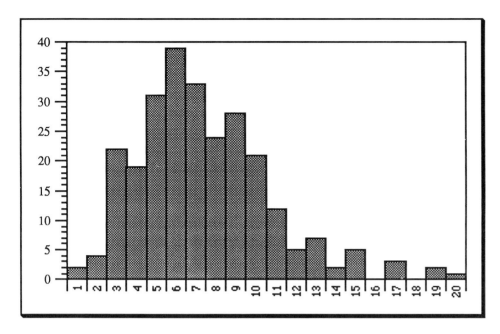

Fig. A.3   Histogram of frequency of occurrence of Mixtec men's names.

quite definitely, not every intersection of such favored names and numbers is used frequently as a name. The specifically selected, or preferred combinations, in order of importance (frequency) are as follows:

1. 3 Wind
2. 1 Crocodile; 4 Motion
3. 10 Reed; 10 Motion; 9 Wind
4. 2 Dog; 1 Motion; 6 Motion; 7 Reed; 7 Flower

The rough order of importance of the day names indicated by the results of the analysis of variance (Table A.3) is well substantiated here, with Motion appearing in four combinations; Wind and Reed in two each; and Crocodile, Flower, and Dog in only one apiece. Day numbers, on the other hand, do not show such a ranking, and there does not appear to be a significant rank order of preference among them, as there seems to be for the day names. This may be a further indication of the priority of the day names in determining the significance of Mixtec names.

Those day names and day numbers that were indicated by the analysis of variance as showing a tendency to be avoided, do indeed exhibit relatively uniform, low frequencies of names in which they are incorporated. The remaining day names and day numbers, neither favored nor avoided, show the expected moderate variation around the global average number of names per day.

If we look at the chronological distribution of these favored men's names throughout the Mixtec sacred calendar (Table A.1), we see that they are spaced highly irregularly. There is a rather dense clumping, or close spacing, of such names from the very end of the 260-day cycle through approximately the first quarter. Throughout the rest of the 260-day cycle these favored names are widely spaced, with the exception of two names very close to each other in the middle of this period of spacing. It is unclear what this might signify, unless it has something to do with increased ritual or symbolic importance of the end of the 260-day cycle and the first part of the new cycle.

Women

Identical analyses were made of the frequencies of Mixtec women's names. A one-way analysis of variance of the counts of women's names by day name revealed differences in the average numbers of names incorporating different day names that were statistically significant at the 5 percent level, but not at the 1 percent level (Table A.6). However, there is no consistent or significant pattern of high variance associated with preference for a day name, as there was in the case of men's names, and it seems prudent in this case to evaluate the level of significance attained in this analysis in the light of the results of the further analyses performed on these data.

A one-way analysis of variance of the frequencies of women's names by day number (Table A.7) revealed no significant differences among averages. There clearly is no pattern of either preference or avoidance of particular day numbers in women's names. Again, we find that patterning, or significance, is stronger in the case of the use of day names than in the use of day numbers.

Looking at the frequency distribution of all women's names, we see a closely normal distribution, with only a slight skew to the left (Fig. A.4). On a normal curve fitted to these data, counts above eight should comprise roughly 2.5 percent, or six to seven of the observations, and counts above nine should represent approximately 0.8 percent, or two observations. We do see, in fact, exactly seven observations falling above eight counts, but these stretch out to the right, resulting in five observations of days on which more than nine individuals were named. This is two-and-a-half times as many observations as we would expect in this range, and it may be worth looking at the specific combinations of day name and day number represented by these particularly favored names.

Putting these five favored names in the context of the combinations of day names and day numbers involved (Table A.8), we see that two of them incorporate the favored day name Serpent (10 Serpent and 11 Serpent). None incorporate the day name Flint, indicated by the analysis of variance as possibly favored. The other frequently encountered

Table A.6   Analysis of Variance of Mixtec Women's Names by Day Name

N= 260 OUT OF 260

SOURCE	DF	SUM OF SQRS.	MEAN SQR.	F-STATISTIC	SIGNIF.
BETWEEN	19	155.30	8.1739	1.7622	.0279
WITHIN	240	1113.2	4.6385		
TOTAL	259	1268.5	(RANDOM EFFECTS STATISTICS)		

ETA= .3499 ETA-SQR.= .1224 (VAR. COMP= .27196 %VAR. AMONG= 5.54)

EQUALITY OF VARIANCES: DF= 19, 24686   F= 1.4534   .0913

DAY-NAME	N	MEAN	VARIANCE	STD. DEV.
CROCODILE	13	3.3846	2.9231	1.7097
WIND	13	3.5385	5.9359	2.4364
HOUSE	13	3.6923	4.0641	2.0160
LIZARD	13	2.4615	2.6026	1.6132
SERPENT	13	5.1538	9.4744	3.0780
DEATH	13	3.3077	3.0641	1.7505
DEER	13	3.4615	5.7692	2.4019
RABBIT	13	3.6154	8.5897	2.9308
WATER	13	3.7692	4.6923	2.1662
DOG	13	2.4615	1.9359	1.3914
MONKEY	13	4.0000	4.5000	2.1213
GRASS	13	4.4615	6.4359	2.5369
REED	13	3.4615	3.6026	1.8980
TIGER	13	3.4615	3.6026	1.8980
EAGLE	13	4.5385	3.7692	1.9415
VULTURE	13	4.0000	4.5000	2.1213
MOTION	13	2.5385	1.4359	1.1983
FLINT	13	5.0769	3.9103	1.9774
RAIN	13	2.5385	2.4359	1.5607
FLOWER	13	4.2308	9.5256	3.0864
GRAND	260	3.6577	4.8978	2.2131

names are 4 Rabbit, 7 Grass, and 7 Flower. In retrospect, all these day names do stand out in the previous analysis by their high variances (in order of decreasing variance: Flower, Serpent, Rabbit, Grass), while the variance of Flint is quite low (Table A.6). The average numbers of names that incorporate these highly variable day names are low because, with

Table A.7   Analysis of Variance of Mixtec Women's Names by Day Number

N= 260 OUT OF 260

SOURCE	DF	SUM OF SQRS.	MEAN SQR.	F-STATISTIC	SIGNIF.
BETWEEN	12	59.485	4.9571	1.0127	.4376
WITHIN	247	1209.0	4.8949		
TOTAL	259	1268.5	(RANDOM EFFECTS STATISTICS)		

ETA= .2165   ETA-SQR.= .0469   (VAR. COMP= .31056 -2 %VAR. AMONG= .06)

EQUALITY OF VARIANCES: DF= 12, 39220   F= 1.7773   .0458

DAY-NO.	N	MEAN	VARIANCE	STD. DEV.
(1)	20	4.3000	3.1684	1.7800
(2)	20	3.3500	4.0289	2.0072
(3)	20	3.0000	5.0526	2.2478
(4)	20	4.0500	6.2605	2.5021
(5)	20	3.2000	3.5368	1.8806
(6)	20	3.3500	3.2921	1.8144
(7)	20	4.1000	10.726	3.2751
(8)	20	3.9000	3.6737	1.9167
(9)	20	3.4500	2.1553	1.4681
(10)	20	4.6500	7.2921	2.7004
(11)	20	3.3000	6.4316	2.5361
(12)	20	3.2500	3.4605	1.8602
(13)	20	3.6500	4.5553	2.1343
GRAND	260	3.6577	4.8978	2.2131

the exception of Serpent, there is for each only a single combination that is particularly favored and thus shows a high count in these data. Similarly, the variances of the day numbers that are incorporated into favored combinations are much higher than the variances of other day numbers (Table A.7).

Consequently, there appear to be no really specific day numbers or day names that are generally preferred for Mixtec women's names, at least in this set of data. Rather, the few specific combinations listed above seem to be somewhat favored above others, although not overwhelmingly so.

Fig. A.4   Histogram of frequency of Mixtec women's names.

The chronological distribution of these few favored names through the Mixtec sacred calendar (Table A.2) is more evenly spaced than that for men, although there is a noticeable lack of preferred names in the middle of the 260-day cycle. Whatever the significance of this distribution—whether, for example, it reflects a different importance of women in a ritual cycle—it is different from the distribution of preferred men's names throughout the 260-day cycle.

Relationship between Men's and Women's Names

Although some general features of the relationship between favored or preferred patterns of naming men and naming women are evident from their separate discussions, some attention should be focused explicitly on this relationship. This is done by extending our analysis to a consideration for each name of the percentage of individuals with that name who are male.

A one-way analysis of variance by day names shows significant differences in the average percentage of men whose names incorporate specific day names (Table A.9). However, on further inspection, it can be seen that the differences among means are essentially all functions of tendencies already observed for certain day names either to be favored or avoided for either men or women. This analysis adds nothing new to what we know already.

Table A.8 Mixtec Women's Names—Observed Frequencies by Day Number and Day Name
(significantly frequent names are indicated in bold type)

	1	2	3	4	5	6	7	8	9	10	11	12	13
Crocodile	4	3	2	2	3	3	2	1	3	7	6	3	5
Wind	4	1	0	8	8	5	4	2	4	4	2	2	2
House	6	2	4	7	5	4	1	5	2	6	1	3	2
Lizard	1	2	4	5	2	2	2	6	2	0	2	2	2
Serpent	7	2	6	3	4	2	4	4	6	**10**	**12**	2	5
Death	5	3	1	5	4	4	7	4	1	2	2	2	3
Deer	8	1	0	3	3	3	2	4	4	8	4	1	4
Rabbit	4	2	2	**11**	2	4	1	5	2	1	3	2	8
Water	3	0	4	5	2	4	5	2	4	8	5	6	1
Dog	3	4	0	3	1	0	3	2	3	4	3	4	2
Monkey	6	4	4	3	2	3	0	7	6	6	5	1	5
Grass	4	7	2	7	3	3	**10**	6	2	3	1	5	5
Reed	6	5	4	2	2	7	1	5	4	3	3	1	2
Tiger	3	7	4	2	1	2	3	4	4	4	3	7	1
Eagle	5	3	3	2	6	8	8	3	4	6	3	4	4
Vulture	4	6	4	3	6	3	6	2	4	8	0	4	2
Motion	1	4	4	2	1	2	2	2	3	4	3	1	4
Flint	3	6	9	4	3	4	7	8	5	3	4	6	4
Rain	4	2	0	2	2	2	2	4	5	1	1	5	3
Flower	5	3	3	2	4	2	**12**	2	1	5	3	4	9

A one-way analysis of variance by day number of the percentage of males named (Table A.10) exhibits no significant favoring or avoiding of day numbers at all. This was the case also for women's names alone, and shows no evident effect from the tendencies revealed earlier for certain day numbers to be favored and others to be clearly avoided for men. This lack of effect tends to reinforce to a degree our earlier interpretation that the day names carry somewhat more weight or significance in any tendencies to preferential naming than do the day numbers.

Finally, inspection of the frequency distribution of the percentage of males named on each day of the Mixtec ritual calendar reveals an almost symmetrical normal distribution, skewed very slightly positively if at all, and certainly not showing any specific high percentages that stand out as differentiable from the regular distribution of values over this curve (Fig. A.5). All in all, there is no evidence for any systematic relationship, positive or negative, between the frequencies of men's names and the frequencies of women's names. In fact, across the entire Mixtec ritual calender, the correlation between them is effectively zero (.003).

Table A.9   Analysis of Variance of Percentage of Mixtec Men's Names by Day Name

N= 260 OUT OF 260

SOURCE	DF	SUM OF SQRS.	MEAN SQR.	F-STATISTIC	SIGNIF.
BETWEEN	19	16782	883.28	2.8989	.0001
WITHIN	240	73126	304.69		
TOTAL	259	89908	(RANDOM EFFECTS STATISTICS)		

ETA= .4320   ETA-SQR.= .1867   (VAR. COMP= 44.507 %VAR. AMONG= 12.75)

DAY-NAME	N	MEAN	VARIANCE	STD. DEV.
CROCODILE	13	68.488	250.08	15.814
WIND	13	69.595	345.84	18.597
HOUSE	13	59.091	211.78	14.553
LIZARD	13	74.328	173.10	13.157
SERPENT	13	55.919	150.67	12.275
DEATH	13	58.688	140.09	11.836
DEER	13	60.901	530.44	23.031
RABBIT	13	61.301	313.05	17.693
WATER	13	58.084	360.99	19.000
DOG	13	73.615	263.71	16.239
MONKEY	13	48.704	610.72	24.713
GRASS	13	50.842	391.70	19.791
REED	13	69.689	288.59	16.988
TIGER	13	65.956	275.81	16.608
EAGLE	13	56.041	251.32	15.853
VULTURE	13	53.401	401.05	20.026
MOTION	13	74.648	295.44	17.188
FLINT	13	51.635	237.80	15.421
RAIN	13	70.253	279.53	16.719
FLOWER	13	65.471	322.07	17.946
GRAND	260	62.333	347.13	18.632

Table A.10   Analysis of Variance of Percentage of Mixtec Men's Names by Day Number

N= 260 OUT OF 260

SOURCE	DF	SUM OF SQRS.	MEAN SQR.	F-STATISTIC	SIGNIF.
BETWEEN	12	3990.1	332.51	.95591	.4918
WITHIN	247	85918	347.84		
TOTAL	259	89908	(RANDOM EFFECTS STATISTICS)		

ETA= .2107   ETA-SQR= .0444   (VAR COMP= -.76675 %VAR AMONG= -0.)

DAY-NO.	N	MEAN	VARIANCE	STD. DEV.
(1)	20	60.890	268.31	16.380
(2)	20	63.951	405.76	20.144
(3)	20	65.858	606.42	24.626
(4)	20	65.561	321.20	17.922
(5)	20	63.736	306.26	17.500
(6)	20	62.318	294.22	17.153
(7)	20	68.799	317.07	17.807
(8)	20	62.949	209.39	14.470
(9)	20	59.106	242.41	15.570
(10)	20	66.366	366.53	19.145
(11)	20	59.849	281.46	16.777
(12)	20	56.099	506.29	22.501
(13)	20	54.843	396.65	19.916
GRAND	260	62.333	347.13	18.632

Summary of Results

After finding that there were no regular cycles of frequency of names for either males or females throughout the 260-day Mixtec calendar, our analysis proceeded to investigate the frequencies of occurrence of men's and women's names in more detail.

Among Mixtec men, analysis first indicated that certain day names and day numbers were "favored," while others were "avoided," as judged by the frequencies of names incorporating them. Such avoidances appear specifically associated with the given day names or day numbers and affect all the combinations (names) in which they appear. However, favored day names and day numbers are not uniformly preferred. The frequencies of names in which they appear are highly variable. It is, in fact, only certain combinations

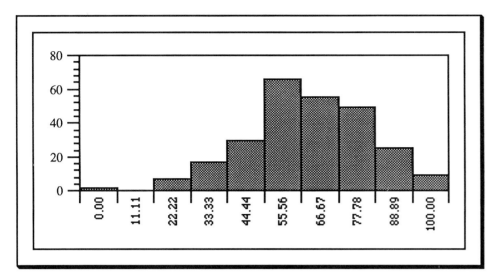

Fig. A.5 Histogram of frequency of percentages of Mixtec male names.

of day names and day numbers that occur in significantly high frequencies, although it seems that the day names are somewhat more important than the day numbers in creating the preferences for these combinations. The analysis identified the small subset of men's names that were so favored or preferred, but these showed no regular or readily interpretable temporal pattern when plotted over the 260-day calendar. Whatever "meaning" these favored names may have, it appears that it is not clearly referable to occurrence or spacing over time.

Among Mixtec women's names, patterning was less marked. There was some indication of preference for, and avoidance of, certain day names, but no significant indication of this with respect to day numbers. A limited subset of specific names, combinations of certain day names and day numbers, was identified as favored in the sense of occurring in significantly high frequencies. Again, it was the day names that appeared to be the more important component of the combinations in this set, and again, these favored combinations showed no interpretable pattern over time when plotted on the 260-day calendar.

Finally, it was found that there is no relationship or correlation in any of these results between men's and women's names, preferences, avoidances, favored combinations, or temporal patterning.

REFERENCES CITED

Acosta, Jorge R.
  1958–59 Exploraciones arqueológicas en Monte Albán, XVIII temporada. *Revista Mexicana de Estudios Antropológicos* 15:7–50.

Acosta, José de
  [1590] 1604 *The Natural and Moral History of the Indies.* 2 volumes. New York: Burt Franklin Reprint.
  [1590] 1962 *Historia Natural y Moral de las Indias,* edited by Edmundo O'Gorman. Mexico: Fondo de Cultura Económica.

Adams, Richard E. W.
  1963 A Polychrome Vessel from Altar de Sacrificios, Peten, Guatemala. *Archaeology* 16(2): 90–92.
  1971 The Ceramics of Altar de Sacrificios. *Papers of the Peabody Museum of Archaeology and Ethnology,* Vol. 63, No. 1. Cambridge, Massachusetts: Harvard University.

Adams, Richard E. W. and Robert C. Aldrich
  1980 A Reevaluation of the Bonampak Murals: A Preliminary Statement on the Paintings and Texts. In *Third Palenque Round Table, 1978,* edited by Merle Greene Robertson, Vol. V, Part 2, pp. 45–59. Austin: University of Texas Press.

Adams, Richard E. W., W. E. Brown, Jr., and T. Patrick Culbert
  1981 Radar Mapping, Archeology, and Ancient Maya Land Use. *Science* 213:1457–1463.

Adelhofer, Otto
  1963 *Codex Vindobonensis Mexicanus I: History and Description of the Codex.* Graz, Austria: Akademische Druck-u. Verlagsanstalt.
  1974 *Codex Vindobonensis Mexicanus I: History and Description of the Codex.* Graz, Austria: Akademische Druck-u. Verlagsanstalt.

Aldred, Cyril
  1973 *Akhenaten and Nefertiti.* New York: The Brooklyn Museum in association with the Viking Press.

Alvarado, Francisco de
  [1593] 1962 *Vocabulario en lengua mixteca, hecho por los padres de la orden de predicadores, que residen en ella, y últimamente recopilado y acabado por el Padre . . . Vicario de Tamazulapa, de la misma orden.* Facsimile edition, edited by Wigberto Jiménez Moreno. Mexico: Instituto Nacional Indigenista e Instituto Nacional de Antropología.

Alvarado Tezozomoc, Fernando
  [1609] 1949 *Crónica Mexicayotl.* Edited and translated by Adrián León. Publicación del Instituto de Historia, Primera Serie, No. 10. Mexico: Universidad Nacional Autónoma de México.
  [1598] 1975 *Crónica Mexicana y Códice Ramírez,* second edition. Mexico: Editorial Porrúa.

Anales de Cuauhtitlán
  [1570] 1945 *Códice Chimalpopoca. Anales de Cuauhtitlán y Leyenda de los Soles.* Edited and translated by Primo Feliciano Velázquez. Publicación del Instituto de Historia, Primera Serie, No. 1. México: Universidad Nacional Autónoma de México, Instituto de Investigaciones Históricas.

Anales de Tlatelolco
  1948 *Anales de Tlatelolco. Unos Anales Históricos de la Nación Mexicana y Códice de Tlatelolco,* edited by Heinrich Berlin and Robert H. Barlow. Fuentes para la Historia de México, No. 2. Mexico: Antigua Librería Robredo de Porrúa e Hijos.

Anderson, Arthur J. O. and Charles E. Dibble
  1952 *Florentine Codex, Book 3—The Origin*

of the Gods. Fray Bernardino de Sahagún's *General History of the Things of New Spain.* Santa Fe, New Mexico: Monographs of The School of American Research.

1953 *Florentine Codex, Book 7—The Sun, Moon, and Stars, and the Binding of the Years.* Fray Bernardino de Sahagún's *General History of the Things of New Spain.* Santa Fe, New Mexico: Monographs of The School of American Research.

1954 *Florentine Codex, Book 8—Kings and Lords.* Fray Bernardino de Sahagún's *General History of the Things of New Spain.* Santa Fe, New Mexico: Monographs of The School of American Research.

Apenes, Ola
    1954 Las páginas 21 y 22 del Códice Borbónico. *Yan: ciencias antropológicas* 2:102–104. Mexico.

Ara, D. de
    [1571] 1986 *Bocabulario en lengua tzeldal.* Manuscript in Newberry Library, Chicago. (see Ruz, Mario H. 1986)

Arana Osnaya, Evangelina
    1961 El idioma de los señores de Tepozcolula. *Anales del Instituto Nacional de Antropología e Historia* XIII: 217–230.

Arana Osnaya, Evangelina and Mauricio Swadesh
    1965 *Los elementos del mixteco antiguo.* México: Instituto Nacional Indigenista e Instituto Nacional de Antropología e Historia.

Armillas, Pedro
    1951 Mesoamerican Fortifications. *Antiquity* 25 (98):77–86.

Arzápalo Marín, Ramón
    1986 The Esoteric and Literary Language of Don Joan Canul in the Ritual of the Bacabs. *New Scholar* 10: 145–158.

Aulie, Enrique
    1961 Nombres de lugares en Chol (Maya). In *Los Mayas del Sur y sus Relaciones con*

los Nahuas Meridionales, pp. 201–205. VIII Mesa Redonda en 1959, San Cristóbal las Casas, Chiapas, Mexico.

Avendaño y Loyola, Fray Andrés de
    1696a *Relación de las entradas que hize a la conversión de los gentiles Itzaex.* Manuscript in Newberry Library, Chicago.
    1696b *Relación de las dos entradas que hize a la conversión de los gentiles Itzaex y Cehaches (1695, 1696).* Translated by Charles P. Bowditch. Manuscript in Tozzer Library, Harvard University, Cambridge, Massachusetts.

Baines, John
    1989 Communication and display: The integration of early Egyptian art and writing. *Antiquity* 63(240):471–482.

Ballesteros Gaibrois, Manuel
    1964 *Códices matritenses de la Historia General de las Cosas de la Nueva España.* Colección Chimalistac de Libros y Documentos acerca de la Nueva España, Volumenes 19, 20. Madrid.

Bancroft, Hubert Howe
    1882–90 *Works.* 39 volumes. San Francisco.

Barbachano, F. C.
    1946 Monografía de los tzotziles de San Miguel Mitontik. *Manuscripts on Middle American Cultural Anthropology No. 6.* Chicago: University of Chicago. (microfilm)

Bard, Kathryn
    1981 Origins of Egyptian Writing and Royal Iconography. Manuscript in possession of author.

Barlow, Robert Hayward
    1945 La Crónica X: versiones coloniales de la historia de los Mexica Tenochca. *Revista Mexicana de Estudios Antropológicos* 7: 65–87. Mexico.
    1946 Materiales para una cronología del imperio de los Mexica. *Revista Mexicana de Estudios Antropológicos* 8:207–215. México.
    1949a The Extent of the Empire of the Culhua Mexica. *Ibero-Americana* 28.

Berkeley: University of California Press.
    1949b El Códice Azcatitlán. *Journal de la Société des Américanistes* 38:101–135. Paris.

Barlow, Robert H. and Byron McAfee, editors
    1949 Diccionario de elementos fonéticos en escritura jeroglífica (Códice Mendocino). *Publicación del Instituto de Historia, Primera Serie, no. 9.* México: Universidad Nacional Autónoma de México.

Barrera Rubio, Alfredo
    1980 Mural Paintings of the Puuc Region in Yucatán. In *Third Palenque Round Table, 1978,* edited by Merle Greene Robertson, Vol. V, Part 2, pp. 173–182. Austin: University of Texas Press.

Barrera Vásquez, Alfredo
    1939 El códice Pérez. *Revista Mexicana de Estudios Mexicanos* 3:69–83. Mexico.
    1943 Horóscopos mayas ó el prognóstico de los 20 signos del tzolkin según los libros de Chilam Balam, de Kaua y de Mani. *Registro de Cultura Yucateca* 1(6):4–33. Mexico.
    1949 The Maya Chronicles. *Carnegie Institution of Washington, Publication 585, Contribution 48.* Washington, D.C.

Barrera Vásquez, Alfredo et al.
    1980 *Diccionario Maya Cordemex. Maya-Español, Español-Maya.* Mérida: Ediciones Cordemex.

Barthel, Thomas S.
    1956 Resultados preliminares del desciframiento de las kohau-rongorongo de la isla de Pascua. *Runa* 7:233–241. Buenos Aires.
    1968 Historisches in dem klassischen Mayainschriften. *Zeitschrift für Ethnologie* 93(1–2):119–156.
    1969 *Intentos de lectura de los afijos de los jeroglíficos en los códices mayas.* Seminario de Estudios de la Escritura Maya, Cuaderno 2. Mexico.
    1980 Mourning and Consolation: Themes of the Palenque Sarcophagus. In *Third Palenque Round Table, 1978,* edited by

Merle Greene Robertson, Vol. V, Part 2, pp. 81–90. Austin: University of Texas Press.

1982 Veritable "Texts" in Teotihuacan Art? *The Masterkey* 56 (1):4–11. Los Angeles: The Southwest Museum.

Becerra, Marcos E.

1933 El antiguo calendario chiapaneco: estudio comparativo entre este i los calendarios precoloniales maya, quiche, nahoa. Manuscript in Tozzer Library, Harvard University, Cambridge. 76 pp.

Beltrán de Santa Rosa, Pedro

1746 *Arte del idioma reducido a sucintas reglas, y semilexicón yucateco.* Mexico (2nd edition, Mérida, 1859).

Berdan, Frances F.

1975 *Trade, Tribute, and Market in the Aztec Empire.* Ph.D. dissertation, University of Texas at Austin.

Berendt, Carl Hermann

1957 Calendario cakchiquel de los indios de Guatemala, 1685. *Antropología e Historia de Guatemala* IX (2):17–29. Guatemala City: Instituto de Antropología e Historia de Guatemala.

Berlin, Heinrich

1947 *Fragmentos desconocidos del Códice de Yanhuitlán y otras investigaciones mixtecas.* Mexico.

1958 El glifo "emblema" en las inscripciones mayas. *Journal de la Société des Américanistes* (n.s.) 47:111–119. Paris.

1959 Glifos nominales en el sarcófago de Palenque. *Humanidades* 2 (10):1–8. Guatemala: Universidad de San Carlos.

1963 The Palenque Triad. *Journal de la Société des Américanistes* 52:91–99.

1965 The Inscription of the Temple of the Cross at Palenque. *American Antiquity* 30(3):330–342.

1968a Estudios epigráficos II. *Antropología e Historia de Guatemala* XX (1):13–24. Guatemala City: Instituto de Antropología e Historia de Guatemala.

1968b The Tablet of the 96 Glyphs at Palenque, Chiapas, Mexico. *Middle American Research Institute, Tulane University, Publication 26*, pp. 135–150. New Orleans.

1973 Beiträge zum Verständnis der Inschriften von Naranjo. *Bulletin de la Société Suisse des Américanistes*, no. 37, pp. 7–14. Geneva: Musée d'Ethnographie.

1977 *Signos y Significados en las Inscripciones Mayas.* Guatemala: Instituto Nacional del Patrimonio Cultural de Guatemala.

Berlo, Janet Catherine

1989 Early Writing in Central Mexico: *In Tlilli In Tlapalli* before A.D. 1000. In *Mesoamerica after the Decline of Teotihuacan A.D. 700–900,* edited by Richard A. Diehl and Janet Catherine Berlo, pp. 19–47. Washington, D.C.: Dumbarton Oaks Research Library and Collection, Trustees for Harvard University.

Bernal, Ignacio

1965 Archaeological Synthesis of Oaxaca. In *Handbook of Middle American Indians, Vol. 3: Archaeology of Southern Mesoamerica, Part 2,* edited by Robert Wauchope and Gordon R. Willey, pp. 788–813. Austin: University of Texas Press.

Berrin, Kathleen, editor

1988 *Feathered Serpents and Flowered Trees: Reconstructing the Murals of Teotihuacan.* San Francisco: Fine Arts Museum.

Beyer, Hermann

1931 The Maya day-signs Been and Kan. *American Anthropologist* 33: 199–208.

1936a Another Maya hieroglyph for day. *American Antiquity* 2: 13–14.

1936b The lunar glyphs of the supplementary series at Quirigua. *El México Antiguo* 3 (11–12): 1–11. Mexico.

1937 Lunar glyphs of the supplementary series at Piedras Negras. *El México Antiguo* 4:75–82. Mexico.

Bittmann Simons, Bente

1968 *Los Mapas de Cuauhtinchan y la Historia Tolteca Chichimeca.* Instituto Nacional de Antropología, Serie Investigación, No. 15. México.

Blanton, Richard E.

1978 *Monte Albán: Settlement Patterns at the Ancient Zapotec Capital.* New York: Academic Press.

Boturini Benaducci, L.

1746 *Idea de una nueva historia general de la América Septentrional.* Madrid.

Bowditch, Charles P.

1900 The Lords of the Night and the Tonalamatl of the Codex Borbonicus. *American Anthropologist* 2: 145–154.

1901 Memoranda on the Maya Calendars used in the Books of Chilam Balam. *American Anthropologist* 3: 129–138.

1910 *The Numeration, Calendar Systems, and Astronomical Knowledge of the Mayas.* Cambridge, Massachusetts. Privately printed.

Brand, Donald D.

1943 An historical sketch of geography and anthropology in the Tarascan region, Part 1. *New Mexico Anthropologist* 6–7(2): 37–108. Albuquerque.

Bray, Warwick

1968 *Everyday Life of the Aztecs.* New York: G. P. Putnam's Sons.

1972 The City State in Central Mexico at the Time of the Spanish Conquest. *Journal of Latin American Studies* 4(2):161–185.

Bricker, Victoria R.

1986 A Grammar of Mayan Hieroglyphs. *Middle American Research Institute, Tulane University, Publication 56.* New Orleans.

Brinton, Daniel Garrison, editor

1882 *The Maya Chronicles.* Brinton's Library of Aboriginal American Literature, Number 1. Philadelphia.

1885 *The Annals of the Cakchiquels.* Brinton's Library of Aboriginal American Literature, Number 6. Philadelphia.

Buck, Sir Peter H. (Te Rangi Hiroa)

1932 Ethnology of Tongareva. *Bernice P. Bishop Museum Bulletin 92.* Honolulu.

Bunzel, Ruth
1952 *Chichicastenango, a Guatemalan Village.* Locust Valley, New York: J. J. Augustin Publisher.

Burgoa, Francisco de
[1670] 1934a *Palestra historial de virtudes y exemplares apostólicos . . .* Publicaciones del Archivo General de la Nación, Vol. 24. Mexico: Talleres Gráficos de la Nación.
[1674] 1934b *Geográfica descripción.* Publicaciones del Archivo General de la Nación, Vols. 25–26. Mexico: Talleres Gráficos de la Nación.

Burkitt, R.
1930–31 The Calendar of Soloma and of other Indian Towns. *Man,* Vol. 30:103–107; Vol. 31:146–150. London.

Burland, Cottie Arthur
1955 *The Selden Roll.* Berlin: Ibero-Americanischen Bibliothek zu Berlin.
1965 *Codex Egerton 2895.* Graz, Austria: Akademische Druck-u. Verlagsanstalt.

Butinov, N. A.
1962 *Korotkoukhie i dlinnoukhie na ostrove Paskhi. Short-ears and Long-ears on Easter Island.* Translated from Russian. Manuscript published for the National Science Foundation and the Smithsonian Institution. Washington, D.C.: Office of Technical Services, U.S. Department of Commerce.

Butinov, N. A. and Y. V. Knorozov
1957 Preliminary Report on the Study of the Written Language of Eastern Island. *Polynesian Society Journal* 66(1):5–17. Wellington, New Zealand.

Calendario Mexicano, Latino y Castellano
1919 *Boletín de la Biblioteca Nacional* XII (5): 195–221. Mexico.

Canseco, Alonso de
[1580] 1905 Relación de Tlacolula y Mitla hecha en los días 12 y 23 de agosto respectivamente. *Papeles de Nueva España, Segunda Serie, Geografía y Estadística,* Vol. 4, edited by Francisco del Paso y Troncoso, pp. 144–154. Madrid: Est. Tipográfico "Sucesores de Rivadeneyra."

Carmack, Robert M.
1973 *Quichean Civilization: The Ethnohistoric, Ethnographic, and Archaeological Sources.* Berkeley: University of California Press.

Carneiro, Robert L.
1970 A Theory of the Origin of the State. *Science* 169:733–738.
1981 The Chiefdom: Precursor of the State. In *The Transition to Statehood in the New World,* edited by Grant D. Jones and Robert R. Kautz, pp. 37–79. Cambridge: Cambridge University Press.
1987 Further Reflections on Resource Concentration and Its Role in the Rise of the State. In *Studies in the Neolithic and Urban Revolution: The V. Gordon Childe Colloquium, Mexico, 1986,* edited by Linda Manzanilla, pp. 245–260. BAR International Series 349. Oxford, England.
1988 The Circumscription Theory. In *American Behavioral Scientist* 31 (4): 497–511. Newbury Park, California: Sage Publications.

Carochi, Horacio
[1645] 1910 *Compendio del arte de la lengua mexicana del Padre Horacio Carochi,* edited by Ignacio de Paredes. Puebla: Talleres de Imprenta "El Escritorio" Zaragoza 8.

Carrasco, Davíd
1982 *Quetzalcoatl and the Irony of Empire: Myths and Prophecies in the Aztec Tradition.* Chicago: University of Chicago Press.

Carrasco Pizana, Pedro
1971 Social Organization of Ancient Mexico. In *Handbook of Middle American Indians, Vol. 10: Archaeology of Northern Mesoamerica, Part 1,* edited by Robert Wauchope (general editor), Gordon F. Ekholm and Ignacio Bernal (volume editors), pp. 349–375. Austin: University of Texas Press.
1974 Sucesión y alianzas matrimoniales en la dinastía teotihuacana. *Estudios de Cultura Náhuatl* 11:235–242.
1984 Royal Marriages in Ancient Mexico. In *Explorations in Ethnohistory: Indians of Central Mexico in the Sixteenth Century,* edited by Herbert R. Harvey and Hanns J. Prem, pp. 41–81. Albuquerque: University of New Mexico Press.

Caso, Alfonso
1928 *Las estelas zapotecas.* Monografías del Museo Nacional de Arqueología, Historia y Etnografía. Publicaciones de la Secretaría de Educación Pública. México: Talleres Gráficos de la Nación.
1932a La tumba 7 de Monte Albán es mixteca. *Universidad de México* 4 (2):117–150.
1932b Monte Albán, richest archaeological find in America. *National Geographic Magazine* LXII:487–512.
1938 *Exploraciones en Oaxaca, quinta y sexta temporadas, 1936–1937.* Instituto Panamericano de Geografía e Historia, Publicación 34. Mexico.
1939 La correlación de los años azteca y cristiano. *Revista Mexicana de Estudios Antropológicos* 3 (1):11–45.
1947 Calendario y escritura de las antiguas culturas de Monte Albán. In *Obras Completas de Miguel Othón de Mendizábal, Un Homenaje.* Vol. 1, pp. 5–102. México: Talleres de la Nación.
1949 El Mapa de Teozacoalco. *Cuadernos Americanos* Año VIII, Vol. 47, No. 5, pp. 145–181. Mexico.
1950 Explicación del reverso del Códice Vindobonensis. *Memoria de El Colegio Nacional,* Vol. V, No. 5, pp. 9–46.
1951 Base para la sincronología mixteca y cristiana. *Memoria de El Colegio Nacional,* Vol. VI, No. 6, pp. 49–66.
1954 *Interpretación del Códice Gómez de Orozco.* Mexico: Talleres de Impresión de

Estampillas y Valores.

1955 Der Jahresanfang bei den mixteken. *Baessler-Archiv* n.s. 3:47–53.

1956 El calendario mixteco. *Historia Mexicana* 5, No. 4, pp. 481–497. Mexico.

1958a Fragmento de Genealogía de los Príncipes Mexicanos (Boban no. 72). *Journal de la Société des Américanistes de Paris,* n.s. vol. 47, pp. 21–31.

1958b El Mapa de Xochitepec. 32nd International Congress of Americanists (Copenhagen), pp. 458–466.

1960 *Interpretation of the Codex Bodley 2858.* Translated by Ruth Morales and John Paddock. Mexico: Sociedad Mexicana de Antropología.

1961 Los lienzos mixtecos de Ihuitlán y Antonio de León. In *Homenaje a Pablo Martínez del Río,* edited by Ignacio Bernal, Jorge Gurría, Santiago Genovés, and Luis Aveleyra Arroyo de Anda, pp. 237–274. Mexico: Instituto Nacional de Antropología e Historia.

1964a *Interpretación del Códice Selden 3135 (A.2)/Interpretation of the Codex Selden 3135 (A.2).* Mexico: Sociedad Mexicana de Antropología.

1964b El Lienzo de Filadelfia. *Homenaje a Fernando Márquez-Miranda,* pp. 135–144. Madrid and Seville, Spain.

1964c Los Señores de Yanhuitlán. *Acta of the 35th International Congress of Americanists,* Vol. 1, pp. 437–448. Mexico.

1965a Zapotec Writing and Calendar. In *Handbook of Middle American Indians, Vol. 3, Archaeology of Southern Mesoamerica, Part 2,* edited by Robert Wauchope (general editor) and Gordon R. Willey (volume editor), pp. 931–947. Austin: University of Texas Press.

1965b Mixtec Writing and Calendar. In *Handbook of Middle American Indians, Vol. 3, Archaeology of Southern Mesoamerica, Part 2,* edited by Robert Wauchope (general editor) and Gordon R. Willey (volume editor), pp. 948–961. Austin: University of Texas Press.

1966a *Interpretación del Códice Colombino/ Interpretation of the Codex Colombino.* Mexico.

1966b The Lords of Yanhuitlán. In *Ancient Oaxaca: Discoveries in Mexican Archeology and History,* edited by John Paddock, pp. 313–335. Stanford: Stanford University Press.

1967 *Los Calendarios Prehispánicos.* Instituto de Investigaciones Históricas, Serie de Cultura Náhuatl, Monografías 6. Mexico: Universidad Nacional Autónoma de México.

1977 *Reyes y reinos de la mixteca,* Vol. 1. Mexico: Fondo de Cultura Económica.

1979 *Reyes y reinos de la mixteca,* Vol. 2. Mexico: Fondo de Cultura Económica.

Caso, Alfonso and Ignacio Bernal
1952 Urnas de Oaxaca. *Memorias del Instituto de Antropología e Historia* 2. Mexico: Instituto Nacional de Antropología e Historia.

Caso, Alfonso and Lorenzo Gamio
1961 Informe de exploraciones en Huamelulpan. Manuscript in Archivo del Instituto Nacional de Antropología, Mexico City.

Caso, Alfonso and Mary Elizabeth Smith
1966 *Interpretación del Códice Colombino/ Interpretation of the Codex Colombino* [by Caso]; *Las Glosas del Códice Colombino/ The Glosses of the Codex Colombino* [by Smith]. Mexico: Sociedad Mexicana de Antropología.

Castillo, Cristóbal del
1908 Fragmentos de la obra general sobre historia de los mexicanos, escrita en lengua náhuatl . . . a fines del siglo XVI. *Biblioteca Náhuatl* 5, Tradiciones migraciones, Cuaderno 2, pp. 43–107. Florence.

Castillo Farreras, Victor M.
1974 Relación Tepepulca de los Señores de Mexico Tenochtitlán y de Acolhuacan *Estudios de Cultura Náhuatl* 11:183–226. Mexico City.

Chase, Arlen F. and Diane Z. Chase
1987 *Investigations at The Classic Maya City of Caracol, Belize: 1985–1987.* Pre-Columbian Art Research Institute, Monograph 3. San Francisco: Pre-Columbian Art Research Institute.

Childe, Vere Gordon
1946 *What Happened in History.* New York: Penguin Books.

1950 The Urban Revolution. *Town Planning Review* 21:3–17.

1951 *Man Makes Himself.* New American Library of World Literature.

Chimalpahin Cuauhtlehuanitzin, Domingo Francisco de San Antón Muñón
1889 *Annales.* Edited and translated by Remi Siméon. Bibliotheque Linguistique Américaine, 12. Paris: Maisonneuve et Ch. Leclerc.

1958 Bas Memorial Breve Acerca de la Fundación de la Ciudad de Culhuacan. Nahuatl text with German translation by Walter Lehmann and Gerdt Kutscher. *Quellenwerke zur alten Geschichte Amerikas aufgezeichnet in den Sprachen der Eingeborenen,* VII. Stuttgart.

1963 *Die Relationen Chimalpahin's zur Geschichte Mexiko's.* Vol. 1, edited by G. Zimmermann. Hamburg: University of Hamburg.

[1606–30] 1965 *Relaciones Originales de Chalco-Amaquemecan.* Edited and translated from Nahuatl, and with an introduction by Silvia Rendón. Biblioteca Americana, Serie Literatura Indígena. Mexico: Fondo de Cultura Económica.

Ciudad Real, Antonio
[1588] 1873 *Relación breve y verdadera de algunas cosas de las muchas que sucedieron al Padre Fray Alonso Ponce en las provincias de la Nueva España.* 2 volumes. Madrid: Imprenta de la Viuda de Calero.

Clark, James Cooper, editor

1912 The Story of "Eight Deer" in Codex Colombino. London: Taylor and Francis.

1938 *Codex Mendoza. The Mexican Manuscript Known as the Collection of Mendoza and Preserved in the Bodleian Library, Oxford.* 3 volumes. London: Waterlow & Sons, Ltd. [Original codex, 1540s]

Clavigero, Francisco Javier
1787 *The History of Mexico.* Translated from Italian by Charles Cullen. 2 volumes. London.

1945 *Historia antigua de México.* Primera edición del original escrito en castellano por el autor. *Colección de Escritores Mexicanos,* edited by Mariano Cuevas, 4 volumes. Mexico: Editorial Porrúa.

Cline, Howard F.
1966 The Oztoticpac Lands Map of Texcoco 1540. *Quarterly Journal of the Library of Congress* 23(2): 77–115. Washington, D.C.

Cline, Susan L.
1986 *Colonial Culhuacan, 1580–1600: A Social History of an Aztec Town.* Albuquerque: University of New Mexico Press.

Closs, Michael P.
1985 The Dynastic History of Naranjo: The Middle Period. In *Fourth Palenque Round Table,* Merle Greene Robertson (general editor) and Virginia M. Fields (volume editor), Vol. 7, pp. 65–78. San Francisco: Pre-Columbian Art Research Institute.

Codex Azcatitlán (see Barlow 1949b)
Codex Becker I/II (see Nowotny 1961)
Codex Bodley (see Caso 1960; Corona Núñez 1964, Vol. II)
Codex Boturini
1944 *Códice Boturini (Tira de la Peregrinación).* Mexico: Librería Anticuaria.
Codex Chimalpopoca (see also Anales de Cuauhtitlán)
1975 *Códice Chimalpopoca: Anales de Cuauhtitlan y Leyenda de los Soles.*

Mexico: Universidad Autónoma de México.
Codex Colombino (see Caso and Smith 1966)
Codex Florentine (see Anderson and Dibble 1950–1969)
Codex Matritense del Real Palacio (see Paso y Troncoso 1906, Vol. 7)
Codex Matritense de la Real Academia de la Historia (see Paso y Troncoso 1907, Vol. 8)
Codex Matritenses (see Sahagún 1964, Ballesteros Gaibrois et al. 1964)
Codex Mendoza (see Clark 1938; Corona Núñez 1964, Vol. I)
Codex Muro (see Smith 1973b)
Codex Nuttall (see Nuttall 1902)
Codex Ramírez (see Alvarado Tezozomoc 1949, 1975)
1944 *Códice Ramírez.* Mexico: Editorial Leyenda.
Codex Ríos (see Codex Vaticanus A)
Codex Sánchez Solís (see Burland 1965)
Codex Selden (see Caso 1964)
Codex Telleriano-Remensis (see Hamy 1899; Kingsborough 1831–1848; Corona Núñez 1964, Vol. I)
Codex Vaticanus A (see *Il manuscritto Messicano Vaticano 3738, detto il codice Rios.* Loubat reproduction. Rome.)
Codex Vienna (see Lehmann and Smital 1929; Adelhofer 1963, 1974; Caso 1950)
Codex Vindobonensis [Vienna] (see Lehmann and Smital 1929; Adelhofer 1963, 1974; Caso 1950)
Codex Xolotl (see Dibble 1951)
Coe, Michael D.
1962 *Mexico.* New York: Frederick A. Praeger.
1965 The Olmec Style and its Distribution. In *Handbook of Middle American Indians, Vol. 3: Archaeology of Southern Mesoamerica, Part 2,* edited by Robert Wauchope and Gordon R. Willey, pp. 739–775. Austin: University of Texas Press.
1968 *America's First Civilization.* New York: American Heritage.

1973 The Iconology of Olmec Art. In *The Iconography of Middle American Sculpture,* pp. 1–12. New York: The Metropolitan Museum of Art.
1984 *Mexico.* Third edition, revised and enlarged. New York: Thames and Hudson.
Coe, Michael D. and Richard A. Diehl
1980 *In the Land of the Olmec.* 2 volumes. Austin: University of Texas Press.
Coe, William R.
1967 *Tikal: A Handbook of the Ancient Maya Ruins.* Philadelphia: University Museum, University of Pennsylvania.
Coggins, Clemency C.
1975 *Painting and Drawing Styles at Tikal: An Historical and Iconographic Reconstruction.* Ph.D. dissertation, Harvard University, Cambridge.
Colección de documentos inéditos . . .
1864–84 *Colección relativos al descubrimiento, conquista y organización de las antiguas posesiones Españolas de América y Oceania sacados de los Archivos del Reino.* 42 volumes. Madrid.
1885–1900 *Colección relativos al descubrimiento, conquista y organización de las antiguas posesiones Españolas de Ultramar,* second series, 13 volumes. Madrid.
Conrad, Geoffrey W. and Arthur A. Demarest
1984 *Religion and Empire: The Dynamics of Aztec and Inca Expansionism.* Cambridge: Cambridge University Press.
Córdova, Fray Juan de
[1578a] 1942 *Vocabulario en lengua zapoteca.* Mexico: Pedro Charte y Antonio Ricardo.
[1578b] 1886 *Arte en lengua zapoteca.* Morelia, Mexico: Pedro Balli.
Corona Núñez, José
1964 Explicaciones. In *Antigüedades de México, basadas en la recopilación de Lord Kingsborough.* 2 volumes. Mexico: Secretaría de Hacienda y Crédito Público.
Coronel, Juan
1620 Arte de la Lengua Maya. In *Diccionario*

de Motul: Maya-Español, edited by Juan
Martínez Hernández (1929). Mérida:
Compañía Tipográfica Yucateca, S.A.

Covarrubias, Miguel
1942 Origen y desarrollo del estilo artístico
"Olmeca." In *Mayas y Olmecas,* pp. 46–
49. Mexico: Sociedad Mexicana de
Antropología.
1946 El arte olmeca o de La Venta.
Cuadernos Americanos V(4):153–179.

Crónica Mexicana (see Alvarado Tezozomoc
1975)

Crónica Mexicayotl (see Alvarado Tezozomoc
1949)

Crónica X (see Barlow 1945)

Dahlgren de Jordán, Barbro
1954 *La Mixteca: su cultura e historia
prehispánicas.* Colección Cultura México
11. Mexico: Imprenta Universitaria.

Dark, Philip and Joyce Plesters
1959 The Palimpsests of Codex Selden:
Recent Attempts to Reveal the Covered
Pictographs. *33rd International Congress
of Americanists,* Vol. II, pp. 530–539. San
José de Costa Rica.

Dávalos Hurtado, Eusebio and Arturo Romano
Pacheco
1954 Estudio preliminar de los restos
osteológicos encontrados en la tumba del
Templo de las Inscripciones, Palenque.
Appendix to "Exploraciones en Palenque:
1952" by Alberto Ruz Lhuillier. In *Anales
del Instituto Nacional de Antropología e
Historia,* Vol. 6, pp. 107–110. Mexico:
Secretaría de Educación Pública.
1973 Estudio preliminar de los restos
osteológicos encontrados en la tumba del
Templo de las Inscripciones, Palenque. In
El Templo de las Inscripciones, edited by
Alberto Ruz Lhuillier, pp. 253–254.
Mexico: Instituto Nacional de
Antropología e Historia.

Davies, C. Nigel
1968 *Los señoríos independientes del imperio
azteca.* Serie Historia, Vol. XIX. Mexico:
Instituto Nacional de Antropología e
Historia.
1973 *Los Mexica: Primeros Pasos Hacia el
Imperio.* Instituto de Investigaciones
Históricas, Serie de Cultura Náhuatl,
Monografías 14. Mexico: Universidad
Nacional Autónoma de México.
1980 *The Toltec Heritage: From the Fall of
Tula to the Rise of Tenochtitlan.* Norman:
University of Oklahoma Press.
1987 *The Aztec Empire. The Toltec
Resurgence.* Norman: University of
Oklahoma Press.

Davies, W. V.
1987 *Egyptian Hieroglyphs.* Berkeley and
Los Angeles: University of California
Press and British Museum.

del Río, Juan
[1580] 1905 Relación de Taliztaca. In *Papeles
de Nueva España: segunda serie,
Geografía y Estadística,* Vol. 4, edited by
Francisco del Paso y Troncoso, pp. 177–
182. Madrid: Est. Tipográfico "Sucesores
de Rivadeneyra."

Demarest, Arthur
1990 *The Vanderbilt University Petexbatún
Regional Archaeological Project. Findings
of the 1990 Season.* A Progress Report to
the National Geographic Society.
Manuscript.

Diakonoff, Igor M.
1974 Structure of Ancient Society and State
in Early Dynastic Sumer. *Monographs of
the Ancient Near East,* Vol. 1, fascicle 3.
Malibu, California: Undena Publications.

Díaz del Castillo, Bernal
[1560s] 1908–16 *The True History of the
Conquest of New Spain.* Translated by
Alfred P. Maudslay, 5 volumes. London:
Hakluyt Society.
1963 *The Conquest of New Spain.* Translated
by J. M. Cohen. Baltimore: Penguin
Books.

Dibble, Charles E.
1940 The Ancient Mexican Writing System.
*Museum of Anthropology, Archaeology
and Ethnology Papers* No. 2:10–31. Salt
Lake City: University of Utah Press.
1942 *Códice en Cruz.* Mexico: Talleres
Linotipográficos Numancia.
1951 *Códice Xolotl.* Publicaciones del
Instituto de Historia, Primera serie, No.
22. Mexico: Universidad Autónoma de
México.
1955 The Aztec Writing System. In *Readings
in Anthropology,* first edition, edited by E.
Adamson Hoebel, Jesse D. Jennings, and
Elmer R. Smith, pp. 296–302. New York:
McGraw-Hill.
1966 The Aztec Writing System. In *Readings
in Anthropology,* second edition, edited by
Jesse D. Jennings and E. Adamson Hoebel,
pp. 270–277. New York: McGraw-Hill.
1971 Writing in Central Mexico. In
*Handbook of Middle American Indians,
Vol. 10: Archaeology of Northern
Mesoamerica,* Part 1, edited by Robert
Wauchope, Gordon F. Ekholm, and Ignacio
Bernal, pp. 322–332. Austin: University of
Texas Press.
1981 *Códice en Cruz.* 2 volumes. Salt Lake
City: University of Utah Press.

Dibble, Charles E. and Arthur J. O. Anderson
1957 *Florentine Codex, Book 4—The
Soothsayers. Book 5: The Omens.* Fray
Bernardino de Sahagún's *General History
of the Things of New Spain.* Santa Fe,
New Mexico: Monographs of The School
of American Research and the Museum of
New Mexico.
1961 *Florentine Codex, Book 10—The
People.* Santa Fe, New Mexico:
Monographs of the School of American
Research and the Museum of New Mexico.
1969 *Florentine Codex, Book 6—Rhetoric
and Moral Philosophy.* Santa Fe, New
Mexico: Monographs of the School of
American Research and the Museum of
New Mexico.

Diringer, David
1962 *Writing.* New York: Praeger.

Drucker, Philip
1952 La Venta, Tabasco: A Study of Olmec

Ceramics and Art. *Smithsonian Institution, Bureau of American Ethnology, Bulletin 153.* Washington, D.C.: Smithsonian Institution.

Drucker, Philip, Robert F. Heizer, and Robert J. Squier
1959 Excavations at La Venta, Tabasco, 1955. *Smithsonian Institution, Bureau of American Ethnology, Bulletin 170.* Washington, D.C.: Smithsonian Institution.

Durán, Fray Diego
1867–80 *Historia de la Nueva España y Islas de Tierra Firme.* 2 volumes. Preface by J. F. Ramírez. Mexico.
1951 *Historia de la Nueva España y Islas de Tierra Firme.* 2 volumes. Mexico: Editora Nacional.
[1581] 1964 *The Aztecs: The History of the Indies of New Spain,* translated with notes by Doris Heyden and Fernando Horcasitas. New York: Orion Press.
[1581] 1967 *Historia de las Indias de Nueva España e Islas de la Tierra Firme,* 2 volumes, edited by Angel María Garibay K. Editorial Porrúa, nos. 36–37 [vols. 1–2]. México: Editorial Porrúa Hnos.
[1570, 1579] 1971 *Book of the Gods and Rites* and *The Ancient Calendar.* Translated by Fernando Horcasitas and Doris Heyden. Norman: University of Oklahoma Press.

Dütting, Dieter
1965 Das Knoten-Graphem bei den Maya. *Zeitschrift für Ethnologie* 90:66–103. Braunschweig.
1970 On the Inscription and Iconography of Kuná-Lacanhá Lintel 1. *Zeitschrift für Ethnologie* 95:196–219. Braunschweig.
1972 Hieroglyphic Miscellanea. *Zeitschrift für Ethnologie* 97:220–256. Braunschweig.
1976 The Great Goddess in Classic Maya Religious Belief. *Zeitschrift für Ethnologie* 101:41–146. Braunschweig.
1978 Birth, Inauguration, and Death in the Inscriptions of Palenque, Chiapas, Mexico.

In *Tercera Mesa Redonda de Palenque, Vol. IV,* edited by Merle Greene Robertson and Donnan Call Jeffers, pp. 183–214. Monterey, California: Herald Printers.
1979 On the Hieroglyphic Inscriptions of Three Monuments from Piedras Negras, Guatemala. *Zeitschrift für Ethnologie* 104:17–63. Braunschweig.
1985 On the Astronomical Background of Mayan Historical Events. In *Fifth Palenque Round Table, 1983,* edited by Merle Greene Robertson (general editor) and Virginia M. Fields (volume editor), Vol. VII: 261–274. San Francisco: Pre-Columbian Art Research Institute.

Edmonson, Munro Sterling
1974/ed. *Sixteenth-Century Mexico: The Work of Sahagún.* A School of American Research Book. Albuquerque: University of New Mexico Press.
1982 *The Ancient Future of the Itza: The Book of Chilam Balam of Tizimin.* Austin: University of Texas Press.
1986 *Heaven Born Merida and Its Destiny: The Book of Chilam Balam of Chumayel.* Austin: University of Texas Press.
1988 *The Book of the Year: Middle American Calendrical Sytems.* Salt Lake City: University of Utah Press.

Elam, J. Michael
1989 Defensible and Fortified Sites. In *Monte Albán's Hinterland, Part II,* Vol. 1, by Stephen A. Kowalewski, Gary M. Feinman, Laura Finsten, Richard E. Blanton, and Linda Nicholas, pp. 385–407. *Memoirs of the Museum of Anthropology, University of Michigan, No. 23.* Ann Arbor.

Ellul, Jacques
1965 *Propaganda: The Formation of Men's Attitudes.* New York: Alfred A. Knopf.
1973 *Propaganda: The Formation of Men's Attitudes.* Reprint. New York: Vintage Books.

Emery, Walter B.
1961 *Archaic Egypt.* New York: Viking

Penguin Books.

Espíndola, Nicolás de
[1580] 1905 Relación de Chichicapa y su Partido. In *Papeles de Nueva España: segunda serie, Geografía y Estadística,* Vol. 4, edited by Francisco del Paso y Troncoso, pp. 115–143. Madrid: Est. Tipográfico "Sucesores de Rivadeneyra."

Falkenstein, Adam
1936 *Archaische Texte aus Uruk.* Leipzig.

Fash, William L., Jr.
1988 A New Look at Maya Statecraft from Copán, Honduras. *Antiquity* 62:157–169.

Flannery, Kent V. and Joyce Marcus
1976 Formative Oaxaca and the Zapotec Cosmos. *American Scientist* 64(4):374–383.
1983a/eds. *The Cloud People: Divergent Evolution of the Zapotec and Mixtec Civilizations.* New York: Academic Press.
1983b The Growth of Site Hierarchies in the Valley of Oaxaca: Part I. In *The Cloud People: Divergent Evolution of the Zapotec and Mixtec Civilizations,* edited by Kent V. Flannery and Joyce Marcus, pp. 53–64. New York: Academic Press.
1990 Borrón, y Cuenta Nueva: Setting Oaxaca's Archaeological Record Straight. In *Debating Oaxaca Archaeology,* edited by Joyce Marcus, pp. 17–69. *Anthropological Papers of the Museum of Anthropology, University of Michigan,* No. 84. Ann Arbor.

Florentine Codex
1950–69 Manuscript in Nahuatl, by Fray Bernardino de Sahagún. Translated by Arthur J. O. Anderson and Charles E. Dibble. (See Anderson and Dibble; Dibble and Anderson 1957, 1961, 1969.)

Follett, Prescott H.F.
1932 War and Weapons of the Maya. *Middle American Research Institute, Tulane University, Publication 4.* New Orleans.

Foncerrada de Molina, Marta
1980 Mural Painting in Cacaxtla and Teotihuacán Cosmopolitism. In *Third*

Palenque Round Table, 1978, edited by Merle Greene Robertson, Vol. V, Part 2, pp. 183–198. Austin: University of Texas Press.

Förstemann, Ernst W.
1880 *Codex Dresdensis.* Die Mayahandschrift der Königlichen öffentlichen Bibliothek zu Dresden. Leipzig: Verlag der A. Naumannseschen Lichtdruckerei.
1902 Commentar zur Madrider Mayahandschrift (Codex Tro-Cortesianus). Danzig: Verlag von L. Sauniers Buchhandlug.

Fragment de l'Histoire des Anciens Mexicains
1981 Geschichte der Azteken: Codex Aubin und vewandte Dokumente. Translated and edited by Walter Lehmann and Gerdt Kutscher. *Quellenwerke zur Alten Geschichte Amerikas aufgezeichnet in den Sprachen der Eingeborenen,* Vol. 13. Berlin: Gebr. Mann Verlag.

Frankfort, Henri
1951 *The Birth of Civilization in the Near East.* Bloomington: Indiana University Press. Reprint, Anchor Books, 1956.
1961 *Ancient Egyptian Religion.* New York: Harper and Row.
1978 *Kingship and the Gods.* Chicago: University of Chicago Press, Phoenix Books.

Frankfort, Henri and H. A. Frankfort
1977 Introduction. In *The Intellectual Adventure of Ancient Man: An Essay on Speculative Thought in the Ancient Near East,* pp. 3–27. Chicago: University of Chicago Press.

Freidel, David A.
1986 Maya Warfare: An example of peer polity interaction. In *Peer Polity Interaction and Socio-Political Change,* edited by Colin Renfrew and John F. Cherry, pp. 93–108. Cambridge: Cambridge University Press.

Fried, Morton H.
1967 *The Evolution of Political Society.* New York: Random House.

Furst, Jill Leslie
1977 The Tree Birth Tradition in the Mixteca, Mexico. *Journal of Latin American Lore* 3 (2):183–226.
1978 Codex Vindobonensis Mexicanus I: A commentary. *Institute for Mesoamerican Studies, Publication No. 4.* Albany: State University of New York at Albany.

García, Fray Gregorio
[1607] 1981 *Origen de los Indios del Nuevo Mundo.* Estudio preliminar de Franklin Pease G. Y. 3rd edition, Biblioteca Americana, Mexico. Fondo de Cultura Económica. (1st ed. 1607, Valencia; 2nd edition, Andrés González de Barcía, Madrid 1729).

Gardiner, Sir Alan
1957 *Egyptian Grammar, Being an Introduction to the Study of Hieroglyphs.* 3rd edition, revised. Oxford: Oxford University Press.
1978 *Egypt of the Pharaohs: an introduction.* Oxford: Oxford University Press.

Garibay K., Angel María
1940 *Llave del Náhuatl.* Otumba, Mexico: Imprenta Mayli.

Gates, W. E.
1931a The 13 Ahaus in the Kaua ms. *Maya Society Quarterly* 1:2–20. Baltimore.
1931b Glyph Studies. *Maya Society Quarterly* 1:32–33. Baltimore.
1931c A Lanquin Kekchi Calendar. *Maya Society Quarterly* 1: 29–32. Baltimore.

Gaxiola, Margarita
1976 *Excavaciones en San Martín Huamelulpan, Oaxaca, 1974.* Tesis profesional, Escuela Nacional de Antropología, Mexico.

Gay, José Antonio
1881 *Historia de Oaxaca.* 2 volumes. Mexico.

Gearing, Frederick
1958 The Structural Poses of Eighteenth Century Cherokee Villages. *American Anthropologist* 60:1148–1157.
1962 Priests and Warriors: Social Structures

for Cherokee Politics in the Eighteenth Century. *American Anthropological Association Memoirs* No. 93. Washington, D.C.: American Anthropological Association.

Gelb, Ignace J.
1963 *A Study of Writing.* Chicago: University of Chicago Press.
1974 *A Study of Writing.* Second edition. Chicago: University of Chicago Press.

Genealogía de los Príncipes Mexicanos
1958 Fragmento de Genealogía de los Príncipes Mexicanos (Boban no. 72), edited by Alfonso Caso. *Journal de la Société des Américanistes de Paris,* n.s. Vol. 47:21–31.

Gibson, Charles
1964 *The Aztecs Under Spanish Rule: A History of the Indians of the Valley of Mexico, 1519–1810.* Stanford: Stanford University Press.

Gillespie, Susan D.
1989 *The Aztec Kings: The Construction of Rulership in Mexica History.* Tucson: University of Arizona Press.

Glass, John B.
1964 *Catálogo de la Colección de Códices.* Mexico: Museo Nacional de Antropología.

Glass, John B. and Donald Robertson
1975 A Census of Native Middle American Pictorial Manuscripts. In *Handbook of Middle American Indians,* edited by Robert Wauchope (general editor), Howard F. Cline (volume editor), and Charles Gibson and H. B. Nicholson (associate editors), Vol. 14, Part 3: 81–252. Austin: University of Texas Press.

Goldman, Irving
1955 Status rivalry and cultural evolution in Polynesia. *American Anthropologist* 57:680–697.
1970 *Ancient Polynesian Society.* Chicago: University of Chicago Press.

Gómez de Orozco, Federico de
1945 Costumbres, fiestas, enterramientos y diversas formas de proceder de los indios

de Nueva España. *Tlalocan* 2 (1):37–63.
Mexico, D.F.

Goodman, J. T.
1897 The Archaic Maya Inscriptions.
Appendix in *Biologia Centrali-Americana*
by Alfred P. Maudslay, 1889–1902.

Gordon, George Byron
1902 The Hieroglyphic Stairway. Ruins of
Copán. *Memoirs of the Peabody Museum
of American Archaeology and Ethnology*,
Vol. 1, No. 6. Cambridge, Massachusetts:
Harvard University.

Gorenstein, Shirley
1973 Tepexi el Viejo: A Postclassic Fortified
Site in the Mixteca-Puebla Region of
Mexico. *Transactions of the American
Philosophical Society* 63, Part 1.
Philadelphia: American Philosophical
Society.

Gossen, Gary H.
1974 *Chamulas in the World of the Sun:
Time and Space in a Maya Oral Tradition.*
Cambridge, Massachusetts: Harvard
University Press.

Graham, Ian
1967 Archaeological Explorations in El Peten,
Guatemala. *Middle American Research
Institute, Tulane University, Publication*
33. New Orleans.

Graham, Ian and Eric von Euw
1975 *Naranjo.* Corpus of Maya Hieroglyphic
Inscriptions 2 (1). Cambridge,
Massachusetts: Peabody Museum, Harvard
University.

Grove, David C.
1981 Olmec Monuments: Mutilation as a
clue to meaning. In *The Olmec and their
Neighbors: Essays in Memory of Matthew
W. Stirling*, edited by Elizabeth P. Benson,
pp. 48–68. Washington, D.C.: Dumbarton
Oaks Research Library and Collection,
Trustees for Harvard University.
1984 *Chalcatzingo: Excavations on the
Olmec Frontier.* London: Thames and
Hudson.

Guiteras Holmes, Calixta
1946 Informe de San Pedro Chenalhó
(Chiapas). *Manuscripts on Middle
American Cultural Anthropology No. 14.*
Chicago: University of Chicago.
(microfilm)

Hamy, E. T.
1899 *Codex Borbonicus. Manuscrit Mexicain
de la Biblioteque du Palais Bourbon.* Paris.

Hassig, Ross
1988 *Aztec Warfare: Imperial Expansion and
Political Control.* Norman: University of
Oklahoma Press.

Haviland, William A.
1977 Dynastic Genealogies from Tikal,
Guatemala: Implications for Descent and
Political Organization. *American
Antiquity* 42: 61–67.
1985 Population and Social Dynamics: The
Dynasties and Social Structure of Tikal.
Expedition 27 (3): 34–41. Philadelphia:
University Museum, University of
Pennsylvania.

Hernández Spina, V.
1854 Kalendaryo conservado hasta el dia por
los sacerdotes del sol en Ixtlauacan, pueblo
descendiente de la nación quiché. In *Maya
Society Quarterly* 1: 72–75 (1932) [article
by E. J. W. Bunting]. Baltimore.

Herrera y Tordesillas, Antonio de
[1601] 1947 *Historia general de los hechos de
los castellanos en las islas y tierra firme
del Mar Océano*, Vol. VI. Madrid:
Academia de la Historia.

Hicks, Frederic
1979 "Flowery War" in Aztec History.
American Ethnologist 6(1):87–92.

Hirth, Kenneth G.
1989 Militarism and Social Organization at
Xochicalco, Morelos. In *Mesoamerica after
the Decline of Teotihuacán A.D. 700–900*,
edited by Richard A. Diehl and Janet
Catherine Berlo, pp. 69–81. Washington,
D.C.: Dumbarton Oaks Research Library
and Collection.

Hodge, Mary G.
1984 Aztec City-States. *Studies in Latin
American Ethnohistory & Archaeology,
Vol. III. Memoirs of the Museum of
Anthropology, University of Michigan,
No. 18.* Ann Arbor.

Hodges, Denise C.
1989 Agricultural Intensification and
Prehistoric Health in the Valley of Oaxaca,
Mexico. *Prehistory and Human Ecology of
the Valley of Oaxaca, Vol. 9. Memoirs of
the Museum of Anthropology, University
of Michigan, Number 22.* Ann Arbor.

Houston, Stephen D.
1984 An Example of Homophony in Maya
Script. *American Antiquity* 49:790–805.
1987 Appendix II: Notes on Caracol
Epigraphy and Its Significance. In
*Investigations at The Classic Maya City of
Caracol, Belize: 1985–1987*, edited by
Arlen F. Chase and Diane Z. Chase,
pp. 85–100. Pre-Columbian Art Research
Institute, Monograph 3. San Francisco:
Pre-Columbian Art Research Institute.

Houston, Stephen D. and Peter Mathews
1985 *The Dynastic Sequence of Dos Pilas,
Guatemala.* Pre-Columbian Art Research
Institute, Monograph 1. San Francisco:
Pre-Columbian Art Research Institute.

Isaac, Barry L.
1983a The Aztec Flowery War: A
Geopolitical Explanation. *Journal of
Anthropological Research* 39:415–432.
1983b Aztec Warfare: Goals and Battlefield
Comportment. *Ethnology* 22:121–131.

Ixtlilxochitl, Fernando de Alva
1891 *Obras Históricas: Relaciones*, Tomo I,
edited by Alfredo Chavero. Mexico:
Secretaría de Fomento.
1892 *Obras Históricas: Historia Chichimeca*,
Tomo II, edited by Alfredo Chavero.
Mexico: Secretaría de Fomento.
1952 *Obras Históricas*, 2 volumes. Mexico:
Editora Nacional.
1975 *Obras Históricas*, Vol. 1, edited by
Edmundo O'Gorman. Mexico: Universidad
Nacional Autónoma de México.
1977 *Obras Históricas*, Vol. 2, edited by

Edmundo O'Gorman. Mexico: Universidad Nacional Autónoma de México.

Jansen, Maarten
1982 *Huisi Tacu. Estudio interpretativo de un libro mixteco antiguo: Codex Vindobonensis Mexicanus I.* Amsterdam: Centrum voor Studie en Documentatie van Latijns Amerika.

Jiménez Moreno, Wigberto
1961 Diferente Principio del Año Entre Diversos Pueblos y Sus Consecuencias Para la Cronología Prehispánica. *El México Antiguo* 9:137–152. Mexico.

Jiménez Moreno, Wigberto and Salvador Mateos Higuera
1940 *Códice de Yanhuitlán.* México: Instituto Nacional de Antropología e Historia.

Jones, Christopher
1977 Inauguration Dates of Three Late Classic Rulers of Tikal, Guatemala. *American Antiquity* 42:28–60.
1988 The Life and Times of Ah Cacau, Ruler of Tikal. In *Primer Simposio Mundial Sobre Epigrafía Maya,* 107–120. Guatemala: Asociación Tikal.

Jones, Christopher and Linton Satterthwaite
1982 The Monuments and Inscriptions of Tikal: The Carved Monuments. *Tikal Report 33A, Monograph of the University Museum, No. 44.* Philadelphia: The University Museum, University of Pennsylvania.

Jonghe, Edouard de
1906 Le calendrier Mexicain. *Journal de la Société des Américanistes* 3 (2): 197–227. Paris.

Justeson, John S.
1975 The Identification of the Emblem Glyph of Yaxha, El Peten. In *Studies in Ancient Mesoamerica, II,* edited by John A. Graham, pp. 123–129. University of California Archaeological Research Facility, Contribution 27. Berkeley: University of California.

Justeson, John S. and Lyle Campbell, editors
1984 *Phoneticism in Mayan Hieroglyphic Writing.* Institute for Mesoamerican Studies, Publication No. 9. Albany: State University of New York.

Karttunen, Frances
1983 *An Analytical Dictionary of Nahuatl.* Austin: University of Texas Press.

Keen, Benjamin
1963 *Life and Labor in Ancient Mexico. The Brief and Summary Relation of the Lords of New Spain,* by Alonso de Zorita. Translated and with an introduction by Benjamin Keen. New Brunswick, New Jersey: Rutgers University Press.

Kelley, David H.
1962a A History of the Decipherment of Maya Script. *Anthropological Linguistics* 4(8):1–48. Bloomington: Indiana University.
1962b Glyphic Evidence for a Dynastic Sequence at Quirigua, Guatemala. *American Antiquity* 27 (3):323–335.
1965 The Birth of the Gods at Palenque. *Estudios de Cultura Maya* 5:93–134. Mexico: Universidad Nacional Autónoma de México.
1968 Kakupacal and the Itzas. *Estudios de Cultura Maya* 7:255–268.
1976 *Deciphering the Maya Script.* Austin: University of Texas Press.

Kemp, Barry J.
1989 *Ancient Egypt. Anatomy of a Civilization.* New York: Routledge, Chapman, and Hall.

King, Mark B.
1988 *Mixtec Political Ideology: Historical Metaphors and the Poetics of Political Symbolism.* Ph.D. dissertation, University of Michigan, Ann Arbor.
1990 Poetics and Metaphor in Mixtec Writing. *Ancient Mesoamerica* 1:141–151. Cambridge: Cambridge University Press.

Kingsborough, Lord Edward King
1831–48 *Antiquities of Mexico.* 9 volumes. London: R. Havell.
1964 *Antigüedades de México.* (See Corona Núñez 1964, Vols.I, II).

Kirch, Patrick Vinton
1984 *The Evolution of the Polynesian Chiefdoms.* Cambridge: Cambridge University Press.

Kirchhoff, Paul
1943 Mesoamérica. *Acta Americana* I:92–107.
1950 The Mexican Calendar and the Founding of Tenochtitlan-Tlatelolco. *Transactions of the New York Academy of Sciences,* Series II, 12 (4): 126–132. New York.
1954/55 Calendarios Tenochca, Tlatelolca y Otros. *Revista Mexicana de Estudios Antropológicos* 14 (1–2):257–267.
1956 Composición étnica y organización política de Chalco según las *Relaciones* de Chimalpahin. *Revista Mexicana de Estudios Antropológicos* 14:297–302.

Kirchhoff, Paul, Lina Odena Güemes, and Luis Reyes García, editors
1976 *Historia tolteca-chichimeca.* Mexico: CISINAH, Instituto Nacional de Antropología e Historia.

Knorozov, Yuri V.
1955 La escritura de los antiguos mayas (ensayo de descifrado). In Russian and Spanish. Reprinted from *Sovetskaya Etnografiya* 1. Moscow: USSR Academy of Sciences Press.
1958a New data on the Maya written language. *Proceedings of the 32nd International Congress of Americanists* (Copenhagen, 1956), pp. 456–475. Copenhagen.
1958b The problem of the study of the Maya hieroglyphic writing. *American Antiquity* 23:284–291.
1967 Selected chapters from *The Writing of the Maya Indians.* Translated by Sophie Coe. Tatiana Proskouriakoff, collaborating editor. Russian Translation Series of the Peabody Museum of Archaeology and Ethnology, Harvard University, Vol. IV. Cambridge, Massachusetts.

Kowalewski, Stephen A., Gary M. Feinman, Laura Finsten, Richard E. Blanton, and Linda M. Nicholas
1989 Monte Albán's Hinterland, Part II: The Prehispanic Settlement Patterns in Tlacolula, Etla, and Ocotlán, the Valley of Oaxaca, Mexico. *Memoirs of the Museum of Anthropology, University of Michigan, No. 23.* 2 volumes. Ann Arbor: Museum of Anthropology.

Kramer, Samuel Noah
1961 *Sumerian Mythology.* New York: Harper and Brothers.
1963 *The Sumerians: Their History, Culture, and Character.* Chicago: University of Chicago Press.

Kubler, George
1969 Studies in Classic Maya Iconography. *Memoirs of the Connecticut Academy of Arts & Sciences,* Vol. XVIII. New Haven, Connecticut.
1972 The Paired Attendants of the Temple Tablets at Palenque. *Sociedad Mexicana de Antropología* XII: 317–328.
1974 Mythological Ancestries in Classic Maya Inscriptions. In *Primera Mesa Redonda de Palenque, Part II,* edited by Merle Greene Robertson, pp. 23–43. Pebble Beach, California: Robert Louis Stevenson School.
1980 Eclecticism at Cacaxtla. In *Third Palenque Round Table, 1978,* edited by Merle Greene Robertson, Vol. V, Part 2, pp. 163–172. Austin: University of Texas Press.

Kubler, George and Charles Gibson
1951 The Tovar Calendar. *Memoirs of the Connecticut Academy of Arts and Sciences,* Vol. XI. New Haven, Connecticut.

La Farge, Oliver
1934 Pre-Columbian Dates and the Maya Correlation Problem. *Maya Research* 1:109–124. New York.
1947 *Santa Eulalia. The Religion of a Cuchumatán Indian Town.* University of Chicago Publications in Anthropology. Chicago: University of Chicago.

La Farge, Oliver and Douglas Byers
1931 The Year Bearer's People. *Middle American Research Institute, Tulane University, Publication 3.* New Orleans.

Lafaye, J.
1972 *Manuskript Tovar.* Graz, Austria.

Landa, Fray Diego de
1566 (see Tozzer 1941)

Langley, James C.
1986 *Symbolic Notation of Teotihuacan: Elements of Writing in a Mesoamerican Culture of the Classic Period.* British Archaeological Reports, International Series, No. 313. Oxford, England.

Laufer, Berthold
1907 A Theory of the Origin of Chinese Writing. *American Anthropologist* 9:487–492.

Leach, Edmund R.
1976 *Culture and Communication: The logic by which symbols are connected.* Cambridge: Cambridge University Press.

Lee, Thomas A., Jr.
1969 The Artifacts of Chiapa de Corzo, Chiapas, Mexico. *Papers of the New World Archaeological Foundation, No. 26.* Provo, Utah: Brigham Young University.

Lehmann, Walter
1905 Die fünf im Kindbett gestorbenen Frauen des Westens und die fünf Götter des Südens in der mexicanischen Mythologie. *Zeitschrift für Ethnologie* XXXVII:848–871. Berlin.

Lehmann, Walter and Ottokar Smital
1929 *Codex Vindobonensis Mexicanus I.* Vienna: Verlag fur Nord u. Sudamerika Kunstanstalt M. Jaffé.

Leigh, Howard
1966 The Evolution of Zapotec Glyph C. In *Ancient Oaxaca: Discoveries in Mexican Archeology and History,* edited by John Paddock, pp. 256–269. Stanford: Stanford University Press.

León, Nicolás

1933 *Códice Sierra.* Mexico: Imprenta del Museo Nacional de Arqueología, Historia, y Etnografía.

León-Portilla, Miguel
1961 *Los antiguos mexicanos a través de sus crónicas y cantares.* México: Fondo de Cultura Económica.
1980 *Toltecáyotl: aspectos de la cultura náhuatl.* México: Fondo de Cultura Económica.

Lerner, Daniel, editor
1951 *Propaganda in War and Crisis.* New York: George W. Stewart.

Lincoln, J. S.
1942 The Maya Calendar of the Ixil of Guatemala. *Carnegie Institution of Washington, Publication 528, Contribution 38.* Washington, D.C.

Lizardi Ramos, César
1954 Los acompañados del Xiuhmolpilli en el Códice Borbónico. *Yan: ciencias antropológicas* 2:95–101. Mexico.

Long, Richard C. E.
1919 The highest known Maya number. *Man* 19:39–42. London.
1923a Maya High Numbers. *Man* 23:66–69. London.
1923b The Burner Period of the Mayas. *Man* 23:173–176. London.
1925 Some Maya time Periods. *Proceedings of the 21st International Congress of Americanists,* pp. 574–580. Göteborg.
1926 The Zouche Codex. *Journal of the Royal Anthropological Institute of Great Britain and Ireland,* Vol. LVI, pp. 239–258. London.
1931 The Correlation of Maya and Christian Chronology. *Journal of Royal Anthropological Society* 61:407–412.

López Austin, Alfredo
1961 *La Constitución Real de México-Tenochtitlan.* Mexico City.
1973 *Hombre-Dios, religión y política en el mundo náhuatl.* México: Universidad Nacional Autónoma de México.

López de Cogolludo, Diego de

1688 *Historia de Yucatán.* Madrid.
1867–68 *Historia de Yucatán.* 2 volumes. Mérida: Manuel Aldana Rivas. Third edition.

López de Molina, Diana
1977 Los murales prehispánicos de Cacaxtla. *Boletín del Instituto Nacional de Antropología e Historia* 20:2–8. Mexico.

López de Molina, Diana and Daniel Molina
1976 Los murales de Cacaxtla. *Boletín del Instituto Nacional de Antropología e Historia* 16:3–8. Mexico.

Lothrop, Samuel K.
1924 Tulum. An Archaeological Study of the East Coast of Yucatan. *Carnegie Institution of Washington, Publication 335.* Washington, D.C.

Lounsbury, Floyd G.
1973 On the Derivation and Reading of the 'Ben-Ich' Prefix. In *Mesoamerican Writing Systems*, edited by Elizabeth P. Benson, pp. 99–143. Washington, D.C.: Dumbarton Oaks Research Library and Collection, Trustees for Harvard University.
1974a Pacal. In *Primera Mesa Redonda de Palenque, Part I*, edited by Merle Greene Robertson, p. ii. Pebble Beach, California: Robert Louis Stevenson School.
1974b The Inscription of the Sarcophagus Lid at Palenque. In *Primera Mesa Redonda de Palenque, Part II*, edited by Merle Greene Robertson, pp. 5–19. Pebble Beach, California: Robert Louis Stevenson School.
1976 A Rationale for the Initial Date of the Temple of the Cross at Palenque. In *The Art, Iconography, and Dynastic History of Palenque, Part III: Proceedings of the Segunda Mesa Redonda de Palenque*, edited by Merle Greene Robertson, pp. 211–224. Pebble Beach, California: Robert Louis Stevenson School.
1978 Maya Numeration, Computation, and Calendrical Astronomy. In *Dictionary of Scientific Bibliography*, edited by Charles Coulson Gillispie, XV: 759–818. New York: Charles Scribner's Sons.
1980 Some Problems in the Interpretation of the Mythological Portion of the Hieroglyphic Text of the Temple of the Cross at Palenque. In *Third Palenque Round Table, 1978*, edited by Merle Greene Robertson, Vol. V, Part 2, pp. 99–115. Austin: University of Texas Press.
1982 Astronomical Knowledge and its Uses at Bonampak, Mexico. In *Archaeoastronomy in the New World*, edited by Anthony F. Aveni, pp. 143–168. New York: Cambridge University Press.
1984 Glyphic Substitutions: Homophonic and Synonymic. In *Phoneticism in Mayan Hieroglyphic Writing*, edited by John S. Justeson and Lyle Campbell, pp. 167–184. Albany: Institute for Mesoamerican Studies, State University of New York.
1985 The Identities of the Mythological Figures in the "Cross Group" of Inscriptions at Palenque. In *Fourth Round Table of Palenque, 1980*, edited by Merle Greene Robertson and Elizabeth P. Benson, Vol. 6, pp. 45–58. San Francisco: Pre-Columbian Art Research Institute.

Ludendorff, Hans
1931 Die astronomische Bedeutung der Seiten 51 und 52 des Dresdener Maya-Kodex. Untersuchungen zur Astronomie der Maya, No. 3. *Sitzungsberichten der Preussischen Akademie der Wissenschaften.* Berlin: W. de Gruyter.
1933 Die astronomischen Inschriften in Yaxchilan. Untersuchungen zur Astronomie der Maya, No. 7. *Sitzungsberichten der Preussischen Akademie der Wissenschaften.* Berlin: W. de Gruyter.
1934 Die astronomische Inschrift aus dem Tempel des Kreuzes in Palenque. Untersuchungen zur Astronomie der Maya, No. 9. *Sitzungsberichten der Preussischen Akademie der Wissenschaften.* Berlin: W. de Gruyter.
1938 Astronomische Inschriften in Palenque. Untersuchungen zur Astronomie der Maya, No. 12. *Sitzungsberichten der Preussischen Akademie der Wissenschaften.* Berlin: W. de Gruyter.
1940 Astronomische Inschriften in Piedras Negras und Naranjo. Untersuchungen zur Astronomie der Maya, No. 13. *Sitzungsberichten der Preussischen Akademie der Wissenschaften.* Berlin: W. de Gruyter.
1942 Astronomische Inschriften in Naranjo. Untersuchungen zur Astronomie der Maya, No. 14. *Sitzungsberichten der Preussischen Akademie der Wissenschaften.* Berlin: W. de Gruyter.

Maler, Teobert
1901–03 Researches in the Central Portion of the Usumatsintla Valley. *Memoirs of the Peabody Museum of Archaeology and Ethnology, Harvard University*, Vol. 2, Nos. 1, 2. Cambridge, Massachusetts.

Mapa de Xochitepec (see Caso 1958b)

Marcus, Joyce
1970 The Role of Writing in Revealing Ideological and Social Systems. Paper prepared for Anthropology 115a, a course taught by Professor Hallam L. Movius, Department of Anthropology, Harvard University, Cambridge.
1973 Territorial Organization of the Lowland Classic Maya. *Science* 180:911–916.
1974a The Iconography of Power among the Classic Maya. *World Archaeology* 6 (1):83–94.
1974b *An Epigraphic Approach to the Territorial Organization of the Lowland Classic Maya.* Ph.D. dissertation, Harvard University, Cambridge.
1976a *Emblem and State in the Classic Maya Lowlands: an epigraphic approach to territorial organization.* Washington, D.C.: Dumbarton Oaks, Center for Pre-Columbian Studies.
1976b The Origins of Mesoamerican Writing. In *Annual Review of*

Anthropology 5:35–67. Palo Alto, California.

1976c The Iconography of Militarism at Monte Albán and Neighboring Sites in the Valley of Oaxaca. In *The Origins of Religious Art and Iconography in Pre-Classic Mesoamerica*, edited by Henry B. Nicholson, pp. 123–139. Los Angeles: Latin American Center, University of California, Los Angeles.

1978 Archaeology and religion: a comparison of the Zapotec and Maya. *World Archaeology* 10 (2):172–191.

1980 Zapotec Writing. *Scientific American* 242 (2):50–64.

1982a The Aztec Monuments of Acalpixcan. In *Prehispanic Settlement Patterns in the Southern Valley of Mexico: The Chalco-Xochimilco Region*, by Jeffrey R. Parsons, Elizabeth M. Brumfiel, Mary H. Parsons, and David J. Wilson. *Memoirs of the Museum of Anthropology, University of Michigan*, No. 14, Appendix 4, pp. 475–485. Ann Arbor.

1982b The Plant World of the Sixteenth- and Seventeenth-Century Lowland Maya. In *Maya Subsistence: Studies in Memory of Dennis E. Puleston*, edited by Kent V. Flannery, pp. 239–273. New York: Academic Press.

1983a On the Nature of the Mesoamerican City. In *Prehistoric Settlement Patterns: Essays in Honor of Gordon R. Willey*, edited by Evon Z. Vogt and Richard M. Leventhal, pp. 195–242. Albuquerque: University of New Mexico Press and Cambridge, Massachusetts: Peabody Museum, Harvard University.

1983b Lowland Maya Archaeology at the Crossroads. *American Antiquity* 48(3):454–488.

1983c The genetic model and the Otomangueans. In *The Cloud People: Divergent Evolution of the Zapotec and Mixtec Civilizations*, edited by Kent V. Flannery and Joyce Marcus, pp. 4–9. New York: Academic Press.

1983d The first appearance of Zapotec writing and calendrics. In *The Cloud People: Divergent Evolution of the Zapotec and Mixtec Civilizations*, edited by Kent V. Flannery and Joyce Marcus, pp. 91–96. New York: Academic Press.

1983e The conquest slabs of Building J, Monte Albán. In *The Cloud People: Divergent Evolution of the Zapotec and Mixtec Civilizations*, edited by Kent V. Flannery and Joyce Marcus, pp. 106–108. New York: Academic Press.

1983f The style of the Huamelulpan stone monuments. In *The Cloud People: Divergent Evolution of the Zapotec and Mixtec Civilizations*, edited by Kent V. Flannery and Joyce Marcus, pp. 125–126. New York: Academic Press.

1983g Stone monuments and tomb murals of Monte Albán IIIa. In *The Cloud People: Divergent Evolution of the Zapotec and Mixtec Civilizations*, edited by Kent V. Flannery and Joyce Marcus, pp. 137–143. New York: Academic Press.

1983h Rethinking the Zapotec Urn. In *The Cloud People: Divergent Evolution of the Zapotec and Mixtec Civilizations*, edited by Kent V. Flannery and Joyce Marcus, pp. 144–148. New York: Academic Press.

1983i Lintel 2 at Xoxocotlán. In *The Cloud People: Divergent Evolution of the Zapotec and Mixtec Civilizations*, edited by Kent V. Flannery and Joyce Marcus, pp. 150–152. New York: Academic Press.

1983j Teotihuacán visitors on Monte Albán monuments and murals. In *The Cloud People: Divergent Evolution of the Zapotec and Mixtec Civilizations*, edited by Kent V. Flannery and Joyce Marcus, pp. 175–181. New York: Academic Press.

1983k Changing patterns of stone monuments after the fall of Monte Albán. In *The Cloud People: Divergent Evolution of the Zapotec and Mixtec Civilizations*, edited by Kent V. Flannery and Joyce Marcus, pp. 191–197. New York: Academic Press.

1983l The reconstructed chronology of the later Zapotec rulers, A.D. 1415–1563. In *The Cloud People: Divergent Evolution of the Zapotec and Mixtec Civilizations*, edited by Kent V. Flannery and Joyce Marcus, pp. 301–308. New York: Academic Press.

1983m Aztec military campaigns against the Zapotec: The documentary evidence. In *The Cloud People: Divergent Evolution of the Zapotec and Mixtec Civilizations*, edited by Kent V. Flannery and Joyce Marcus, pp. 314–318. New York: Academic Press.

1983n Monte Albán's Tomb 7. In *The Cloud People: Divergent Evolution of the Zapotec and Mixtec Civilizations*, edited by Kent V. Flannery and Joyce Marcus, pp. 282–285. New York: Academic Press.

1983o A Synthesis of the Cultural Evolution of the Zapotec and Mixtec. In *The Cloud People: Divergent Evolution of the Zapotec and Mixtec Civilizations*, edited by Kent V. Flannery and Joyce Marcus, pp. 355–360. New York: Academic Press.

1983p Zapotec Religion. In *The Cloud People: Divergent Evolution of the Zapotec and Mixtec Civilizations*, edited by Kent V. Flannery and Joyce Marcus, pp. 345–351. New York: Academic Press.

1984 Mesoamerican Territorial Boundaries: Reconstructions from Archaeology and Hieroglyphic Writing. *Archaeological Review from Cambridge* 3 (2):48–62. Cambridge.

1987 *The Inscriptions of Calakmul. Royal Marriage at a Maya City in Campeche, Mexico*. Technical Report of the Museum of Anthropology, University of Michigan, No. 21. Ann Arbor.

1988 Comment on William T. Sanders' and Deborah L. Nichols' article entitled "Ecological Theory and Cultural Evolution in the Valley of Oaxaca." *Current*

Anthropology 29(1): 60–61. New York: Wenner-Gren Foundation for Anthropological Research.

1989a Zapotec Chiefdoms and The Nature of Formative Religions. In *Regional Perspectives on the Olmec*, edited by Robert J. Sharer and David C. Grove, pp. 148–197. Santa Fe, New Mexico: School of American Research Advanced Seminar Series, and Cambridge: Cambridge University Press.

1989b From Centralized Systems to City-States: Possible Models for the Epiclassic. In *Mesoamerica After the Decline of Teotihuacan A.D. 700–900*, edited by Richard A. Diehl and Janet Catherine Berlo, pp. 201–208. Washington, D.C.: Dumbarton Oaks Research Library and Collection, Trustees for Harvard University.

1991 First Dates. *Natural History* 4:26–29. New York: American Museum of Natural History.

n.d.a Royal Families, Royal Texts: Examples from the Zapotec and Maya. In *Mesoamerican Elites: An Archaeological Assessment*, edited by Arlen F. Chase and Diane Z. Chase. Norman: University of Oklahoma Press.

n.d.b Religión maya. In *Historia General de Guatemala*, Tomo I, Sección 1.5.9.4., edited by Jorge Luján Muñoz. Guatemala City.

n.d.c Ancient Maya Political Organization. In *Lowland Maya Civilization in the Eighth Century A.D.*, edited by Jeremy A. Sabloff and John S. Henderson. Washington, D.C.: Dumbarton Oaks Research Library and Collection, Trustees for Harvard University.

n.d.d *Ancient Zapotec Monuments and Political History.* Manuscript.

Marcus, Joyce and Kent V. Flannery
1978 Ethnoscience of the Sixteenth-Century Valley Zapotec. In *The Nature and Status of Ethnobotany*, edited by Richard I. Ford.

Anthropological Papers of the Museum of Anthropology, University of Michigan, No. 67, pp. 51–79. Ann Arbor.

1983 The Postclassic Balkanization of Oaxaca. In *The Cloud People: Divergent Evolution of the Zapotec and Mixtec Civilizations*, edited by Kent V. Flannery and Joyce Marcus, pp. 217–226. New York: Academic Press.

n.d. Ancient Zapotec Ritual and Religion: An Application of the Direct Historical Approach. In *The Ancient Mind*, edited by Colin Renfrew and Ezra Zubrow. Cambridge: Cambridge University Press.

Marcus, Joyce, Kent V. Flannery, and Ronald Spores
1983 The Cultural Legacy of the Oaxacan Preceramic. In *The Cloud People: Divergent Evolution of the Zapotec and Mixtec Civilizations*, edited by Kent V. Flannery and Joyce Marcus, pp. 36–39. New York: Academic Press.

Markman, Charles W.
1981 Prehispanic Settlement Dynamics in Central Oaxaca, Mexico. A View from the Miahuatlán Valley. *Vanderbilt University Publications in Anthropology*, No. 26. Nashville.

Martínez Gracida, Manuel
1883 *Colección de Cuadros Sinópticos de los pueblos, haciendas y ranchos del Estado libre y soberano de Oaxaca*. Oaxaca: Gobierno del Estado de Oaxaca.

1888 Catálogo etimológico de los nombres de los pueblos, haciendas y ranchos del estado de Oaxaca. *Boletín de la Sociedad Mexicana de Geografía y Estadística*, 4a época, 1(5–6):285–438.

Martínez Hernández, Juan, editor
1927 *Crónicas mayas*. Mérida: Compañia Tipográfica Yucateca.

[1585?] 1929 *Diccionario de Motul: Maya-Español*. Atribuido a Fray Antonio de Ciudad Real y Arte de la Lengua Maya por Fray Juan Coronel. Mérida: Compañia Tipográfica Yucateca, S.A.

Mata, Fray Juan de
[1580] 1905 Relación de Teozapotlan. In *Papeles de Nueva España: segunda serie, Geografía y Estadística*, edited by Francisco del Paso y Troncoso, Vol. 4, pp. 190–195. Madrid: Est. Tipográfico "Sucesores de Rivadeneyra."

Mathews, Peter
1980 Notes on the Dynastic Sequence of Bonampak, Part 1. In *Third Palenque Round Table, 1978*, edited by Merle Greene Robertson, Vol. V, Part 2, pp. 60–73. Austin: University of Texas Press.

Mathews, Peter and Linda Schele
1974 Lords of Palenque—The Glyphic Evidence. In *Primera Mesa Redonda de Palenque, Part 1*, edited by Merle Greene Robertson, pp. 63–76. Pebble Beach, California: Robert Louis Stevenson School.

Matrícula de Tributos
1890 In *Monumentos del Arte Mexicano*, by Antonio Peñafiel, Vol. 2, Plates 228–259. Berlin.

Maudslay, Alfred P.
1889–1902 Archaeology. In *Biologia Centrali-Americana: Contributions to the Knowledge of the Fauna and Flora of Mexico and Central America*. 6 volumes. London: R. H. Porter and Dulau & Co.

Miller, Arthur G.
1973 *The Mural Painting of Teotihuacán*. Washington, D.C.: Dumbarton Oaks Research Library and Collection, Trustees for Harvard University.

Miller, Jeffrey H.
1974 Notes on a Stelae Pair Probably from Calakmul, Campeche, Mexico. In *Primera Mesa Redonda de Palenque, Part I*, edited by Merle Greene Robertson, pp. 149–162. Pebble Beach, California: Robert Louis Stevenson School.

Miller, Mary Ellen
1986 *The Murals of Bonampak*. Princeton, New Jersey: Princeton University Press.

Millon, Clara

1973 Painting, Writing, and Polity in Teotihuacan, Mexico. *American Antiquity* 38:294–314.

1988 A Reexamination of the Teotihuacan Tassel Headdress Insignia. In *Feathered Serpents and Flowering Trees: Reconstructing the Murals of Teotihuacan*, edited by Kathleen Berrin, pp. 114–134. San Francisco: The Fine Arts Museum.

Millon, René

1988 Where *Do* They All Come From? The Provenance of the Wagner Murals from Teotihuacán. In *Feathered Serpents and Flowering Trees: Reconstructing the Murals of Teotihuacan*, edited by Kathleen Berrin, pp. 78–113. San Francisco: The Fine Arts Museum.

Molina, Fray Alonso de

[1571] 1944 *Vocabulario en Lengua Castellana y Mexicana y Mexicana y Castellana*. Colección de Incunables Americanos, Vol. IV. Madrid: Ediciones Cultura Hispánica.

[1571] 1977 *Vocabulario en Lengua Castellana y Mexicana y Mexicana y Castellana*. Edición facsimile. México, D.F.: Editorial Porrúa, S.A.

Moortgat, A.

1969 *The Art of Ancient Mesopotamia*. London: Phaidon.

Morán, Francisco

1935 *Arte y Diccionario en lengua Cholti, a manuscript copied from the Libro Grande of Fray Pedro* (sic) *Moran of about 1625*. Baltimore: The Maya Society.

Morley, Frances R. and Sylvanus G. Morley

1938 The Age and Provenance of the Leyden Plate. *Carnegie Institution of Washington, Publication 509, Contributions to American Anthropology and History*, Vol. V, No. 24, pp. 5–22. Washington, D.C.

Morley, Sylvanus Griswold

1915 An Introduction to the Study of the Maya Hieroglyphs. *Smithsonian Institution, Bureau of American Ethnology, Bulletin 57*. Washington, D.C.: Government Printing Office.

1920 The Inscriptions at Copan. *Carnegie Institution of Washington, Publication 219*. Washington, D.C.

1922 The Foremost Intellectual Achievement of Ancient America. The Hieroglyphic Inscriptions on the Monuments in the Ruined Cities of Mexico, Guatemala, and Honduras are Yielding the Secrets of the Maya Civilization. In *The National Geographic Magazine*, Vol. XLI, No. 2: 109–130. Washington, D.C.

1933 The Calakmul Expedition. *Scientific Monthly* 37:193–206. Lancaster, Pennsylvania.

1937–38 The Inscriptions of Petén. *Carnegie Institution of Washington, Publication 437*. 5 volumes. Washington, D.C.

1946 *The Ancient Maya*. Stanford: Stanford University Press.

Morley, Sylvanus G. and George W. Brainerd

1956 *The Ancient Maya*. Third edition. Stanford: Stanford University Press.

Morley, Sylvanus G., George W. Brainerd, and Robert J. Sharer

1983 *The Ancient Maya*. Fourth edition. Stanford: Stanford University Press.

Moser, Chris

1977 Ñuiñe Writing and Iconography of the Mixteca Baja. *Vanderbilt University Publications in Anthropology 19*. Nashville: Department of Anthropology, Vanderbilt University.

Motolinía, Toribio de Benavente

1903 Memoriales. In *Documentos históricos de México*, edited by L. García Pimentel, Vol. 1. Mexico.

1971 *Memoriales o libro de las cosas de la Nueva España y de los naturales de ella*. Mexico: Universidad Nacional Autónoma de México.

Motul Dictionary (see Martínez Hernández 1929)

Nicholson, Henry B.

1957 Topiltzin Quetzalcoatl of Tollan: A Problem in Mesoamerican Ethnohistory. Ph.D. dissertation, Harvard University.

1961 The Chapultepec Cliff Sculpture of Motecuhzoma Xocoyotzin. *El México Antiguo* IX:379–444. Mexico: Sociedad Alemana Mexicanista.

1971 Religion in Pre-Hispanic Central Mexico. In *Handbook of Middle American Indians*, Vol. 10: Archaeology of Northern Mesoamerica, Part 1, edited by Robert Wauchope (general editor) and Gordon F. Ekholm and Ignacio Bernal (volume editors), pp. 395–446. Austin: University of Texas Press.

1973 Phoneticism in the Late Pre-Hispanic Central Mexican Writing System. In *Mesoamerican Writing Systems, a Conference at Dumbarton Oaks, October 30th and 31st, 1971*, edited by Elizabeth P. Benson, pp. 1–46. Washington, D.C.: Dumbarton Oaks Research Library and Collection, Trustees for Harvard University.

1974 Tepepolco, the Locale of the First Stage of Fray Bernardino de Sahagún's Great Ethnographic Project: Historical and Cultural Notes. In *Mesoamerican Archaeology: New Approaches*, edited by Norman Hammond, pp. 145–154. Austin: University of Texas Press.

1978a Western Mesoamerica: A.D. 900–1520. In *Chronologies in New World Archaeology*, edited by R. E. Taylor and Clement W. Meighan, pp. 285–329. New York: Academic Press.

1978b The Deity 9 Wind "Ehecatl-Quetzalcoatl" in the Mixteca Pictorials. *Journal of Latin American Lore* 4(1):61–92.

Nissen, Hans Jorg

1988 *The Early History of the Ancient Near East, 9000–2000 B.C.* Translated by Elizabeth Lutzeier with Kenneth J. Northcott. Chicago: University of Chicago Press.

Norman, V. Garth

1973 Izapa Sculpture. Part 1: Album. *Papers*

of the New World Archaeological
Foundation, Number 30. Provo, Utah:
New World Archaeological Foundation,
Brigham Young University.

1976 Izapa Sculpture. Part 2: Text. *Papers of
the New World Archaeological
Foundation, Number 30.* Provo, Utah:
New World Archaeological Foundation,
Brigham Young University.

Nowotny, Karl Anton

1948 Erläuterungen zum Codex
Vindobonensis (Vorderseite). *Archiv für
Völkerkunde* 3:156–200.

1959a Die Hieroglyphen des Codex
Mendoza: Der Bau einer
mittelamerikanischen Wortschrift.
*Mitteilungen aus dem Museum für
Völkerkunde und Vorgeschichte,* Vol.
XXV, pp. 97–113. Hamburg.

1959b Die Bilderfolge des Codex
Vindobonensis und verwandter
Handschriften. *Archiv für Völkerkunde*
12:210–221.

1961 *Codices Becker I/II.* Graz, Austria:
Akademische Druck-u. Verlangsanstalt.

1963 *Der Bau der mexikanischen
Hieroglyphen.* VI Congres International
des Sciences Anthropologiques et
Ethnologiques, Paris, 30 juillet-6 aout
1960, tome II, Ethnologie (premier
volume), pp. 451–455. Paris: Musée de
l'Homme.

1967 Die mexikanische Bilderschrift.
Studium Generale 20 (9):584–594. Berlin:
Springer-Verlag.

Noyes, Ernest

1932 Fray Alonso Ponce in Yucatán, 1588.
*Middle American Research Institute,
Tulane University,* Publication 4: 297–
372. New Orleans.

Nuttall, Zelia

1902 *Codex Nuttall. Facsimile of an ancient
Mexican codex belonging to Lord Zouche
of Harynworth, England.* Cambridge,
Massachusetts: Peabody Museum of
American Archaeology and Ethnology,
Harvard University.

1904 The Periodical Adjustments of the
Ancient Mexican Calendar. *American
Anthropologist* 6: 486–500. Lancaster,
Pennsylvania.

Oppenheim, A. Leo

1964 *Ancient Mesopotamia.* Chicago:
University of Chicago Press.

Orozco y Berra, Manuel

1877 El cuauhxicalli de Tizoc. *Anales del
Museo Nacional,* Vol. 1:3–39. Mexico.

1877–81 Códice Mendozino. Ensayo de
descifración geroglífica. *Anales del Museo
Nacional,* Vols. 1, 2. Mexico.

1880 *Historia antigua y de la conquista de
México.* 4 volumes + atlas. Mexico:
Tipográfico de G.A. Esteva.

Paddock, John

1966a Monte Albán: ¿sede de imperio?
*Revista Mexicana de Estudios
Antropológicos* 20:117–146.

1966b *Ancient Oaxaca: Discoveries in
Mexican Archeology and History.*
Stanford: Stanford University Press.

1982 Confluence in Zapotec and Mixtec
Ethnohistories: The 1580 Mapa de
Macuilxochitl. In Native American
Ethnohistory, edited by Joseph W.
Whitecotton and Judith Bradley
Whitecotton, *University of Oklahoma
Papers in Anthropology,* Vol. 23, No. 2,
pp. 345–357. Norman.

1983a Comments on the Lienzos of
Huilotepec and Guevea. In *The Cloud
People: Divergent Evolution of the
Zapotec and Mixtec Civilizations,* edited
by Kent V. Flannery and Joyce Marcus,
pp. 308–313. New York: Academic Press.

1983b Lord 5 Flower's Family. Rulers of
Zaachila and Cuilapan. *Vanderbilt
University Publications in Anthropology,*
No. 29. Nashville.

Pahl, Gary W.

1977 The Inscriptions of Río Amarillo and
Los Higos: Secondary Centers of the
Southeastern Maya Frontier. In *Journal of*

Latin American Lore 3 (1): 133–154.

Parmenter, Ross

1966 "Break-through" on the Lienzo de
Filadelfia. *Expedition* Vol. VIII-2:14–22.
Philadelphia: University Museum,
University of Pennsylvania.

Paso y Troncoso, Francisco del, editor

1898 *Códice del Palais Bourbon de París.*
Florence, Italy.

1905–06 *Relaciones Geográficas. Papeles de
Nueva España, segunda serie, Geografía y
Estadística,* Vols.I-VII. Madrid: Est.
Tipográfico "Sucesores de Rivadeneyra."

1906 *Fray Bernardino de Sahagún: Historia
de las Cosas de Nueva España.* (Vol. 7
includes Códice Matritense del Real
Palacio.) Madrid: Hauser y Menet.

1907 *Fray Bernardino de Sahagún: Historia
de las Cosas de Nueva España.* (Vol. 8
includes Códice Matritense de la Real
Academia de la Historia.) Madrid: Hauser
y Menet.

Peñafiel, Antonio

1885 *Nombres geográficos de México.
Catálogo alfabético de los nombres de
lugar pertenecientes al idioma "Nahuatl."
Estudio jeroglífico de la Matrícula de los
Tributos del Códice Mendocino.* 2
volumes. México: Secretaría de Fomento.

1897 *Nomenclatura geográfica de México.
Etimologías de los nombres de lugar
correspondientes a los principales idiomas
que se hablan en la república.* 2 volumes.
México: Secretaría de Fomento.

1900 *Códice Mixteco. Lienzo de Zacatepec.*
Mexico: Tipográfica de la Secretaría de
Fomento.

1910 *Principio de la época colonial.
Destrucción del Templo Mayor de México
antiguo y los monumentos encontrados en
la ciudad en las excavaciones de 1897 y
1902.* Mexico: Secretaría de Fomento.

Pike, Kenneth L.

1945 Tone Puns in Mixteco. *International
Journal of American Linguistics* XI:129–
139.

1948 *Tone Languages*. University of Michigan Publication in Linguistics, Vol. IV. Ann Arbor.

Pineda, E.
1845 Descripción geográfica del Departamento de Chiapas y Soconusco. Manuscript in Tozzer Library, Harvard University, Cambridge.

Pío Pérez, Juan
1898 *Coordinación alfabética de las voces del idioma Maya que se hallan en el arte y obras del Padre Fr. Pedro Beltrán de Santa Rosa, con las equivalencias castellanas que en las mismas se hallan.* Mérida.

Pohl, John M. D. and Bruce E. Byland
1990 Mixtec Landscape Perception and Archaeological Settlement Patterns. *Ancient Mesoamerica* 1:113–131.

Pomar, Juan Bautista de
[1582] 1941 Relación de Tezcoco. In *Nueva Colección de documentos para la Historia de México*, second edition, edited by Joaquín García Icazbalceta, Vol. 3, pp. 1–64. Mexico: Editorial Salvador Chávez Hayhoe.

Postgate, J. N.
1984 Cuneiform Catalysis: The first information revolution. *Archaeological Review from Cambridge* 3 (2): 4–18. Cambridge.

Prem, Hanns J.
1967 Die Namenshieroglyphen der Matrícula von Huexotzinco (ms. Mex. 387 der Bib. Nat. Paris). Ph.D. dissertation, University of Hamburg, Germany.
1970 Aztec Hieroglyphic Writing System—Possibilities and Limits. *Verhandlungen des XXXVIII Internationalen Amerikanistenkongresses*, Stuttgart-München 12, bis 18. August 1968, Band II:159–165. München.

Proskouriakoff, Tatiana
1946 *An Album of Maya Architecture. Carnegie Institution of Washington, Publication 558.* Washington, D.C.: Carnegie Institution of Washington.

1960 Historical Implications of a Pattern of Dates at Piedras Negras, Guatemala. *American Antiquity* 25 (4):454–475.
1961 Portraits of Women in Maya Art. *Essays in Pre-Columbian Art and Archaeology*, edited by Samuel K. Lothrop et al., pp. 81–99. Cambridge, Massachusetts: Harvard University Press.
1962 Civic and Religious Structures of Mayapan. In Mayapan, Yucatan, Mexico, by Harry E.D. Pollock, Ralph L. Roys, Tatiana Proskouriakoff, and A. Ledyard Smith, *Carnegie Institution of Washington, Publication 619*, pp. 87–164. Washington, D.C.: Carnegie Institution of Washington.
1963 Historical Data in the Inscriptions of Yaxchilan, Part I. *Estudios de Cultura Maya* 3:149–167. Mexico: Universidad Nacional Autónoma de México.
1964 Historical Data in the Inscriptions of Yaxchilan, Part II. *Estudios de Cultura Maya* 4:177–201. Mexico: Universidad Nacional Autónoma de México.
1968 The Jog and the Jaguar Signs in Maya Writing. *American Antiquity* 33(2):247–251.
1973 The Hand-grasping-fish and Associated Glyphs on Classic Maya Monuments. In *Mesoamerican Writing Systems, A Conference at Dumbarton Oaks, October 30th and 31st, 1971*, edited by Elizabeth P. Benson, pp. 165–178. Washington, D.C.: Dumbarton Oaks Research Library and Collection, Trustees for Harvard University.

Rabin, Emily
1981 Chronology of the Mixtec Historical Codices: An Overview. Paper presented at the annual meeting of the American Society for Ethnohistory, Colorado Springs, Colorado.

Rappaport, Roy A.
1979 *Ecology, Meaning, and Religion.* Richmond, California: North Atlantic Books.

Redford, Donald B.
1987 *Akhenaten: The Heretic King.* Princeton, New Jersey: Princeton University Press.

Redmond, Elsa M.
1983 A Fuego y Sangre: Early Zapotec Imperialism in the Cuicatlán Cañada, Oaxaca. *Studies in Latin American Ethnohistory & Archaeology*, Vol. I. *Memoirs of the Museum of Anthropology, University of Michigan*, No. 16. Ann Arbor.

Redmond, Elsa and Charles S. Spencer
1983 The Cuicatlán Cañada and the Period II Frontier of the Zapotec State. In *The Cloud People: Divergent Evolution of the Zapotec and Mixtec Civilizations*, edited by Kent V. Flannery and Joyce Marcus, pp. 117–120. New York: Academic Press.

Relación de la Genealogía . . . (see Pomar)
1941 *Nueva Colección de Documentos para la Historia de México*, edited by Joaquín García Icazbalceta, Vol. 3:240–256. Mexico: Editorial Chávez Hayhoe.

Relaciones de Yucatán
1898–1900 In *Colección de documentos inéditos relativos al descubrimiento, conquista y organización de las antiguas posesiones españolas de ultramar.* Vols. I, II (Vols. 11, 13). Madrid: Real Academia de la Historia.

Reyes, Fray Antonio de los
[1593] 1976 Arte en lengua mixteca. *Vanderbilt University Publications in Anthropology*, No. 14. Nashville.

Rice, Don S. and Prudence M. Rice
1981 Muralla de León: A Lowland Maya Fortification. *Journal of Field Archaeology* 8:271–288.

Riese, Berthold
1984 Relaciones clásico-tardías entre Copán y Quiriguá. Algunas evidencias epigráficas. *Yaxkin* 7 (1):23–30. Tegucigalpa.
1988 Epigraphy of the Southeast Zone in Relation to Other Parts of Mesoamerica. In *The Southeast Classic Maya Zone*,

edited by Elizabeth H. Boone and Gordon R. Willey, pp. 67–94. Washington, D.C.: Dumbarton Oaks Research Library and Collection.

Ríos 1900 (see Codex Vaticanus A)

Roys, Ralph Loveland

1922 A New Maya Historical Narrative. *American Anthropologist* 24:44–60.

1933 The Book of Chilam Balam of Chumayel. *Carnegie Institution of Washington, Publication 438.* Washington, D.C.

1940 Personal Names of the Maya of Yucatan. *Carnegie Institution of Washington, Publication 523, Contribution 31.* Washington, D.C.

1943 The Indian Background of Colonial Yucatan. *Carnegie Institution of Washington, Publication 548.* Washington, D.C.

1946 The Book of Chilam Balam of Ixil. *Carnegie Institution of Washington, Division of Historical Research, Notes on Middle American Archaeology and Ethnology,* No. 75. Washington, D.C.

1949 The Prophecies for the Maya *tuns* or years in the books of Chilam Balam of Tizimin and Mani. *Carnegie Institution of Washington, Publication 585, Contribution 51.* Washington, D.C.

1957 The Political Geography of the Yucatan Maya. *Carnegie Institution of Washington, Publication 613.* Washington, D.C.

1962 Literary Sources for the History of Mayapan. In Mayapan, Yucatan, Mexico, by Harry E. D. Pollock, Ralph L. Roys, Tatiana Proskouriakoff, and A. Ledyard Smith, *Carnegie Institution of Washington, Publication 619,* pp. 24–86. Washington, D.C.

1965 Lowland Maya Society at Spanish Contact. In *Handbook of Middle American Indians,* Vol. 3, edited by Robert Wauchope and Gordon R. Willey, pp. 659–678. Austin: University of Texas Press.

1967 *The Book of Chilam Balam of Chumayel.* Norman: University of Oklahoma Press.

Ruppert, Karl and John H. Denison, Jr.

1943 Archaeological Reconnaissance in Campeche, Quintana Roo, and Petén. *Carnegie Institution of Washington, Publication 543.* Washington, D.C.

Ruppert, Karl, J. Eric S. Thompson, and Tatiana Proskouriakoff

1955 Bonampak, Chiapas, Mexico. *Carnegie Institution of Washington, Publication 602.* Washington, D.C.: Carnegie Institution of Washington.

Ruz, Mario Humberto

[1571] 1986 Vocabulario de lengua tzeldal según el orden de Copanabastla. *Fuentes para el Estudio de la Cultura Maya, No. 4.* Centro de Estudios Mayas. Mexico: Universidad Nacional Autónoma de México.

Ruz Lhuillier, Alberto

1954 Exploraciones en Palenque: 1952. In *Anales del Instituto Nacional de Antropología e Historia* 6:107–110. Mexico: Secretaría de Educación Pública.

1958 Exploraciones arqueológicas en Palenque: 1953–1956. In *Anales del Instituto Nacional de Antropología e Historia* 10:69–299. Mexico: Secretaría de Educación Pública.

1973 El Templo de las Inscripciones, Palenque. *Colección Científica 7.* Mexico City.

1977 Gerontocracy at Palenque? In *Social Process in Maya Prehistory: Studies in Honour of Sir J. Eric S. Thompson,* edited by Norman Hammond, pp. 287–295. London: Academic Press.

Sabloff, Jeremy A.

1990 *The New Archaeology and the Ancient Maya.* New York: Scientific American Library Series.

Sáenz, César A.

1961 Tres estelas en Xochicalco. *Revista Mexicana de Estudios Antropológicos*

17:39–65.

1962 Las estelas de Xochicalco. *Proceedings of the 35th International Congress of Americanists* 2:69–82. Mexico City.

1968 Cuatro Piedras con Inscripciones en Xochicalco, México. *Anales de Antropología* 5: 181–198. Mexico: Universidad Nacional Autónoma de México.

Sahagún, Fray Bernardino de

1938 Historia general de las cosas de Nueva España. Mexico: Editorial Pedro Robredo.

1949 Sterbende Gotter und Christliche Heilsbotschaft; Wechselreden Indianischer Vornehmer und Spanischer Glaubensapostel in Mexiko 1524: "Coloquios y doctrina christiana" des Fray Bernardino de Sahagún aus dem Jahre 1564, edited by Walter Lehmann. *Quellenwerke zur Alten Geschichte Amerikas Aufgezeichnet in den Sprachen der Eingeborenen* (Latein-Amerikanischen Bibliothek, Berlin). III. Stuttgart.

[1569–79] 1950–69 *Florentine Codex: General History of the Things of New Spain.* Translated by Arthur J. O. Anderson and Charles E. Dibble. 12 volumes. Salt Lake City: University of Utah and School of American Research.

1956 *Historia General de las Cosas de Nueva España.* 4 volumes. Edited by Angel María Garibay. Mexico: Editorial Porrúa.

1964 *Códices Matritenses de la Historia General de las Cosas de la Nueva España,* edited by Manuel Ballesteros Gaibrois, 2 volumes. Madrid: Ediciones José Porrúa Turanzas.

Sahlins, Marshall D.

1958 *Social Stratification in Polynesia.* Seattle: University of Washington Press.

Sánchez de Aguilar, Pedro

[1639] 1900 Informe contra idolorum cultores del Obispado de Yucatan. *Anales del Museo Nacional de México,* época 1, Vol. 6:15–122. Second edition. México.

Sanders, William T. and Deborah L. Nichols

1988 Ecological Theory and Cultural Evolution in the Valley of Oaxaca. *Current Anthropology* 29(1):33–80.

Satterthwaite, Linton
1958 The Problem of Abnormal Stela Placements at Tikal and Elsewhere. *Tikal Report 3*, pp. 61–83. *University Museum Monographs*, No. 15. Philadelphia: University Museum, University of Pennsylvania.
1965 Calendrics of the Maya Lowlands. In *Handbook of Middle American Indians, Vol. 3: Archaeology of Southern Mesoamerica*, edited by Robert Wauchope and Gordon R. Willey, pp. 603–631. Austin: University of Texas Press.

Saville, Marshall H.
1899 Exploration of Zapotecan Tombs in Southern Mexico. *American Anthropologist* 1:350–362.

Schele, Linda
1979 Genealogical documentation on the tri-figure panels at Palenque. In *Third Palenque Round Table*, edited by Merle Greene Robertson and Donnan Call Jeffers, Vol. IV, pp. 41–70. Monterey, California: Herald Printers.
1982 *Maya Glyphs: The Verbs*. Austin: University of Texas Press.

Schele, Linda and David Freidel
1990 *A Forest of Kings*. New York: William Morrow and Company.

Schele, Linda and Jeffrey H. Miller
1983 The Mirror, the Rabbit, and the Bundle: "Accession" Expressions from the Classic Maya Inscriptions. *Studies in Pre-Columbian Art & Archaeology, No. 25*. Washington, D.C.: Dumbarton Oaks Research Library and Collection.

Schele, Linda and Mary Ellen Miller
1986 *The Blood of Kings: Dynasty and Ritual in Maya Art*. Fort Worth, Texas: Kimbell Art Museum.

Schmandt-Besserat, Denise
1977 An Archaic recording System and the Origin of Writing. *Syro-Mesopotamian Studies* 1:31–70.
1980 The Envelopes that Bear the First Writing. *Technology and Culture* 21:357–385.

Schulz, R. P. C.
1942 Apuntes sobre cálculos relativos al calendario de los indígenas de Chiapas. *El México Antiguo* 6: 6–14. Mexico.

Seler, Eduard
1900–01 *The Tonalamatl of the Aubin Collection*. Berlin and London.
1901–02 *Codex Fejervary-Mayer*. Berlin and London.
1902–03 *Codex Vaticanus 3773*. Berlin and London.
1902–23 *Gesammelte Abhandlungen zur Amerikanischen Sprach- und Alterthumskunde*. 5 volumes. Berlin: A. Asher & Co. (Second edition, 1960–1961, Graz, Austria.)
1904 The Mexican chronology with special reference to the Zapotec calendar. *Smithsonian Institution, Bureau of American Ethnology, Bulletin 28*, pp. 11–55. Washington, D.C.: Government Printing Office.
1904–1909 *Codex Borgia*. 3 volumes. Berlin.
1906 Das Dorfbuch von Santiago Guevea. *Zeitschrift für Ethnologie XXXVIII*, pp. 121–155.
1908 Das Dorfbuch von Santiago Guevea. In *Gesammelte Abhandlungen zur Amerikanischen Sprach- und Alterthumskunde*, Vol. 3, pp. 157–193. Graz, Austria.
1963 *Comentarios al Códice Borgia*. 3 volumes. Mexico City: Fondo de Cultura Económica. Originally published in 1904–1909 as *Codex Borgia: Eine altmexikanische Bilderschrift der Bibliothek der Congregatio de Propaganda Fide*. Berlin, Germany.

Serna, J. de la
1900 Manual de Ministros de Indios. *Anales del Museo Nacional de México*, primera época, Vol. VI. Mexico.

Service, Elman R.
1962 *Primitive Social Organization: an evolutionary perspective*. New York: Random House.
1975 *The Origins of Civilization and the State*. New York: W. W. Norton and Company.

Shanks, Michael and Christopher Tilley
1987 *Re-Constructing Archaeology: Theory and Practice*. New Studies in Archaeology Series, edited by Colin Renfrew and Jeremy Sabloff. Cambridge: Cambridge University Press.

Sharer, Robert J.
1978 Archaeology and History at Quiriguá, Guatemala. *Journal of Field Archaeology* 5(1):51–70.
1990 *Quiriguá: A Classic Maya Center & Its Sculptures*. Durham, North Carolina: Carolina Academic Press.

Sharer, Robert J. and David C. Grove, editors
1989 *Regional Perspectives on the Olmec*. Cambridge: Cambridge University Press.

Shook, Edwin M.
1960 Tikal Stela 29. *Expedition* 2 (2):29–35. Philadelphia: University Museum, University of Pennsylvania.

Smith, Mary Elizabeth
1963 The Codex Colombino: A Document of the South Coast of Oaxaca. *Tlalocan* IV (3):276–288.
1966 Las Glosas del Códice Colombino/The Glosses of Codex Colombino. In *Interpretación del Códice Colombino/Interpretation of the Codex Colombino*, by Alfonso Caso. Pp. 51–84, 149–176. Mexico: Sociedad Mexicana de Antropología.
1973a *Picture Writing from Ancient Southern Mexico. Mixtec Place Signs and Maps*. Norman: University of Oklahoma Press.
1973b The Relationship between Mixtec Manuscript Painting and the Mixtec Language: A Study of Some Personal Names in Codices Muro and Sánchez

Solís. In *Mesoamerican Writing Systems: A Conference at Dumbarton Oaks*, edited by Elizabeth P. Benson, pp. 47–98. Washington, D.C.: Dumbarton Oaks Research Library and Collections.

1983a Codex Selden: A manuscript from the Valley of Nochixtlán? In *The Cloud People: Divergent Evolution of the Zapotec and Mixtec Civilizations*, edited by Kent V. Flannery and Joyce Marcus, pp. 248–255. New York: Academic Press.

1983b Regional Points of View in the Mixtec Codices. In *The Cloud People: Divergent Evolution of the Zapotec and Mixtec Civilizations*, edited by Kent V. Flannery and Joyce Marcus, pp. 260–266. New York: Academic Press.

1983c The Mixtec Writing System. In *The Cloud People: Divergent Evolution of the Zapotec and Mixtec Civilizations*, edited by Kent V. Flannery and Joyce Marcus, pp. 238–245. New York: Academic Press.

Soustelle, Jacques
1964 *The Daily Life of the Aztecs on the Eve of the Spanish Conquest*. Translated from the French by Patrick O'Brian. Harmondsworth, Middlesex, England: Penguin Books, Ltd.

Spencer, Charles S.
1982 *The Cuicatlán Cañada and Monte Albán: A Study of Primary State Formation*. New York: Academic Press.

Spencer, Charles S. and Elsa M. Redmond
1983 A Middle Formative Elite Residence and Associated Structures at La Coyotera, Oaxaca. In *The Cloud People: Divergent Evolution of the Zapotec and Mixtec Civilizations*, edited by Kent V. Flannery and Joyce Marcus, pp. 71–74. New York: Academic Press.

Spinden, Herbert Joseph
1913 A Study of Maya Art. *Memoirs of the Peabody Museum of American Archaeology and Ethnology*, Vol. 6. Cambridge, Massachusetts: Harvard University.

1924 The Reduction of Mayan Dates. *Papers of the Peabody Museum of American Archaeology and Ethnology*, Vol. 6, no. 4. Cambridge, Massachusetts: Harvard University.

1935 Indian Manuscripts of Southern Mexico. *Annual Report of the Board of Regents of the Smithsonian Institution for the year ending June 30, 1933*, pp. 429–451. Washington, D.C.: U.S. Government Printing Office.

Spores, Ronald
1965 The Zapotec and Mixtec at Spanish Contact. In *Handbook of Middle American Indians, Vol. 3: Archaeology of Southern Mesoamerica, Part 2*, edited by Robert Wauchope and Gordon R. Willey, pp. 962–987. Austin: University of Texas Press.

1967 *The Mixtec Kings and their People*. Norman: University of Oklahoma Press.

1972 An Archaeological Settlement Survey of the Nochixtlán Valley, Oaxaca. *Vanderbilt University Publications in Anthropology*, No. 1. Nashville: Vanderbilt University.

1974a Marital Alliance in the Political Integration of Mixtec Kingdoms. *American Anthropologist* 76:297–311.

1974b Stratigraphic Excavations in the Nochixtlan Valley, Oaxaca. *Vanderbilt University Publications in Anthropology*, No. 11. Nashville: Vanderbilt University.

1983 The Origin and Evolution of the Mixtec System of Social Stratification. In *The Cloud People: Divergent Evolution of the Zapotec and Mixtec Civilizations*, edited by Kent V. Flannery and Joyce Marcus, pp. 227–238. New York: Academic Press.

1984 *The Mixtecs in Ancient and Colonial Times*. Norman: University of Oklahoma Press.

Spores, Ronald and Kent V. Flannery
1983 Sixteenth-Century Kinship and Social Organization. In *The Cloud People: Divergent Evolution of the Zapotec and*

Mixtec Civilizations, edited by Kent V. Flannery and Joyce Marcus, pp. 339–342. New York: Academic Press.

Starr, Frederick
1902 Notes upon the ethnography of southern Mexico, Part II. *Davenport Academy of Natural Sciences* 9:63–172. Davenport.

Stephens, John L.
1843 *Incidents of Travel in Yucatan*. 2 volumes. New York: Harper.

Stirling, Matthew W.
1940 An Initial Series from Tres Zapotes, Vera Cruz, Mexico. *National Geographic Society, Contributed Technical Papers on Mexican Archaeology* 1 (1): 1–15. Washington, D.C.: National Geographic Society.

Stross, Brian
1983 The Language of Zuyua. *American Ethnologist* 10 (1):150–164.

Stuart, David
1985 The Yaxha Emblem Glyph as *Yax-ha*. *Research Reports on Ancient Maya Writing*, No. 1. Washington, D.C.: Center for Maya Research.

1988 Blood Symbolism in Maya Iconography. In *Maya Iconography*, edited by Elizabeth P. Benson and Gillett G. Griffin, pp. 175–221. Princeton, New Jersey: Princeton University Press.

Stuart, David and Stephen D. Houston
1989 Maya Writing. *Scientific American* 261(2):82–89.

Sugiyama, Saburo
1989 Burials Dedicated to the Old Temple of Quetzalcoatl at Teotihuacan, Mexico. *American Antiquity* 54 (1):85–106.

Sullivan, Thelma D.
1972 The Arms and Insignia of the Mexica. *Estudios de Cultura Náhuatl* 10:155–193.

1980 Tlatoani and Tlatocayotl in the Sahagun Manuscripts. *Estudios de Cultura Náhuatl* 14:225–238.

1982 Tlazolteotl-Ixcuina: The Great Spinner and Weaver. *The Art and Iconography of*

Late Post-Classic Central Mexico, edited by Elizabeth Boone, pp. 7–35. Washington, D.C.: Dumbarton Oaks Research Library and Collection, Trustees for Harvard University.

Swadesh, Morris
1967 Lexicostatistic classification. In *Handbook of Middle American Indians, Vol. 5: Linguistics*, edited by Robert Wauchope (general editor) and Norman A. McQuown (volume editor), pp. 79–115. Austin: University of Texas Press.

Tedlock, Barbara
1982 *Time and the Highland Maya*. Albuquerque: University of New Mexico Press.

Teeple, John E.
1925a Maya Inscriptions: Glyphs C, D, and E of the Supplementary Series. *American Anthropologist* 27:108–115.
1925b Maya Inscriptions: Further Notes on the Supplementary Series. *American Anthropologist* 27: 544–549.
1926 Maya Inscriptions: The Venus Calendar and Another Correlation. *American Anthropologist* n.s. 28: 402–408.
1928 Maya Inscriptions: VI. The Lunar Calendar and its Relation to Maya history. *American Anthropologist* 30:391–407.
1930 Maya Astronomy. *Carnegie Institution of Washington, Publication 403, Contribution 2*. Washington, D.C.: Carnegie Institution of Washington.

Termer, Franz
1930 Zur Ethnologie und Ethnographie des nördlichen Mittelamerika. *Ibero-Amerikanisches Archiv* 4 (4). Berlin and Bonn.

Thompson, Edward H.
1904 Archaeological Researches in Yucatán. *Memoirs of the Peabody Museum of American Archaeology and Ethnology*, Vol. 3, No. 1. Cambridge, Massachusetts: Harvard University.

Thompson, J. Eric S.
1932 A Maya Calendar from Alta Vera Paz, Guatemala. *American Anthropologist* 34: 449–454.
1934 Sky-Bearers, Colors and Directions in Maya and Mexican Religion. *Carnegie Institution of Washington, Publication 436. Contributions to American Anthropology No. 10*. Washington, D.C.
1944 The Fish as a Maya Symbol for Counting and Further Discussions of Directional Glyphs. *Carnegie Institution of Washington, Theoretical Approaches to Problems No. 2*. Washington, D.C.
1950 *Maya Hieroglyphic Writing: An Introduction*. Carnegie Institution of Washington, Publication 589. Washington, D.C.
1954 *The Rise and Fall of Maya Civilization*. Norman: University of Oklahoma Press.
1962 *A Catalog of Maya Hieroglyphs*. Norman: University of Oklahoma Press.
1970 *Maya History and Religion*. Norman: University of Oklahoma Press.
1972 A Commentary on the Dresden Codex, a Maya Hieroglyphic Book. *Memoirs of the American Philosophical Society*, Vol. 93. Philadelphia.
1977 A proposal for constituting a Maya subgroup, cultural and linguistic, in the Petén and adjacent regions. In *Anthropology and History in Yucatan*, edited by Grant D. Jones, pp. 3–42. Austin: University of Texas Press.

Torquemada, Fray Juan de
1723 *Los veintiún libros rituales y monarchía indiana con el origen y guerras de los indios occidentales, de sus poblaciones, descubrimiento, conquista, comercio y otras cosas maravillosas de la misma tierra*. 3 volumes. Nicolás Rodríquez Franco, Madrid. Reprinted in 1943–1944 as *Monarquía Indiana* by Editorial Salvador Chávez Hayhoe, Mexico. 3 volumes.
[1615] 1969 *Los Veinte i un Libros Rituales i Monarchia Indiana*. 3 volumes. Mexico: Editorial Porrúa.

1975–83 *Monarquía Indiana*. 7 volumes. Mexico: Universidad Nacional Autónoma de México.

Tozzer, Alfred Marston
1907 *A Comparative Study of the Mayas and Lacandones*. New York and London: Macmillan.
1912 The Value of Ancient Mexican Manuscripts in the Study of the General Development of Writing. *Smithsonian Institution Annual Report, 1911*, pp. 493–506. Washington, D.C.
1941 Landa's Relación de las cosas de Yucatán. A translation edited with notes by A. M. Tozzer. *Papers of the Peabody Museum of American Archaeology and Ethnology, Vol. XVIII*. Cambridge, Massachusetts: Harvard University.
1957 Chichen Itza and its Cenote of Sacrifice: A Comparative Study of Contemporaneous Maya and Toltec. *Memoirs of the Peabody Museum of Archaeology and Ethnology, Harvard University*, Vols. XI, XII. Cambridge, Massachusetts: Harvard University.

Troike, Nancy
1974 *The Codex Colombino-Becker*. Ph.D. dissertation, University of London.
1978 Fundamental Changes in the Interpretations of the Mixtec Codices. *American Antiquity* 43(4):553–568.

Vaillant, George C.
1950 *Aztecs of Mexico*. New York: Doubleday.

Vayda, Andrew Peter
1960 Maori Warfare. *Polynesian Society Maori Monograph* 2. Wellington, New Zealand.
1961 Expansion and warfare among swidden agriculturalists. *American Anthropologist* 63:346–358.
1976 *War in Ecological Perspective*. New York: Plenum Press.

Veytia, Mariano
1907 *Los Calendarios Mexicanos*. Mexico: Imprenta y Taller del Museo Nacional.

Villagutierre Soto-Mayor, Juan de
1701 *Historia de la conquista de la Provincia de el Itzá, Reducción, y Progressos de la de El Lacandón, y Otras Naciones de Indios Barbaros, de la Mediación del Reyno de Guatimala, a las Provincias de Yucatán, en la América Septentrional.* Madrid.
1933 Historia de la conquista de la provincia de el Itzá, reducción y progresos de la de el Lacandón. *Biblioteca "Goathemala" de la Sociedad de Geografía e Historia*, Vol. 9. Guatemala: Tipografía Nacional.

Vogt, Evon Z.
1969 *Zinacantán: A Maya Community in the Highlands of Chiapas.* Cambridge, Massachusetts: Harvard University Press.

Watterson, Barbara
1981 *Introducing Egyptian Hieroglyphs.* Edinburgh: Scottish Academic Press.
1985 *More About Egyptian Hieroglyphs. A Simplified Grammar of Middle Egyptian.* Edinburgh: Scottish Academic Press.

Webster, David L.
1976a Lowland Maya Fortifications. *Proceedings of the American Philosophical Society* 120:361–371. Philadelphia: American Philosophical Society.
1976b Defensive Earthworks at Becan, Campeche, Mexico: Implications for Maya Warfare. *Middle American Research Institute, Tulane University, Publication* 41. New Orleans.
1977 Warfare and the Evolution of Maya Society. In *The Origins of Maya Civilization*, edited by Richard E. W. Adams, pp. 335–372. Albuquerque: University of New Mexico Press.
1978 Three Walled Sites of the Northern Maya Lowlands. *Journal of Field Archaeology* 5:375–390.
1979 Cuca, Chaccob, Dzonot Ake—Three Walled Northern Maya Centers. *Occasional Papers in Anthropology No. 11.* University Park: Department of Anthropology, Pennsylvania State University.

n.d. Unpublished manuscript on Maya warfare.

White, Leslie A.
1948 Ikhnaton: The Great Man vs. the Culture Process. *Journal of the American Oriental Society* 68(2): 91–114.

Whitecotton, Joseph W.
1977 *The Zapotecs: Princes, Priests, and Peasants.* Norman: University of Oklahoma Press.
1990 Zapotec Elite Ethnohistory: Pictorial Genealogies from Eastern Oaxaca. *Vanderbilt University Publications in Anthropology, No. 39.* Nashville.

Whitecotton, Joseph W. and Judith Bradley Whitecotton
1982 Native American Ethnohistory. *University of Oklahoma Papers in Anthropology*, Vol. 23, No. 2. Norman.

Willey, Gordon R.
1971 *An Introduction to American Archaeology, Vol. 2: South America.* Englewood Cliffs, New Jersey: Prentice-Hall.

Wilson, John A.
1951 *The Burden of Egypt.* Chicago: University of Chicago Press.
1975 *The Culture of Ancient Egypt* (originally published as *The Burden of Egypt*). Chicago: University of Chicago Press.

Winter, Edward H.
1955 *Bwamba of Africa.* Cambridge: Heffer.

Winter, Irene J.
1986 After the Battle is Over: The Stele of the Vultures and the Beginning of Historical Narrative in the Art of the Ancient Near East. In *Pictorial Narrative in Antiquity and the Middle Ages*, edited by Herbert L. Kessler and Marianna Shreve Simpson, Studies in the History of the Art, Vol. 16. Washington, D.C.: National Gallery of Art.

Wright, Henry T.
1977 Recent Research on the Origins of the State. *Annual Review of Anthropology* 6:379–397.
1984 Prestate Political Formations. In *On the Evolution of Complex Societies: Essays in Honor of Harry Hoijer*, edited by William Sanders, Henry Wright, Robert McC. Adams, and Timothy K. Earle, pp. 41–77. Malibu, California: Undena Publications.

Wright, Henry T. and Gregory A. Johnson
1975 Population, Exchange, and Early State Formation in southwestern Iran. *American Anthropologist* 77:267–289.

Ximénez, Francisco
[1722] 1929–31 Historia de la Provincia de San Vicente de Chiapa y Guatemala de la Orden de Predicadores. *Biblioteca "Goathemala" de la Sociedad de Geografía e Historia*, Vols.I-III. Guatemala.

Ximénez Ortíz, Juan
[1579] 1905 Relación de Iztepexi. In *Papeles de Nueva España: segunda serie, Geografía y Estadística*, edited by Francisco del Paso y Troncoso, Vol. 4, pp. 9–23. Madrid: Est. Tipográfico "Sucesores de Rivadeneyra."

Zantwijk, Rudolf van
1982 La Entronización de Acamapichtli de Tenochtitlán y las Características de su Gobierno. *Estudios de Cultura Náhuatl* 15:17–26.
1985 *The Aztec Arrangement: The Social History of pre-Spanish Mexico* (with foreword by Miguel León-Portilla). Norman: University of Oklahoma Press.

Zárate, Bartolomé de
[1581] 1905 Relación de Guaxilotitlán. In *Papeles de Nueva España: segunda serie, Geografía y Estadística*, edited by Francisco del Paso y Troncoso, Vol. 4, pp. 196–205. Madrid: Est. Tipográfico "Sucesores de Rivadeneyra."

Zorita, Alonso de
[1570–80] 1963 *Life and Labor in Ancient Mexico.* Translated by Benjamin Keen. New Brunswick, New Jersey: Rutgers University Press.

INDEX